CONNECT FEATURES

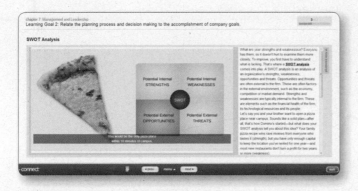

Interactive Presentations

Interactive Presentations cover each chapter's core learning objectives with narrated, animated presentations that pause frequently to check for comprehension. Interactive Presentations harness the full power of technology to appeal to all learning styles. Interactive Presentations are a great way to improve online or hybrid sections, but also extend the learning opportunity for traditional classes, such as in facilitating a "flipped classroom."

Interactive Applications

Interactive Applications offer a variety of automatically graded exercises that require students to **apply** key concepts. Whether the assignment includes a *click and drag*, *video case*, case analysis, or *decision generator*, these applications provide instant feedback and progress tracking for students and detailed results for the instructor.

eBook

Connect Plus includes a media-rich eBook that allows you to share your notes with your students. Your students can insert and review their own notes, highlight the text, search for specific information, and interact with media resources. Using an eBook with Connect Plus gives your students a complete digital solution that allows them to access their materials from any computer.

Tegrity

Make your classes available anytime, anywhere. With simple, one-click recording, students can search for a word or phrase and be taken to the exact place in your lecture that they need to review.

EASY TO USE

Learning Management System Integration

McGraw-Hill Campus is a one-stop teaching and learning experience available to use with any learning management system. McGraw-Hill Campus provides single sign-on to faculty and students for all McGraw-Hill material and technology from within the school website. McGraw-Hill Campus also allows instructors instant access to all supplements and teaching materials for all McGraw-Hill products.

Blackboard users also benefit from McGraw-Hill's industry-leading integration, providing single sign-on to access all Connect assignments and automatic feeding of assignment results to the Blackboard grade book.

POWERFUL REPORTING

Connect generates comprehensive reports and graphs that provide instructors with an instant view of the performance of individual students, a specific section, or multiple sections. Since all content is mapped to learning objectives, Connect reporting is ideal for accreditation or other administrative documentation.

marketing

Fourth Edition

Dhruv Grewal, PhD
Babson College

Michael Levy, PhD
Babson College

McGraw Hill Education

marketing,
fourth edition

SENIOR VICE PRESIDENT, PRODUCTS & MARKETS **KURT L. STRAND**
VICE PRESIDENT, GENERAL MANAGER, PRODUCTS & MARKETS **MICHAEL J. RYAN**
VICE PRESIDENT, CONTENT PRODUCTION & TECHNOLOGY SERVICES **KIMBERLY MERIWETHER DAVID**
MANAGING DIRECTOR **PAUL DUCHAM**
EXECUTIVE BRAND MANAGER **SANKHA BASU**
EXECUTIVE DIRECTOR OF DEVELOPMENT **ANN TORBERT**
SENIOR DEVELOPMENT EDITOR **KELLY L. DELSO**
MARKETING MANAGER II **DONIELLE XU**
DIRECTOR, CONTENT PRODUCTION **TERRI SCHIESL**
CONTENT PROJECT MANAGER **CHRISTINE A. VAUGHAN**
CONTENT PROJECT MANAGER **DANIELLE CLEMENT**
SENIOR BUYER **MICHAEL R. MCCORMICK**
DESIGN **LISA KING**
LEAD CONTENT LICENSING SPECIALIST **KERI JOHNSON**
TYPEFACE **10/12 TIMES LT STD**
COMPOSITOR **APTARA®, INC.**
PRINTER **R. R. DONNELLEY**

COVER IMAGES

Front cover: © Tomacco/Getty Images; Courtesy mySugr/GmbH. — K. Rose; Courtesy Left Brain Right Brain LLC. Used with permission; © William Andrew/Getty Images; © K. Rousonelos; © Robert Churchill/the Agency Collection/Getty Images; © Ryan McVay/Getty Images; Images used with permission of Chili's® Grill & Bar; © Sam Edwards/OJO Images/Getty Images; Courtesy L.L. Bean. Used with permission; © YinYang/Getty Images; © Brent Jones; M&M's is a registered trademark of Mars, Incorporated. This trademark and advertisement are used with permission. Mars, Incorporated is not associated with McGraw-Hill Higher Education. *Back cover:* © Alejandro Rivera/Getty Images

---

brief contents

contents

section two
UNDERSTANDING
THE MARKETPLACE

section three
TARGETING THE MARKETPLACE

section four
VALUE CREATION

section six
VALUE DELIVERY: DESIGNING THE CHANNEL AND SUPPLY CHAIN

marketing

red mango

chapter one

I t's nearing the end of the spring semester, and it's a hot day. Leaving the sweltering classroom, you and your friends decide to go grab a frozen dessert. But now the hard negotiations really begin: ice cream or frozen yogurt? Ben & Jerry's or Red Mango? Someone wants coconut-based instead of milk-based ice cream. Another friend insists it's time for everyone to try gelato. Each of these frozen desserts offers a cool treat, and various companies provide multiple options. So what's the difference among them, and what makes customers loyal to one choice over another?

Let's think about the options available for your frozen dessert indulgence: ice cream, frozen custard, gelato, frozen yogurt, sherbet, sorbet, water ice, single-serving desserts such as popsicles, milkshakes, and blended treats that combine frozen dairy products with bits of cookies or candies.[1] In addition to their wide variety of flavors, they also come in reduced-fat, soy, coconut, organic, fair-trade, probiotic, nutrition-enhanced, and gluten-free versions.

overview of marketing

LEARNING OBJECTIVES

After reading this chapter, you should be able to:

LO 1-1 Define the role of marketing in organizations.

LO 1-2 Describe how marketers create value for a product or service.

LO 1-3 Understand why marketing is important, both within and outside the firm.

In the grocery store, Unilever and Nestlé/Dreyer's are the undisputed leaders of the frozen dessert market. The former manufactures or distributes Breyer's, Ben & Jerry's, Good Humor, Klondike, and Popsicle;[2] the latter is responsible for Häagen-Dazs, Skinny Cow, and Edy's as well as Dreyer's and Nestlé brands. Frozen yogurt sales are a relatively small but growing part of the $25 billion frozen dessert market. This

continued on p. 4

> ## TO BUILD AND MAINTAIN A LOYAL CUSTOMER BASE, EACH FROZEN DESSERT BRAND MUST DISTINGUISH ITSELF FROM ITS COMPETITORS BY OFFERING PRODUCTS, SERVICES, AND AMBIANCE THAT ARE SO APPEALING THAT CUSTOMERS SHUN COMPETITORS.

continued from p. 3

growth trend has spawned intense competition among existing frozen yogurt shops and inspired new brands to set up shop.

To build and maintain a loyal customer base, each frozen dessert brand must distinguish itself from its competitors by offering products, services, and ambiance that are so appealing that customers shun competitors. Since it opened in 2007, for example, Red Mango has attracted loyal fans devoted to its tart-flavored yogurt, which contains probiotics and thus promises to aid digestion. Stores offer a limited number of exotic flavors, many of which are seasonal, and a wide array of high-end toppings.[3] The minimalism in the flavor choices is part of the company's brand image, as reflected in the stark, bright store layouts. That is, this popular new chain offers consistency across its products and its store images, even as it promises that customers can eat healthy, low-fat, hormone-free milk products, and still indulge in unusual yogurt flavors and interesting toppings.[4]

In contrast, the more traditional dessert idea offered by TCBY allows consumers to help themselves to yogurt flavors like cake batter, red velvet cake, and peanut butter and then pile on candy, cookies, fruit, sauces, and sprinkles.[5] Because the stores calculate the costs of each dessert by weight rather than by serving size, customers feel free to create towering frozen creations that they might have felt awkward ordering. It also results in a higher per-serving cost.[6]

From the moment the Vermont-based Ben & Jerry's opened its doors in 1978, offering super-premium ice cream, sorbet, and frozen yogurt, it committed to operating in a way that would contribute to the quality of life, both locally and globally.[7] Through the Ben & Jerry Foundation, the company funds community-oriented projects.

As these examples show, newcomers must constantly try to find a foothold in the market. Already established businesses must grow and change their product offerings and corporate citizenry to keep pace with customer needs and

Red Mango's tart-flavored yogurt contains probiotics and thus promises to aid digestion. By the way, it tastes great!

tastes. Red Mango stresses health and style; TCBY gives customers more choices and more control over portions; Ben & Jerry's takes a stand on social issues. Yet what's common to both new and established frozen dessert brands is their traditional approach to marketing: Each company succeeds because it provides good value to its customers. ∎

LO 1-1   Define the role of marketing in organizations.

WHAT IS MARKETING?

Unlike other subjects you may have studied, marketing already is very familiar to you. You start your day by agreeing to do the dishes in exchange for a freshly made cup of coffee. Then you fill up your car with gas. You attend a class that you have chosen and paid for. After class, you pick up lunch (and maybe a frozen dessert) at the cafeteria, which you eat while reading a book on your iPad. Then you leave campus to have your hair cut and take in a movie. On your bus ride back to school, you pass the time by buying a few songs from Apple's iTunes. In each case, you have acted as the buyer and made a decision about whether you should part with your time and/or money to receive a particular service or product. If, after you return home, you decide to sell some clothes you don't wear much anymore on eBay, you have become a seller. And in each of these transactions, you were engaged in marketing.

The American Marketing Association states that "**marketing** is the activity, set of institutions, and processes for creating,

capturing, communicating, delivering, and exchanging offerings that have value for customers, clients, partners, and society at large."[8] What does this definition really mean? Good marketing is not a random activity; it requires thoughtful planning with an emphasis on the ethical implications of any of those decisions on society in general. Firms develop a **marketing plan** (Chapter 2) that specifies the marketing activities for a specific period of time. The marketing plan also is broken down into various components—how the product or service will be conceived or designed, how much it should cost, where and how it will be promoted, and how it will get to the consumer. In any exchange, the parties to the transaction should be satisfied. In our previous example, you should be satisfied or even delighted with the song you downloaded, and Apple should be satisfied with the amount of money it received from you. Thus, the core aspects of marketing are found in Exhibit 1.1. Let's see how these core aspects look in practice.

▼ **EXHIBIT 1.1**   Core Aspects of Marketing

- Marketing helps create value.
- Marketing is about satisfying customer needs and wants.
- Marketing entails an exchange.
- Marketing requires product, price, place, and promotion decisions.
- Marketing can be performed by both individuals and organizations.
- Marketing occurs in many settings.

(center) Marketing

▼ EXHIBIT 1.2 Exchange: The Underpinning of Seller–Buyer Relationships

Marketing Is about Satisfying Customer Needs and Wants

Understanding the marketplace, and especially consumer needs and wants, is fundamental to marketing success. In the broadest terms, the marketplace refers to the world of trade. More narrowly, however, the marketplace can be segmented or divided into groups of people who are pertinent to an organization for particular reasons. For example, the marketplace for soft drinks may include most people in the world, but as Pepsi and Coke battle each other worldwide, they divide the global population into a host of categories: men versus women, calorie-conscious or not, people who prefer carbonated versus noncarbonated drinks, and multiple categories of flavor preferences, among others.[9] If you manufacture a beverage with zero calories, you want to know for which marketplace segments your product is most relevant, then make sure that you build a marketing strategy that targets those groups. Certain diet- and health-conscious customers may prefer Diet Coke or Diet Pepsi; others may opt for bottled water products like Dasani or Aquafina.

Although marketers would prefer to sell their products and services to everyone, it is not practical to do so. Because marketing costs money, good marketers carefully seek out potential customers who have both an interest in the product and an ability to buy it. For example, most people need some form of transportation, and many people probably would like to own the new hybrid from Lexus. Starting at more than $110,000, the Lexus LS 600h L is one of the most sophisticated hybrid cars on the market. But Lexus is not actually interested in everyone who wants an LS 600h L, because not everyone can afford to spend that much on a car. Instead, Lexus defines its viable target market as those consumers who want and can afford such a product.[10] Although not all companies focus on such a specific, and wealthy, target, all marketers are interested in finding the buyers who are most likely to be interested in their offerings.

Marketing Entails an Exchange

Marketing is about an **exchange**—the trade of things of value between the buyer and the seller so that each is better off as a result. As depicted in Exhibit 1.2, sellers provide

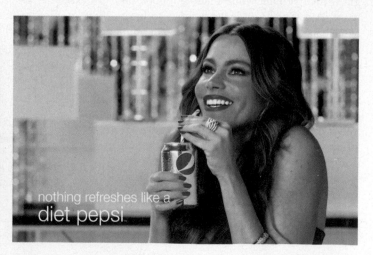

Coke and Pepsi are constantly battling to be number one.

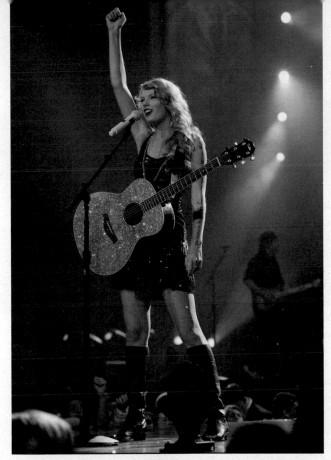

Purchasing a Taylor Swift song from the iTunes store entails an exchange. The customer gets the song, and Apple gets money and information.

products or services, then communicate and facilitate the delivery of their offering to consumers. Buyers complete the exchange by giving money and information to the seller. Suppose you learn about a new Taylor Swift album by hearing one of her songs on SiriusXM Satellite radio. The same day, a friend tweets on her Twitter account that she loves the new album, and you visit the Taylor Swift Facebook fan page, which is full of recommendations. From there, you click into the iTunes Store, where you can purchase the song you heard, multiple songs, or the entire new album. You begin with the song you heard, which you continue to love after hearing it several times. Therefore, you go back to iTunes and take advantage of its offer to complete the album by downloading the rest of the songs to your iTunes library. Your billing information is already in the company's system, so you do not have to enter your credit card number or other information. Furthermore, iTunes creates a record of your purchase, which it uses, together with your other purchase trends, to create personalized recommendations of other albums or songs that you might like. Thus, Apple uses the valuable information you provide to facilitate future exchanges and solidify its relationship with you.

Marketing Requires Product, Price, Place, and Promotion Decisions

Marketing traditionally has been divided into a set of four interrelated decisions and consequent actions known as the **marketing mix**, or **four Ps**: product, price, place, and promotion (as defined in Exhibit 1.3).[11] The four Ps comprise the controllable set of decisions/ activities that the firm uses to respond to the wants of its target markets. But what does each of these activities in the marketing mix entail?

Product: Creating Value Although marketing is a multifaceted function, its fundamental purpose is to create value by developing a variety of offerings, including *goods, services,* and *ideas,* to satisfy customer needs.[12] Take, for example, a frozen dessert. Not too long ago, consumers perceived milk-based ice cream as their primary option. But as we recognized in the chapter opener, numerous other options have evolved, including frozen yogurt, coconut-based frozen desserts,

Nondairy options such as coconut milk, frozen desserts, and sorbets are becoming more popular.

> # When people buy tickets—whether for airline travel, a sporting event, or the theater—they are paying not for the physical ticket stub but of course for the experience they gain.

sorbets, and even liquid nitrogen–frozen concoctions.[13] Coconut-based frozen desserts are extremely popular dessert options for folks with milk allergies; sorbets and sherbets appeal to people who like something lighter to cleanse their palates. The dessert is a *good,* the *service* might involve your enjoyment of it in a yogurt shop, and there might even be an *idea* driving your experience—that frozen yogurt desserts can be healthy for you too.

Goods are items that you can physically touch. Nike shoes, Pepsi-Cola, Budweiser, Kraft cheese, Tide, an iPad, and countless other products are examples of goods. As we describe at the start of Chapter 2, Nike primarily makes shoes but also adds value to its products by, for example, offering custom designs under its Nike ID brand that increase their fashionable appeal and enlisting popular celebrities such as Rafael Nadal to add their names to the designs.

Unlike goods, **services** are intangible customer benefits that are produced by people or machines and cannot be separated from the producer. When people buy tickets—whether for airline travel, a sporting event, or the theater—they are paying not for the physical ticket stub but of course for the experience they gain. Hotels, insurance agencies, and spas similarly provide services. Getting money from your bank, whether through an ATM or from a teller, is another example of using a service. In this case, cash machines usually add value to the banking experience because they are conveniently located, fast, and easy to use. Many offerings in the market combine goods and services.[14] When you go to an optical center, you get your eyes examined (a service) and purchase new contact lenses (a good). If you enjoy Beyoncé, you can attend a concert that can be provided only at that particular time and place (a service) and that gives you the chance to purchase a

Seeing Beyoncé in concert is a service, but buying a CD of her music is a product.

Rafael Nadal adds value to the Nike brand.

Beyoncé concert T-shirt (a good). If you manage to get your shirt signed by Beyoncé herself, you obtain a customized good that puts the finishing touch on and even extends a satisfying service experience.

Ideas include concepts, opinions, and philosophies; intellectual concepts such as these also can be marketed. Groups promoting bicycle safety go to schools, give talks, and sponsor bike helmet poster contests for the members of their primary market: children. Then their secondary target market segment, parents and siblings, gets involved through their interactions with the young contest participants. The exchange of value occurs when the children listen to the sponsors' presentation and wear their helmets while bicycling, which means they have adopted, or become purchasers, of the safety idea that the group marketed.

Price: Capturing Value

Everything has a price, although it doesn't always have to be monetary. Price, therefore, is everything the buyer gives up—money, time, energy—in exchange for the product.[15] Marketers must determine the price of a product carefully on the basis of the potential buyer's belief about its value. For example, United Airlines can take you from New York to Denver. The price you pay for that

minimizing systemwide costs and satisfying the service levels required by the customers. Many marketing students initially overlook the importance of marketing channel management because a lot of these activities are behind the scenes. But without a strong and efficient marketing channel system, merchandise isn't available when customers want it. Then customers are disappointed, and sales and profits suffer.

In the frozen desserts domain, for example, marketing channel considerations have pushed a growing number of businesses to adopt multiple convenient locations and self-service delivery systems. Rather than requiring a large, free-standing store, TCBY or Yogurtini have set up smaller kiosk-type storefronts. In these more conveniently located places (which also require fewer staff and therefore reduce costs for the company), consumers get to choose exactly what to put on their desserts. As a consequence, the company does not have to determine the right

> **goods** Items that can be physically touched.
>
> **services** Any intangible offering that involves a deed, performance, or effort that cannot be physically possessed; intangible customer benefits that are produced by people or machines and cannot be separated from the producer.
>
> **ideas** Intellectual concepts—thoughts, opinions, and philosophies.

> ## Price is everything the buyer gives up—money, time, energy—in exchange for the product.

service depends on how far in advance you book the ticket, the time of year, and whether you want to fly coach or business class. If you value the convenience of buying your ticket at the last minute for a ski trip between Christmas and New Year's Day and you want to fly business class, you can expect to pay four or five times as much as you would for the cheapest available ticket. That is, you have traded off a lower price for convenience. For marketers, the key to determining prices is figuring out how much customers are willing to pay so that they are satisfied with the purchase and the seller achieves a reasonable profit.

Place: Delivering the Value Proposition

The third P, place, represents all the activities necessary to get the product to the right customer when that customer wants it.

Place more commonly deals specifically with retailing and marketing channel management. *Marketing channel management,* also known as *supply chain management,* is the set of approaches and techniques that firms employ to efficiently and effectively integrate their suppliers, manufacturers, warehouses, stores, and other firms involved in the transaction (e.g., transportation companies) into a seamless value chain in which merchandise is produced and distributed in the right quantities, to the right locations, and at the right time while

Dishing It Out
Do-it-yourself is a hot idea in the frozen-yogurt business. Here's a look at what customers bring to the counter at self-serve chain Yogurtini

Average ounces in an order 14

Average check size $5.46

CHECK-OUT

Top three flavors classic vanila, birthday-cake batter and signature blueberry tartini

Most popular toppings strawberries and M&Ms

amounts or variations to offer; the customer makes that decision.[16]

Promotion: Communicating the Value Proposition Even the best products and services will go unsold if marketers cannot communicate their value to customers. Promotion is communication by a marketer that informs, persuades, and reminds potential buyers about a product or service to influence their opinions and elicit a response. Promotion generally can enhance a product's or service's value, as is the case with Halle Berry's perfume, Closer. It is formulated to provoke attraction between the opposite sexes. Social & Mobile Marketing 1.1 considers how Facebook communicates its value by encouraging networks of users and businesses beyond its site.

Halle Berry is using proactive appeals in her fragrance promotions.

Marketing Can Be Performed by Both Individuals and Organizations

Imagine how complicated the world would be if you had to buy everything you consumed directly from producers or manufacturers. You would have to go from farm to farm buying your food and then from manufacturer to manufacturer to purchase the table, plates, and utensils you needed to eat that food. Fortunately, marketing intermediaries, such as retailers, accumulate merchandise from producers in large amounts and then sell it to you in smaller amounts. The process by which businesses sell to consumers is known as **B2C (business-to-consumer)** marketing, whereas the process of selling merchandise or services from one business to another is called **B2B (business-to-business)** marketing. With the advent of various Internet auction sites (e.g., eBay) and social media, consumers have started marketing their products and services to other consumers. This third category, in which consumers

sell to other consumers, is **C2C** marketing. These marketing transactions are illustrated in Exhibit 1.4.

Individuals can also undertake activities to market themselves. When you apply for a job, for instance, the research you do about the firm, the résumé and cover letter you submit with your application, and the way you dress for an interview and conduct yourself during it are all forms of marketing activities. Accountants, lawyers, financial planners, physicians, and other professional service providers also constantly market their services one way or another.

Marketing Affects Various Stakeholders

Most people think of marketing as a way to facilitate the sale of products or services to customers or clients. But marketing can also affect several other stakeholders (e.g., supply chain

▼ **EXHIBIT 1.4** Marketing Can Be Performed by Both Individuals and Organizations partners, society at large). Partners in the supply chain include wholesalers, retailers, or other intermediaries such as transportation or warehousing companies. All of these entities are involved in marketing to one another. Manufacturers sell merchandise to retailers, but the retailers often have to convince manufacturers to sell to them. After many years of not carrying Ralph Lauren products, JCPenney has co-introduced a line of clothing and home furnishings called American Living, sold exclusively at JCPenney, that does not bear the Ralph Lauren name.

Marketing also can aim to benefit an entire industry or society at large. The dairy industry has used a very successful, award-winning campaign with its slogan, "Got Milk," aimed at different target segments. This campaign has not only created high levels of awareness about the benefits of drinking milk but also increased milk consumption in various target segments, perhaps in response to the use of various celebrities, from David Beckham and Ray Rice to Hayden Panettiere and Demi Lovato. This campaign benefits the entire dairy industry and promotes the health benefits of drinking milk to society at large.

B2C (business-to-consumers) The process in which businesses sell to consumers.

B2B (business-to-business) The process of selling merchandise or services from one business to another.

C2C (consumer-to-consumer) The process in which consumers sell to other consumers.

Social & Mobile Marketing 1.1
Facebook Networks the Web[17]

Facebook would prefer it if you checked your account daily (or even hourly). Its nearly 1 billion users, more than half of whom do log in daily, spend an average of 55 minutes per day on the site. It is the second most frequently visited site in the United States. Facebook also is expanding the network in which it operates by making it easier for users to share information outside of Facebook.

Social plug-ins are those Like buttons you see on a business's website that encourage a social experience outside of Facebook. Social plug-ins make it easier for the user to share content from other websites with friends with a single click; if users like the content, whether an article, a restaurant, or a band, this preference is shared automatically on their Facebook newsfeed. Friends in turn can link easily to the liked site, such that the system benefits both the external company and Facebook—and users. Companies thus place Like buttons on their web pages to drive more traffic to Facebook and then enjoy more return traffic from Facebook to their own web pages.

Around 2.5 million websites contain Like buttons, but 10,000 more are added every day. And users like the Like button too. Only 13 percent of users ever write reviews on websites, but a much higher percentage of people are willing to click Like. It is easy, and it gives Facebook users a simple way to communicate with friends and possibly extend their social influence.

Businesses can use Facebook users' information to target potential customers. In addition, Yelp can use your preferences to give you personalized information on restaurants or music venues because Yelp can access songs that you "like" on Pandora, and also the restaurants that you "like" on Yelp.com. Even IMBD, the comprehensive site for movie lovers, is getting in on the game, gathering Facebook users' favorite movies and television shows. By getting to know all those 1 billion users, Facebook offers incredibly relevant and increasingly useful information to advertisers—which is why its annual advertising revenues of more than $1 billion continue to grow.

Chili's can use the "Likes" of its Facebook page to get information on its customers.

The dairy industry's "Got Milk" ad campaign has created high levels of awareness about the benefits of drinking milk and has increased milk consumption by using celebrities such as soccer star David Beckham and singer/songwriter/actress Demi Lovato.

Marketing Helps Create Value

Marketing didn't get to its current prominence among individuals, corporations, and society at large overnight. To understand how marketing has evolved into its present-day, integral business function of creating value, let's look for a moment at some of the milestones in marketing's short history (see Exhibit 1.5).

Production-Oriented Era Around the turn of the twentieth century, most firms were production oriented and believed that a good product would sell itself. Henry Ford, the founder

of Ford Motor Co., once famously remarked, "Customers can have any color they want so long as it's black." Manufacturers were concerned with product innovation, not with satisfying the needs of individual consumers, and retail stores typically were considered places to hold the merchandise until a consumer wanted it.

Sales-Oriented Era Between 1920 and 1950, production and distribution techniques became more sophisticated, and the Great Depression and World War II conditioned

▼ **EXHIBIT 1.5** Marketing Evolution: Production, Sales, Marketing, and Value

Turn of the century — 1920 — 1950 — 1990

Production | Sales | Marketing | Value-based marketing

customers to consume less or manufacture items themselves, so they planted victory gardens instead of buying produce. As a result, manufacturers had the capacity to produce more than customers really wanted or were able to buy. Firms found an answer to their overproduction in becoming sales oriented; they depended on heavy doses of personal selling and advertising.

Market-Oriented Era After World War II, soldiers returned home, got new jobs, and started families. At the same time, manufacturers turned from focusing on the war effort toward making consumer products. Suburban communities, featuring cars in every garage, sprouted up around the country, and the new suburban fixture, the shopping center, began to replace cities' central business districts as the hub of retail activity and a place to just hang out. Some products, once in limited supply because of World War II, became plentiful. And the United States entered a buyers' market—the customer became king! When consumers again had choices, they were able to make purchasing decisions on the basis of factors such as quality, convenience, and price. Manufacturers and retailers thus began to focus on what consumers wanted and needed

> *Around the turn of the twentieth century, most firms were production oriented and believed that a good product would sell itself.*

before they designed, made, or attempted to sell their products and services. It was during this period that firms discovered marketing.

Value-Based Marketing Era Most successful firms today are market oriented.[18] That means they generally have transcended a production or selling orientation and attempt to discover and satisfy their customers' needs and wants. Before the turn of the twenty-first century, better marketing firms recognized that there was more to good marketing than simply discovering and providing what consumers wanted and needed; to compete successfully, they would have to give their customers greater value than their competitors did. (The importance of value is appropriately incorporated into the AMA definition of marketing discussed earlier.)

Value reflects the relationship of benefits to costs, or what you *get* for what you *give*.[19] In a marketing context, customers seek a fair return in goods and/or services for their hard-earned money and scarce time. They want products or services that meet their specific needs or wants *and* that are offered at a price that they believe is a good value. A creative way to provide value to customers is to engage in **value cocreation**.[20] In this case, customers can act as collaborators to create the product or service. When clients work with their investment advisors, they cocreate their investment portfolios; when Nike allows customers to custom design their sneakers, they are cocreating. Adding Value 1.1 examines how companies are adding value to smartphones by developing smart accessories.

In the next section, we explore the notion of value-based marketing further. Specifically, we look at various options for attracting customers by providing them with better value than the competition does. Then we discuss how firms compete on the basis of value. Finally, we examine how firms transform the value concept into their value-driven activities.

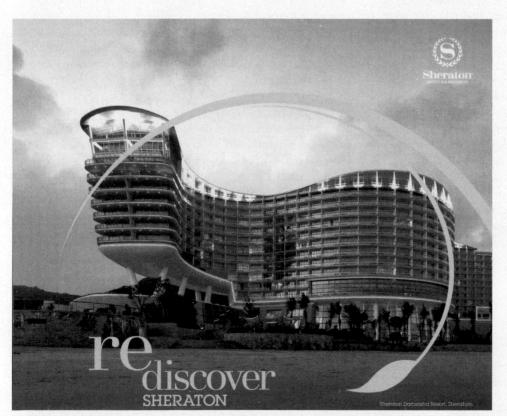

re*discover*
SHERATON

Sheraton Dameisha Resort, Shenzhen

In deciding whether to stay at a Sheraton, potential customers trade off the benefits they will receive with the money it will cost them.

Adding Value   1.1

Smartphones? Try Smart Glasses, Smart Monitors, Smart...

It might be hard to imagine, but just a few short years ago, the idea of being able to talk to someone while away from home was a massive added value. Then the value added became being able check e-mail on a phone. Such offerings seem incredibly basic today, though. Obviously, the smart market is a dynamic and rapidly changing one in which the definition of what constitutes value also changes constantly.

Some of the most modern smart gadgets seek to make it easier for people to engage in their day-to-day activities. An app by Mercedes-Benz allows car owners to unlock their doors or open the trunk with their phones. Alternatively, an external device, Hone, attaches to keychains and allows smartphone users to activate a visual and audio signal so that they can find their car keys wherever they left them (e.g., in the freezer, tucked in a drawer) the last time they came home with arms full of groceries and dropped that keychain somewhere mysterious.[21]

For exercise fans, the Nike+ FuelBand calculates steps taken, calories burned, and time spent exercising, then syncs the information gathered from the wrist band with a mobile app that combines all the information in one place. The UP band, by Jawbone, tracks all this information as well as sleep times and food intake.[22] Thus, it can tell users how long they took to fall asleep and how many hours of deep sleep they actually got. Then it promises to summarize this information in Insights, which suggest recommendations based on individual trends. If a person sleeps poorly after snacking late in the day, UP will recommend no more eating after 8:00 p.m., for example. For even more adventurous exercisers, the Crash Sensor, a device made to mount onto a bicycle helmet, alerts emergency contacts if a crash occurs and provides coordinates so that emergency crews can find a hiker lost in the wilderness.[23]

Other smart tools are a little more forward thinking, moving us into a future world in which connecting to anyone anywhere doesn't even require our thumbs. Perhaps the most widely talked about version is Google Glass, the technology that puts the web in the corner

Smartphones and related connected devices/apps, such as Google Glass, are revolutionizing the marketplace.

of users' vision and allows them to connect, using just eye movement. This revolutionary innovation appears likely to change virtually everything (pun intended). However, its rollout has been slow thus far, and the company has sought to avoid just moving smartphone apps to Glass. Google thus has created guidelines for developing Glassware: keep the information concise, keep alerts relevant, make tasks easy, and make information provision timely.[24]

Nearly as ubiquitous as the chatter about the device are the concerns about it. Critics have questioned how Google Glass might alter social interactions, cause accidents by people focused on the web rather than where they are walking, and even rewire our cognitive capacities.[25] The promise of Google Glass is so intriguing, though, that consumers are lining up to pay around $1,500 for the potential to mess with their brain matter.

---

 check yourself

1. What is the definition of marketing?
2. Marketing is about satisfying _____ and _____.
3. What are the four components of the marketing mix?
4. Who can perform marketing?
5. What are the various eras of marketing?

LO 1-2   Describe how marketers create value for a product or service.

How Do Marketing Firms Become More Value Driven?

Firms become value driven by focusing on four activities. First, they share information about their customers and competitors across their own organization and even with other firms, such as the manufacturers and transportation companies that help them get their product or service to the marketplace. Second, they strive to balance their customers' benefits and costs. Third, they concentrate on building relationships with customers. Fourth, they take advantage of new technologies and connect with their customers by using social and mobile media.

Sharing Information

In a value-based, marketing-oriented firm, marketers share information about customers and competitors (see Chapter 9, Marketing Research) and integrate it across the firm's various departments. The fashion designers for J.Crew, for instance, collect purchase information and research customer trends to determine what their customers will want to wear in the next few weeks; simultaneously, the logisticians—those persons in charge of getting the merchandise to the stores—use the same purchase history to forecast sales and allocate appropriate merchandise to individual stores. Sharing

relational orientation A method of building a relationship with customers based on the philosophy that buyers and sellers should develop a long-term relationship.

customer relationship management (CRM) A business philosophy and set of strategies, programs, and systems that focus on identifying and building loyalty among the firm's most valued customers.

Balancing Benefits with Costs

Value-oriented marketers constantly measure the benefits that customers perceive against the cost of their offerings. They use available customer data to find opportunities to satisfy their customers' needs better, keep costs down, and develop long-term loyalties. For example, IKEA does not have highly paid salespeople to sell its furniture, but its simple designs mean customers can easily choose a product and assemble it themselves.

> ## Sharing and coordinating information represents a critical success factor for any firm.

and coordinating such information represents a critical success factor for any firm. Imagine what might happen if J.Crew's advertising department were to plan a special promotion but not share its sales projections with those people in charge of creating the merchandise or getting it to stores.

Building Relationships with Customers

During the past couple of decades, marketers have begun to develop a **relational orientation** as they have realized that they need to think about their customers in terms of relationships rather than transactions.[26] To build relationships, firms focus on the lifetime profitability of the relationship, not how much money is made during each transaction. Thus, Apple makes its innovations compatible with existing products to encourage consumers to maintain a long-term relationship with the company across all their electronic needs.

This relationship approach uses a process known as **customer relationship management (CRM)**, a business

Collecting and sharing information among departments at J.Crew is important for its success.

Furniture retailer IKEA focuses on what its customers value—low prices and great design.

Apple makes its new products compatible with existing ones to maintain a long-term relationship with its customers.

philosophy and set of strategies, programs, and systems that focus on identifying and building loyalty among the firm's most valued customers.[27] Firms that employ CRM systematically collect information about their customers' needs and then use that information to target their best customers with the products, services, and special promotions that appear most important to them.

Connecting with Customers by Using Social and Mobile Media

Marketers are steadily embracing new technologies, such as social and mobile media, to allow them to connect better with their customers and thereby serve their needs more effectively. Businesses take social and mobile media seriously, including these advanced tools in the development of their marketing strategies. Approximately three-quarters of U.S. companies now use social media tools for marketing purposes, and 46 percent of Internet users worldwide interact with social media on a daily basis.[28] The explosive growth of mobile phones in India and China means that more than 77 percent of the world's population subscribes to mobile services.[29]

Yet even with this astounding penetration, only

Marketers connect with customers by using social and mobile media.

10 percent of the world's population uses Facebook—which means 90 percent still has not signed up. The United States and United Kingdom may be approaching saturation, but there is still huge growth potential for social networks. Before users can sign up for Facebook, though, they need access to high-speed Internet.[30] Other countries continue to experience higher Facebook growth rates as they gain greater Internet access and as Facebook becomes available in more languages (around 70 currently). Brazil and Russia have only about 40 percent Internet penetration, and only 33 percent of Chinese people and less than 7 percent of consumers in India have access to the Internet.[31]

Beyond social media sites, online travel agencies such as Expedia, Travelocity, Orbitz, Priceline, and Kayak have become the first place that users go to book travel arrangements; 46 percent of online hotel bookings take place through one of these portals.[32] Customers who book hotels using travel agencies become loyal to the agency that gives them the lowest prices, rather than to any particular hotel brand. So hotels are using social media and mobile applications to lure customers back to their specific brands by engaging in conversations with them on Facebook and allowing fans of the page to book their hotel reservations through Facebook. Some hotel chains have mobile applications that allow customers to make changes to their reservations, shift check-in and check-out times, and add amenities or services to their stays. The hotels know a lot about their customers because they collect information about their previous visits, including the type of room they stayed in, their preferences (from pillows to drinks consumed from the minibar), and the type of room service they prefer.

Several restaurant chains are exploiting location-based social media applications such as Foursquare, Scvngr, Yelp, Google Maps, and Loopt. These customers tend to be more loyal and can help spread the word to others about the restaurant.[33] By using location-based applications on mobile phones, restaurants connect with their customers immediately; customers using these apps visit restaurants nearly twice as often as those who don't. The result is that users are driving the way brands and stores are interacting with social media.

Buffalo Wild Wings suggests that its diners check in to its locations by using their phones. The target customers for this chain are young and tech savvy, and with its in-house games and sports broadcasts, Buffalo Wild Wings is uniquely situated to encourage customers to connect and bring their friends along. It offers contests and encourages frequent visits to win. Customers can earn free chicken wings or soft drinks within their first three visits. Other contests encourage patrons to upload photos of the crowd's reaction to a big play. Moreover, customers can develop their own challenges from their bar stools. Approximately 10,000 people participated in 33,000 challenges, and 5000 rewards were given out in the first week of Buffalo Wild Wings' contests by using location-based applications.[34]

Now that we've examined what marketing is and how it creates value, let's consider how it fits into the world of commerce as well as into society in general.

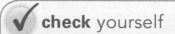

check yourself

1. Does providing a good value mean selling at a low price?

2. What are the benefits of long-term relationships with customers?

3. How are marketers connecting with customers using social and mobile media?

LO 1-3 Understand why marketing is important, both within and outside the firm.

SOCIAL MEDIA STATS & FACTS OF 2013

TWO FACTORS DRIVING SOCIAL MEDIA IN 2013

Mobile – with the number of people accessing the internet via a mobile phone increasing by 60.3% to 818.4 million in the last 2 years.

60.3%

Older Users Adoption – On Twitter the ages 55-64 are the fastest growing, with 79% growth rate since 2012. On G+ and Facebook ages 45-54 are the fastest growing, with 46% and 56% growth rate.

79%

f FACEBOOK

Facebook **continues to grow** and make money via ads and mobile users. The latest facts and figures from its earnings call for the first quarter of 2013.

1 BILLION

Daily active users **665M**

Monthly mobile users **751M**

Monthly active users **1.1B**

% Mobile Ad Revenue

23%

30%

Mobile ads (2012)

Mobile ads (2013 Q1)

🐦 TWITTER

Twitter is the **fastest** growing social network in the world by active users. Twitter's fastest growing age demographic **is 55 to 64 year olds,** registering an increase in active users of 79%.

Monthly active users **288M**

44% Growth from June 2012 - March 2013

21% Twitter has 288 million monthly active users. That means that 21% of the world's internet population are using Twitter every month.

TWEET!

📺 YOUTUBE

YouTube reaches more U.S. adults ages 18-34 **than any cable network.** Hours of video watched **DOUBLED** from last May when only 3B hrs were watched.

Unique monthly visiters **1B**

Hours of video watched a month **6B**

Social media is growing by leaps and bounds.

WHY IS MARKETING IMPORTANT?

Marketing once was only an afterthought to production. Early marketing philosophy went something like this: "We've made it; now how do we get rid of it?" However, marketing not only has shifted its focus dramatically, it also has evolved into a major business function that crosses all areas of a firm or organization, as illustrated in Exhibit 1.6. Marketing advises production about how much of the company's product to make and then tells logistics when to ship it. It creates long-lasting, mutually valuable relationships between the company and the firms from which it buys.[35] It identifies those elements that local customers value and makes it possible for the firm to expand globally. Marketing has had a significant impact on consumers as well. Without marketing, it would be difficult for any of us to learn about new products and services. Understanding marketing can even help you find a job after you finish school.

Marketing Expands Firms' Global Presence

A generation ago, Coca-Cola was available in many nations, but Levi's and most other U.S. brands weren't. Blue jeans were primarily an American product—made in the United States for the U.S. market. But today most jeans, including those of Levi Strauss & Co., are made in places other than the United

supply chain
The group of firms that make and deliver a given set of goods and services.

marketing channel
The set of institutions that transfer the ownership of and move goods from the point of production to the point of consumption; consists of all the institutions and marketing activities in the marketing process.

entrepreneurs
A person who organizes, operates, and assumes the risk of a new business venture.

▼ **EXHIBIT 1.6** Importance of Marketing

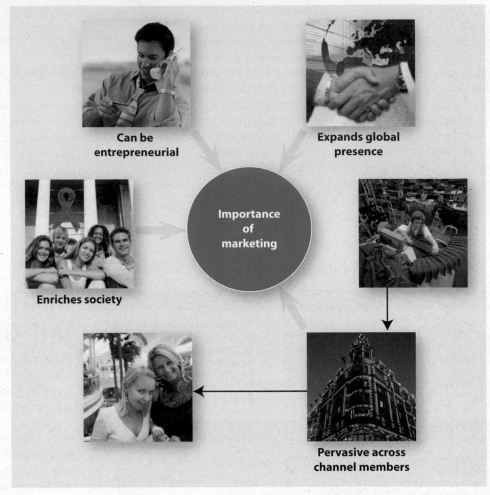

Can be entrepreneurial

Expands global presence

Enriches society

Importance of marketing

Pervasive across channel members

States and are available nearly everywhere. Thanks to MTV and other global entertainment venues, cheap foreign travel, and the Internet, you share many of your consumption behaviors with college students in countries all over the globe. The best fashions, music, and even food trends disseminate rapidly around the world. Take a look at your next shopping bag. Whatever it contains, you will find goods from many countries—produce from Mexico, jeans from Japan, electronics from Korea. Global manufacturers and retailers continue to make inroads into the U.S. market. The Dutch grocery store giant Ahold is among the top five grocery store chains in the United States, although you may never have heard of it because it operates under names such as Stop & Shop, GIANT, and Peapod in the United States.[36] As marketing helps expand firms' global presence, it also enhances global career opportunities for marketing professionals.

Marketing Is Pervasive across Marketing Channel Members

Firms do not work in isolation. Manufacturers buy raw materials and components from suppliers, which they sell to wholesalers, retailers, or other businesses after they have turned the materials into products (see Exhibit 1.7). Every time materials or products are bought or sold, they are transported to a different location, which sometimes requires that they be stored in a warehouse operated by yet another organization. Such a group of firms that make and deliver a given set of goods and services is known as a **supply chain** or a **marketing channel**. All the various channel members (e.g., suppliers, manufacturers, wholesalers, and retailers) of the supply chain are firms that are likely to provide career opportunities to marketing professionals.

Effectively managing supply chain relationships often has a marked impact on a firm's ability to satisfy the consumer, which results in increased profitability for all parties. Consider Levi Strauss & Co. and its close relationship with its major retailers. Not too many years ago, only about 40 percent of orders from the jeans manufacturer to its retailers arrived on time, which made it very difficult for retailers to keep all sizes in stock and therefore keep customers, who are generally not satisfied with anything less than the correct size, happy. Today, Levi's uses an automatic inventory replenishment system through which it manages the retailers' inventory itself. When a

> ## SOCIALLY RESPONSIBLE FIRMS RECOGNIZE THAT INCLUDING A STRONG SOCIAL ORIENTATION IN BUSINESS IS A SOUND STRATEGY THAT IS IN BOTH ITS OWN AND ITS CUSTOMERS' BEST INTEREST.

▼ **EXHIBIT 1.7** Supply Chain

| Raw material | Manufacturer | Retailer | Consumer |

customer buys a pair of jeans, the information is transferred directly from the retailer to Levi's, which then determines which items the retailer needs to reorder and automatically ships the merchandise. The relationship benefits all parties: Retailers don't have to worry about keeping their stores stocked in jeans and save money because they don't have to invest as much money in inventory. Because Levi's has control of the jeans inventory, it can be assured that it won't lose sales because its retailers have let their inventory run down. Finally, customers benefit by having the merchandise when they want it—a good value.

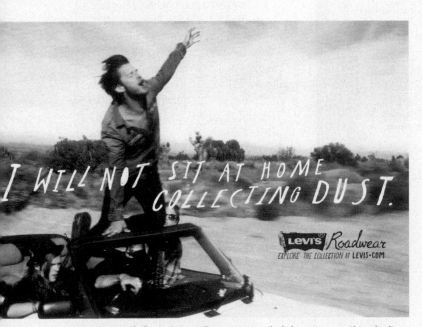

Levi Strauss & Co. helps retailers manage their inventory so they don't run out of stock.

Marketing Enriches Society

Should marketing focus on factors other than financial profitability—such as good corporate citizenry? Many of America's best-known corporations seem to think so because they have undertaken various marketing activities in this direction, such as developing greener products, making healthier food options and safer products, and improving their supply chains to reduce their carbon footprint. At a more macro level, firms are making socially responsible activities an integral component of everything they do.

Socially responsible firms recognize that including a strong social orientation in business is a sound strategy that is in both its own and its customers' best interest. It shows the consumer marketplace that the firm will be around for the long run and can be trusted with the marketplace's business. In a volatile market, investors view firms that operate with high levels of corporate responsibility and ethics as safe investments. Similarly, firms have come to realize that good corporate citizenship through socially responsible actions should be a priority because it will help their bottom line in the long run.[37] In a world in which consumers constantly hear about negative examples of ethics, the need for companies to live up to their ethical promises becomes even more important; Ethical & Societal Dilemma 1.1 outlines the challenges companies face when they attempt to go green.

Marketing Can Be Entrepreneurial

Whereas marketing plays a major role in the success of large corporations, it also is at the center of the successes of numerous new ventures initiated by **entrepreneurs**, or people who organize, operate, and assume the risk of a business venture.[38] Key to the success of many such entrepreneurs is that they launch ventures that aim to satisfy unfilled needs. Some examples of

Going Green

The Ben & Jerry's ice cream brand was built on more than fabulous flavors. With every double scoop of Chunky Monkey, owners Ben Cohen and Jerry Greenfield were also inviting customers to help make the world better. They donated 7.5 percent of profits to charity, paid employees a living wage and good benefits, and bought their Brazil nuts from a cooperative of indigenous Amazon farmers.[39] Combining a delicious ice cream with this socially responsible focus on the triple bottom line of profits, people, and planet appealed to consumers and investors alike.

It also drew suitors. In 2000, the corporate giant Unilever purchased Ben & Jerry's at a purchase price that Cohen and Greenfield could not reject. Doing so would have deprived their shareholders of a fair profit. Facing questions about whether the ice cream company's social responsibility mission would survive, Unilever took steps to preserve some of the promises and features of the original brand. Although it was forced to drop the "all-natural" label from packaging and began using processed ingredients, like partially hydrogenated soybean oil, it has attempted to shift its procurement practices to fair-trade sources. Charitable donations from its foundation total $1.8 million annually. These activities continue because the corporation views them as good business practices. But Unilever has set forth no permanent commitment to broad social responsibility goals.

Corporations that want to factor social responsibility explicitly into their bottom-line calculations also can undergo a certification process to become a B Corp, or benefit corporation.[40] The standards for this classification include bylaws that require a business to consider the impact of its actions on its workforce, the community, and the environment. Procter & Gamble (P&G) has staked its claim and commitment to

Going green is certainly in.

environmental sustainability and social responsibility by retooling its business practices—without donning an outside seal of approval. Other companies use the Green Seal® stamp to certify that their manufacturing processes meet environmental standards. Procter & Gamble's Professional Green Guarantee instead is a company-specific promise that all its products, packaging, and operations are environmentally and humanly safe.[41]

In a recent sustainability overview, P&G stated that its goal was "to touch and improve lives, now and for generations to come."[42] It has enlisted both suppliers and social responsibility experts in pursuit of those goals. Its first annual Supplier Environmental Scorecard rated the 310 suppliers that agreed to participate, according to their emissions and resource consumption.[43] Thus far, P&G's self-set goals appear within reach: It has reduced its nonrenewable energy consumption by 16 percent, cut landfill-bound waste by 57 percent, decreased carbon emissions by 12 percent, and lowered water consumption by 22 percent.

Consider, for example, P&G's new renewable packaging for Pantene Nature Fusion. By switching to bottles made of plant-based plastic, the production of the shampoo involves 70 percent less greenhouse gas emissions. Made of sugar cane, this next-generation packaging also sucks CO_2 out of landfilled or recycled plastic, yielding an overall carbon emission reduction of 170 percent for this product.[44] Who wouldn't want to participate in such positive changes for the planet? Each consumer who buys Pantene, with its upbeat matrix of green and blue leaves on the white plastic bottle, gains the promise of being part of the solution.

Since these firms recognize the benefit of becoming more socially responsible, and their activities resonate with their customers, why don't all firms make enriching society a core value and major activity?

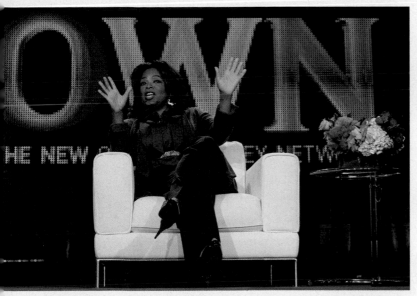

When you think of Oprah Winfrey, think big: Harpo Productions, Inc.; O, The Oprah Magazine; O at Home magazine; Harpo Films; the OWN television network; not to mention her philanthropic work with the Oprah Winfrey Foundation.

opportunity (i.e., the unfilled need), conduct a thorough examination of the marketplace, and develop and communicate the value of their product and services to potential consumers.

✓ **check** yourself

1. List five functions that illustrate the importance of marketing.
2. A firm doing the right thing emphasizes the importance of marketing to _____.

successful ventures (and their founders) that understood their customers and added value include

· Ben & Jerry's (Ben Cohen and Jerry Greenfield)

· Hayley Barna and Katia Beauchamp (Birchbox)

· Amazon (Jeff Bezos)

· Netflix (Reed Hastings)

· OWN (Oprah Winfrey)

An extraordinary entrepreneur and marketer, Oprah Winfrey was a self-made billionaire before she turned 50 years of age. Winfrey went from being the youngest person and first African-American woman to anchor news at WTVF-TV in Nashville, Tennessee, to being only the third woman in history to head her own production studio. Under the Oprah banner are a variety of successful endeavors, including Harpo Films, Oprah's Book Club, Oprah.com, the Oxygen television network, and OWN (the Oprah Winfrey Network). In addition to producing two of the highest-rated talk shows ever on television, *The Oprah Winfrey Show* and *Dr. Phil*, Harpo Studios has produced films such as *Beloved*. Oprah's philanthropic contributions are vast and varied. Through the Oprah Winfrey Foundation and Oprah's Angel Network, people worldwide have raised more than $80 million for scholarships, schools, women's shelters, and youth centers.[45] Although her signature televised talk show has ended, her influence persists.

Great and distinguished entrepreneurs have visions of how certain combinations of products and services can satisfy unfilled needs. They find and understand a marketing

check it out!

mhhe.com/GrewalM4e
for study materials, including quizzes and videos.

two

developing marketing strategies and a marketing plan

In athletic competitions, the goal is clear: Win! For companies that design, produce, and sell athletic equipment to help runners, players, and competitors achieve their best performance, the idea of victory is similar. However, the competition that takes place between companies aiming to appeal most to their valuable customers—whoever they are—is a little more complicated than who crosses a finish line first.

When it comes to Nike and adidas, for example, the competitive contest spans a wealth of product lines, target markets, and marketing approaches. Thus, the firms must carefully and precisely determine the marketing strategies and plans that they use to appeal to customers and ensure their survival and success.

LEARNING OBJECTIVES

After reading this chapter, you should be able to:

LO 2-1   Define a marketing strategy.

LO 2-2   Describe the elements of a marketing plan.

LO 2-3   Analyze a marketing situation using SWOT analysis.

LO 2-4   Describe how a firm chooses which consumer group(s) to pursue with its marketing efforts.

LO 2-5   Outline the implementation of the marketing mix as a means to increase customer value.

LO 2-6   Summarize portfolio analysis and its use to evaluate marketing performance.

LO 2-7   Describe how firms grow their business.

Created by runners in Oregon, Nike began in the early 1970s as an American company, focused mainly on the American market.[1] Its first running

continued on p. 24

adidas spokesperson and NBA star Dwight Howard at an Adidas Crazy Light Challenge event in Tokyo, Japan.

continued from p. 23

shoes featured a then-innovative design with a waffle-patterned sole. The customers were mainly elite runners, determined to find the lightest shoe they could. But as *Forrest Gump* recounted, running also was gaining popularity among casual athletes, and just like Forrest, many members of this community sported Nikes on their feet.

By 1984, the company had gone public, and it had found Michael Jordan. Thus the entire market—and the very concept of sponsorship—changed forever. The Air Jordan line of basketball shoes turned Nike into a massive success, with broad appeal to sports fans of virtually all ages and profiles. Nike continues to affiliate with high-profile, elite basketball players, including 48 NBA All-Stars such as Dwayne Wade, Kobe Bryant, and LeBron James.[2]

Basketball shoes may be the most well-known site for the brand's famous swoosh logo, but Nike also has branched into other related sectors. For example, it owns Cole-Haan, which makes dress and casual street shoes.[3] It produces other components of athletic uniforms for both professionals (e.g., team jerseys) and casual buyers (e.g., tracksuits, gym bags). It also purchased Umbro, another sports brand that has appealed mainly to soccer enthusiasts in the past.

This purchase of Umbro suggests that Nike is taking on its main competitor, adidas, directly in a market that previously had been dominated by adidas. As a European company, started in Germany in the early twentieth century, adidas began by designing mainly soccer (or in Europe, football) shoes as well as some track and field footwear.

Today it has spread into other sports, though its focus on international sponsorships of the Olympic Games and the World Cup continues to reflect its origins. Yet it also seems determined to challenge Nike's dominance on the basketball court. With young stars such as Derrick Rose and Dwight Howard as spokespeople, adidas has initiated an advertising offensive, mocking Nike's shoes as heavier, less technologically advanced, and bland.[4] It also purchased a third competitor in the market, Reebok, in 2005, in a clear effort to gain U.S. market share.

Although their primary markets continue to differ, Nike and adidas are involved in a turf war in more and more segments. Faced with the resulting challenges, they have struggled to enhance their reputations for innovation while also keeping their costs low. For example, Nike introduced its iPod-focused partnership with Apple. With the Nike+ sensor inserted in their shoes, runners can program their iPods to play a collection of songs that matches their distance or time goals.[5] The sensor also keeps track of their speed and distance, and Nike saves the data and provides platforms for social interactions among runners in the same area. Not to be outdone, adidas has moved to introduce the micro-A smart shoe, whose sensors determine the athlete's performance, together with the environmental conditions, then adjust the cushioning and airflow in the shoe to match the conditions.

To produce these high-tech versions of their footwear, both companies outsource production to countries other than their home base.[6] Nike suffered a major public relations scandal in the 1990s when activists uncovered human rights abuses in some Nike factories. Since then, it has worked actively to improve its reputation, led the way in mandating regulations for overseas

continued from p. 24

factories, and donated heavily to philanthropic causes. Although its move to international production is more recent, adidas regards its presence in less developed areas as an inroad to consumers in these markets; its sponsorship of the Beijing Olympics also represented its strong push for dominance in China.

Nike maintains a strong lead in this race: It commands approximately 33 percent of the worldwide market, whereas adidas owns only 22 percent.[7] A count in recent Olympic track and field trials showed that Nike was sponsoring nearly 60 percent of the U.S. athletes present, whereas adidas shoes appeared on less than 13 percent of these elite feet.[8] But this competition is less a 100-yard dash than a super-marathon. When it comes to their race for market share, Nike and adidas have miles to go, and a strong competitor is always in their sights. ■

marketing strategy
A firm's target market, marketing mix, and method of obtaining a sustainable competitive advantage.

sustainable competitive advantage Something the firm can persistently do better than its competitors.

> [A competitive advantage acts like a wall that the firm has built around its position in a market.]

In this chapter, we start by discussing a *marketing strategy*, which outlines the specific actions a firm intends to implement to appeal to potential customers. Then we discuss how to do a *marketing plan*, which provides a blueprint for implementing the marketing strategy. The chapter concludes with a discussion of strategies firms use to grow.

LO 2-1 Define a marketing strategy.

WHAT IS A MARKETING STRATEGY?

A **marketing strategy** identifies (1) a firm's target market(s), (2) a related marketing mix—its four Ps—and (3) the bases on which the firm plans to build a sustainable competitive advantage. A **sustainable competitive advantage** is an advantage over the competition that is not easily copied and thus can be maintained over a long period of time. A competitive advantage acts like a wall that the firm has built around its position in a market. This wall makes it hard for outside competitors to contact customers inside—otherwise known as the marketer's target market. Of course, if the marketer has built a wall around an attractive market, competitors will attempt to break down the wall. Over time, advantages will erode because of these competitive forces, but by building high, thick walls, marketers can sustain their advantage, minimize competitive pressure, and boost profits for a longer time. Thus, establishing a sustainable competitive advantage is key to long-term financial performance.

For Nike, its thickest wall is from its strong brand, based on years of technological breakthroughs, which has created a loyal customer base. These customers know the Nike swoosh well and consider the brand as a first option when they need running, basketball, or even just casual athletic shoes. This appeal reflects Nike's careful targeting and marketing mix implementation. In terms of the four Ps, Nike is constantly trying to come up with new versions of its relatively basic product, namely, shoes and related apparel. To sell these varied products, it relies on multiple channels: online, in dedicated Nike stores and superstores, and through independent retailers such as FootLocker. Its pricing spans a broad range, from lower end, simpler options for casual shoes to the most expensive, technically sophisticated, highly reputed lines associated with big name athletes. And these popular athletes are central to its promotion efforts. Thus it remains dominant in most athletic fields, and it feels confident about expanding further.

There are four macro, or overarching, strategies that focus on aspects of the marketing mix to create and deliver value and develop sustainable competitive advantages, as we depict in Exhibit 2.1:[9]

- **Customer excellence:** Focuses on retaining loyal customers and excellent customer service.

- **Operational excellence:** Achieved through efficient operations and excellent supply chain and human resource management.

- **Product excellence:** Having products with high perceived value and effective branding and positioning.

- **Locational excellence:** Having a good physical location and Internet presence.

▼ **EXHIBIT 2.1** Macro Strategies For Developing Customer Value

pairs of shoes every year for 20 years. She is not a $100 customer; combining all purchases for her family over the years, she is at least a $10,000 shoe customer—and that doesn't even count the shorts, shirts, and socks she adds on to her purchases. Viewing customers with a lifetime value perspective, rather than on a transaction-by-transaction basis, is key to modern customer retention programs.[11] We will examine how the lifetime value of a customer is calculated in Chapter 10, Appendix 10A, available online.

Marketers also use several methods to build customer loyalty. One way involves developing a clear and precise positioning strategy. With its long history in the sport, adidas is clearly positioned as a provider of soccer cleats, far more so than Nike. That positioning helps explain why Nike might have bought Umbro. But Nike also left the Umbro brand name alone so that it could continue to appeal to players of one of the fastest growing sports in the world.

Customer Excellence

Customer excellence is achieved when a firm develops value-based strategies for retaining loyal customers and provides outstanding customer service.

Retaining Loyal Customers Sometimes, the methods a firm uses to maintain a sustainable competitive advantage help attract and maintain loyal customers. For instance, having a strong brand, unique merchandise, and superior customer service all help solidify a loyal customer base. In addition, having loyal customers is, in and of itself, an important method of sustaining an advantage over competitors.

Loyalty is more than simply preferring to purchase from one firm instead of another.[10] It means that customers are reluctant to patronize competitive firms. Loyal customers buy Nike apparel for all their sporting and casual endeavors, even if adidas goes on sale or opens a new store right around the corner from their house.

More and more firms thus realize the value of achieving customer excellence through focusing their strategy on retaining loyal customers. Nike doesn't think in terms of selling a single pair of fashionable shoes for $100; instead, it focuses on satisfying the customer who buys track shoes for herself, Cole-Haan dress shoes for her spouse, soccer shoes for her daughter, and basketball shoes for her son. Conservatively, she might buy five

Another method of achieving customer loyalty creates an emotional attachment through loyalty programs. These loyalty programs, which constitute part of an overall customer relationship management (CRM) program, prevail in many industries, from airlines to hotels to movie theaters to retail stores. With such programs, firms can identify members through the loyalty card or membership information the consumer provides when he or she makes a purchase. Using that purchase information, analysts determine which types of merchandise certain groups of customers are buying and thereby tailor their offering to meet the needs of their loyal customers better. For instance, by analyzing their databases, banks develop profiles of customers who have defected in the past and use that information to identify customers who may defect in the future. Once it identifies these customers, the firm can implement special retention programs to keep them.

Customer Service Marketers also may build sustainable competitive advantage by offering excellent customer service,[12] though consistency in this area can prove difficult. Customer service is provided by employees, and invariably, humans are less consistent than machines. On every visit, for example, Starbucks must attempt to ensure that every single barista greets customers in a friendly way and makes drinks consistently. But what happens when a barista comes to work in a bad mood or

Starbucks' friendly and knowledgeable baristas form a basis for competitive advantage.

simply forgets to add nutmeg to a drink? Firms that offer good customer service must instill its importance in their employees over a long period of time so that it becomes part of the organizational culture. Although it may take considerable time and effort to build a reputation for customer service, once a marketer has earned a good service reputation, it can sustain this advantage for a long time because a competitor is hard pressed to develop a comparable reputation.

Operational Excellence

Firms achieve **operational excellence**, the second way to achieve a sustainable competitive advantage, through their efficient operations, excellent supply chain management, and strong relationships with their suppliers.

All marketers strive for efficient operations to get their customers the merchandise they want, when they want it, in the required quantities, and at a lower delivered cost than that of their competitors. By so doing, they ensure good value to their customers, earn profitability for themselves, and satisfy their customers' needs. In addition, efficient operations enable firms either to provide their consumers with lower-priced merchandise or, even if their prices are not lower than those of the competition, to use the additional margin they earn to attract customers away from competitors by offering even better service, merchandise assortments, or visual presentations.

Firms achieve efficiencies by developing sophisticated distribution and information systems as well as strong relationships with vendors. Like customer relationships, vendor relations must be developed over the long term and generally cannot be easily offset by a competitor.[13] Furthermore, firms with strong

Netflix customers can receive videos instantly via the iPad, TV, or computer.

relationships may gain exclusive rights to (1) sell merchandise in a particular region, (2) obtain special terms of purchase that are not available to competitors, or (3) receive popular merchandise that may be in short supply.

The supply chain for Netflix represented a remarkable innovation when the company first started: With its high-tech distribution centers, it got movies to most of its subscribers overnight. Its current streaming services expand offering even further, allowing subscribers to access various movies and television shows immediately through gaming devices (e.g., Wii), tablets (e.g., iPad), Internet-enabled televisions, or computers. Its supply chain thus continues to evolve and become increasingly efficient. The case study at the end of this chapter provides additional information about the methods Netflix has used to become a dominant player in the movie rental industry—as well as some of the challenges it has faced recently.

Product Excellence

Product excellence, the third way to achieve a sustainable competitive advantage, occurs by providing products with high perceived value and effective branding and positioning. Some firms have difficulty developing a competitive advantage through their merchandise and service offerings, especially if competitors can deliver similar products or services easily. However, others have been able to maintain their sustainable competitive advantage by investing in their brand itself; positioning their product or service using a clear, distinctive brand image; and constantly reinforcing that image through their merchandise, service, and promotion. For instance, *Bloomberg Businessweek*'s top global brands—such as Coca-Cola, IBM, Microsoft, Google, GE, McDonalds, Intel, Apple, Disney, and HP—are all leaders in their respective industries, at least in part because they have strong brands and a clear position in the marketplace.[14]

Locational Excellence

Location is particularly important for retailers and service providers. Many say, "The three most important things in retailing are location, location, location." For example, most people will not walk or drive very far when looking to buy a cup of coffee. A competitive advantage based on location is sustainable because it is not easily duplicated. Starbucks has developed a strong competitive advantage with its location selection. The high density of stores it has established in some markets makes it very difficult for a competitor to enter that market and find good locations. Of course, when McDonald's entered the fancy coffee drink battle, it did not need to worry too much about finding new locations; its stores already appear nearly everywhere!

Multiple Sources of Advantage

In most cases, a single strategy, such as low prices or excellent service, is not sufficient to build a sustainable competitive advantage. Firms require multiple approaches to build a wall around their position that stands as high as possible. For example, Southwest Airlines consistently has positioned itself as a carrier that provides good service at a good value—customers get to their destination on time for a reasonable price without having to pay extra for checked luggage. At the same time, its customers don't expect food service or seat assignments. But they do expect—and even more important, get—on-time flights that are reasonably priced. By developing its unique capabilities in several areas, Southwest has built a very high wall around its position as the value player in the airline industry, which has resulted in a huge cadre of loyal customers.

> "A written marketing plan provides a reference point for evaluating whether the firm has met its objectives."

check yourself

1. What are the various components of a marketing strategy?

2. List the four macro strategies that can help a firm develop a sustainable competitive advantage.

LO 2-2   Describe the elements of a marketing plan.

THE MARKETING PLAN

Effective marketing doesn't just happen. Firms like Nike and adidas carefully plan their marketing strategies to react to changes in the environment, the competition, and their customers by creating a marketing plan. A **marketing plan** is a written document composed of an analysis of the current marketing situation, opportunities and threats for the firm, marketing objectives and strategy specified in terms of the four Ps, action programs, and projected or pro-forma income (and other financial) statements.[15] The three major phases of the marketing plan are planning, implementation, and control.[16]

Although most people do not have a written plan that outlines what they are planning to accomplish in the next year, and how they expect to do it, firms do need such a document. It is important for everyone involved in implementing the plan to know what the overall objectives for the firm are and how they will be met. Other stakeholders, such as investors and potential investors, also want to know what the firm plans to do. A written marketing plan provides a reference point for evaluating whether the firm has met its objectives.

A marketing plan entails five steps, depicted in Exhibit 2.2. In Step 1 of the **planning phase**, marketing executives, in conjunction with other top managers, define the mission and/or vision of the business. For the second step, they evaluate the situation by assessing how various players, both in and outside the organization, affect the firm's potential for success (Step 2). In the **implementation phase**, marketing managers identify and evaluate different opportunities by engaging in a process known as segmentation, targeting, and positioning (STP) (Step 3). They then are responsible for implementing the marketing mix using the four Ps (Step 4). Finally, the **control phase** entails evaluating the performance of the marketing strategy using marketing metrics and taking any necessary corrective actions (Step 5).

As indicated in Exhibit 2.2, it is not always necessary to go through the entire process for every evaluation (Step 5). For instance, a firm could evaluate its performance in Step 5, then go directly to Step 2 to conduct a situation audit without redefining its overall mission.

We first discuss each step involved in developing a marketing plan. Then we consider ways of analyzing a marketing situation as well as identifying and evaluating marketing opportunities. We also examine some specific strategies marketers use to grow a business. Finally, we consider how the implementation of the marketing mix increases customer value.

Step 1: Define the Business Mission

The **mission statement**, a broad description of a firm's objectives and the scope of activities it plans to undertake,[17] attempts to answer two main questions: What type of business are we? What do we need to do to accomplish our goals and objectives? These fundamental business questions must be answered at the highest corporate levels before marketing executives can get involved. Most firms want to maximize

marketing plan A written document composed of an analysis of the current marketing situation, opportunities and threats for the firm, marketing objectives and strategy specified in terms of the four Ps, action programs, and projected or pro forma income (and other financial) statements.

planning phase The part of the strategic marketing planning process when marketing executives, in conjunction with other top managers, (1) define the mission or vision of the business and (2) evaluate the situation by assessing how various players, both in and outside the organization, affect the firm's potential for success.

implementation phase The part of the strategic marketing planning process when marketing managers (1) identify and evaluate different opportunities by engaging in segmentation, targeting, and positioning (see *STP*) and (2) implement the marketing mix using the four Ps.

control phase The part of the strategic marketing planning process when managers evaluate the performance of the marketing strategy and take any necessary corrective actions.

mission statement A broad description of a firm's objectives and the scope of activities it plans to undertake; attempts to answer two main questions: What type of business is it? What does it need to do to accomplish its goals and objectives?

▼ **EXHIBIT 2.2** The Marketing Plan

stockholders' wealth by increasing the value of the firms' stock and paying dividends.[18] Let's look at Nike and adidas.

· **Nike's Mission Statement:** "To bring inspiration and innovation to every athlete* in the world," and then with its asterisk, defines an athlete by quoting one of its founders: "If you have a body, you are an athlete."[19]

· **adidas's Mission Statement:** "The adidas group strives to be the global leader in the sporting goods industry with brands built on a passion for sport and a sporting lifestyle."[20]

For both of these firms, marketing is primarily responsible for enhancing the value of the company's offering for its

customers and other constituents, whether in pursuit of a profit or not. Another key goal or objective often embedded in a mission statement relates to how the firm is building its sustainable competitive advantage.

However, owners of small, privately held firms frequently have other objectives, such as achieving a specific level of income and avoiding risks. Nonprofit organizations instead have nonmonetary objectives like Teach for America's:

· **Teach for America's** mission is to build the movement to eliminate educational inequity by enlisting our nation's most promising future leaders in the effort.[21]

Both Nike's and adidas's ads reflect their mission statements. Nike's ads (left) consistently inspire athletes to excel; adidas's ads (right) emphasize passion for sports.

Step 2: Conduct a Situation Analysis

After developing its mission, a firm should perform a **situation analysis**, using a **SWOT** analysis that assesses both the internal environment with regard to its **S**trengths and **W**eaknesses and the external environment in terms of its **O**pportunities and **T**hreats. In addition, it should assess the opportunities and uncertainties of the marketplace due to changes in **C**ultural, **D**emographic, **S**ocial, **T**echnological, **E**conomic, and **P**olitical forces (CDSTEP). These factors are discussed in more detail in Chapter 4. With this information, firms can anticipate and interpret change, so they can allocate appropriate resources.

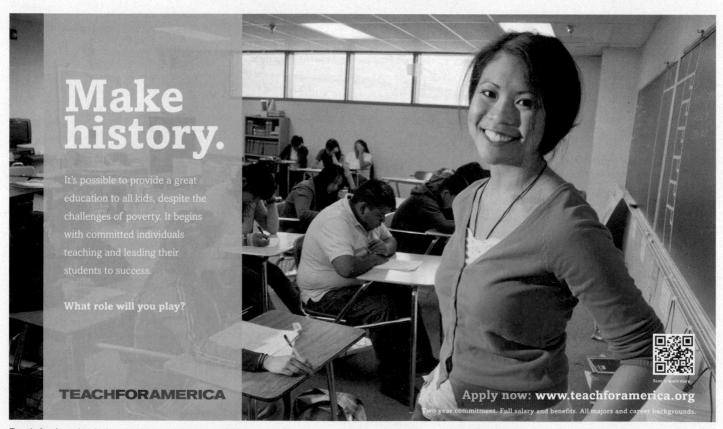

Make history.

It's possible to provide a great education to all kids, despite the challenges of poverty. It begins with committed individuals teaching and leading their students to success.

What role will you play?

TEACHFORAMERICA

Apply now: **www.teachforamerica.org**
Two year commitment. Full salary and benefits. All majors and career backgrounds.

Teach for America helps provide education to all kids.

		Environment	**Evaluation**
		Positive	*Negative*
Nike	**Internal**	**Strengths** Strong brand Strong celebrity endorsers Innovative products	**Weakness** Overreliance on footwear
	External	**Opportunity** Emerging countries Other fashion segments	**Threats** Cheaper imports Imitation products Retail becoming price competitive
adidas	**Internal**	**Strengths** Strong brand Portfolio of brands Strong global presence	**Weakness** Management of numerous brands
	External	**Opportunity** Emerging countries	**Threats** Cheaper imports Imitation products Recessionary forces

situation analysis
Second step in a marketing plan; uses a SWOT analysis that assesses both the internal environment with regard to its **S**trengths and **W**eaknesses and the external environment in terms of its **O**pportunities and **T**hreats.

Consider how Nike might conduct a SWOT analysis, as outlined in Exhibit 2.3. We focus on Nike here, but we also recognize that its marketing managers might find it helpful to perform parallel analyses for competitors, such as adidas. Because a company's strengths (Exhibit 2.3, upper left) refer to the positive internal attributes of the firm, in this example we might include Nike's great brand recognition and the visibility of the celebrities who wear its products. Furthermore, its introduction of the Nike+ iPod was the first of its kind, continuing the innovative tradition that has marked Nike since it first came up with waffle-soled running shoes. Its name recognition makes consumers more likely to try out these innovations when they appear on the market—especially when they see their favorite athlete wearing similar apparel on the court or in the field.

Yet every firm has its weaknesses, and Nike is no exception. Weaknesses (Exhibit 2.3, upper right) are negative attributes of the firm. Nike relies heavily—perhaps even too heavily—on its athletic shoe lines, especially for running and basketball. The NBA lockout for the 2012 season put undue stress on its sales in this segment. Not only would players and teams stop buying, but as the old saying goes, "Out of sight, out of mind." If the players are not on the court, their fans aren't thinking about them, and then sales will suffer.[22] In response to the popular emergence of other options, such as toning and barefoot models, Nike has largely suggested they are fads that will not last, stressing instead its traditional athletic shoe models.[23]

Opportunities (Exhibit 2.3, lower left) pertain to positive aspects of the external environment. Among Nike's opportunities, it appears determined to pursue dominance in other, sometime niche, sports markets. For the Olympic Games, it introduced footwear for less familiar sports, including fencing, wrestling, and equestrian events.[24] This goal also aligns with another notable opportunity for Nike, that is, growth in global markets. It sells products in 170 countries worldwide through independent distributors, Nike stores, the website, and licenses.[25] It aims to expand further, and it has devoted significant resources to improving its prominence among European football players and fans.[26]

Finally, threats (Exhibit 2.3, lower right) represent the negative aspects of the company's external environment. For example, its widespread market dominance makes Nike the primary target for all its competitors,[27] from adidas to New

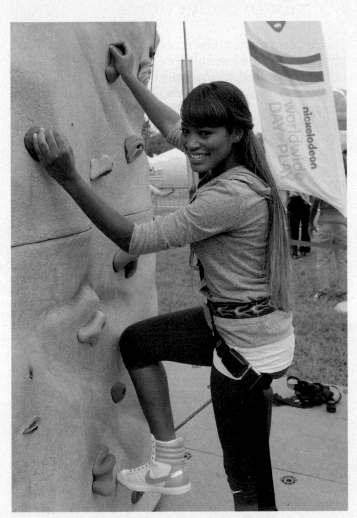

Keke Palmer is wearing her Nikes at a Nickelodeon event.

Nike's strengths include its innovative product tradition. It was the first to introduce the Nike+ iPod, a sensor that when inserted into shoes gives the runner instant feedback on factors such as running time, distance, pace, and calories burned.

Step 3: Identifying and Evaluating Opportunities Using STP (Segmentation, Targeting, and Positioning)

After completing the situation audit, the next step is to identify and evaluate opportunities for increasing sales and profits using **STP** (segmentation, targeting, and positioning). With STP, the firm first divides the marketplace into subgroups or segments, determines which of those segments it should pursue or target, and finally decides how it should position its products and services to meet the needs of those chosen targets best. (More details on the STP process can be found in Chapter 8.)

Segmentation Many types of customers appear in any market, and most firms cannot satisfy everyone's needs. For

> Hertz uses a variety of demographics—gender, age, income, interests—to identify customers who might want the Fun, Prestige, Green, and SUV/Minivan collections.

Balance to Li Ning, China's largest shoe maker. All of these firms want to take market share from Nike, which means it must constantly be a little bit on the defensive. Furthermore, a perpetual threat for any apparel company is staying fashionable, as Nike itself acknowledges: "We must . . . respond to trends and shifts in consumer preferences by adjusting the mix of existing product offerings, developing new products, styles and categories, and influencing sports and fitness preferences through aggressive marketing. Failure to respond in a timely and adequate manner could have a material adverse effect on our sales and profitability. This is a continuing risk."[28]

LO 2-4   Describe how a firm chooses which consumer group(s) to pursue with its marketing efforts.

instance, among Internet users, some do research online, some shop, some look for entertainment, and many do all three. Each of these groups might be a **market segment** consisting of consumers who respond similarly to a firm's marketing efforts. The process of dividing the market into groups of customers with different needs, wants, or characteristics—who therefore might appreciate products or services geared especially for them—is called **market segmentation**.

Let's look at Hertz, the car rental company. The example in Exhibit 2.4 reveals that some of the segments that Hertz targets includes its Fun Collection, including the Corvette ZHZ and Chevrolet Camaro, to single people and couples wanting to have a bit of fun. Its Prestige Collection, which features the Cadillac Escalade and Infiniti QX56, targets business customers and families who prefer a luxurious ride. With its Green collection of cars such as the Toyota Prius and Ford Fusion, Hertz appeals to environmentally conscious customers, and with its SUV/Minivan collection, it brings in families. It also offers commercial vans for service customers.[29] Thus, Hertz uses a variety of demographics—gender, age, income, interests—to identify customers who might want the Fun, Prestige, Green, and SUV/Minivan collections, but it also applies psychological or behavioral factors, such as a preference for style or a need to move possessions across town, to identify likely consumers of the Fun Collection and its commercial vans.

▼ **EXHIBIT 2.4** Hertz Market Segmentation

	Segment 1	Segment 2	Segment 3	Segment 4	Segment 5
Segments	Single people and couples wanting to have a bit of fun	Business customers and families who prefer a luxurious ride	Environmentally conscious customers	Families	Commercial customers
	Fun Collection	Prestige Collection	Green Collection	SUV/Minivan & crossover	Commercial Van/Truck
Cars Offered	Corvette ZHZ	Infiniti QX56	Toyota Prius	Toyota Rav 4	
	Chevrolet Camaro	Cadillac Escalade	Ford Fusion	Ford Explorer	Ford Cargo Van

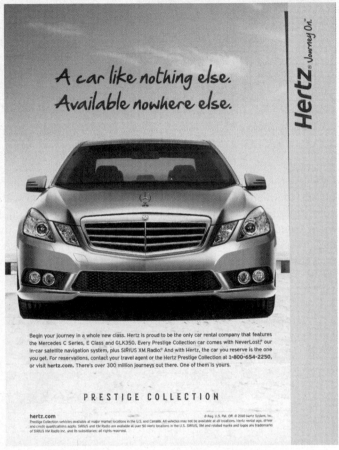

Hertz targets several markets. Its Fun Collection (left) appeals to single people and couples wanting to have fun; its Prestige Collection (right) appeals to its business customers and families who prefer a luxurious ride.

Go back to our Nike example; let's look at how it segments its customers based on gender and how the products are used. Nike focuses on the following segments: running, basketball, football (soccer), men's training, women's training, action sports, sportswear, and golf.

Targeting After a firm has identified the various market segments it might pursue, it evaluates each segment's attractiveness and decides which to pursue using a process known as **target marketing or targeting**. For example, Hertz realizes that its primary appeal for the SUV/Minivan collection centers on young families, so the bulk of its marketing efforts for this business is directed toward that group.

Soft drink manufacturers also divide their massive markets into submarkets or segments. Coca-Cola, for instance, makes several types of Coke, including regular, Coke II, and Cherry Coke. Among its diet colas, it targets Coke Zero to men and Diet Coke to women, because men prefer not to be associated with diets. It also markets Sprite to those who don't like dark colas, Fruitopia and Minute Maid for more health-conscious consumers, and Dasani bottled water for purists.

Positioning Finally, when the firm decides which segments to pursue, it must determine how it wants to be positioned within those segments. **Market positioning** involves the process of defining the marketing mix variables so that

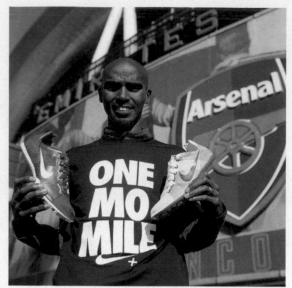

Nike targets different segments, such as women's fitness, golf, and running.

target customers have a clear, distinctive, desirable understanding of what the product does or represents in comparison with competing products. Hertz positions itself as a quality car (and truck) rental company that is the first choice for each of its target segments. In its marketing communications, it stresses that customers will get peace of mind when they rent from

Strategies section later in the chapter. Firms typically are most successful when they focus on opportunities that build on their strengths relative to those of their competition. In Step 4 of the marketing plan, the firm implements its marketing mix and allocates resources to different products and services.

> **Firms typically are most successful when they focus on opportunities that build on their strengths relative to those of their competition.**

Hertz, the market leader in the car rental business, and be able to enjoy their journey (e.g., leisure consumers) and reduce travel time (e.g., business consumers).[30]

To segment the coffee drinker market, Starbucks uses a variety of methods, including geography (e.g., college campuses versus shopping/business districts) and benefits (e.g., drinkers of caffeinated versus decaffeinated products). After determining which of those segments represent effective targets, Starbucks positions itself as a firm that develops a variety of products that match the wants and needs of the different market segments—espresso drinks, coffees, teas, bottled drinks, pastries, and cooler foods.

After identifying its target segments, a firm must evaluate each of its strategic opportunities. A method of examining which segments to pursue is described in the Growth

For example, Pizza Hut decided to jump on changing consumer desires for rapid access to its offering by constantly expanding its mobile applications, but it also found its positioning as a convenient option appealing to more markets than it even expected, as Social & Mobile Media 2.1 reveals.

LO 2-5 Outline the implementation of the marketing mix as a means to increase customer value.

Step 4: Implement Marketing Mix and Allocate Resources

When the firm has identified and evaluated different growth opportunities by performing an STP analysis, the real action begins. It has decided what to do, how to do it, and how many resources should be allocated to it. In the fourth step of the planning process, marketers implement the actual marketing mix—product, price, promotion, and place—for each product and service on the basis of what they believe their target markets will value. At the same time, marketers make important decisions about how they will allocate their scarce resources to their various products and services.

Product and Value Creation **Products**, which include services, constitute the first of the four Ps. Because the key to the success of any marketing program is the creation of value, firms attempt to develop products and services that customers perceive as valuable enough to buy. Dyson fans and fan heaters draw in and redirect surrounding air without potentially dangerous or fast spinning blades or visible heating elements. Although more expensive than conventional fans and space heaters, these sculpturally beautiful appliances are perceived by consumers to be a valuable alternative to products that haven't significantly changed since the early 1900s.

Price and Value Capture Recall that the second element of the marketing mix is price. As part of the exchange

> **products** Anything that is of value to a consumer and can be offered through a voluntary marketing exchange.

Social & Mobile Marketing 2.1
Truly Mobile Pizza[31]

The pizza delivery business has always been mobile in one sense, but Pizza Hut is making sure that it spreads convenience into mobile commerce as well. This first-mover introduced its mobile website in 2007, an iPhone application in 2009, and apps for the iPad, Android, Windows Mobile 7 in 2010, and an application for Xbox 360 in 2013.

The decision to go mobile was based on a few insights that Pizza Hut gleaned from its market research. In particular, if it did not offer mobile access quickly, its competitors might be first to do so in the competitive pizza delivery market. The Pizza Hut app lets customers order food through a user-friendly experience, but it also makes sure to identify the closest store locations for delivery or pick-up service to emphasize further convenience.

Without much information about who the consumers who would use the app were, Pizza Hut anticipated more orders from college-aged men, who do not like to cook and want their food on demand, but also are not willing to stop a video game to take the time to order food through more traditional channels. The assumption seemed reasonable—but it also was dead wrong. Further market research, based on the introduction of the app, has shown that there are just as many pizza connoisseurs with iPhones who are older than 55 as there are 13–24-year-olds ordering the pies.

Pizza Hut's mobile app makes ordering pizza a piece of cake.

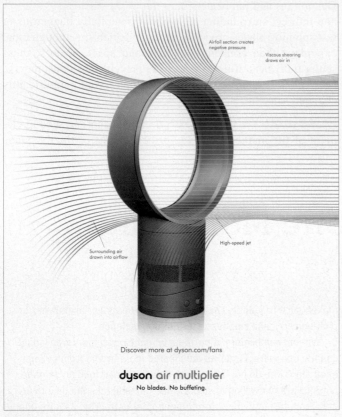

Dyson creates value with its innovative products.

process, a firm provides a product or a service, or some combination thereof, and in return, it gets money. Value-based marketing requires firms to charge a price that customers perceive as giving them a good value for the product they receive. Clearly, it is important for a firm to have a clear focus in terms of what products to sell, where to sell them, and what methods to use in selling them. But pricing is the only activity that actually brings in money and therefore influences revenues. If a price is set too high, it will not generate much volume. If a price is set too low, it may result in lower-than-optimal margins and profits. Therefore, price should be based on the value that the customer perceives. Dyson fans can retail for $150 or more while conventional fans retail for around $25. Customers thus can decide just what they want from their fan and choose the one at the price they prefer.

Place and Value Delivery
For the third P, place, the firm must be able, after it has created value through a product and/or

service, to make the product or service readily accessible when and where the customer wants it. Recently, Tesco took an innovative step along these lines when it opened HomePlus virtual stores in several South Korean subway stations. The virtual stores in subway stations look like grocery stores—except that they are just LCD screens! The virtual markets allow customers to shop with just their smartphones.[32] Adding Value 2.1 takes a closer look at how Tesco HomePlus provides consumers great value.

Promotion and Value Communication
The fourth and last P of the marketing mix is promotion. Marketers communicate the value of their offering, or the value proposition, to their customers through a variety of media including television, radio, magazines, sales forces, and the Internet. A relatively new promotion channel relies on daily deal websites such as Groupon or LivingSocial to get the word out. Many smaller companies find that these sites give them greater name recognition than they ever could have achieved on their own.

But when a well-known company uses the sites, the effect is even more remarkable. For example, Whole Foods offered a certificate for $20 worth of goods at a cost of only $10 on LivingSocial.com. Consumers snatched up the deal at a rate of 115,000 per hour.[33] Whole Foods capped the offer at 1 million deals, so it exposed itself to costs of around $10–15 million (if we include the fees it had to pay to LivingSocial to post the deal) in this attempt to get more grocery shoppers to visit its stores.

Step 5: Evaluate Performance Using Marketing Metrics
The final step in the planning process includes evaluating the results of the strategy and implementation program using marketing metrics. A **metric** is a measuring system that quantifies a trend, dynamic, or characteristic. Metrics are used to explain why things happened and to project the future. They make it possible to compare results across regions, strategic business units (SBUs), product lines, and time periods. The firm can determine why it achieved or did not achieve its performance goals with the help of these metrics. Understanding the causes of the performance, regardless of whether that performance exceeded, met, or fell below the firm's goals, enables firms to make appropriate adjustments.

Typically, managers begin by reviewing the implementation programs, and their analysis may indicate that the strategy (or even the mission statement) needs to be reconsidered. Problems can arise both when firms successfully implement poor strategies and when they poorly implement good strategies.

> **Understanding the causes of the performance, regardless of whether that performance exceeded, met, or fell below the firm's goals, enables firms to make appropriate adjustments.**

Adding Value 2.1

Online Retail Meets Bricks and Mortar: Tesco's HomePlus Virtual Stores

South Korea is known for its tech innovations, introduced by highly creative companies and embraced by a forward-thinking consumer public. But the top app in this tech-savvy nation isn't associated with some space-age fantasy. Instead, it pertains to a seemingly perpetual, distinctly old-fashioned task: grocery shopping.

The international retailer Tesco chose Korea as the site to open its HomePlus virtual stores back in 2011. Virtual stores began appearing on LCD screens in subway stations.[34] Shoppers on their way to or home from work could scan the barcodes or QR codes for the items they wanted to purchase with their smartphones. The virtual stores are laid out in a grid, similar to a brick-and-mortar store, which helped shoppers feel familiar with the radically new approach. Furthermore, the app allows them to schedule home delivery so that fresh produce, food for their pets, replenished cleaning supplies, and maybe even dinner for themselves can be waiting on their doorstep when they get home.

The remarkable success of this app has prompted Tesco to expand the placement of HomePlus stores to bus depots and other commuter routes.[35] Within about six months of the introduction, nearly 1 million consumers had downloaded and used the HomePlus app.

Despite the success and popularity of HomePlus, Tesco continues to keep its physical stores open, with no plans to eliminate them. Two main features demand this dual approach. First, Korea is somewhat special in terms of its significant embrace and acceptance of virtual tools and high-tech options. In many other countries, including Tesco's U.K. home market, and in rural areas where access to public spaces such as bus stops is just as challenging as getting to the local store, acceptance may be less widespread. Even in Korea, consumers tend to use HomePlus for dry goods but still like to be able to touch and feel vegetables and fruit before buying them.

Second, for many people, shopping is an enjoyable pastime that gets them out of their houses or offices for a brief time. Noting this persistent preference, Tesco is seeking to integrate virtual offerings better into some of its stores. For example, it is considering plans to add interactive tablets in its in-store cafes. Customers could take a break, have a cup of tea, and type in a few ingredients that sound appealing to them. The tablets then might produce recipes that match the ingredients, along with a map, showing the customers just where to find each needed item.[36]

The HomePlus Virtual Stores have created a whole new way of providing the third P, place, and value delivery.

Who Is Accountable for Performance? At each level of an organization, the business unit and its manager should be held accountable only for the revenues, expenses, and profits that they can control. Thus, expenses that affect several levels of the organization (such as the labor and capital expenses associated with operating a corporate headquarters) shouldn't be arbitrarily assigned to lower levels. In the case of a store, for example, it may be appropriate to evaluate performance objectives based on sales, sales associate productivity, and energy costs. If the corporate office lowers prices to get rid of merchandise and therefore profits suffer, then it's not fair to assess a store manager's performance based on the resulting decline in store profit.

> # THE METRICS USED TO EVALUATE A FIRM VARY DEPENDING ON (1) THE LEVEL OF THE ORGANIZATION AT WHICH THE DECISION IS MADE AND (2) THE RESOURCES THE MANAGER CONTROLS.

Performance evaluations are used to pinpoint problem areas. Reasons performance may be above or below planned levels must be examined. If a manager's performance is below planned levels, was it because the sales force didn't do an adequate job, because the economy took a downward turn, because competition successfully implemented a new strategy, or because the managers involved in setting the objectives aren't very good at making estimates? The manager should only be held accountable in the case of the inadequate sales force job or setting inappropriate forecasts.

When it appears that actual performance is going to be below the plan because of circumstances beyond the manager's control, the firm can still take action to minimize the harm. For our chapter exemplar Nike, two situations have arisen recently over which the firm had little control—a global recession and a scandal involving a spokesperson. Many consumers cut their spending on things like apparel in the modern recession. And the Tiger Woods infidelity scandal left Nike in an awkward position. According to researchers at Carnegie Mellon University, for the 10 years prior to the scandal, Woods's endorsement had earned Nike's golf ball division approximately $60 million in additional profits. In the year following widespread media reports of his infidelity, Nike lost approximately 105,000 customers and $1.3 million in profit.[37]

In remarkable cases such as this, marketing managers must ask themselves several relevant questions: How quickly were plans adjusted? How rapidly and appropriately were pricing and promotional policies modified? In short, did I react to salvage an adverse situation, or did my reactions worsen the situation? For the Woods scandal, it appears that marketing managers made the right decision by keeping him as an endorser, despite their short-term losses. The same researchers estimate that "even in the midst of the scandal, the overall profit was greater by $1.6 million for Nike with Tiger Woods than without him."[38]

Performance Objectives and Metrics

Many factors contribute to a firm's overall performance, which makes it hard to find a single metric to evaluate performance. One approach is to compare a firm's performance over time or to competing firms, using common financial metrics such as sales and profits. Another method of assessing performance is to view the firm's products or services as a portfolio. Depending on the firm's relative performance, the profits from some products or services are used to fuel growth for others.

Financial Performance Metrics

Some commonly used metrics to assess performance include revenues, or sales, and profits. For instance, sales are a global measure of a firm's activity level. However, a manager could easily increase sales by lowering prices, but the profit realized on that merchandise (gross margin) would suffer as a result. An attempt to maximize one metric may lower another. Managers must therefore understand how their actions affect multiple performance metrics. It's usually unwise to use only one metric because it rarely tells the whole story.

In addition to assessing the absolute level of sales and profits, a firm may wish to measure the relative level of sales and profits. For example, a relative metric of sales or profits is its increase or decrease over the prior year. In addition, a firm may compare its growth in sales or profits relative to other benchmark companies (e.g., Coke may compare itself to Pepsi).

The metrics used to evaluate a firm vary depending on (1) the level of the organization at which the decision is made and (2) the resources the manager controls. For example, although the top executives of a firm have control over all of the firm's resources and resulting expenses, a regional sales manager only has control over the sales and expenses generated by his or her salespeople.

Let's look at Nike's sales revenue and profits (after taxes) and compare them with those of adidas (Exhibit 2.5).

Tiger Woods is back.

▼ **EXHIBIT 2.5** Performance Metrics: Nike vs. adidas

		2011	2012	% Change
Nike	Net Sales	$20.9B	$24.1B	15.30%
	Net Profit	$ 2.1B	$ 2.2B	4.80%
	Net Profit/Net Sales	10.00%	9.10%	−9.00%
adidas	Net Sales	$ 17.6B	$ 19.7B	12.00%
	Net Profit	$809.8M	$694.9M	−14.20%
	Net Profit/Net Sales	4.60%	3.50%	−23.90%

Furthermore, as the corporate consciousness of the importance of social responsibility grows, firms are starting to report corporate social responsibility metrics in major areas, such as their impact on the environment, their ability to diversify their workforce, energy conservation initiatives, and their policies on protecting the human rights of their employees and the employees of their suppliers. Ethical & Societal Dilemma 2.1 examines how dietary supplement and energy drink manufacturers and retailers are wrestling with how best to market their products.

LO 2-6   Summarize portfolio analysis and its use to evaluate marketing performance.

Portfolio Analysis

In portfolio analysis, management evaluates the firm's various products and businesses—its portfolio—and allocates resources according to which products are expected to be the most profitable for the firm in the future. Portfolio analysis is typically performed at the **strategic business unit (SBU)** or **product line** level of the firm, though managers also can use it to analyze brands or even individual items. An SBU is a division of the firm itself that can be managed and operated somewhat independently from other divisions and may have a different mission or objectives. For example, Goodyear is one of the largest tire firms in the world, selling its products on six continents in over 180 countries and with sales of approximately $18 billion. Its four SBUs are organized by geography: North America, Europe, Middle East, Africa, Latin America, and Asia/Pacific.[39]

A product line, in contrast, is a group of products that consumers may use together or perceive as similar in some way. One line of product for Goodyear could be car, van, SUV, and light truck while another line could be racing tires or aviation tires.

One of the most popular portfolio analysis methods, developed by the Boston Consulting Group (BCG), requires firms to classify all their products or services into a two-by-two matrix, as depicted in Exhibit 2.6.[40] The circles represent brands, and their sizes are in direct proportion to the brands' annual sales. The horizontal axis represents the relative market share.

In general, **market share** is the percentage of a market accounted for by a specific entity [41] and is used to establish the product's strength in a particular market. It is usually discussed in units, revenue, or sales. A special type of market

▼ **EXHIBIT 2.6** Boston Consulting Group Matrix

ethical & societal dilemma

Dangerous Consumption: Is the Consumer or the Company to Blame?

A 22-year-old soldier, with no history of health issues, collapsed while out for a training run, soon after ingesting a dietary supplement he had purchased from GNC.[42] A 14-year-old girl from Maryland drank two 24-ounce Monster Energy Drinks in one day and went into cardiac arrest.[43] Another teen, who drank two cans of Monster Energy every day for three years, ultimately suffered cardiac arrhythmia as well.[44] In response to these tragic deaths, several lawsuits are alleging that the manufacturers and retailers should be held liable.

Energy drinks that contain high levels of caffeine increasingly have come under attack as potential health threats, especially to the youthful consumers that the companies target. Alleging that the companies fail to disclose the risks of drinking such high doses of caffeine, these lawsuits seek to force Monster, Rockstar, and other competitors to carry warnings on their labels. Another lawsuit is attempting to ban the marketing of such products to children under the age of 18 years—a ban supported by the American Medical Association.[45]

The Jack3d dietary supplement contains dimethylalimine (DMAA), a stimulant that promises to increase endurance and stamina among athletes. On the GNC website, promotions of the brand assert that it provides "ultra-intense muscle-gorging

strength, energy, power and endurance." In this case, legislators—together with the family of the soldier who died after taking Jack3d—argue that retailers such as GNC should be held responsible for the effects of the products they sell. By creating a sort of scientific or expert image, GNC may signal that the products it sells have been

tested and confirmed as safe. Instead, GNC's legal status as a retailer and not a producer of supplements has generally meant that in the past it could not be held responsible for any damages imposed by the products it sells.[46] GNC is defending this position, noting that as a retailer, it

must depend on the guarantees offered by the supplement vendors that the ingredients used are safe.

The makers of energy drinks appear to be taking a different tack. Both Rockstar and Monster have repositioned their products, transforming them from dietary supplements to beverages. This move means more than just changing their locations on store shelves. By calling the products beverages instead of dietary supplements, energy drink makers avoid the requirement that they must transmit any reports of health damages or deaths to the U.S. Food and Drug Administration (FDA).[47] However, they face the new requirement that they must list all nutrition information, including caffeine content, on the cans.

Dietary supplements continue to be largely unregulated by national agencies such as the FDA or the U.S. Department of Agriculture (USDA). Furthermore, these products, similar to energy drinks, do not fit obviously into existing product categories, which makes it difficult to determine which federal agency, if any, has responsibility for ensuring their safety. The product makers and retailers argue vigorously that no evidence confirms that the ingredients in their products are harmful. That is, despite the allegations, no one can prove that the three young people died because they ingested the products.

---

share metric, **relative market share**, is used in this application because it provides managers with a product's relative strength, compared with that of the largest firm in the industry.[48] The vertical axis is the **market growth rate**, or the annual rate of growth of the specific market in which the product competes. Market growth rate thus measures how attractive a particular market is. Each quadrant in the matrix has been named on the basis of the amount of resources it generates for and requires from the firm.

Stars. Stars (upper left quadrant) occur in high-growth markets and are high market share products. That is, stars often require a heavy resource investment in such things as promotions and new production facilities to fuel their rapid growth. As their market growth slows, stars will migrate from heavy users of resources to heavy generators of resources and become cash cows.

Cash Cows. Cash cows (lower left quadrant) are in low-growth markets but are high market share products. Because these products have already received heavy investments to develop their high market share, they have excess resources that can be spun off to those products that need it. For example, the firm may decide to use the excess resources generated by Brand C to fund products in the question mark quadrant.

Question Marks. Question marks (upper right quadrant) appear in high-growth markets but have relatively low market shares; thus, they are often the most managerially intensive products in that they require significant resources to maintain and potentially increase their market share. Managers must decide whether to infuse question marks with resources generated by the cash cows, so that they can become stars, or withdraw resources and eventually phase out the products. Brand A, for instance, is currently a question mark, but by infusing it with resources, the firm hopes to turn it into a star.

Dogs. Dogs (lower right quadrant) are in low-growth markets and have relatively low market shares. Although they may generate enough resources to sustain themselves, dogs are not destined for stardom and should be phased out unless they are needed to complement or boost the sales of another product or for competitive purposes. In the case depicted in Exhibit 2.6, the company has decided to stop making Brand B.

Now let's look at Apple and some of its products.[49] The four that we will focus our attention on are:

- iPhone
- iPod
- iMac Desktop
- iPad

EVERYTHING WE'VE LEARNED HELPING THE MUSTANG HOLD ITS HORSES, INSPIRES WHAT WE ROLL INTO YOUR TIRES.

EAGLE® F1 ULTRA-HIGH PERFORMANCE STOPPING POWER.   **GOODYEAR** MORE DRIVEN

Goodyear, one of the largest tire firms in the world, organizes its strategic business units by geography.

In which Boston Consulting quadrant do these two products fit?

Let's consider each of these products and place them in the BCG matrix based on these data. The iPhone is clearly a star—a high growth rate (87 percent). In fact, by the end of 2011, Apple returned to its position as the top selling smartphone in the industry, with 16.2 million units sold in their fourth quarter alone, making its relative market share 100 percent.[50]

Apple's iPod is a different story. With a staggering absolute market share consistently above 75 percent, its relative market share is also 100 percent, and with more than 300 million iPods sold in a little over 10 years, it is definitely an important product for Apple. Unfortunately, the MP3 market is contracting (the market shrank by 10 percent from 2010 to 2011). Combine the lack of growth with a large relative market share, and it is likely that the iPod is a cash cow for Apple.[51]

Although popular with graphic designers, the growth rate of the Mac Desktop has slowed to a pitiful 4 percent. Given that it also has a small relative market share in the desktop market, the iMac can be tentatively classified as a dog. Should Apple get rid of the iMac? For at least two reasons, this is probably a bad idea. First, it risks alienating graphic designers and other Apple loyalists who depend on the iMac. Since these customers may also enjoy other Apple products, their dissatisfaction might adversely affect sales of these other products. Second, discontinuing the iMac would leave a gaping hole in its

portfolio, and would therefore hurt its brand image as a computer company.

Then we have the iPad with an incredible sales growth rate from 2010 to 2011 of 333 percent and sales of approximately 55 million units as of early 2012. In 2010, its absolute market share was 95.5 percent, making it the market leader with a relative market share of 100 percent. However, it is also experiencing increasing competition from Android tablets and the Kindle Fire. Looking at 2011 as a whole, the iPad captured 66.6 percent of the tablet market (2 out of every 3 tablets sold was an iPad). But by the end of 2011, its absolute market share had dropped to 57 percent.[52] Where on the BCG matrix would you classify the iPad? Would you argue that a 57 percent absolute market share places it in the star category, or would you be more conservative and put it as a question mark, citing the steady erosion of absolute market share? Will Apple be able to continue to grow and maintain its market share leader position by releasing a new version of the iPad?

Although quite useful for conceptualizing the relative performance of products or services and using this information to allocate resources, the BCG approach and others like it are often difficult to implement in practice. In particular, it is difficult to measure both relative market share and industry growth. Furthermore, other measures easily could serve as substitutes to represent a product's competitive position and the market's relative attractiveness. Another issue for marketers is the potentially

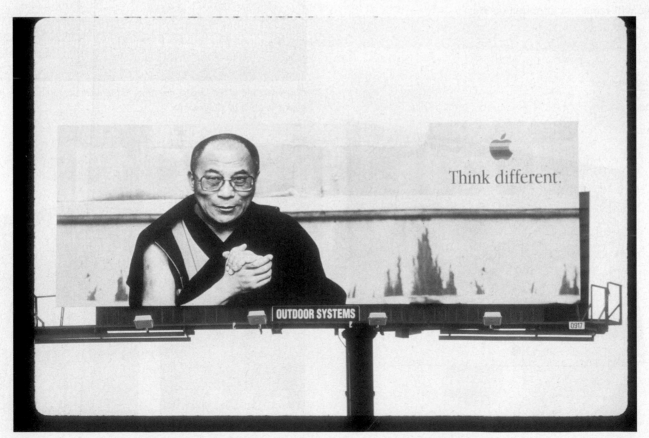

Like the Dalai Lama, Apple approaches the world by thinking differently.

self-fulfilling prophecy of placing a product or service into a quadrant. As we have shown in our Apple iPad example, whether it is classified as a star or a question mark has profound implications on how it is treated and supported within the firm. Question marks require more marketing and production support.

Because of these limitations, many firms have tempered their use of matrix approaches to achieve a more balanced approach to evaluating products and services and allocating their resources. Instead of assigning allocation decisions to the top levels of the organization, many firms start at lower management levels and employ checks and balances to force managers at each level of the organizational hierarchy to negotiate with those above and below them to reach their final decisions.

Strategic Planning Is Not Sequential

The planning process in Exhibit 2.2 suggests that managers follow a set sequence when they make strategic decisions. Namely, after they've defined the business mission, they perform the situation analysis, identify strategic opportunities, evaluate alternatives, set objectives, allocate resources, develop the implementation plan, and, finally, evaluate their performance and make adjustments. But actual planning processes can move back and forth among these steps. For example, a situation analysis may uncover a logical alternative, even though this alternative might not be included in the mission statement, which would mean that the mission statement would need to be revised. The development of the implementation plan also might reveal that insufficient resources have been allocated to a particular product for it to achieve its objective. In that case, the firm would need either to change the objective or increase the resources; alternatively, the marketer might consider not investing in the product at all.

Now that we have gone through the steps of the marketing plan, let's look at some growth strategies that have been responsible for making many marketing firms successful.

 check yourself

1. What are the five steps in creating a marketing plan?
2. What tool helps a marketer conduct a situation analysis?
3. What is STP?
4. What do the four quadrants of the portfolio analysis represent?

LO 2-7   Describe how firms grow their business.

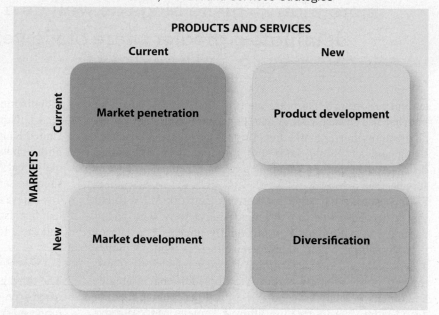

GROWTH STRATEGIES

Firms consider pursuing various market segments as part of their overall growth strategies, which may include the four major strategies in Exhibit 2.7.[53] The rows distinguish those opportunities a firm possesses in its current markets from those it has in new markets, whereas the columns distinguish between the firm's current marketing offering and that of a new opportunity. Let's consider each of them in detail.

Market Penetration

A **market penetration strategy** employs the existing marketing mix and focuses the firm's efforts on existing customers. Such a growth strategy might be achieved by attracting new consumers to the firm's current target market or encouraging

To increase market penetration with its young target audience, MTV produces reality shows like "America's Best Dance Crew."

current customers to patronize the firm more often or buy more merchandise on each visit. A market penetration strategy generally requires greater marketing efforts, such as increased advertising and additional sales and promotions or intensified distribution efforts in geographic areas in which the product or service already is sold.

To penetrate its target market, TV network MTV found that it needed new ways to engage its viewers. The young audience to which MTV traditionally appeals consists of text-messaging, video-gaming multitaskers who no longer accept plain video programming on their televisions. Thus, the network is working hard to develop additional strategies and outlets to retain viewers as well as to encourage them to spend more time interacting with its content. MTV discovered that interactions with the audience through alternative channels increase ratings for its shows. Therefore, in addition to producing and airing reality shows such as *America's Best Dance Crew* and *Jersey Shore*, MTV has partnered with a video game producer Yoostar to offer "Yoostar on MTV" for Xbox 360. The game provides a massive library of constantly updated shows, music videos, and recordings of live events. Using the green screen technology contained in the game, fans of these shows can insert themselves into scenes they've already seen their more famous teen peers undergo. Of course, the game also allows them to upload their completed performance to Facebook, Twitter, or a Yoostar dedicated website.[54] On MTV's website, dedicated forums, blogs, and activities for each show also encourage viewers to connect with characters in their shows. Not only can viewers talk about the characters as if they were friends, but they can buy the products they wear and download the music played during the show.[55]

Market Development

A **market development strategy** employs the existing marketing offering to reach new market segments, whether domestic or international. International expansion generally is riskier than domestic expansion because firms must deal with differences in government regulations, cultural traditions, supply chains, and language. However, many U.S. firms, including MTV, enjoy a competitive advantage in global markets—such as Mexico, Latin America, Europe, China, and Japan—because, especially among young people, U.S. culture is widely emulated for consumer products.

For example, because of rising prosperity worldwide and rapidly increasing access to cable television that offers U.S. programming, fashion trends from the United States have spread to young people in emerging countries. Since its

founding in 1981, MTV has expanded well beyond the United States, with niche sites in more than 20 countries, including the United Kingdom, Japan, Brazil, and India. It is available in 562 million households in 161 countries and 33 languages.[56] Thus, the global MTV generation prefers soft drinks to tea, athletic shoes to sandals, French fries to rice, and credit cards to cash. To achieve such growth, MTV leveraged its existing media content but also delivers culturally relevant content using local DJs and show formats.

Product Development

The third growth strategy option, a **product development strategy**, offers a new product or service to a firm's current target market. Consider MTV's dynamic line-up: The network

MTV's Real World Las Vegas *cast members: Heather Marter, Dustin Zito, Naomi Defensor, and Jasmine Reynaud.*

constantly develops new pilots and show concepts to increase the amount of time viewers can spend watching MTV. For example, each version of *The Real World* reality series and new series such as *Ridiculousness* and *Friendzone* all represent new programs designed to attract and retain existing viewers. Along with its new TV series, MTV develops new online products to engage consumers through more than 25 niche blogs as well as a website that it uses to dominate a greater share of viewers' minds and time. These various MTV-branded niche sites pertain to social, political, and environmental issues that appeal to different segments in its target market. The sites further encourage viewers to get involved in real-world issues (not *The Real World* issues) through mobile technologies. By visiting the sites, MTV promises that consumers can share mobile content, educate themselves, and take action on important issues.[57]

Diversification

A **diversification strategy**, the last of the growth strategies from Exhibit 2.7, introduces a new product or service to a market segment that currently is not served. Diversification opportunities may be either related or unrelated. In a **related diversification** opportunity, the current target market and/or marketing mix shares something in common with the new opportunity.[58] In other words, the firm might be able to purchase from existing vendors, use the same distribution and/or management information system, or advertise in the same newspapers to target markets that are similar to their current consumers. MTV has pursued related diversification by introducing TV series that focus on more positive social messages instead of on wealth, celebrities, and excessive youth culture (e.g., *The Hills, My Super Sweet 16*). In series such as *I Used to Be Fat* and *Made,* recognizable and seemingly similar teens still appeal to viewers and provide a healthy dose of drama. However, the plotlines of these shows focus on how people overcome adversity or struggle with everyday challenges to attain some level of happiness.[59]

In contrast, in an **unrelated diversification**, the new business lacks any common elements with the present business. Unrelated diversifications do not capitalize on either core strengths associated with markets or with products. Thus, they would be viewed as very risky. For instance, if Nike ventured into the child day care service industry, it would be an unrelated diversification because it is so different from its core business, and therefore very risky. ■

✔ **check** yourself

1. What are the four growth strategies?
2. What type of strategy is growing the business from existing customers?
3. Which strategy is the riskiest?

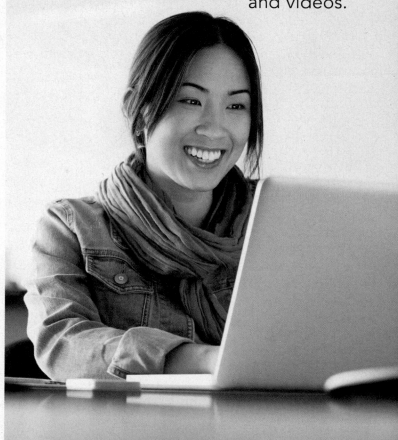

check it out!

mhhe.com/GrewalM4e
for study materials, including quizzes and videos.

three

social and mobile
marketing

Social media have revolutionized how companies communicate with, listen to, and learn from customers. Its influence is far-reaching, whether firms are selling online or in stores, providing services or products, or dealing primarily with consumers or business customers. Modern listening and analysis tools (such as those provided by IBM or Salesforce.com, a company that specializes in customer relationship management software and cloud computing) allow firms to identify salient, pertinent trends and customer input through social media.

Despite its potential importance, social media strategies remain haphazard, uncertain, and not particularly effective in many firms. Gatorade, however, offers a stellar example of a carefully designed plan for connecting effectively with customers, controlling social media buzz, and responding to trends as they arise. Although Gatorade's basic marketing

LEARNING OBJECTIVES

After reading this chapter, you should be able to:

LO 3-1   Describe the 4E framework of social media marketing.

LO 3-2   Understand the types of social media.

LO 3-3   Understand the types of mobile applications.

LO 3-4   Recognize and understand the three components of a social media strategy.

LO 3-5   Understand the methods for marketing yourself using social media.

strategy continues to include famous athletic spokepersons, it constantly seeks new ways to use these superb athletes to help ensure consumers' connections with the brand.

Residing in the marketing department at Gatorade's Chicago headquarters is its Social Media Mission Control center, which hosts massive monitors that track social media referring to Gatorade and its competitors. One monitor stays on

continued on p. 48

Gatorade's Chicago Social Media Mission Control center hosts massive monitors that track social media referring to Gatorade and its competitors.

continued from p. 47

blog trends; another summarizes the topics and sentiments expressed in tweets, all in real time.[1]

One day not too long ago, social media chatter indicated consumers' highly favorable responses to a just-released commercial featuring a new song by rapper David Banner. Gatorade

discussions, (2) monitor the sports landscape, (3) engage in proactive social media outreach, (4) track media performance, (5) track brand attitudes, and (6) track sports trends and buzz. Through the insights it gathers from consumers, Gatorade can influence not only its marketing communications but also its products and brand.[2]

> [The diffusion of technology used to bring us social media has been accelerating since the Internet came on the scene in the mid- to late-1990s.]

worked immediately with Banner to develop the snippet into a full-length song, which it distributed within a day through its Facebook and Twitter sites. Mission Control also is responsible for connecting fans with athletes associated with Gatorade. During the Super Bowl, it hosted discussions through the Ustream social media site.

According to Gatorade (and its owner, PepsiCo.), Mission Control actually has six main missions: (1) monitor online

In addition to this innovative and unique mission control center, Gatorade takes care of old-school social media too. Its Facebook page contains little explicit advertising for the brand. Instead, it posts provocative questions in an attempt to get fans to engage in conversations with the brand and one another. Its Twitter feed consists mainly of inspirational sayings and quotes. On YouTube, Gatorade offers easy access to some of its most famous commercials from over the years—ads that have taken on an iconic cult following, including old favorites describing how to "Be Like Mike" and more recent versions that challenge, "Is It In You?"[3]

When consumers search for Gatorade on popular search engines, they also see page after page of company-sponsored results rather than outside comments.[4] As this outcome reveals, Gatorade has done the preliminary work, through search engine optimization and brand building, to control what people see online. Although no company can prevent negative comments online (such as common complaints about Gatorade's taste), Gatorade has managed to ensure that those negative comments are hidden under a wave of positive, company-approved messages. Consumers must look harder to find the criticisms.

In this sense, Gatorade prepared itself for social media marketing well before any of these tools were readily available. Then, it applied its strong reputation and a proactive attitude toward social media to design its groundbreaking Social Media Mission Control center. As a result, Gatorade accounts for an astounding 75 percent of the social buzz related to sports drinks.[5] ■

social media Media content used for social interactions such as YouTube, Facebook, and Twitter.

LO 3-1 Describe the 4E framework of social media marketing.

THE 4E FRAMEWORK FOR SOCIAL MEDIA

As we will see throughout the book and as we saw in the chapter opener, social media is becoming an integral component of any integrated marketing communications strategy. The term **social media** refers to content distributed through online and mobile technologies to facilitate interpersonal interactions. These media use various firms that offer services or tools to help consumers and firms build connections. Through these connections, marketers and customers share information of all forms—from their thoughts about products or images to uploaded pictures, music, and videos.

The diffusion of technology used to bring us social media has been accelerating since the Internet came on the scene in the mid- to late-1990s, as depicted in Exhibit 3.1. The ideas were exciting, but ultimately, there was little to engage people. After the crisis of Y2K at the turn of the twentieth century, when computers failed to implode as a result of their inability to change their internal clocks to the new century, and after the bursting of the dot-com bubble, social media got a bit more serious and professional. Sites recognized that they had to offer surfers

▼ **EXHIBIT 3.1** Technology Evolution over the Life of the Social Web

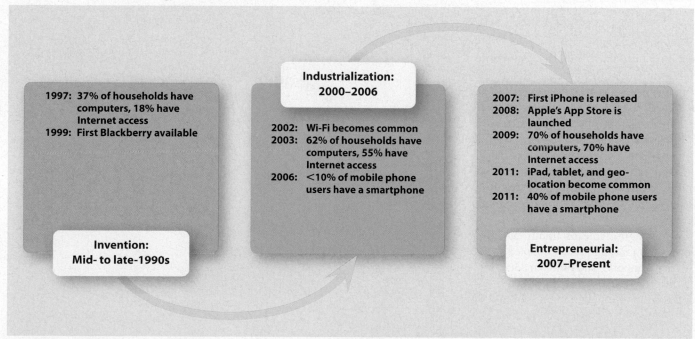

Industrialization:
2000–2006

1997: 37% of households have computers, 18% have Internet access
1999: First Blackberry available

2002: Wi-Fi becomes common
2003: 62% of households have computers, 55% have Internet access
2006: <10% of mobile phone users have a smartphone

2007: First iPhone is released
2008: Apple's App Store is launched
2009: 70% of households have computers, 70% have Internet access
2011: iPad, tablet, and geo-location become common
2011: 40% of mobile phone users have a smartphone

Invention:
Mid- to late-1990s

Entrepreneurial:
2007–Present

Source: Adapted from: Coca-Cola Retailing Research Council and the Integer Group, "Assessing the Social Networking Landscape," in *Untangling the Social Web: Insights for Users, Brands, and Retailers,* January 2012.

THE CHANGES AND ADVANCES IN SOCIAL, MOBILE, AND ONLINE TECHNOLOGIES HAVE CREATED A PERFECT STORM, FORCING FIRMS TO CHANGE HOW THEY COMMUNICATE WITH THEIR CUSTOMERS. "

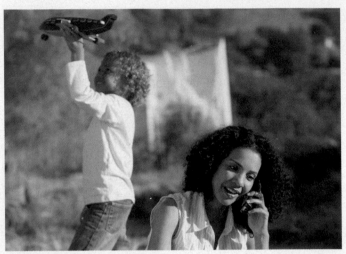

Today, multi-tasking is a way of life.

- Help them **E**xperience products, whether directly or indirectly.

- Give them an opportunity to **E**ngage with their social network.

Excite the Customer

Marketers use many kinds of social media–related offers to excite customers, including mobile applications and games to get the customers excited about an idea, product, brand, or company. Firms actively use social networks such as Facebook and Google+ to communicate deals that are likely to excite consumers, such as a Groupon price promotion that is communicated through the social networks of already interested consumers.

To excite customers, an offer must be relevant to its targeted customer. Relevancy can be achieved by providing something exciting, educational, or experiential if they were to keep them coming back. Today, we have entered the entrepreneurial era, in which companies work to find ways to earn profits from the ways that consumers use and enjoy social media.

The changes and advances in social, mobile, and online technologies have created a perfect storm, forcing firms to change how they communicate with their customers. Traditional ways to market their products, using brick-and-mortar stores, traditional mass media (e.g., print, television, radio), and other sales promotional vehicles (e.g., mail, telemarketing) are no longer sufficient for many firms. The presence of social, mobile, and online marketing is steadily expanding relative to these more traditional forms of integrated marketing communication (IMC).

The changing role of traditional media, sales promotions, and retail, coupled with the new social, mobile, and online media, has led to a different way of thinking about the objectives of marketing communications using the 4E framework (see Exhibit 3.2):

- **E**xcite customers with relevant offers.

- **E**ducate them about the offering.

▼ **EXHIBIT 3.2** The 4E Framework for Social Media

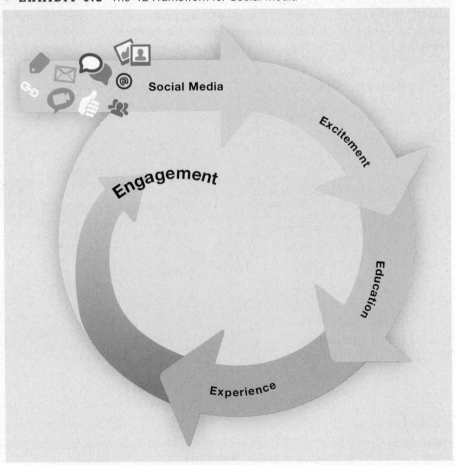

Campaign	Description
True Blood	To get fans excited for its most recent season of *True Blood,* HBO released a Facebook app called Immortalize Yourself. The app allowed vampire lovers and avid fans to break through the barrier of the television by inserting images of themselves and their friends into *True Blood* video clips. As science fiction fans have long dreamed, they could appear to be actually part of the action—fangs and all.
Heinz	Modern consumers often feel that they lack the time or ability to remember when they should send greeting cards or check in with a sick friend. Instead, they send birthday wishes via Facebook. Therefore, the condiment company expanded the notion by developing a Facebook campaign that allowed users to pay $3 to send a sick friend a can of tomato or chicken soup, inscribed with the friend's name with the greeting "Get Well Soon." How thoughtful did they look—simply by clicking a button!
Volkswagen	A lot of companies ask customers to like their site. Although clicking the Facebook thumbs-up icon is easy, Volkswagen decided to make it exciting as well. Customers in the Netherlands who visited Facebook and voted for their favorite classic car—the T1 or the Beetle— were entered automatically in a drawing for a Fanwagen. This special edition of the winning car model was fully loaded with social media features, including the ability to view Facebook news feeds in the car and display a relationship status on the license plate.
Flair	*Flair* fashion magazine turned the popular question, "Where did you find that fabulous item?" into the Fashion Tag Facebook app. People have long looked to others, especially relevant members of a social group, for fashion inspiration. With the Fashion Tag app, users can ask about where to find the great looks, including both clothing and accessories, featured in friends' pictures.
Intel–Toshiba	Movies are great, but they would be better if the characters would just listen to the advice viewers give them! Intel and Toshiba understand; they developed the interactive movie, *The Inside Experience,* starring Emmy Rossum. The actress posted clues about her abducted character's whereabouts on Facebook, Twitter, and YouTube, and viewers worked together to solve the central mystery of the film and thus save her character. Anyone who had ever complained about an unbelievable plot twist or disappointing ending had his or her own chance to determine how the show would end.

Source: Adapted from "Like This, Follow That: It's the 10 Best Social Media Campaigns of the Year," *Ad Age,* December 12, 2011.

personalized offers, which are determined through insights and information obtained from customer relationship management and/or loyalty programs. To obtain these insights and information, the firm might use online analytic tools such as Google analytics or a listening system such as those provided by Salesforce.com, described in the chapter opener and later in this chapter.

In some cases, location-based software and applications help bring the offer to the customers when they are making a purchase decision. For instance, Staples may provide a loyal customer a relevant coupon, based on previous purchases, through his or her mobile phone while the customer is in the store—a very relevant and hopefully exciting experience. Exhibit 3.3 highlights some illustrative and successful social media campaigns because they are exciting and relevant to their audiences. Social and Mobile Media 3.1 highlights how Dove launched an innovative campaign that generated high levels of excitement while educating customers about the difference between how women perceive themselves and how others see them.

Educate the Customer

An imperative of well-designed social media marketing offers is that they have a clear call to action: to draw customers through their computers, tablets, and mobile devices into online websites or traditional retail stores. When potential customers arrive at the websites or stores, the marketer has a

Staples excites its customers by giving them instant rewards through their mobile phones while they are in the store.

Social & Mobile Marketing 3.1
Social Media That Goes Beyond the Surface

Dove's nearly decade-long Campaign for Real Beauty has been the subject of innumerable advertising analyses. From its inspiring messages to its embrace of nontraditional-looking models, the Unilever brand's approach to marketing its skin care products has broken various boundaries.

With its latest iteration of that campaign, it also broke through to the social media stratosphere. The Real Beauty Sketches advertisement recounts women's encounters with a sketch artist, who draws them (sight unseen) on the basis of their self-descriptions. In the videos, he then draws them again, on the basis of someone else's description. The differences in the resulting sketches have been instructive about the self-criticisms that modern women apply to themselves and their appearance.

The emotional tone and resonant meaning of the videos led to them becoming the most watched advertisement on YouTube within just a month of their release, at which time they had prompted 114 million views.[6] The effect also was not limited to the ads themselves. An article about the campaign, posted on the popular Mashable.com site, prompted more than 500,000 shares within 24 hours of being posted.[7]

Most explanations for the incredibly viral nature of these videos focus on the powerful emotions they evoke. Like the women featured in the ads themselves, millions of female consumers regarded this reminder to embrace their own personal beauty as inspirational

and motivational. Many male consumers were similarly moved, whether because they imagined their daughters facing similar levels of self-criticism or simply because they empathized with the notion. The resurgently popular actor and activist George Takei even weighed in, commenting on his Facebook page that even though it was an ad, "it brought tears to my eyes through its powerful message"—and thereby garnered tens of thousands of likes.

Such popularity is bound to spark some backlash. Some of it was humorous; a spoof of the ad with men describing themselves quickly earned millions of views on YouTube on its own. But in addition, some critics decried the persistent notion, which they asserted the commercials reinforced, that women needed to be judged on their looks at all.[8] On a Tumblr site, one commentator noted that rather than focusing on the women's strength, intelligence, or courage, the ads continued to encourage them to define their self-worth by how attractive someone else regarded them as being.[9]

Despite the critics, it's hard to argue that the advertising campaign was anything less than a spectacular success. It encouraged millions of consumers to share and comment on it, with little additional effort from Dove. When the campaign also won a prestigious Titanium Grand Prix at the Cannes annual advertising awards, it garnered even more coverage and interest among people compelled by the ads themselves.[10]

> Although most of the top videos on YouTube are funny, silly, or otherwise entertaining, the site's most useful contributions may be the vivid information it provides about a firm's goods and services.

golden opportunity to educate them about its value proposition and communicate the offered benefits. Some of this information may be new, but in some cases, education is all about reminding people about what they already know. Therefore, by engaging in appropriate education, marketers are expanding the overlap of the benefits that they provide with the benefits that customers require. In this sense, the second E of the 4E framework constitutes a method to develop a sustainable competitive advantage.

Several social media tools are critical in helping marketers educate their potential customers, such as blogs and blogging tools (e.g., WordPress and Twitter), HubSpot (all-in-one

marketing software), YouTube and Google+, as well as some less known options such as Roost or Schedulicity. Adding Value 3.1 highlights how HubSpot can be used to educate one's customers better.

Experience the Product or Service

Although most of the top videos on YouTube are funny, silly, or otherwise entertaining, the site's most useful contributions may be the vivid information it provides about a firm's goods and services—how they work, how to use them, and where they can

Adding Value 3.1

Educating Customers Using HubSpot[11]

Today's marketers reach customers via a new set of inbound marketing tools that includes blogging, tweeting, websites, search engine optimization, and analytics. However, effectively using these disconnected strategies requires time and technical savvy. To simplify matters, HubSpot helps its clients post content on websites, Twitter, and other social media platforms and tracks the results with its proprietary software.

Canadian Mountain Holidays Heli-Skiing & Summer Adventures (CMH) provides helicopter transport, lodging, and guides for ski, snowboard, and hiking vacations. The adventure company had tried out a number of web-based tactics but found its approaches cumbersome and inefficient. They had no ability to analyze the effectiveness of their efforts. However, after using HubSpot's analytics to help them coordinate and disseminate their social media messages and then analyze the results for three years, CMH documented a 387 percent increase in traffic from social marketing and a 772 percent increase in leads.

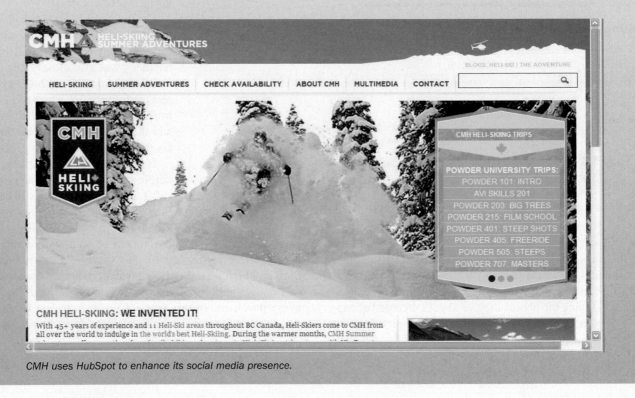

CMH uses HubSpot to enhance its social media presence.

be obtained. YouTube and similar sites can come relatively close to simulating real experiences. Such benefits are very common for products that have long been sold online—so much so that we might forget that it used to be difficult to assess these products before buying them. But today, consumers can download a chapter of a new book to their tablet before buying it. They can try out a software option for a month before buying it. They often can listen to a few seconds or even an entire song before purchasing from iTunes. The diffusion of such products has expanded to feature a wealth of new channels and media options.

For other offerings, such as services, social media again offer experience-based information that was not previously available unless consumers bought and tried the product or service. Need help choosing a new nail polish color or applying a new makeup trend? Check blogs such as Temptalia (http://www.temptalia.com/category/tutorials), which offers both advice and tutorials. Relied too long on clip-on ties? Head over to Tie-a-Tie (http://www.tie-a-tie.net/) to find pictures, videos, and step-by-step instructions on how to manage a Windsor, Pratt, or bowtie knot as well as advice on what to wear to an interview.

Home Depot has long been a source for do-it-yourselfers (DIYers). But if eager customers forget what the salesclerk said about installing a newly purchased water heater, they can check the retailer's website (http://www6.homedepot.com/how-to/index.html) to get detailed, in-depth instructions. They also will find a section that enables them to chat with other users who might have run into similar problems in their own installation projects.

creators Hip, cool contributors who sit at the cutting edge and plan to stay there. Social media give them new ways to post and share their creative, clever ideas.

bonders Social butterflies who use social media to enhance and expand their relationships, which they consider all-important in their lives.

professionals People who are constantly on the go, busy, and want to appear efficient, with everything together, so they use social media to demonstrate just how smart they are.

sharers A type of consumer that uses social media sites and wants to help by being constantly well informed, so that they can provide genuine insights to others.

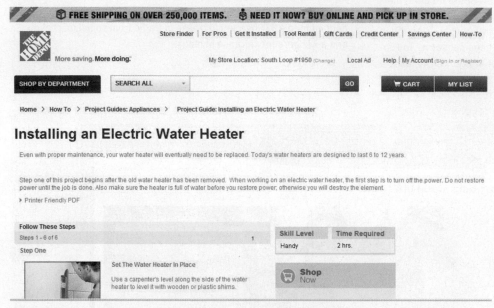

Need information on how to install a water heater? Go to Home Depot's website.

Nikon's Digital Learning Center (see http://www.flickr.com /groups/nikondigitallearningcenter/; http://www.flickr.com /Nikon) provides Flickr members with "tutorials, practical photography tips and advice from Nikon photo professionals to assist them in taking the photos they've always dreamed of capturing."[12] Beyond just providing static photography tips that

customers actively engage with firms and their own social networks. Such engagement can be negative or positive. Positively engaged consumers tend to be more profitable consumers, purchasing 20 to 40 percent more than less engaged customers.[13]

On the other hand, Dave Carroll, a traveling musician whose guitar was roughly handled by United baggage handlers, was also closely engaged (in a negative manner) with the company and other users. He spent considerable time and effort to release three songs and their videos, just to convince others that they should not fly United.

But that story also offers an example of positive engagement. Carroll's music, face, and story gained international recognition as an example of how just one social media user could have a huge negative influence on a giant company. To leverage this fame, Carroll has established a website and blog in which he talks about his experiences. His book offers automatic links to copies of his famous United songs with every purchase. In this sense, Carroll is trying to move beyond the excitement and education he initially elicited from

[Positively engaged consumers tend to be more profitable consumers, purchasing 20 to 40 percent more than less engaged customers.]

could be found in a book, Nikon created a two-way dialogue with customers, inviting professional photographers to provide instruction and host question-and-answer sessions and encouraging users to post their own photos. The more than 64,000 members of the learning center thus learn from others' experiences, even as they create their own.

Engage the Customer

In a sense, the first three Es set the stage for the last one: engaging the customer. With engagement comes action, the potential for a relationship, and possibly even loyalty and commitment. Through social media tools such as blogging and microblogging,

other people. Now he wants to engage those same people as consumers—of his book.

Next we'll look at the role of various social media tools in shaping the 4E framework for social media.

 check yourself

1. What are the 4Es?
2. What social media elements work best for each of the 4Es?

LO 3-2 Understand the types of social media.

CATEGORIES OF SOCIAL MEDIA

Consider your own Facebook site. Are all your real-life friends your online friends too? Do you actually know all the friends registered on your online site? In all likelihood, you host online friends you've never met, and your circle of virtual friends may be larger than the number of people you see regularly or talk to personally. Accordingly, the audience for marketers could be bigger on social media sites than through other, more traditional forms of media. Such a huge potential audience has gotten the attention of marketers.

Marketers rely on the three types of social media: social network sites, media-sharing sites, and thought-sharing sites (or blogs) (see Exhibit 3.4) to achieve three objectives. First, members promote themselves to gain more friends. Second, the sites promote to get more members. Third, outside companies promote their products and services to appeal to the potential consumers who are active on the sites.

Social Network Sites

Social network sites are an excellent way for marketers to create *excitement,* the first of the 4 Es. People can interact with friends (e.g., Facebook) or business acquaintances (e.g., LinkedIn). Although the amount of time people spend on such sites varies, research indicates that they are widely used.[14] Specifically, Exhibit 3.5 shows how much social networks are used by different types of consumers based on their motivations and habits. Note that the vast majority of people in this study use social network sites between one and four hours every day!

- **Creators**, those hip, cool contributors, sit at the cutting edge and plan to stay there. Social media give them new ways to post and share their creative, clever ideas.

- **Bonders** are social butterflies who use social media to enhance and expand their relationships, which they consider all-important in their lives.

▼ **EXHIBIT 3.4** Types of Social Media

- **Professionals**, who are constantly on the go and busy, want to appear efficient, with everything together, so they use social media to demonstrate just how smart they are.

- **Sharers** really want to help others, and the best way to do so is by being constantly well informed so that they can provide genuine insights to others.

All four segments use various types of social networking, as the following sections detail.

▼ **EXHIBIT 3.5** Length of Time Using Social Networking Sites Daily

Source: Coca-Cola Retailing Research Council and the Integer Group, "Social Networking Personas: A Look at Consumer and Shopper Mind Sets," in *Untangling the Social Web: Insights for Users, Brands, and Retailers,* March 2012.

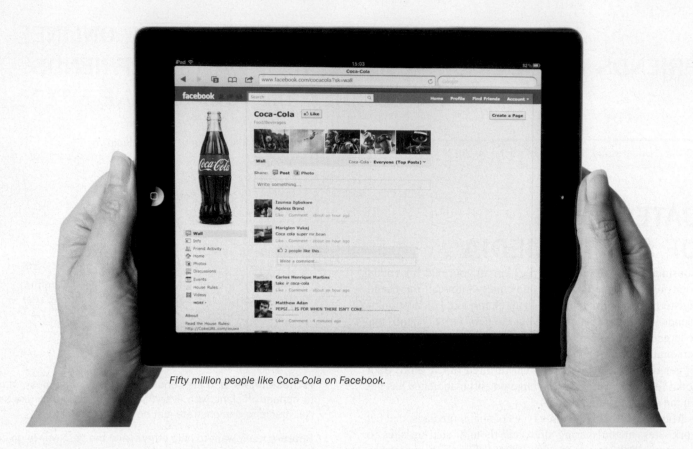

Fifty million people like Coca-Cola on Facebook.

Facebook On this well-known social network platform, more than 800 million active users give companies a forum for interacting with their fans. Thus Facebook not only assures individual users a way to connect with others but gives marketers the ability to target their audience carefully. Companies have access to the same features that regular users do, including a wall where they can post company updates, photos, and videos or participate in a discussion board. Through this form of free exposure, the company can post content and information regarding products, events, news, or promotions that might be exciting to their customers. Only the fans of their page generally have access to such information, so the company can specifically target its fans.

Successful companies on Facebook attempt to excite their customers regularly. On the fan page for the discount clothing retailer Forever 21, for example,[15] when a fan clicks to indicate that he or she likes a certain post, the message is relayed to a news feed. Then every friend of that user sees what he or she likes, creating an exciting and huge multiplier effect.[16]

Another, albeit more controversial example, was when Burger King launched a Facebook campaign in which customers could earn a free Whopper if they delisted 10 friends from their account. The so-called Whopper Sacrifice was intended to show what someone would give up for a Whopper, and the campaign attracted the participation of more than 200,000 active users. After a Whopper Sacrifice, the ex-friends received notification, which was also published on the Facebook mini-feed and thus helped spread the word even more quickly. As the campaign caught on though, Facebook disabled it. Thus, the Facebook page for Burger King read: "Facebook has disabled Whopper Sacrifice after your love for the Whopper sandwich proved to be stronger than 233,906 friendships." By affecting 233,906 people, who were either defriended or actually did the defriending, Burger King created a notable form of excitement—despite being shut down quickly.[17]

Display advertising with Facebook ads targets specific groups of people, according to their profile information, browsing histories, and other preferences. If online users reveal an interest in ski equipment or Burton snowboards, marketers can target both groups. Thus, Facebook offers a variation on more traditional forms of promotion, with the promise of more accurate targeting and segmentation. But being effective and relevant on Facebook is not simply a matter of shifting an offline ad into social network sites, as Adding Value 3.2 recognizes.

> "Facebook not only assures individual users a way to connect with others but gives marketers the ability to target their audience carefully."

Adding Value 3.2

Effective Friending

The use of social networking in marketing is so new that inexperienced marketers have launched poorly conceived Facebook campaigns with the hope that any strategy that includes social media is good enough. But good enough is rarely sufficient in a competitive marketplace, and some brands have hurt their images by launching campaigns that are out of step with social media culture.

When a group of industry professionals discussed the ingredients necessary to attract positive attention from Facebook's 800 million users,[18] they agreed that a successful campaign must tell a story. Ideally, the story should involve and engage users in the plotline. Equally important, these creative heavyweights highlighted the need to connect the campaign to the real world, as Heinz did with its campaign that allowed users to send personalized cans of soup to sick friends (recall Exhibit 3.3).

Making good use of consumer data available on Facebook can also improve campaign success by giving marketers the ability to home in on target audiences and track consumer response. After months of flat reactions to a Facebook promotion of its environmentally friendly cleaners, Clorox launched new initiatives designed to educate people about and increase sales of its Green Works products. The campaign targeted only those women whose Facebook profiles featured the words "clean" or "green."[19] At the same time, Clorox aimed to enhance the experience of other potential users by inviting consumers to nominate green heroes in their community to receive a $15,000 grant. In yet another effort, Clorox offered a $3-off coupon to people who connected to the Green Works web page. The result was a record-breaking engagement rate for the company, demonstrating that social media, when used properly, can be a valuable marketing tool.

Clorox's Facebook promotion is designed to educate people about and increase sales of its Green Works products.

> **More than 12 million of LinkedIn's users are small-business owners, making it an excellent resource for entrepreneurs to network.**

LinkedIn A professional instead of casual or friendship-based site, LinkedIn allows users to share their professional lives. With more than 150 million users, it is a place where users can post their résumés, network with other professionals, and search for jobs.[20] It is *not* the place where you will see games such as Mafia Wars or FarmVille; instead, users post to question-and-answer forums, do job searches, and post personal intellectual property, such as presentations they have given.

The professional networking benefits of LinkedIn are particularly beneficial for small-business owners. More than 12 million of LinkedIn's users are small-business owners, making it an excellent resource for entrepreneurs to network with

> ## WITHIN SIX WEEKS OF ITS LAUNCH, GOOGLE+ HAD ADDED 16 GAMES TO ITS LINEUP, INCLUDING ANGRY BIRDS AND ZYNGA POKER. THE GOAL WAS TO EXCITE USERS WHO LOVE TO PLAY.

like-minded firms, identify the best vendors, or build brand reputation by participating in LinkedIn's professional association groups. With more than 150,000 company profiles on LinkedIn, it also offers a great place to prospect for new business customers and keep an eye on and get key information about competitors.[21]

Google+ The launch of Google+ represents an attempt to compete with the excitement of Facebook. Its effect on social media and gaming communities was nearly immediate. Within six weeks of its launch, Google+ had added 16 games to its lineup, including Angry Birds and Zynga Poker. The goal was to excite users who love to play, especially games that let them interact with one another—the people who made such a massive success out of Facebook's FarmVille game.[22] If Google+ can attract players effectively, it hopes they never go back to Facebook. With this tactic, Google+ attracted more than 20 million unique visitors within weeks of its launch. But advertisers, users, and gaming companies continue to watch closely to discover how the Google+ network will fare. Are users going to be loyal to Google+, or are they just signing on to check out the newest thing from an Internet giant?[23]

Adding Value 3.3 highlights how social network tools help small businesses expand by teaching their customers about what they can provide.

Media-Sharing Sites

The World Wide Web has the ability to connect people more easily and in more ways than have ever been possible before. Media-sharing sites explicitly rely on this capability to enable users to share content they have generated, from videos on YouTube to pictures on Flickr and so on. In terms of the 4E framework, companies use such sites to highlight how consumers can *experience* their goods or services as well as encourage consumers to *engage* with the firm, its other social media outlets, and other consumers.

Instagram With Instagram, people who have downloaded the app (more than 100 million and counting) can take a photo of themselves or their surroundings.[24] The app enables them to add fun filters, such as causing the picture to look as if it were taken by an old Polaroid camera. Then they can upload the artistic creation to various social networking sites, including Twitter, Tumblr, or Facebook.

The name of this app evokes the founders' idea of its use: a sort of modern-day, immediate telegram.[25] It was effective enough that it attracted the attention of some of the most famous names in media sharing, including Justin Beiber, Kim Kardashian, and Tony Hawk—which increased its popularity even more. Recognizing the value of a mobile option, Facebook purchased Instagram in 2012. For the first time, the social media giant promised not to absorb its purchase but to allow Instagram to continue functioning much as it had been all along.[26]

Instagram recently added video-sharing capabilities as well, although another app had beat it to that punch. Vine, which was purchased by Twitter in 2012, lets users capture and share 6-second videos. Advertisers already have embraced this option, finding that the short time limit appeals to consumers. People are ready to share a quick video, far more so than a longer commercial, which enhances the chances of a Vine marketing campaign going viral.[27]

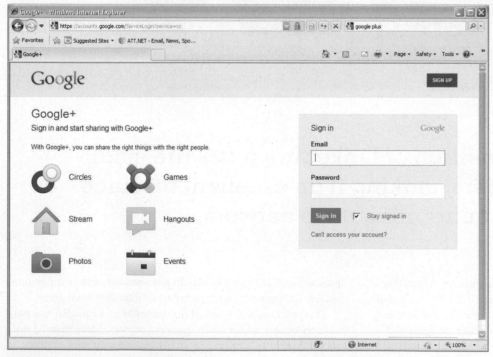

Google+ is Google's answer to Facebook.

Adding Value   3.3

Social Networks Help Small Businesses Grow

Any small business, especially a new one, comes right up against the bottom line. A skeletal staff and tight budgets may make it tough to take on a new task such as social media management. Yet some small-business owners have found that social networks are an essential tool to reach customers and put their products on the map.

Specializing in luxury watches like Cartier and Rolex that sell for at least $4,000 each, Melrose Jewelers has used social networks to connect with its primary customer base: young, upwardly mobile consumers who are technologically savvy.

Its social media activity, including Facebook (with 100,000 likes), a blog, and YouTube, increased sales by 71 percent the first year. One Facebook campaign, a personality quiz that helped customers decide which watch best suited them, attracted $100,000 in sales. Facebook's customer testimonials also helped build credibility with older customers.[28]

Negri Electronics, a high-end cell phone vendor, uses Google+ for customer communication. Google+ circles enable the owner to send specialized messages to each customer group. Google+ also has made Web searching more social, because the +1 feature allows the owner to prioritize web pages for circle members. The owner of Mansfield Fine Furniture disagrees, though. After six months in business, he has about a dozen customers who have purchased his pieces, which range in price from $500 to $5,000 each. He finds Facebook still yields a more robust customer response because Google+ is not yet widely used.[29]

YouTube On this video-sharing social media platform, users upload, share, and view videos. This medium gives companies a chance to express themselves in a different way than they have in the past. YouTube videos also show up in Google searches, making it an appealing vehicle for retailers.[30] The site's demographics indicate visitors are affluent, of the age range most appealing to retailers, and racially reflective of the wider U.S. population.[31]

YouTube also provides an effective medium for hosting contests and posting instructional videos. The Home Depot attracts more than 4,400 viewers with an array of videos detailing new products available in stores as well as instructional do-it-yourself videos such as "How To Tips for Mowing Your Lawn" or "How To Repair a Toilet."[32] These videos maintain the core identity of the Home Depot brand while adding value for consumers, who learn useful ways to improve their homes. As a good example of IMC, Home Depot reinforces its brand image and makes itself more relevant to the consumer's life.

Companies can broadcast from their own channel, that is, a YouTube site that contains content relevant only to the company's own products.[33] For example, Home Shopping Network (HSN) offers consumers an interesting vehicle to use the 4E framework—*excite, educate, experience,* and *engage*—using a multichannel strategy with its television channel as its central focus. As competition in this field has increased, HSN has added to its communication arsenal an e-commerce site and Facebook and MySpace pages. But perhaps the most powerful tool it has added is its dedicated YouTube channel, which it exploits to reach target shoppers in an exciting way that maximizes the value of its media content. Products promoted on HSN, such as Tori Spelling's jewelry line,[34] are available on YouTube almost immediately after they appear on television. Then HSN marketers can use the information gathered from YouTube to target its direct mail campaigns. For example, it could send jewelry promotions to households that

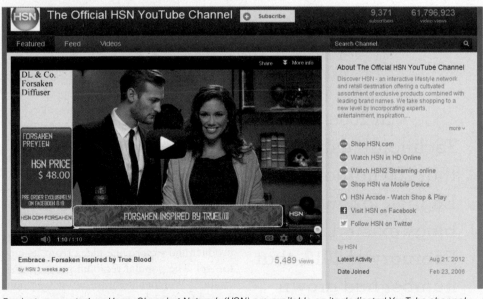

Products promoted on Home Shopping Network (HSN) are available on its dedicated YouTube channel almost immediately after they appear on television.

viewed the YouTube video clip for a necklace from the Tori Spelling Collection. Consumer responses are monitored 24/7 and measured against hourly sales goals. There's thus never a dull moment.

Flickr and Other Photo Sites Whereas YouTube allows users to share videos, Flickr, Picasa, TwitPic, Photobucket, and Imgur allow them to share photos. They tend to be less popular as marketing tools, yet some innovative companies have found ways to engage with customers such as by hosting picture posting competitions or using photos to communicate core tenets and values.[35]

The U.K. brand Innocent, known for selling pure 100 percent fruit smoothies, uses Flickr to communicate its quirky brand image. Its photo posting competitions, such as the Funny Shaped Fruit Competition (http://www.flickr.com/groups/funnyshapedfruit/), provide significant entertainment value. But it also uses Flickr for more serious purposes, such as to post photos related to its Big Knit charity promotion.[36]

Thought-Sharing Sites

Thought-sharing sites consist of different types of blogs: corporate, professional, personal, and micro. In terms of the 4E framework, blogs are particularly effective at *educating* and *engaging* users and, in many cases, enhance their *experience* with the products and services being discussed.

Blogs Once upon a time, confined to a journal or diary in a person's room, the **blog** (from "web log") on the Internet has allowed us to make our thoughts open to the world through thought-sharing websites. For corporations, the comment section allows marketing managers to create a two-way dialogue directly with the end users. The wide availability of free blogging tools such as WordPress, Blogger, and TypePad, which enable non–technically oriented people to create their own blogs, has made blogging a very popular pastime. In 2009, Technorati estimated that 200 million English language blogs existed, and by February of 2012, that number had grown to 450 million.[37]

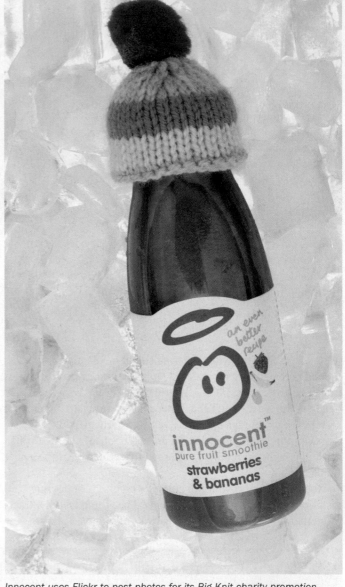

Innocent uses Flickr to post photos for its Big Knit charity promotion.

Companies have responded to this interest and now have several ways to include blogging in their social media marketing strategy. Blogs provide firms the opportunity to *educate* their customers about their offerings, and to *engage* them by responding to their communications, both positive and negative. The reach that marketers have to their customers from blogs can be categorized by the level of control they offer. **Corporate blogs**, which are created by the companies themselves, have the highest level of control because, to a large degree, they can control the content posted on them. Of course, blogs also allow customers to respond to posts, so the content can

> In 2009, Technorati estimated that 200 million English language blogs existed, and by February of 2012, that number had grown to 450 million.

never be completely controlled, but marketing managers have a good opportunity to pepper their blogs with the messages they wish their customers to see. The best corporate blogs illustrate the importance of engaging customers around the core brand tenets without being overly concerned with a hard sell.

Starbucks (http://mystarbucksidea.force.com/apex/ideaHome) uses its blog for new product development by generating new product and *experience* ideas from its customers. The popular regional grocery store chain.[37] Wegman's (http://www.wegmans.com/blog/) blogs to generate loyalty and generate sales by sharing employees' ideas about entertaining, nutrition, and recipes. General Electric (http://www.gereports.com/) *educates* customers through its blog by telling entertaining stories geared at getting customers to realize it sells more than just light bulbs.[38]

From a marketing perspective, **professional blogs** are those written by people who review and give recommendations on products and services. Marketers often offer free products or provide modest remuneration to top-rated professional bloggers in the hopes of getting a good product review. Marketers have less control over professional bloggers than they do their own corporate blogs. But consumers seem to trust professional bloggers' reviews much more than corporate blogs and other more traditional media such as advertising. Such trust may be fleeting, however, as more consumers realize that professional bloggers are often compensated for positive reviews. "Mommy Blogs," a particularly popular type of professional blog, feature advice and product recommendations from one mother to many

for hacked Twitter accounts or ill-considered tweets. And Twitter can also act as an international, rapidly spread complaint forum.[40]

A central problem for companies is ownership of relevant Twitter handles and responsibility for outgoing Twitter communication. If Twitter control is shared by a lot of people, the message usually gets muddled. But if only one or two people are in charge, the need to respond to the vast number of incoming tweets might become overwhelming. Different companies thus manage their Twitter strategies in various ways.

Whole Foods tries to develop a broader engagement with customers by interacting with its 2.1 million Twitter followers. It instituted a weekly Twitter chat, for an hour every Thursday, during which Whole Foods representatives discuss topics such as holiday menu planning and healthy eating. Many Whole Foods stores also have their own Twitter accounts to answer questions directly related to their stores.

[As much as Twitter can help build a firm's brand image, it can also tarnish it instantly.]

others. Dooce, written by Heather Armstrong, has more than 1.5 million mommy followers.[39]

Finally, **personal blogs** are written by people who receive no products or remuneration for their efforts. Thus, of the various types of blogs, marketers have the lowest level of control over this type. However, personal blogs are useful for monitoring what is going on in the marketplace and for responding to customer complaints or compliments.

Microblogs As the name implies, a **microblog** differs from a traditional blog in size—short sentences, short videos, or individual images. On the most popular microblogging site, Twitter, users are limited to 140-character messages. Twitter provides another option for companies to *educate* their customers by providing corporate and product information and to *engage* them by providing a platform for two-way communications. Even companies that may have once resisted social media are now realizing that Twitter offers an important communications channel.

As much as Twitter can help build a firm's brand image, though, it can also tarnish it instantly. Firms have to watch out

In contrast, Best Buy hires an army of specialists to manage its Twitter accounts: not just the main account @Best Buy, but also @BestBuy_Deals, @GeekSquad, and @BestBuyNews. The specialists who work Best Buy's help desk also will answer questions through Twitter, at @Twelpforce. Users who tweet the help desk receive an almost instant response from one of Best Buy's 3,000 employees who have signed up to participate on the task force, which further helps showcase the broad spectrum of expertise available through Best Buy.[41]

For small companies with limited marketing budgets, the use of tweeted promotional messages are particularly appealing. A local bakery tweeted, "Two new scones: Lemon Blueberry and Chorizo Cheddar!" and received responses from 400 Twitter followers—a huge captive audience for a local entity.

Of course, some of the most famous Twitter users are celebrities, who have their own brands to manage and marketing goals to reach. Think about how teen idol Justin Bieber and his management team have relied on Twitter and other social media to reach his target audience, as we describe in Adding Value 3.4.

Adding Value

3.4

Never Say Never Once Social Media Catch Fire

Teen idol Justin Bieber was just a boy who liked to sing when his mother uploaded some of their homemade videos onto YouTube in 2007. Within a year, the 13-year-old Canadian had been discovered, signed a contract with the record producer Usher, and was well on his way to a blockbuster career. In 2010, he performed for President Obama. His "Baby" video registered the most views on YouTube, with more than 408 million downloads.[42] His phenomenal success worldwide points to the power of social media—especially for anyone trying to reach a global market of adolescent girls.

Bieber's vast social media platform reaches millions of followers worldwide, including around 40 million fans on his Facebook site, and more than 21,000 new members join every day. His music on MySpace has registered more than 108 million plays.[43] Yet Bieber's success was not, at first, guaranteed. When music producer Scooter Braun spotted him on YouTube and took his videos to the record companies, they declined. But Braun believed in his young client's boy-next-door-look and convincing R&B sound. So he decided to continue the YouTube uploads of Bieber performing in any venue they could find.[44] By the time Bieber surpassed 10 million YouTube views, he had also started working with Usher. *My World,* his first album, pushed Bieber's YouTube numbers past 100 million views.[45]

He and his management team never looked back. In 2011, Bieber broke YouTube records by reaching 2 billion views.[46] Twitter helped build so much buzz that one New York concert had to be cancelled after 5,000 fans suddenly swarmed the venue in a kind of flash mob.[47] Bieber also has over 14 million Twitter followers; his account represents 3 percent of the total traffic on Twitter,[48] where his fan clubs thrive. One of the biggest began in Australia and soon had 90,000 followers tweeting from @JBSource. Besieged by media requests, the singer granted the two girls leading that club his only interview, rather than meet with the major media. The interview became the most watched video of Bieber's tour. Teenagers want to see Bieber meet and talk with someone like them, Braun later explained, not look for information on a dot-com news site.[49]

The Bieber team also has continued to use social media to promote his records and concerts. When the song "Never Say Never" was released, a web video campaign registered 2.8 million views and 400,000 personalized videos, logging more audience engagement than ever before.[50] In perhaps the perfect convergence of a product, a marketing medium, and the moment, Justin Bieber has ridden social media all the way to the top. Whatever you might think of his singing, it makes for great marketing, especially in the age of instantaneous connection.

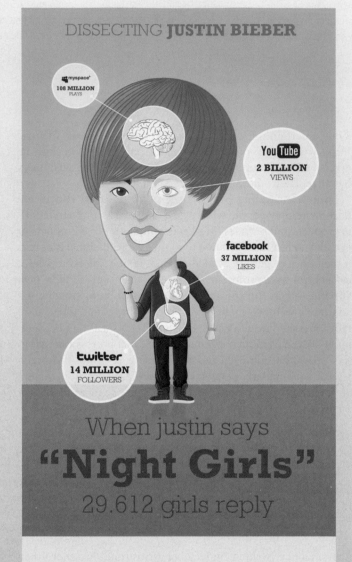

DISSECTING **JUSTIN BIEBER**

myspace
108 MILLION
PLAYS

You Tube
2 BILLION
VIEWS

facebook
37 MILLION
LIKES

twitter
14 MILLION
FOLLOWERS

When justin says

"Night Girls"

29.612 girls reply

1994	•	Justin Drew Bieber (pronounced / ˈdʒʌstɪn ˈbiːbər/) is born
2007	•	Justin's mother posts a video on YouTube of Justin singing 'So Sick' by Ne-Yo
2008	•	Justin is signed by Usher
2009	•	Sings for U.S President Barack Obama
2010	•	'Baby' is the most viewed (and disliked) Youtube video of the year (with 408 million views)
2010	•	Justin is accounted for 3% of all Twitter traffic
2010	•	"justin bieber syphilis" hits #1 on google trends
2010	•	Justin becomes Proactiv spokesperson
2011	•	Is the first to reach 2 billion views on Youtube

Crisp

GOING MOBILE AND SOCIAL

Although 97 percent of consumers access social media through their computers, 37 percent access these media via their mobile phones, 3 percent through iPads, and 2 percent through e-readers.[51] Also, of the more than 100 million people that have smartphones in the U.S., approximately half of them make purchases on these devices. Thus, mobile marketing is significant and growing. In this huge market, consumers generally are younger and wealthier than others, who own older-model mobile phones (or none at all). For example, more than 50 percent of mobile retail consumers earn at least $75,000 annually. In terms of the 4E framework, mobile marketing is particularly useful for creating *excitement* with consumers at the time of sale as we now explain. Several applications have been developed to market goods and services better to these attractive consumers. We briefly discuss a few types: price check apps, fashion apps, and location apps.

Price Check Apps When out shopping, smartphone users no longer have to go from store to store or stop home to go online and compare prices. Using a price checking app, such as at Amazon, or Stylish Girl, customers can scan a product in a store and instantly compare the prices online to see whether a better deal is available. Although price checking can encourage competition, as we discuss in Ethical and Societal Dilemma 3.1, companies can stray into grey ethical areas depending on how they promote their apps.

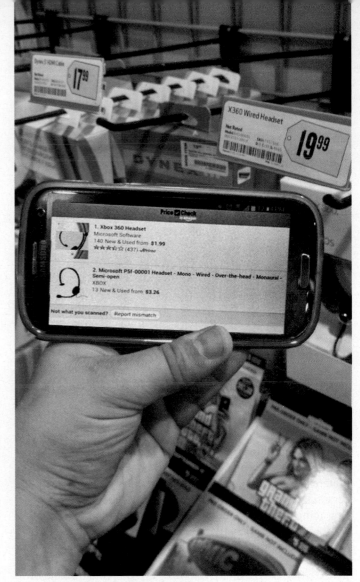

Price check apps enable users to compare prices online to find the best deal.

ethical & societal dilemma   3.1

Internet vs. Brick-and-Mortar Stores

Smartphone price check apps help consumers save money by using a scanned bar code, search query, or photo and spoken product name to search multiple merchants for the best price for a particular item. The results tend to favor online merchants, which don't have to bear the cost of brick-and-mortar stores. But Amazon took price checking a step further: Just in time for holiday shopping, the company sliced off an additional 5 percent for shoppers using Amazon's Price Check app in a physical store.[52] The app only revealed Amazon's price, and the discount, which applied to toys, electronics, and DVDs, could be used for up to three items at a maximum savings of $5 per item.

Retailers complained that the app rewarded consumers for using brick-and-mortar stores as showrooms where shoppers could experience an item in a comfortable environment, learn about it from sales staff, decide to buy it, and then receive a discount for purchasing it online—oftentimes while the customer was still in the store. Although the discount didn't apply to books, it triggered outrage and a call for an Amazon boycott from bookstores already hurt by the Internet retailer's low prices and ability to avoid collecting state sales tax.[53] Critics called the promotion predatory and claimed Amazon was compromising the personality and economic stability of communities.

Retailers compete for customers, particularly during the holiday season, and Amazon's promotion helped shoppers save money. But should Amazon have considered the showroom effect on brick-and-mortar stores? On a broader scale, how aggressive can a marketer be before triggering backlash that can harm the company's reputation?

Realizing that online price checking could be damaging to business, retailers are responding in kind. Lowe's arms its employees with smartphones to help them instantly search the in-store and nearby inventories and place orders online if products are out of stock to ensure that no customer ever leaves empty handed.[54] Target is working with vendors to create exclusive in-store items, to match online retailer pricing, and to develop a subscription-based online pricing strategy that gives regular buyers special discounts.[55]

Fashion Apps

The consumers who are most likely to use mobile media also are likely to buy from technology and fashion-oriented firms, whether they are fashion or technology retailers, sell fashion magazine content, or brand information. Style.com offers a mobile application for people to access the same content available on the *Style.com* magazine website, including blogs, reviews, couture shows, and video feeds.[56] Other apps provide a more in-depth look at a particular brand. Louis Vuitton's NOWNESS app combines magazine content with brand promotion. Pose is not brand-specific; instead, this photo-sharing app shares various style and fashion views and tips. Pinterest allows people to pin merchandise, services, recipes, or ideas onto a virtual bulletin board. For instance, Pinterest users can pin clothing and accessories that match their personal taste; others can browse their pinboards to discover new things and make comments. Marketers therefore can receive unlimited exposure to their products and services as like-minded people share pinned items and services.

Location-Based Gamified Apps

Smartphone owners are increasingly using location-based apps. Customers can

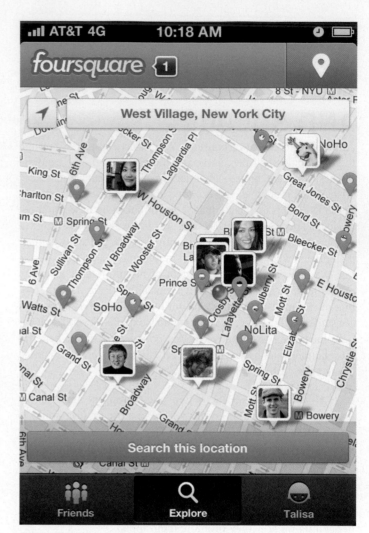

Users of Foursquare can check in at their favorite restaurants and stores, sharing their location on Facebook.

download several free apps that use the GPS function of their phone to share what they are doing, where they are, and when they're doing it. Companies use these apps to build loyalty by making patronage a game, a process known as **gamification**.

Users of Foursquare can check in at their favorite restaurants and stores, sharing their location on Facebook. They can compete with other users for the title of Mayor by achieving the most number of check-ins at a retail location in a 60-day period. Another spin on location-based gamification is SCVNGR. This app takes location-based gaming and direct sales to the next level. Users logging on to the app are provided with a list of stores near them participating in SCVNGR. By completing challenges at these stores, ranging from simply checking in to bumping phones with other SCVNGR users at the establishment to making a portrait of the person sitting across from them out of food and taking a picture of it, users accrue points that unlock in-app badges and real-world coupons such as free coffee. Another interesting app is Snapette, which focuses on shoes and bags and aims to help customers find the merchandise they want according to their immediate location.

Fashion apps allow customers to find the look they want without going to stores and trying on clothes.

In the past two decades, marketers have developed websites and other methods to communicate information about and to sell their goods and services. Their quest for new ways to improve, integrate, and enhance these outcomes has resulted in a confluence of social, mobile, and online marketing. Social network and mobile applications and the associated relevant offers are ideal for stimulating *excitement* in the offers. In particular, mobile location-based apps are exciting because they provide customers with highly relevant offers when they are in close proximity to the retailer or service provider, or they can even be used to provide competitive offers. Media-sharing sites (e.g., YouTube and Flickr) are excellent social media tools that provide customers visual *experiences* of customers or professionals who are using these goods and services. They also provide customers an opportunity to *engage* with the firms as well as their own social network by posting their own experiences (i.e., uploading videos) and sharing their thoughts (blogs and Twitter posts). Finally, thought-sharing sites like blogs are excellent

LO 3-4 Recognize and understand the three components of a social media strategy.

HOW DO FIRMS ENGAGE THEIR CUSTOMERS USING SOCIAL MEDIA?

Now that we have an understanding of the various social and mobile media that are at the firm's disposal, it is important to determine how firms should go about engaging customers through social and mobile media. The three-stage process found in Exhibit 3.6 is **listen** to what customers have to say, **analyze** the information available through various touch points, and finally implement (or **do**) social media tactics to excite customers.

> Customers appear willing to provide their opinions about just about anything, including their interests and purchases—both their own and those of their friends.

for providing customer *education,* as was highlighted by how HubSpot adds value for its clients.

check yourself

1. What is an example of a social network, a media-sharing site, a thought-sharing site, and a mobile application?

2. At which of the 4E dimensions do social networks, media-sharing sites, thought-sharing sites, and mobile applications excel?

Listen

From a market research point of view, companies can learn a lot about their customers by listening (and monitoring) what they say on their social networks, blogs, review sites, and so on. Customers appear willing to provide their opinions about just about anything, including their interests and purchases—both their own and those of their friends. Writing blogs and providing opinions via polls about such diverse topics as BOTOX treatments, ASICS running sneakers, or a particular play of an NFL team during the playoffs all constitute new ways that customers communicate with one another—and with marketers who are paying attention.

▼ **EXHIBIT 3.6** Social Media Engagement Process

SENTIMENT ANALYSIS IS FUNDAMENTALLY TRANSFORMING HOW COMPANIES INTERACT WITH AND ENGAGE THEIR CUSTOMERS. "

Marketers can analyze the content found on sites such as Facebook, Twitter, online blogs, and reviews to assess the favorableness or unfavorableness of the sentiments, using a technique known as **sentiment analysis**. Sentiment analysis allows marketers to analyze data from these sources to collect consumer comments about companies and their products. The data are then analyzed to distill customer attitudes and preferences, including reactions to specific products and IMC campaigns. Scouring millions of sites with sentiment analysis techniques provides new insights into what consumers really think. Companies plugged into such real-time information and insights can become more nimble, allowing for numerous quick changes, such as in a product roll-out, a new advertising campaign, or reacting to customer complaints.

There are several companies that specialize in monitoring social media.[57] For example, Salesforce.com offers social media listening and engagement tools to help its clients such as GE, Kodak, Microsoft, and PepsiCo connect with their customers.[58] Using sentiment analysis techniques, it processes a constant stream of online consumer opinion from blogs, Facebook, and other networking sites, including 400 million Twitter tweets a day. The Salesforce.com tools for managing consumer sentiment data allow companies to identify opinion trends that might warrant an online corporate response. For instance, Salesforce.com may identify negative consumer sentiment; it then provides services to help its client respond. Reacting to

attitudes uncovered in sentiment analysis allows companies to counteract negative opinions, maybe influence those perceptions, and perhaps win customer loyalty.[59]

As an example of how a firm like Salesforce.com can help its clients engage their customers, consider the New York–based nonprofit Let's Get Ready that helps low-income high school students get into college.[60] When it decided to compete for Chase American Giving Awards funding, Let's Get Ready needed broader support. Salesforce.com helped the organization find Web-based conversations among individuals and groups who might share its educational mission. It further helped Let's Get Ready reach out to potential supporters, share information about its work, and ask for votes. The campaign worked: Let's Get Ready placed second, winning $500,000 for free SAT preparation and college admission counseling to motivated students. Sentiment analysis thus is fundamentally transforming how companies interact with and engage their customers.

Analyze

Fortunately, the companies that help facilitate listening also provide analytic tools to assess what customers are saying about the firm and its competitors. Three main categories of analysis are used for understanding data collected from social media.[61]

First, it is important to determine the amount of traffic using their sites, visiting their blogs, or tweeting about them. Measures used for this purpose include **hits** (total requests for a page), visits to a particular site or page, unique visitors to the site, and **page views** (the number of times any pages gets viewed by any visitor).

Second, although knowing how many people are using a firm's social media is important, it is even more critical to learn who those visitors are, what they are doing, and what engages and excites them. To analyze these factors, social media marketers use metrics such as the **bounce rate**, which refers to the percentage of times a visitor leaves the site almost immediately, such as after viewing only one page. Analyzing which pages are the most frequent entry and exit locations

Salesforce.com analyzes customer sentiment for its customers, which enables them to identify opinion trends that might warrant an online corporate response.

sentiment analysis A technique that allows marketers to analyze data from social media sites to collect consumer comments about companies and their products.

hits A request for a file made by web browsers and search engines. Hits are commonly misinterpreted as a metric for website success, however the number of hits typically is much larger than the number of people visiting a website.

page views The number of times an Internet page gets viewed by any visitor.

bounce rate The percentage of times a visitor leaves the website almost immediately, such as after viewing only one page.

click paths Shows how users proceed through the information on a website—not unlike how grocery stores try to track the way shoppers move through their aisles.

conversion rates Percentage of consumers who buy a product after viewing it.

keyword analysis An evaluation of what keywords people use to search on the Internet for their products and services.

provide direction on how to make a website more effective. In addition, following visitors' **click paths** shows how users proceed through the information—not unlike how grocery stores try to track the way shoppers move through their aisles. A firm can use this information to provide users with an easier navigation experience through the site so they can more quickly find what they are looking for. The data analysis can also reveal **conversion rates**, a measure that indicates what percentage of visitors or potential customers act as the marketer hopes, whether by clicking, buying, or donating. Click paths and conversion rates can also reveal what users might have wanted, but not found, on the site.

Third, some companies want to analyze data that comes from other sites, such as measuring where people have come from to get to the company's site. Did

> **Even the greatest analysis has little use if firms fail to implement what they have learned from analyzing their social and mobile media activity.**

they search through Google or Amazon? Did they receive a referral from a friend? Which keywords did they use to find the firm? Firms can use **keyword analysis** to determine what keywords people use to search on the Internet for their products and services. With this information, they can refine their websites by choosing keywords to use on their site that their customers use. Then they can assess the ROI of the investment made by improving the site. This would be done by calculating the incremental profit increase divided by the investment on the site improvement. For social media, it is more challenging to determine ROI than for more traditional IMC applications because the revenue generated by social media is often not directly related to the expenditure. So, instead of traditional ROI measures, firms often examine questions like: Does having more Twitter followers correlate with having higher sales? Do Facebook fans of the company buy more than nonfans? [62]

These analyses require well-trained marketing managers, marketing analytic software, and perhaps some help with consulting specialists (e.g., IBM, SAS, or PriceWaterhouseCoopers). But almost everyone seems to be turning to Google Analytics these days because it offers a sophisticated, in-depth form of analysis, all for free. Not only does Google Analytics track the elements that are shown in Exhibit 3.7, but it also is highly customizable. [63]

Do

Even the greatest analysis has little use if firms fail to implement what they have learned from analyzing their social and mobile media activity. That is, social media may be all about relationships, but ultimately, firms need to use their connections to increase

▼ **EXHIBIT 3.7** Analytics

Type of Analytic	How It's Used	Competitors Offering Similar Analytics
Content	Understand what's popular and what's not on a firm's website, including page load times and site navigation.	Adobe SiteCatlyst, Clickstream, Coremetrics, IBM SurfAid, Mtracking, VisiStat
Social	Track effectiveness of social media programs, including information on social media referred conversion rates and engagement metrics.	Facebook Insights, Twitter Web Analytics, Webtrends
Mobile	Track website access from mobile devices, track which ads direct people to a firm's app, understand what mobile platform performs best.	AppClix, Bango, Flurry, Localytics, Medialets, Webtrends
Conversion	Moving beyond page views and visitor counts, conversion analytics measures sales, downloads, video plays, or any other action important to a firm.	Clicktale, KeyMetric, Latitude
Advertising	Track the effectiveness of social, mobile, search and display ads, divide ad effectiveness by device, platform, or type.	AdTech, MediaMelon MediaCloud, Metronome, Snoobi, YieldMetrics,

Source: http://www.google.com/analytics/features/index.html.

▼ **EXHIBIT 3.8** How to Do a Social Media Marketing Campaign

their business.[64] They might launch a new Facebook campaign, actively blog, or provide mobile offers.

When Facebook first introduced its new Page format, many users balked, complaining about having to reformat all their posts. But Macy's jumped on the chance to refresh its image among its Facebook followers, tell a better story, and

To illustrate how firms might go about undertaking such campaigns, consider the steps involved in developing and implementing a Facebook marketing campaign (Exhibit 3.8).[66] These steps are not unlike the steps used in any integrated marketing communications (IMC) program. (See Chapters 18 and 19 for more details.) Assume a marketer was developing a

> ## "The firm has to determine exactly what it hopes to promote and achieve through its campaign."

develop a testing lab for new promotions and offers. On Pinterest, Macy's also is testing communication tactics that might enable it to piggyback on women's posts about things that inspire them. If one user notes her dream of a beach vacation, Macy's might contact her with an offer for bathing suits—even in the dead of winter. In a recent marketing research survey, the retailer discovered—to its surprise—that 40 percent of the responses came through mobile devices. If customers are responding to surveys through their smartphones, what might they do with mobile promotions?[65] Macy's aims to find out.

Although Macy's appears to have undertaken a broad-based approach, deciding which tactics to employ and when is key. The social media marketer needs to act like an orchestra conductor, waving a wand to make sure that hundreds of musicians, playing a variety of instruments, come together to create some beautiful music. A well-developed marketing strategy involves a host of social and mobile tools, working in conjunction with the firm's traditional IMC tactics, to move the consumer up the purchase decision hierarchy from awareness to purchase to loyalty.

Facebook marketing campaign for a new product that the company has designed.

1. **Identify strategy and goals.** The firm has to determine exactly what it hopes to promote and achieve through its campaign. Does it want to increase awareness of the product? Is it hoping more potential customers might visit and like its Facebook page? Is its focus mainly on increasing sales of the product? Depending on what it aims to achieve, it might focus on developing a Facebook page, creating a Facebook app, or hosting a Facebook event.

2. **Identify target audience.** The next step is to determine whom it is targeting. As Exhibit 3.9 shows, Facebook enables the firm to perform targeting that is based on location, language, education, gender, profession, age, relationship status, likes/dislikes, and friends or connections. The marketer's aim is to find an audience big enough to reach those who might adopt the company's product without being so big that the marketer ends up trying to appeal to someone way outside of the target audience.

3. **Develop the campaign: experiment and engage.** Now that the firm knows whom it is targeting, the next step is to

▼ **EXHIBIT 3.9** Example Facebook Targeting Choices

2. Targeting

Location

Country: (?) [New York]

○ Everywhere
○ By State/Provience (?)
◉ By City (?)

Demographics

Age: (?) [24 ⬍] – [35 ⬍]

Demographics

Age: (?) [24 ⬍] – [35 ⬍]

☐ Require exact age match

Sex: (?) ◉ All   ○ Men   ○

Interests

Precise interests: (?) [Cooking]

Switch to Broad Category Targeting (?)

Estimated Reach (?)

266,920 people

- who live in the **United States**
- who live within **50 miles of New York, NY**
- between the ages of **24** and **35 inclusive**
- who are in the category **Cooking**

Source: From http://www.facebook.com/business/ads/. Reprinted with permission.

develop the communication, including the copy and images. Here again, the process is not very different from any other IMC campaign. There should be a call to action that is clear and compelling. Strong, eye-catching images and designs are important. And the campaign must appeal to the right customers. However, an aspect that is more critical with social media than other forms of IMC is that the images and messages need to be updated almost constantly. Because people expect changing content online, it would be inappropriate to run the same campaign for several months, as the firm might if it were advertising on television, for example.

4. **Develop the budget.** Budgeting is key. Facebook allows advertisers to set a daily budget: Once their costs (usually per click) reach a certain level, the ad disappears for the rest of the day. Of course, this option can be risky if the firm is getting great feedback, and all of a sudden, a compelling ad disappears. Therefore, similar to the campaign content, budgets demand nearly constant review. For example, if a competitor lowers its price significantly, it might be necessary to follow suit to avoid being excluded from customers' consideration sets.

5. **Monitor and change.** The final step is to review the success of the campaign and make changes as necessary. Facebook's Ad Manager offers various metrics and reports, such as number of clicks on ads, audience demographics, and ad performance for specific time periods.

Adding Value 3.5 examines how Applebee's <u>listens</u> to its customers, <u>analyzes</u> the information it has collected, and implements (<u>does</u>) a social media program.

LO 3-5   Understand the methods for marketing yourself using social media.

MANAGING YOUR INDIVIDUAL BRAND VALUE IN A SOCIAL MEDIA WORLD

The branding concepts examined in Chapter 11 apply in unique ways in the social media world, in which context people engage in self-branding in new and exciting ways. Recall that brands attempt to build awareness, aim to develop loyalty, and exert an impact. If one applies these concepts to individual brand equity, one might think of individual brand management in some of the following ways.

Adding Value 3.5
Applebee's Listens, Analyzes, and Does Social Media

National brands are recognizing the need to create specific social media pages tailored to local audiences. Applebee's has tried to be true to its "Eating good in the neighborhood" tagline by maintaining a local focus and encouraging franchisees to stay connected to their local communities. Social media has been instrumental in providing franchisees further opportunities to do so. However, with 2,000 restaurants and 44 franchisees, executives were worried that all of the different messages could dilute the brand or differ from Applebee's corporate-driven initiatives. Therefore, the company hired Expion to help manage its social engagement initiatives across franchises and to extend social media development from the brand to the store level. Franchisees are allowed, and encouraged, to develop their own local social media pages. However, each franchisee must go through an

approval process, run by corporate headquarters, to post comments and photos before they appear online. Reviews are usually approved (or denied) within several hours. In addition, corporate headquarters can send out mass updates such as new menu items or promotional initiatives, which appear to customers as if they are coming from the local store. If customers post negative comments, local and regional managers are alerted immediately.

The new system appears to be paying off: Its Facebook fans have jumped in number from 180,000 to more than 1,000,000. For now, Applebee's is mostly focusing on Facebook content rather than building YouTube or Twitter sites. The goal is to focus on one component of social media to build credibility and trust sufficiently before trying to reach customers through multiple social media outlets.[67] In this sense, listening entails more than just asking questions and putting the response data into a spreadsheet. It also involves entering into social engagement initiatives by joining various conversations, making judgments about the data, and then applying the lessons provided by those data to improve further listening activities.[68]

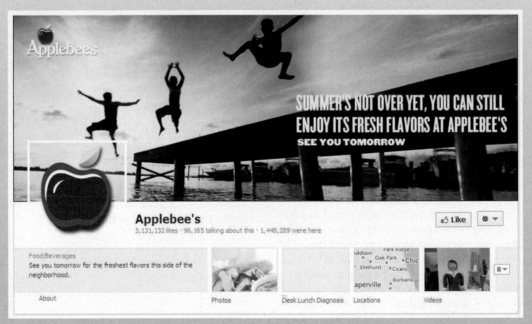

Applebee's is concentrating its social media strategy on Facebook. Its new system has been so successful that its Facebook fans have jumped from 180,000 to over a million.

Measures of individual social media effectiveness or equity use metrics such as **social reach**, which refers to how many people a person influences (e.g., number of individuals in the person's social networks such as Facebook and LinkedIn); **influence**, which is the extent to which the person influences others (e.g., how much do the people in a person's network read that person's content); and **extended network**, or the influence of the person's extended network, that is, the cumulative number of members (10,000) = 100 members each having 100 members of their own.

Several firms have developed metrics to assess a person's social impact (e.g., Klout, PeerIndex, Twitalyzer, and Kred). For example, Klout combines these three elements—social reach, influence, and extended network—to define a Klout score that can range from 0 to 100. The average score earned by regular people that aren't either celebrities or heavily involved in social media, such as bloggers, is around 20. Justin Bieber is the only person ever to earn a perfect 100.

Although Klout offers a good general view of social influence, various other options exist for more specific or detailed analyses, such as PeerIndex (http://www.peerindex.net), Tweet-level (http://tweetlevel.edelman.com/), Twitalyzer (http://twitalyzer.com/), How Sociable (http://www.howsociable.com/), Postrank (http://www.postrank.com/), or TwitterGrader (http://twittergrader.com/).[69] Links shared through Twitter or Facebook also affect search rankings on search engines such as Google or Bing, such that greater influence increases the chances that people can find a more influential source of information or fashion.[70]

In a sense, social media are like high school:[71] In both places, people self-select into groups or cliques. Many people define their self-worth based on how many friends they can count. People's expressions and actions determine their reputation—whether negatively or positively. The environment can be either inclusive or exclusive—and sometimes both. Users seek out others, both as individuals and as groups. Wallflowers are ignored; fun, active, exciting contributors attract attention.

But remember, "No matter how brilliant and talented you are, you won't be sufficiently appreciated . . . until the broader public recognizes you."[72] Thus, beyond creating an online presence, people with true influence also use networks of contacts they make in various realms, give presentations and speeches, publish books and articles as well as blogs, submit themselves for prestigious awards, and try to get on television or other national news outlets.

3. *Blogger.* These highly sought-after jobs provide great flexibility and freedom. By posting articles on relevant websites, bloggers can earn $35–$75 hourly.

4. *Social media marketing specialist.* These well-paid professionals distribute promotional channels using a range of social media channels, which requires strong online marketing skills.

5. *Search engine marketing associate.* Focusing on search engines, these online marketers rely on their knowledge of optimization techniques to increase the organic search rankings for a website.

6. *Online customer service representative.* Customers like to provide feedback, often online, and the best service companies make sure that someone is on hand to respond.

Regardless of the exact job title, social media jobs are increasing. On the Monster.com job search site for example, the number of social media–related jobs recently jumped by

social reach A metric used to determine to how many people a person influences (e.g., number of individuals in the person's social networks such as Facebook and LinkedIn).

influence In a social media context, the extent to which the person influences others (e.g., how much do the people in a person's network read that person's content).

extended network In social media, it is the total number of people a person or entity reaches or has influence over.

> Beyond creating an online presence, people with true influence also use networks of contacts they make in various realms.

Even if a person's goal is not necessarily to become the premier expert on a particular topic, social influence can have significant effects on other elements of his or her life, such as hiring success.[73] Employers can check these social presence scores or impact factors, along with other sources of information, to assess how well connected, creative, and active a potential hire is. This source is particularly critical for the rapidly expanding field of social media jobs for marketers.

A student who graduates with a marketing degree likely has a good foundation for one of the following social media jobs:[74]

1. *Social media strategist.* In this quite high-paying social media job, people create social media marketing campaigns, then measure the results, using an effective strategic plan.

2. *Community manager.* These positions are responsible for handling corporate forums and blogs, increasing traffic to the site, and broadening their company's community.

approximately 75 percent.[75] They also offer good salaries and the promise of continued growth, as Exhibit 3.10 shows.

Getting such jobs implies that candidates truly have influence, and these social media impact scores offer some idea about what personal branding really means.[76] First, influence by itself has little impact. Rather, a person needs to leverage his or her personal brand to induce some action, whether that entails convincing friends to support a cause the person likes or convincing a company to hire that person for an internship. Second, just as it does for a product or service brand, building a personal brand takes time as well as consistent effort. It would be impossible to become really influential by exhibiting a flurry of activity for a couple of days and then taking a month-long break. Third, there is a big difference between being active and being influential. Simply retweeting comments from other creators is insufficient to achieve true influence. To be influential, a personal brand must follow the 4Es: You need to excite, educate, give experience, and engage your followers.

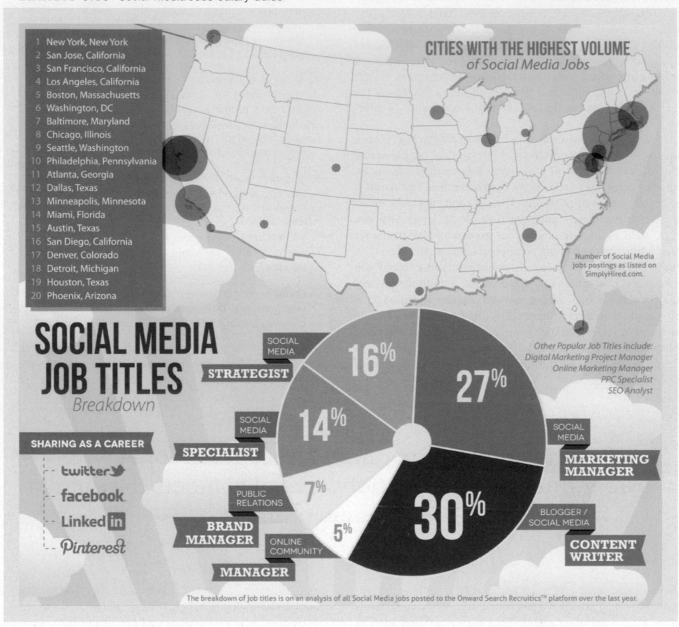

Moreover, just like any other marketing tactic, personal branding needs to take ethical considerations under advisement. For example, we might think carefully about the spread of metrics especially amid reports about the ways they are being used, perhaps without people's knowledge. For example, at the Palms Casino Resort Hotel, clerks check the Klout scores of guests as they check in and then offer upgrades to those with the highest scores.[77] Is that great marketing or an ethically questionable exploitation?

The importance of such scores also implies the potential for abuse. What if firms game the system, such that the only search engine results you see are those that have developed influence because the companies have paid legions of followers to tweet about their offering?[78] Are you really getting the best choices then?

On a more personal note, it has been pretty well established that embarrassing pictures on Facebook can be detrimental to your future career. But what about just basic posts and influence efforts? Despite the benefits of building your social influence, the more information available about you online, the more information potential employers and others have. One study even suggests that human resource managers should assess social media sources to determine whether a potential hire is agreeable (pleasant in interactions or caustic in humor?), emotionally stable (did an interpersonal fight go viral?), or conscientious.[79] Such information also is available for use in legal cases.[80] You thus may be liable for everything you do to enhance your social influence. So think before you post, tweet, or blog: Is this something you want to answer for in court or even just in the court of public opinion? ■

 check yourself

1. What are the three steps in developing social media engagement strategies?
2. How do firms examine customer sentiments?
3. What are the steps in developing a social media campaign?
4. Why might it be important to develop a personal social media presence?

check it out!

mhhe.com/GrewalM4e
for study materials,
including quizzes
and videos.

chapter four

marketing ethics

There is so much to like about fish as a key ingredient to a balanced diet. It is relatively lower in saturated fats, it contains essential omega-3 acids and high levels of protein, and it encourages brain development—hence its reputation as brain food. But as more and more consumers turn to fish as an increasing part of their diet, the practices associated with providing those fish meet more and more ethical challenges.

A primary concern is overfishing. Predictions based on current production levels suggest that oceans will be essentially devoid of fish by 2048.[1] Thus fisheries have moved on to alternative tactics to meet demand, including fish farming and the pursuit of alternatives to some of the most popular, and thus most overfished, breeds. To make these alternatives more appealing, some producers simply rename an existing breed. A lot more people are willing to order orange roughy from a waiter than ask for slimehead—the original common name of this fish.[2] Others go less ethical routes and substitute an unknown or less popular fish for similar tasting options, without consumers' knowledge or agreement.

In Florida for example, grouper sandwiches are a popular local delicacy. But an investigation in dozens of restaurants, in which investigators actually took samples from their plates and tested the DNA of the fish they had been served, revealed only three were actually grouper.[3]

A more recent exposé by the *Boston Globe* showed that the same type of fraud was rampant in Boston-area restaurants.[4] The summary report noted that "consumers routinely and unwittingly overpay for less desirable, sometimes undesirable, species—or buy seafood that is simply not what it is advertised to be. In many cases, the fish was caught thousands of miles away and frozen, not hauled in by local fishermen, as the menu claimed. It may be perfectly palatable—just not what the customer ordered."

LEARNING OBJECTIVES

After reading this chapter, you should be able to:

LO 4-1 Identify the ethical values marketers should embrace.

LO 4-2 Distinguish between ethics and social responsibility.

LO 4-3 Identify the four steps in ethical decision making.

LO 4-4 Describe how ethics can be integrated into a firm's marketing strategy.

LO 4-5 Describe the ways in which corporate social responsibility programs help various stakeholders.

continued on p. 76

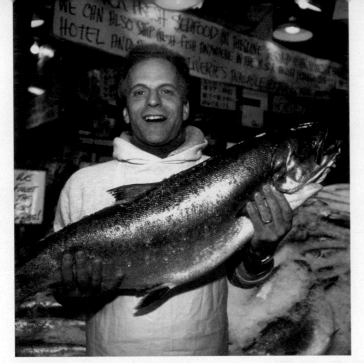

Is this really a grouper or something else?

continued from p. 75

The regulations on fish labeling and naming remain relatively flexible, meaning that in many cases, the restaurants are not breaking any laws. And investigators in all these instances admit that sometimes the restaurants serving the wrong fish simply don't know the difference. But other scenarios clearly show an intent to defraud, as fish sellers and restaurants enjoy the benefits of increased demand and higher profit margins when they lie about what is in the fish. The outcome damages consumers, who do not get what they paid for. But it also threatens fishermen, who struggle to sell legitimate catches for reasonable prices, and innocent restaurants, whose reputations come under fire.

In a sense, this ethical scandal began with a sincere attempt to solve the problem. Increased fishing resulted from the desire to improve healthy diets. Relabeling might have represented an effort to encourage diners to try less endangered, more plentiful fish options and avoid overfishing endangered populations. But when consumers are forced to ask, "Is this grouper really grouper, or is it 'grouper'?" then the situation has become unethical. The result remains an ongoing ethical crisis for consumers—and the fish they eat. ∎

> [**As these examples show, sometimes the ethical dilemma has as much to do with defining our terms as with what the products contain.**]

Which is the more important corporate objective: making a profit or obtaining and keeping customers?[5] Although firms cannot stay in business without earning a profit, using profit as the sole guiding light for corporate action can lead to short-term decisions that cause the firm to lose customers in the long run. The balancing act may turn out to be the quest to place the company on the firmest footing possible.

This question leads into the primary ethical dilemma facing managers, that is, how to balance shareholder interests with the needs of society. In our opening example, overall societal health can benefit from greater access to fish as part of a healthy diet. But in attempting to provide this benefit, many producers have focused more on earning profits rather than ensuring they are transparent in their labeling and sales practices. How might a better balance arise in this setting?

Perhaps the fishing industry could take a cue from the European toy industry. New regulations enforced by the European Union places the responsibility for content and safety on toy producers, importers, and distributors.[6] They are responsible to document that the products in any toys imported into the EU contain no dangerous materials, avoid potential allergens, and cannot cause choking risks.

Or maybe that's the wrong place to look; in the United States, new regulations similarly have been designed to prevent the sort of massive toy recalls that Mattel had to undertake when hundreds of millions of its most popular toys—including Barbie dolls, Matchbox cars, and Laughing Elmo—turned out to be safety risks.[7] In the process, manufacturers, regulators, retailers, parents, and various other groups have been battling over the definition of "children's products."[8] Is a stuffed bear with a Valentine's Day theme a product for children or one for adults?

As these examples show, sometimes the ethical dilemma has as much to do with defining our terms as with what the products

In one month, Mattel recalled more than 20 million potentially dangerous products.

GRANTLAND®

Panel 1: "YOUR POSITION MEANS THAT YOU SHOULD TAKE ANY REPORT OF WRONGDOING VERY SERIOUSLY."

Panel 2: "YOU MEAN BECAUSE I'M A MANAGER?" "YES—"

Panel 3: "THAT, AND THE POSITION YOU'LL BE IN IF THERE'S AN INVESTIGATION." "WHAT'S THAT?"

Panel 4: "ALL BY YOURSELF."

Source: Copyright Grantland Enterprises; www.grantland.net.

contain. But even if the question seems to be one of terminology, if customers believe they can no longer trust a company or that the company is not acting responsibly, they will no longer support that company by purchasing its products or services or investing in its stock. For marketers, the firm's ability to build and maintain consumer trust by conducting ethical, transparent, clear transactions must be of paramount importance.

principles must be a continuous and dynamic process.[9] The nearby cartoon illustrates the importance of making good ethical decisions. Because the marketing profession is often singled out among business disciplines as the root cause of a host of ethical lapses (e.g., unethical advertising, the promotion of shoddy products), anyone involved in marketing must recognize the ethical implications of their actions. These can involve

> " Because the marketing profession is often singled out among business disciplines as the root cause of a host of ethical lapses, anyone involved in marketing must recognize the ethical implications of their actions. "

In this chapter, we start by examining what marketing ethics is and why behaving ethically is so important to successful marketing and to long-term profits. We then discuss how firms can create an ethical climate among employees and how their individual behavior can affect the ability of the firm to act ethically. To help you make ethical marketing decisions, we provide a framework for ethical decision making and then examine some ethical issues within the context of the marketing plan (from Chapter 2). Finally, we present some scenarios that highlight typical ethical challenges marketing managers often must face.

THE SCOPE OF MARKETING ETHICS

Business ethics refers to the moral or ethical dilemmas that might arise in a business setting. **Marketing ethics**, in contrast, examines those ethical problems that are specific to the domain of marketing. Firms' attempts to apply sound ethical

societal issues, such as the sale of products or services that may damage the environment; global issues, such as the use of child labor (see Chapter 8 as well); and individual consumer issues, such as deceptive advertising[10] or the marketing of dangerous products.[11]

ETHICAL ISSUES ASSOCIATED WITH MARKETING DECISIONS

Unlike other business functions such as accounting or finance, people in marketing interact directly with the public. Because they are in the public eye, it should not be surprising that marketing and sales professionals sometimes rank poorly in ratings of the most trusted professions. In a recent Gallup survey, most professions were rated much higher than advertising or sales professions—lobbyists came in last, and car salespeople fared only slightly better, about the same as congresspeople[12] (see Exhibit 4.1.) For marketers, who depend on the long-term trust of their customers, this low ranking is very disappointing.

Yet there is some good news too.[13] Although many consumers remain highly skeptical of business, and especially of marketing, the marketing function interacts with a vast number of entities outside the firm on a regular basis. Therefore, it has a tremendous opportunity to build public trust. Creating an ethical climate that establishes the health and well-being of consumers as the firm's number one priority just makes good business sense.

Creating an Ethical Climate in the Workplace

The process of creating a strong **ethical climate** within a marketing firm (or in the marketing division of any firm) includes having a set of values that guides decision making and behavior such as Johnson & Johnson's Credo. General Robert Wood Johnson wrote and published the first "Credo" for Johnson & Johnson (J&J) in 1943[14]—a one-page document

Nurses and doctors are among the most trusted professionals.

▼ **EXHIBIT 4.1** Attitudes about Ethical Standards of Various Professions

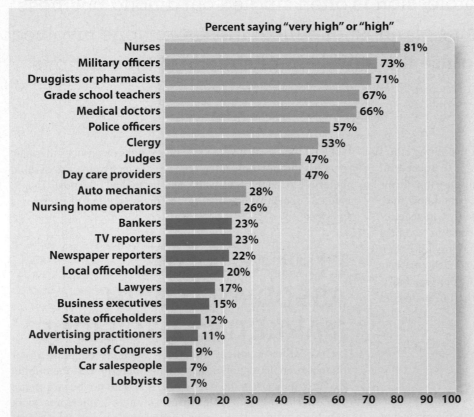

Percent saying "very high" or "high"

Profession	Percent
Nurses	81%
Military officers	73%
Druggists or pharmacists	71%
Grade school teachers	67%
Medical doctors	66%
Police officers	57%
Clergy	53%
Judges	47%
Day care providers	47%
Auto mechanics	28%
Nursing home operators	26%
Bankers	23%
TV reporters	23%
Newspaper reporters	22%
Local officeholders	20%
Lawyers	17%
Business executives	15%
State officeholders	12%
Advertising practitioners	11%
Members of Congress	9%
Car salespeople	7%
Lobbyists	7%

outlining the firm's commitments and responsibilities to its various stakeholders. The J&J Credo can be summarized as follows:

> We believe our first responsibility is to doctors, nurses, patients, mothers, fathers, and all others who use our products and services. We are responsible to our employees. We must respect their dignity and recognize their merit. Compensation must be fair and adequate and working conditions clean, orderly, and safe. We are responsible to the communities in which we live and work and to the world community as well. Our final responsibility is to our stockholders. When we operate according to these principles, the stockholders should realize a fair return.

Today, J&J continues to follow this credo in its daily business practices, as was evidenced by the infamous Tylenol recall. In the 1980s, seven people taking Tylenol died of cyanide poisoning. Without worrying initially about whether the poison got into the products during production or on the shelf, J&J immediately and voluntarily withdrew all Tylenol from the market until it could ensure its products' safety.

> # EVERYONE WITHIN A FIRM MUST SHARE THE SAME UNDERSTANDING OF ITS ETHICAL VALUES AND HOW THEY TRANSLATE INTO THE BUSINESS ACTIVITIES OF THE FIRM.

Even more recently, J&J responded to new limits on acetaminophen dosages (the active ingredient in Tylenol) by reassuring consumers that they were safe—as long as they followed the dosage instructions on the packaging.[15] In advertising communications that touted Tylenol as "the safest brand of pain reliever you can choose," J&J also was careful to remind people that taking more than the recommended dosage could cause them serious liver damage.

But not all firms operate according to the principles in J&J's credo. For instance, Merck & Co. withdrew its highly successful drug Vioxx from the marketplace in 2004 because of evidence that it increased the chance of heart attacks and strokes in patients taking the drug.[16] The move came at least four years after studies showed that patients taking Vioxx had an increased incidence of cardiovascular problems compared to an older drug. Although Merck continued to monitor these ongoing studies, it did not act nor did it initiate new studies. In another pharmaceutical example, AstraZeneca, the maker of the schizophrenia drug Seroquel, faced sanctions and fines for misrepresenting the appropriate uses of the drug to medical practitioners. Eventually, AstraZeneca agreed to pay $520 million to settle the claims of its unethical, "off-label" marketing efforts.[17] Would Merck and AstraZeneca have performed more ethically had they been working with J&J's credo for ethical behavior?[18]

Everyone within a firm must share

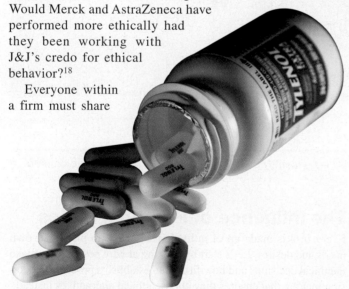

Johnson & Johnson, makers of Tylenol, continues to act in accordance with its original 1943 credo to be responsible to everyone who uses its products and services.

the same understanding of its ethical values and how they translate into the business activities of the firm. They also need to share a consistent language to discuss them. Once the values are understood, the firm must develop explicit rules and implicit understandings that govern all the firm's transactions. Top management must commit to establishing an ethical climate, and employees throughout the firm must be dedicated to that climate because the roots of ethical conflict often are the competing values of individuals. Each individual holds his or her own set of values, and sometimes those values result in inner turmoil or even conflicts between employees. For instance, a salesperson may believe that it is important to make a sale because her family depends on her for support, but at the same time, she may feel that the product she is selling is not appropriate for a particular customer. Once the rules are in place, there must be a system of controls that helps resolve such dilemmas and rewards appropriate behavior—that is, behavior consistent with the firm's values—and punishes inappropriate behavior.

Among the most important controls is policing potential violations of human rights and child labor laws. Many firms have had to defend themselves publicly against allegations of human rights, child labor, or other abuses involving the factories and countries in which their goods are made.[19] Fewer imported goods are produced in sweatshop conditions today, though. Some firms even are proactive in enforcing the labor practices of their suppliers. Limited Brands was one of the first U.S. apparel manufacturers to develop and implement policies requiring observance by vendors and their subcontractors and suppliers of core labor standards as a condition of doing business. Among other things, this requirement ensures that each supplier pays minimum wages and benefits; limits overtime to local industry standards; does not use prisoners, forced labor, or child labor; and provides a healthy and safe environment.[20] Many other companies that produce or sell goods made in low-wage countries conduct similar self-policing. Self-policing allows companies to avoid painful public revelations. Adding Value 4.1 examines how Walmart is pushing its vendors to be environmentally responsible.

Like companies that develop and apply their ethical codes, many professions, including the marketing profession, also have their own codes of ethics that firms and individuals in the profession agree to abide by. The

Adding Value 4.1

It Isn't Easy to Sell to Walmart[21]

Walmart is known for its low prices and for driving its vendors nearly to tears to get them. Now it is pressuring its vendors to supply it with environmentally friendly merchandise with labels to prove it. In the future, merchandise sold at Walmart will have the environmental equivalent of nutrition labels, providing information on the product's carbon footprint, the amount of water and air pollution used to produce it, and other environmental issues. To measure how a vendor's products are doing, it has developed a sustainability index that simultaneously takes several issues into consideration.

Walmart required its top 200 factories to become 20 percent more energy-efficient by 2012. Results are promising; for example, Jiangsu Redbud Dyeing Technology in China has cut coal consumption by one-tenth and is attempting to cut its toxic emissions to zero.

Walmart hasn't always been touted as a good corporate citizen. In the 1990s, it came to light that workers at some factories producing clothing for Walmart were subjected to inhumane conditions. More recently, two governmental organizations accused Walmart of buying from 15 factories that engage in abuse and labor violations, including child labor, 19-hour shifts, and below-subsistence wages. It and other companies have also been accused of dumping hazardous waste in Oklahoma City.

Some wonder why Walmart is attempting to position itself as the retail industry's sustainability leader. Certainly initiatives that show that it is a good corporate citizen enhance its image. But it expects it to be good for business as well. Its customers, especially those born from 1980 to 2000, are increasingly concerned about how the products they use affect the environment and the people who produce them. Also, Walmart believes that many of these initiatives will help streamline supply chain processes and therefore provide additional financial benefits to its suppliers and customers.

generally accepted code in marketing, developed by the American Marketing Association, flows from universal norms of conduct to the specific values to which marketers should aspire.[22] It indicates that the basic ethical values marketers should aspire to are honesty, responsibility, fairness, respect, openness, and citizenship. Each subarea within marketing, such as marketing research, advertising, pricing, and so forth, has its own code of ethics that deals with the specific issues that arise when conducting business in those areas.

Now let's examine the ethical role of the individuals within the firm and how individuals contribute to the firm's ethical climate.

LO 4-1 Identify the ethical values marketers should embrace.

The Influence of Personal Ethics

Every firm is made up of individuals, each with his or her own needs and desires. Let's start by looking at why people may make *un*ethical decisions and how firms can establish a process for decision making that ensures they choose ethical alternatives instead.

Why People Act Unethically Every individual is a product of his or her culture, upbringing, genes, and various other influences. In spite of these factors, people continue to grow emotionally in their understanding of what is and is not ethical behavior. As a six-year-old child, you might have thought nothing of taking your brother's toy and bonking him on the head with it. As an adult, you probably have outgrown this behavior. But all of us vary in the way we view more complex situations, depending on our ethical understandings.

Consider product recalls of toys, for example. How can certain manufacturers engage in such egregious behavior as using lead paint on toys marketed toward young children? What makes people take actions that create so much harm? Are all the individuals who contributed to that behavior just plain immoral? These simple questions have complex answers.

As another example, imagine that a brand manager for a car company discovers from conversations with a member of the development team that the hot new energy-efficient hybrid model that is set to go into full production shortly has a potentially dangerous design flaw. There are two options for the brand manager: delay production and remedy the design flaw, which pushes production off schedule, delays revenue, and may result in layoffs and loss of the manager's bonus; or stay on schedule, put the flawed design into production, achieve planned revenues and bonus, and hope it does not result in injuries to consumers and loss of revenue for the firm due to recalls later on. This type of dilemma occurs nearly every day in thousands of business environments.

When asked in a survey whether they had seen any unethical behavior among their colleagues, chief marketing officers responded that they had observed employees participating in high pressure, misleading, or deceptive sales tactics (45 percent); misrepresenting company earnings, sales, and/or revenues (35 percent); withholding or destroying information that could hurt company sales or image

(32 percent); and conducting false or misleading advertising (31 percent).[23] Did all the marketers in these situations view their actions as unethical? Probably not. There may have been extenuating circumstances. In marketing, managers often face the choice of doing what is beneficial for them and possibly the firm in the short run and doing what is right and beneficial for the firm and society in the long run.

For instance, a manager might feel confident that earnings will increase in the next few months and therefore believe it benefits himself, his branch, and his employees to exaggerate current earnings just a little. Another manager might feel considerable pressure to increase sales in a retail store, so she brings in some new merchandise, marks it at an artificially high price, and then immediately puts it on sale, deceiving consumers into thinking they are getting a good deal because they viewed the initial price as the real price. These decisions may have been justifiable at the time, but they have serious consequences for the company.

To avoid such dire consequences, the short-term goals of each employee must be aligned with the long-term goals of the firm. In our hybrid car example, the brand manager's short-term drive to receive a bonus conflicted with the firm's long-term aim of providing consumers with safe, reliable cars. To align personal and corporate goals, firms need to have a strong ethical climate, explicit rules for governing transactions including a code of ethics, and a system for rewarding and punishing inappropriate behavior.

In the next section, we add the concept of corporate social responsibility to our discussion of ethics.

> "In marketing, managers often face the choice of doing what is beneficial for them and possibly the firm in the short run and doing what is right and beneficial for the firm and society in the long run."

What is the real price? Did the manager bring the T-shirts in at an artificially high level and then immediately mark them down?

LO 4-2 Distinguish between ethics and social responsibility.

Ethics and Corporate Social Responsibility

Although no single, established definition of the concept exists,[24] **corporate social responsibility** generally entails voluntary actions taken by a company to address the ethical, social, and environmental impacts of its business operations and the concerns of its stakeholders. The AMA's definition refers to it as the serious consideration of "the impact of the company's actions and operating in a way that balances short-term profit needs with society's long-term needs, thus ensuring the company's survival in a healthy environment."[25] This notion

Nothing *stirs you* like The Original

DANNON® Fruit on the Bottom Strawberry

Try these and other great flavors!

©2010 The Dannon Company, Inc.

Dannon is both ethical and socially responsible. It has an ethical commitment to make healthy food. It is socially responsible since it is involved in many activities and charities that help people.

communities, holds annual Children's Day outreach programs, and reduces its environmental footprints.

Being socially responsible generally means going above and beyond the norms of corporate ethical behavior. For example, a firm's employees may conduct their activities in an ethically acceptable manner, but the firm may still not be considered socially responsible because its activities have little or no impact on anyone other than its closest stakeholders: its customers, employees, and stockholders (Exhibit 4.2, upper right quadrant).

Employees at some firms that are perceived as socially responsible can nevertheless take actions that are viewed as unethical (Exhibit 4.2, lower left quadrant). For instance, a firm might be considered socially responsible because it makes generous donations to charities but is simultaneously involved in questionable sales practices. After the 2010 oil spill in the Gulf of Mexico, BP committed to donating millions of dollars to help economically affected states promote tourism.[27] Ethically, how do we characterize a firm that obtains its profits through illicit actions but then donates a large percentage of those profits to charity? The worst situation, of course, is when firms behave both unethically and in a socially unacceptable manner (Exhibit 4.2, lower right quadrant).

Consumers and investors increasingly appear to want to purchase products and services from and invest in companies that

> After the 2010 oil spill in the Gulf of Mexico, BP committed to donating millions of dollars to help economically affected states promote tourism.

goes beyond the individual ethics that we've discussed so far, but for a company to act in a socially responsible manner, the employees of the company must also first maintain high ethical standards and recognize how their individual decisions lead to optimal collective actions of the firm. Firms with strong ethical climates tend to be more socially responsible.

However, it is important to distinguish between ethical business practices and corporate social responsibility programs. Ideally, firms should implement programs that are socially responsible, *and* its employees should act in an ethically responsible manner. (See Exhibit 4.2, upper left quadrant.) Dannon yogurt, for example, has long supported internal research into healthy eating, which supports its ethical commitment to bring "health food to as many people as possible."[26] It is also socially responsible, in that it donates food and money to the hunger-relief charity Feeding America, encourages employees to volunteer in their

Oil spills are a major catastrophe for all parties.

Ethics versus Social Responsibility

	Socially Responsible	**Socially Irresponsible**
Ethical	Both ethical and socially responsible	Ethical firm not involved with the larger community
Unethical	Questionable firm practices, yet donates a lot to the community	Neither ethical nor socially responsible

act in socially responsible ways. They also may be willing to pay more if they can be assured the companies truly are ethical.[28] According to a recent poll conducted by *Time Magazine*, even in economically constrained settings, 38 percent of U.S. consumers actively tried to purchase from companies they considered responsible. The magazine thus cites the rise of the "ethical consumer" and the evolution of the social contract "between many Americans and businesses about what goes into making the products we buy."[29]

With such ethical consumers making up more and more of the market, many large companies have recognized that they must be perceived as socially responsible by their stakeholders to earn their business. Other companies began their operations with such a commitment, as Adding Value 4.2 describes.

We cannot expect every member of a firm always to act ethically. However, a framework for ethical decision making can help move people to work toward common ethical goals.

Adding Value 4.2

The Barefoot Entrepreneur[30]

Blake Mycoskie doesn't just want his customers to buy his shoes; he wants to turn them into benefactors. In this innovative approach to marketing, his company, TOMS Shoes, does not just engage in charitable acts; the charitable acts are the company. There is no separating TOMS from the social responsibility it embraces.

In 2006, Mycoskie started manufacturing a revised version of a traditional Argentinean shoe called alpargatas and selling them to consumers outside their generally impoverished source nation. The combination of the comfortable shoes and the extreme poverty he observed led to a simple code: "You buy a pair of TOMS, and I give a pair to a child on your behalf. One for One."

His Shoe Drops, during which Mycoskie brings thousands of pairs of shoes to poorer children in underdeveloped nations, have led to the distribution of literally millions of pairs of shoes: The millionth pair was given away in September 2010. As the company has grown, it also has added lines of vegan and recycled shoes. Most recently, it expanded into sunglasses, where the One for One philosophy dictates that for every pair sold, TOMS provides eye care, such as medicine treatment, glasses, or surgery, to someone else in the world at risk of losing his or her sight.

Each year, TOMS also hosts One Day Without Shoes, a campaign to raise awareness about how difficult it can be to function, even in developed nations, without shoes. In the 2010 iteration,

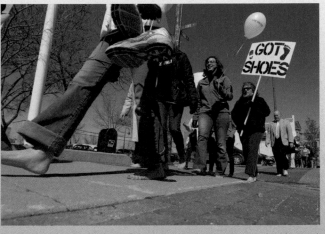

When you buy a pair of TOMS shoes, they give a pair to a child in need.

one-quarter of a million people participated, leaving their shoes at home for the entire day. The company also partners with groups such as Insight Argentina, an organization offering volunteer activities in Argentina to help that area address its most pressing social issues.

Detractors argue that by shipping in the shoes to be donated, TOMS may do some harm by reducing demand for locally produced products. But since TOMS has given away more than 1 million pairs of shoes, that means consumers have bought just as many—at an average price of $55 per pair. Clearly, the value they find in these cloth shoes goes well beyond the simple linen and canvas parts that go into making them.

Step 1	Step 2	Step 3	Step 4
Identify issues	Gather information and identify stakeholders	Brainstorm and evaluate alternatives	Choose a course of action

LO 4-3   Identify the four steps in ethical decision making.

A Framework for Ethical Decision Making

Exhibit 4.3 outlines a simple framework for ethical decision making. Let's consider each of the steps.

Step 1: Identify Issues

The first step is to identify the issue. For illustrative purposes, we'll investigate the use (or misuse) of data collected from consumers by a marketing research firm. One of the issues that might arise is the way the data are collected. For instance, are the respondents told about the real purpose of the study? Another issue might be whether the results will be used in a way that might mislead or even harm the public, such as selling the information to a firm to use in soliciting the respondents.

Step 2: Gather Information and Identify Stakeholders

In this step, the firm focuses on gathering facts that are important to the ethical issue, including all relevant legal information. To get a complete picture, the firm must identify all the individuals and groups that have a stake in how the issue is resolved.

Stakeholders typically include the firm's employees and retired employees, suppliers, the government, customer groups, stockholders, and members of the community in which the firm operates. Beyond these, many firms now also analyze the needs of the industry and the global community as well as one-off stakeholders such as future generations and the natural environment itself. In describing its sustainability and transparency efforts, for example, the electronics firm Philips notes that it tries to communicate with and consider "anyone with an interest in Philips."[31]

Step 3: Brainstorm Alternatives

After the marketing firm has identified the stakeholders and their issues and gathered the available data, all parties relevant to the decision should come together to brainstorm any alternative courses of action. In our example, these might include halting the market research project, making responses anonymous, instituting training on the AMA Code of Ethics for all researchers, and so forth. Management then reviews and refines these alternatives, leading to the final step.

Step 4: Choose a Course of Action

The objective of this last step is to weigh the various alternatives and choose a course of action that generates the best solution for the stakeholders, using ethical practices. Management will rank the alternatives in order of preference, clearly establishing the advantages and disadvantages of each. It is also crucial to investigate any potential legal issues associated with each alternative. Of course, any illegal activity should immediately be rejected.

To choose the appropriate course of action, marketing managers will evaluate each alternative by using a process something like the sample ethical decision-making metric in Exhibit 4.4. The marketer's task here is to ensure that he or she

> To choose the appropriate course of action, marketing managers will evaluate each alternative by using a process something like the sample ethical decision-making metric.

has applied all relevant decision-making criteria and to assess his or her level of confidence that the decision being made meets those stated criteria. If the marketer isn't confident about the decision, he or she should reexamine the other alternatives. Using Exhibit 4.4, you can gauge your own ethical response. If your scores tend to be in the green area (1 and 2), then the situation is not an ethically troubling situation for you. If, in contrast, your scores tend to be in the red area (6 and 7), it is ethically troubling and you know it. If your scores are scattered or in the yellow area, you need to step back and reflect on how you wish to proceed.

In using such an ethical metric or framework, decision makers must consider the relevant ethical issues, evaluate the alternatives, and then choose a course of action that will help them avoid serious ethical lapses.

Next, let's illustrate how the ethical decision-making metric in Exhibit 4.4 can be used to make ethical business decisions.

> REPORTS SHOWING THAT CHILDREN RARELY EAT ENOUGH VEGETABLES HAVE COMBINED WITH STUDIES THAT INDICATE SCHOOL KIDS HAVE A LIMITED AMOUNT OF TIME TO EAT THEIR LUNCHES.

▼ **EXHIBIT 4.4** Ethical Decision-Making Metric

Test	Decision						
	Yes		Maybe			No	
	1	2	3	4	5	6	7
The Publicity Test Would I want to see this action that I'm about to take described on the front page of the local paper or in a national magazine?							
The Moral Mentor Test Would the person I admire the most engage in this activity?							
The Admired Observer Test Would I want the person I admire most to see me doing this?							
The Transparency Test Could I give a clear explanation for the action I'm contemplating, including an honest and transparent account of all my motives, that would satisfy a fair and dispassionate moral judge?							
The Person in the Mirror Test Will I be able to look at myself in the mirror and respect the person I see there?							
The Golden Rule Test Would I like to be on the receiving end of this action and all its potential consequences?							

Source: Adapted from Tom Morris, *The Art of Achievement: Mastering the 7 Cs of Success in Business and in Life* (Kansas City, MO: Andrew McMeel Publishing, 2002). http://edbrenegar.typepad.com/leading_questions/2005/05/real_life_leade.html.

Myra Jansen, the head cook at Lincoln High School in Anytown, USA, has had enough. Reports showing that children rarely eat enough vegetables have combined with studies that indicate school kids have a limited amount of time to eat their lunches. The combination has led to increasing obesity rates and troublesome reports about the long-term effects. Jansen has therefore decided that the tater-tots and hotdogs are out. Vegetables and healthy proteins are in.

The problem, of course, is getting the kids to eat raw vegetables, plant proteins, and lean meat. For many teenagers, recommending that they eat healthy food at lunch is akin to calling detention a play date. But Myra has a plan: She's going to reformulate various menu items using different ingredients and just never tell the students. Thus the regular hot dogs will be replaced with turkey or soy dogs. The tater-tots will contain the more nutrient-dense sweet potatoes instead of the vitamin-deficient regular spuds they used to be made out of. She is convinced she can make such switches for most of the menu items, and none of the children need to know.

Most of the kitchen staff is onboard with the idea and even have suggested other possible menu switches that would benefit the students by ensuring that they receive a well-balanced meal at school. School board members, when apprised of the idea, got very excited and praised Myra for her innovative thinking. But the community liaison for the school, whose job it is to communicate with parents and other members of the community, is not so sure. Salim Jones is nervous about how students will react when they learn that they have been deceived. He also has two small children of his own, one of whom has a severe wheat allergy. Thus the Joneses are extremely cautious about eating out, always asking for a detailed, specific list of ingredients for anything they order.

Using his training in ethical decision making, Salim sits down to evaluate his alternatives, beginning with identifying possible options available to the school district as well as the various stakeholders who might be affected by the decision. He comes up with the following list:

1. Switch out the food without telling students.

2. Leave menus as they are.

3. Switch out the food ingredients but also tell students exactly what is in each item in the cafeteria.

To make a clear recommendation to the board about what would be the best ethical choice, Salim decides to evaluate each alternative using a series of questions similar to those in Exhibit 4.4.

Question 1: Would I want to see this action described on the front page of the local paper? The school board's reaction caused Salim to think that the larger community would appreciate the effort to improve students' health. Thus, option 1 appears best for these stakeholders, and possibly for society, which may reduce the prevalence of obesity among these students. However, he shudders to think about how angry students might be if they learned they had been tricked. They also likely are accustomed to their menu as it is, and therefore, they would prefer option 2.

Question 2: Would the person I admire most engage in this activity, and would I want him or her to see me engage in this activity? For most of his life, Salim has held up Mahatma Gandhi as his ideal for how to act in the world. For Mahatma Gandhi, truth was an absolute concept, not something that could be changed depending on the situation. Therefore, Salim believes Mahatma Gandhi would strongly disapprove of option 1. However, Mahatma Gandhi also worried about the ethics of eating and took care to avoid food choices that had negative effects on society, so he might reject option 2 as well.

Question 3: Can I give a clear explanation for my action, including an honest account of my motives? In thinking about his children, Salim realizes that he is prioritizing their needs, more so than the needs of other children, such as those who struggle with weight issues. That is, he worries that his daughter might unknowingly be exposed to wheat in a school cafeteria, so he prefers option 3.

Question 4: Will I be able to look at myself in the mirror and respect what I see? By bringing up the ethics of this decision, even when it seems as if everyone else has agreed with it, Salim feels confident that he has taken the right first step. The option chosen is still important, but it is a group decision, and Salim thinks he is doing his part.

Question 5: Would I want to be on the receiving end of this action and its consequences? Salim struggles most with this question. He remembers the kind of junk foods he chose when he was in college and the 20 pounds he put on as a result. He wishes now that his parents had given him rules to follow about what to eat at school. But he also remembers how rebellious he was and knows that he probably would not have followed those rules. And at the same time, he hates the idea that someone could give him food to eat with falsified ingredients.

On the basis of this exercise, Salim decides that he wants to recommend option 3 to the school board. When he does so,

Myra Jansen protests loudly: "This is ridiculous! I know better what kids should be eating, and I know too that some community liaison has no idea what they are willing to eat. You've got to trick them to get them to eat right." Another school board member agrees, noting, "They're just kids. They don't necessarily have the same rights as adults, so we are allowed to decide what's best for them. And hiding the healthy ingredients to get the kids to eat healthy foods is what's best."

So what does the school board decide?

 check yourself

1. Identify the stages in the ethical decision-making framework.

LO 4-4 Describe how ethics can be integrated into a firm's marketing strategy.

INTEGRATING ETHICS INTO MARKETING STRATEGY

Ethical decision making is not a simple process, though it can get easier as decision makers within the firm become accustomed to thinking about the ethical implications of their actions from a strategic perspective. In this section, we examine how ethical decision making can be integrated into the marketing plan introduced in Chapter 2. The questions vary at each stage of the strategic marketing planning process. For instance, in the planning stage, the firm will decide what level of commitment to its ethical policies and standards it is willing to declare publicly. In the implementation stage, the tone of the questions switches from "can we?" serve the market with the firm's products or services in an ethically responsible manner to "should we?" be engaging in particular marketing practices. The key task in the control phase is to ensure that all potential ethical issues raised during the planning process have been addressed and that all employees of the firm have acted ethically. Let's take a closer look at how ethics can be integrated at each stage of the strategic marketing planning process.

Planning Phase

Marketers can introduce ethics at the beginning of the planning process simply by including ethical statements in the firm's mission or vision statements (recall our discussion of various mission statements in Chapter 2). Johnson & Johnson has its Credo; other firms use mission statements that include both ethical and social responsibility precepts for shaping the organization. For instance, the mission statement for natural

Since 1982, Newman's Own has given over $280 million to charities such as Newman's Hole in the Wall Gang camps for children with life-threatening diseases.

skin care company Burt's Bees is to "create natural, Earth-friendly personal care products formulated to help you maximize your well-being and that of the world around you,"[32] which reflects not only what is good for its customers but for society in general.

For General Electric, the complexity of its organization and the wealth of ethical issues it faces necessitated an entire booklet, "The Spirit and the Letter." This booklet outlines not only a statement of integrity from the CEO and a code of conduct but also detailed policies for dealing with everything from international competition laws to security and crisis management to insider trading. In addition, GE publishes an annual citizenship report to determine the scope of its impacts, "produced for the benefit of all stakeholders, including GE employees—the people whose actions define GE every day."[33]

During the planning stage, ethical mission statements can take on another role as a means to guide a firm's SWOT analysis. Newman's Own, for example, has what most would

Own—over $280 million since 1982—have been donated to thousands of charities, especially Newman's Hole in the Wall Gang camps for children with life-threatening diseases.[34]

The unique mission of the company and the entrepreneurial flair of the founders made this nonprofit a smashing, ongoing success. Employees of Newman's Own have the great satisfaction of giving back to society, various charities benefit from the donations, and customers enjoy good food with a clear conscience.

Implementation Phase

In the implementation phase of the marketing strategy, when firms are identifying potential markets and ways to deliver the 4Ps to them, firms must consider several ethical issues. Sometimes a firm's choice of target market and how it pursues it can lead to charges of unethical behavior. For instance, Molson Brewery launched a Facebook campaign targeted toward college students in which it asked them to post party pictures, which it would use to identify the "top party school."

[Profits from Newman's Own—over $280 million since 1982—have been donated to thousands of charities, especially Newman's Hole in the Wall Gang camps for children with life-threatening diseases.]

consider a simple but powerful purpose: The company would sell salad dressing (initially; it expanded later to many other product lines) and use the proceeds to benefit charities. This simple idea began in Paul Newman's basement, when he and a friend produced a batch of salad dressing to give as holiday gifts. When they also decided to check with a local grocer to see if it would be interested in the product, they found they could sell 10,000 bottles in two weeks. Thus Newman's Own, a nonprofit organization, quickly grew to include dozens of products. Today, Newman's Own and Newman's Own Organic products are sold in 15 countries and include dozens of lines, from coffee to popcorn to dog food. Profits from Newman's

This effort not only encouraged underage, illegal drinking but also deeply irritated universities across both Canada and the United States, which had little interest in being thus identified. Although these student groups might have been responsive to the firm's efforts, it did not represent an appropriate target market. Marketing through social media has some particular ethical concerns associated with it, as Social & Mobile Marketing 4.1 shows.

Once the strategy is implemented, controls must be in place to be certain that the firm has actually done what it has set out to do. These activities take place in the next phase of the strategic marketing planning process.

Social & Mobile Marketing 4.1
Who Tweeted Me to Buy a Ford Fiesta?[35]

Auto manufacturers have long paid celebrities to be spokespeople for their lines of vehicles. But maybe customers really want to hear from people like themselves rather than a celebrity paid millions of dollars to promote a car. Although car companies can save a lot of money by paying normal people less than they pay celebrities, they do not want just anyone to promote their products. They want social media gurus or popular Twitter and blog figures with legions of followers.

Marketing campaigns by Lexus, Ford, and Land Rover all promote their products socially on the web. Ford recruited 100 people with strong online followings to test drive the Ford Focus and then talk about their experiences online. Ford previously had been successful with its Ford Fiesta campaign, in which anyone who test drove the newly introduced car posted YouTube videos, Flickr photos, and Twitter tweets—adding up to more than 7 million views on YouTube and 4 million mentions on Twitter. As a result, over 130,000 people visited the Ford Fiesta website, 83 percent of whom had never owned a Ford before. The campaign certainly received a lot of attention, though the actual sales conversion has not been disclosed.

Influential online informants also can have negative influences though. Even if a firm pays a blogger or tweeter, no rule can force him or her to write positive reviews. But the likelihood is that a paid blogger will be more positive than an unpaid, disinterested reviewer. Thus the Federal Trade Commission (FTC) has created guidelines for blogging and tweeting, saying that those who post messages must disclose any compensation they may have received for talking about the product. They also must disclose if there is a connection, such as an employee/employer relationship, between the endorser and the marketer of the product that might affect how people evaluate the endorsement.

Ford Fiesta's social media campaign draws attention to its traditional media ads.

Are these FTC guidelines strong enough to let potential customers know that the message being received through social media is a paid form of promotion, not unlike an ad on TV?

> Systems must be in place to check whether each potentially ethical issue raised in the planning process was actually successfully addressed.

Control Phase

During the control phase of the strategic marketing planning process, managers must be evaluated on their actions from an ethical perspective. Systems must be in place to check whether each potentially ethical issue raised in the planning process was actually successfully addressed. Systems used in the control phase must also react to change. The emergence of new technologies and new markets ensures that new ethical issues continually arise. Social & Mobile Marketing 4.2 uncovers many of these new privacy issues.

Many firms have emergency response plans in place just in case they ever encounter a situation similar to the Tylenol tampering emergency or an industrial accident at a manufacturing plant. Ethics thus remains an ongoing crucial component of the strategic marketing planning process and should be incorporated into all the firm's decision making down the road.

Social & Mobile Marketing 4.2
Check-Ins and Facebook Photos Can Be Dangerous

The rise of social media has been a boon for many marketers: When consumers like a brand on Facebook, tweet about a consumption experience on Twitter, and check in on Foursquare, they are providing the company free marketing. But they are also giving criminals and unethical marketers an easy means to take advantage of them. Thus the vast benefits of social media combine some threats to consumers.

Consider these examples: On your commute in to work each day, you might pay for your train fare with a monthly transit card that identifies you as the specific user. Say you are running a bit late one day and decide to blame the trains, instead of admitting you slept in late. Conceivably, your boss could check the data gathered when you swiped your card and confront you with the fact that you didn't even get on the train until 9:15. Or your mother could check to see that you got on at a different stop than usual and ask where exactly you spent the night.

These possibilities may seem harmful to your reputation or pride more than anything else. However, when people post their vacation plans or softball schedules on Facebook, they also inform potential burglars exactly when they will be away from their homes. Checking in on Foursquare gives criminals an immediate indication; if you check in at a restaurant, chances are you will not be home for another couple of hours. To highlight this issue, the mashup website Please Rob Me (www.pleaserobme.com) randomly taps people's posts on Facebook and Twitter to identify those who have clearly broadcast that they are not at home.

Now imagine that an unscrupulous marketer fails to protect information about the items you have bought from it. With just a few clicks of a mouse and some technology savvy, criminals know not only when your house will be empty but also exactly what kinds of valuables they might steal when they break in.

Many users have grown more aware of such concerns and work to avoid such obvious releases of their information. But smartphone cameras stamp each photo taken with latitude and longitude information. Thus, even if you never mention the location of your favorite haunts, stalkers can obtain information about where you are likely to be, based on the photos you have posted on Facebook, especially if they are uploaded in real time.

The "Check in" feature on several apps, including Facebook and Foursquare, provide friends with information about where you are or where you have been at a given time.

The need for a new kind of privacy is thus a critical issue for marketers and consumers alike. Ethical marketers must find a way to collect the priceless data that customers make available through social media while avoiding collecting details that violate people's right to **locational privacy**—defined as a person's ability to move normally in public spaces with the expectation that his or her location will not be recorded for subsequent use.[36]

check yourself

1. What ethical questions should a marketing manager consider at each stage of the marketing plan?

LO 4-5 Describe the ways in which corporate social responsibility programs help various stakeholders.

CORPORATE SOCIAL RESPONSIBILITY

In 1906, Upton Sinclair published *The Jungle*, his novel exposing the horrific conditions in U.S. meat-packing plants, which prompted President Theodore Roosevelt and Congress to force meat companies to take responsibility for the safety of their products. The notion of societal marketing and corporate social responsibility has changed significantly since then, and recent decades have seen its prevalence increase rapidly. Today, companies are undertaking a wide range of corporate social responsibility initiatives, such as establishing corporate charitable

foundations, supporting and associating with existing nonprofit groups, supporting minority activities, and following responsible marketing, sales, and production practices. Social responsibility is even one of the key measures that *Fortune* magazine uses to create its list of the most admired companies (see Exhibit 4.5).

One of *Fortune*'s most admired companies, McDonald's, concentrates its sustainability efforts in several areas.[37] Some specific highlights include:

- Nutrition and well-being. It promotes awareness of fruit, vegetable, and low-fat or fat-free dairy options for children through advertising and promotions. For example, McDonald's France and Italy introduced "free fruit" campaigns, during which fruit bags were given free with every Happy Meal on selected days.

- Sustainable supply chain. It is committed to sourcing all of its food and packaging from sustainable sources, with an initial focus on beef, poultry, coffee, palm oil, fish, and fiber.

- Environmental responsibility. It has developed better, more reliable energy-related metrics, which are used to measure energy savings. It is implementing energy-efficient lighting, occupancy sensors, and energy-efficient equipment.

- Community. It supports the Ronald McDonald House charities by, for instance, having raised $170 million during McHappy Day/Give a Hand events since 2002.

▼ **EXHIBIT 4.5** Top 20 Admired Companies and Illustrative CSR Programs

Rank	Company	Illustration of CSR Program
1	Apple	Actively working to reduce carbon footprint: http://www.apple.com/environment/
2	Google	Google.org funds for pro-profit entrepreneurship in Africa, Google China Social Innovation Cup for College Students
3	Berkshire Hathaway	Donates billions of dollars to the Bill and Melinda Gates Foundation
4	Southwest Airlines	Employees donate volunteer hours to Ronald McDonald Houses throughout the U.S.
5	Procter & Gamble	Live, Learn, and Thrive improves the lives of children worldwide.
6	Coca-Cola	Spent $102 million through The Coca-Cola Campaign focusing on water stewardship, healthy and active lifestyles, community recycling, and education
7	Amazon.com	Developed nonprofit Simple Pay Donation system to help nonprofits raise money easily
8	FedEx	Delivered 440 tons of relief supplies at no charge to Hurricane Katrina victims
9	Microsoft	Developed a system with the American Red Cross for vital information on people's welfare in a disaster's aftermath
10	McDonald's	99% of fish come from MSC-fisheries, transitioning to sustainable food and packaging sources, Ronald McDonald House charities
11	Walmart Stores	Green strategy to reduce packaging and use energy efficient lighting
12	IBM	KidSmart Early Learning, Smarter Cities Challenge, MentorPlace, TryScience programs
13	General Electric	Ecomagination campaign, GE Volunteers Foundation
14	Walt Disney	Disney's Planet Challenge, worldwide animal and conservation fund
15	3M	Pollution Prevention Pays (3Ps) program focuses on conserving resources
16	Starbucks	Develops ecologically friendly growing practices, LEED certified stores
17	Johnson & Johnson	Funds nonprofits that fight AIDS/HIV around the world
18	Singapore Airlines	Provided air travel for Australian social workers to Dhaka in Bangladesh for a project to prevent hearing loss in textile workers at no charge
19	BMW	Light Up Hope and BMW Children's Safety programs
20	American Express	Partners with National Trust for Historic Preservation through the WMF to preserve sites in the U.S. and worldwide.

Source: From *Fortune Magazine*, March 19, 2012, "World's Most Admired Companies." Copyright © 2012 Time Inc. Used under license.

Source: http://www.aboutmcdonalds.com/mcd/sustainability/2011_sustainability_scorecard.html.

McDonald's Global Sustainability Scorecard is found in Exhibit 4.6.

Some economists and social commentators suggest that CSR is unnecessary, that the goal of any corporation in a capitalist economy is single and simple: Make money.[38] How does it benefit the company or its shareholders if a company worries about such unquantifiable issues as being a good citizen? But the fallout from the recent global economic crisis seems to have pushed economists to repudiate this school of thought.

When companies embrace CSR, they appeal not only to their shareholders but to their key stakeholders (Exhibit 4.7), including their own employees, consumers, the marketplace, and society at large. Thus the insurance provider Aflac differentiates its goal, "to be a profitable company," from its calling "to be an ethical partner to our stakeholders—one that plays by the rules and demonstrates leadership in the arena of business ethics."[39]

▼ **EXHIBIT 4.7** Key CSR Stakeholders

Let's consider each of these stakeholder categories to understand the meaning and effects of corporate social responsibility in the modern marketing arena as well as how CSR ultimately can benefit the firm that undertakes it.

Employees Perhaps the most basic corporate social responsibility to employees is to ensure a safe working environment, free of threats to their physical safety, health, or well-being. In some cases, though, this basic level of safety seems insufficient to achieve responsibility to workers. Aflac regards its pay-for-performance structure a key element of its responsibility to its employees, with the notion that everyone, from call center operators to the CEO, faces the same compensation standards. In this sense, it ensures equality of treatment and fairness in compensation. In doing so, Aflac earns a reputation as a good place to work and increases the number of people who apply for jobs there. These happy employees also should provide better service to customers, which in turn ensures better outcomes for the firm.

In addition to focusing on employees, more and more firms realize that happy employee families make happy and productive employees. Consequently, firms are focusing their efforts on outreach programs aimed at their employees' families.

Customers Especially as changes in the marketing environment emerge, firms must consider the effects on the customers who currently patronize them and future customers whom they are targeting. Corporate social responsibility programs must take such shifts and trends into account and react to them quickly. A few of the trends that are receiving the most attention include respecting and protecting privacy in an electronic world and ensuring the healthiness of products, especially those aimed at children. Moreover, CSR often increases consumer awareness of the firm, which can lead to better brand equity and sales in the long run.

America on the Move (AOM) has helped launch a variety of initiatives to help develop a healthier way of life through an active lifestyle, such as walking an extra 2,000 steps and eating 100 fewer calories every day.[40] Pepsi has cooperated with AOM to improve many of its products and their labels, such as reducing the saturated fat in its Frito-Lay's Ruffles.[41] The goal of such programs is to increase consumer awareness of the need to eat healthier choices. These efforts ultimately benefit consumers too, who not only gain additional consumption choices but also suffer less risk of the dangers associated with pollution or unhealthy foods.

Marketplace When one firm in the industry leads the way toward CSR, its partners and competitors often have no choice but to follow—or run the risk of not doing business or being left behind. To address issues such as global warming, water scarcity, and energy, GE uses a program it calls ecomagination, which encompasses a business strategy composed of four commitments: to double investments in clean R&D, increase revenues from ecomagination products, reduce greenhouse gas emissions, and inform the public about these issues.[42] When confronted with such initiatives, other energy companies are forced to make a decision: continue as they have been doing or adopt more responsible practices themselves. In either case, the

Pepsi cooperated with AOM to improve many of its products, such as reducing the saturated fat in its Frito-Lay's Ruffles.

initiating firm enjoys an advantage by gaining a reputation for being on the cutting edge of CSR efforts.

Society Firms expend considerable time and energy engaging in activities aimed at improving the overall community and the physical environment. According to a McKinsey & Co. survey, 95 percent of CEOs believe that society increasingly expects companies to take on public responsibilities.[43] That is, in a broad sense, companies cannot ignore societal demands for them to act responsibly. A firm that fails to do so causes damage to all the preceding stakeholders as well as to itself. Perhaps the most famous recent example is BP, which failed to offer adequate protections to the workers on the Deep Horizon deep sea oil rig, ensure that consumers could enjoy waters free of oil contamination, or live up to marketplace standards for safety. As a result, society as a whole suffered, as did BP's corporate reputation, profits, and outlook for the future. ∎

 check yourself

1. How has corporate social responsibility evolved since the turn of the twenty-first century?

2. Provide examples of each of the stakeholders that firms should consider in their corporate social responsibility efforts.

GE is the industry leader in CSR with its ecomagination program.

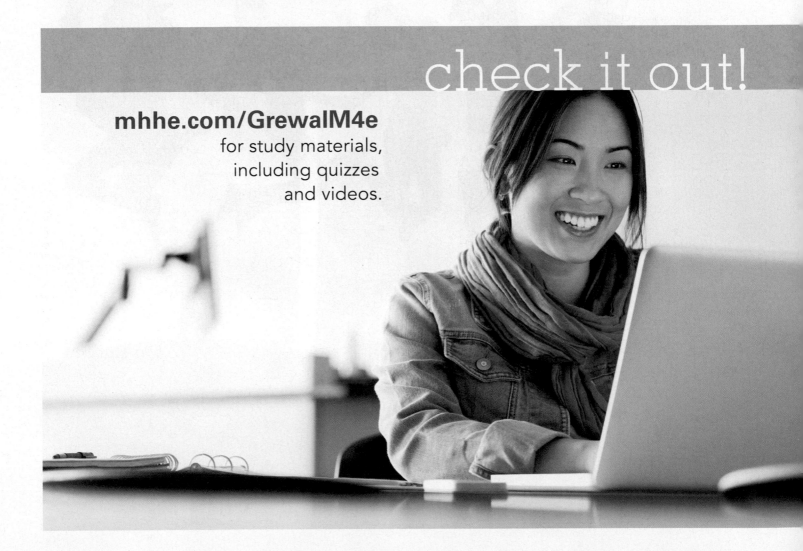

check it out!

mhhe.com/GrewalM4e
for study materials,
including quizzes
and videos.

analyzing
the marketing
environment

When it comes to being cool, no one wants to be left behind. Adolescents beg their parents (or save money themselves) to buy the latest music, and their parents take care never to be seen in last season's fashions. But the drive for coolness is not limited just to consumers. Many businesses also need to stay on the cutting edge, without being left behind, to stay current in their environment.

To help them, services such as The Cool Hunter and Trend Hunters collect, summarize, and describe the latest and greatest ideas in various realms. Imagine a construction firm that needs to know what kinds of materials people will want in their homes. It can visit the Architecture page on The Cool Hunter website to realize that more and more

LEARNING OBJECTIVES

After reading this chapter, you should be able to:

LO 5-1   Outline how customers, the company, competitors, and corporate partners affect marketing strategy.

LO 5-2   Explain why marketers must consider their macroenvironment when they make decisions.

LO 5-3   Describe the differences among the various generational cohorts.

LO 5-4   Identify various social trends that affect marketing.

modern homes feature curved glass exterior walls.[1] If customers want them, then construction firms, designers, and architects had better learn how to make them.

The Cool Hunter (or TCH, for those in the know) functions not only as a resource for other firms but also as its

continued on p. 96

Cool hunters help firms interpret the latest ideas and trends.

continued from p. 95
own example of how to analyze and respond to the marketing environment. For example, on a recent Lifestyle page, it noted the seemingly constantly growing interest in getting back to nature, especially among people who live in urban settings. Thus the site offers glamour shots of trees and plant life, bringing a sense of nature to visitors' computer screens.[2]

Yet the site also rejects the notion that it is simply a trendspotter. Rather, TCH promises that its goal is to be the authority on all things cool. Of course, readers of the site can also contract with its affiliated creative agency, ACCESS, to have it create a new campaign or run an event.

In contrast, Trend Hunters specifically and exclusively targets brands that want more information about what is happening in their environment. It relies on contributions by thousands of trend hunters, each of whom writes up a short description of the trends he or she has noticed. Although some of the most prolific hunters are employed by the company, thousands more post for the fame, glory, pride of having

their posts published and, they hope, featured on a front page of the site.[3]

The site takes responsibility for filtering the massive number of trends posted. Using crowd filtering, it condenses the 120,000 micro-trends posted by its approximately 80,000 trend hunters into 40,000 of the best micro-trends. Then its professional staff identifies around 1,200 insights that it provides to its professional clients, which they can use to anticipate and predict the shifts in their markets.

For example, Trend Hunters has noted how one obvious and literal element of the marketing environment, billboards, has changed radically. Consumers and passersby no longer notice most billboards; instead, according to Trend Hunters, the best bet is to create shocking, attention-grabbing, in-your-face versions. One featured example makes the post of the billboard look like a fork, with a piece of steak on the end, to advertise a beef producer. Although the visual image is arresting, the trend does not stop there: During rush hours (7:00–10:00 a.m. and 4:00–7:00 p.m.), it also sprays a beef scent into the air.[4]

> ## BECAUSE THE CONSUMER IS THE CENTER OF ALL MARKETING EFFORTS, VALUE-BASED MARKETING AIMS TO PROVIDE GREATER VALUE TO CONSUMERS THAN COMPETITORS OFFER.

continued from p. 96

As another example of this trend, Trend Hunters highlights guerilla advertising, such as a social awareness campaign that draws chalk outlines of bodies on sidewalks, within which are listed statistics and information about homelessness in that city.[5] In another effort, guerilla gardeners plant tiny gardens inside unpaved potholes, to bring commuters'

attention to street conditions and, perhaps, the need to obey speed limits.[6]

Despite their different targets and aims, both these sites reflect a similar drive: the need to know what is cool, trendy, and hot in the surrounding market. This need is nearly universal, which explains why marketers spend so much time and effort analyzing their marketing environments. ■

LO 5-1 Outline how customers, the company, competitors, and corporate partners affect marketing strategy.

A MARKETING ENVIRONMENT ANALYSIS FRAMEWORK

As our opening of this chapter has illustrated, marketers continue to find changes in what their customers demand or expect and adapt their product and service offerings accordingly. By paying close attention to customer needs and continuously monitoring the business environment in which the company operates, a good marketer can identify potential opportunities.

Exhibit 5.1 illustrates factors that affect the marketing environment. The centerpiece, as always, is consumers. Consumers may be influenced directly by the immediate actions of the focal company, the company's competitors, or corporate partners that work with the firm to make and supply products and services to consumers. The firm, and therefore consumers indirectly, is influenced by the macroenvironment, which includes various impacts of culture, demographics, and social, technological, economic, and political/legal factors. We discuss each of these components in detail in this chapter and suggest how they might interrelate.

Because the consumer is the center of all marketing efforts, value-based marketing aims

to provide greater value to consumers than competitors offer. Therefore, the marketing firm must consider the entire business process, all from a consumer's point of view.[7] Consumers' needs and wants, as well as their ability to purchase, depend on a host of factors that change and evolve over time. Firms use various tools to keep track of competitors' activities and consumer trends, including sites such as The Cool Hunters and Trend Hunters, and they rely on various methods to communicate with their corporate partners. Furthermore, they monitor their macroenvironment to determine how such factors influence consumers and how they should respond to them. Sometimes, a firm can even anticipate trends.

▼ **EXHIBIT 5.1** Understanding the Marketing Environment

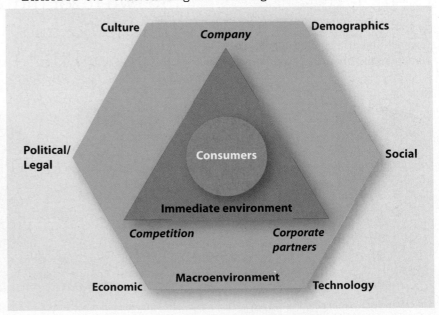

▼ **EXHIBIT 5.2** Understanding the Immediate Environment

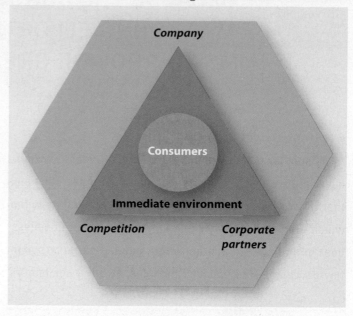

THE IMMEDIATE ENVIRONMENT

Exhibit 5.2 illustrates the factors that affect consumers' immediate environment: the company's capabilities, competitors, and corporate partners.

Company Capabilities

In the immediate environment, the first factor that affects the consumer is the firm itself. Successful marketing firms focus on satisfying customer needs that match their core competencies. The primary strength of Pepsi is the manufacture, distribution, and promotion of carbonated beverages, but it has also successfully leveraged its core competency in the bottled water arena with its Aquafina brand, after recognizing the marketplace trend toward and consumer desire for bottled water. Marketers can use an analysis of the external environment, like the SWOT analysis described in Chapter 2, to categorize an opportunity as either attractive or unattractive. If it appears attractive, they can assess it in terms of their existing competencies.

Competitors

Competition also significantly affects consumers in the immediate environment. It is therefore critical that marketers understand their firm's competitors, including their strengths, weaknesses, and likely reactions to the marketing activities that their own firm undertakes. No one would want to get caught in the war between the two razor giants, Gillette Co. and Energizer USA, which makes Schick razors, as each manufacturer works to add ever more blades to its disposable razors.[8] Gillette accused Schick of engaging in false and misleading advertising when ads claimed that its Hydro razor would hydrate skin. Schick's parent company countered with the complaint that Gillette's Fusion ProGlide Razor ads attempt to deceive when they assert that the blades are "Gillette's thinnest blades ever." All these efforts represent the companies' recognition of what their closest competitor is doing as well as their attempts to halt tactics they consider damaging. But at the same time, each razor company touts its benefits over its competitors because the ultimate goal, of course, is to appeal to consumers.

> No one would want to get caught in the war between the two razor giants, Gillette Co. and Energizer USA.

Corporate Partners

Few firms operate in isolation. For example, automobile manufacturers collaborate with suppliers of sheet metal, tire manufacturers, component part makers, unions, transport companies, and dealerships to produce and market their automobiles successfully. Parties that work with the focal firm are its corporate partners.

Gillette and Schick are actively engaged in fierce competition for the razor market.

Consider an example that demonstrates the role these partners play and how they work with the firm to create a single, efficient manufacturing system. Unlike most outdoor clothing manufacturers that use synthetic nonrenewable materials, Nau makes outdoor and ski clothing from renewable sources such as corn and recycled plastic bottles. It was founded by a team of entrepreneurs who left companies such as Nike and Patagonia. To develop clothing from sustainable materials that were rugged and beautiful, these founders turned to manufacturing partners around the world to develop new fabrics, such as PLA (polyactic acid), a fast-wicking biopolymer made from corn. To complement the new fabrics, the company uses only organic cotton and wool from "happy sheep," provided by partners in the ranching industry that embrace animal-friendly practices. Thus, not only does Nau represent the cutting-edge of sustainability and green business;

Nau works with its corporate partners to develop a socially responsible strategy.

it also clearly demonstrates how "going green" can prompt companies to work more closely with their partners to innovate.[9] Its collaborative attitude has gotten Nau a mention on a trend-spotting site similar to those mentioned in the chapter's opening vignette.[10]

✓ check yourself

1. What are the components of the immediate environment?

Culture

We broadly define **culture** as the shared meanings, beliefs, morals, values, and customs of a group of people.[11] Transmitted by words, literature, and institutions, culture is passed down from generation to generation and learned over time. You participate in many cultures: Your family has a cultural heritage, so perhaps your mealtime traditions include eating rugelach, a traditional Jewish pastry, or sharing corned beef and cabbage to celebrate your Irish ancestry on St. Patrick's Day. Your school

> ## "Our various cultures influence what, why, how, where, and when we buy."

LO 5-2 Explain why marketers must consider their macroenvironment when they make decisions.

MACROENVIRONMENTAL FACTORS

In addition to understanding their customers, the company itself, their competition, and their corporate partners, marketers must understand the **macroenvironmental factors** that operate in the external environment, namely, the culture, demographics, social issues, technological advances, economic situation, and political/regulatory environment, or CDSTEP, as shown in Exhibit 5.3.

or workplace also shares its own common culture. In a broader sense, you also participate in the cultural aspects of the town and country in which you live. The challenge for marketers is to have products or services identifiable by and relevant to a particular group of people. Our various cultures influence what, why, how, where, and when we buy. Two dimensions of culture that marketers must take into account as they develop their marketing strategies are the culture of the country and that of a region within a country.

Country Culture The visible nuances of a country's culture, such as artifacts, behavior, dress, symbols, physical settings, ceremonies, language differences, colors and tastes, and food preferences, are easy to spot. But the subtler aspects of

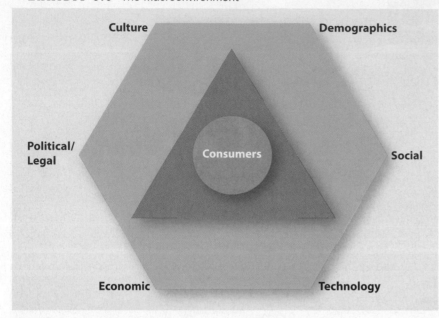

Mini and other global automobile manufacturers have successfully bridged the cultural gap by producing advertising that appeals to the same target market across countries. The pictures and copy are the same. The only thing that changes is the language.

Regional Culture The region in which people live in a particular country has its own **regional culture** that affects many aspects of people's life, for instance, the way they might refer to a particular product category. In the soft drink market, 38 percent of Americans refer to carbonated beverages as "soda," whereas another 38 percent call them "pop," and an additional 19 percent call any such beverage a "Coke," even when it is Pepsi.[12] Eat lunch in Indiana, and you'll have the best luck ordering a "pop" from the Midwesterner who owns the restaurant, but if you then head to Atlanta for dinner, you'd better order your "Coke," regardless of the brand you prefer. Head

country culture generally are trickier to identify and navigate. Sometimes the best answer is to establish a universal appeal within the specific identities of country culture. BMW's to Massachusetts, and the term is "soda," but if you move to Texas, you might be asked if you'd like a Dr Pepper—a generic term for carbonated beverages in the Lone Star state because it

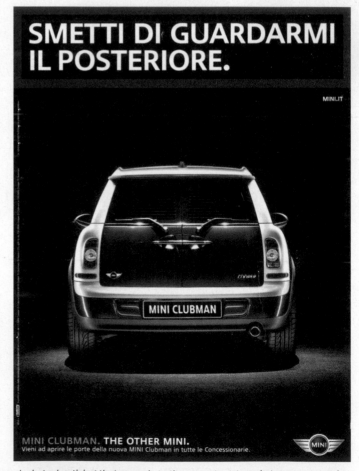

Some firms, such as BMW's Mini, have successfully bridged the cultural gap by producing advertising that appeals to the same target market across countries.

country culture Entails easy-to-spot visible nuances that are particular to a country, such as dress, symbols, ceremonies, language, colors, and food preferences, and more subtle aspects, which are trickier to identify.

regional culture The influence of the area within a country in which people live.

demographics Information about the characteristics of human populations and segments, especially those used to identify consumer markets such as by age, gender, income, and education.

generational cohort A group of people of the same generation—typically have similar purchase behaviors because they have shared experiences and are in the same stage of life.

Generation Z (Gen Z) Also known as the *Digital Natives*, because people in this group were born into a world that already was full of electronic gadgets and digital technologies, such as the Internet and social networks.

Digital Native Also known as *Generation Z*, people in this group were born into a world that already was full of electronic gadgets and digital technologies, such as the Internet and social networks.

was first formulated there in 1885.[13] Imagine the difficulty these firms have in developing promotional materials that transcend these regional differences.

Demographics

Demographics indicate the characteristics of human populations and segments, especially those used to identify consumer markets. Typical demographics such as age—which includes generational cohorts—gender, race, and income are readily available from market research firms such as Symphony/Information Resources Inc. Many firms undertake their own market research as well. For example, with its ExtraCard loyalty program, CVS collects massive amounts of data about shoppers who visit all its stores. It uses this information to target offers for, say, cosmetics to young female shoppers. But it also uses these data to benefit its communities. When the data gathered show that consumers—especially elderly customers of the pharmacy chain—are not refilling their prescriptions at the expected rate, CVS proactively interacts with these at-risk populations to encourage adherence to their medical plans.[14]

Demographics thus provide an easily understood snapshot of the typical consumer in a specific target market, as the next few sections detail.

LO 5-3 Describe the differences among the various generational cohorts.

Generational Cohorts Consumers in a **generational cohort**—a group of people of the same generation—have similar purchase behaviors because they have shared experiences and are in the same stage of life. For instance, Baby Boomers (people born after World War II, 1946–1964) and Generation Yers (people born between 1977 and 2000) both gravitate toward products and services that foster a casual lifestyle; however, they tend to do so for different reasons. The aging Baby Boomers, who grew up with jeans and khakis and brought casual dressing into the business arena, are often trying to maintain their youth. Yers, in contrast, typically wear jeans for status.

Applying age as a basis to identify consumers is quite useful to marketers, as long as it is used in conjunction with other consumer characteristics. For example, most media are characterized by the consumers who use it.[15] Age groups can identify appropriate magazine and television shows in which firms should advertise as well as lists for direct mail and telemarketing campaigns. Age is also useful for identifying the best social media outlets (e.g., Twitter, Facebook). Although there are many ways to cut the generational pie, we discuss four major groups, as listed in Exhibit 5.4.

Generation Z. **Generation Z** is also known as the **Digital Natives** because people in this group were born into a world that already was full of electronic gadgets and digital technologies such as the Internet and social networks.[16] These technologies are being developed and adopted at an unprecedented rate. Whereas it took 38 years for the radio to be adopted by 50 million people and 13 years for television, it only took 2 years for the same number of consumers to sign up for Facebook. Because of the technologies available to them, these digital natives will be more globally connected than previous generations. They thus might have a better appreciation for diverse cultures, but Gen Z consumers also were also born into a world confronted by both national and international terrorism, often facilitated by technology, and widespread environmental concerns.

▼ **EXHIBIT 5.4** Generational Cohorts

Generational cohort	Gen Z	Gen Y	Gen X	Baby boomers
Range of birth years	2001–2014	1977–2000	1965–1976	1946–1964
Age in 2014	0–13	14–37	38–49	50–68

Generation Z children are being raised by and have a lot in common with their Generation X parents, whom we discuss later. Gen Z and their parents increasingly watch the same television channels, such as Nickelodeon, especially when it shows nostalgic shows that the parents remember and the children enjoy anew. Both groups also like video games, leading the industry to develop family-oriented games on communal consoles, such as the Nintendo Wii. Finally, because Gen Z kids still go shopping with their parents, they are developing an affinity for the same brands, prompting retailers such as The Gap (GapKids, babyGap) and JCrew (Crewcuts) to develop special product lines to accommodate their demands. But at a certain point, such accommodation might cross the line into exploitation, as Ethical & Societal Dilemma 5.1 suggests.

Generation Y. **Generation Y**, also called **Millennials**, includes more than 60 million members in the United States alone, born between 1977 and 2000. Children of the Baby Boomers, this group is the biggest cohort since the original postwar World War II boom. It also varies the most in age, ranging from teenagers to adults who have their own families.[17] Now that Gen Y is entering the workplace, it is becoming apparent that its

Tweens are always connected.

members have different expectations and requirements than those of other cohorts. Gen Y puts a strong emphasis on balancing work and life—these young adults want a good job, but they also want to live in a location that supports their lifestyle.

difficult to tell the difference in appearance between Gen Ys in the United States and other developed countries, based solely on their uniforms of jeans, sneakers, and T-shirts.

Generation X. The next group, **Generation X** (Xers), includes those born between 1965 and 1976 and represents some 41 million Americans. Vastly unlike their Baby Boomer parents, Xers are the first generation of latchkey children (those who grew up in homes in which both parents worked), and 50 percent of them have divorced parents. This influence has led them to act like helicopter parents with their own children, working to shield their offspring from any threats or disappointment.[19] Unlike most previous generations, they are unlikely to enjoy greater economic prosperity than their parents.[20]

Although fewer in number than Generation Y or Baby Boomers,[21] Gen Xers possess considerable spending power because they tend to get married later and buy houses later in life. They're much less interested in shopping than their parents and far more cynical, which tends to make them astute consumers. They demand convenience and tend to be less likely to believe advertising claims or what salespeople tell them. Because of their experience as children of working parents, who had little time to shop, Xers developed shopping savvy at an early age and knew how to make shopping decisions by the time they were teenagers. As a result, they grew more

> Gen Y puts a strong emphasis on balancing work and life—these young adults want a good job, but they also want to live in a location that supports their lifestyle.

They also consider marriage secondary, and not obviously necessary, to being good parents themselves.[18]

The younger edge of this group (often referred to as tweens) has never lived without the Internet or easy access to cell phones, which makes them technologically savvy. As a result, these Gen Yers look and consume rather similarly across countries. They have similar lifestyles, music, and entertainment. MTV and CNN are available in most developed countries. It is

knowledgeable about products and more risk averse than other generational cohorts.

Baby Boomers. After World War II, the birth rate in the United States rose sharply, resulting in a group known as the **Baby Boomers**, the 78 million Americans born between 1946 and 1964. Now that the oldest Boomers are collecting Social Security, it is clear that this cohort will be the largest population

ethical & societal dilemma

The Next Target: Infants?

By the time a child is three years old, he or she can recognize an average of 100 brand logos.[22] Marketers can make use of this information to ensure that their logos and advertising communication are prominent on packaging, as well as on the toys themselves to ensure that children demand their brand from gift-giving parents.

The influence does not stop with toys, though. More and more companies are placing advertisements in schools and on buses.[23] And even though Facebook and similar sites officially require users to be at least 13 years of age, recent reports suggest that nearly 8 million Facebook visitors actually are younger than 12.[24] Although initially, most social media sites adopted this age restriction so that they could avoid meeting regulations associated with youthful users, it appears they are switching tactics in response to this widespread usage among young digital natives. Facebook has hired several lobbyists to encourage Congress to change the rules, including the 1998 Children's Online Privacy Protection Act.[25]

For Facebook and similar sites, inviting children to join offers two main advantages. First, it encourages their brand loyalty to the site itself. If a child creates a Facebook profile at the age of 10, she is unlikely to take it down by the time she is 15 or 18 or 26 years old. Second, by making the concept of sharing information more familiar to users from a very young age, Facebook helps encourage the type of behaviors it needs from consumers for it to survive. If digital natives have few expectations of privacy but instead share all their preferences online, advertisers enjoy greater access to their ideas and thoughts.

Brands can then use this information to market their own products to children. As the exhibit shows, the makers of sugary drinks have done so extensively. Despite concerns about childhood obesity and the ethicality of marketing nutritionally void foods to children, no laws prevent brands from hosting Facebook pages or creating a Twitter account to appeal to children.

Of course, access also potentially extends to sexual predators and others who might do harm to children. Some findings suggest that at least 1 million children are harassed or bullied through Facebook each year.[27] Thus the question becomes: Is expanding demographic target markets to ever younger children a boon for marketers? Or is it rather a danger to children?

▼ Ranking of Brand Followers[26]

Brand	Number of Facebook Fans	Number of Twitter Followers
Coke (regular)	30,747,955	3,000,026
Red Bull	20,462,113	223,494
Monster Energy Drink	11,238,533	75,485
Dr Pepper	9,680,095	43,810
Mountain Dew	5,517,588	39,917
Pepsi (regular)	4,449,173	89,371
Sprite	3,740,522	15,397
Gatorade	3,704,295	329,616
Vitamin Water	2,539,549	13,884
Lipton Brisk Iced Tea	849,800	26,625

Note: Data as of June 15, 2011.

Is expanding demographic target markets to ever younger children a boon for marketers? Or is it rather a danger to children?

of 50-plus consumers the United States has ever seen. Although the Baby Boomer generation spans 18 years, experts agree that its members share several traits that set them apart from those born before World War II. First, they are individualistic. Second, leisure time represents a high priority for them. Third, they believe that they will always be able to take care of themselves, partly evinced by their feeling of economic security, even though they are a little careless about the way they spend their money. Fourth, they have an obsession with maintaining their youth. Fifth and finally, they will always love rock 'n roll.

> **"Retailers recognize the immense buying power of the aging Baby Boomers, so they cater directly to them with larger fonts in signage, staff available to read the small print on product packaging, and seating options in stores."**

The move from suits and ties to jeans and T-shirts in business is a direct result of Baby Boomers imposing their values on the workplace as they have moved into upper management positions.[28] Boomers, who wore tie-dyed shirts, ripped jeans, and long hair in their younger days, have pushed their casual lifestyles into the workplace and virtually every aspect with which they are associated. Recognizing the opportunity, Levi-Strauss developed its Dockers line of casual shirts and khakis.

Food companies have also targeted Baby Boomers with healthier options for cereals, frozen entrees, and snacks that have no cholesterol, low fat, and no sugar. General Mills has added extra calcium to Yoplait Original yogurt in an attempt to help women increase their daily calcium requirements.[29] It has reduced the sodium in products like Cheerios, Progresso soups, and its Chex Snack Mix line. Finally, General Mills has created a new version of Total cereal containing omega-3 fatty acids, which are good for heart health.

Retailers also recognize the immense buying power of the aging Baby Boomers, so they cater directly to them with larger fonts in signage, staff available to read the small print on product packaging, and seating options in stores.[30] They note that their older customers, even the ones with moderate incomes, are more focused on quality than price and make decisions on what merchandise to carry accordingly. Finally, and perhaps surprisingly, Baby Boomers are heavy Internet users and tend to do research before purchasing online.

Income Income distribution in the United States has grown more polarized—the highest-income groups are growing, whereas many middle- and lower-income groups' real purchasing power keeps declining. Although the trend of wealthy households outpacing both poor and middle classes is worldwide, it is particularly prominent in the United States. The average weekly income of the richest 1–10 percent of the population is more than $1,895; the average weekly income for the United States as a whole was $774 in 2013. And the poorest 10 percent of the population earned less than $374 per week. Furthermore, the number of people who earn less than the poverty line ($23,550 for a family of four in 2013) continues to grow.[31] The wealthiest 1 percent control 34.6 percent of Americans' total net worth; the bottom 90 percent control only 26.9 percent in comparison.[32] The increase in wealthy

No matter how old they get, Baby Boomers will always love rock 'n roll.

families may be due to the maturing of the general population, the increase in dual-income households, and the higher overall level of education. It also may prompt some ethical concerns about the distribution of wealth. However, the broad range in incomes creates marketing opportunities at both the high and low ends of the market.

Although some marketers choose to target only affluent population segments, others have had great success delivering value to middle- and low-income earners. Consider, for example, the toys presented by the specialty retailer Hammacher Schlemmer versus the mass appeal of Walmart's toy sections. Toy buyers at Walmart are looking for inexpensive products; those at Hammacher Schlemmer go to great lengths to find unusual toys such as the Fuel Cell Car and Experiment Kit, pictured, or the Gigantic Inflatable Climbing Iceberg.[33]

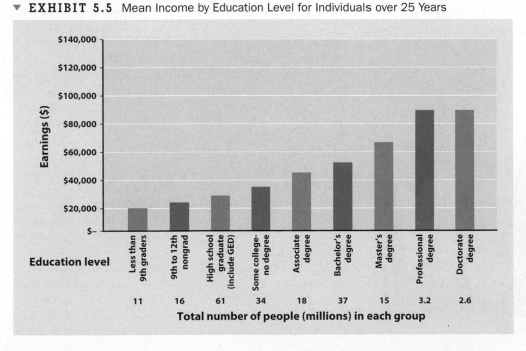

The Fuel Cell Car and Experiment Kit appeals to an affluent customer at specialty retailer, Hammacher Schlemmer.

Another aspect of the income demographic relates to the concept of value. Why are customers searching for value more today than in recent decades? During the first three decades after World War II, most American families experienced real income growth, but starting in the late 1970s and continuing through to today, that growth has stagnated. Family incomes have stayed slightly ahead of inflation (the general rate of price increases), but their health care costs, property taxes, and tuition bills have risen much faster than inflation.

Education Studies show that higher levels of education lead to better jobs and higher incomes.[34] (See Exhibit 5.5.) According the U.S. Bureau of Labor Statistics, employment that requires a college or secondary degree accounts for nearly half of all projected job growth in the near future. Moreover, average annual earnings are higher for those with degrees than for those without. Those who did not graduate from high school have an average annual salary of about $23,000; high school grads earn around $32,500; those with a bachelor's degree earn nearly $54,000.[35]

For some products, marketers can combine education level with other data such as occupation and income and obtain pretty accurate predictions of purchase behavior. For instance, a full-time college student with a part-time job may have relatively little personal income but will spend his or her disposable dollars differently than would a high school graduate who works in a factory and earns a similar income. College students tend

▼ **EXHIBIT 5.5** Mean Income by Education Level for Individuals over 25 Years

Education level	Less than 9th graders	9th to 12th nongrad	High school graduate (include GED)	Some college- no degree	Associate degree	Bachelor's degree	Master's degree	Professional degree	Doctorate degree
Earnings ($)	$20,000	$24,000	$29,000	$36,000	$45,000	$53,000	$67,000	$90,000	$90,000
Total number of people (millions) in each group	11	16	61	34	18	37	15	3.2	2.6

to play sports and go to nightclubs, whereas high school graduates are more likely watch sports and go to bars. Marketers need to be quite cognizant of the interaction among education, income, and occupation.

Gender

Years ago, gender roles appeared clear, but those male/female roles have been blurred. This shift in attitude and behavior affects the way many firms design and promote their products and services. More firms are careful about gender neutrality in positioning their products and attempt to transcend gender boundaries, especially through increased interactions with their customers. On the basis of its research with men for example, the children's stroller company Bugaboo International designed a high-tech, black-and-chrome contraption with dirt bike tires.

Rather than rely on stereotypical feminine appeals, Nike also has recognized the increasing numbers of women who engage in physically challenging activities. For the annual Women's Marathon in San Francisco, Nike registered 20,000 competitors in just three weeks. In addition to encouraging women to take up the challenge, with the tagline Run to Be, Nike provides special events for women along the

The Hispanic market is so large in some areas of the United States that marketers develop entire marketing programs just to meet Hispanics' needs.

Nike sponsors numerous women's running events all over the world.

course, such as a chocolate mile, pedicure stations, and free massages—though it also notes that men are welcome to participate. Every participant also receives a finisher's necklace from Tiffany & Co.[36]

Ethnicity[37]

Because of immigration and increasing birth rates among various ethnic and racial groups, the United States continues to grow more diverse. Approximately 80 percent of all population growth in the next 20 years is expected to come from African American, Hispanic, and Asian communities. Minorities now represent approximately one-quarter of the population; by 2050, they will represent about 50 percent, and nearly 30 percent of the population will be Hispanic.[38] The United Nations also estimates that approximately 1 million people per year will immigrate from less developed nations to the United States over the next 40 years.[39] Many foreign-born Americans and recent immigrants tend to concentrate in a handful of metropolitan areas, such as New York, Los Angeles, San Francisco, and Chicago.

Among the different groups, Hispanic buying power is projected to reach $1.3 trillion in 2015, a cumulative increase of around 25 percent compared with 2010.[40] The 50 million Hispanic consumers in the United States have increasing influences on mainstream U.S. culture. Many families have been in the United States for multiple generations, and the consumer behavior of these highly acculturated Hispanics differs little from that of other groups of Americans. For example, they use credit cards, are minimally influenced by advertising and product placements, exhibit greater sensitivity to in-store promotions, and are likely to shop online and from catalogs. Marketers have generally taken a separate approach to reaching the Hispanic market, recognizing that promotions targeted toward Mexican Americans may not appeal to Hispanics of Cuban or Argentinean descent. When appealing to younger, more assimilated Hispanics, firms are gearing their marketing to appeal to the whole U.S. market, regardless of ethnicity.[41]

The 2010 U.S. Census counts 42 million African American U.S. households, who are more affluent and suburban than previous studies suggested. They also tend to be younger, such that 47 percent are between the ages of 18 and 49 years (i.e., a key age demographic for many marketers). The number of black

The United States is like a salad bowl, made up of people from every corner of the world.

households earning more than $75,000 has increased by 47 percent since 2005, and by 2015, trends indicate that a majority of black Americans will live in the suburbs.[42] For example, in the Atlanta metropolitan area, the city lost 8 percent of its African American households, while the surrounding suburbs gained a remarkable 40 percent.[43] For this demographic segment, especially as it moves increasingly to the suburbs, Home Depot has developed particular appeals featuring national figures such as Tom Joyner and Steve Harvey.

Finally, Asian Americans make up only about 5.6 percent of the U.S. population, but they also represent the fastest-growing minority population, tend to earn more, have more schooling, and be more likely to be professionally employed or own a business. However, as with Hispanics, marketers cannot assume they can use a single strategy to appeal to all minority groups. For example, the Chinese, Japanese, Indian, Korean, and Southeast Asian subgroups, such as the Vietnamese and Cambodian, all speak different languages and come from different regional and country cultures.

LO 5-4 Identify various social trends that affect marketing.

Social Trends

Various social trends appear to be shaping consumer values in the United States and around the world, including a greater emphasis on thrift, health and wellness concerns, greener consumers, privacy concerns, and time-poor societies.

Thrift American society has become a consumer society, and yet the economic impacts of a recession and housing crash have prompted many people to embrace the idea of spending less as a virtuous pursuit. Bloggers describe their efforts to get by on less, whether their plan involves spending only $1 per day on food or refusing to buy new clothing (other than underwear) for a year.[44] Another recent trend has even gotten the reality television treatment, as Adding Value 5.1 describes.

Not everyone is quite so extreme though; consumers across the board appear to be attempting to save more, spend less on luxuries, and manage to get by without dipping into their savings. Frequently called the lipstick effect, some shoppers enjoy the thrill of treating themselves to small luxuries, such as a Chanel lipstick, but forgo larger luxury items such as a vacation. According to some consumer psychologists, in an uncertain economic setting, it's just too hard to be frugal all the time.[45]

As consumers have become more savvy and conscientious about bargain shopping and searching for deals, innovative entrepreneurs such as Groupon and LivingSocial developed

Get your kids to eat better without ever raising your voice.

Childhood obesity is a growing issue and a big concern. And we're doing something to combat it. Our SUBWAY FRESH FIT FOR KIDS™ meal fits into the American Heart Association's approach to a healthy lifestyle. And best of all, it's a fast, tasty way to give kids a "better for them" meal. Finally there's fast food you can feel good about.

American Heart Association *Proud sponsor of the American Heart Association's Jump Rope for Heart.*

Subway appeals to customers wanting healthier quick service food alternatives.

Adding Value 5.1

Clever Thrift or Middle-Class Hoarding?

A $400 grocery tab reduced to $6. Discounts and coupons combined to make the purchases of some staples absolutely free. And garages are filled to the ceiling with nonperishable products. These are the signs of extreme couponing.

As presented most notably on the reality show *Extreme Couponing,* extreme coupon shoppers refuse ever to pay full price. Devoting hours to their planning and coupon clipping, they carefully time their purchases to ensure they only buy items when they go on sale. Then they combine the sale with a coupon or combine multiple coupons for the same item. When they find a good deal, they buy as much as they possibly can and stock up at home, which means they won't need to buy those items again for months.[46]

The effort to get everything at extremely low prices, or even for free, can get a little uncomfortable to watch though. The couponers featured on the show load up multiple carts, driving shoppers lined up behind them, as well as the checkout clerks, into near panic. Then they lug all their purchases home to stash throughout their homes. Some of these extreme shoppers admit to being driven by a sense of fear. Even if they lose their jobs, there are hundreds of jars of peanut butter in their basement, so they won't starve.

The practice requires a middle-class, suburban lifestyle to start though. People living in apartments in the city cannot store the bulk quantities required. Even for consumers in the suburbs, inventory costs might become a concern, just as they are for retailers. If a consumer is fortunate enough to have a spare bedroom that no one is using, it's easy to fill it with groceries. But not everyone has that luxury.[47]

Couponers haven't died; they've morphed into a new species on steroids called Extreme Couponers.

Furthermore, extreme couponers create bottlenecks in store check-out lines, cause stock-outs, and create inventory and supply chain problems for many retailers, especially grocers. In addition to increases in coupon enthusiasts, retailers are also noticing an increase in fraudulent coupons and coupon misuse. In response, some stores have updated their coupon policies. Target's restated policy prevents customers from combining two buy-one-get-one-free coupons to get both items for free. Rite-Aid restricts the number of coupons customers can use for a specific item. Walgreens updated its current coupon policy to give management the right to limit the number of coupons consumers can use.[48]

> In the past 20 years, child obesity has doubled and teenage obesity tripled in the United States, leading to skyrocketing rates of high blood pressure, high cholesterol, early signs of heart disease, and Type 2 diabetes among children.

business plans to satisfy the desire for a deal. These websites deliver daily e-mails to consumers that are tailored to consumers' preferences, shopping habits, and locations. Millions of subscribers have signed up for varying deal sites and enjoy significant discounts and exposure to new products and services. Yet after receiving dozens of deal messages a day, consumers have become somewhat inoculated to bargains. Consumer expectations of what constitutes a good deal have changed rapidly over the past several years, which means marketers need some new ideas about how to appeal to them.[49]

Health and Wellness Concerns Health concerns, especially those pertaining to children, are prevalent, critical, and widespread. In the past 20 years, child obesity has doubled and teenage obesity tripled in the United States, leading to skyrocketing rates of high blood pressure, high cholesterol, early signs of heart disease, and Type 2 diabetes among children. The U.S. Centers for Disease Control and Prevention also estimate that approximately one-third of U.S. adults are obese, and the incidence of diabetes has reached 8.3 percent—with much higher rates for people still undiagnosed or classified as having prediabetes.[50] It is also increasing at alarming rates in other countries and among consumers who adopt more Western diets.

New advertising guidelines therefore require marketers to produce food in reasonably proportioned sizes. Advertised food items must provide basic nutrients, have less than 30 percent of their total calories from fat, and include no added sweeteners. The advertising also cannot be aired during children's programming, and companies cannot link unhealthy foods with cartoon and celebrity figures. For example, Burger King no longer uses SpongeBob SquarePants to promote burgers and fries.[51]

As the same time, consumers' interest in improving their health has opened up several new markets and niches focused on healthy living. For example, consumer spending on yoga classes, mats, and clothing has increased consistently, leading to a 9.5 percent sales jump between 2006 and 2011.[52] Yoga studios actually combine multiple modern trends: As the economy sours, people face increasing stress, which they hope to reduce through yoga. In addition, yoga studios are relatively inexpensive to open and operate, so entrepreneurs and

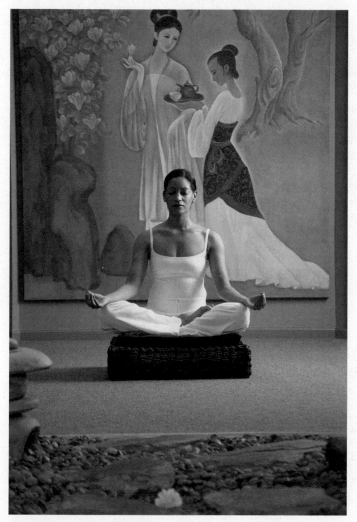

The practice of yoga is growing as more consumers embrace a healthy lifestyle.

consumers appreciate the value for the money they offer. And of course, Americans remain consistently on the lookout for exercise mechanisms that can help them shed pounds and match media images of athletic prowess. Thus competition is growing in this industry, and some studios have begun combine their basic yoga classes with additional offers to attract clients, such as food services, acupuncture, or massages.[53]

Greener Consumers **Green marketing** involves a strategic effort by firms to supply customers with environmentally friendly merchandise.[54] Many consumers, concerned about everything from the purity of air and water to the safety of beef and salmon, believe that each person can make a difference in the environment. For example, nearly half of U.S. adults now recycle their soda bottles and newspapers, and European consumers are even more green. Germans are required by law to recycle bottles, and the European Union does not allow beef raised on artificial growth hormones to be imported.

Demand for green-oriented products has been a boon to the firms that supply them. (A case that discusses a primary example may be found online at www.mhhe.com/grewalM4e.) Marketers encourage consumers to replace older versions of washing machines and dishwashers with water- and energy-saving models and to invest in phosphate-free laundry powder and mercury-free and rechargeable batteries. New markets emerge for recycled building products, packaging, paper goods, and even sweaters and sneakers as well as for more efficient appliances, lighting, and heating and cooling systems in homes and offices. Jumping on the green bandwagon, Frito-Lay's SunChip line of snack foods uses solar power at one of its eight production facilities to harness the sun's energy to produce its products.[55] Ethical & Social Dilemma 5.2 examines some of the challenges companies face in making green products.

These green products and initiatives suggest a complicated business model. Are they good for business? Some green options are more expensive than traditional products and initiatives. Are consumers interested in or willing to pay the higher prices for green products? Are firms really interested in improving the environment? Or are they disingenuously marketing products or services as environmentally friendly, with the goal of gaining public approval and sales rather than actually improving the environment? This type of exploitation is common enough that it even has produced a new term: **greenwashing**. Consumers need to question whether a firm is spending significantly more money and time advertising being green and operating with consideration for the environment than actually spending these resources on environmentally sound practices.

Privacy Concerns More and more consumers worldwide sense a loss of privacy. At the same time that the Internet

ethical & societal dilemma

Green Cereal?

It may seem at times that massive conglomerates are slow to change, but some companies are clearly learning some lessons when it comes to responsible sourcing. Just a few years ago, Nestlé suffered terrible consumer backlash when it agreed to purchase a small amount of palm oil (used in its chocolate candies) from a company that cleared rainforests to access the palms.[56]

Wary of such reactions, General Mills (GM) quickly promised that all the palm oil used in any of its products and packaging would come from responsible, sustainable sources by 2015. Recent estimates suggest that such moves are achieving some success. The rate of Amazonian deforestation in 2012 was lower than at any other point since the Brazilian government started tracking this statistic in 1988.[57] But neither GM nor any of its competitors in the consumer packaged goods industry has reached the goal of complete sustainability goal quite yet.

Determined not to limit itself to palm oil, GM also committed to improving the trade conditions for vanilla farmers that supply the raw material for the traditional, favorite flavor of its Häagen-Dazs ice cream. With a two-year investment of $125 million in Madagascar, GM plans to train small vanilla farmers in sustainable methods that also increase crop quality, such as yield improvements and

The demand for palm oil can often lead to rain forests, such as this one, being clear cut.

curing techniques. Ideally, these tactics also will enhance the earnings of local farmers and their communities.[58]

Next, GM helped found—in collaboration with the USDA and EPA—the U.S. Food Waste Challenge.[59] This initiative seeks not only to reduce the environmental impacts of waste collected in landfills but also to address spreading food insecurity concerns. By reducing the waste and loss of food products, the collaborators hope to feed more people or at least use the edible remainders for productive uses such as animal feed.

These examples reflect GM's overall sustainability mission and efforts. It has released Global Responsibility Reports

annually for more than 40 years. It also touts its efforts widely, through its blog, press releases, and other communications. In this sense, GM runs the risk that skeptical consumers will come to believe it publicizes its good works to cover up bad behavior. But as the CEO of General Mills has readily acknowledged, "we're finding opportunities to collaborate with business, government and non-governmental organizations on important systemic solutions. While we're proud of our progress, we also know there is still much more to be done. We are committed to continued progress in these areas. Our business requires it and future generations depend on it."[60]

---

has created an explosion of accessibility to consumer information, improvements in computer storage facilities and the manipulation of information have led to more and better security and credit check services. Yet controversies still erupt, and some observers suggest hackers are just getting more effective. In 2011, for example, multiple multinational corporations suffered security breaches, including the defense contractor Lockheed Martin, NASA, the Fox Network, and Sony. In the last case, a group of hackers stole the personal information of 102 million PlayStation users.[61]

The Federal Trade Commission (FTC), responding to consumer outcries regarding unwanted telephone solicitations, has registered the phone numbers of more than 200 million phone numbers in the Do Not Call Registry. This action was designed to protect consumers against

> " In the majority of families, both parents work, and the kids are busier than ever. "

intrusions that Congress determined to be particularly invasive.[62] Unfortunately, the Do Not Call Registry may have eliminated many honest telemarketers, leaving the wires open for the crooked groups who often use nontraceable recordings to reach potential customers at home. In the end, most companies are moving resources away from telephone campaigns and refocusing them elsewhere.

A Time-Poor Society Reaching a target market has always been a major challenge, but it is made even more complicated by several trends that increase the difficulty of grabbing those markets' attention. In the majority of families, both parents work, and the kids are busier than ever. Since 1973, the median number of hours that people say they work has jumped from 41 to 49 a week. During that same period, reported leisure time has dropped from

26 to 19 hours a week.[63] Among younger consumers, the trend is to cope with a lack of leisure time by multitasking—watching television or listening to music while talking on the telephone or doing homework. Their divided attention simply cannot focus as well on advertisements that appear in those media.

Marketers must respond to the challenge of getting consumers' attention by adjusting. Noting that many viewers of cooking shows spent little time cooking themselves, the Bravo television network partnered with the Healthy Choice line to sell *Top Chef* branded frozen dinners in grocery stores. Consumers can purchase meals similar to those prepared on the show, such as barbecued steak with red potatoes or roasted chicken Marsala with mushrooms. On the Bravo website of course, they also can try their hand at cooking themselves, maybe on the weekends, by ordering a related line of knives, aprons, cookbooks and other equipment.[64]

Retailers are doing their part by making their products available to customers whenever and wherever they want. For instance, many retailers have become full-fledged multichannel retailers that offer stores, catalogs, and Internet shopping options. In addition, retailers such as Office Depot and Walgreens have extended their hours of operation so that their customers can shop during hours they aren't working. Automated processes such as self-checkout lanes and electronic kiosks speed the shopping process and provide customers with product and ordering information. Grocery stores and home improvement centers have been particularly aggressive in developing strategies to help time-poor customers, as Adding Value 5.2 describes.

To find and develop such methods to make life easier for consumers in the time-poor society, marketers often rely on technology, another macroenvironmental factor and the topic of the next section.

Technological Advances

Technological advances have accelerated during the past decade, improving the value of both products and services. Consumers have constant access to the Internet everywhere through services such as WiFi, 3G, and 4G. Smartphones using the Apple, RIM, Android, and Symbian operating systems allow for greater computing, data storage, and communication. Tablet computers, starting with the iPad, have extended mobile computing even further by offering a larger mobile interface in environments that traditionally limited access.

These examples of advanced technology make consumers increasingly dependent on the help they can provide, especially in terms of making decisions and communicating with others.

Adding Value 5.2

Grocery Retailers Help Time-Poor Consumers

Traditional methods of shopping for and preparing food have always been time-consuming. Restaurants, and particularly fast-food restaurants, have helped lighten this burdensome task for decades. But as consumers become more time-pressed and as traditional grocery stores are feeling increased competition from superstores such as Walmart and Target and warehouse stores such as Costco and Sam's Club, some grocery retailers are developing innovative methods of helping consumers put food on their families' tables.

Through its Signature Café line, for example, Safeway provides entrees, side dishes, sandwiches, and pizzas—offerings popular enough that it has earned approximately $100 million in sales of these items each year since introducing them.[65] Even Walgreens, a chain not traditionally known for fresh food items, is slowly introducing fresh foods to its stores. In a somewhat different approach, Walgreens has decided to initiate its program in "food deserts"— that is, urban neighborhoods traditionally underserved when it comes to fresh fruit and vegetable options.[66]

Walgreens also is rolling out another new program to help customers get all their necessary tasks done in a day. With its Web Pickup service, customers in selected markets can shop online, then pick up their orders in around an hour at their local store.[67]

Self-checkout lanes speed the shopping process, but do they improve customer service?

Whole Foods already provides ready-made meals, but it also began to worry about the efficiency with which customers could get in and out of stores when they were in a hurry. So this chain streamlined the checkout process by organizing checkout lines like a bank. One line is formed, and customers are helped at the next available register.

Social & Mobile Marketing 5.1
Foursquare's Promise and Facebook's Response

The location-based mobile platform Foursquare not only awards badges to frequent customers to reflect their status in certain locations, but it also helps people find the locations their friends are frequenting and gives them helpful tips about local bars, restaurants, parks, museums, grocery stores, and movie theaters—such as where to park or what not to order. For the 250,000 companies that appear on the platform,[68] Foursquare also provides an effective means to attract, appeal to, and retain loyal customers.

A Foursquare user who checks in to a local restaurant, for example, accumulates points and rewards in the form of badges. These badges earn the user discounts and coupons on future visits to the restaurant as long as he or she keeps checking in at the site. The more a user visits, the more incentives she or he receives. To up the ante even more, customers can earn additional points for bringing along a friend on their next visit and getting that friend to check in at the same time. The social aspects of Foursquare go still further: Users often leave reviews of the venues they visit and then plan ahead to determine the places they will go next, according to what other similar users have said about a location.

For the companies, these uses provide remarkable insights into target markets.[69] They know who is visiting when, how often, and with whom. Finally, because the concept is based on rewarding frequent visitors, companies know they are devoting their best efforts to their best, most loyal customers.

By gathering the vast information from all its users, both consumers and sellers, Foursquare can issue on-target recommendations of other places to go. Did you visit a coffee shop on Elm Street? Foursquare thinks you might find the tea house on Oak Lane interesting as well. If another fellow fan of the local pizza joint also tends to check in at the movie theater down the street, Foursquare can suggest you might like it too.

But Foursquare isn't the only game in town. Facebook also allows users to check in at locations and has the advantage of a much larger social network—more than 800 million users, compared with Foursquare's 10 million or so.[70] Thus Facebook fans can tag friends who are with them, to show how many people are showing up at a particular location. This tool means Facebook can learn about its users and the places they or their friends like to go to. Marketers then can use this information to learn more about their customers, including the places they prefer and how those preferences align with their other interests—as communicated by their Facebook profile.

Foursquare allows you to "Check In" and share what you're doing with your friends.

Thus Netflix suggests which movies we should watch, Pandora outlines the music we should listen to, and Amazon tells us what we should read. Near field communication technology takes payments, coupons, and loyalty card data from customers as they walk by the scanner. The next wave of mobile applications is likely to involve wireless payments, such that customers' phones also serve as m-wallets.

From the firm's perspective, the technology called RFID (radio frequency identification device) enables it to track an item from the moment it was manufactured, through the distribution system, to the retail store, and into the hands of the final consumer. Because they are able to determine exactly how much of each product is at a given point in the supply chain, retailers can also communicate with their suppliers and collaboratively plan to meet their inventory needs.

As Social & Mobile Marketing 5.1 shows, mobile devices enhance the customer's experience by making it easier to interact with the manufacturer or retailer or other customers, and they add a new channel of access, which makes customers more loyal and more likely to spend more with a particular retailer.

Walgreens' applications, in addition to the Web Pickup service we described previously, allow customers to order prescriptions or review their prescription history, check the in-store inventories, and print photos. Steve Madden, the footwear retailer, attracts more than 10 percent of its web traffic from mobile devices—which earns it more than $1 million in mobile sales annually. Furthermore, these shoppers spend an average of seven minutes on Steve Madden's mobile site.[71] Whereas customers view an average of seven web pages during online visits, they browse only four or five pages in a mobile setting.

Mobile applications are not just about shopping with a phone. By 2015, people will access the web more often through smartphones than through laptops and desktops combined. But mobile experiences cannot be identical to web experiences because the interface is different, thus the way users employ the sites differ. In particular, the smaller screen on mobile devices means that less information must convey the same brand image.

Economic Situation

Marketers monitor the general economic situation, both in their home country and abroad, because it affects the way consumers buy merchandise and spend money. Some major factors that influence the state of an economy include the rate of inflation, foreign currency exchange rates, and interest rates.

Inflation refers to the persistent increase in the prices of goods and services. Increasing prices cause the purchasing power of the dollar to decline; in other words, the dollar buys less than it used to.

In a similar fashion, **foreign currency fluctuations** can influence consumer spending. For instance, in the summer of 2002, the euro was valued at slightly less than US$1. By the middle of 2013, it was worth $1.32 but only after it had risen to an all-time high of $1.60 in 2008.[72] As the euro becomes more expensive compared with the dollar, merchandise made in Europe and other countries tied to the euro becomes more costly to Americans, whereas products made in the United States cost less for European consumers. In contrast, the current European financial crisis indicates shrinking value of the euro relative to the U.S. dollar, in which case Europeans might buy fewer American goods.

This crisis that is shaking European economies and the Euro Zone as a whole has several other potential impacts on the U.S. economy. European consumers purchase approximately 22 percent of U.S. exports, a rate that could easily drop if Greece, Italy, and other at-risk economies fail. In addition, global financial markets are closely connected, such that when one falls, everyone suffers.[73]

Finally, **interest rates** represent the cost of borrowing money. When customers borrow money from a bank, they agree

Tourists from other countries flock to the United States to shop because the value of the dollar is low compared to their own currency.

to pay back the loan, plus the interest that accrues. The interest, in effect, is the cost to the customers or the fee the bank charges those customers for borrowing the money. Likewise, if a customer opens a savings account at a bank, he or she will earn interest on the amount saved, which means the interest becomes the fee the consumer gets for loaning the money to the bank. If the interest rate goes up, consumers have an incentive to save more because they earn more for loaning the bank their money; when interest rates go down, however, consumers generally borrow more.

How do these three important economic factors—inflation, foreign currency fluctuations, and interest rates—affect firms' ability to market goods and services? Shifts in the three economic factors make marketing easier for some and harder for others. For instance, when inflation increases, consumers probably don't buy less food, but they may shift their expenditures from expensive steaks to less expensive hamburgers. Grocery stores and inexpensive restaurants win, but expensive restaurants lose. Consumers also buy less discretionary merchandise, though off-price and discount retailers often gain ground at the expense of their full-price competitors. Similarly, the sales of expensive jewelry, fancy cars, and extravagant vacations decrease, but the sale of low-cost luxuries, such as personal care products and home entertainment, tends to increase.

Political/Regulatory Environment

The **political/regulatory environment** comprises political parties, government organizations, and legislation and laws. Organizations must fully understand and comply with any legislation regarding fair competition, consumer protection, or

If Greece's economy continues to erode, what will be its impact on the value of the U.S. dollar vis-á-vis the euro?

goal; the 1914 Clayton Act that supports the Sherman Act by prohibiting the combination of two or more competing corporations through pooling ownership of stock and restricting pricing policies such as price discrimination, exclusive dealing, and tying clauses to different buyers; and the 1936 Robison-Patman Act that specifically outlaws price discrimination toward wholesalers, retailers, or other producers and requires sellers to make ancillary services or allowances available to all buyers on proportionately equal terms. These laws have been specifically used to increase competition, such as the deregulation of the telephone and energy industries, in which massive conglomerates such as Ma Bell, the nickname for AT&T, were broken into smaller, competing companies.

Legislation has also been enacted to protect consumers in a variety of ways. First, regulations require marketers to abstain from false or misleading advertising practices that might mislead consumers, such as claims that a medication can cure a disease when in fact it causes other health risks. Second, manufacturers are required to refrain from using any harmful or hazardous materials (e.g., lead in toys) that might place a consumer at risk. Third, organizations must adhere to fair and reasonable business practices when they communicate with consumers. For example, they must employ reasonable debt collection methods and disclose any finance charges, and they are limited with regard to their telemarketing and e-mail solicitation activities. A summary of the most significant legislation affecting marketing interests appears in Exhibit 5.6.

industry-specific regulation. Since the turn of the century, the government has enacted laws that promote both fair trade and competition by prohibiting the formation of monopolies or alliances that would damage a competitive marketplace, fostering fair pricing practices for all suppliers and consumers.

The government enacts laws focused on insuring that companies compete fairly with one another. Although enacted in the early part of the twentieth century, they remain the backbone of U.S. legislation protecting competition in commerce. These laws include the 1890 Sherman Antitrust Act that prohibits monopolies and other activities that would restrain trade or competition and makes fair trade within a free market a national

▼ **EXHIBIT 5.6** Consumer Protection Legislation

Year	Law	Description
1906	Federal Food and Drug Act	Created the Food and Drug Administration. Prohibited the manufacture or sale of adulterated or fraudulently labeled food and drug products.
1914	Federal Trade Commission	Established the Federal Trade Commission (FTC) to regulate unfair competitive practices and practices that deceive or are unfair to consumers.
1966	Fair Packaging and Labeling Act	Regulates packaging and labeling of consumer goods; requires manufacturers to state the contents of the package, who made it, and the amounts contained within.
1966	Child Protection Act	Prohibits the sale of harmful toys and components to children. Sets the standard for child-resistant packaging.
1967	Federal Cigarette Labeling and Advertising Act	Requires cigarette packages to display this warning: "Warning: The Surgeon General Has Determined that Cigarette Smoking Is Dangerous to Your Health."
1972	Consumer Product Safety Act	Created the Consumer Product Safety Commission, which has the authority to regulate safety standards for consumer products.
1990	Children's Television Act	Limits the number of commercials shown during children's programming.
1990	Nutrition Labeling and Education Act	Requires food manufacturers to display nutritional contents on product labels.
1995	Telemarketing Sales Rule	Regulates fraudulent activities conducted over the telephone. Violators are subject to fines and actions enforced by the FTC.
2003	Controlling the Assault of Non-Solicited Pornography and Marketing Act of 2003 (CAN-SPAM Act)	Prohibits misleading commercial e-mail, particularly misleading subject and from lines.
2003	Amendment to the Telemarketing Sales Rule	Establishes a National Do Not Call Registry, requiring telemarketers to abstain from calling consumers who opt to be placed on the list.
2003	Do Not Spam Law	Laws created to reduce spam or unwarranted e-mails.
2010	Financial Reform Law	Created the Consumer Financial Protection Bureau whose aim will be to enforce appropriate consumer-oriented regulations on a number of financial firms, such as banks, mortgage businesses, and payday and student lenders. It also set up the Financial Services Oversight Council to act as an early warning system.

Responding to the Environment

As the examples throughout this chapter show, many companies engage in tactics and marketing strategies that attempt to respond to multiple developments in the wider environment. For example, responding to pressures from the Federal Communications Commission (political and regulatory environment), the economic status of consumers (economic situation), increasing access to faster broadband capabilities (technological advances), and calls for greater social responsibility (social trends), 14 cable companies agreed to provide low-cost Internet access to impoverished families.[74] This remarkable agreement allows the cable companies to promote their social responsibility. But it also ensures that families whose children are eligible for free lunch programs can gain access to the services, opportunities, and options available only online.

We noted the remarkable growth in health and wellness markets, including yoga, previously. Lululemon was one company that was quick to notice the trend and respond with great success. Its yoga pants average $98 per pair—a high price point in the market—but its image as a small, niche brand with a yoga-centric philosophy has helped it succeed.[75]

In a constantly changing marketing environment, the marketers that succeed are the ones that respond quickly, accurately, and sensitively to their consumers. ■

 check yourself

1. What are the six key macroenvironmental factors?
2. Differentiate between country culture and regional culture.
3. Identify the different generational cohorts.
4. What are some important social trends shaping consumer values and shopping behavior?

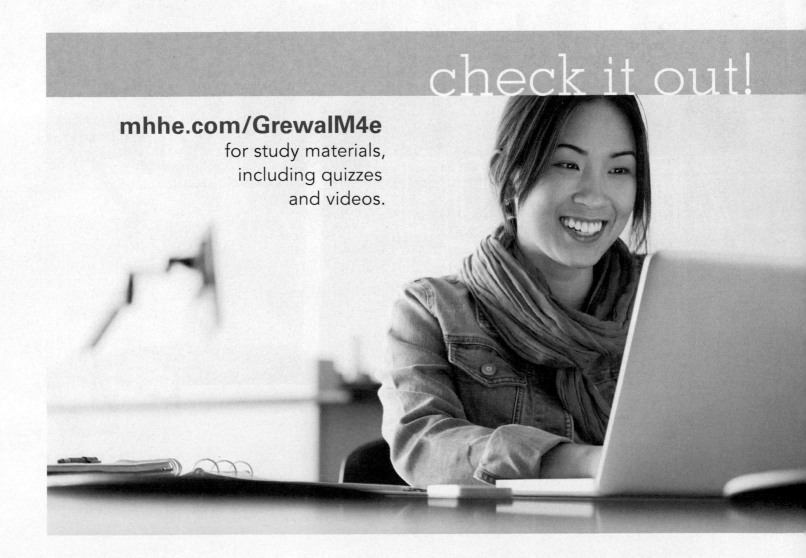

check it out!

mhhe.com/GrewalM4e
for study materials,
including quizzes
and videos.

chapter SIX

consumer behavior

As first-year students arrive on college campuses to begin the fall semester, they often are greeted by smiling upper-class students, offering to help them locate their rooms or unload their cars.[1] Other experienced students are on hand to assist newcomers with the purchase of a laptop or to invite them to one of the highlights of back-to-school week, a combined party and late-night shopping excursion. Thoughtful people helping rookies settle in? Maybe.

These goodwill ambassadors are also student marketers, paid by companies such as American Eagle Outfitters, Hewlett-Packard, and Red Bull, to hawk products on campus and through social networks. Even the first big college party is a marketing event in this case, sponsored by Target. Bused by the retail giant to a local superstore, first-year students dance to music spun by a DJ, collect free samples of junk food, and win prizes such as

LEARNING OBJECTIVES

After reading this chapter, you should be able to:

LO 6-1 Articulate the steps in the consumer buying process.

LO 6-2 Describe the difference between functional and psychological needs.

LO 6-3 Describe factors that affect information search.

LO 6-4 Discuss postpurchase outcomes.

LO 6-5 List the factors that affect the consumer decision process.

LO 6-6 Describe how involvement influences the consumer decision process.

refrigerators and cases of soda—all while shopping for more room furnishings for their dorms.

Using students to promote goods to their peers and classmates gives manufacturers the credibility of word-of-mouth advertising and direct contact with a market segment worth about $36 billion a year. Students promoting the brand and those experiencing it for

continued on p. 118

The Zipcar/Ford alliance is designed to appeal to college students and get them hooked on Ford products.

continued from p. 117

the first time can become fans and spread the word to their families and high school friends. They can also form a habit and continue purchasing the same brand of toothpaste, smartphone, or jeans as they build their careers and families. This potential to attract new consumers and influence their lifetime shopping behavior, just by marketing to college students, is so significant that two companies that seemingly should function as competitors, Ford Motor Company and Zipcar, have joined forces to take advantage of the opportunities.[2]

A Zipcar, available by the hour for a low rental fee, theoretically might eliminate a student's need to own a car. It thus might steal a customer from Ford. But a Zipcar rental also may be an opportunity for a young driver to test a car model and become comfortable driving it. This familiarity can translate, over time, into a purchase or even repeat purchases. This

logic motivated Ford to provide Zipcar with up to 1,000 Ford Focus sedans for use on 250 U.S. college and university campuses.[3] With its advanced technology features and fuel efficiency, the Focus is particularly alluring to younger drivers. But Ford further sweetened the deal for students by offering $10 off Zipcar's annual membership fee and a $1 per hour discount on the hourly rental fee for students renting a Ford. Zipcar is also purchasing a few Ford Escape sport utility vehicles, which will be available at discounted fees too.

The alliance helps Ford tap into the spending that college students allow themselves. It also gives them a relatively low-cost way to control the early driving experiences of future car buyers, because the deal means that more than half of all Zipcar vehicles available on U.S. campuses will be Fords. The manufacturer's 20 or so rivals are left to divvy up the remains. The relationship helps Zipcar by increasing its presence on college campuses, but also by increasing the number of U.S. cars it can advertise as being in the company's fleet.

As these events and developments show, companies such as Target, Zipcar, and Ford recognize the value of reaching young buyers to shape both their current and future consumer behavior. By using peer-to-peer endorsements and other approaches that resonate with college students, these companies are creating life-long customers, whose behaviors will continue to benefit the firms. ■

[To understand consumer behavior, we must ask *why* people buy goods or services.]

We are all consumers, and we take this status for granted. But we are also complex and irrational creatures who cannot always explain our own choices and actions. This inability makes the vitally important job of marketing managers even more difficult, in that they must be able to explain consumers' behavior to give marketers as clear an understanding of their customers as possible.

To understand consumer behavior, we must ask *why* people buy goods or services. Using principles and theories from

sociology and psychology, marketers have been able to decipher many consumer choices and develop basic strategies for dealing with consumers' behavior. Generally, people buy one product or service instead of another because they perceive it to be the better value for them; that is, the ratio of benefits to costs is higher for the product or service than for any other.[4]

However, benefits can be subtle and less than rationally assessed, as we shall see. Consider Katie Smith, who is considering a dress purchase for a job interview. She requires something fashionable but professional looking and doesn't want to spend a lot of money. In making the decision about where she should buy the dress, Katie asks herself:

· Which alternative gives me the best overall value—the most appropriate, yet fashionable dress at the lowest price?

· Which alternative is the best investment—the dress that I can get the most use of?

Because Katie might have several reasons to choose a particular store or dress, it is critical for companies such as Ann Taylor or Macy's to key in on the specific benefits that are most important to her. Other factors that might influence Katie go beyond her conscious awareness, which means that the retailers need to be even more well-versed in her decision process than she is.[5] Only then can they create a marketing mix that will satisfy Katie.

In this chapter, we explore the process that consumers go through when they buy products and services. Then we discuss the psychological, social, and situational factors that influence this consumer decision process. Throughout the chapter, we emphasize what firms can do to influence consumers to purchase their products and services.

LO 6-1 Articulate the steps in the consumer buying process.

THE CONSUMER DECISION PROCESS

The consumer decision process model represents the steps that consumers go through before, during, and after making purchases.[6] Because marketers often find it difficult to determine how consumers make their purchasing decisions, it is useful for us to break down the process into a series of steps and examine each individually, as in Exhibit 6.1.

Need Recognition

The consumer decision process begins when consumers recognize they have an unsatisfied need, and they would like to go from their actual, needy state to a different, desired state. The greater the discrepancy between these two states, the greater the **need recognition** will be. For example, your stomach tells you that you are hungry, and you would rather not have that particular feeling. If you are only a little hungry, you may pass it off and decide to eat later. But if your stomach is growling and you cannot concentrate, the *need*—the difference between your actual (hungry) state and your desired (not hungry) state—is greater, and you'll want to eat immediately to get to your desired state. Furthermore, your hunger conceivably could be satisfied by a nice healthy salad, but what you really want is a bowl of ice cream. *Wants* are goods or services that are not necessarily needed but are desired.[7] Regardless of the level of your hunger, your desire for ice cream will never be satisfied by any

▼ **EXHIBIT 6.1** The Consumer Decision Process

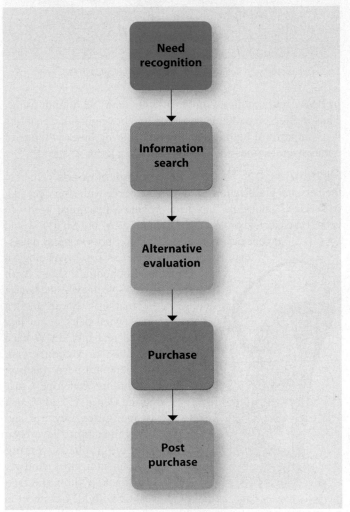

type of salad. Consumer needs like these can be classified as functional, psychological, or both.[8]

LO 6-2 Describe the difference between functional and psychological needs.

Functional Needs **Functional needs** pertain to the performance of a product or service. For years, BMW has made functionally superior motorcycles. BMW's K1600 model has an inline-six cylinder motor, something previously available only

Does this motorcycle satisfy functional or psychological needs?

in BMW automobiles, combined with a stiff aluminum frame. Thus it offers remarkable power on a lightweight bike, enabling it to outperform both the best luxury touring bikes in terms of comfort and serious sporty motorcycles in terms of speed.

Psychological Needs
Psychological needs pertain to the personal gratification consumers associate with a product and/or service.[9] Shoes, for instance, provide a functional need—to keep feet clean and protect them from the elements. So why would anyone pay more than $1000 for shoes that may do neither? Because they seek to satisfy psychological needs. Christian Louboutin's shoes, with their signature red sole, may be the hottest shoe on the market.[10] Sarah Jessica Parker sports several pairs in *Sex and the City* and in real life; BMW even featured the shoe in a commercial. Virtually every modern fashion icon, including Penelope Cruz, Catherine Deneuve, Lady Gaga, Ashley Olsen, Beyoncé, and Angelina Jolie, have been photographed wearing Louboutin shoes. And yet a black python-and-lace shoe with a 14-cm heel is not a particularly practical

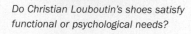

Do Christian Louboutin's shoes satisfy functional or psychological needs?

means of spending $1500. As a result of all the media attention though, there is a strong demand for Louboutin shoes by women who love exciting (and expensive) shoes.

These examples highlight that the vast majority of goods and services are likely to satisfy both functional and psychological needs, albeit to different degrees. Whereas the functional characteristics of BMW K1600 are its main selling point, it also maintains a fashionable appeal for bikers and comes in several colors to match buyers' aesthetic preferences. In contrast, Christian Louboutin shoes satisfy psychological needs that overshadow the functional needs, though they still ultimately serve the function of a shoe.

Consider another, slightly more realistic example: You can get a $15 haircut at SuperCuts or spend $80 or more to get basically the same thing at an upscale salon. Are the two haircuts objectively different? The answer might vary depending on which you believe represents a good haircut and a good value: One person might value getting a really good deal; another might enjoy the extra attention and amenities associated with a fancy salon.

A key to successful marketing is determining the correct balance of functional and psychological needs that best appeals to the firm's target markets. Marriott is carefully balancing this fine line. In the modern economic environment, Marriott is focusing on what matters most to guests. Many hotel consumers just step on the newspapers delivered to their doors, without ever picking them up to read. The various Marriott brands—including Courtyard, Residence Inn, Fairfield Inn, and the Ritz-Carlton—therefore have discontinued deliveries of approximately 50,000 papers daily. The cost savings enable Marriott to avoid massive layoffs, which supports its core value of taking care of employees and thereby encouraging them to treat customers well. The switch to Edy's brand ice cream, instead of Häagen-Dazs, saves money and facilitates employees' jobs because the less dense dessert is easier to scoop. Yet even as it cuts costs, Marriott recognizes the need to attract more customers, so it offers free nights and discounted rates, including $85 in Medan, Indonesia, and $120 at a casino and beach resort in Curaçao.

Search for Information

The second step, after a consumer recognizes a need, is to search for information about the various options that exist to satisfy that need. The length and intensity of the search are

Mariott focuses on what is really important to its customers. But it saves money by switching from Häagen-Dazs to Edy's brand ice cream.

based on the degree of perceived risk associated with purchasing the product or service. If the way your hair is cut is important to your appearance and self-image, you may engage in an involved search for the right salon and stylist. Alternatively, an athlete looking for a short buzz cut might go to the closest, most convenient, and cheapest barber shop. Regardless of the required search level, there are two key types of information search: internal and external.

Internal Search for Information In an **internal search for information**, the buyer examines his or her own memory and knowledge about the product or service, gathered through past experiences. For example, every time Katie wants to eat salad for lunch, she and her friends go to Sweet Tomatoes, but if she's craving dessert, she heads straight to The Cheesecake Factory. In making these choices, she relies on her memory of past experiences when she has eaten at these restaurant chains.

External Search for Information In an **external search for information**, the buyer seeks information outside his or her personal knowledge base to help make the buying decision. Consumers might fill in their personal knowledge gaps by talking with friends, family, or a salesperson. They can also scour commercial media for unsponsored and (it is hoped) unbiased information, such as that available through *Consumer Reports,* or peruse sponsored media such as magazines, television, or radio. Sometimes consumers get commercial exposures to products or services without really knowing it. New media such as blogs are steadily becoming a major source of external insformation to consumers, as Adding Value 6.1 notes.

The Internet provides more information than that contained in blogs though.[11] For example, while watching an episode of CW's *Gossip Girl,* Katie saw the character Vanessa wearing a fantastic outfit consisting of a peasant blouse and leggings. She pulled her laptop over, went to Google, and searched for Shop the Look and Gossip Girl. She found a number of websites that carry news items and pictures of the characters. These websites also identify the prices for the various items worn by its characters. A long list of items included both the blouse and the leggings. The

You can find the clothing worn by Gossip Girl *characters online.*

blouse was designed by Joie and available for sale for $248, and the leggings by LnA cost $105.[12] But Katie is also a savvy shopper, so she searched lna leggings on Google and found that through the company's site, she could get a cropped version on sale for only $45.[13] Satisfied with that purchase, she began flipping through a magazine and saw Reese Witherspoon wearing a pair of jeans she loved. This time, she navigated directly to www.TrueFit.com, which featured those very jeans, designed by 7 for All Mankind, on its homepage.[14] Katie entered her measurements and style preferences, and the website returned recommendations of jeans that would be a good fit for her.

All these types of search are examples of external searches for information. Katie used the television show's dedicated site to find a style she liked; she referred to a magazine for additional style tips; and she found jeans that will be a perfect fit for her using the web. All these events took place without Katie leaving her home to go to the store or try on dozens of pairs of pants.

LO 6-3 Describe factors that affect information search.

Factors Affecting Consumers' Search Processes It is important for marketers to understand the many factors that affect consumers' search processes. Among them are the following three factors.

The Perceived Benefits versus Perceived Costs of Search. Is it worth the time and effort to search for information about a product or service? For instance, most families spend a lot of time researching the housing market in their preferred area before they make a purchase because homes are a very expensive and important purchase with significant safety and enjoyment implications. They likely spend much less time researching which inexpensive dollhouse to buy for the youngest member of the family.

The Locus of Control. People who have an **internal locus of control** believe they have some control over the outcomes of their actions, in which case they generally engage in more search activities. With an **external locus of control**, consumers believe that fate or other external factors control all outcomes. In that case, they believe it doesn't

Adding Value 6.1

How Fashion Blogs Sell Clothes

Sweatpants and T-shirts used to dominate fashion on college campuses. Now students and young professionals are upgrading their wardrobes, seeking ways to stay current with the rapid change in trends while expressing individuality through how they dress.[15] Where do they find their inspiration?

The time-honored approaches are to page through a fashion magazine, keep an eye on how peers dress, or consult with a friend. Now blogs are replacing magazines and expanding style choices, literally putting the world of fashion at a customer's fingertips. These blogs combine the sense of reliability that comes from peer-to-peer advice with the rapid access to information that today's shoppers have come to expect. The result is a marketing channel that is exerting increasing influence over consumer behavior.[16]

Fashion blogs use the Internet to connect designers and styles to the shoppers who are most likely to buy them, but they feature two distinct differences from passive websites: editors who control what appears on the site and contributors who post comments on what they see. One popular blog written by college women, College Fashion, provides fashion tips on subjects ranging from the must-have updates for a fall wardrobe to the top designers for teens and twenty-somethings.[17] Quizzes help site visitors decide which colors would suit their mood on a given day or which celebrity most inspires their style.[18] Clearly the editor's sense of style helps build followers, but the blog also creates a sense of community, providing a place where fashion-conscious young women can contribute their own point of view or proudly announce a new purchase.

At the other end of the fashion blog spectrum are professional sites, such as Refinery29, which offers separate editions for New York, Los Angeles, Chicago, San Francisco, and Washington DC. Multiple editors juggle blogs about various topics of interest, including diet tips and hair and makeup trends. As an added feature, the site goes beyond a discussion format, providing a members-only shopping site with exclusive offers from popular names in fashion, beauty, and decor. In addition to being able to peruse the site to see what's new, members receive e-mails announcing hot designers, stores, and websites.

Professional fashion blogs such as Refinery29 offer a members—only shopping site as well as tips on diet, hair, and makeup trends.

Marketers are recognizing the value of these blogs to reach customers. Like College Fashion, Refinery29 and its competitor, FabSugar, host advertisements—yet another way for retailers to reach target markets. FabSugar, which contains posts on fashion, entertainment, sex and culture, food, money, pets, and even pregnancy and parenting, is considered one of the top 20 most influential fashion blogs.[19] With projected revenues of $8 million in its sixth year of business, Refinery29's blog demonstrates the ability of this marketing channel to generate both followers and sales.[20]

---

matter how much information they gather; if they make a wise decision, it isn't to their credit, and if they make a poor one, it isn't their fault. People who do a lot of research before purchasing individual stocks have an internal locus of control; those who purchase mutual funds are more likely to believe that they can't predict the market and probably have an external locus of control. These beliefs have widespread effects. For example, when people believe that they can choose their own consumption goals (internal locus of control), they work harder to achieve them than if those goals feel imposed upon them (external locus of control).[21] Social & Mobile Marketing 6.1 discusses how consumers are gaining a greater internal locus of control over their health by using smartphone apps.

Actual or Perceived Risk. Five types of risk associated with purchase decisions can delay or discourage a purchase: performance, financial, social, physiological, and psychological. The higher the risk, the more likely the consumer is to engage in an extended search.

Performance risk involves the perceived danger inherent in a poorly performing product or service. An example of performance risk is the possibility that Katie Smith's new interview dress is prone to shrinking when dry cleaned.

Financial risk is risk associated with a monetary outlay and includes the initial cost of the purchase as well as the costs of using the item or service.[22] Katie is not only concerned that her new dress will provide her with the

performance risk Involves the perceived danger inherent in a poorly performing product or service.

financial risk Risk associated with a monetary outlay; includes the initial cost of the purchase, as well as the costs of using the item or service.

professional appearance she is seeking but also that the cost of dry cleaning will not be exorbitant. Retailers recognize buying professional apparel can be a financial burden and therefore offer guarantees that the products they sell will perform as expected. Their suppliers are also well aware that dry cleaning is

Social & Mobile Marketing 6.1
The Future of Health Is Mobile[23]

A host of new applications and mobile links make it easier than ever for consumers to maintain their own health and well-being with just a few clicks. Whether the condition is chronic or new, these health-related offerings seek to make it easier for health care consumers to understand their options, consider solutions, and recognize when to seek immediate medical care. They also facilitate providers' efforts to stay up to date with the latest treatments and advances. Consider a few examples:

- An award-winning app, mySugr turns the tedious task of glucose monitoring into a game for diabetics. They earn points for each data entry they make that helps them tame a monster named Diabetes. The app also supports food logging with a snapshot feature, provides immediate data analyses, produces a summary report that users can send their doctors, and maintains the data in a central location.

- Doctor Mole allows people to take a selfie (i.e., self-portrait) of any suspicious skin growth. Using augmented reality technology, the app applies the well-established criteria for assessing the risk associated with each mole (i.e., asymmetry, borders, color, diameter). Thus users can determine whether they have a potentially cancerous malignancy or just a new freckle.

- With BurnMed, users draw on a displayed image of a body to indicate the extent of the burn suffered, whether by themselves, a friend, or a patient. That is, this app seeks to target both laypeople and medical practitioners. In a lay setting, users can determine the seriousness of a burn they might have suffered at home. In a medical practice, emergency staff can quickly determine the appropriate treatment when faced with a crisis such as a tanker explosion that burns hundreds of victims.

- The vCath training tool is expressly for medical students who need to learn to insert neuro-surgical catheters. In patients, this step is critical and risky, such that students have little leeway for practicing their technique. This app enables them to do so virtually, as many times as they wish, before confronting any live patients.

Smartphone apps empower consumers to take control of their health in exciting new ways.

Along with these dedicated apps, various hospitals and doctors are experimenting with software that reminds patients to take their medicine or when their next appointments are. By encouraging positive behaviors, these technology advances should lead to greater consumer health and happiness as well as benefits for society as a whole.

social risk The fears that consumers suffer when they worry others might not regard their purchases positively.

physiological risk The fear of an actual harm should a product not perform properly.

safety risk See *psychological risk*.

psychological risks Associated with the way people will feel if the product or service does not convey the right image.

universal sets Includes all possible choices for a product-category.

retrieval sets Includes those brands or stores that the consumer can readily bring forth from memory.

evoked set Comprises the alternative brands or stores that the consumer states he or she would consider when making a purchase decision.

evaluative criteria Consist of a set of salient, or important, attributes about a particular product.

expensive and can limit the life of the garment, so many offer easy-to-care-for washable fabrics.

Social risk involves the fears that consumers suffer when they worry others might not regard their purchases positively. When buying a dress, consumers like Katie consider what their friends would like. Alternatively, because this job interview is so important, Katie might make a conscious effort to assert a distinctive identity or make a statement by buying a unique, more stylish, and possibly more expensive dress than her friends would typically buy.

Physiological risk could also be called **safety risk**. Whereas performance risk involves what might happen if a product does not perform as expected, physiological (or safety) risk refers to the fear of an actual harm should the product not perform properly. Although physiological risk is typically not an issue with apparel, it can be an important issue when buying other products, such as a car. External agencies and government bodies publish safety ratings for cars to help assuage this risk. Consumers compare the safety records of their various choices because they recognize the real danger to their well-being if the

purchase, read several fashion magazines and sought her friends' opinions because she wanted people to think she looked great in the dress, and she wanted to get the job!

Recent research suggests that psychological risks might help explain why consumers enjoy supersizing their menu options. Especially when consumers feel powerless or more vulnerable, they equate larger sizes—whether in televisions, houses, or menu items—with improved status. That is, consumers who feel powerless choose bigger food portions to gain a sense of status.[24]

Evaluation of Alternatives

Once a consumer has recognized a problem and explored the possible options, he or she must sift through the choices available and evaluate the alternatives. Alternative evaluation often occurs while the consumer is engaged in the process of information search. For example, Katie Smith would rule out various stores because she knows they won't carry the style she needs for the job interview. Once in the store, she would try on lots of dresses and eliminate those that don't fit, don't look good on her, or aren't appropriate attire for the occasion. Consumers forgo alternative evaluations altogether when buying habitual (convenience) products; you'll rarely catch a loyal Pepsi drinker buying Coca-Cola.

Attribute Sets
Research has shown that a consumer's mind organizes and categorizes alternatives to aid his or her decision process. **Universal sets** include all possible choices for a prod-

> *Recent research suggests that psychological risks might help explain why consumers enjoy supersizing their menu options. Especially when consumers feel powerless or more vulnerable, they equate larger sizes— whether in televisions, houses, or menu items—with improved status.*

automobile they purchase fails to perform a basic task, such as stopping when the driver steps on the brakes or protecting the passengers in the cabin even if the car flips.

Another major physiological risk pertains to growing concerns about health risks associated with the food and beverages we consume. McDonald's has come under a lot of associated scrutiny recently, especially in response to *Supersize Me* and related media (see Ethical & Societal Dilemma 6.1).

Finally, **psychological risks** are those risks associated with the way people will feel if the product or service does not convey the right image. Katie Smith, thinking of her dress

uct category, but because it would be unwieldy for a person to recall all possible alternatives for every purchase decision, marketers tend to focus on only a subset of choices. One important subset is **retrieval sets**, which are those brands or stores that can be readily brought forth from memory. Another is a consumer's **evoked set**, which comprises the alternative brands or stores that the consumer states he or she would consider when making a purchase decision. If a firm can get its brand or store into a consumer's evoked set, it has increased the likelihood of purchase and therefore reduced search time because the consumer will think specifically of that brand when considering choices.

ethical & societal dilemma

The Obesity Epidemic and Fast Foods

Filmmaker Morgan Spurlock has shown us that a steady fast-food diet can be downright dangerous. Thirty days of eating nothing but McDonald's hamburgers, fries, and shakes turned Spurlock—who started the experiment as a healthy 32-year-old man—into an overweight, depressed, and dysfunctional guy with soaring cholesterol levels and liver trouble.

Today, 42 percent of low-income women in the United States are obese,[25] and there is a growing consensus that an overreliance on fast food and junk food has contributed significantly to this health problem. Although marketing is certainly a major factor in attracting customers to McDonald's and other fast-food restaurants, health experts also have shown that multiple other factors also drive obesity-promoting habits.[26]

In particular, working moms with little time to cook appreciate the convenience of fast foods. Families on a tight budget like these low-cost menus. And the fast-food industry has learned to cater to America's taste for foods high in sugar, salt, and fat, which turn into near-addictive desires. Combine those high-calorie habits with a sedentary or car-dependent lifestyle that rarely includes exercise, and you have a prescription for obesity.

In the film Super Size Me, *filmmaker Morgan Spurlock ate nothing but McDonald's food for thirty days. He gained weight, became depressed, and developed high cholesterol and liver trouble.*

The problem is especially serious among children. One Harvard School of Public Health physician noted that children aged 2 to 19 years consume 7 trillion calories through sugar-sweetened beverages a year, fueling a $24 billion industry for kids.[27] It's just one major factor in the 17 percent obesity rate among U.S. youth.

Efforts to revise food labels so that they clearly tell consumers whether a meal or a supermarket item contains unhealthy ingredients have been blocked successfully by the food industry. But McDonald's—the focus of significant pressures from both health advocates and parents as well as the defendant in at least one lawsuit alleging that its high-fat menu caused obesity-related health damage to two children (*Pelman v. McDonald's Corp.,* 237 F. Supp. 2d 512 [S.D.N.Y. January 22, 2003])—has decided to change some of its ways.

The company has announced a planned 20 percent reduction in the calorie count of its Happy Meals. But it declined to voluntarily jettison the toys that come along with the Happy Meal, a marketing hook that has long made this item one of the most popular on the kids' menu. Lawmakers and parents seeking to break the childhood link between toys and fast food have demanded that such toy giveaways be banned. San Francisco was the first city to enforce such a law; in response, the restaurant chain chose to charge a dime for each toy, so that it could comply with the regulation but still make the toys easily accessible to its youthful customers.[28] McDonald's also has rejected calls to eliminate French fries altogether, along with its traditional soda. But the company says it will include apple slices with every order and reduce salt content by 2015.

Some critics are not impressed. Changes like a one-ounce reduction in French fries won't help kids much. But McDonald's small concessions should generate huge publicity for the company.

Katie Smith knows that there are a lot of apparel stores (universal set). However, only some have the style that she is looking for, such as Macy's, Ann Taylor, The Gap, and Banana Republic (retrieval set). She recalls that Ann Taylor is where her mother shops and The Gap is a favorite of her younger sister. But she is sure that Banana Republic and Macy's carry business attire she would like, so only those stores are in her evoked set.

When consumers begin to evaluate different alternatives, they often base their evaluations on a set of important attributes or evaluative criteria. **Evaluative criteria** consist of salient, or important, attributes about a particular product. For example, when Katie is looking for her dress, she might consider things like the selling price, fit, materials and construction quality, reputation of the brand, and the service support that the retailer offers. At times, however, it becomes difficult to evaluate different brands or stores because there are so many choices,[29] especially when those choices involve aspects of the garment that are difficult to evaluate, such as materials and construction quality.

Ann Taylor is part of the <u>retrieval set</u> of stores available to women for business apparel, but Banana Republic is in the <u>evoked set</u> for young women looking for business apparel.

Consumers use several shortcuts to simplify the potentially complicated decision process: determinant attributes and consumer decision rules. **Determinant attributes** are product or service features that are important to the buyer and on which competing brands or stores are perceived to differ.[30] Because many important and desirable criteria are equal among the various choices, consumers look for something special—a determinant attribute—to differentiate one brand or store from another. Determinant attributes may appear perfectly rational, such as health and nutrition claims offered by certain foods and beverages, or they may be more subtle and psychologically based, such as the red soles on a pair of Christian Louboutin heels. Ethical & Societal Dilemma 6.2 highlights the use of determinant attributes describing food and beverages marketed as natural when in fact they are not.

Consumer Decision Rules

Consumer decision rules are the set of criteria that consumers use consciously or subconsciously to quickly and efficiently select from among several alternatives. These rules are typically either compensatory or noncompensatory.

Compensatory. A **compensatory decision rule** assumes that the consumer, when evaluating alternatives, trades off one characteristic against another, such that good characteristics compensate for bad characteristics.[31] For instance, Hanna Jackson is looking to buy breakfast cereal and is considering several factors such as taste, calories, price, and natural/organic claims. But even if the cereal is priced a little higher than Hanna was planning to spend, a superb overall rating offsets, or compensates for, the higher price.

Although Hanna probably would not go through the formal process of making the purchasing decision based on the **multi-attribute model** described in Exhibit 6.2, this exhibit illustrates how a compensatory model would work.[32] Hanna assigns weights to the importance of each factor. These weights must add up to 1.0. So, for instance, taste is the most important, with a weight of .4, and calories are least important, with a weight of .1. She assigns weights to how well each of the cereals might perform, with 1 being very poor and 10 being very good. Hanna thinks Cheerios has the best taste, so she assigns it a 10. Then she multiplies each performance rating by its importance rating to get an overall score for each cereal. The rating for

▼ **EXHIBIT 6.2** Compensatory Purchasing Multi-Attribute Model for Buying Cereal

	Taste	Calories	Natural /Organic Claims	Price	Overall Score
Importance Weight	0.4	0.1	0.3	0.2	
Cheerios	10	8	6	8	8.2
Post	8	9	8	3	7.1
Kashi	6	8	10	5	7.2

determinant attributes Product or service features that are important to the buyer and on which competing brands or stores are perceived to differ.

consumer decision rules The set of criteria that consumers use consciously or subconsciously to quickly and efficiently select from among several alternatives.

compensatory decision rule At work when the consumer is evaluating alternatives and trades off one characteristic against another, such that good characteristics compensate for bad ones.

multi-attribute model A compensatory model of customer decision making based on the notion that customers see a product as a collection of attributes or characteristics. The model uses a weighted average score based on the importance of various attributes and performance on those issues.

ethical & societal dilemma 6.2

Wearing the "Healthy" Label: Natural and Organic Foods

With competition for shelf space always at a premium, today's supermarket aisles are more crowded than ever. Much of the new competition comes from natural and organic foods, which comprised more than 4 percent of the $673 billion U.S. food industry in 2010.[33]

For a consumer facing a dizzying array of choices, these natural foods offer a unique appeal: They promise to improve personal and planetary health. Organic and natural food companies claim that their foods are safer and more nutritious because they are produced with only natural ingredients.

Consumers generally believe that these claims mean the food contains no artificial or highly processed ingredients.[34] Yet Snapple's "natural" bottled iced tea contains high-fructose corn syrup, a highly processed, and recently controversial, form of sugar. In California, most organic strawberry farmers use seeds and plants from nurseries that are not organic, including growers producing fruit for Driscoll Strawberry Associates, the largest berry distributor in the world.[35] The farmers argue that once their plants bear fruit, they halt their use of chemical pesticides and herbicides, so the berries themselves are still organic. These companies thus might be contradicting consumer expectations, but they are not actually violating federal requirements.

The U.S. Department of Agriculture (USDA) regulates the production of organic foods. Products bearing the USDA Organic label must be grown using organic, not conventional, farming methods.[36] That regulation means using natural fertilizers, such as manure or compost; beneficial insects or birds to control insects rather than chemical insecticides; and crop rotation or other manual methods to control weeds rather than chemical herbicides. Animals raised for meat production must be given organic feed and access to the outdoors rather than antibiotics, growth hormones, and other medications.

Yet the USDA's National Organic Program (NOP) regulations do not explicitly govern the production of seeds and planting stock. Advocates who want to see sustainable production methods used throughout the food-growing process have called on the USDA to outlaw the use of chemical fumigants, including methyl bromide, a widely used pesticide and soil sterilizer known to deplete the ozone layer.[37] Furthermore, the NOP regulations have not been updated since 2002; they allow conventional agricultural stock to be used whenever organically grown seeds and plants are not commercially available.

Nor does the USDA regulate the production of foods labeled natural, except for meats and poultry,[38]

which must be minimally processed and free of artificial colors, flavors, sweeteners, preservatives, and ingredients. No such specifics govern other foods that choose to carry the natural label rather than an organic claim.

For the consumer, the organic and natural food experience is also about perception. Some shoppers may believe these foods deliver healthful benefits, but studies also reveal that simply identifying a grocery item as a health food may affect their eating experience. Students given snacks labeled health bars reported feeling hungry afterward and craving foods they enjoyed more. In another study, respondents widely perceived "that 'healthy' isn't going to meet enjoyment goals," which likely reflects consumers' assumption that healthy foods won't taste good.[39]

How healthy is Snapple?

> CONVERSION RATES TEND TO BE LOWER FOR CONSUMERS USING AN INTERNET CHANNEL BECAUSE THEY ARE ABLE TO LOOK AT PRODUCTS AND THROW THEM IN THEIR CART BUT STILL DELAY THEIR PURCHASE DECISION.

Cheerios in this example is the highest of the three cereals [(.4 × 10) + (.1 × 8) + (.3 × 6) + (.2 × 8) = 8.2)]. This multiattributes model allows the trade-off between the various factors to be incorporated explicitly into a consumer's purchase decision.

Noncompensatory. Sometimes however, consumers use a **noncompensatory decision rule**, in which they choose a product or service on the basis of one characteristic or one subset of a characteristic, regardless of the values of its other attributes.[40] Thus, though Cheerios received the highest overall score of 8.2, Hanna might still pick Kashi because she is particularly sensitive to claims of natural or organic contents, and this brand earned the highest score on this attribute (i.e., a 10).

Once a consumer has considered the possible alternatives and evaluated the pros and cons of each, he or she can move toward a purchase decision.

Purchase and Consumption

After evaluating the alternatives, customers are ready to buy. However, they don't always patronize the store or purchase the brand or item on which they had originally decided. It may not be available at the retail store, for example. Retailers therefore turn to the **conversion rate** to measure how well they have converted purchase intentions into purchases. One method of measuring the conversion rate is the number of real or virtual abandoned carts in the retailer's store or website.

Retailers use various tactics to increase the chances that customers will convert their positive evaluations into purchases. They can reduce the number of abandoned carts by making it easier to purchase merchandise. Most important, they should have plenty of stock on hand of the merchandise that customers want. They can also reduce the actual wait time to buy merchandise by opening more checkout lanes and placing them conveniently inside the store. To reduce perceived wait times, they might install digital displays to entertain customers waiting in line.[41]

For different types of companies, the conversion rate also refers to rentals (e.g., Netflix) or to outright purchases (e.g., haute couture), though some of these lines appear to be blurring as consumers seek new ways to access the items they want. At Rent the Runway, fashion- and budget-conscious shoppers gain temporary possession of the latest fashions from big names, including Badgley Mischka, Kate Spade, and Vera Wang. As if they were dealing with movies on DVDs, members rent haute couture dresses, handbags, jewelry, and even wedding gowns; pay anywhere between $50 and $400 for their chosen items;

receive the glam wear in the mail within a few days; and then return the items after their fabulous affair has ended.[42] At the same time, Warner Bros. is working on a new idea to get movie renters to start buying more of its offerings. It purchased Flixster, the movie buff website, and initiated UltraViolet, a movie storage service that enables viewers to purchase a movie once and then access it on any of their connected devices (e.g., computer, tablet, smartphone, web-ready television).[43]

But conversion rates still tend to be lower for consumers using an Internet channel because they are able to look at products and throw them in their cart but still delay their purchase decision. To encourage customers to make purchase decisions, Zappos.com and Overstock.com create urgency by alerting customers when an item they have put it in their shopping cart is almost sold out. Other sites, such as Gilt, offer items for specified 36-hour periods or until they run out, and Neiman Marcus runs two-hour, online-only sales. Many retailers send reminder e-mails to visitors about items in carts they have abandoned.[44]

LO 6-4   Discuss postpurchase outcomes.

Postpurchase

The final step of the consumer decision process is postpurchase behavior. Marketers are particularly interested in postpurchase behavior because it entails actual rather than potential customers. Satisfied customers, whom marketers hope to create, become loyal, purchase again, and spread positive word of mouth, so they are quite important. There are three possible positive postpurchase outcomes as illustrated in Exhibit 6.3: customer satisfaction, postpurchase cognitive dissonance, and customer loyalty (or disloyalty).

Customer Satisfaction Setting unrealistically high consumer expectations of the product through advertising, personal selling, or other types of promotion may lead to higher initial sales, but it eventually will result in dissatisfaction if the product fails to achieve high performance expectations. (For a related discussion about communication gaps, see Chapter 13.) This failure can lead to dissatisfied customers and the potential for negative word of mouth.[45] Setting customer expectations too low is an equally dangerous strategy. Many retailers don't put their best foot forward. For instance, no matter how good the merchandise and service may be, if a store is not clean and appealing from the entrance, customers are not likely to enter.

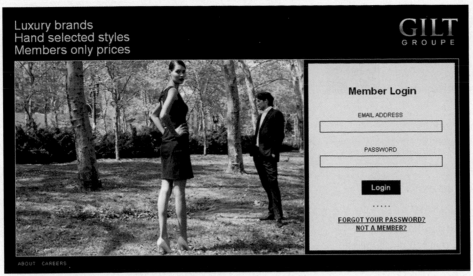

Gilt.com encourages customers to buy now by offering a limited number of items for short time period.

noncompensatory decision rule At work when consumers choose a product or service on the basis of a subset of its characteristics, regardless of the values of its other attributes.

conversion rate Percentage of consumers who buy a product after viewing it.

postpurchase cognitive dissonance The psychologically uncomfortable state produced by an inconsistency between beliefs and behaviors that in turn evokes a motivation to reduce the dissonance; buyers' remorse.

▼ **EXHIBIT 6.3** Components of Postpurchase Outcomes

Marketers can take several steps to ensure postpurchase satisfaction though, such as to:

- Build realistic expectations, not too high and not too low.

- Demonstrate correct product use—improper usage can cause dissatisfaction.

- Stand behind the product or service by providing money-back guarantees and warranties.

- Encourage customer feedback, which cuts down on negative word of mouth and helps marketers adjust their offerings.

- Periodically make contact with customers and thank them for their support. This contact reminds customers that the marketer cares about their business and wants them to be satisfied. It also provides an opportunity to correct any problems. Customers appreciate human contact, though it is more expensive for marketers than e-mail or postal mail contacts.

Postpurchase Cognitive Dissonance **Postpurchase cognitive dissonance** is an internal conflict that arises from an inconsistency between two beliefs or between beliefs and behavior. For example, you might have buyer's remorse after purchasing an expensive TV because you question after all whether a high-price TV is appreciably better quality than a similar size TV at a lower price—or whether you need a television at all, considering your ability to stream content through your computer. Thus, postpurchase cognitive dissonance generally occurs when a consumer questions the appropriateness of a purchase after his or her decision has been made.

Postpurchase cognitive dissonance is especially likely for products that are expensive, are infrequently purchased, do not work as intended, and are associated with high levels of risk. Marketers direct efforts at consumers after the purchase is made to address this issue.[46] General Electric sends a letter to purchasers of its appliances, positively reinforcing the message that the customer made a wise decision by mentioning the high quality that went into the product's design and production. Some clothing manufacturers include a tag on their garments to offer the reassurance that because of their special manufacturing process, perhaps designed to provide a soft, vintage appearance, there may be variations in color that have no effect on the quality of the item. After a pang of dissonance, satisfaction may then set in.

Let's check back in with our friend Katie to recognize these effects. When Katie purchased her interview dress at Macy's, she tried it on for some of her friends. Her boyfriend said he loved it, but several of her girlfriends seemed less impressed. Katie thought it made her look more mature. Because of these mixed signals, some dissonance resulted and manifested itself as an uncomfortable, unsettled feeling. To reduce the dissonance, Katie could:

- Take back the dress.

- Pay attention to positive information, such as looking up ads and articles about this particular dress designer.

- Seek more positive feedback from friends.

- Seek negative information about dresses made by designers not selected.

After a while, satisfaction with her experience probably will result.

Customer Loyalty
In the postpurchase stage of the decision-making process, marketers attempt to solidify a loyal relationship with their customers. They want customers to be satisfied with their purchase and buy from the same company again. Loyal customers will buy only certain brands and shop at certain stores, and they include no other firms in their evoked set. As we explained in Chapter 2, such customers are therefore very valuable to firms, and marketers have designed customer relationship management (CRM) programs specifically to retain them.

Undesirable Consumer Behavior
Although firms want satisfied, loyal customers, sometimes they fail to attain them. Passive consumers are those who don't repeat purchase or recommend the product to others. More serious and potentially damaging, however, is negative consumer behavior, such as negative word of mouth and rumors.

Negative word of mouth occurs when consumers spread negative information about a product, service, or store to others. When customers' expectations are met or even exceeded, they often don't tell anyone about it. But when consumers believe that they have been treated unfairly in some way, they

Whirlpool posts both good and bad comments on Twitter. It believes that posting negative comments opens up discussions and emphasizes the proactive measures the company is taking to remedy service or product failures.

usually want to complain, often to many people. The Internet has provided an effective method of spreading negative word of mouth to millions of people instantaneously through personal blogs, Twitter, and corporate websites. To lessen the impact of negative word of mouth, firms provide customer service representatives—whether online, on the phone, or in stores—to handle and respond to complaints. Many companies also allow customers to post comments and complaints to proprietary social media sites.

For example, Whirlpool set up Facebook pages for its appliance brands, Maytag, KitchenAid, and Whirlpool. Customers may share their thoughts on these sites without fear that their negative feedback will be deleted from the site. Whirlpool believes that it should keep the bad to open up discussions and emphasize the proactive measures the company is taking to remedy service or product failures.[47] If a customer believes that positive action will be taken as a result of the complaint, he or she is less likely to complain to family and friends or through the Internet. (A detailed example of word of mouth appears in Chapter 13.)

Stores collect customer information for their CRM programs from customer credit cards.

 check yourself

1. Name the five stages in the consumer decision process.

2. What is the difference between a need and a want?

3. Distinguish between functional and psychological needs.

4. What are the various types of perceived risk?

5. What are the differences between compensatory and noncompensatory decision rules?

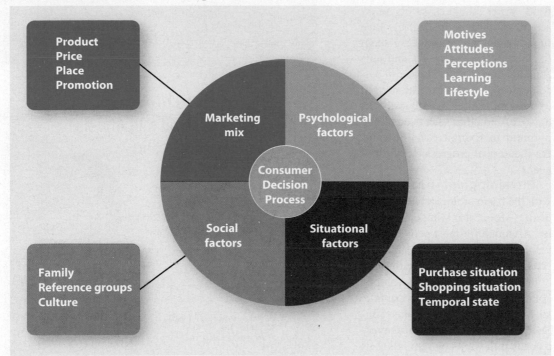

Product
Price
Place
Promotion

Motives
Attitudes
Perceptions
Learning
Lifestyle

Marketing mix

Psychological factors

Consumer Decision Process

Social factors

Situational factors

Family
Reference groups
Culture

Purchase situation
Shopping situation
Temporal state

negative word of mouth Occurs when consumers spread negative information about a product, service, or store to others.

motive A need or want that is strong enough to cause the person to seek satisfaction.

Maslow's Hierarchy of Needs A paradigm for classifying people's motives. It argues that when lower-level, more basic needs (physiological and safety) are fulfilled, people turn to satisfying their higher-level human needs (social and personal); see *physiological, safety, social,* and *personal needs.*

> A motive is a need or want that is strong enough to cause the person to seek satisfaction.

LO 6-5 List the factors that affect the consumer decision process.

FACTORS INFLUENCING THE CONSUMER DECISION PROCESS

The consumer decision process can be influenced by several factors, as illustrated in Exhibit 6.4. First are the elements of the marketing mix, which we discuss throughout this book. Second are psychological factors, which are influences internal to the customer, such as motives, attitudes, perception, and learning. Third, social factors, such as family, reference groups, and culture, also influence the decision process. Fourth, there are situational factors, such as the specific purchase situation, a particular shopping situation, or temporal state (the time of day), that affect the decision process.

Every decision people make as consumers will take them through some form of the consumer decision process. But, like life itself, this process does not exist in a vacuum.

Psychological Factors

Although marketers can influence purchase decisions, a host of psychological factors affect the way people receive marketers' messages. Among them are motives, attitudes, perception, learning, and lifestyle. In this section, we examine how such psychological factors can influence the consumer decision process.[48]

Motives In Chapter 1, we argued that marketing is all about satisfying customer needs and wants. When a need, such as thirst, or a want, such as a Diet Pepsi, is not satisfied, it motivates us, or drives us, to get satisfaction. So, a **motive** is a need or want that is strong enough to cause the person to seek satisfaction.

People have several types of motives. One of the best known paradigms for explaining these motive types was developed by Abraham Maslow more than 30 years ago, called **Maslow's Hierarchy of Needs.**[49] Maslow categorized five groups of

physiological needs Those relating to the basic biological necessities of life: food, drink, rest, and shelter.

safety needs One of the needs in the PSSP hierarchy of needs; pertain to protection and physical well-being.

love needs Needs expressed through interactions with others.

esteem needs Needs that enable people to fulfill inner desires.

self-actualization When a person is completely satisfied with his or her life.

needs, namely, physiological (e.g., food, water, shelter), safety (e.g., secure employment, health), love (e.g., friendship, family), esteem (e.g., confidence, respect), and self-actualization (people engage in personal growth activities and attempt to meet their intellectual, aesthetic, creative, and other such needs). The pyramid in Exhibit 6.5 illustrates the theoretical progression of those needs.

Physiological needs deal with the basic biological necessities of life—food, drink, rest, and shelter. Although for most people in developed countries these basic needs are generally met, there are those in both developed and less-developed countries who are less fortunate. However, everyone remains concerned with meeting these basic needs.[50] Marketers seize every opportunity to convert these needs into wants by reminding us to eat at Taco Bell, drink milk, sleep on a Beautyrest mattress, and stay at a Marriott.

Safety needs pertain to protection and physical well-being. The marketplace is full of products and services that are designed to make you safer, such as airbags in cars and burglar alarms in homes, or healthier, such as vitamins and organic meats and vegetables.

Love needs relate to our interactions with others. Haircuts and makeup make you look more attractive, and deodorants prevent odor. Greeting cards help you express your feelings toward others.

▼ **EXHIBIT 6.5** Maslow's Hierarchy of Needs

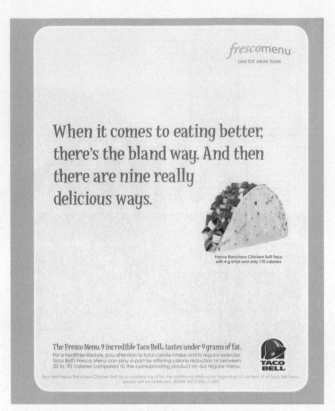

Taco Bell satisfies physiological needs.

Ads for crime prevention satisfy safety needs.

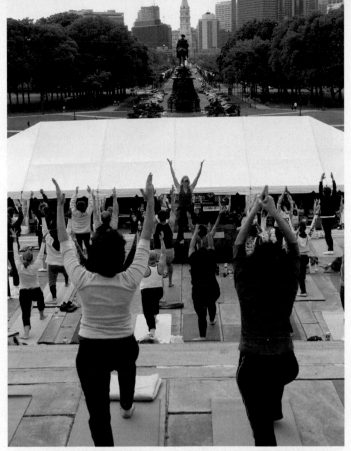

Yoga satisifies esteem needs by helping people satisy their inner desires.

people up the needs hierarchy and offering information on as many of the pyramid of needs as they can.

Attitude We have attitudes about almost everything. For instance, we like this class, but we don't like the instructor. We like where we live, but we don't like the weather. An **attitude** is a person's enduring evaluation of his or her feelings about and behavioral tendencies toward an object or idea. Attitudes are learned and long lasting, and they might develop over a long period of time, though they can also abruptly change. For instance, you might like your instructor for much of the semester—until she returns your first exam. The one thing attitudes have in common for everyone is their ability to influence our decisions and actions.

An attitude consists of three components. The **cognitive component** reflects a person's belief system, or what we believe to be true; the **affective component** involves emotions, or what we feel about the issue at hand, including our like or dislike of something; and the **behavioral component** pertains to the actions we undertake based on what we know and feel. For example, Matt and Lisa Martinez see an advertisement for the latest *Pirates of the Caribbean* movie, showing Johnny Depp dueling with Geoffrey Rush. The ad lists quotes from different movie critics who call it a great and exciting film. Matt and Lisa therefore come to believe that the critics must be correct and that the new *Pirates of the Caribbean* will be a good movie (cognitive component). Later they catch an interview with Johnny Depp, who talks about making the movie and his enjoyment playing Captain Jack Sparrow. Therefore, Matt and Lisa start to believe the movie will be fun and engaging, because they appreciate action adventures and have enjoyed previous Johnny Depp films (affective component). After weighing their various options—which include various other movies, other entertainment options such as attending a concert instead, or just staying home—Matt and Lisa decide to go see the movie (behavioral component).

Esteem needs allow people to satisfy their inner desires. Yoga, meditation, health clubs, and many books appeal to people's desires to grow or maintain a happy, satisfied outlook on life.

Finally, **self-actualization** occurs when you feel completely satisfied with your life and how you live. You don't care what others think. You drive a Ford Fusion because it suits the person you are, not because some celebrity endorses it or because you want others to think better of you.

Which of these needs applies when a consumer purchases a magazine? Magazines such as *Weight Watchers,* for instance, help satisfy physiological needs like how to eat healthy but also esteem needs like how to be happy with one's life.[51] Magazines such as *Family Circle* provide tips on how to make the home a safer place to live, and magazines such as *Weddings* help satisfy love and belonging needs because they provide instructions on how to prepare gracious invitations for friends and family, for example. Many of these magazines fulfill several needs simultaneously, of course. Good marketers add value to their products or services by nudging

Which categories of Maslow's hierarchy of needs do these magazines fulfill?

Ideally, agreement exists among these three components. But when there is incongruence among the three—if Matt and Lisa read positive reviews and like action films but do not find Johnny Depp an appealing actor—cognitive dissonance might occur. Matt and Lisa might decide their reviews and their liking of action films will outweigh their dislike of Johnny Depp and go see the movie. If they then find the movie unenjoyable because Johnny Depp is the primary star, they may feel foolish for having wasted their money.

Such dissonance is a terrible feeling, which people try to avoid, often by convincing themselves that the decision was a good one in some way.[52] In this example, Matt and Lisa might focus on the special effects and the romantic elements of the movie while mentally glossing over the parts that featured the actor they did not enjoy. In this way, they can convince themselves that the parts they liked were good enough to counterbalance the part they didn't like, and thus, they make their movie-going experience a positive event overall.

Although attitudes are pervasive and usually slow to change, the important fact from a marketer's point of view is that they can be influenced and perhaps changed through persuasive communications and personal experience. Marketing communication—through salespeople, advertisements, free samples, or other such methods—can attempt to change what people believe to be true about a product or service (cognitive) or how they feel toward it (affective). If the marketer is successful, the cognitive and affective components work in concert to affect behavior. Continuing with our example, suppose that prior to viewing the movie ad, Matt and Lisa thought that *Cowboys & Aliens* would be the next movie they would go see, but they had heard good things about *Pirates of the Caribbean*. The ad positively influenced the cognitive component of their attitude toward *Pirates of the Caribbean*, making it consistent with their affective component.

Perception

Perception Another psychological factor, **perception**, is the process by which we select, organize, and interpret information to form a meaningful picture of the world. Perception in marketing influences our acquisition and consumption of goods and services through our tendency to assign meaning to such things as color, symbols, taste, and packaging. Culture, tradition, and our overall upbringing determine our perception of the world. For instance, Lisa Martinez has always wanted an apartment in the Back Bay neighborhood of Boston because her favorite aunt had one, and they had a great time visiting for Thanksgiving one year. However, from his past experiences, Matt has a different perception. Matt thinks Back Bay apartments are small, expensive, and impractical for a couple thinking about having children—though they would be convenient for single people who work in downtown Boston. The city of Boston has

Based on positive review (cognitive component) and positive feelings (affective component), many people went to see the latest Pirates of the Caribbean *movie (behavioral component) and came away with a positive attitude.*

worked hard in recent years to overcome the long-standing negative perceptual bias that Matt and many others hold by working with developers to create larger, modern, and more affordable apartments and using promotion to reposition the perception of apartments in the Back Bay for young couples.[53]

Learning

Learning **Learning** refers to a change in a person's thought process or behavior that arises from experience and takes place throughout the consumer decision process. For instance, after Katie Smith recognized that she needed a dress for her job interview, she started looking for ads and searching for reviews and articles on the Internet. She learned from each new piece of information, so her thoughts about the look she wanted in a dress were different from those before she had read anything. She liked what she learned about the clothing line from Macy's. She learned from her search, and it became part of her memory to be used in the future, possibly so she could recommend the store to her friends.

Learning affects both attitudes and perceptions. Throughout the buying process, Katie's attitudes shifted. The cognitive component came into play for her when she learned Macy's had one of the most extensive collections of career apparel. Once she was in the store and tried on some dresses, she realized how much she liked the way she looked and felt in them, which involved the affective component. Then she purchased it, which involved the behavioral component. Each time she was exposed to information about the store or the dresses, she learned something different that affected her perception. Before she tried them on, Katie hadn't realized how easy it would be to find exactly what she was looking for; thus, her perception of Macy's line of dresses changed through learning.

Lifestyle

Lifestyle refers to the way consumers spend their time and money to live. For many consumers, the question of whether the product or service fits with their actual lifestyle, which may be fairly sedentary, or their perceived lifestyle, which might be outdoorsy, is an important one. Some of the many consumers sporting North Face jackets certainly need the high-tech, cold weather gear because they are planning their next hike up Mount Rainier and want to be sure they have sufficient protection against the elements. Others, however, simply like the image that the jacket conveys—the image that they might be leaving for their own mountain-climbing expedition any day now—even if the closest they have come has been shoveling their driveway.

A person's perceptions and ability to learn are affected by their social experiences, which we discuss next.

Social Factors

The consumer decision process is influenced from within by psychological factors, but also by the external, social environment, which consists of the customer's family, reference groups, and culture.[54] (Refer to Exhibit 6.4.)

Family

Many purchase decisions are made about products or services that the entire family will consume or use. Thus, firms must consider how families make purchase decisions and understand how various family members might influence these decisions.

When families make purchase decisions, they often consider the needs of all the family members. In choosing a restaurant, for example, all the family members may participate in the decision making. In other situations, however, different members of the family may take on the purchasing role. For example, the husband and teenage child may look through car magazines and *Consumer Reports* to search for information about a new car. But once they arrive at the dealership, the husband and wife, not the child, decide which model and color to buy, and the wife negotiates the final deal.[55]

Children and adolescents play an increasingly important role in family buying decisions. Kids in the United States spend over $200 billion a year on personal items such as snacks, soft drinks, entertainment, and apparel. They directly influence the purchase of another $300 billion worth of items such as food, snacks, beverages, toys, health and beauty aids, clothing, accessories, gifts, and school supplies. Their indirect influence on family spending is even higher—$600 billion for items such as

lifestyle A component of *psychographics;* refers to the way a person lives his or her life to achieve goals.

reference group One or more persons whom an individual uses as a basis for comparison regarding beliefs, feelings, and behaviors.

recreation, vacations, technology, and even the family car.[56] Even grandparents contribute to the economic impact of children in the United States. It is estimated that grandparents spend $52 billion dollars on purchases for grandchildren.[57]

Influencing a group that holds this much spending power is vitally important. Traditional food retailers are already caught in a squeeze between Walmart, which lures low-end customers, and specialty retailers like Whole Foods, which target the high end. Knowing how children influence food buying decisions is a strategic opportunity for traditional supermarkets and their suppliers to exploit. Currently, the age cohorts referred to as Gen X and Millennials (remember from Chapter 5 that these groups were born anywhere between 1966 and 1994) tend to shop at Target, Kmart, and Walmart more and spend more at those stores than other generational groups.[58] Getting this group to prefer one store, chain, or product over another can make a difference in the bottom line as well as in the chances for survival in a difficult marketplace.

Reference Groups

A **reference group** is one or more persons whom an individual uses as a basis for comparison

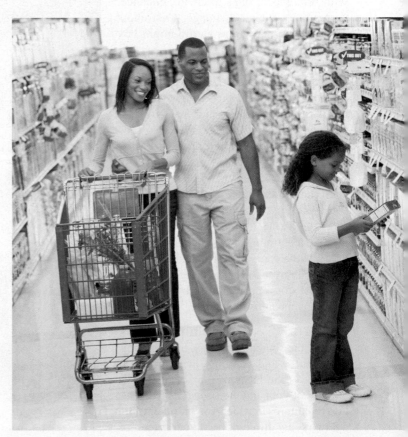

Children influence parents' purchasing decisions.

regarding beliefs, feelings, and behaviors. A consumer might have various reference groups, including family, friends, co-workers, or famous people the consumer would like to emulate. These reference groups affect buying decisions by (1) offering information, (2) providing rewards for specific purchasing behaviors, and (3) enhancing a consumer's self-image.

Reference groups provide information to consumers directly through conversation or indirectly through observation. For example, Katie received valuable information from a friend about where she should shop for her interview dress. On another occasion, she heard a favorite cousin who is a fashionista praising the virtues of shopping at Macy's, which solidified her decision to go there.

Some reference groups also influence behaviors by rewarding behavior that meets with their approval or chastising behavior that doesn't. For example, smokers are often criticized or even ostracized by their friends and made to smoke outside or in restricted areas.

Consumers can identify and affiliate with reference groups to create, enhance, or maintain their self-image. Customers who want to be seen as earthy might buy Birkenstock sandals, whereas those wanting to be seen as high fashion might buy Christian Louboutin shoes, as we discussed previously in this chapter. If they purchase a gift for someone else and that gift conflicts with their self-image, they also seek to reestablish their preferred affiliation quickly by purchasing something more in line with their identity.[59]

Some stores, such as Abercrombie & Fitch, play on these forms of influence and hire sales associates they hope will serve as a reference group for customers who shop there. These cool, attractive, and somewhat aloof employees are encouraged to wear the latest store apparel—thereby serving as living mannequins to emulate.[60]

Culture We defined **culture** in Chapter 5 as the shared meanings, beliefs, morals, values, and customs of a group of people. As the basis of the social factors that affect your buying decisions, the culture or cultures in which you participate are not markedly different from your reference groups. That is, your cultural group might

Famous people, like Sarah Jessica Parker, can be part of your reference group, influencing your purchases.

be as small as your reference group at school or as large as the country in which you live or the religion to which you belong. Like reference groups, cultures influence consumer behavior. For instance, the culture at Katie's college is rather fashion conscious. This influences, to some extent, the way she spends, how she dresses, and where she shops.

Situational Factors

Psychological and social factors typically influence the consumer decision process the same way each time. For example, your motivation to quench your thirst usually drives you to drink a Coke or a Pepsi, and your reference group at the workplace coerces you to wear appropriate attire. But sometimes, **situational factors**, or factors specific to the situation, override, or at least influence, psychological and social issues. These situational factors are related to the purchase and shopping situation as well as to temporal states.[61]

Purchase Situation Customers may be predisposed to purchase certain products or services because of some underlying psychological trait or social factor, but these factors may change in certain purchase situations. For instance, Samantha Crumb considers herself a thrifty, cautious shopper—someone who likes to get a good deal. But her best friend is getting married, and she wants to buy the couple a silver tray. If the tray were for herself, she would probably go to Crate & Barrel or possibly even Walmart. But since it is for her best friend, she went to Tiffany & Co. Why? To purchase something fitting for the special occasion of a wedding.

Shopping Situation Consumers might be ready to purchase a product or service but be completely derailed once they arrive in the store. Marketers use several techniques to influence consumers at this choice stage of the decision process. Consider the following techniques.

Store Atmosphere. Some retailers and service providers have developed unique images that are based at least in part on their internal environment, also known as their atmospherics.[62] Research has shown that, if used in concert with other aspects of a

The Cheesecake Factory has developed atmospherics that are not only pleasant, but consistent with their image, menu, and service.

retailer's strategy, music, scent, lighting, and even color can positively influence the decision process.[63] Restaurants such as Outback Steakhouse and The Cheesecake Factory have developed internal environments that are not only pleasant but also consistent with their food and service.

Some Wegmans and Whole Foods stores have built bars and restaurants inside their stores, where customers can stop and relax, have a glass of wine or a bite to eat, but still get their shopping done for the week. Whole Foods has cutting edge culinary centers that offer cooking classes in over 30 stores. Other grocery store chains are following suit; the Brewers Yard Kroger in Ohio has a band play in the store on Friday nights. Still other grocery stores offer flat-screen televisions, comfortable chairs, free Wi-Fi hotspots, in-store cooking classes, or wine tasting events to create interactive atmospheres that will appeal to customers.[64]

Salespeople. Well-trained sales personnel can influence the sale at the point of purchase by educating consumers about product attributes, pointing out the advantages of one item over another, and encouraging multiple purchases. The salesperson at Tiffany & Co., for instance, explained to Samantha why one platter was better than another and suggested some serving pieces to go with it.

Jordan's Furniture, a New England–based chain, has worked hard to make furniture shopping fun by offering in-store entertainment and food outlets. But after going through all the effort to make the store atmospheres inviting, Jordan's also realized that the quality of its salespeople could mean all the difference between a consumer just visiting the store for fun or making a purchase. It

In-store demonstrations entice people to buy.

therefore initiated an extensive training program for its entire sales staff to guarantee that salespeople were knowledgeable about anything and everything customers may want to know. The regular training modules take place during workshops at the individual stores, usually before hours over three consecutive days. The sessions focus on various topics, including the differences between solid wood and veneers or the introduction of a new fabric line by a certain manufacturer.

Crowding. Customers can feel crowded because there are too many people, too much merchandise, or lines that are too long. If there are too many people in a store, some people become distracted and may even leave.[65] Others have difficulty purchasing if the merchandise is packed too closely together. This issue is a particular problem for shoppers with mobility disabilities.

In-Store Demonstrations. The taste and smell of new food items may attract people to try something they normally wouldn't. Similarly, some fashion retailers offer trunk shows, during which their vendors show their whole line of merchandise on a certain day. During these well-advertised events, customers are often enticed to purchase that day because they get special assistance from the salespeople and can order merchandise that the retailer otherwise does not carry.

Promotions. Retailers employ various promotional vehicles to influence customers once they have arrived in the store. An unadvertised price promotion can alter a person's preconceived buying plan. Multi-item discounts, such as buy 1, get 1 free sales, are popular means to get people to buy more

Adding Value 6.2

Judging a Product by Its Cover[66]

In stores, customers spend just 3 to 10 seconds standing in front of products as they decide whether to buy them. Regardless of the significant time and money put into marketing products in places outside store walls, customers evaluate most products based mainly on their appearance in the store. That means that packaging is tremendously important.

Packaging must sell itself to the customer, over and above any competitors on the shelf. Redesigned packages offer the excitement of exhibiting something new, but they also might alienate customers who find them unfamiliar. Yet increasing the visibility of any package on the shelf helps increase sales—which may be why Pringles keeps packaging its chips in tubes that differ greatly from the formless bags farther down the aisle.

But not all product packaging can, or should, remain the same, the way Pringles has. Doublemint Gum undertook its first packaging redesign in 2006—nearly a century after its 1914 product launch. The move was designed to help the chewing gum appeal to a younger audience, even while it maintained its loyal base of older consumers. Another aging brand, Kraft's Macaroni & Cheese, similarly redesigned its packaging, which it launched originally in 1937.

For Nonni's Biscotti, the most recent package redesign involved adding a window to the front of the box, so customers could see the texture of the baked treats. The biscotti, stacked vertically

Nonni's redesigned its biscotti packages to include a window so customers could see the products.

instead of horizontally, now help give a grander impression of the product. Furthermore, by adding decorative touches to make the packaging more visually appealing, Nonni's could encourage customers to leave the box right on their countertops, easily accessible to snackers.

---

than they normally would.[67] Because many people regard clipping coupons from the newspaper as too much trouble, some stores make coupons available in the store, on the Internet, or on their cell phones. Another form of promotion is offering a free gift with the purchase of a good or service. This type of promotion is particularly popular with cosmetics.

Packaging. It is difficult to make a product stand out in the crowd when it competes for shelf space with several other brands. This problem is particularly difficult for consumer packaged goods, such as groceries and health and beauty products (see Adding Value 6.2). Marketers therefore spend millions of dollars designing and updating their packages to be more appealing and eye catching.[68]

Temporal State Our state of mind at any particular time can alter our preconceived notions of what we are going to purchase. For instance, some people are morning people, whereas others function better at night. A purchase situation may thus have different appeal levels depending on the time of day and the type of person the consumer is. Mood swings can alter consumer behavior.[69] Suppose Samantha received a parking ticket just prior to shopping at Tiffany & Co. It is likely that she would be less receptive to the salesperson's influence than if

she came into the store in a good mood. Her bad mood might even cause her to have a less positive postpurchase feeling about the store. Since retailers can't affect what happens outside the store very much, they should do everything possible to make sure their customers have a positive shopping experience once they are in the store.

The factors that affect the consumer decision process—the marketing mix, psychological factors, social factors, and situational factors—are all affected by the level of consumer involvement, the subject of the next section.

 check yourself

1. What are some examples of specific needs suggested by Maslow's Hierarchy of Needs?

2. Which social factors likely have the most influence on (a) the purchase of a new outfit for a job interview and (b) the choice of a college to attend?

3. List some of the tactics stores can use to influence consumers' decision processes.

involvement
Consumer's interest in
a product or service.

▼ **EXHIBIT 6.6** Elaboration Likelihood Model

who is researching buying a dress for a job interview) will scrutinize all the information provided (price, fabric quality, construction) and process the key elements of the message more deeply. As an involved consumer, Katie likely ends up judging the ad as truthful and forming a favorable impression of the product, or else she regards the message as superficial and develops negative product impressions (i.e., her research suggests the product is not as good as it is being portrayed).

In contrast, a low-involvement consumer will likely process the same advertisement in a less thorough manner. Such a consumer might pay less attention to the key elements of the message (price, fabric quality, construction) and focus on heuristic elements such as brand name (Macy's I·N·C) or the presence of a celebrity endorser. The impressions of the low-involvement consumer are likely to be more superficial.

LO 6-6   Describe how involvement influences the consumer decision process.

INVOLVEMENT AND CONSUMER BUYING DECISIONS

Consumers make two types of buying decisions depending on their level of involvement: extended problem solving; and limited problem solving, which includes impulse buying and habitual decision making. **Involvement** is the consumer's degree of interest in the product or service.[70] Consumers may have different levels of involvement for the same type of product. One consumer behavior theory, the elaboration likelihood model, illustrated in Exhibit 6.6, proposes that high- and low-involvement consumers process different aspects of a message or advertisement.

If both types of consumers viewed ads for career dresses, the high-involvement consumer (e.g., Katie,

What type of buying decision does each of these products represent?

[Consumers may have different levels of involvement for the same type of product.]

> ## LIMITED PROBLEM SOLVING USUALLY RELIES ON PAST EXPERIENCE MORE THAN ON EXTERNAL INFORMATION.

Extended Problem Solving

The buying process begins when consumers recognize that they have an unsatisfied need. Katie Smith recognized her need to buy a new dress for a job interview. She sought information by asking for advice from her friends, reading fashion magazines, and conducting research online. She visited several stores to determine which had the best options for her.

Picking up a hamburger at a drive-through fast-food restaurant like In-N-Out Burger requires little thought. It is a habitual decision.

Finally, after considerable time and effort analyzing her alternatives, Katie purchased a dress at Macy's. This process is an example of **extended problem solving**, which is common when the customer perceives that the purchase decision entails a lot of risk. The potential risks associated with Katie's decision to buy the dress include financial (did I pay too much?) and social (will my potential employer and friends think I look professional?) risks. To reduce her perceived risk, Katie spent a lot of effort searching for information before she actually made her purchase.

Limited Problem Solving

Limited problem solving occurs during a purchase decision that calls for, at most, a moderate amount of effort and time. Customers engage in this type of buying process when they have had some prior experience with the product or service and the perceived risk is moderate. Limited problem solving usually relies on past experience more than on external information. For many people, an apparel purchase, even a dress for a job interview, could require limited effort.

A common type of limited problem solving is **impulse buying**, a buying decision made by customers on the spot when they see the merchandise.[71] When Katie went to the grocery store to do her weekly shopping, she saw a display case of popcorn and Dr Pepper near the checkout counter. Knowing that some of her friends were coming over to watch a movie, she stocked up. The popcorn and soda were an impulse purchase. Katie didn't go through the entire decision process; instead, she recognized her need and jumped directly to purchase without spending any time searching for additional information or evaluating alternatives. The grocery store facilitated this impulse purchase by providing easily accessible cues (i.e., by offering the popcorn and soda in a prominent display, at a great location in the store, and at a reasonable price).

Some purchases require even less thought. **Habitual decision making** describes a purchase decision process in which consumers engage in little conscious effort. On her way home from the grocery store, for example, Katie drove past an In-N-Out Burger and swung into the drive-through for a cheeseburger and Diet Coke. She did

extended problem solving A purchase decision process during which the consumer devotes considerable time and effort to analyzing alternatives; often occurs when the consumer perceives that the purchase decision entails a lot of risk.

limited problem solving Occurs during a purchase decision that calls for, at most, a moderate amount of effort and time.

impulse buying A buying decision made by customers on the spot when they see the merchandise.

habitual decision making A purchase decision process in which consumers engage with little conscious effort.

not ponder the potential benefits of going to Wendy's instead for lunch. Rather, she simply reacted to the cue provided by the sign and engaged in habitual decision making. Marketers strive to attract and maintain habitual purchasers by creating strong brands and store loyalty (see Chapters 11 and 12) because these customers don't even consider alternative brands or stores. ■

 check yourself

1. How do low- versus high-involvement consumers process the information in an advertisement?
2. What is the difference between extended versus limited problem solving?

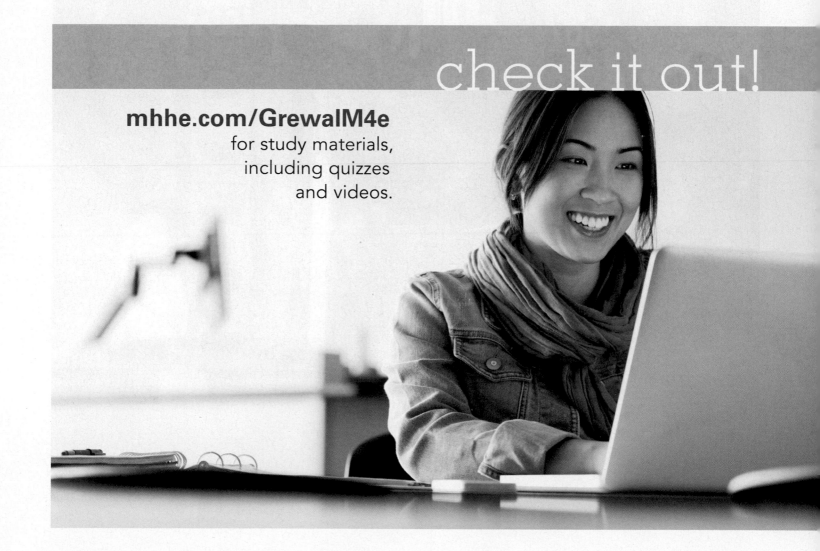

check it out!

mhhe.com/GrewalM4e
for study materials,
including quizzes
and videos.

chapter seven

business-to-business marketing

I f you are like most people, jeans are a staple of your wardrobe. However, when you pull on a pair, you probably don't wonder about where they were made, how much material they contain, or the impact they have on the environment. But for Levi Strauss & Co., one of the oldest names in jeans, these questions remain important to the company's long-term survival.[1]

In particular, Levi's is a major consumer of cotton: A single pair of its 501 jeans uses nearly two pounds of cotton,[2] and the vast majority of all Levi's products are made with cotton. Cotton needs water to grow, and jeans continue to require water throughout their life cycle, whether as part of the stone-wash softening process or in the laundry. By the time your latest pair of jeans has reached the end of its life cycle, it will have used more than 900 gallons of water.[3]

A decade ago, this water consumption was of less concern. But changes in

LEARNING OBJECTIVES

After reading this chapter, you should be able to:

LO 7-1 Describe the ways in which business-to-business (B2B) firms segment their markets.

LO 7-2 List the steps in the B2B buying process.

LO 7-3 Identify the roles within the buying center.

LO 7-4 Describe the different types of organizational cultures.

LO 7-5 Detail different buying situations.

rainfall patterns caused by global climate change are directly tying Levi's future to water: Less water means less moisture for cotton crops, and less cotton means Levi's will either have to incorporate more synthetics into its clothing—a significant change to its brand—or pay more for scarce raw materials. If the company pays more, the increased prices will be passed along to customers, possibly resulting in Levi's

continued on p. 144

Levi's works with its suppliers to implement sustainable water use in the production of its jeans.

continued from p. 143

loyalists moving to other brands. A third alternative, reducing the cost of other garment materials such as buttons and zippers, affects both the brand and quality standards, though it can help control the end cost charged to consumers.

To address these challenges, Levi's is working with suppliers to implement more sustainable water use and other environmental practices as well as more responsible practices with regard to workers throughout its supply chain. These partnerships are challenging to instigate and oversee because cotton

The company has also partnered with other large consumers of cotton, including IKEA, adidas, and The Gap; environmental organizations such as the World Wildlife Federation; and a cotton industry association to study growing practices that reduce water and pesticide use. In one such study, conducted on a farm in India, cotton plants using a new drip irrigation system were taller and bore more flowers than those using traditional methods. The drip system reduced water use by about 70 percent and shortened the duration of electricity use for the system from three days to three hours. It also distributed fertilizer more evenly. Levi Strauss, IKEA, and adidas thus agreed to set aggressive goals for increasing the amount of this better cotton in their products. In addition, Levi Strauss has introduced a line of stone-washed denim that does not use water.

In conjunction with other members of the apparel industry and outdoor-wear makers such as Target, Nike, Patagonia, and REI, Levi's has adopted a software tool, the Eco Index, that helps clothing manufacturers determine the environmental and human impact of their products.[6] These efforts go beyond water

> "The distinction between a B2B and a B2C transaction is not the product or service itself; rather, it is the ultimate user of that product or service."

is raised in more than 100 countries and grown primarily on small, family-owned farms.[4] Levi's began, more than 20 years ago, by creating a Terms of Engagement code of conduct that spells out what the company requires from its business partners in terms of social, ethical, legal, and environmental practices and employment standards. The agreement covers such issues as working ages, health and safety, and child labor as well as wages, benefits, and disciplinary practices.[5]

use to include every step of the garment's life cycle—from raw material production to disposal—and help companies make the most responsible decisions when sourcing and distributing their wares.

Whether working with small farm owners in foreign countries or major retailers in the United States, Levi's efforts to be a responsible consumer have one thing in common: It involves business-to-business relationships among companies. ■

Business-to-business (B2B) marketing refers to the process of buying and selling goods or services to be used in the production of other goods and services for consumption by the buying organization and/or resale by wholesalers and retailers. Therefore, a typical B2B marketing transaction involves manufacturers (e.g., Levi's, Siemens, IBM, Ford) selling to wholesalers that, in turn, sell products as retailers. B2B transactions can also involve service firms (e.g., UPS, Oracle, Accenture) that market their services to other businesses but not to the ultimate consumer (e.g., you). The distinction between a B2B and a business-to-consumer (B2C) transaction is not the product or service itself; rather, it is the ultimate user of that product or service. Another key distinction is that B2B transactions tend to be more complex and involve multiple members of both the buying organization (e.g., buyers, marketing team, product developers) and the selling organization (e.g., sellers, R&D support team), whereas B2C often entails a simple transaction between the retailer and the individual consumer.

The demand for B2B sales is often derived from B2C sales in the same supply chain. More specifically, **derived demand** reflects the link between consumers' demand for a company's output and the company's purchase of necessary inputs to manufacture or assemble that particular output. For example, if more customers want to purchase staplers (a B2C transaction), a company that produces them must purchase

business-to-business (B2B) marketing The process of buying and selling goods or services to be used in the production of other goods and services, for consumption by the buying organization, or for resale by wholesalers and retailers.

derived demand The linkage between consumers' demand for a company's output and its purchase of necessary inputs to manufacture or assemble that particular output.

more metal from its supplier to make additional staplers (a B2B transaction).

Similar to organizations that sell directly to final consumers in B2C transactions, B2B firms focus on serving specific types of customer markets by creating value for those customers.[7] For example, Intel created and produces processors that are critical to the speed of many modern computers sold by Dell or Compaq as well as smart televisions with the Sony brand name and, in the future, Android phones marketed by Google.[8] Also like B2C firms, many B2B companies find it more productive to focus their efforts on key industries or market segments. Siemens has identified core sectors, including health care, energy, technology, and software, that might benefit from its expertise. Through its market leadership in the field of water treatment, Siemens provides technology that enables its customers, whether corporate or civic, to provide emergency water

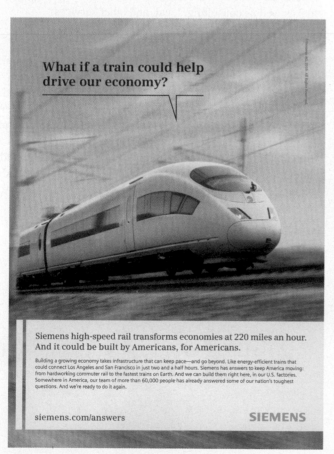

What if a train could help drive our economy?

Siemens high-speed rail transforms economies at 220 miles an hour. And it could be built by Americans, for Americans.

Building a growing economy takes infrastructure that can keep pace—and go beyond. Like energy-efficient trains that could connect Los Angeles and San Francisco in just two and a half hours. Siemens has answers to keep America moving: from hardworking commuter rail to the fastest trains on Earth. And we can build them right here, in our U.S. factories. Somewhere in America, our team of more than 60,000 people has already answered some of our nation's toughest questions. And we're ready to do it again.

siemens.com/answers   SIEMENS

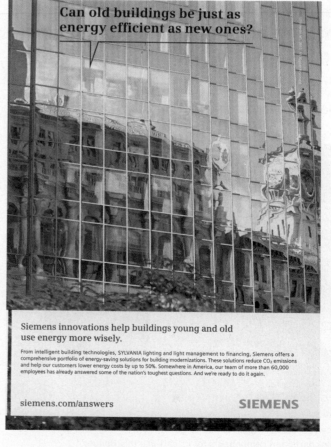

Can old buildings be just as energy efficient as new ones?

Siemens innovations help buildings young and old use energy more wisely.

From intelligent building technologies, SYLVANIA lighting and light management to financing, Siemens offers a comprehensive portfolio of energy-saving solutions for building modernizations. These solutions reduce CO₂ emissions and help our customers lower energy costs by up to 50%. Somewhere in America, our team of more than 60,000 employees has already answered some of the nation's toughest questions. And we're ready to do it again.

siemens.com/answers   SIEMENS

Siemens serves multiple B2B target markets.

supplies, institute water treatment processes, and adopt waste-water reuse systems.[9]

In this chapter, we look at the different types of B2B markets and examine the B2B buying process, with an eye toward how it differs from the B2C buying process we discussed in Chapter 6. Several factors influence the B2B buying process, and we discuss these as well.

LO 7-1   Describe the ways in which business-to-business (B2B) firms segment their markets.

B2B MARKETS

The most visible types of B2B transactions are those where manufacturers and service providers sell to other businesses. However, resellers, institutions, and governments also may be involved in B2B transactions. Therefore, in the next sections, we describe each of these B2B organizations (see Exhibit 7.1).

Manufacturers and Service Providers

Manufacturers buy raw materials, components, and parts that allow them to make and market their own goods and ancillary services. For example, the German-based Volkswagen Group, the largest auto manufacturer in Europe, owns and distributes the Audi, Bentley, Bugatti, Lamborghini, Seat, Skoda, Scania VW, and VW Commercial Vehicles brands.[10] Whereas formerly, purchasing agents spent 70 percent of their time searching for, analyzing, validating, and forwarding information about parts and components, today they can use VWSupplyGroup.com to communicate with suppliers for all transactions, from procurement to logistics. The VW Group system is used by 45,600 suppliers, who were engaged in transactions worth 2.13 billion Euros (or nearly US $3 billion) in 2010.[11] Purchasing agents receive product descriptions directly from suppliers online, which means search processes that used to take two hours now require about nine minutes. Users of the system receive alerts of potential parts shortages before they occur and thus can focus on efficiencies instead of redundant paperwork.

IBM provided the consulting services necessary to design the Volkswagen Group's system. IBM, which was once a major manufacturer of computers and related products, now generates over 90 percent of its profits from its software, consulting, and financing businesses—all of which are considered services. Like Volkswagen Group, it requires a host of B2B products and services to support these businesses. For instance, the airlines that IBM consultants and service providers rely on to shuttle them around the globe also use a mix of products such as airplanes and fuel as well as consulting, legal, and other services.

Resellers

Resellers are marketing intermediaries that resell manufactured products without significantly altering their form. For instance, **wholesalers** and **distributors** buy Xerox products and sell them to retailers (B2B transaction), then retailers in turn resell those Xerox products to the ultimate consumer (B2C transaction). Alternatively, these retailers may buy directly from Xerox. Thus, wholesalers, distributors, and retailers are all resellers. Retailers represent resellers and engage in B2B transactions when they buy merchandise for

German-based Volkswagen Group communicates directly with suppliers to acquire parts and components for its cars like this Bentley.

▼ **EXHIBIT 7.1** B2B Markets

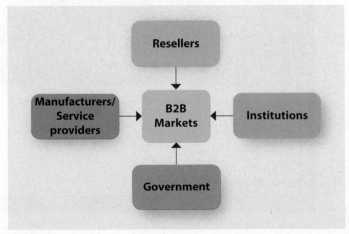

their stores, fixtures, capital investments, leasing locations, and financing operations.

Institutions

Institutions, such as hospitals, educational organizations, and religious organizations, also purchase all kinds of goods and services. A public school system might have a $40 million annual budget for textbooks alone, which gives it significant buying power and enables it to take advantage of bulk discounts. However, if each school makes its own purchasing decisions, the system as a whole cannot leverage its combined buying power. Public institutions also engage in B2B relationships to fulfill their needs for capital construction, equipment, supplies, food, and janitorial services. For example, as Social & Mobile Marketing 7.1 highlights, iPads are playing increasing roles in educational institutions and businesses, which suggests that institutions need to start making purchasing decisions about them too.

Social & Mobile Marketing   7.1
iPads Go to Work

Since being introduced in 2010, iPads have rocketed into widespread use for gaming, online access, music, videos, and e-mail. Tech-savvy business executives and educators also have noted some advantages of these devices that could make them useful at work, as well as at play. Tablet computers weigh less and cost less than laptop computers. Uploaded e-books can be more up to date and are less expensive than physical textbooks.[12] And in both the classroom and the workplace, the use of iPads extends the enthusiastic adoption of technology that is already occurring naturally in social contexts.

These devices, educators have learned, go beyond delivery of course materials by saving additional funds for schools and increasing the value for students. Students can watch videos or tutorials, take notes, or use interactive programs that demonstrate particular skills. They can scroll effortlessly through documents or between texts to reach a section relevant to the current class discussion. Part-time and distance students can communicate more readily with their classmates, potentially enhancing collaboration and team-based learning.[13] Visual learners, children with autism spectrum disorders or learning disabilities, and students who have grown up using electronic devices in various facets of their lives all can benefit from the interactive nature of iPads. And all students benefit from developing comfort with technology, a vital skill set in tomorrow's workforce.

The iPad is finding fans in the workplace as well. Executives, staff members, and clients at companies as diverse as Wells Fargo Bank, the business management software developer SAP, and Daimler's Mercedes-Benz have adopted the device. Airplane pilots have begun replacing paper binders full of flight manuals, navigation charts, and other materials with iPads.[14] Siemens Energy has equipped some of its wind turbine service technicians with iPads so that they have convenient access to manuals, checklists, and cameras, even from atop a 300-foot tower. Thus iPad's manufacturer Apple claims that 80 percent of *Fortune* 100 companies are either using the device or have launched pilot projects to try it.[15]

Whether in the classroom or in the workplace, iPads are not without their disadvantages. Schools may save money in textbook costs

80 percent of Fortune 100 companies are either using the iPad or have launched pilot projects to try it.

but will need funding for repairs and wireless infrastructure. Tablets may enhance learning, but they cannot replace teachers or peer-to-peer interactions. Academic and business users find that the virtual keyboard is challenging for composing longer text, sharing applications is burdensome, and multitasking is impossible. Some companies are put off by iPad security breaches; others reject Apple's traditional focus on the consumer market, often at the expense of business sales.[16] Despite these challenges though, the iPad has gained a strong foothold in both the classroom and the workplace.[17]

request for proposals (RFP) A process through which buying organizations invite alternative suppliers to bid on supplying their required components.

web portal An Internet site whose purpose is to be a major starting point for users when they connect to the Web.

Government

In most countries, the central government is one of the largest purchasers of goods and services. For example, the U.S. federal government spends about $3.7 trillion annually on procuring goods and services.[18] If you add in the amount state and local governments spend, these numbers reach staggering proportions. Specifically, with its estimated outlay of over 526.6 billion dollars for fiscal year 2014, the Pentagon represents a spending force to be reckoned with,[19] especially when it comes to aerospace and defense (A&D) manufacturers, some of the Pentagon's greatest suppliers of products. Policy Studies Inc. (PSI), for instance, offers consulting, technology, and outsourced services to government agencies involved in criminal justice, health care, and human services. One of its most visible services is its child support enforcement programs for state and local government agencies.[20]

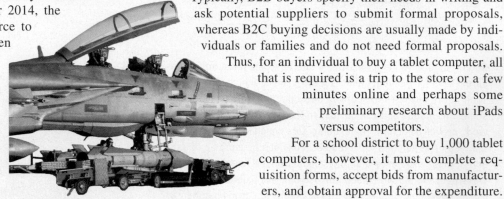

The U.S. government spends over $5 billion a year on aerospace and defense for everything from nuts and bolts to this F-14 Tomcat jetfighter.

 check yourself

1. What are the various B2B markets?

LO 7-2   List the steps in the B2B buying process.

THE BUSINESS-TO-BUSINESS BUYING PROCESS

The B2B buying process (Exhibit 7.2) parallels the B2C process, though it differs in many ways. Both start with need recognition, but the information search and alternative evaluation steps are more formal and structured in the B2B process. Typically, B2B buyers specify their needs in writing and ask potential suppliers to submit formal proposals, whereas B2C buying decisions are usually made by individuals or families and do not need formal proposals. Thus, for an individual to buy a tablet computer, all that is required is a trip to the store or a few minutes online and perhaps some preliminary research about iPads versus competitors.

For a school district to buy 1,000 tablet computers, however, it must complete requisition forms, accept bids from manufacturers, and obtain approval for the expenditure. The final decision rests with a committee, as is the case for most B2B buying decisions, which often demand a great deal of consideration. Finally, in B2C buying situations, customers evaluate their purchase decision and sometimes experience postpurchase dissonance. However, formal performance evaluations of the vendor and the products sold generally do not occur, as they do in the B2B setting. Let's examine all six stages in the context of a school district buying tablets for middle school students as a resource.

> The information search and alternative evaluation steps are more formal and structured in the B2B process.

▼ **EXHIBIT 7.2** Business-to-Business Buying Process

Need recognition → Product specification → RFP process → Proposal analysis and supplier selection → Order specification → Vendor/performance assessment using metrics

> ## ALTHOUGH THERE ARE GENERAL PORTALS SUCH AS YAHOO OR MSN, B2B PARTNERS CONNECT TO SPECIALIZED OR NICHE PORTALS TO PARTICIPATE IN ONLINE INFORMATION EXCHANGES AND TRANSACTIONS.

The first step in the B2B decision process is to recognize that the middle schools need to purchase 1,000 tablets.

Stage 1: Need Recognition

In the first stage of the B2B buying process, the buying organization recognizes, through either internal or external sources, that it has an unfilled need. The Salt Lake City, Utah, school district wants to introduce computer tablets into its middle-school resource programs to help build literacy and matching skills for students. A group of educators has reviewed pedagogical literature that describes how these devices can help students learn better because they can directly interact with the materials rather than only hearing information or seeing it on a whiteboard. Using this information, they have convinced the school board to provide sufficient funding. They are ready to purchase 1000 tablets.

Stage 2: Product Specification

After recognizing the need and considering alternative solutions, including laptop computers, the school district wrote a list of potential specifications that vendors might use to develop their proposals. The school's specifications include screen size, battery life, processor speed, how the device connects to the Internet, and delivery date. In addition, the district has requested that a bundle of educational apps be preloaded on the tablets, that all other apps be removed, and that each tablet come equipped with a screen protector, power cord, cover, stand, keyboard, and headphones. The school district has also requested a three-year service contract that includes replacement within 24 hours for any tablets that are returned to the vendor for servicing.

Stage 3: RFP Process

The **request for proposals (RFP)** is a common process through which organizations invite alternative vendors or suppliers to bid on supplying their required components or specifications. The purchasing company may simply post its RFP

needs on its website or work through various B2B web portals or inform their preferred vendors directly.[21] Because the school district likely does not have a preferred vendor, it issues an RFP and invites various tablet suppliers, technology companies, and other interested parties to bid on the contract.

Smaller companies may lack the ability to attract broad attention to their requests, so they might turn to a **web portal**, an Internet site whose purpose is to be a major starting point for users when they connect to the web. Although there are general portals such as Yahoo or MSN, B2B partners connect to specialized or niche portals to participate in online information exchanges and transactions. These exchanges help streamline procurement or distribution processes. Portals can provide tremendous cost savings because they eliminate periodic negotiations and routine paperwork, and they offer the means to form a supply chain that can respond quickly to the buyer's needs.

Small to medium-sized companies looking for skilled service workers also can use portals such as Guru.com, started to help freelance professionals connect with companies that need their services, whether those services entail graphic design and cartooning or finance and accounting advice. Currently, 724,000 professionals list their offerings on this service-oriented professional exchange, and more than 30,000 companies regularly visit the site to post work orders. Guru.com thus provides value to both companies and freelancers by offering not only a site for finding each other but also dispute resolution, escrow for payments, and a means to rate freelancer quality.[22]

Stage 4: Proposal Analysis, Vendor Negotiation, and Selection

The buying organization, in conjunction with its critical decision makers, evaluates all the proposals it receives in response to its RFP. Thus the school district reviews all proposals it receives, together with the school board, representatives from the teachers' union, and perhaps interested parents. Many firms narrow the process to a few suppliers, often those with which they have existing relationships, and discuss key terms of the sale, such as price, quality, delivery, and financing. Some firms have a policy that requires them to negotiate with several suppliers, particularly if the product or service represents a critical component or aspect of the business. This policy keeps suppliers on their toes; they know that the buying firm can always shift a greater portion of its business to an alternative supplier if it offers better terms.

The school district evaluates proposals on the basis of the amount of experience the vendor has with tablet computers and similar technology products because it wants to make sure that its investment is reliable in the short term and flexible enough to accommodate new apps or updates. In addition, the district wants to be sure the technology will remain relevant in the longer term and not become obsolete. The vendor's ability to meet its specifications also is important because if a battery needs to recharge in the middle of the school day, for example, a student may not have access to the device and may thus fall behind classmates. The vendor's financial position also provides an important indication of whether the vendor will be able to stay in business.

Stage 5: Order Specification

In the fifth stage, the firm places its order with its preferred supplier (or suppliers). The order includes a detailed description of the goods, prices, delivery dates, and, in some cases, penalties for noncompliance. The supplier then sends an acknowledgement that it has received the order and fills it by the specified date. In the case of the school's tablets, the terms are clearly laid out regarding when and how the vendor is expected to perform any preventive maintenance, who the contact person is for any problems with delivery or the tablets themselves, and under what circumstances the vendor will be expected to provide a replacement for a malfunctioning tablet. Issues such as maintenance and replacement are important to the school because it cannot afford to keep an inventory of extra tablets on hand.

Stage 6: Vendor Performance Assessment Using Metrics

Just as in the consumer buying process, firms analyze their vendors' performance so they can make decisions about their future purchases. The difference is that in a B2B setting, this analysis is typically more formal and objective. Let's consider how the school district might evaluate the tablet vendor's performance, as in Exhibit 7.3, using the following metrics: delivery (based on

promised delivery date), quality, customer service, and issue resolution.

1. The buying team develops a list of issues that it believes are important to consider in the vendor evaluation.

2. To determine the importance of each issue (column 1), the buying team assigns an importance score to each (column 2). The more important the issue, the higher its score, but the importance scores must add up to 1. In this case, the buying team believes that customer service and quality are most important, whereas the issue resolution and delivery are comparatively less important.

3. In the third column, the buying team assigns numbers that reflect its judgments about how well the vendor performs. Using a five-point scale, where 1 equals poor performance and 5 equals excellent performance, the school district decides that the tablet vendor performs quite well on all issues except product quality.

4. To calculate an overall performance score in the fourth column, the team combines the importance of each issue and the vendor's performance scores by multiplying them. Because the tablet vendor performed well on the most important issues, when we add the importance/performance scores in column 4, we find that the overall evaluation is pretty good—4.2 on a five-point scale.

 check yourself

1. Identify the stages in the B2B buying process.
2. How do you perform a vendor analysis?

LO 7-3 Identify the roles within the buying center.

THE BUYING CENTER

In most large organizations, several people are responsible for buying decisions. These **buying center** participants can range from employees who have a formal role in purchasing decisions (i.e., the purchasing or procurement department) to members of the design team that is specifying the particular equipment or raw material needed to employees who will be using a new machine that is being ordered. All these employees are likely to play different roles in the buying process, which vendors must understand and adapt to in their marketing and sales efforts.

▼ **EXHIBIT 7.3** Evaluating a Vendor's Performance

(1) Key Issues	(2) Importance Score	(3) Vendor's Performance	(4) Importance × Performance (2) × (3)
Customer Service	.40	5	2.0
Issue Resolution	.20	4	0.8
Delivery	.10	5	0.5
Quality	.30	3	0.9
Total	1.0		4.2

We can categorize six buying roles within a typical buying center (see Exhibit 7.4). One or more people may take on a certain role, or one person may take on more than one of the following roles: (1) "**initiator**, the person who first suggests buying the particular product or service; (2) **influencer**, the person whose views influence other members of the buying center in making the final decision; (3) **decider**, the person who ultimately determines any part of or the entire buying decision—whether to buy, what to buy, how to buy, or where to buy; (4) **buyer**, the person who handles the paperwork of the actual purchase; (5) **user**, the person who consumes or uses the product or service; and (6) **gatekeeper**, the person who controls information or access, or both, to decision makers and influencers."[23]

To illustrate how a buying center operates, consider purchases made by a hospital. Where do hospitals obtain their x-ray machines, syringes, and bedpans? Why are some medical procedures covered in whole or in part by insurance, whereas others are not? Why might your doctor recommend one type of allergy medication instead of another?

The Initiator—Your Doctor

When you seek treatment from your physician, he or she initiates the buying process by determining the products and services that will best address and treat your illness or injury. For example, say that you fell backward off your snowboard and, in trying to catch yourself, shattered your elbow. You require surgery to mend the affected area, which includes the insertion of several screws to hold the bones in place. Your doctor promptly notifies the hospital to schedule a time for the procedure and specifies the brand of screws she wants on hand for your surgery.

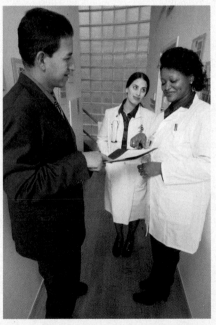

From an ethical perspective, what information should pharmaceutical sales representatives provide to doctors?

The Influencer—The Medical Device Supplier, the Pharmacy

For years, your doctor has been using ElbowMed screws, a slightly higher-priced screw. Her first introduction to ElbowMed screws came from the company's sales representative, who visited her office to demonstrate how ElbowMed screws were far superior to those of its competition. Your doctor recognized ElbowMed as a good value. Armed with empirical data and case studies, ElbowMed's sales rep effectively influenced your doctor's decision to use that screw.

The Decider—The Hospital

Even though your doctor requested ElbowMed screws, the hospital ultimately is responsible for deciding whether to buy ElbowMed screws. The hospital supplies the operating room, instrumentation, and surgical supplies, and therefore, the hospital administrators must weigh a variety of factors to determine whether the ElbowMed screw is not only best for the patients but also involves a cost that is reimbursable by various insurance providers.

The Buyer

The actual buyer of the screw will likely be the hospital's materials manager, who is charged with buying and maintaining inventory for the hospital in the most cost-effective manner. Whereas ElbowMed screws are specific to your type of procedure, other items, such as gauze and sutures, may be purchased through a group purchasing organization (GPO), which obtains better prices through volume buying.

The User—The Patient

Ultimately though, the buying process for this procedure will be greatly affected by the user, namely, you and your broken elbow. If you are uncomfortable with the procedure or have read about alternative procedures that you prefer, you may decide that ElbowMed screws are not the best treatment.

The Gatekeeper—The Insurance Company

Your insurer may believe that ElbowMed screws are too expensive and that other screws deliver equally effective results and therefore refuse to reimburse the hospital in full or in part for the use of the screws.

In the end, the final purchase decision must take into consideration every single buying center participant. Ethical & Societal Dilemma 7.1 examines the unethical, illegal, but also international practice of influencing the influencers through expensive gifts and payments.

user The person who consumes or uses the product or service purchased by the buying center.

gatekeeper The buying center participant who controls information or access to decision makers and influencers.

ethical & societal dilemma

Is It Business or Bribery?

In some parts of the world, accepting money, offering expensive gifts, or distributing payments to government and business officials to influence business decisions is considered an acceptable business practice.[24] In the United States though, these practices are considered unethical and illegal. As the world moves to a more global economy, pressure is mounting to level the playing field by eliminating bribery. Yet countries that have traditionally relied on business bribery argue that criminalizing this activity will negatively affect their ability to compete.[25] How do executives doing business on an international scale respond when a behavior that could earn them a lucrative contract in one country could earn them jail time in another?

Whenever businesses cooperate with one another or companies intersect with governments, the opportunity exists for bribery. An extravagant gift or economic incentive may mean one contractor lands a lucrative contract. A private exchange of money between an executive and a public official may result in the official driving a new car while the executive's company bypasses a restriction that could hinder its

growth. These types of interactions occur behind closed doors and between two people, yet they can have significant repercussions, including unsafe infrastructure, bridges, and buildings, if they occur in the context of large business transactions. Increasingly, the world's economies thus are pushing for an end to foreign bribery.

One tactic they are using is a public report by Transparency International that compares corruption rates of countries and industries.[26] This investigation reveals unexpected trends, such as evidence that bribes passing from one business to another are almost as common as bribes slipped to public officials. By highlighting those business sectors or countries perceived as the worst offenders, the Bribery Index also aims to bring about change, whether through embarrassment or economic repercussions that result when companies refuse to do business in corrupt economies. Finally, this report highlights suggestions for reducing corruption and incentives for improvement.

The 2011 Transparency International Bribery Index, as summarized in the graph, reveals that all the world's 28 largest economies engage in bribery; China and Russia emerged as those most likely to be using money and gifts to influence decisions.

Although in some parts of the world bribes are part of doing business, in the US they are unethical and illegal.

Although these figures are relatively unchanged from the 2008 report, both countries have recently begun enforcing legal repercussions for companies and individuals that engage in international business bribery.

The report also highlights positive results of reduced corruption: A business survey conducted in Europe found that two-thirds of respondents believe that a company with a reputation for ethical behavior enjoys a commercial advantage.[27] Findings such as these, along with improved transparency added to business practices, international anti-corruption standards, monitoring and enforcement of anti-corruption business policies and laws, and empowerment of whistleblowers, may also help reduce international bribery rates.

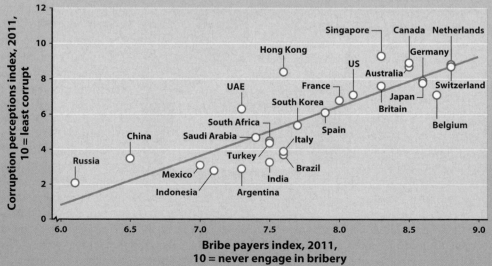

Perceived corruption levels by country and companies' propensity to bribe

*Y-axis: Corruption perceptions index, 2011, 10 = least corrupt*

X-axis: Bribe payers index, 2011, 10 = never engage in bribery

Source: © *The Economist Newspaper Limited*, London.

organizational culture Reflects the set of values, traditions, and customs that guide a firm's employees' behavior.

autocratic buying center A buying center in which one person makes the decision alone, though there may be multiple participants.

democratic buying center A buying center in which the majority rules in making decisions.

consultative buying centers A buying center in which one person makes the decision but he or she solicits input from others before doing so.

consensus buying center A buying center in which all members of the team must reach a collective agreement that they can support a particular purchase.

LO 7-4 Describe the different types of organizational cultures.

Organizational Culture

A firm's **organizational culture** reflects the set of values, traditions, and customs that guide its employees' behavior. The firm's culture often comprises a set of unspoken guidelines that employees share with one another through various work situations. For example, Walmart buyers are not allowed to accept even the smallest gift from a vendor, not even a cup of coffee. This rule highlights its overall corporate culture: It is a low-cost operator whose buyers must base their decisions only on the products' and vendors' merits.

Organizational culture can have a profound influence on purchasing decisions, and corporate buying center cultures thus might be divided into four general types: autocratic, democratic, consultative, and consensus (as illustrated in Exhibit 7.5). Knowing which buying center culture is prevalent in a given organization helps the seller decide how to approach that particular client, how and to whom to deliver pertinent information, and to whom to make sales presentations.

In an **autocratic buying center**, though there may be multiple participants, one person makes the decision alone, whereas the majority rules in a **democratic buying center**. **Consultative buying centers** use one person to make a decision but solicit input from others before doing so. Finally,

> "Cultures act like living, breathing entities that change and grow, just as organizations do."

in a **consensus buying center**, all members of the team must reach a collective agreement that they can support a particular purchase.[28]

Cultures act like living, breathing entities that change and grow, just as organizations do. Even within some companies, culture may vary by geography, by division, or by functional department. Whether you are a member of the buying center or a supplier trying to sell to it, it is extremely important to understand its culture and the roles of the key players in the buying process. Not knowing the roles of the key players could waste a lot of time and could even alienate the real decision maker.

Building B2B Relationships

In B2B contexts, there are a multitude of ways to enhance relationships, and these methods seem to be advancing and evolving by the minute. For example, blogs and social media can build awareness, provide search engine results, educate potential and existing clients about products or services, and warm up a seemingly cold corporate culture.[29] An expert who offers advice and knowledge about products increases brand awareness, and a blog is a great medium for this information. Web analytics, such as traffic on the website and the number of comments, can offer tangible evaluations, but a better measure is how often the blog gets mentioned elsewhere, the media attention it receives, and the interaction, involvement, intimacy, and influence that it promotes.

The LinkedIn.com social network is mainly used for professional networking in the B2B marketplace (see Social & Mobile Marketing 7.2). Twitter, the micro blogging site, is also valuable for B2B marketers because they can communicate with other businesses as often as they want. Companies such as HootSuite make it easier for companies using Twitter to manage their followers, update their posts, track analytics, and even schedule tweets, just as they would to manage a traditional marketing campaign.[30]

The majority of B2B marketers use white papers for their marketing efforts, and the majority of B2B buyers regularly read them prior to making a purchase.[31] When executives confront an unfulfilled business need, they normally turn to white papers. Their B2B partner may have a technologically advanced solution, but buyers have to understand the solution before they can consider a purchase. A good white paper provides information about the industry and its challenges in an educational context, rather than a promotional sense, to avoid seeming like

▼ **EXHIBIT 7.5** Organizational Buying Culture

Social & Mobile Marketing 7.2
Making the Most of LinkedIn

Business-to-business (B2B) marketing may seem relatively impersonal, but even in formalized, standardized buying situations, personal relationships count. Thus social media, with a bit of a tweak, play a key role in this setting, just as well as they do in consumer contexts. Perhaps the best example is LinkedIn, the social media site for business professionals. Launched in 2003, the site has been attracting roughly 1 million members weekly. As of March 2011, its worldwide membership surpassed the 100 million mark. The site is available in six languages and 200 countries, which means that it can help B2B interactions overcome geographical boundaries.[32]

In particular, LinkedIn can boast that executives from all the *Fortune* 500 companies have memberships on its site. Accordingly, its promise for networking, whether individually or for the company, is virtually unsurpassed. Such networking entails several key groups: [33]

- Customers and prospective customers. LinkedIn allows a firm or its representatives to introduce themselves to possible buyers, using a credible and easily accessible format. The Q&A option on LinkedIn pages also allows customers to ask questions and suppliers to demonstrate their expertise.
- Investors. The LinkedIn page offers tangible evidence of the firm's existence and its promise, which is critical information for outsiders who might be willing to invest in its development.
- Suppliers. By starting their own group on LinkedIn, B2B buyers might better identify which suppliers in the market are best matched with their needs and most interested in providing the resources they need.
- Employees and prospective employees. LinkedIn is a great source for finding employees who are diligent, professional,

LinkedIn is perhaps the best social media site for networking with business professionals.

interested, and qualified. Furthermore, if a firm retains its links to former employees, it can gain a good source of referrals—assuming those employees left on good terms.

- Analysts. The job of an analyst is to find detailed information about a company and then recommend it, or not, to the market. LinkedIn gives firms a means to provide that information in a credible but still firm-controlled context.

The site also provides sophisticated analytics for keeping track of all these networking opportunities. Users can see who visited their pages, which descriptions they viewed, and even compare their LinkedIn performance against competitors' pages.[34]

---

simply propaganda. That is, the goal of white papers is to provide valuable information that a businessperson can easily understand and that will help the company address its problems with new solutions.

LO 7-5   Detail different buying situations.

THE BUYING SITUATION

The type of buying situation also affects the B2B decision process. Most B2B buying situations can be categorized into three types: new buys, modified rebuys, and straight rebuys. (See Exhibit 7.6.) To illustrate the nuances among these three

▼ **EXHIBIT 7.6** Buying Situations

buying situations, consider how colleges and universities develop relationships with some of their suppliers. Most universities negotiate with sports apparel manufacturers, such as Nike, Reebok, and New Balance, to establish purchasing agreements for their sports teams. Those with successful sports teams have been very successful in managing these relationships, to the benefit of both the team and the company.[35] Large universities that win national championships, such as the University of Alabama or USC, can solicit sponsorships in exchange for free athletic equipment, whereas less popular teams or smaller schools typically must accept an upfront sponsorship and then agree to buy from that vendor for a specified period of time. In exchange for this sponsorship, the vendors gain the right to sell apparel with the university logo and require the school's team to purchase only their equipment. Many apparel companies make a significant por-

fits each player to achieve the best fit possible.

With another sort of example, Adding Value 7.1 highlights how Hubspot helps buyers become more informed about products before engaging in the B2B buying process.

Another example of a new buy occurs in the fashion industry, where runway shows offer wholesale buyers an opportunity to inspect new lines of clothing and place orders. Designer sales often occur during private meetings with buyers, both before and after runway shows. Buyers meet with the designers, discuss the line, and observe a model wearing the clothing. The buyer's challenge then is to determine which items will sell best in the retail stores he or she represents while trying to imagine what the item will look like in regular, as

> ## Most universities negotiate with sports apparel manufacturers, such as Nike, Reebok, and New Balance, to establish purchasing agreements for their sports teams.

tion of their revenue through sponsorship deals that grant them the right to sell apparel with popular university logos.

In a **new buy** situation, a customer purchases a good or service for the first time,[36] which means the buying decision is likely to be quite involved because the buyer or the buying organization does not have any experience with the item. In the B2B context, the buying center is likely to proceed through all six steps in the buying process and involve many people in the buying decision. Typical new buys might range from capital equipment to components that the firm previously made itself but now has decided to purchase instead. For example, a small college might need to decide which apparel company to approach for a sponsorship. For smaller colleges, finding a company that will sponsor multiple sports teams—such as women's soccer as well as men's basketball—is a priority, though it also must balance other considerations, such as the length of the contract. Some vendors offer perks to attract new buyers; New Balance offers teams that sign up for long-term contracts custom fittings for their players' shoes. Each season, a sales team from New Balance visits the school and custom

opposed to model, sizes. Buyers must also negotiate purchases for orders that may not be delivered for as much as six months. Buyers can suggest modifications to make the clothing more or less expensive or more comfortable for their customers. Buyers and designers recognize the significant value of this relationship, which occasionally prompts buyers to purchase a few items from

Schools such as the University of Alabama negotiate with sports apparel manufacturers, such as Nike, to get free athletic equipment. The manufacturers, in turn, get to sell apparel with the university logo.

Adding Value 7.1
Getting the Message Out with Inbound Marketing[37]

Search engines, company web pages, social media sites, and the blogosphere have transformed the way businesses learn about and shop for products and services. Unlike a decade ago, when a prospective customer had little knowledge of a vendor's products at first contact, today's customers have searched the Internet using relevant keywords and reviewed company websites by the time they speak with a vendor. As a result, they are well-informed and seriously interested in a purchase, adding new efficiency to B2B transactions. But this development only works if companies have the marketing savvy to use today's technology to their advantage.

Two entrepreneurs noticed that small companies and start-ups without the skills to use these tools effectively get lost in the noise, even if prospective customers are searching for vendors in their niche. Furthermore, companies that enlist marketing firms are disadvantaged if those firms rely solely on traditional best practices, such as print advertising, telemarketing, and trade shows. To help these businesses, the two launched a software marketing program, HubSpot, designed to help companies transform their marketing approach. The idea was to abandon intrusive outbound marketing, which people are increasingly able to screen out, and replace it with inbound marketing. Inbound marketing, defined as any marketing tactic that relies on earning customer interest rather than buying it, is built on the understanding that Facebook, Twitter, online user reviews, smartphones, blogs, and websites are the true force behind the way actors in today's marketplace actually learn and shop.

HubSpot's software contains easy-to-use tools that help companies get noticed, convert website visitors to customers, and analyze the effectiveness of marketing efforts across channels. Among the tools in the first category, for example, is a keyword grader that helps companies create content and a list of relevant keywords to improve search engine odds and ranking. Using the lead conversion tools, marketers without technical skills can create landing pages with customizable lead capture forms, auto-response e-mails, and thank-you pages. These tools can also be used to send customized e-mails to new leads on a self-selected schedule. The marketing analytics tools allow HubSpot's customers to track competitors, evaluate the impact of a blog, and compare the effectiveness of all marketing channels to provide important insight into the behaviors of customers and the value of each channel to the bottom line.

HubSpot's approach has been successful for both the founders and their customers. The company, launched in June 2006, reached 3,500 customers in four years and is the second fastest growing software-as-a-service (SAS) company in history.

One customer, the nonprofit National Institute for Fitness and Sport (NIFS), wanted to increase its visibility with corporate and retirement fitness centers. After experiencing difficulty driving traffic to the company website—and after an expensive marketing company campaign proved ineffective—NIFS turned to HubSpot. The results were increases in traffic and leads by more than 200 percent and an increase in social media traffic of 16 percent. According to NIFS's director of media, the fitness company "picked up a number of requests for proposals from businesses that never would have paid attention to us initially because we were able to raise where we sit in the search engines."[38]

Companies such as HubSpot are taking advantage of changes that have already occurred in the marketplace to reduce costs and improve the effectiveness of marketing. As technology evolves and more business and individual shoppers use online information to make their purchasing decisions, businesses will have to adapt their marketing strategies to encompass new technologies and new shopping behaviors.

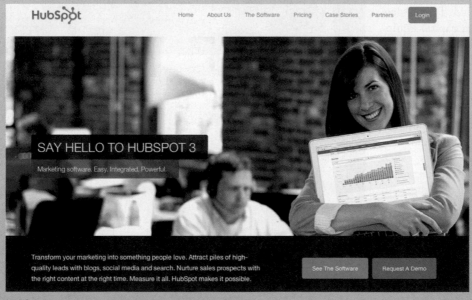

HubSpot helps its customers get noticed on the Internet.

a designer, even if those items do not exactly fit the store's core customers' tastes. Doing so ensures that the buyer will have access to the designer's collection for the next season.[39]

In a **modified rebuy**, the buyer has purchased a similar product in the past but has decided to change some specifications, such as the desired price, quality level, customer service level, options, or so forth. Current vendors are likely to have an advantage in acquiring the sale in a modified rebuy situation as long as the reason for the modification is not dissatisfaction with the vendor or its products. The Ohio State University's sports department might ask adidas to modify the specifications for its basketball shoes after noticing some improvements made to the addidas shoes used by the University of Michigan.

Straight rebuys occur when the buyer or buying organization simply buys additional units of products that had previously been purchased. Many B2B purchases are likely to fall in the straight rebuy category. For example, sports teams need to re-purchase a tremendous amount of equipment that is not covered by apparel sponsorships, such as tape for athletes' ankles or weights for the weight room. The purchase of bottled water also typically involves a straight rebuy from an existing supplier.

These varied types of buying situations call for very different marketing and selling strategies. The most complex and difficult is the new buy because it requires the buying organization to make changes in its current practices and purchases. As a result, several members of the buying center will likely become involved, and the level of their involvement will be more intense than in the case of modified and straight rebuys. In new buying situations, buying center members also typically spend more time at each stage of the B2B buying process, similar to the extended decision-making process that consumers use in the B2C process. In comparison, in modified rebuys, the buyers spend less time at each stage of the B2B buying process, similar to limited decision making in the B2C process (see Chapter 6).

In straight rebuys, however, the buyer is often the only member of the buying center involved in the process. Like a consumer's habitual purchase, straight rebuys often enable the buyer to recognize the firm's need and go directly to the fifth step in the B2B buying process, skipping the product specification, RFP process, and proposal analysis and supplier selection steps.

Thus, in various ways, B2B marketing both differs from and mirrors the consumer behavior (B2C) process we detailed in Chapter 6. The differences in the six stages of the buying process make sense in view of the many unique factors that come into play. The constitution of the buying center (initiator, influencer, decider, buyer, user, and gatekeeper), the culture of the purchasing firm (autocratic, democratic, consultative, or consensus), and the context of the buying situation (new buy, modified rebuy, straight rebuy) all influence the B2B buying process in various ways, which means that sellers must be constantly aware of these factors if they want to be successful in their sales attempts. Finally, just as it has done seemingly everywhere we look, the Internet has radically changed some elements of the B2B world, increasing the frequency of both private electronic exchanges and auctions. ■

modified rebuy
Refers to when the buyer has purchased a similar product in the past but has decided to change some specifications, such as the desired price, quality level, customer service level, options, or so forth.

straight rebuys
Refers to when the buyer or buying organization simply buys additional units of products that have previously been purchased.

 check yourself

1. What factors affect the B2B buying process?
2. What are the six buying roles?
3. What is the difference between new buy, rebuy, and modified rebuy?

global marketing

From the Maharaja Mac in India to the Prosperity Burger prepared especially for the Chinese New Year celebrations, McDonald's has built a global fast-food empire under its golden arches. Only 31 percent of McDonald's revenue now comes from sales in the United States, and most of its international growth has come from the surging economies of Brazil, Russia, China, and India.[1] A pioneer in overseas franchising, McDonald's has spared no effort in its attempts to penetrate foreign markets. In China, it recently announced that within four years, it plans to open one new outlet daily to meet its immediate goal of 2,000 stores.[2] In Brazil, it created Latin America's first environmentally certified fast-food restaurant. A vast market defined by stark cultural differences, India has required a more modest approach that would allow McDonald's to develop its real estate and supply infrastructure, train its local workforce and management at its

LEARNING OBJECTIVES

After reading this chapter, you should be able to:

LO 8-1   Describe the components of a country market assessment.

LO 8-2   Understand the marketing opportunities in BRIC countries.

LO 8-3   Identify the various market entry strategies.

LO 8-4   Highlight the similarities and differences between a domestic marketing strategy and a global marketing strategy.

famed Hamburger University, and adjust the menu for vegetarian customers.[3] Although the McAloo Tikki Burger has been a great success, the company has opened just 210 restaurants in India since 1996.

But McDonald's growth strategy relies on more than just added locations. In crowded cities, with real estate prices too high to build drive-through restaurants, the company has hired droves of motorbike drivers to bring Big

continued on p. 160

continued from p. 159

globalization Refers to the processes by which goods, services, capital, people, information, and ideas flow across national borders.

Macs to customers. This nimble delivery approach is now a mainstay in cities from Beijing to Kuwait City. Online ordering will be next, though the challenge will be to reduce the cost of call centers to support this new distribution model.[4]

Despite growth in these rapidly transitioning economies, Europe still generates the bulk of foreign sales for McDonald's. Most new growth comes from Russia, where the company has 245 locations and controls 70 percent of the booming fast-food business. Even as fast-food competitors face potential market saturation in the United States, Russian demand for quick burgers appears to be insatiable.[5] Driving this Russian appetite has been the growth of a newly affluent middle class, with money to spend to dine out. Infrastructure development in Russia also has been a boon as cities open malls with food courts, highways are constructed with drive-through locations, and specialty suppliers of frozen food and packaging have appeared.

In the early years of Russian expansion, few private businesses existed to supply all the ingredients McDonald's needed to produce Big Macs and fries. The company solved the

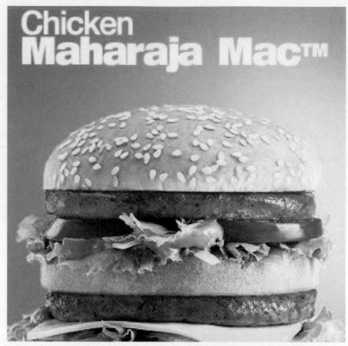

Chicken **Maharaja Mac**™

The Chicken Maharaja Mac is a popular choice at McDonald's in India.

problem by building an enormous food processing plant outside Moscow. But it also worked to cultivate relationships with local Russian vendors and contractors to which it eventually could outsource its supply chain. Today, a grower who began selling cucumbers to McDonald's in 1990 has become the Pickle King of Russia, dominating the processed foods market.[6] ■

Increasing globalization affects not only massive U.S. corporations that actively search out new markets but also small and medium-sized businesses that increasingly depend on goods produced globally to deliver their products and services. Few people really think about how globalization affects their daily lives, but just take a minute to read the labels on the clothing you are wearing right now. Chances are that most of the items, even if they carry U.S. brand names, were manufactured in another part of the world.

In the United States, the market has evolved from a system of regional marketplaces to national markets to geographically regional markets (e.g., Canada and the United States together) to international markets and finally to global markets. **Globalization** refers to the processes by which goods, services, capital, people, information, and ideas flow across national borders. Global markets are the result of several fundamental changes such as reductions or eliminations of trade barriers by country governments, the decreasing concerns of distance and time with regard to moving products and ideas across countries, the standardization of laws across borders, and globally integrated production processes.[7]

Each of these fundamental changes has paved the way for marketing to flourish in other countries. The elimination of trade barriers and other governmental actions, for instance, allows goods and ideas to move quickly and efficiently around the world, which in turn facilitates the quick delivery of goods to better meet the needs of global consumers.

As a consequence, consumers have easy access to global products and services. When we walk into a toy store, we expect to find Legos from Denmark. In the local sporting goods store, we anticipate finding running shoes made in China by the German firm, adidas. In the grocery store, we demand out-of-season produce such as blueberries from Chile in January. Or consider how a $12 digital camera for your keychain, made in Taiwan, could be produced, transported halfway around the world, and sold for so little money at your local Target. These are the questions we will be examining in this chapter.

We begin by looking at how firms assess the potential of a given market, with particular attention to the BRIC countries (Brazil, Russia, India, and China.) Then we examine how firms make decisions to go global and choose how and what they will

These 25-foot-tall replicas of the New York skyline are made completely out of Legos and are on display at the Times Square Toys"R"Us in New York City. How do Legos get from their manufacturer in Denmark to toy stores in the United States?

> The greater the wealth of people in a country, the better the opportunity a firm will have in that particular country.

sell globally. Then we explore how to build the marketing mix for global products.

LO 8-1   Describe the components of a country market assessment.

ASSESSING GLOBAL MARKETS

Because different countries, with their different stages of globalization, offer marketers a variety of opportunities, firms must assess the viability of various potential market entries. As illustrated in Exhibit 8.1, we examine four sets of criteria necessary to assess a country's market: economic analysis, infrastructure and technological analysis, government actions or inactions, and sociocultural analysis. Information about these four areas offers marketers a more complete picture of a country's potential as a market for products and services.

Economic Analysis Using Metrics

The greater the wealth of people in a country, generally, the better the opportunity a firm will have in that particular country. A firm conducting an economic analysis of a country market must look at three major economic factors, using well-established metrics: the general economic environment, the market size and population growth rate, and real income.

Evaluating the General Economic Environment
In general, healthy economies provide better opportunities for global marketing expansions, and there are several ways a firm

trade deficit Results when a country imports more goods than it exports.

trade surplus Occurs when a country has a higher level of exports than imports.

gross domestic product (GDP) Defined as the market value of the goods and services produced by a country in a year; the most widely used standardized measure of output.

gross national income (GNI) Consists of GDP plus the net income earned from investments abroad (minus any payments made to nonresidents who contribute to the domestic economy).

purchasing power parity (PPP) A theory that states that if the exchange rates of two countries are in equilibrium, a product purchased in one will cost the same in the other, expressed in the same currency.

▼ **EXHIBIT 8.1** Components of a Country Market Assessment

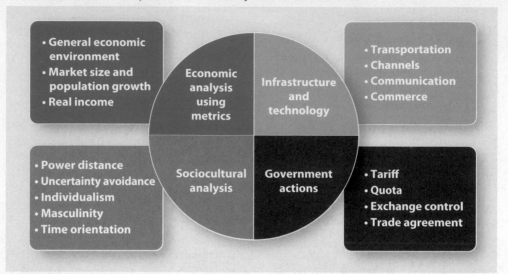

can use metrics to measure the relative health of a particular country's economy. Each way offers a slightly different view, and some may be more useful for some products and services than for others.

To determine the market potential for its particular product or service, a firm should use as many metrics as it can obtain. One metric is the relative level of imports and exports. The United States, for example, suffers a **trade deficit**, which means that the country imports more goods than it exports.[8] For U.S. marketers, this deficit can signal the potential for greater competition at home from foreign producers. Firms would prefer to manufacture in a country that has a **trade surplus**, or a higher level of exports than imports, because it signals a greater opportunity to export products to more markets.

The most common way to gauge the size and market potential of an economy, and therefore the potential the country has for global marketing, is to use standardized metrics of output. **Gross domestic product (GDP)**, the most widely used of these metrics, is defined as the market value of the goods and services produced by a country in a year. **Gross national income (GNI)** consists of GDP plus the net income earned from investments abroad (minus any payments made to nonresidents who contribute to the domestic economy). In other words, U.S. firms that invest or maintain operations abroad count their income from those operations in the GNI but not the GDP.[9]

Another frequently used metric of an overall economy is the **purchasing power parity (PPP)**, a theory that states that if the exchange rates of two countries are in equilibrium, a product purchased in one will cost the same in the other, if expressed in the same currency.[10] A novel metric that employs PPP to assess the relative economic buying power among nations is *The*

Economist's Big Mac Index, which suggests that exchange rates should adjust to equalize the cost of a basket of goods and services, wherever it is bought around the world. Using McDonald's Big Mac as the market basket, Exhibit 8.2 shows that the cheapest burger is in India, where it costs $1.89, compared with an average American price of $4.07. In Brazil, the same burger costs $6.16. This index thus implies that the Indian rupee is 53 percent undervalued, whereas the Brazilian real is 52 percent overvalued, in comparison with the U.S. dollar.[11]

▼ **EXHIBIT 8.2** Big Mac Index

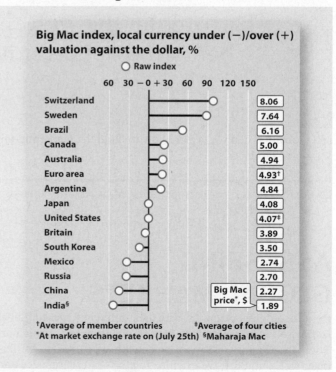

Big Mac index, local currency under (−)/over (+) valuation against the dollar, %

○ Raw index

	Big Mac price*, $
Switzerland	8.06
Sweden	7.64
Brazil	6.16
Canada	5.00
Australia	4.94
Euro area	4.93[†]
Argentina	4.84
Japan	4.08
United States	4.07[‡]
Britain	3.89
South Korea	3.50
Mexico	2.74
Russia	2.70
China	2.27
India[§]	1.89

[†]Average of member countries   [‡]Average of four cities
*At market exchange rate on (July 25th) [§]Maharaja Mac

Source: © *The Economist Newspaper* Limited, London.

> ## THE COUNTRIES WITH THE HIGHEST PURCHASING POWER TODAY MAY BECOME LESS ATTRACTIVE IN THE FUTURE FOR MANY PRODUCTS AND SERVICES BECAUSE OF STAGNATED GROWTH.

These various metrics help marketers understand the relative wealth of a particular country, though they may not give a full picture of the economic health of a country because they are based solely on material output. Nor is a weak dollar always a bad thing. For U.S. exporters, a weak dollar means greater demand for their products in foreign countries because they can sell at a lower price.[12] Although an understanding of the macroeconomic environment is crucial for managers facing a market entry decision, of equal importance is the understanding of economic metrics of market size and population growth rate.

Evaluating Market Size and Population Growth Rate
Global population has been growing dramatically since the turn of the twentieth century, at least. From a marketing perspective, however, growth has never been equally dispersed.

"Minute Maid Pulpy Super Milky" combines fruit juice, milk powder, whey protein, and coconut bits for the Chinese market.

Today, less developed nations, by and large, are experiencing rapid population growth, while many developed countries are experiencing either zero or negative population growth. The countries with the highest purchasing power today may become less attractive in the future for many products and services because of stagnated growth. And as we discussed previously, the BRIC countries are likely to be the source of most market growth.

In response, consumer goods companies are paying close attention to the strong demand in BRIC nations. Thus, Procter & Gamble, which enjoys a strong advantage in the Chinese market, also is expanding aggressively into India and Brazil (as well as sub-Saharan Africa).[13] With 1.33 billion people, China offers such promise that international companies such as PepsiCo and Coca-Cola cannot afford not to focus their efforts there. Each company plans to invest more than $2.5 billion immediately in China, with the goal of achieving at least double-digit annual growth. Pepsi also plans to build a research and development center for its Asian products to ensure that it correctly targets this new consumer market. In some cases, the companies will sell the same products in China and in the United States; in other situations, they are creating new products to meet Chinese consumers' tastes. The "Minute Maid Pulpy Super Milky" combines fruit juice, milk powder, whey protein, and coconut bits. Pepsi offers cucumber-flavored and crispy prawn–flavored potato chips.[14] As another example, the Nano, a $2000 car, is being introduced as the world's cheapest car to capitalize on the 1.16 billion people living in India. The car weighs half the weight of the Honda Accord and gets 56 miles to the gallon.[15]

Another aspect related to market size and population growth pertains to the distribution of the population within a particular region; namely, is the population located primarily in rural or urban areas? This distinction determines where and how products and services can be delivered. Long supply chains, in which goods pass through many hands, are often necessary to reach rural populations in less developed countries and therefore add to the products' cost. As we noted previously, India's 1.16 billion people live overwhelmingly in rural areas, though the population is moving toward urban areas to meet the demands of the growing industrial and service centers located in major cities such as Bangalore and New Delhi. This population shift, perhaps not surprisingly, is accompanied by rapid growth in the middle class. Furthermore, relatively careful banking policies and minimal dependence on exports

Developed for the Indian market, the Nano is the world's cheapest car—about $2,000.

have helped protect India from the global financial crisis. The business impacts of these combined trends of increasing urbanization, a growing middle class, a degree of protectionism by the central government, and a youthful populace make India an absolutely enormous market for consumer goods.

Evaluating Real Income Firms can make adjustments to an existing product or change the price to meet the unique needs of a particular country market. Such shifts are particularly common for low-priced consumer goods. For instance, Procter & Gamble developed a single-use shampoo packet for consumers in less developed nations that cannot afford an entire bottle at one time. To increase consumption of Coca-Cola in rural India, the company lowered its price to the equivalent of about 10 cents per bottle; Cadbury International introduced Dairy Milk Shots for the equivalent of about 4 cents.[16] Textbook publishers sell paperback versions of U.S. books for a fraction of their U.S. price to countries where students would not otherwise be able to afford a text. But pricing adjustments aren't only for inexpensive products. Fashion and jewelry manufacturers also make downward adjustments to their prices in countries where the incomes of their target markets cannot support higher prices.

Even as multinationals battle for dominance in emerging economies, local marketers also are becoming increasingly price competitive in selling their wares. Local marketers already have strong familiarity with their markets, existing distribution channels, and good name recognition. These smaller firms can often exhibit greater flexibility in their pricing to hold on to market share. The best outcome for everyone involved is not just a higher share of an existing market but rather the ongoing development of the market for everyone.[17]

Analyzing Infrastructure and Technological Capabilities

The next component of any market assessment is an infrastructure and technological analysis. **Infrastructure** is defined as the basic facilities, services, and installations needed for a

> **Marketers are especially concerned with four key elements of a country's infrastructure: transportation, distribution channels, communications, and commerce.**

To adjust for India's lower income, Cadbury International sells its Dairy Milk Shots for the equivalent of about four cents.

community or society to function, such as transportation and communications systems, water and power lines, and public institutions such as schools, post offices, and prisons.

Marketers are especially concerned with four key elements of a country's infrastructure: transportation, distribution channels, communications, and commerce. First, there must be a system to transport goods throughout the various markets and to consumers in geographically dispersed marketplaces— trains, roads, refrigeration. Second, distribution channels must exist to deliver products in a timely manner and at a reasonable cost. Third, the communications system, particularly media access, must be sufficiently developed to allow consumers to find information about the products and services available in the marketplace. Fourth, the commercial infrastructure, which consists of the legal, banking, and regulatory systems, allows

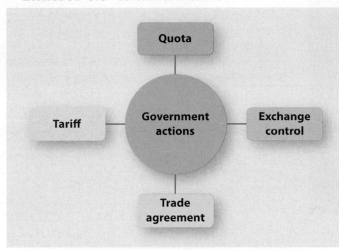

markets to function. In the next section, we focus on how issues pertaining to the political and legal structures of a country can affect the risk that marketers face in operating in a given country.

Analyzing Government Actions

Governmental actions, as well as the actions of nongovernmental political groups, can significantly influence firms' ability to sell goods and services because they often result in laws or other regulations that either promote the growth of the global market or close off the country and inhibit growth. These issues include tariffs, quotas, exchange controls, and trade agreements. (See Exhibit 8.3.)

Tariffs
A **tariff** (also called a **duty**) is a tax levied on a good imported into a country. In most cases, tariffs are intended to make imported goods more expensive and thus less competitive with domestic products,[18] which in turn protects domestic industries from foreign competition. In other cases, tariffs might be imposed to penalize another country for trade practices that the home country views as unfair. When China entered the World Trade Organization, it agreed to a safeguard provision imposed by the United States, which stated that U.S. companies harmed by Chinese imports could ask for protection from a surge of Chinese alternatives.

Quotas
A **quota** designates the maximum quantity of a product that may be brought into a country during a specified time period. The United States, for instance, allows 1.2 million tons of sugar to be imported (the quota) without a tariff because the country generally consumes more than it produces.[19] It then monitors consumption closely to protect domestic sugar farmers. If demand exceeds supply, it increases the quota.

Tariffs and quotas can have fundamental and potentially devastating impacts on a firm's ability to sell products in another country. Tariffs artificially raise prices and therefore lower demand, and quotas reduce the availability of imported merchandise. Conversely, tariffs and quotas benefit domestically made products because they reduce foreign competition.

Exchange Control
Exchange control refers to the regulation of a country's currency **exchange rate**, the measure of how much one currency is worth in relation to another.[20] A designated agency in each country, often the central bank, sets the rules for currency exchange, though in the United States, the Federal Reserve sets the currency exchange rates. In recent years, the value of the U.S. dollar has changed significantly compared with other important world currencies. When the dollar falls, it has a twofold effect on U.S. firms' ability to conduct global business. For firms that depend on imports of finished products, raw materials that they fabricate into other products, or services from other countries, the cost of doing business goes up dramatically. At the same time, buyers in other countries find the costs of U.S. goods and services much lower than they were before.

Trade agreements affect the global marketing environment. Here, Uraguayan president, Jose Mujica, delivers a speech during a press conference after the Mercosur Extraordinary Summit at Planalto Palace in Brasilia, Brazil on July 31, 2012.

The European Union has resulted in lowering trade barriers and strengthening global relationships among member nations.

Trade Agreements Marketers must consider the **trade agreements** to which a particular country is a signatory or the **trading bloc** to which it belongs. A trade agreement is an intergovernmental agreement designed to manage and promote trade activities for a specific region, and a trading bloc consists of those countries that have signed the particular trade agreement.[21] Some major trade agreements cover two-thirds of the world's international trade: the European Union (EU), the North American Free Trade Agreement (NAFTA), Central America Free Trade Agreement (CAFTA), Mercosur, and the Association of Southeast Asian Nations (ASEAN).[22] These trade agreements are summarized in Exhibit 8.4. The EU represents the highest level of integration across individual nations, whereas the other agreements vary in their integration levels.

Analyzing Sociocultural Factors Understanding another country's culture is crucial to the success of any global marketing initiative. Culture, or the shared meanings, beliefs, morals, values, and customs of a group of people,

exists on two levels: visible artifacts (e.g., behavior, dress, symbols, physical settings, ceremonies) and underlying values (thought processes, beliefs, and assumptions).[24] Visible artifacts are easy to recognize, but businesses often find it more difficult to understand the underlying values of a culture and appropriately adapt their marketing strategies to them.[25]

For example, IKEA stores across the globe are open seven days a week—except in France. French law prevents retailers from selling on Sundays, and when IKEA tried to challenge the law by keeping one of its stores open, it provoked a lawsuit from a French workers' union. Although IKEA would love to sell over the whole weekend, when it earns approximately one-quarter of its weekly revenues, neither the workers' unions nor French consumers are likely to change their ways any time soon; leaving Sunday as a day of relaxation constitutes a fundamental foundation of French culture.[26] For the Swiss, a similar prohibition against Sunday retailing may soon fall to the wayside though. If stores remain closed, Switzerland will continue to lose tourism revenues because most foreign visitors, who tend to visit on the weekend,

▼ **EXHIBIT 8.4** Trade Agreements

Name	Countries
European Union	There are 27 member countries of the EU: Austria, Belgium, Bulgaria, Cyprus, Czech Republic, Denmark, Estonia, Finland, France, Germany, Greece, Hungary, Ireland, Italy, Latvia, Lithuania, Luxembourg, Malta, Netherlands, Poland, Portugal, Romania, Slovakia, Slovenia, Spain, Sweden, and the United Kingdom.[23] There are five official candidate countries to join the EU: Croatia, Macedonia, Turkey, Iceland, and Montenegro.
NAFTA	United States, Canada, and Mexico.
CAFTA	United States, Costa Rica, the Dominican Republic, El Salvador, Guatemala, Honduras, and Nicaragua.
Mercosur	Full members: Argentina, Brazil, Paraguay, Uruguay, and Venezuela.
ASEAN	Brunei Darussalam, Cambodia, Indonesia, Laos, Malaysia, Myanmar, Philippines, Singapore, Thailand, and Vietnam.

France is the only place on the globe IKEA is not open on Sundays. Notice times for "Dimanche", the French word for Sunday, is absent from the store hours sign.

trade agreements
Intergovernmental agreements designed to manage and promote trade activities for specific regions.

trading bloc
Consists of those countries that have signed a particular trade agreement.

are accustomed to shopping on Sundays. Opening retail stores on Sundays could mean increased consumption and wages for workers who work more hours as well as employment for more people. But the loss of a day traditionally designated for family time and relaxation might be something the country cannot abide.[27] There may be no completely right answer to this dilemma, but global marketers clearly must be aware of the regulations and cultural norms of the countries they enter.

One important cultural classification scheme that firms can use is Geert Hofstede's cultural dimensions concept, which sheds more light on these underlying values. Hofstede believes cultures differ on five dimensions:[28]

1. **Power distance:** Willingness to accept social inequality as natural.

2. **Uncertainty avoidance:** The extent to which the society relies on orderliness, consistency, structure, and formalized procedures to address situations that arise in daily life.

3. **Individualism:** Perceived obligation to and dependence on groups.

4. **Masculinity:** The extent to which dominant values are male oriented. A lower masculinity ranking indicates that men and women are treated equally in all aspects of society; a higher masculinity ranking suggests that men dominate in positions of power.

5. **Time orientation:** Short- versus long-term orientation. A country that tends to have a long-term orientation values long-term commitments and is willing to accept a longer time horizon for, say, the success of a new product introduction.

To illustrate two of the five dimensions, consider the data and graph in Exhibit 8.5. Power distance is on the vertical axis and individualism is on the horizontal axis. Several Latin American countries, including Brazil, cluster high on power distance but low on individualism; the United States, Australia, Canada, and the United

> IKEA stores across the globe are open seven days a week— except in France.

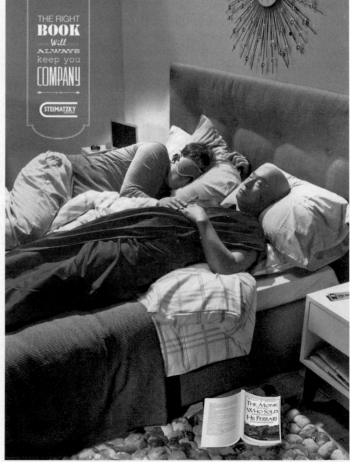

These ads from Steimatzky, the oldest and largest chain bookstore chain in Israel, depict ads that are highly feminine (left) and masculine (right).

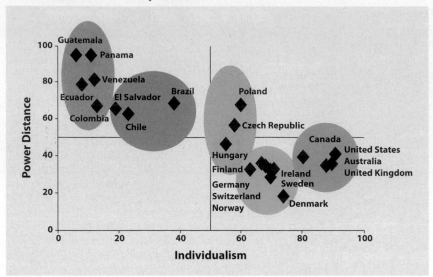

▼ **EXHIBIT 8.5** Country Clusters

Source: Based on data available at http://www.geert-hofstede.com. Data from: Geert Hofstede, *Culture's Consequences,* 2nd ed. (Thousand Oaks, CA: Sage, 2001), Reprinted with permission of Geert Hofstede.

that the situation or context means much more than mere words. For instance, business relationships in China often are formalized by just a handshake, and trust and honor are often more important than legal arrangements.

Overall, culture affects every aspect of consumer behavior: why people buy; who is in charge of buying decisions; and how, when, and where people shop. After marketing managers have completed the four parts of the market assessment, they are better able to make informed decisions about whether a particular country possesses the necessary characteristics to be considered a potential market for the firm's products and services. In the next section, we detail the market entry decision process, beginning with a discussion of the various ways firms might enter a new global market. Adding Value 8.1 gets the discussion started with one illustrative example.

Kingdom, in contrast, cluster high on individualism but low on power distance. Using this information, firms should expect that if they design a marketing campaign that stresses equality and individualism, it will be well accepted in English-speaking countries, all other factors being equal, but not be as well received in Latin American countries.

We also find that China scores very high on its time orientation but low in individualism; India has medium to high levels on all five dimensions; and Russia posts notably high

LO 8-2 Understand the marketing opportunities in BRIC countries.

The Appeal of the BRIC Countries

Changes in technology, especially communications, have been a driving force for growth in global markets for decades. The

> [**Sounds and images from across the globe are delivered to TV sets, radios, and computers in real time, which enables receivers in all parts of the world to observe how others live, work, and play.**]

uncertainty avoidance and power distance scores. Hofstede is careful to warn that these scores are informative only in a comparative sense, but marketers clearly can use them to design strategies for the varied, promising, BRIC growth markets.[29]

Another means of classifying cultures distinguishes them according to the importance of verbal communication.[30] In the United States and most European countries, business relationships are governed by what is said and written down, often through formal contracts. In countries such as China and South Korea, however, most relationships rely on nonverbal cues, so

telegraph, radio, television, computer, and Internet have increasingly connected distant parts of the world. Today, communication is instantaneous. Sounds and images from across the globe are delivered to TV sets, radios, and computers in real time, which enables receivers in all parts of the world to observe how others live, work, and play.

Perhaps the greatest change facing the global community in recent years has been the growth and expansion of four countries that together have come to be known as the BRIC countries: Brazil, Russia, India, and China. Let's examine each in turn.

Adding Value 8.1

Brightening Smiles across the Globe

Known best for its toothpaste, the Colgate-Palmolive Company provides oral, personal, and home care products and pet nutrition products to consumers around the globe.[31] Colgate's strategic plan includes international growth, and the company has built brand loyalty and market share in emerging markets as well as a global leadership position for the sales of toothpaste and toothbrushes. The roots of this success lie in Colgate's commitment to understanding local tastes, educating consumers about the importance of better oral hygiene, developing relationships with dental professionals, and supporting communities.

In India, for example, Colgate researchers spent two days in a rural village studying the habits and values of inhabitants. The main insight: Mothers hoped desperately for better lives for their children. The resulting campaign stressed the health implications of good oral care habits and offered opportunities for scholarships. In other countries, similar interactions with locals have spawned ideas for new products, including a highly energy-efficient toothbrush manufacturing plant in China that adheres to the highest standards of environmental protection. Visits with storeowners in rural Russia led to new packaging options for use in small, crowded shops.

In addition to consumers and store owners, Colgate builds bonds with dental professionals, who are in a position to endorse the brand and provide product samples. These relationships have prompted significant numbers of dentists and hygienists in Brazil, India, and China to recommend Colgate over any other brand to patients. In the United States, Colgate is creating new ties with hygienists by providing oral health education tools and inviting their participation in the company's oral health advisory board.

Colgate's commitment to community support stems from its global values of caring, continuous improvement, and global teamwork. In the United Kingdom, the company teamed with the international retailer Tesco in a customizable Share a Smile program that benefits local communities. A partnership in the African country of Malawi promoted healthy oral care habits.

Using Bollywood actors Shahid Kapoor and Genelia D'Souza, Colgate promotes Max Fresh as part of its international growth strategy, which is based on building brand loyatly and market share in emerging markets like India.

By paying close attention to the unique sociocultural characteristics of various countries and honing its global product strategies, Colgate is able to compete successfully in global and emerging markets, despite the aggressive competition in consumer product markets and the challenging economic conditions worldwide.

Brazil[32] Long a regional powerhouse, Brazil's ability to weather, and even thrive, during the most recent economic storm has transformed it into a global contender. Currently, Brazil is the world's seventh largest economy, but predicted growth rates indicate it will move into the fifth spot within a few years. This growth has been aided by a large, literate population and the impositions of social programs that have allowed more than half of the 190 million Brazilians to enter the middle class. This large South American democracy welcomes foreign investors.

Russia[33] The relations between the United States and Russia are a little more complicated than for Brazil. Since the fall of the former Soviet Union, Russia has undergone multiple up- and downturns in its economy. However, its overall growth prospects appear promising, especially as a consumer market. Long denied access to consumer goods, the well-educated population exhibits strong demand for U.S. products and brands. In particular, the number of Russian Internet users, presently at 60 million, is growing at a rate of approximately 15 percent annually. Russia is likely to become Europe's largest online

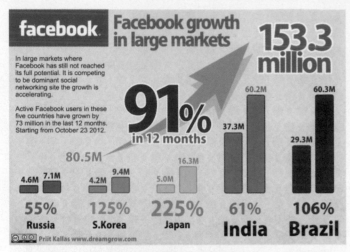

facebook

Facebook growth in large markets

153.3 million

In large markets where Facebook has still not reached its full potential. It is competing to be dominant social networking site the growth is accelerating.

Active Facebook users in these five countries have grown by 73 million in the last 12 months. Starting from October 23 2012.

91% in 12 months

80.5M

4.6M 7.1M	4.2M 9.4M	5.0M 16.3M	37.3M 60.2M	29.3M 60.3M
55% Russia	**125%** S.Korea	**225%** Japan	**61%** India	**106%** Brazil

Priit Kallas www.dreamgrow.com

Facebook and the use of social media marketing are a growing phenomena worldwide.

Source: http://www.dreamgrow.com/social-media-trends-2013-1-5-billion-people-using-facebook/.

market in the next few years. The country also is negotiating to enter the WTO to improve trade relations with other countries. Russia still faces an aging population and low birth rates. If these trends persist, Russia's population could decline by one-third in the next half-century. At the same time, corruption is widespread, creating ethical dilemmas for firms trying to market their goods and services.

India[34]

With more than 1.1 billion people, or approximately 15 percent of the world's population, together with expanding middle and upper classes, India is one of the world's fastest growing markets. With a median age of 25 years, India has one of the youngest populations in the world. Its young inhabitants increasingly are adopting global attitudes while living in growing urban centers and shopping at large malls. The well-educated modern generation is largely fluent in English, and

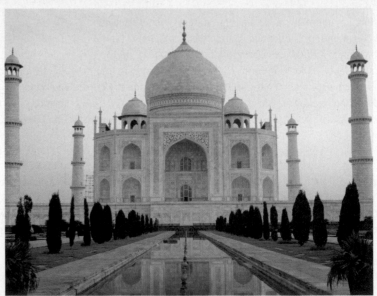

In which of the BRIC countries does each of these classic structures reside?

Like other countries in which McDonald's thrives, Brazil has a strong and growing middle class.

the highly skilled workforce holds great attraction for firms that hope to expand using local talent, especially in technical fields.

India's retail environment is still dominated by millions of small stores and lacks modern supply chain management facilities and systems.[35] Recent changes by the Indian government, however, have the potential to significantly modernize the retail landscape. Foreign retailers that carry multiple brands, like Walmart, are now allowed to own up to 51 percent of joint ventures in India, whereas previously these retailers were permitted only to enter into wholesale joint ventures. Also, retailers that carry only their own brand, like Nike, can now own 100 percent of their Indian businesses, whereas in the past they were only allowed to own up to 51 percent of a partnership with an Indian company.

China[36] For most of the twentieth century, China experienced foreign occupation, civil unrest, major famine, and a strict one-party Communist regime. However, since 1978, China's leadership, while maintaining communist political ideals, has embraced market-oriented economic development, which has led to startlingly rapid gains. For many Chinese, recent developments have dramatically improved their living standards and their levels of personal freedom. Increasing liberalization in the economy has prompted a large increase in China's gross domestic product (GDP); it is now the second-largest economy and the third-largest market for U.S. exports. The U.S. ambassador to China, Gary Locke, has noted: "Everyone that has exported to

The retail landscape in India is changing. Consumers, particularly young ones, are attracted to large modern malls.

Relaxed Indian governmental restrictions now allow foreign retailers that carry their own brand, like Levi's, to own 100 percent of their Indian businesses.

exporting Producing goods in one country and selling them in another.

China reports that what may have started off small builds over time, such that we've seen phenomenal increases in U.S. exports from the United States to China. In fact exports were up some 32 percent last year alone."[37] It makes an excellent target for consumer goods, assuming they can be produced at the right price.

Yet the country continues to suffer from drastically unequal economic distribution, which has led to a significant migrant workforce that subsists on part-time, low-paying jobs. These workers were hit hard by the global financial crisis, which reduced demand for Chinese exports for the first time in years. Furthermore, actual growth of the 1.3 billion-strong Chinese population slowed as a result of government population controls that limit each family to one child. Although China's median age is slightly younger than that of the United States currently, at 34.1 years, the application of the one-child policy means that China is one of the most rapidly aging countries in the world.

Even as vast numbers of U.S. companies actively target the massive Chinese market or explore options for entering it, Ethical & Societal Dilemma 8.1 highlights some challenges that one famous potential entrant faces before it makes this choice.

 check yourself

1. What metrics can help analyze the economic environment of a country?
2. What types of government actions should we be concerned about as we evaluate a country?
3. What are five important cultural dimensions?
4. Why are each of the BRIC countries viewed as potential candidates for global expansion?

ethical & societal dilemma 8.1

Can Social Networking and Censorship Coexist?

By Facebook CEO Mark Zuckerberg's own admission, Facebook grew exponentially for years without a strategic plan for international growth.[38] As the company has matured, however, Facebook has refocused its attention on developing a strategy for China. But attempting to combine the inherent openness of social networking with China's censorship rules presents significant challenges. Add in local competitors and human rights advocacy groups concerned with government backlash against users, and Facebook may be looking at the same fate that has befallen other Western technology companies trying to expand to the East—including such marketing geniuses as Google, eBay, and Twitter.[39]

Successful entry into the Chinese market requires a particular blend of timing, skill, cultural understanding, and political savvy, and these factors may not be quite in alignment for Facebook yet. The timing may be wrong because China's autocratic leaders have

enforced greater controls on social networking and blogging in response to the Arab Spring uprisings. Nor do Facebook executives appear to have a full grasp of the political and cultural nuances of business in China, despite a good track record of respecting local cultural values, such as when it agreed to block content about Nazism in Germany or drawings of Muhammad in Pakistan. And even if Facebook were to navigate these challenges safely, China has a strong, enduring preference for companies owned and run by its own people.

Zuckerberg can (and does) claim that his company will employ diplomacy in China, but censorship issues are highly complex. For instance, how would Facebook respond to retaliation against users who criticize the government?[40] For Google, whose mission statement simply advises, "Don't Be Evil," such questions became all too pertinent when hackers in China gained access to the e-mail accounts of prominent

CEO Mark Zuckerberg (center) claims that Facebook will employ diplomacy in China, but censorship issues are highly complex.

human rights activists. When Western companies have cooperated with the Chinese government, some operations have led to the imprisonment of online activists.

Censorship has global repercussions too. Blocking a comment generated by someone outside of China, such that readers within China cannot see it, will affect access globally. But the question is about more than whether users can enjoy all the fun of Facebook. When a post on Facebook can lead to jail time, it becomes a question of basic human rights.

CHOOSING A GLOBAL ENTRY STRATEGY

When a firm has concluded its assessment analysis of the most viable markets for its products and services, it must then conduct an internal assessment of its capabilities. As we discussed in Chapter 2, this analysis includes an assessment of the firm's access to capital, the current markets it serves, its manufacturing capacity, its proprietary assets, and the commitment of its management to the proposed strategy. These factors ultimately contribute to the success or failure of a market expansion strategy, whether at home or in a foreign market. After these internal market assessments, it is time for the firm to choose its entry strategy.

A firm can choose from many approaches when it decides to enter a new market, which vary according to the level of risk the firm is willing to take. Many firms actually follow a progression in which they begin with less risky strategies to enter their first foreign markets and move to increasingly risky strategies as they gain confidence in their abilities and more control over their operations, as illustrated in Exhibit 8.6. We examine these different approaches that marketers take when entering global markets, beginning with the least risky.

Exporting

Exporting means producing goods in one country and selling them in another. This entry strategy requires the least financial

Rolex exports its watches to countries all over the world from its factory in Switzerland.

risk but also allows for only a limited return to the exporting firm. Global expansion often begins when a firm receives an order for its product or service from another country, in which case it faces little risk because it has no investment in people, capital equipment, buildings, or infrastructure.[41] By the same token, it is difficult to achieve economies of scale when everything has to be shipped internationally. The Swiss watchmaker Rolex sells relatively small numbers of expensive watches all

▼ **EXHIBIT 8.6** Global Entry Strategies

KFC and Pizza Hut are successful global franchisors.

over the world. Because its transportation costs are relatively small compared with the cost of the watches, the best way for it to service any market is to export from Switzerland.

Franchising

Franchising is a contractual agreement between a firm, the **franchisor**, and another firm or individual, the **franchisee**. A franchising contract allows the franchisee to operate a business—a retail product or service firm or a B2B provider—using the

Strategic Alliance

Strategic alliances refer to collaborative relationships between independent firms, though the partnering firms do not create an equity partnership; that is, they do not invest in one another. Therefore, when Cisco Systems Inc. of San Jose, California, and Tata Consultancy Services of Mumbai, India, entered into their strategic alliance, they both continued to develop market-ready infrastructure and network solutions for

> "In addition to sharing financial burdens, a local partner offers the foreign entrant greater understanding of the market and access to resources such as vendors and real estate."

name and business format developed and supported by the franchisor. Many of the best-known retailers in the United States are also successful global franchisors, including McDonald's, Pizza Hut, Starbucks, Domino's Pizza, KFC, and Holiday Inn, all of which have found that global franchising entails lower risks and requires less investment than does opening units owned wholly by the firm. However, when it engages in franchising, the firm has limited control over the market operations in the foreign country, its potential profit is reduced because it must be split with the franchisee, and, once the franchise is established, there is always the threat that the franchisee will break away and operate as a competitor under a different name.

customers, but they relied on each other to provide the training and skills that one or the other might have lacked. At the same time, Cisco maintains alliances with various other companies, including Microsoft, Nokia, IBM, and Accenture.

Joint Venture

A **joint venture** is formed when a firm entering a market pools its resources with those of a local firm. As a consequence, ownership, control, and profits are shared. In addition to sharing financial burdens, a local partner offers the foreign entrant greater understanding of the market and access to resources such as vendors and real estate.

Some countries require joint ownership of firms entering their domestic markets, as is the case with the new regulations affecting multi-line retailers entering India, although many of these restrictions are loosening as a result of WTO negotiations and ever-increasing globalization pressures. Problems with this entry approach can arise when the partners disagree or if the government places restrictions on the firm's ability to move its profits out of the foreign country and back to its home country.

In some cases, joint ventures span several markets, as when the Japanese electronics superstar Sony teamed up with the Swedish communication firm Ericsson. A truly global venture, its central management was located in London, and it maintained R&D facilities in India, the United States, Sweden, Japan, China, Germany, and the United Kingdom. The widespread success of this venture ultimately led Sony to pursue complete ownership of the Sony Ericsson mobile handset line.[42] Adding Value 8.2 highlights an interesting joint venture led by Virgin Galactic to provide space tourism to millionaires all over the world.

Direct Investment

Direct investment requires a firm to maintain 100 percent ownership of its plants, operation facilities, and offices in a foreign country, often through the formation of wholly owned subsidiaries. This entry strategy requires the highest level of investment and exposes the firm to significant risks, including the loss of its operating and/or initial investments. This risk

Adding Value 8.2

Just the Perfect Thing for a Millionaire with Everything: A Trip to Space![43]

The title of this chapter might be too limiting. At least one modern marketing organization promises to go extra-global in its reach; it offers consumers the chance to experience space travel. Virgin Galactic—the space tourism arm of Sir Richard Branson's Virgin conglomerate—promises that someday soon, passengers (which it refers to as astronauts) can enjoy the thrill of rides that will break the sound barrier and enable them to experience weightlessness.

The venture continues to make strides toward achieving its goal of space tourism, including a recent demonstration in which a carrier rocket towed SpaceShip Two up to 46,000 feet, after which its rocket propelled itself another 10,000 feet, moving at approximately 1.2 times the speed of sound. This initial, 16-second test flight represented the first time the vehicle had maneuvered under its own power and the control of pilots rather than simply gliding after being released.

Virgin Galactic is a global joint venture made up of firms on two continents. Virgin remains headquartered in the United Kingdom. The aerospace firm Scales Composites (owned by the United States' Northrop Grumman) designed SpaceShip Two to expand the seating capacity beyond the two-seater SpaceShip One to carry eight (two pilots, six passengers). In addition, these two firms initially collaborated in a U.S.-based joint venture, The Spaceship Company, over which Virgin Galactic has since acquired full control.

For $200,000, you can purchase a trip to space.

Despite missing several self-set deadlines for when commercial space tourism would be available, Virgin Galactic persists in its optimism that the first flights will take place by 2014. Already, nearly 600 consumers have purchased tickets—at a cost of approximately $200,000 each—for early suborbital flights lasting about two and a half hours each. They include Russian oligarchs, Danish royalty, and Ashton Kutcher.

The market for this high-end offering thus is both global and specific. Anyone of any nationality from any region of the world can experience the thrill of heading into space as long as they consider it reasonable and affordable to spend nearly a quarter of a million dollars for a service that lasts about as long as the average Hollywood movie.

A PRODUCT, SERVICE, OR EVEN A RETAILER OFTEN MUST BE POSITIONED DIFFERENTLY IN DIFFERENT MARKETS.

The joint venture between Sony and Ericsson was so successful that Sony purchased the Ericsson mobile handset line.

helps explain why Sony and Ericsson worked together on a joint venture for more than a decade before agreeing to make the Sony Ericsson line a wholly owned subsidiary of Sony. A dramatic economic downturn caused by a natural disaster, war, political instability, or changes in the country's laws can increase a foreign entrant's risk considerably. Many firms believe that in certain markets, these potential risks are outweighed by the high potential returns. With this strategy, none of the potential profits must be shared with other firms. In addition to the high potential returns, direct investment offers the firm complete control over its operations in the foreign country.

As we noted, each of these entry strategies entails different levels of risk and rewards for the foreign entrant. But even after a firm has determined how much risk it is willing to take, and therefore how it will enter a new global market, it still must establish its marketing strategy, as we discuss in the next section.

check yourself
1. Which entry strategy has the least risk and why?
2. Which entry strategy has the most risk and why?

LO 8-4 Highlight the similarities and differences between a domestic marketing strategy and a global marketing strategy.

CHOOSING A GLOBAL MARKETING STRATEGY

Just like any other marketing strategy, a global marketing strategy includes two components: determining the target markets to pursue and developing a marketing mix that will sustain a competitive advantage over time. In this section, we examine marketing strategy as it relates specifically to global markets.

Target Market: Segmentation, Targeting, and Positioning

Global segmentation, targeting, and positioning (STP) are more complicated than domestic STP for several reasons. First, firms considering a global expansion have much more difficulty understanding the cultural nuances of other countries. Second, subcultures within each country also must be considered. Third, consumers often view products and their role as consumers differently in different countries.[44] A product, service, or even a retailer often must be positioned differently in different markets.

For example, Ford has enjoyed U.S. success with its venerable F-Series trucks for many years,[45] but this vehicle is not as appealing to the Indian market, where small cars are more popular. So Ford targeted India's small-car market segment with a new model, the Figo. This small vehicle's technology and architecture were proven in other markets in advance, and its features derived from consumer research and testing on India's roads. Many small-car buyers are first-time automobile owners, so the model also focuses on value for money, offering fuel efficiency, low maintenance costs, and technology enhancements that improve ride and handling on India's rough roads

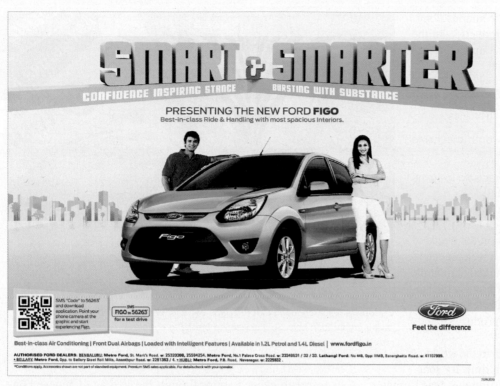

Ford has introduced the Figo to first-time value-driven owners in India.

and crowded streets.[46] Within 15 months of introducing this model, Ford announced it had sold 100,000 Figos in India and planned to expand its Figo exports to 50 additional developing countries.[47] Ford also focuses on other market segments in India with models such as the Ikon, designed to appeal to upwardly mobile urban men looking to purchase an affordable luxury car, and the Fusion, which incorporates the benefits of a sedan and a utility vehicle and targets young families.[48]

Ford's segmentation, targeting, and positioning strategy thus have been successful in India. But the company must continually monitor economic and social trends to protect its position within the market and adjust its products and marketing strategies to meet the changing needs of global markets. In this sense, global marketing is no different from local or national marketing.

Segments and target markets can and should be defined by more than just geography. For example, when Yahoo determines its segmentation and positioning strategies, it relies on research into a segment familiar throughout the world: moms. By working with a global market research firm, Yahoo investigates how moms in Russia, Colombia, China, the United States, Mexico, India, the United Kingdom, Argentina, and France understand and use social media and other modern technologies. This study of global moms also aims to determine how digital technology affects family interactions, such as mealtimes, special occasions, and scheduling.[49] Looking on with great interest is the global product brand Procter &

Gamble, which ran a global Proud Sponsor of Moms campaign during the 2012 Summer Olympics.[50]

When any firm identifies its positioning within the market, it then must decide how to implement its marketing strategies using the marketing mix. Just as firms adjust their products and services to meet the needs of national target markets, they must alter their marketing mix to serve the needs of global markets.

The Global Marketing Mix

During the early stages of globalization, in the 1950s and 1960s, large U.S. firms were uniquely positioned in the global marketplace because they had the skills necessary to develop, promote, and market brand name consumer products. In the 1970s and 1980s, however, Japanese firms dominated the global marketplace because they could exploit their skills in production, materials management, and new product development. Today, retailers such as Zara, financial services firms such as Citicorp, and software firms such as Microsoft are dominating the newest stage of globalization by exploiting their technological skills, while

Thank you, Mom.

Proctor & Gamble targeted moms on a global basis with their Proud Sponsor of Moms campaign, which ran during the 2012 Summer Olympics.

Asian and South and Central American countries dominate the manufacturing of consumer products.[51] In the following, we explore the four Ps (product, price, promotion, and place) from a global perspective.

Global Product or Service Strategies

There are three potential global product strategies:

- Sell the same product or service in both the home country market and the host country.

- Sell a product or service similar to that sold in home country but include minor adaptations.

- Sell totally new products or services.

The strategy a firm chooses depends on the needs of the target market. The level of economic development, as well as differences in product and technical standards, helps determine the need for and level of product adaptation. Cultural differences such as food preferences, language, and religion also play a role in product strategy planning.

Russia, one of the largest new markets in the world, is notable for its past development, including its long-standing embrace of communism. Consumption was limited, with few foreign options available. However, as this BRIC country moves toward a market-based economy, consumers are happily learning to spend the money they have, even though average monthly income levels hover at around $650. As the retail market expands rapidly, companies closely examine these latest consumers. They have disposable income because they generally live mortgage free; receive heavily subsidized electricity and gas; have very little debt (because credit was not available under communism); and have little interest in saving, because history has taught them that they were likely to lose any pensions they might have saved. Yet the shift to a market economy also has been marked by terrible levels of corruption, unnecessary bureaucracy, significant income disparity, bribery, and uncertain legislation.[52] (For further discussion of a country moving from a communist to a market economy, see the case study at www.mhhe.com/grewalM4e.)

In such varied cultural settings, bringing even the simplest consumer goods to new markets can be challenging. For example, Campbell discovered that though Russia and China are two of the largest markets for soup in the world, cooks in those countries have unique demands. Chinese consumers drink 320 billion bowls of soup each year, and Russian buyers consume 32 billion servings, compared with only 14 billion bowls of soup served in the United States. However, Chinese cooks generally refuse

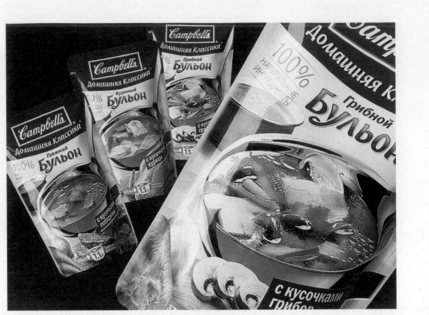

Campbell's research found that Russians eat a lot of soup, and they want time-saving preparation help. So it developed broths to enable cooks to prepare soups with their own flair.

> " Chinese consumers drink 320 billion bowls of soup each year, and Russian buyers consume 32 billion servings, compared with only 14 billion bowls of soup served in the United States. "

to resort to canned soup; though the average Chinese consumer eats soup five times each week, he or she also takes great pride in preparing it personally with fresh ingredients. In contrast, Russian consumers, though they demand very high quality in their soups, had grown tired of spending hours preparing their homemade broths. To identify opportunities in these markets, Campbell sent teams of social anthropologists to study how Chinese and Russian cooks prepare and consume soup. When it faced further hurdles, it entered into a joint venture with the Swire soup company in China. But its efforts in Russia never panned out, forcing Campbell to withdraw after around four years. That is, even with extensive, devoted efforts by an industry giant, global marketing remains a challenge.[53]

The level of economic development also affects the global product strategy because it relates directly to consumer behavior. Consumers in developed countries tend to demand more attributes in their products than do consumers in less developed countries. In the United States, Honda does not offer its line of urban motorcycles, available in Mexico, China, and India, because the product line resembles a motor scooter more than a motorcycle, which does not tend to appeal to American consumers. Motorcycles sold in the United States have more horsepower and bigger frames and come with an array of options that are not offered in other countries.

glocalization
The process of firms standardizing their products globally, but using different promotional campaigns to sell them.

reverse innovation
When companies initially develop products for niche or underdeveloped markets, and then expand them into their original or home markets.

The level of economic development affects the global product strategy. Consumers in the United States prefer larger motorcycles with more amenities, such as the Honda Goldwing on the left with the air bag deploying. Motorcycles in India are generally smaller.

> In parts of Europe, including Belgium, Italy, Spain, Greece, and France, sales are allowed only twice a year, in January and June or July.

Referred to as **glocalization**, some firms also standardize their products globally but use different promotional campaigns to sell them. The original Pringles potato chip product remains the same globally, as do the images and themes of the promotional campaign, with limited language adaptations for the local markets, though English is used whenever possible. However, the company changes Pringles' flavors in different countries, including paprika-flavored chips sold in Italy and Germany.[54]

Global expansion can move in various directions. In **reverse innovation**, for example, companies initially develop products for niche or underdeveloped markets and then expand them into their original or home markets. For example, General Electric realized that adapting medical diagnostic equipment that had been developed in the United States to sell it in India was ineffective. Few Indian medical providers had sufficient resources to pay $20,000 for the massive machinery. Therefore, GE undertook innovation specific to the Indian market to develop a battery-operated, portable EKG (electrocardiogram) machine for $500. Then it realized that the small, affordable machines would appeal as well to U.S. emergency medical personnel in the field and therefore globalized its offer.[55]

Firms also can just market an existing product "as is" in all foreign markets. Ford Motor Co., for example, envisions a world car that will sell everywhere, as we discuss in Adding Value 8.3.

Global Pricing Strategies
Determining the selling price in the global marketplace is an extremely difficult task.[56] Many countries still have rules governing the competitive marketplace, including those that affect pricing. For example, in parts of Europe, including Belgium, Italy, Spain, Greece, and France, sales are allowed only twice a year, in January and June or July. In most European countries, retailers can't sell below cost, and in others they can't advertise reduced prices in advance of sales or discount items until they have been on the shelves more than a month. For firms such as Walmart and other discounters, these restrictions threaten their core competitive positioning as the lowest-cost provider in the market. Other issues, such as tariffs, quotas, antidumping laws, and currency exchange policies, can also affect pricing decisions.[57]

Competitive factors influence global pricing in the same way they do home country pricing, but because a firm's products or services may not have the same positioning in the global marketplace as they do in their home country, market prices must be adjusted to reflect the local pricing structure. Spain's fashion retailer Zara, for instance, is relatively inexpensive in

Spain's fashion retailer Zara is priced higher in the United States than in Spain because it ships its merchandise to the United States from Spain by air.

Adding Value

8.3

Is One World Car Enough for All of Us?[58]

Gertrude Stein famously wrote, "A rose is a rose is a rose." But in the world of global marketing, that line has never seemed to hold particularly true. Is a car the same as a car the same as a car, the world over?

Previous developments would suggest not. Consider, for example, our discussion of the Nano, the 1300-pound mini-car that has enjoyed great success in India. Or recall how Ford had to give up on the idea of moving F-150 trucks overseas. In the United States, where car buyers love huge SUVs, roads have plenty of room for several cars side by side, and the car culture is well developed, so bigger is often thought of as better. In other areas of the world, huge automobiles are unlikely to prompt much excitement.

Ford CEO Alan Mulally seems determined to find a car that everyone will appreciate whether they live in New Delhi, New York, or Newfoundland. He chose the name Fiesta, despite some concerns that the previous iteration of this name was an unpopular, unattractive subcompact in the 1970s. Yet the name also is recognizable, and it does not suffer from any negative translations or connotations in various languages (e.g., Volkswagen's Bora model sounded too much like "boring" in English, so it changed the name to Jetta). Therefore, whatever market it appeared in, the one-world car would be the Fiesta.

This choice offers several benefits for the automaker; in particular, it saves on some of its marketing costs. That is, Ford needs only one logo for the Fiesta and perhaps, even one set of marketing communications in various international markets. In addition, it prevents consumer confusion, which is common in an online world when a company uses the same name for different lines. For example, the Ford Fusion is a sedan in Europe but an SUV in the United States. An online shopper who clicks the wrong link would be terribly confused.

The universal Fiesta first entered the European market and soon became the top-selling small car on that continent. A few years later, Ford rolled out the same car in the United States after investing heavily in determining which features would appeal across the board. For example, it attempted to make the Fiesta aesthetically pleasing across cultures, without increasing costs. Within a year, the Fiesta was the top ranking affordable small car in the U.S. market too.

The Ford Fiesta is designed to be sold similiarly throughout the world. This ad from the U.K. could easily be used in the U.S.

the EU but is priced about 40 percent higher in the United States, putting it right in the middle of its moderately priced competition.[59] Zara is dedicated to keeping production in Spain, but it also must get its fashions to the United States quickly, so it incurs additional transportation expenses, which it passes on to its North American customers. Finally, as we discussed previously in this chapter, currency fluctuations affect global pricing strategies.

> # The number of firms with which the seller needs to deal to get its merchandise to the consumer determines the complexity of a channel.

Global Distribution Strategies Global distribution networks form complex value chains that involve middlemen, exporters, importers, and different transportation systems. These additional middlemen typically add cost and ultimately increase the final selling price of a product. As a result of these cost factors, constant pressure exists to simplify distribution channels wherever possible.

The number of firms with which the seller needs to deal to get its merchandise to the consumer determines the complexity of a channel. In most developing countries, manufacturers must go through many types of distribution channels to get their products to end users, who often lack adequate transportation to shop at central shopping areas or large malls. Therefore, consumers shop near their homes at small, family-owned retail outlets. To reach these small retail outlets, most of which are located far from major rail stations or roads, marketers have devised a variety of creative solutions. Unilever's strategy in India is a prime example of how a global company can adapt its distribution network to fit local conditions. Unilever trained 45,000 Indian women to serve as distributors, who in turn extended Unilever's reach to nearly 100,000 villages and their 3 million residents, all across India. The program generates $250 million each year just in villages that otherwise would be too costly to serve.[60]

Global Communication Strategies The major challenge in developing a global communication strategy is identifying the elements that need to be adapted to be effective in the global marketplace. For instance, literacy levels vary dramatically across the globe. Consider again the BRIC nations: In India, approximately 39 percent of the adult population is illiterate (and for Indian women, the illiteracy rate surpasses 50 percent), compared with 11 percent in Brazil, 7.8 percent in China, and less than 1 percent in Russia.[61] Media availability also varies widely; some countries offer only state-controlled media. Advertising regulations differ too. In an attempt at standardization, the EU recently recommended common guidelines for its member countries regarding advertising to children and is currently initiating a multiphase ban on junk food advertising.[62]

Differences in language, customs, and culture also complicate marketers' ability to communicate with customers in various countries. Language can be particularly vexing for advertisers. For example, in the United Kingdom, a thong is only a sandal, whereas in the United States, it can also be an undergarment. To avoid the potential embarrassment that language confusion can cause, firms spend millions of dollars to develop brand names that have no preexisting meaning in any known language, such as Accenture (a management consulting firm) or Avaya (a subsidiary of Lucent Technologies, formerly Bell Labs).

Within many countries there are multiple variants on a language or more than one language. For example, China has three main languages; the written forms produce meaning through the characters used but the spoken forms depend on tone and pronunciation. Some firms choose names that sound similar to their English-language names, such as Nike, whose Chinese brand name is pronounced *nai ke*. Others focus on the meanings of the characters, such that Citibank is known as *hui qi yinhang,* which means "star-spangled banner bank." Still other firms, such as Mercedes-Benz, have adapted their names for each language: *peng zee* in Cantonese for Hong Kong, *peng chi* in Mandarin for Taiwan, and *ben chi* in Mandarin for mainland China. Naming is a constant challenge in China, especially to avoid the threat that a brand name evokes unwanted connotations, such as when Microsoft realized that the sound of its search engine name, Bing, meant "virus" in China—not the best image for an online company![63]

Even with all these differences, many products and services serve the same needs and wants globally with little or no

Nike's Chinese brand name is pronounced nai ke, which is very similar to the English pronunciation, and means "enduring and persevering."

EVEN AMONG ENGLISH SPEAKERS, THERE CAN BE SIGNIFICANT DIFFERENCES IN THE EFFECTIVENESS OF ADVERTISING CAMPAIGNS.

adaptation in their form or message. Firms with global appeal can run global advertising campaigns and simply translate the wording in the advertisements and product labeling. Furthermore, as Social & Mobile Marketing 8.1 highlights, social networks grant various brands, including Lady Gaga, access to a global market.

Other products require a more localized approach because of cultural and religious differences. In a classic advertisement for Longines watches, a woman's bare arm and hand appear, with a watch on her wrist. The advertisement was considered too risqué for Muslim countries, where women's bare arms are never displayed in public, but the company simply changed the advertisement to show a gloved arm and hand wearing the same watch.

Even among English speakers, there can be significant differences in the effectiveness of advertising campaigns. Take the popular "What Happens in Vegas Stays in Vegas" advertising campaign, which has been very successful and spawned numerous copycat slogans in the United States. Essentially, the U.S. mass market thought the provocative campaign pushed the envelope, but just far enough to be entertaining. However, when the Las Vegas tourism group extended its advertising to the

Social & Mobile Marketing 8.1
Lady Gaga Is More Popular than Barack Obama

Lady Gaga's nearly unsurpassed status in modern pop culture has arrived as the result of her shock tactics, carefully orchestrated media blitz, and expert use of varied social media channels—not to mention some serious musical talent.

Granted, wearing a dress made of meat and creating music videos that veer close to pornography will get anyone's attention, even through traditional media settings. And indeed, nearly 12,000 traditional media stories mentioned her in 2010.[64] But Lady Gaga's worldwide domination involves far more.

From the time she first arrived on the scene in 2008, Gaga has been available to her fans nearly all the time, in a vast array of forums. In the early days, she was constantly available for interviews, and she made content, including videos and photos, available for music bloggers to post. Her iPhone application, Haus of Gaga, acts as a portal for her fans, widely known as Little Monsters, to stay easily connected through exclusive content,

Lady Gaga can mix fashion with her music and get away with it.

videos, news, and chats. She personally manages her daily posts, even when she is backstage at a concert. Gaga keeps her fans interested by speaking to them directly via social media. Her Facebook page is managed by her with the help of others, and she handles her Twitter account on her own. This authentic one-to-one contact has strengthened her personal connection with her fans.[65]

Through these efforts, she has become the most popular living thing on Facebook, with more than 35 million Facebook fans; has more Twitter followers than anyone else, at 10 million, even more than Barack Obama; and has prompted more than 1 billion views on her YouTube channel. She is strategic in her decisions on what she wears and what she does, knowing that people will be talking about it later. Gaga makes sure that she feeds her fans the content she wants them to talk about—namely, just what unexpected thing she has done most recently.

182 SECTION 2 | Understanding the Marketplace

United Kingdom, it found that the ad campaign was not nearly as effective. After conducting focus groups, the group found that British consumers did not find the advertisements edgy enough for their more irreverent British tastes. In response, the advertising agency began studying British slang and phrases to find ways to make the campaign even sexier and more provocative.[66]

check it out!

mhhe.com/GrewalM4e
for study materials,
including quizzes
and videos.

chapter nine

segmentation, targeting,
and positioning

K nown for its highly watched fashion shows, Angel models, and assortment of sexy intimate apparel and sleepwear, Victoria's Secret has reached annual net sales of more than $4 billion and opened more than 1,000 stores.[1] Most of the undergarments that Victoria's Secret sells attempt to conjure romance and seduction, which means they are likely to involve discretionary expenses. Yet women need bras and panties, so the offerings also represent basic necessities.

Determining who its customers are and then balancing the discrepancies between their needs and wants is part of what makes Victoria's Secret so successful. Given the changes in the economy, the company introduced lower-priced offerings, simultaneously reducing inventory.[2] The chain's Everyday line of bras retail for $29.50, about half the price of other styles. Its popular Seven-Way bra functions well with various clothing silhouettes, so that women do not need to purchase separate bras to wear with T-shirts, strapless tops, racer-back shirts, sheer clothing, and so on. After discontinuing it briefly to encourage sales of the various alternatives, Victoria's Secret was quick to expand the line, such that women could buy multi-use bras across various product lines, including its BioFit and Showstopper selections.[3]

continued on p. 186

LEARNING OBJECTIVES

After reading this chapter, you should be able to:

LO 9-1 Outline the different methods of segmenting a market.

LO 9-2 Describe how firms determine whether a segment is attractive and therefore worth pursuing.

LO 9-3 Articulate the differences among targeting strategies: undifferentiated, differentiated, concentrated, or micromarketing.

LO 9-4 Determine the value proposition.

LO 9-5 Define positioning and describe how firms do it.

Victoria's Secret created different product lines to appeal to various consumer segments.

continued from p. 185

Moving beyond these long-running offerings, Victoria's Secret Pink product line, launched in 2004, is designed to appeal to younger shoppers with brightly colored sweatshirts, T-shirts, pajamas, pillows and bedding, sandals, and swimwear as well as undergarments.[4] The Wear Everywhere bra costs $32 for a package of two, and rather than going for glamorous or sexy, Pink clothing is intended to be comfortable and cute.

In Chapter 1, we learned that marketing is about satisfying consumers' wants and needs. Chapter 2 noted how companies analyze their markets to determine the different kinds of products and services people want. But it is not sufficient just to produce such an offering. Firms must also position their offerings in the minds of customers in their target market in such a way that these consumers understand why the thing the company is providing meets their needs better than other, competitive offerings.

This process requires a marketing plan, as we discussed in Chapter 2. As you should recall, the third step of this plan is identifying and evaluating opportunities by performing an STP (segmentation, targeting, and positioning) analysis. This chapter focuses on that very analysis.

The Pink line also aims to expand the reach of Victoria's Secret through cobranding. Pink offers merchandise imprinted with the logos and names of most major U.S. colleges and universities (though it stumbled when it mistakenly printed the University of Michigan slogan, "Hail to the Victors," beneath the Spartan logo of rival Michigan State University).[5] With these options, the brand may attract more male consumers, who enjoy purchasing gifts for their significant others that are both feminine and indicative of support for a favorite National Football League or Major League Baseball team.[6]

Even with these extensions though, Victoria's Secret remains true to its core offering: appealing to women who are more concerned with curves than cost. Its Miraculous push-up bra promises to add two cup sizes to a wearer's bust. And its annual fashion show is a widely anticipated event that features top models sporting ornate, handmade wings (to invoke the image of angels) along with minuscule lingerie. There is nothing cozy or price-conscious on display on the runway. Instead, Miranda Kerr hoisted a heavy, clam-shaped set of wings, surrounding her diamond-encrusted bra worth $2.5 million.[7]

Using price points to segment its market; customizing color, fabrics, and styles to appeal to various target audiences; associating its brand with supermodels, baseball and football teams, and colleges; reaching different shoppers through different stores and assortments; and promoting products through multiple selling channels all help Victoria's Secret, and its varied customers, feel quite in the pink. ■

LO 9-1   Outline the different methods of segmenting a market.

THE SEGMENTATION, TARGETING, AND POSITIONING PROCESS

In this chapter, we discuss how a firm conducts a market segmentation or STP analysis (see Exhibit 9.1). We first outline a firm's overall strategy and objectives, methods of segmenting

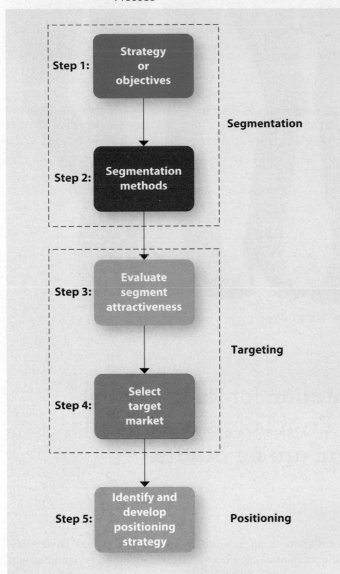

Step 1: **Strategy or objectives**

Step 2: **Segmentation methods**

Segmentation

Step 3: **Evaluate segment attractiveness**

Step 4: **Select target market**

Targeting

Step 5: **Identify and develop positioning strategy**

Positioning

a firm could start with a strategy but then modify it as it gathers more information about various segments' attractiveness.

Step 1: Establish Overall Strategy or Objectives

The first step in the segmentation process is to articulate the vision or objectives of the company's marketing strategy clearly. The segmentation strategy must be consistent with and derived from the firm's mission and objectives as well as its current situation—its strengths, weaknesses, opportunities, and threats (SWOT). Coca-Cola's objective, for instance, is to increase sales in a mature industry. The company knows its strengths are its brand name and its ability to place new products on retailers' shelves, but its primary weakness is that it may not have a product line for newer market segments. Identifying this potentially large and profitable market segment,

Coke Zero targets health-conscious men.

before many of its mainstream competitors can do so, offers a great opportunity. However, following through on that opportunity could lead to a significant threat: competitive retaliation. Coca-Cola's recent choice to pursue health-conscious men with products such as Coke Zero is consistent with its overall strategy and objectives. (See the case study on this text's website for more discussion of Coke's strategy.)

Now let's take a look at methods for segmenting a market.

Step 2: Segmentation Methods

The second step in the segmentation process is to use a particular method or combination of methods to segment the market.

Marketers use geographic, demographic, psychographic, benefits, and behavioral segmentation methods.

the market, and which segments are worth pursuing. Then we discuss how to choose a target market or markets by evaluating each segment's attractiveness and, on the basis of this evaluation, choose which segment or segments to pursue. Finally, we describe how a firm develops its positioning strategy.

Although the STP process in Exhibit 9.1 implies that the decision making is linear, this need not be the case. For instance,

This step also develops descriptions of the different segments, which helps firms better understand the customer profiles in each segment. With this information, they can distinguish customer similarities within a segment and dissimilarities across segments. Marketers use geographic, demographic, psychographic, benefits, and behavioral segmentation methods, as Exhibit 9.2 details.

Denizen jeans by Levi's are made exclusively for Target. What segmentation method is Target using?

> "Kellogg's uses age segmentation for its breakfast cereals: Cocoa Krispies and Fruit Loops are for kids; Special K and All-Bran are for adults."

Soft-drink marketers, for instance, divide the carbonated beverage landscape into caffeinated or decaffeinated, regular (with sugar) or diet, and cola versus something else. This segmentation method is based on the *benefits* that consumers derive from the products.

Geographic Segmentation

Geographic segmentation organizes customers into groups on the basis of where they live. Thus, a market could be grouped by country, region (northeast, southeast), or areas within a region (state, city, neighborhoods, zip codes). Not surprisingly, geographic segmentation is most useful for companies whose products satisfy needs that vary by region.

Firms can provide the same basic goods or services to all segments even if they market globally or nationally, but better marketers make adjustments to meet the needs of smaller geographic groups.[8] A national grocery store chain such as Safeway or Kroger runs similar stores with similar assortments in various locations across the United States. Within those similar stores, though, a significant percentage of the assortment of goods will vary by region, city, or even neighborhood, depending on the different needs of the customers who surround each location.

Demographic Segmentation

Demographic segmentation groups consumers according to easily measured,

▼ **EXHIBIT 9.2** Methods for Describing Market Segments

Segmentation Method	Sample Segments
Geographic	Continent: North America, Asia, Europe, Africa Within U.S.: Pacific, mountain, central, south, mid-Atlantic, northeast
Demographic	Age, gender, income
Psychographic	Lifestyle, self-concept, self-values
Benefits	Convenience, economy, prestige
Behavioral	Occasion, loyalty

objective characteristics such as age, gender, income, and education. These variables represent the most common means to define segments because they are easy to identify and demographically segmented markets are easy to reach. Kellogg's uses age segmentation for its breakfast cereals: Cocoa Krispies and Fruit Loops are for kids; Special K and All-Bran are for adults. It also tends to adopt a gender-based segmentation, such that marketing communications about Special K almost exclusively appeal to women.

Gender plays a very important role in how most firms market products and services.[9] For instance, TV viewing habits vary significantly between men and women. Men tend to channel surf—switching quickly from channel to channel—and watch prime-time shows that are action oriented and feature physically attractive cast members. Women, in contrast, tend to view shows to which they can personally relate through the situational plot or characters and those recommended by friends. Print media is similar: A company such as Lululemon, which sells fitness clothing for both men and women, therefore considers the gender appeal of various magazines when it buys advertising space.

However, demographics may not be useful for defining the target segments for other companies. They are poor predictors of the users of activewear, such as jogging suits and athletic shoes. At one time, firms such as Nike assumed that activewear would be purchased exclusively by young, active people, but the health and fitness trend has led people of all ages to buy such merchandise. And even relatively inactive consumers of all ages, incomes, and education find activewear more comfortable than traditional street clothes.

Rethinking some stereotypical ideas about who is buying thus has become a relatively common trend among firms that once thought their target market was well defined. Adding Value 9.1 highlights how Skechers has broadened its appeal by aiming marketing communications at various segments of potential consumers.

geographic segmentation The grouping of consumers on the basis of where they live.

demographic segmentation The grouping of consumers according to easily measured, objective characteristics such as age, gender, income, and education.

Adding Value 9.1
Skechers Broadening Its Appeal

In its earliest days, Skechers was mostly a lifestyle brand, with hip styles and vibrant designs that appealed to young trendsetters and hipsters, both men and women. When its Shape-Up line arrived in 2010, it offered promises that even if they were a little older and perhaps not quite as in shape as Christina Aguilera, women could improve muscle tone in their legs and buttocks by wearing the rocker-shaped shoe. It began running advertisements in *AARP the Magazine* as well as in *Cosmopolitan* and *GQ*.[10] It hired Kris Jenner as a spokesperson, along with her daughter Kim Kardashian. This success among older women prompted further extensions, including Shape-Ups for men and girls.[11]

Skechers has expanded into more athletic arenas to market itself as an alternative for sports, not just lifestyle. Joe Montana appears in televised ads, and the 2012 Super Bowl featured a prominent commercial with Mark Cuban, the outspoken owner of the Dallas Mavericks, introducing Skechers' latest GOrun line of shoes.[12]

The comparison of its Super Bowl commercials is telling. Whereas in 2011, the ad featured Kim Kardashian, which prominently focused on her physique, the 2012 version puts a small dog in sneakers. Thus the company is trying to appeal to multiple segments.

Skechers creates shoes that appeal to several target markets, including kids.

psychographics
Used in segmentation; delves into how consumers describe themselves; allows people to describe themselves using those characteristics that help them choose how they occupy their time (behavior) and what underlying psychological reasons determine those choices.

Psychographic Segmentation

Of the various methods for segmenting, or breaking down, the market, **psychographics** is the one that delves into how consumers actually describe themselves. Usually marketers determine (through demographics, buying patterns, or usage) into which segment an individual consumer falls. Psychographics studies how people self-select, as it were, based on the characteristics of how they choose to occupy their time (behavior) and what underlying psychological reasons determine those choices.[13] For example, a person might have a strong need for inclusion or belonging, which motivates him or her to seek out activities that involve others, which in turn influences the products he or she buys to fit in with the group. Determining psychographics involves knowing and understanding three components: self-values, self-concept, and lifestyles.

Self-values are goals for life, not just the goals one wants to accomplish in a day. They are the overriding desires that drive how a person lives his or her life. Examples might be the need for self-respect, self-fulfillment, or a specific sense of belonging.

> "A person who has a goal to belong may see, or want to see, himself as a fun-loving, gregarious type whom people wish to be around."

This motivation causes people to develop self-images of how they want to be and then images of a way of life that will help them arrive at these ultimate goals. From a marketing point of view, self-values help determine the benefits the target market may be looking for from a product. The underlying, fundamental, personal need that pushes a person to seek out certain products or brands stems from his or her desire to fulfill a self-value.

People's self-image, or **self-concept**, is the image people ideally have of themselves.[14] For instance, a person who has a goal to belong may see, or want to see, himself as a fun-loving, gregarious type whom people wish to be around. Marketers often make use of this particular self-concept through communications that show their products being used by groups of laughing people who are having a good time. The connection emerges between the group fun and the product being shown and connotes a lifestyle that many consumers seek.

Lifestyles, the third component of people's psychographic makeup, are the way we live.[15] If values provide an end goal and self-concept is the way one sees oneself in the context of that goal, lifestyles are how we live our lives to achieve goals.

One of the most storied lifestyles in American legend is the Harley way of life. The open road, wind in your hair, rebelling against conventions—the image nearly always depicted men like Dennis Hopper in *Easy Rider*. But the notions of freedom, rebellion, and standing out from a crowd vastly appeal to all sorts of people. In response, Harley-Davidson has shifted its STP methods to define four main target markets: core (white men older than 35 years), young adults (both genders, 18–34 years), women (white and older than 35 years), and diverse (men and women, African American and Hispanic, older than 35 years).[16]

For women, for example, it encourages lifestyle events such as Garage Parties, women's-only social gatherings hosted in the evenings at dealerships to teach women the basics of motorcycling. The company publication *We Ride* focuses solely on female Hogs, and the HD-1 Customization website offers a separate process for women to build their cycles to match their build, power preferences, and color desires.[17]

The most widely used tool to support such psychographic segmentation efforts is **Value and Lifestyle Survey, VALS™**, owned and operated by Strategic Business Insights (SBI).[18] Consumers can be classified into the eight segments shown in Exhibit 9.3 based on their answers to the questionnaire

Marketers such as Benetton want their ads to appeal to people's self-concepts: "I'm like them (or I want to be like them), so I should buy their products."

(http://www.strategicbusinessinsights.com/vals/presurvey .shtml). The vertical dimension of the VALS framework indicates level of resources, including income, education, health, energy level, and degree of innovativeness. The upper segments have more resources and are more innovative than those on the bottom.

The horizontal dimension shows the segments' primary psychological motivation for buying. Consumers buy products and services because of their primary motivations—that is, how they see themselves in the world and how that self-image governs their activities. The three primary motivations of U.S. consumers are ideals, achievement, and self-expression. People who are primarily motivated by ideals are guided by knowledge and principles. Those who are motivated by achievement look for products and services that demonstrate success to their peers. Consumers who are primarily motivated by self-expression desire social or physical activity, variety, and risk.

VALS also enables firms to identify target segments and their underlying motivations. It shows correlations between psychology and lifestyle choices. For instance, a European luxury automobile manufacturer used VALS to identify online, mobile applications that would appeal to affluent, early-adopter consumers within the next five years.[19] The VALS

analysis enabled the company to prioritize the most promising applications to develop. In another case, VALS was used to help a medical center identify customers most interested and able to afford cosmetic surgery. Based on the underlying motivations of its target customers, the center and its ad agency developed an ad campaign so successful that it had to be pulled early to avoid overbooking at the surgical center.

Firms are finding that psychographic segmentation schemes like VALS are often more useful for predicting consumer behavior than are demographics. This is because people who share demographics often have very different psychological traits. Take, for example, Jack and John, both 30-year-old, married, college graduates. Demographically, they are the same, but Jack is

self-values Goals for life, not just the goals one wants to accomplish in a day; a component of *psychographics* that refers to overriding desires that drive how a person lives his or her life.

self-concept The image a person has of him- or herself; a component of *psychographics*.

lifestyles A component of *psychographics;* refers to the way a person lives his or her life to achieve goals.

Value and Lifestyle Survey (VALS™) A psychographic tool developed by SRI Consulting Business Intelligence; classifies consumers into eight segments: innovators, thinkers, believers, achievers, strivers, experiencers, makers, or survivors.

Using lifestyle segmentation, Harley-Davidson has four main target markets: On the left is its core segment, consisting of white men older than 35 years. On the right are white women older than 35 years.

> # BECAUSE MARKETING IS ALL ABOUT SATISFYING CONSUMERS' NEEDS AND WANTS, DIVIDING THE MARKET INTO SEGMENTS WHOSE NEEDS AND WANTS ARE BEST SATISFIED BY THE PRODUCT BENEFITS CAN BE A VERY POWERFUL TOOL.

▼ **EXHIBIT 9.3** VALS Framework

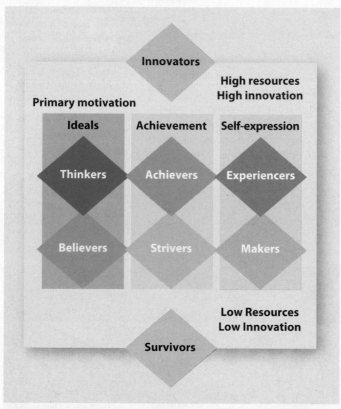

Source: Reprinted with permission of Strategic Business Insights (SBI); www.strategicbusinessinsights.com/VALS.

risk-averse and John is a risk taker. Jack is socially conscious and John is focused on himself. Lumping Jack and John together as a target does not make sense because the ways they think and act are totally different from each other.

There are limitations to using psychographic segmentation, however. Psychographics are more expensive as a means to identify potential customers. With demographics, for example, a firm like Nike can easily identify its customers as, say, men or women and then direct its marketing strategies to each group differently. The problem is that not all men are alike, as we saw with Jack and John. Women are not all alike either! To identify VALS Thinkers or Makers, companies use the VALS questionnaire in surveys or focus groups. Then VALS provides segment descriptions, linkages with consumer product and media data, communication styles, and zip code locations.[20]

Benefit Segmentation **Benefit segmentation** groups consumers on the basis of the benefits they derive from products or services. Because marketing is all about satisfying consumers' needs and wants, dividing the market into segments whose needs and wants are best satisfied by the product benefits can be a very powerful tool.[21] It is effective and relatively easy to portray a product's or service's benefits in the firm's communication strategies. Social & Mobile Marketing 9.1 describes how Heinz is using social media to convey the specific benefits of its new balsamic vinegar ketchup.

Hollywood in particular is a constant and effective practitioner of benefit segmentation. Although all movies may seem

It is just as easy to identify Thinkers (left) as it is Makers (right). A person is given the VALS questionnaire, and the VALS program at SRIC-BI runs the answers through the computer for scoring to determine the VALS type.

Hollywood uses benefit segmentation to segment moviegoers. Fans of Men in Black *go because they love action movies.*

to provide the same service—entertainment for a couple of hours—film producers know that people visit the theater or rent films to obtain a vast variety of benefits, and market them accordingly. Need a laugh? Try the latest comedy from Adam Sandler or Melissa McCarthy. Want to cry and then feel warm and fuzzy? Go to a romantic movie starring Katherine Heigl, for by the time you leave the theater, you are likely to feel quite happy because the lead characters will have faced obstacles, overcome them, and ultimately found love.

Behavioral Segmentation **Behavioral segmentation** divides customers into groups on the basis of how they use the product or service. Some common behavioral measures include occasion and loyalty.

Occasion. Behavioral segmentation based on when a product or service is purchased or consumed is called **occasion segmentation**. Men's Wearhouse uses this type of segmentation to develop its merchandise selection and its promotions. Sometimes men need a suit for their everyday work, but other suits are expressly for special occasions such as a prom or a wedding. Snack food companies such as Frito-Lay also make and promote snacks for various occasions—individual servings of potato chips for a snack on the run but 16-ounce bags for parties.

Loyalty. Firms have long known that it pays to retain loyal customers. Loyal customers are those who feel so strongly that the firm can meet their relevant needs best that any competitors are virtually excluded from their consideration; that is, these customers buy almost exclusively from the firm. These loyal customers are the most profitable in the long term.[22] In light of the high cost of finding new customers and the profitability of loyal customers, today's companies are using **loyalty segmentation** and investing in retention and loyalty initiatives to retain their most profitable customers.

Airlines definitely believe that not all customers are created equal. At United Airlines, customers who have flown the most miles with the company, the Premier Executive 1K, receive guaranteed reservations even on sold-out flights, priority check-in, special seating priorities, dedicated reservation services and priority waitlist status.[23] According to Hollywood, flying 10 million miles, like George Clooney's character in *Up in the Air,* even gets you a dedicated customer service line.[24] None of these special services are available to the occasional flyer.

benefit segmentation The grouping of consumers on the basis of the benefits they derive from products or services.

behavioral segmentation A segmentation method that divides customers into groups based on how they use the product or service. Some common behavioral measures include occasion and loyalty.

occasion segmentation A type of behavioral segmentation based on when a product or service is purchased or consumed.

loyalty segmentation Strategy of investing in loyalty initiatives to retain the firm's most profitable customers.

Using Multiple Segmentation Methods Although all segmentation methods are useful, each has its unique advantages and disadvantages. For example, segmenting by demographics and geography is easy because information about who the customers are and where they are located is readily available, but these characteristics don't help marketers determine their customers' needs. Knowing what benefits customers are seeking or how the product or service fits a particular lifestyle is important for designing an overall marketing strategy, but such segmentation schemes present a problem for marketers

Airlines use a loyalty segmentation strategy to attract frequent fliers. It costs less for frequent flyer members with more miles to have access to airlines' elite lounges.

Social & Mobile Marketing 9.1
Trials of a Bottle of Ketchup[25]

When you sell a product whose recipe has not ever really changed, it can be hard to create much excitement or buzz. But the rarity of changes also means that virtually any move you make provokes commentary. When Heinz Ketchup changed its label in 2009, replacing the picture of a gherkin that had been there since the 1890s with a ripe tomato, there were some complaints. But the brand also enjoyed a bit more press than was usual, which helped it emphasize a key selling point: that all its ketchup was made from tomatoes the company had grown from seed.

The change in that case was related to packaging, not the contents of the bottle. To build buzz about an entirely new flavor—Heinz Tomato Ketchup Blended with Balsamic Vinegar—Heinz realized it needed an entirely new approach. As consumer goods firms have learned from several examples of failed flavor changes (e.g., New Coke), it's never a good idea to eliminate old favorites. Rather, Heinz left traditional bottles on shelves and offered a limited release of the balsamic version to its faithful fan base. To define those customers, it went beyond simple purchase counts or segmentation based on any demographic considerations. It prioritized people who followed the Heinz Ketchup Facebook page.

For those who had already indicated their loyalty, Heinz granted the right to order a $2.49 bottle of the limited-edition ketchup (with a $2 shipping fee), compared with $1.89 for the regular flavor. If consumers purchased a bottle online through Facebook, they received

Heinz extensively used Facebook to introduce its new Ketchup Blended with Balsamic Vinegar.

25 cents off and a free sample of the new Heinz Dip 'N Squeeze Ketchup package. Heinz Ketchup Blended with Balsamic Vinegar was available for purchase on Facebook from November 14 through December, when it also became available at select retailers (including Walmart, Safeway, and other regional stores). The limited edition offering would be available in stores through March, then offered permanently, depending on the demand.

At least, that was the plan. On November 14, the Facebook launch of Heinz Ketchup Blended with Balsamic Vinegar was disrupted by unforeseen technical difficulties. Heinz received an overwhelming response from consumers placing orders for the balsamic ketchup via Facebook, which led to the technical difficulties. The plan was to resume the offering within 24 hours. The online buzz began, but not quite in the way Heinz had hoped. Consumers complained directly on the page. Heinz responded to fans on the Facebook page, notifying them of the technical difficulties. Everyone who contacted Heinz on the Heinz Ketchup Facebook wall on November 14 and 15 received a free bottle with their order plus free shipping. On a social network, even a few hours' delay seems like an eternity.

The Heinz Ketchup Facebook page received 86,000 new likes during the balsamic ketchup promotion period. Clearly, these potential customers do not fit into the other segmentation schemes. They have self-selected into a segment based on a perceived *benefit*.

attempting to identify specifically which customers are seeking these benefits. Thus, firms often employ a combination of segmentation methods, using demographics and geography to identify and target marketing communications to their customers, then using benefits or lifestyles to design the product or service and the substance of the marketing message.

One very popular mixture of segmentation schemes is geodemographic segmentation. Based on the adage "birds of a feather flock together," **geodemographic segmentation** uses a combination of geographic, demographic, and lifestyle characteristics to classify consumers. Consumers in the same neighborhoods tend to buy the same types of cars, appliances, and apparel and shop at the same types of retailers. Two of the

most widely used tools for geodemographic segmentation are PRIZM (Potential Rating Index by Zip Market), developed by Nielsen Claritas (www.mybestsegments.com), and ESRI's (www.esri.com) Tapestry. Using detailed demographic data and information about the consumption and media habits of people who live in each U.S. block tract (zip code + 4), PRIZM can identify 66 geodemographic segments or neighborhoods. Each block group then can be analyzed and sorted by more than 60 characteristics, including income, home value, occupation, education, household type, age, and several key lifestyle variables. The information in Exhibit 9.4 describes two PRIZM clusters.

Geodemographic segmentation can be particularly useful for retailers because customers typically patronize stores close to

geodemographic segmentation The grouping of consumers on the basis of a combination of geographic, demographic, and lifestyle characteristics.

▼ **EXHIBIT 9.4** PRIZM Clusters

Segment Name	Bohemian Mix	Big Sky Families
Segment Number	16	33
Demographics Traits:		
Urbanicity:	Urban	Rural
Median household income:	$55,665	$57,074
Age ranges:	<55	25–44
Presence of kids:	Family mix	HH w/kids
Homeownership:	Renters	Mostly owners
Employment levels:	White collar, Mix	Blue collar, Service, Mix
Education levels:	College grad	Some college
Ethnic diversity:	White, Black, Asian, Hispanic	White
Lifestyle Traits:		
	Shop at Express, 3mo	Own horse
	Own/lease new Volkswagen	Buy children's clothes, 6mos
	Go Snowboarding, 1yr	Own satellite dish
Food & Drink:		
	Drink Corona Extra beer, 1wk	Use baby foods, 1wk
	Buy from Au Bon Pain, 1mo	Buy from family restaurant, child decides, 6mo
	Buy from Dunkin Donuts, 1mo	Buy from Hardee's, 1mo
Media Usage:		
	Read *The New Yorker,* last issue	Read *Hunting,* last issue
	Visit Internet Movie Database (imdb.com), 1mo	Visit nascar.com, 1mo
	Write a blog online, 1mo	Watch The Disney Channel, 1wk

Source: Reprinted with permission of The Nielsen Company.

their neighborhood. Thus, retailers can use geodemographic segmentation to tailor each store's assortment to the preferences of the local community. If a toy store discovers that one of its stores is surrounded by Big Sky Families, it might adjust its offering to include less expensive toys. This kind of segmentation is also useful for finding new locations; retailers identify their best locations and determine what types of people live in the area surrounding those stores, according to the geodemographic clusters. They can then find other potential locations where similar segments reside.

check yourself

1. What are the various segmentation methods?

LO 9-2 Describe how firms determine whether a segment is attractive and therefore worth pursuing.

Step 3: Evaluate Segment Attractiveness

The third step in the segmentation process involves evaluating the attractiveness of the various segments. To undertake this

evaluation, marketers first must determine whether the segment is worth pursuing, using several descriptive criteria: Is the segment identifiable, substantial, reachable, responsive, and profitable (see Exhibit 9.5)?

Identifiable Firms must be able to identify who is within their market to be able to design products or services to meet their needs. It is equally important to ensure that the segments are distinct from one another because too much overlap between segments means that distinct marketing strategies aren't necessary to meet segment members' needs. Thus, Conde Nast is able to identify its market for *Modern Bride* magazine by purchasing mailing lists of people who have bridal registries. It also knows that *Modern Bride* customers tend to be distinct from those who subscribe to *GQ*.

Substantial Once the firm has identified its potential target markets, it needs to measure their size. If a market is too small or its buying power insignificant, it won't generate sufficient profits or be able to support the marketing mix activities. As China's economy started growing, there were not enough middle-class car buyers to push foreign automakers to design an entry-level vehicle. It was only after that number reached substantial numbers that it became worthwhile for them to market to these identified consumers.

▼ **EXHIBIT 9.5** Evaluation of Segment Attractiveness

undifferentiated targeting strategy (mass marketing)
A marketing strategy a firm can use if the product or service is perceived to provide the same benefits to everyone, with no need to develop separate strategies for different groups.

differentiated targeting strategy
A strategy through which a firm targets several market segments with a different offering for each.

> [If, through the firm's distinctive competencies, it cannot provide products or services to that segment, it should not target it.]

Reachable The best product or service cannot have any impact, no matter how identifiable or substantial the target market is, if that market cannot be reached (or accessed) through persuasive communications and product distribution. The consumer must know the product or service exists, understand what it can do for him or her, and recognize how to buy it. If Victoria's Secret fails to tell women that it is offering some less luxurious, more affordable options, shoppers will just walk right past the store and buy basic bras from the Macy's store in the same mall, for example.

Responsive For a segmentation strategy to be successful, the customers in the segment must react similarly and positively to the firm's offering. If, through the firm's distinctive competencies, it cannot provide products or services to that segment, it should not target it. For instance, General Motors (GM) has introduced a line of cars to the large and very lucrative luxury car segment. People in this market typically purchase Porsches, BMWs, Audis, and Lexuses. In contrast, GM has been somewhat successful competing for the middle-priced family-oriented car and light truck segments. Thus, though the luxury car segment meets all the other criteria for a successful segment, GM took a big risk in attempting to pursue this market.

Profitable Marketers must also focus their assessments on the potential profitability of each segment, both current and future. Some key factors to keep in mind in this analysis include

Can General Motors compete with other luxury car companies for the very lucrative luxury car segment?

market growth (current size and expected growth rate), market competitiveness (number of competitors, entry barriers, product substitutes), and market access (ease of developing or accessing distribution channels and brand familiarity). Some straightforward calculations can help illustrate the profitability of a segment:[26]

Segment profitability = (Segment size
× Segment adoption percentage
× Purchase behavior
× Profit margin percentage)
− Fixed costs

where

Segment size = Number of people in the segment

Segment adoption percentage = Percentage of customers in the segment who are likely to adopt the product/service

Purchase behavior = Purchase price × number of times the customer would buy the product/service in a year

Profit margin percentage = (Selling price − variable costs) ÷ selling price

Fixed costs = Advertising expenditure, rent, utilities, insurance, and administrative salaries for managers

To illustrate how a business might determine a segment's profitability, consider Camillo's start-up lawn service. He is trying to determine whether to target homeowners or businesses in a small Midwestern town. Exhibit 9.6 estimates the profitability of the two segments. The homeowner segment is much larger than the business segment, but there are already several lawn services with established customers. There is much less competition in the business segment. So, the segment adoption rate for the homeowner segment is only 1 percent,

▼ **EXHIBIT 9.6** Profitability of Two Market Segments for Camillo's Lawn Service

	Homeowners	Businesses
Segment size	75,000	1,000
Segment adoption percentage	1%	20%
Purchase behavior Purchase price Frequency of purchase	$100 12 times	$500 20 times
Profit margin percentage	60%	80%
Fixed costs	$400,000	$1,000,000
Segment profit	$140,000	$600,000

compared with 20 percent for the business segment. Camillo can charge a much higher price to businesses, and they use lawn services more frequently. The profit margin for the business segment is higher as well because Camillo can use large equipment to cut the grass and therefore save on variable labor costs. However, the fixed costs for purchasing and maintaining the large equipment are much higher for the business segment. Furthermore, he needs to spend more money obtaining and maintaining the business customers, whereas he would use less expensive door-to-door flyers to reach household customers. On the basis of these informed predictions, Camillo decides the business segment is more profitable for his lawn service.

This analysis provides an estimate of the profitability of two segments at one point in time. It is also useful to evaluate the profitability of a segment over the lifetime of one of its typical customers, as Social & Mobile Marketing 9.2 highlights in a different context, namely, the modern music business.

To address such issues, marketers consider factors such as how long the customer will remain loyal to the firm, the defection rate (percentage of customers who switch on a yearly basis), the costs of replacing lost customers (advertising, promotion), whether customers will buy more or more expensive merchandise in the future, and other such factors.

Now that we've evaluated each segment's attractiveness (Step 3), we can select the target markets to pursue (Step 4).

LO 9-3 Articulate the differences among targeting strategies: undifferentiated, differentiated, concentrated, or micromarketing.

Step 4: Select Target Market

The fourth step in the STP process is to select a target market. The key factor likely to affect this decision is the marketer's ability to pursue such an opportunity or target segment. Thus, as we mentioned in Chapter 2, a firm assesses both the attractiveness of the target market (opportunities and threats based on the SWOT analysis and the profitability of the segment) and its own competencies (strengths and weaknesses based on SWOT analysis) very carefully.

Determining how to select target markets is not always straightforward. Exhibit 9.7 illustrates several targeting strategies, which we discuss in more detail next.

Undifferentiated Targeting Strategy, or Mass Marketing
When everyone might be considered a potential user of its product, a firm uses an **undifferentiated targeting strategy**. (See Exhibit 9.7.) Clearly, such a targeting strategy focuses on the similarities in needs of the customers as opposed to the differences. If the product or service is perceived to provide

▼ **EXHIBIT 9.7** Targeting Strategies

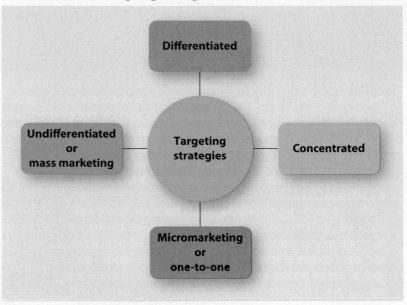

similar benefits to most consumers, there simply is little need to develop separate strategies for different groups.

Although not a common strategy in today's complex marketplace, an undifferentiated strategy is used for many basic commodities such as salt or sugar. However, even those firms that offer salt and sugar now are trying to differentiate their products. Similarly, everyone with a car needs gasoline. Yet gasoline companies have vigorously moved from an undifferentiated strategy to a differentiated one by targeting their offerings to low-, medium-, and high-octane gasoline users.

Differentiated Targeting Strategy
Firms using a **differentiated targeting strategy** target several market segments with a different offering for each (see again Exhibit 9.2). Condé Nast has more than 20 niche magazines focused on different aspects of life—from *Vogue* for fashionistas to *Bon Appetit* for foodies to *GQ* for fashion-conscious men to *The*

Condé Nast has more than 20 niche magazines focused on different aspects of life.

The music business has long been a microcosm that demonstrates changing technology. From record albums to eight-tracks to CDs to digital downloads, its history summarizes the history of changing customer demand and reinventions of the offerings. And that history shows no signs of changing as the industry once again leads the way in shifting its approach by reimagining what it means to sell to customers.

The industry keeps learning the lesson that major record labels are unnecessary if a band can attract fans on its own. But that can be challenging as a band gets started, so companies such as Topspin offer assistance. With Topspin web applications, bands have a route to upload and sell recordings, along with tickets to shows and merchandise. The company handles the accounting and customer contact details, while also offering detailed advice and suggestions about how best to build a fan base.

Perhaps the most notable of Topspin's recommendations is the notion that bands should reject the $.99 single download model popularized by iTunes. Rather than encouraging fans to buy one single for less than a dollar, bands should give away their product for free in the hope of encouraging those fans to buy a $15 T-shirt, a $50 deluxe set of recordings, or even a $100 concert ticket.

Whereas the recent trend has been to unbundle music—that is, rather than buying the entire album, consumers can pick and choose which singles they prefer—Topspin encourage rebundling. Thus it combines free digital downloads with offers for physical products such as posters as well as services such as ticket sales. The average value of transactions on the Topspin website, even when the music is available for free, is $26. If the measure includes sales when customers bought tickets, the average jumps to $88.

The chief executive of Topspin summarizes the idea succinctly:

> You are talking to your fans so you probably know what they want but if you're not sure, ask them! Create something of value for them. It could be as simple as a T-shirt or vinyl or as elaborate as a box set or an in-person experience. But remember not everyone has the same level of fandom or depth of pocketbook. Every day there are people coming to your website who are just entering the "Awareness" phase and there's nothing you're going to do to get them to open their wallet for you. Offer something free, something in the $10 price range, something in the $25 price range, something in the $50 price range, and something in the superfan price range. It turns out the Internet isn't about "going digital" after all, it's about consumer choice. Give your fans a valuable product that fits their budget and level of fandom and they will be happy to support you.

Another digital firm takes a different approach to help musicians evaluate the attractiveness of their fans and potential customers. With the FanTrail application, those musicians set up an easily accessible site for fans. The sites include features such as LoveMail—a function that allows the artist to record a message that gets sent automatically to registered fans' smartphones. Then with the LoveMeter function, that same artist can determine just how active each fan is, measured in terms of purchases and check-ins at concerts. The messages can be precisely targeted, based on fans' location or LoveMeter ranking, which allows artists to reward their biggest, most loyal fans with invitations to secret shows, advance ticket sales, and so forth.

Ian Rogers, CEO of Topspin, believes that if you give customers a valuable product, even if it is free music at first, they will be happy and support you as your fandom and depth of pocketbook increases.

New Yorker for literature lovers to *Golf Digest* for those who walk the links.

Firms embrace differentiated targeting because it helps them obtain a bigger share of the market and increase the market for their products overall. Readers of *Golf Digest* probably are unlike readers of *Architectural Digest* in their interests, as well as in their demographics, such as gender, age, and income. Providing products or services that appeal to multiple segments helps diversify the business and therefore lowers the company's (in this case, Conde Nast's) overall risk. Even if one magazine suffers a circulation decline, the impact on the firm's profitability can be offset by revenue from another publication that continues to do well. But a differentiated strategy is likely to be more costly for the firm.

Concentrated Targeting Strategy

When an organization selects a single, primary target market and focuses all its energies on providing a product to fit that market's needs, it is using a **concentrated targeting strategy**.

Entrepreneurial start-up ventures often benefit from using a concentrated strategy, which allows them to employ their limited resources more efficiently. Newton Running, for instance, has concentrated its targeting strategy to runners—but not all runners. It focuses only on those who prefer to land on their forefeet while running, a style that recently has been suggested as more natural, efficient, and less injury-prone than the style encouraged by more traditional running shoes with their heel-first construction and substantial cushioning. In comparison, though it also is known for its running shoes, Nike uses a differentiated targeting strategy (recall the opening vignette about Nike in Chapter 2). It makes shoes for segments that include basketball and football players and skateboarders as well as fashion-conscious white-collar workers with its subsidiary brand Cole-Haan.

Micromarketing[28] Take a look at your collection of belts. Have you ever had one made to match your exact specifications? (If you're interested, try www.leather-goodsconnection.com.) When a firm tailors a product or service to suit an individual customer's wants or needs, it is undertaking an extreme form of segmentation called **micromarketing** or **one-to-one marketing**.

Such small producers and service providers generally can tailor their offerings to individual customers more easily. But it is far more difficult for larger companies to achieve this degree of segmentation. Major players such as Dell (computers) and Lands' End (shirts) tried to capitalize on Internet technologies to offer custom products. Lands' End let customers choose from a variety of options in the fabric, type of collar, sleeve, shape, and based on the customer's specific measurements—but it halted this service when it could not manage to achieve profitable sales. Dell still allows customers to choose the size, color, and speed of their laptops, though it has backed off its promotions and limits the choice of software included. These adjustments demonstrate the difficulty of micromarketing.

The Internet clearly helps facilitate such a segmentation strategy.[29] Companies can cater to very small segments, sometimes as small as one customer at a time, relatively efficiently and inexpensively (e.g., mortgage and insurance sites provide personalized quotes). An Internet-based company can offer one-to-one service more inexpensively than can other venues, such as retail stores or telephone-based businesses. For example,

> "Readers of *Golf Digest* probably are unlike readers of *Architectural Digest* in their interests, as well as in their demographics, such as gender, age, and income."

Newton Running has concentrated its targeting strategy on runners who seek to land on the forefront.

www.mymms.com allows customers to customize their candy.

made especially for them, which means they'll meet the person's needs exactly. If a tailor measures you first and then sews a suit that fits your shoulders, hips, and leg length exactly, it probably will fit better than an off-the-rack suit that you pick up at a department store. But such products and services are typically more expensive than ready-made offerings and often take longer to obtain. You can purchase a dress shirt in your size at Macy's and wear it out of the store. Ordering a tailored shirt from an online site that allows you to enter in your measurements might take five to six weeks to receive delivery. And if you visited an old-fashioned tailor, the processes of measuring you, ordering the material, and sewing the pants might take several months—at a much higher cost.

frequent fliers of American Airlines can check prices and choose special services online at a fraction of the cost that the company would incur for a phone consultation with a ticket agent.

The Internet also simplifies customer identification. **Cookies**, or small text files a website stores in a visitor's browser, provide a unique identification of each potential customer who visits and details how the customer has searched the site. Marketers also can ask visitors to fill out an online registration form. Using such information, the company can make a variety of recommendations to customers. Amazon.com is renowned for the algorithms it uses to provide recommendations for related products to customers as they browse the site, which match customer profiles to those of other customers. The marketing strategy therefore is customized in real time, using known and accurate data about the customer. Staples offers merchandise at different prices in different parts of the country—simply by asking customers to enter their zip codes.

Customers can even do the work themselves, both to create items for themselves and to find the perfect gifts for others.[30] Mars Chocolate North America's MY M&M's® Brand site (www.mymms.com) lets customers customize their own M&M's® Chocolate Candies with personalized greetings, including messages for birthday parties, sporting events, graduations, and weddings—as well as wedding proposals! Both online and in stores, Build-A-Bear lets young (or not so young) customers design their very own stuffed furry friend with unique clothes, accessories, sounds, and the name printed on its birth certificate.

Some consumers appreciate such custom-made goods and services because they are

LO 9-4   Determine the value proposition.

Step 5: Develop Positioning Strategy

The last step in developing a market segmentation strategy is positioning. Market positioning involves a process of defining the marketing mix variables so that target customers have a clear, distinctive, desirable understanding of what the product does or represents in comparison with competing products.

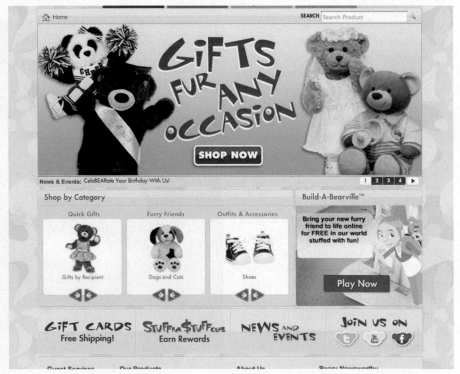

Build-A-Bear lets customers design their own stuffed furry friend with unique clothes, accessories, sounds, and the name printed on its birth certificate.

The positioning strategy can help communicate the firm's or the product's **value proposition**, which communicates the customer benefits to be received from a product or service and thereby provides reasons for wanting to purchase it.

To visualize the value proposition, examine the Circles for a Successful Value Proposition framework in Exhibit 9.8A.[31] The first circle represents the customer needs and wants, the second circle represents the benefits that the company provides (i.e., its capabilities), and the final circle represents the benefits provided by competitors. The best situation is if a firm's product or service offering overlaps with customer needs and wants but suffers no overlap with competitors' offerings (Exhibit 9.8A). The shaded portion reflects the value proposition, or the intersection of what the customer needs and wants with what the firm can offer. Unfortunately, even if the situation depicted in Exhibit 9.8A existed, the product or service then would be successful, so it likely would not be sustainable because competitors would attempt to copy the important product or service attributes and therefore begin to encroach on the firm's value proposition. Maintaining a unique value proposition can be sustained in the long term only in monopoly situations or possibly monopolistic competition situations.

In Exhibit 9.8B, the intersection of customer needs, the benefits provided by our focal firm, and the benefits provided by a competing firm reveal seven specific spaces where a product or service might be located. Let's look at each one in turn, using the offerings of the airline industry as hypothetical examples to understand each space.

Space 1. Representing the firm's value proposition, this space reveals which customer needs are effectively met by the benefits that the firm provides but not by the benefits provided by competitors. That is, there is no overlap between competitors. When airline customers prefer a cattle-call approach to seating, which allows them to choose their own seats on the plane as long as they get an early check-in, they turn to Southwest, and Southwest alone, for their flights.

> ## The best situation is if a firm's product or service offering overlaps with customer needs and wants but suffers no overlap with competitors' offerings.

▼ **EXHIBIT 9.8** Circles for a Successful Value Proposition

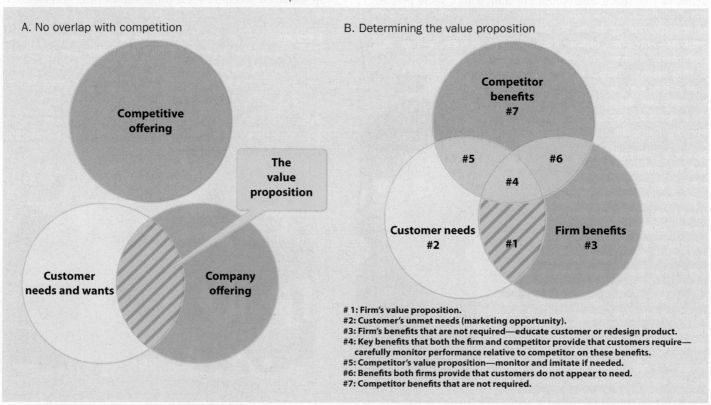

A. No overlap with competition

- Competitive offering
- The value proposition
- Customer needs and wants
- Company offering

B. Determining the value proposition

- Competitor benefits #7
- #5
- #6
- #4
- Customer needs #2
- #1
- Firm benefits #3

1: Firm's value proposition.
#2: Customer's unmet needs (marketing opportunity).
#3: Firm's benefits that are not required—educate customer or redesign product.
#4: Key benefits that both the firm and competitor provide that customers require—carefully monitor performance relative to competitor on these benefits.
#5: Competitor's value proposition—monitor and imitate if needed.
#6: Benefits both firms provide that customers do not appear to need.
#7: Competitor benefits that are not required.

Space 2. These customer needs are unmet. It represents an important marketing opportunity in that the firm could create new products or augment existing services to satisfy these needs better. A direct route between two cities that currently are not connected by any airline represents a prime example of such a space.

Space 3. Customers express little need or desire for these company benefits. The firm thus has several options. It might educate customers about the importance and benefits that it provides with this space, to encourage customers to develop a sense of their need. Alternatively, it could reengineer its approach to stop providing these unwanted benefits, which likely would enable it to save money. For example, when airlines realized that passengers cared little about the appearance of a piece of lettuce underneath the in-flight sandwiches they were served, they saved millions of dollars they had previously spent on unwanted produce.

Space 4. These needs are being met by the benefits of the firm as well as by competitors. Many customers make frequent trips between major cities, like New York and Washington, DC, and many airlines offer multiple direct flights each day between these hubs. Each firm therefore works to compete effectively, such as by offering convenient flight times or striving to increase its on-time rates to make it easier for customers to compare firms on these specific features.

Space 5. This space constitutes the competitor's value proposition: The needs of customers that are met by benefits a competitor provides but not by the benefits provided by our focal firm. For example, only a few airlines host separate lounges for their best customers; a lower-cost airline cannot compete in this space. However, if more and more customers start to make demands for these benefits, the focal firm needs to monitor developments carefully and match some benefits if possible.

Space 6. Although both the focal firm and its competitors provide these benefits, they somehow are not meeting customer needs. The stringent security screening requirements aim to increase passenger safety, but they also represent a significant inconvenience that many fliers associate with airlines rather than federal regulators. Expending significant efforts to educate customers by the focal firm about these needs would also benefit competitors, so they likely are lower in the priority list of spending.

Space 7. Finally, some competitor benefits are either undesired or unnecessary among customers. Similar to Space 3,

the competitor could invest money to educate customers about the importance of these benefits and highlight their needs through advertising and promotional campaigns. If so, the focal firm should recognize that this need is moving to Space 5. Alternatively, the competitor could reengineer its products to eliminate these benefits, in which case it requires no response from the focal firm.

Regardless of their existing space though, firms must constantly and closely monitor their competitors' offerings. If competitors offer features that the firm does not, it is important to determine their importance to customers. Important attributes should be considered for inclusion in the firm's offering—or else they will provide a unique value proposition for competitors.

In Exhibit 9.9, we highlight the elements of developing and communicating a firm's value proposition. The main value proposition components are:

1. Target market

2. Offering name or brand

3. Product/service category or concept

4. Unique point of difference/benefits

Let's focus on a couple of well-known products, Gatorade and 7-Up, and their potential value propositions (brackets added to separate the value proposition components):

- **Gatorade:**[32] To [athletes around the world] [Gatorade] is the [sports drink] that [represents the heart, hustle, and soul of athleticism and gives the fuel for working muscles, fluid for hydration, and electrolytes to help replace what is lost in sweat before, during, and after activity to get the most out of your body].

- **7UP:**[33] To [non-cola consumers] [7UP] is a [non-caffeinated soft drink] that [is light, refreshing, lemon-lime flavored, and has a crisp, bubbly, and clean taste].

What are the value propositions for Gatorade and 7UP?

▼ **EXHIBIT 9.9** Value Proposition Statement Key Elements

	Gatorade	7UP
Target market:	To **athletes around the world**	To **non-cola consumers**
Offering name or brand:	**Gatorade**	**7UP**
Product/service category or concept:	is the **sports drink**	is a **non-caffeinated soft drink**
Unique point of difference/ benefits:	representing the **heart, hustle, and soul of athleticism and gives the fuel for working muscles, fluid for hydration, and electrolytes to help replace what is lost in sweat before, during, and after activity to get the most out of your body.**	that is **light, refreshing, lemon-lime flavored and has a crisp, bubbly, and clean taste.**

LO 9-5 Define positioning and describe how firms do it.

Positioning Methods

Firms position products and services based on different methods such as the value proposition, salient attributes, symbols, and competition.

The positioning strategy can help communicate the firm's or the product's value proposition, the unique value that a product or service provides to its customers, and how it is better than and different from those of competitors. Firms thus position their products and services according to value and salient attributes. **Value** is a popular positioning method because the relationship of price to quality is among the most important considerations for consumers when they make a purchase decision.

Remember that value does not necessarily mean low priced. The watchmaker Patek Philippe uses the advertising tagline, "You never actually own a Patek Philippe. You merely take care of it for the next generation," to encourage buyers to consider its arm candy an investment.[34] The long-running campaign takes on added effectiveness in the modern economic downturn, especially as a way to market a luxury brand in a necessity-focused economy. Other brands that rely on a similar idea of luxury value include Hermès, Chanel, and Mercedes-Benz.

Another common positioning strategy focuses on the product attributes that are most important to the target market. Volvo, the car company traditionally positioned for the safety-conscious driver, wants to stretch its safety image to one focused on driving performance and excitement. The company expects the positioning adjustment to be a long and concentrated effort because so many of Volvo's boxier vehicles remain on the road today, which reinforces its more conservative image. Volvo's goal is not

French retailer Hermès is positioned as a luxury brand, which makes its customers less price-sensitive for its products like this handmade Birkin bag which retails for $9,000.

to abandon the safety notions associated with the brand but rather to expand its image to compete with other top luxury brands.[35]

A well-known symbol can also be used as a positioning tool. What comes to mind when you think of Colonel Sanders, the Jolly Green Giant, the Gerber Baby, or Tony the Tiger? Or consider the Texaco star, the Nike swoosh, or the Ralph Lauren polo player? These symbols are so strong and well known that they create a position for the brand that distinguishes it from its competition. Many such symbols are registered trademarks that are legally protected by the companies that developed them.

Firms can choose to position their products or services against a specific competitor or an entire product/service classification. For instance, 7UP positioned its product as the Uncola to differentiate it from caramel-colored cola beverages such as Pepsi and Coke. Goodrich tires were promoted as the other guys, or the ones without the blimp, to set them apart from Goodyear tires.

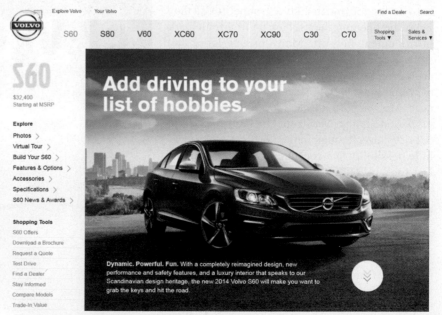

Volvo is repositioning its cars from safe to safe plus performance.

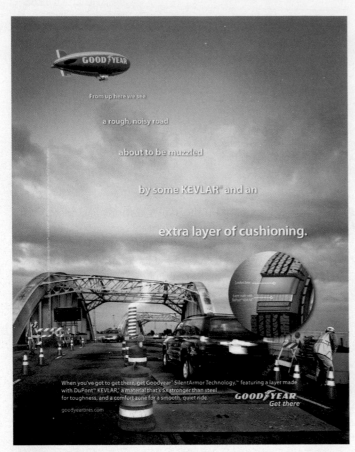

Goodrich positions its tires as the ones without the blimp to set them apart from Goodyear.

steps. Before you read about these steps, though, examine Exhibit 9.10 (Charts A–D), a hypothetical perceptual map of the soft drink industry. A **perceptual map** displays, in two or more dimensions, the position of products or brands in the consumer's mind. We have chosen two dimensions for illustrative purposes: strong versus light taste (vertical) and fun versus healthy (horizontal). Also, though this industry is quite complex, we have simplified the diagram to include only a few players in the market. The position of each brand is denoted by a small circle, and the numbered circles denote consumers' **ideal points**—where a particular market segment's ideal product would lie on the map. The larger the numbered circle, the larger the market size.

To derive a perceptual map such as shown in Exhibit 9.10, marketers follow six steps.

1. **Determine consumers' perceptions and evaluations of the product or service in relation to competitors'.** Marketers determine their brand's position by asking consumers a series of questions about their and competitors' products. For instance, they might ask how the consumer uses the existing product or services, what items the consumer regards as alternative sources to satisfy his or her needs, what the person likes or dislikes about the brand in relation to competitors, and what might

Marketers must be careful, however, that they don't position their product too closely to their competition. If, for instance, their package or logo looks too much like a competitor's, they might be opening themselves up to a trademark infringement lawsuit. Many private-label and store brands have been challenged for using packaging that appears confusingly similar to that of the national brand leaders in a category. Similarly, McDonald's sues anyone who uses the Mc prefix, including McSleep Inns and McDental Services, even though in the latter case there was little possibility that consumers would believe the fast-food restaurant company would branch out into dental services.

Positioning Using Perceptual Mapping

Now that we have identified the various methods by which firms position their products and services, we discuss the actual steps they go through to establish that position. When developing a positioning strategy, firms go through six important

Gatorade uses athletes to compete for target markets in Exhibit 9.10.

make that person choose one brand over another. Exhibit 9.10A depicts the six products using two dimensions (light taste–sweet taste; and less natural–healthy).

2. **Identify the market's ideal points and size.** On a perceptual map, marketers can represent the size of current and potential markets. For example, Exhibit 9.10B uses differently sized ovals that correspond to the market size. Ideal point 1 represents the largest market, so if the firm does not already have a product positioned close to this point, it should consider an introduction. Point 3 is the smallest market, so there are relatively few customers who want a healthy, light-tasting drink. This is not to suggest that this market should be ignored; however, the company might want to consider a niche, rather than mass, market strategy for this group of consumers.

3. **Identify competitors' positions.** When the firm understands how its customers view its brand relative to competitors', it must study how those same competitors position themselves. For instance, POWERade positions itself closely to Gatorade, which means they appear next to each other on the perceptual map and appeal to target market 2 (see Exhibit 9.10C). They are also often found next to each other on store shelves, are similarly priced, and are viewed by customers as sports drinks. Gatorade also knows that its sports drink is perceived to be more like POWERade than like its own Propel

perceptual map
Displays, in two or more dimensions, the position of products or brands in the consumer's mind.

ideal points
The position at which a particular market segment's ideal product would lie on a *perceptual map*.

▼ **EXHIBIT 9.10A** Perceptual Maps

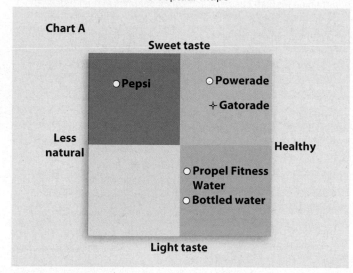

▼ **EXHIBIT 9.10C** Perceptual Maps

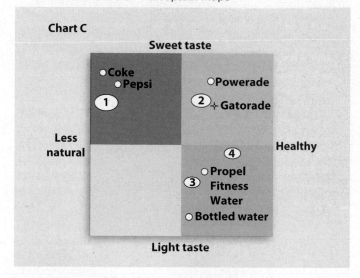

▼ **EXHIBIT 9.10B** Perceptual Maps

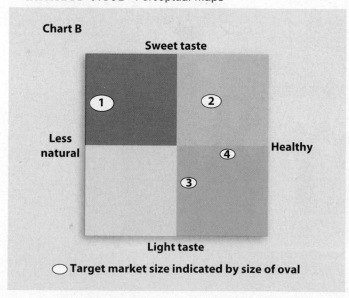

▼ **EXHIBIT 9.10D** Perceptual Maps

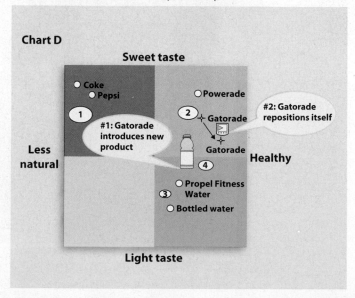

Fitness Water (located near target market 3) or Coke (target market 1).

4. **Determine consumer preferences.** The firm knows what the consumer thinks of the products or services in the marketplace and their positions relative to one another. Now it must find out what the consumer really wants, that is, determine the ideal product or service that appeals to each market. For example, a huge market exists for traditional Gatorade, and that market is shared by POWERade. Gatorade also recognizes a market, depicted as the ideal product for segment 4 on the perceptual map, of consumers who would prefer a less sweet, less calorie-laden drink that offers the same rejuvenating properties as Gatorade. Currently, no product is adequately serving market 4.

Adding Value 9.2
Striving to Encourage the Strivers to Stay[36]

The InterContinental Hotels Group owns several well-known brands, including the Holiday Inn and Crowne Plaza hotel chains. It conducted a $1 billion overhaul of the Holiday Inn brand—only to realize that the Crowne Plaza image was outdated, unfocused, and apparently unappealing to customers. In particular, it identified a target market of young travelers, or strivers, whose needs Crowne Plaza was not meeting.

Using a combination of promotions and advertisements aimed directly at this target market, Crowne Plaza has worked to highlight its key attractions and events likely to captivate their interest. For example, noting that young travelers are highly likely to book their rooms online and through mobile applications, Crowne Plaza allows people to book same-day reservations through their Android, Blackberry, or iPhone applications.

Beyond age and usage, strivers are interesting in terms of their international character. Richard Solomons, the chief executive of the InterContinental Group, noted the chain's recognition that "there is a big customer base in China that wants a brand that gives them the comfort of being part of an international group but is designed in our China office, by our China team, for our Chinese customers." This group also has specific demands for service, including spaces for entertaining for both business and social contacts in their hotels. By including such spaces in the designs of Crowne Plaza hotels, the brand appeals directly to such customers, without doing anything that would damage its image among strivers from other cultures.

The turbulent state of the hotel industry also suggests that Crowne Plaza will need to reconsider some of its offerings, including whether to shut down underperforming sites. Careful marketing research has suggested that segmentation will increase as customers express increasingly specific preferences and demands.

At the same time, there are some appeals that seem almost universal. All the redesigned hotels therefore will feature a pancake-making machine, available for customers' use any time of the day. It may seem like just a pancake, but it's also fun, different, and playful, and that's exactly the image Crowne Plaza is pursuing.

Repositioning isn't easy! But Crowne Plaza is attempting to reposition itself with an exciting image to appeal to young travelers.

5. **Select the position.** Continuing with the Gatorade example, the company has some choices to appeal to the "less sweet sports drink" target market 4. It could develop a new product to meet the needs of market 4 (see Exhibit 9.10D, option 1). Alternatively, it could adjust or reposition its marketing approach—its product and promotion—to sell original Gatorade to market 4 (option 2). Finally, it could ignore what target market 4 really wants and hope that consumers will be attracted to the original Gatorade because it is closer to their ideal product than anything else on the market.

6. **Monitor the positioning strategy.** Markets are not stagnant. Consumers' tastes shift, and competitors react to those shifts. Attempting to maintain the same position year after year can spell disaster for any company. Thus, firms must always view the first three steps of the positioning process as ongoing, with adjustments made in step four as necessary.

Despite the apparent simplicity of this presentation, marketers should recognize that changing their firm's positioning is never an easy task. Some firms might try to change their image in response to a shift in the target market, such as when Skechers realized that older consumers wanted hip lifestyle shoes too. Crowne Plaza has attempted to reposition itself in the other direction, namely, to gain a more vital, exciting image among younger travelers, as Adding Value 9.2 describes. ■

 check yourself

1. What is a perceptual map?
2. Identify the six positioning steps.

check it out!

mhhe.com/GrewalM4e
for study materials,
including quizzes
and videos.

marketing research

When used in games and movies, virtual reality allows people to participate in scenarios they might never encounter in daily life. Special 3D glasses and realistically rendered images create the sensation of being there—whether "there" is in the midst of a military operation, climbing Mt. Everest, or playing a challenging game of tennis. When applied to marketing research, this same technology provides manufacturers with valuable information about how consumers are likely to respond to new products and product displays. Used properly, virtual shopping tools provide more accurate information about customer behaviors than traditional research methods and are more efficient than field testing.[1]

Virtual store testing is not especially new. Companies such as Procter & Gamble (P&G) have been using these

LEARNING OBJECTIVES

After reading this chapter, you should be able to:

LO 10-1 Identify the five steps in the marketing research process.

LO 10-2 Describe the various secondary data sources.

LO 10-3 Describe the various primary data collection techniques.

LO 10-4 Summarize the differences between secondary data and primary data.

LO 10-5 Examine the circumstances in which collecting information on consumers is ethical.

tools to conduct market research for more than a decade.[2] But as the technology has evolved, P&G's reliance on it to create, test, and improve package designs, shelf displays, and store layouts has increased.[3] Today, more than three-quarters of global manufacturers' business initiatives rely on virtual solution tools.

continued on p. 210

continued from p. 209

For P&G, virtual reality centers on life-sized, 3D images of new products as they might appear on a retailer's shelves, which helps create a fully interactive world. As consumers peruse the shelves, sophisticated software analyzes their reactions, providing insight into common responses to packaging and messaging. Product development teams use this information to make improvements early in the design process, which in turn increases the speed to market, reduces the number of costly physical prototypes, and maximizes the chances of success when the product actually goes live.

The technology also allows P&G to create virtual store environments for analyzing product placement strategies. Marketing researchers supply retailers with information and customer feedback from these tests to help them improve customer satisfaction and build sales. The approach can be used for a single product such as a new type of fabric refresher aimed at sports enthusiasts. Or it can be used to research an entire line of new products in a private environment, which enables an innovating firm to protect its strategic marketing decisions from snooping competitors.[4]

Today's refinements in virtual reality for marketing research are making the software easier to use for both business decision makers and communicators. The technology has also evolved to provide remarkably realistic graphics and interactivity, which improve insights into consumer responses.[5] Such advanced forms of market research are helping firms such as Procter & Gamble understand how to serve their customers and business partners better. And better service means better profits. ■

> # The largest U.S.-based marketing research firm, the ACNielsen Company, earns annual worldwide revenues of almost $5 billion.

As the P&G example shows, **marketing research** is a prerequisite of successful decision making. It consists of a set of techniques and principles for systematically collecting, recording, analyzing, and interpreting data that can aid decision makers involved in marketing goods, services, or ideas.[6] When marketing managers attempt to develop their strategies, marketing research can provide valuable information that will help them make segmentation, positioning, product, place, price, and promotion decisions.

Firms invest billions of dollars in marketing research every year. The largest U.S.-based marketing research firm, the ACNielsen Company, earns annual worldwide revenues of almost $5 billion.[7] Why do marketers find this research valuable? First, it helps reduce some of the uncertainty under which they currently operate. Successful managers know when research might help their decision making and then take appropriate steps to acquire the information they need. Second, marketing research provides a crucial link between firms and their environments, which enables them to be customer oriented because they build their strategies by using customer input and continual feedback. Third, by constantly monitoring their competitors, firms can anticipate and respond quickly to competitive moves.

If you think market research is applicable only to corporate or retailing ventures though, think again. Not-for-profit organizations and governments also use research to serve their constituencies better. The political sector has been slicing and dicing the voting public for decades to determine relevant messages for different demographics. Politicians desperately want to understand who makes up the voting public to determine how to reach them. But not only do they want to know your political views; they also want to understand your media habits, such as what magazines you subscribe to, so they can target you more effectively.

To do so, they rely on the five-step marketing research process we outline in this chapter. We also discuss some of the ethical implications of using the information that these databases can collect.

THE MARKETING RESEARCH PROCESS

Managers consider several factors before embarking on a marketing research project. First, will the research be useful; will it provide insights beyond what the managers already know and reduce uncertainty associated with the project? Second, is top management committed to the project and willing to abide by the results of the research? Related to both of these questions is

▼ **EXHIBIT 10.1** The Marketing Research Process

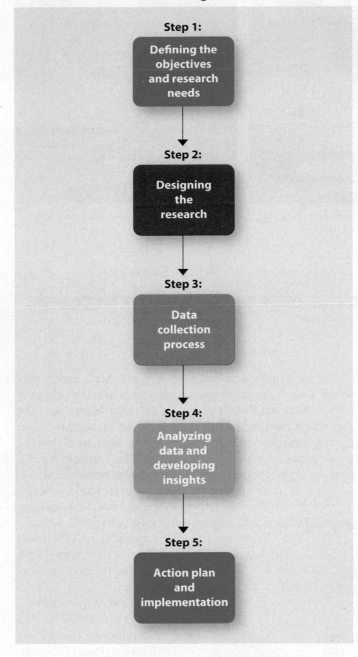

Step 1:
Defining the objectives and research needs

Step 2:
Designing the research

Step 3:
Data collection process

Step 4:
Analyzing data and developing insights

Step 5:
Action plan and implementation

need arises. For example, marketers may establish a specific research objective, which they follow with data collection and preliminary analysis. If they uncover new information during the collection step or if the findings of the analysis spotlight new research needs, they might redefine their objectives and begin again from a new starting point. Another important requirement before embarking on a research project is to plan the entire project in advance. By planning the entire research process prior to starting the project, researchers can avoid unnecessary alterations to the research plan as they move through the process.

LO 10-1   Identify the five steps in the marketing research process.

Marketing Research Process Step 1: Defining Objectives and Research Needs

Because research is both expensive and time-consuming, it is important to establish in advance exactly what problem needs to be solved. To do so, marketers must clearly define the objectives of their marketing research project.

Consider the following scenario: McDonald's wants a better understanding of its customers' experience. It also needs to understand how customers view the experience at Wendy's, a main competitor. Finally, McDonald's hopes to gain some insight into how it should set a price for and market its latest combo meal of a hamburger, fries, and drink. Any one of these questions could initiate a research project. The complexity of the project that the company eventually undertakes depends on how much time and resources it has available as well as the amount of in-depth knowledge it needs.

Researchers assess the value of a project through a careful comparison of the benefits of answering some of their questions and the costs associated with conducting the research. When researchers have determined what information they need to address a particular problem or issue, the next step is to design a research project to meet those objectives.

Marketing Research Process Step 2: Designing the Research

The second step in the marketing research project involves design. In this step, researchers identify the type of data needed and determine the research necessary to collect it. Recall that the objectives of the project drive the type of data needed, as outlined in Step 1.

Let's look at how this second step works, using the McDonald's customer experience. McDonald's needs to ask its

the value of the research. Marketing research can be very expensive, and if the results won't be useful or management does not abide by the findings, it represents a waste of money. Third, should the marketing research project be small or large? A project might involve a simple analysis of data that the firm already has, or it could be an in-depth assessment that costs hundreds of thousands of dollars and takes months to complete.

The marketing research process itself consists of five steps (see Exhibit 10.1). Although we present the stages of the marketing research process in a step-by-step progression, of course research does not always, or even usually, happen that way. Researchers go back and forth from one step to another as the

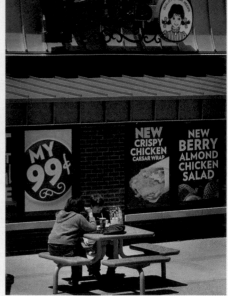

If McDonald's were to do research to better understand its customers' experience, it would study both the McDonald's experience and that of its major competitors, like Wendy's.

> ## Data collection begins only after the research design process.

customers about their McDonald's experience. However, because people don't always tell the whole truth in surveys, the company also may want to observe customers to see how they actually enter the stores, interact with employees, and consume the product. The project's design might begin with available data, such as information that shows people with children often come into the restaurants at lunchtime and order Happy Meals. Then McDonald's market researchers can start to ask customers specific questions about their McDonald's experience.

Marketing Research Process Step 3: Data Collection Process

Data collection begins only after the research design process. Based on the design of the project, data can be collected from secondary or primary data sources. **Secondary data** are pieces of information that have been collected prior to the start of the focal research project. Secondary data include both external and internal data sources. **Primary data**, in contrast, are those data collected to address specific research needs. Some common primary data collection methods include focus groups, in-depth interviews, and surveys.

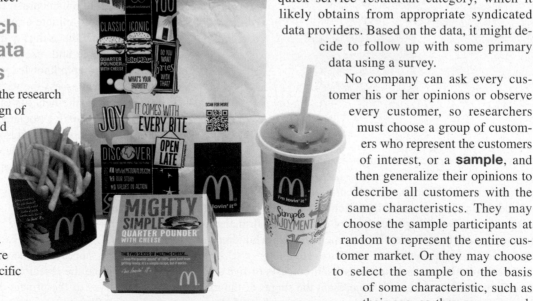

McDonald's assesses its customers' market experience by examining available data and then asks customers about their experience with products such as Value Meals.

For our hypothetical fast food scenario, McDonald's may decide to get relevant secondary data from external providers such as National Purchase Diary Panel and ACNielsen. The data might include the prices of different ingredients, sales figures, growth or decline in the category, and advertising and promotional spending. McDonald's is likely to gather pertinent data about sales from its franchisees. However, it also wants competitor data, overall food consumption data, and other information about the quick service restaurant category, which it likely obtains from appropriate syndicated data providers. Based on the data, it might decide to follow up with some primary data using a survey.

No company can ask every customer his or her opinions or observe every customer, so researchers must choose a group of customers who represent the customers of interest, or a **sample**, and then generalize their opinions to describe all customers with the same characteristics. They may choose the sample participants at random to represent the entire customer market. Or they may choose to select the sample on the basis of some characteristic, such as their age, so they can research how seniors experience buying Value Meals.

Marketing researchers use various methods of asking questions to measure the issues they are tackling. In our hypothetical McDonald's scenario, assume the research team has developed a questionnaire (see Exhibit 10.2), using a few different types of questions. Section A measures the customer's experience in McDonald's, Section B measures the customer's experience in Wendy's, Section C measures the customer's habits at McDonald's, and Section D measures customer demographics.[8]

Marketing Research Process Step 4: Analyzing Data and Developing Insights

The next step in the marketing research process—analyzing and interpreting the data—should be both thorough and methodical. To generate meaningful information, researchers analyze and make use of the collected data. In this context, **data** can be defined as raw numbers or other factual information that, on their own, have limited value to marketers. However, when the data are interpreted, they become **information**, which results from organizing, analyzing, and interpreting data and putting them into a form that is useful to marketing decision makers. For example, a checkout scanner in the grocery store collects sales data about individual consumer purchases. Not until those data are categorized and examined do they provide information about which products and services were purchased together or how an in-store promotional activity translated into sales.

For the McDonald's example, we can summarize the results of the survey (from Exhibit 10.2) in Exhibit 10.3. Both McDonald's and Wendy's scored the same on the cleanliness of their restaurants, but McDonald's had lower prices, whereas Wendy's food

secondary data Pieces of information that have already been collected from other sources and usually are readily available.

primary data Data collected to address specific research needs.

sample A group of customers who represent the customers of interest in a research study.

data Raw numbers or facts.

information Organized, analyzed, interpreted data that offer value to marketers.

▼ **EXHIBIT 10.2** A Hypothetical Fast Food Survey

Please Evaluate Your Experience at McDonald's					
A. McDonald's	Strongly Disagree 1	Disagree 2	Neither Agree or Disagree 3	Agree 4	Strongly Agree 5
McDonald's food tastes good	❑	❑	❑	☑	❑
McDonald's is clean	❑	❑	❑	☑	❑
McDonald's has low prices	❑	❑	❑	☑	❑
B. Wendy's	Strongly Disagree 1	Disagree 2	Neither Agree or Disagree 3	Agree 4	Strongly Agree 5
Wendy's food tastes good	❑	❑	❑	☑	❑
Wendy's is clean	❑	❑	❑	☑	❑
Wendy's has low prices	❑	❑	❑	☑	❑

C. McDonald's				
In the last month, how many times have you been to McDonald's?	Never ❑	1–2 times ❑	3–4 times ❑	More than 5 times ❑ ✓
On average, how much do you spend each visit at McDonald's?	$ _____			
What is your favorite item at McDonald's?	_____			

D. Please tell us about yourself				
What is your age?	under 16 ❑	17–24 ❑	25–35 ❑	36+ ❑
What is your gender?	Male ❑	Female ❑		

Please take a few minutes to tell us about your experience at McDonald's and Wendy's. For each question, please respond by checking the box that applies or writing your response in the space provided.

tasted better. McDonald's thus may want to improve the taste of its food, though without raising prices too much, to compete more effectively with Wendy's.

Marketing Research Process Step 5: Action Plan and Implementation

In the final phase in the marketing research process, the analyst prepares the results and presents them to the appropriate decision makers, who undertake appropriate marketing strategies. A typical marketing research presentation includes an executive summary, the body of the report (which discusses the research objectives, methodology used, and detailed findings), the conclusions, the limitations, and appropriate supplemental tables, figures, and appendixes.[9]

In the McDonald's hypothetical scenario, according to the research findings, the company is doing fine in terms of cleanliness (comparable to its competitors) and is perceived to have lower prices, but the taste of its food could be improved. Using this analysis and the related insights gained, McDonald's might consider hiring some gourmet chefs as consultants to improve the menu and offerings.[10] It then could highlight its efforts to improve the taste of the food and the additional offerings available in restaurants through

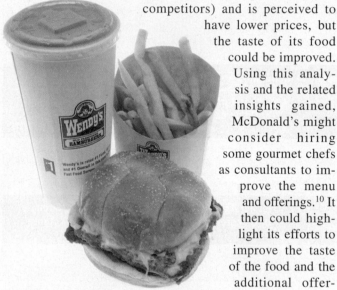

McDonald's marketing research will show how to better compete against Wendy's.

marketing communications and promotions. McDonald's also should consider undertaking additional pricing research to determine whether its lower prices enhance sales and profits or whether it could increase its prices and still compete effectively with Wendy's.

Now let's take a closer look at sources of secondary and primary data.

check yourself

1. What are the steps in the marketing research process?
2. What is the difference between data and information?

LO 10-2 Describe the various secondary data sources.

SECONDARY DATA

A marketing research project often begins with a review of the relevant secondary data. Secondary data might come from free or very inexpensive external sources such as census data, information from trade associations, and reports published in magazines. Although readily accessible, these inexpensive sources may not be specific or timely enough to solve the marketer's research needs and objectives. Firms also can purchase more specific or applicable secondary data from specialized research firms. Finally, secondary sources can be accessed through internal sources, including the company's sales invoices, customer lists, and other reports generated by the company itself.

In political settings, such secondary data can be critical for candidates running for office. Both major political parties thus have developed proprietary databases that contain vast information about voters, broken down by demographic and geographic information. Before a local politician, canvasser, or poll taker even knocks on doors in a neighborhood, he or she likely knows which houses are inhabited by retirees, who has a subscription to *The Wall Street Journal* or *The New York Times,* for whom the residents said they voted in the last election, or whether they served in the military. All these traits can give hints about the voters' likely concerns, which a good politician can address immediately upon knocking on the door. Such research also can dictate tactics for designing broader campaign materials or zero in on very specific issues. One gubernatorial candidate in Illinois successfully targeted suburban neighborhoods that housed lots of pets and their owners by running advertisements in which he criticized his opponent's vote for legislation that made it easier for shelters to euthanize strays.[11]

▼ **EXHIBIT 10.3** Survey Results for McDonald's and Wendy's

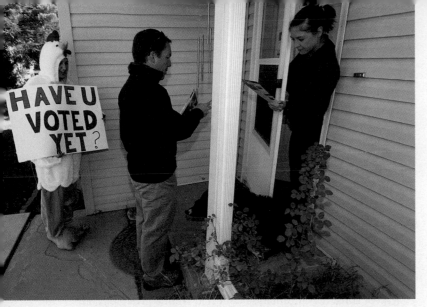

Secondary data is useful to politicians so they know who they are talking to before they knock on a voter's door.

syndicated data Data available for a fee from commercial research firms such as Information Resources Inc. (IRI), National Purchase Diary Panel, and ACNielsen.

some purpose other than the research question at hand, they may not be completely relevant or timely. The U.S. census is a great source of demographic data about a particular market area, and it can be easily accessed at a low cost. However, the data are collected only at the beginning of every decade, so they quickly become outdated. Right now, firms are fortunate because the 2010 census is relatively current and up to date. If an entrepreneur wanted to open a retail flooring store in 2014, though, the data would already be four years old, and the housing market might be much stronger than it was in 2010. Researchers must also pay careful attention to how other sources of inexpensive secondary data were collected. Despite the great deal of data available on the Internet, easy access does not ensure that the data are trustworthy.

Inexpensive External Secondary Data

Some sources of external secondary data can be quickly accessed at a relatively low cost. The U.S. Bureau of the Census (www.census.gov), for example, provides data about businesses by county and zip code. If you wanted to open a new location of a business you are already operating, these data may help you determine the size of your potential market.

Often, however, inexpensive data sources are not adequate to meet researchers' needs. Because the data initially were acquired for

> "Despite the great deal of data available on the Internet, easy access does not ensure that the data are trustworthy."

Syndicated External Secondary Data

Although the secondary data described previously are either free or inexpensively obtained, marketers can purchase external secondary data called **syndicated data**, which are available for a fee from commercial research firms such as SymphonyIRI Group, the National Purchase Diary Panel, and ACNielsen. Exhibit 10.4 contains information about various firms that provide syndicated data.

▼ **EXHIBIT 10.4** Syndicated Data Providers and Some of Their Services

Name	Services Provided
ACNielsen (www.acnielsen.com)	With its *Market Measurement Services,* the company tracks the sales of consumer packaged goods, gathered at the point of sale in retail stores of all types and sizes.
SymphonyIRI Group (www.symphonyiri.com)	*InfoScan* store tracking provides detailed information about sales, share, distribution, pricing, and promotion across a wide variety of retail channels and accounts.
J.D. Power and Associates (www.jdpower.com)	Widely known for its automotive ratings, it produces quality and customer satisfaction research for a variety of industries.
Mediamark Research Inc. (www.mediamark.com)	Supplies multimedia audience research pertaining to media and marketing planning for advertised brands.
National Purchase Diary Panel (www.npd.com)	Based on detailed records consumers keep about their purchases (i.e., a diary), it provides information about product movement and consumer behavior in a variety of industries.
NOP World (www.nopworld.com)	The *mKids US* research study tracks mobile telephone ownership and usage, brand affinities, and entertainment habits of American youth between 12 and 19 years of age.
Research and Markets (www.researchandmarkets.com)	Promotes itself as a one-stop shop for market research and data from most leading publishers, consultants, and analysts.
Roper Center for Public Opinion Research (www.ropercenter.uconn.edu)	The *General Social Survey* is one of the nation's longest running surveys of social, cultural, and political indicators.
Simmons Market Research Bureau (www.smrb.com)	Reports on the products American consumers buy, the brands they prefer, and their lifestyles, attitudes, and media preferences.
Yankelovich (www.yankelovich.com)	The *MONITOR* tracks consumer attitudes, values, and lifestyles shaping the American marketplace.

Firms like Kellogg's use scanner data to assess the success of new products such as its Special K Popcorn Chips.

Scanner data are used in quantitative research obtained from scanner readings of UPC labels at check-out counters. Whenever you go into your local grocery store, your purchases are rung up using scanner systems. The data from these purchases are likely to be acquired by leading marketing research firms, such as SymphonyIRI or ACNielsen, which use this information to help leading consumer packaged goods firms (e.g., Kellogg's, Pepsi, Kraft) assess what is happening in the marketplace. For example, a firm can use scanner data to determine what would happen to its sales if it reduced the price of its least popular product by 10 percent in a given month. In the test market in which it lowers the price, do sales increase, decrease, or stay the same?

Panel data are information collected from a group of consumers, organized into panels, over time. Data collected from panelists often include their records of what they have purchased (i.e., secondary data) as well as their responses to survey questions that the client gives to the panel firm to ask the panelists (i.e., primary data). Secondary panel data thus might show that when Diet Pepsi is offered at a deep discount, 80 percent of usual Diet Coke consumers switch to Diet Pepsi. Primary panel data could give insights into what they think of each option. We discuss how marketing researchers use scanner and panel data to answer specific research questions further in the primary data section.

Consumer packaged goods firms that sell to wholesalers often lack the means to gather pertinent data directly from the retailers that sell their products to consumers, which makes syndicated data a valuable resource for them. Some syndicated data providers also offer information about shifting brand preferences and product usage in households, which they gather from scanner data and consumer panels.

Overall, though, both panel and scanner data provide firms with a comprehensive picture of what consumers are buying or not buying. The key difference between scanner research and panel research is how the data is aggregated. Scanner research typically focuses on weekly consumption of a particular product at a given unit of

Syndicated external secondary data are obtained from scanner data obtained from scanner readings of UPC codes at check-out counters (left) and from panel data collected from consumers that electronically record their purchases (right).

analysis (e.g., individual store, chain, region); panel research focuses on the total weekly consumption by a particular person or household. Both types are valuable, and Adding Value 10.1 describes just how SymphonyIRI provides them to its customers.

scanner data A type of syndicated external secondary data used in quantitative research that is obtained from scanner readings of UPC codes at check-out counters.

panel data Information collected from a group of consumers.

Adding Value 10.1
SymphonyIRI and the Value of Information

SymphonyIRI was previously known as Information Resources Inc. Regardless of its name, though, the company has long provided market research and analytical services for the consumer packaged goods, health care, and retail industries. Ninety-five percent of the *Fortune* Global 500 in the consumer packaged goods and retail industries use SymphonyIRI market research to make their business decisions.[12] For its clients—which include Anheuser-Busch, ConAgra, CVS, Johnson & Johnson, and PepsiCo—SymphonyIRI collects, monitors, and manages a variety of data in some of the most active research markets in the world, including the United States and Europe.

SymphonyIRI tracks a host of data to deliver detailed findings that are designed to grow and enhance clients' operations. To identify trends in private-label sales, for instance, it collects sales data from the scanners at the checkout from almost 95,000 retail stores throughout the United States and Europe,[13] then cross-references these data with data collected from a panel of 70,000 households that SymphonyIRI has armed with personal scanners to track their household purchases.

For example, in a report tracking the increase in private-label brands (see Chapter 11) in the consumer packaged goods industry, SymphonyIRI summarizes how consumer attitudes have changed. If a grocery store chooses to offer its own brand of detergent, it must engage in competition with various branded detergents, such as Tide, Cheer, and All. In the past, private-label products often were positioned as more affordable versions of popular brands and tended to target and attract price-conscious consumers. However, according to SymphonyIRI's findings, recent trends indicate private-label sales are growing across consumer segments, especially as middle-class consumers look for ways to conserve costs in struggling global economies.[14]

Another report highlights the market researcher's findings about the types of trips modern shoppers make and how that determines what they buy. With data that hold interest for both manufacturers and retailers, SymphonyIRI shows that consumer packaged goods shoppers take four types of trips: quick, pantry stock-up, special purpose, or fill-in. The first two account for nearly two-thirds of grocery shoppers' purchases, which means that marketers need to find ways to appeal to people moving fast as well as those seeking bargains to fill their shelves at home. SymphonyIRI also suggests low-cost, high-value solutions for retailers and manufacturers that can best appeal to these various kinds of shoppers.[15]

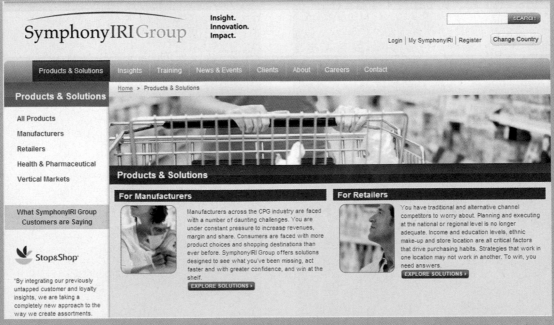

Symphony IRI provides market research and analytical services to the consumer packaged goods, health care, and retail industries.

> # THE PURPOSE OF CONVERTING DATA TO INFORMATION IS TO DESCRIBE, EXPLAIN, PREDICT, AND/OR EVALUATE A PARTICULAR SITUATION. "

Internal Secondary Data

Internally, companies also generate a tremendous amount of secondary data from their day-to-day operations. One of the most valuable resources such firms have at their disposal is their rich cache of customer information and purchase history. However, it can be difficult to make sense of the millions and even billions of pieces of individual data, which are stored in large computer files called **data warehouses**. For this reason, firms find it necessary to use data mining techniques to extract valuable information from their databases.

Data mining uses a variety of statistical analysis tools to uncover previously unknown patterns in the data or relationships among variables. Some retailers try to customize their product and service offerings to match the needs of their customers. For instance, the U.K. grocer Tesco uses its loyalty card to collect massive amounts of information about its individual customers. Every time a loyalty card member buys something, the card is scanned, and the store captures key purchase data, specific to that member. But these specific data are basically useless until Tesco mines and analyzes them to identify three income groups: upscale, middle income, and less affluent. With this mined information, Tesco has been able to create appealing private-label product offerings for each group, according to their preferences, and began targeting promotions to each customer according to his or her income classification. Since 2000, Tesco's market share has grown by more than 20 percent.[16]

Data mining can also enable a home improvement retailer such as Lowe's to learn that 25 percent of the time its customers buy a garden hose, they also purchase a sprinkler. With such information, the retailer may decide to put the garden hoses next to the sprinklers in the store. Outside the retail realm, an investment firm might use statistical techniques to group clients according to their income, age, type of securities purchased, and prior investment experience. This categorization identifies different segments to which the firm can offer valuable packages that meet their specific needs. The firm also can tailor separate marketing programs to each of these segments. Data mining thus can be useful for a broad range of situations and organizations. By analyzing the enormous amount of

Marketers use data mining techniques to determine what items people buy at the same time so they can be promoted and displayed together.

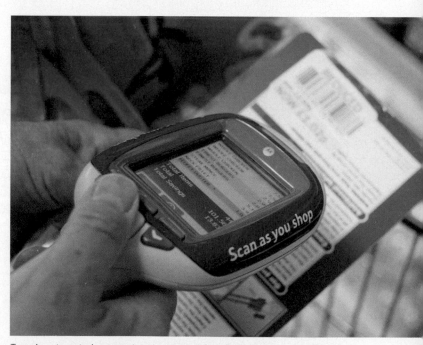

Tesco's automated payment system uses a handheld device that allows consumers to scan items as they shop. This device allows customers to keep track of the cost of their shopping as they progress through the store.

information that it possesses about its customers, companies have developed statistical models that help identify when a customer is dissatisfied with his or her service. Once the company identifies an unhappy customer, it can follow up and proactively address that customer's issues. By mining customer data and information, the company also reduced its churn levels. **Churn** is the number of participants who discontinue use of a service, divided by the average number of total participants. With this knowledge, the company can focus on what it does best. The purpose of converting data to information is to describe, explain, predict, and/or evaluate a particular situation.

PRIMARY DATA COLLECTION TECHNIQUES

In many cases, the information researchers need is available only through primary data or data collected to address specific research needs. Depending on the nature of the research problem, the primary data collection method can employ a *qualitative* or a *quantitative* research method.

As its name implies, **qualitative research** is used to understand the phenomenon of interest through broad open-ended

> Qualitative research is more informal than quantitative research methods and includes observation, following social media sites, in-depth interviews, focus groups, and projective techniques.

Overall, firms hope to use data mining to generate customer-based analytics that they can apply to their strategic decision making and thereby make good customers better and better customers their best. Firms can also use secondary data to assess the profitability of their customers by determining the customer lifetime value (CLV).

✔ check yourself

1. What is the difference between internal and external secondary research?

LO 10-3 Describe the various primary data collection techniques.

responses. It provides initial information that helps the researcher more clearly formulate the research objectives. Qualitative research is more informal than quantitative research methods and includes observation, following social media sites, in-depth interviews, focus groups, and projective techniques (see Exhibit 10.5, left side).

Once the firm has gained insights from doing qualitative research, it is likely to engage in **quantitative research**, which are structured responses that can be statistically tested. Quantitative research provides information needed to confirm insights and hypotheses generated via qualitative research or secondary data and helps managers pursue appropriate courses of action. Formal studies such as specific experiments, scanner and panel data, or some combination of these are quantitative in nature. (See Exhibit 10.5, right side.) We now examine each of these primary data collection techniques in order.

▼ **EXHIBIT 10.5** Qualitative versus Quantitative Data Collection

Observation

Observation entails examining purchase and consumption behaviors through personal or video camera scrutiny. For example, researchers might observe customers while they shop or when they go about their daily lives, during which processes they use a variety of products. Observation can last for a very brief period of time (e.g., two hours watching teenagers shop for clothing in the mall), or it may take days or weeks (e.g., researchers live with families to observe their use of products). When consumers are unable to articulate their experiences, observation research becomes particularly useful; how else could researchers determine which educational toys babies choose to play with or confirm details of the buying process that consumers might not be able to recall accurately?

Observation may be the best method, and sometimes the only way, to determine how consumers might use a product, and therefore be useful for designing and marketing them. By watching women wash their hair in a rural town in China, Procter & Gamble recognized the fallacy of its assumption that the poorest consumers were only interested in functionality of a product—how to get hair clean. One woman struggled to find ways to wash her long hair effectively, even in the face of severe water shortages, rather than cut off what

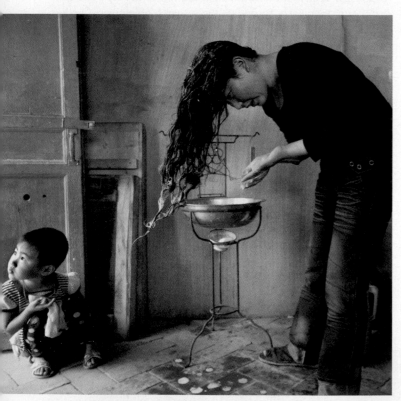

By watching women in rural China wash their hair, Procter & Gamble learned that even their poorest customers wanted beautiful hair, but it has to be packaged affordably.

she considered the source of her beauty. Based on its research, P&G has added value by selling Rejoice shampoo inexpensively ($1.50) to a market that was using alternative options such as laundry detergent. Other observations pushed P&G to develop a more skin-sensitive laundry detergent after noting how many people in developing markets wash their clothes by hand.[17]

These insights might be helpful, both for the company that gathers them and for consumers who ultimately benefit from better products. But Ethical & Societal Dilemma 10.1 also raises a key question: Should people be informed that they are being watched?

Social Media

Social media sites are a booming source of data for marketers. Marketers have realized that social media can provide valuable information that could aid their marketing research and strategy endeavors. In particular, contributors to social media sites rarely are shy about providing their opinions about the firm's own products or its competitors' offerings. If companies can monitor, gather, and mine these vast social media data, they can learn a lot about their customers' likes, dislikes, and preferences. They then might cross-reference such social media commentary with consumers' past purchases to derive a better sense of what they want. Customers also appear keen to submit their opinions about their friends' purchases, interests, polls, and blogs.

Blogs in particular represent valuable sources of marketing research insights. Marketers are paying attention to online reviews about everything from restaurants to running shoes to recycling.[18] On the Videogum blog, the bylined writers invite constant commentary from a community of readers, who go by the collective nickname Monsters. Their reviews are tongue-in-cheek and a little mischievous, but they also offer justifications and reasons for why the movie *Drive* was one of the best of the year, and then why its star Ryan Gosling also qualifies as one of the 10 best actors.[19] *The Truth About Cars* blog is known for its unflinchingly objective reviews of various makes and models as well as discussions about the industry as a whole, marketing tactics, and global competition, among other topics.[20]

Part of what makes blogs so valuable is also what makes them challenging for firms. Bloggers are usually, but not always, unaffiliated with the companies that produce the items they review, which means they have no reason to hold back from negative commentary. When ConAgra tried a hidden camera experiment with a group of food bloggers, it suffered significant backlash throughout the blogosphere. It invited the writers to a dinner, supposedly with a gourmet chef, then fed them a frozen lasagna meal to gauge their responses. Not only did the victims of the prank find it less than funny, they also blasted ConAgra for exposing them, without their permission, to the preservatives and processed ingredients contained in the frozen dinners.[21]

ethical & societal dilemma

Watching Consumers

How does sitting in a mall or standing in a store checking out the people in the corner add up to bona fide market research? Well, for Paco Underhill and his company Envirosell, that's just another day on the job.

Envirosell's wide-ranging projects encompass firms in a broad variety of industries. According to its mission statement, Envirosell focuses "on how people, products and spaces interrelate. Our research environments, once rooted in bricks and mortar retail, now span to cover spaces as huge and chaotic as train stations and airports. We've worked in libraries, doctor offices, model homes, showrooms, and every kind of food service imaginable. Our clients are merchants, consumer goods manufacturers, banks, trade associations, not for profits, government agencies and the full spectrum of design, advertising and marketing agencies."[22]

For Staples, for example, it observed consumers in 12 stores, videotaping their movements through the stores for eight hours each research day, as a means to better understand how consumers actually shopped around the various departments to gather products, view signs, and interact with sales associates. Envirosell researchers also conduct interviews with shoppers. On the basis of the results of these studies, Staples rolled out a new store format that focuses on solving customer problems by combining service with self-service rather than just selling individual items. Staples' sales associates can now provide a higher level of service in those areas that demand it, and the new store format gives customers the tools to be self-sufficient if they choose to browse on their own.

Using observational research, marketing research can identify information that would not be accessible to them through more traditional marketing research means—a respondent to a simple questionnaire or people involved in an interview probably would not be able to provide insightful information about the patterns they follow when walking through a store or a mall. But the method also extends into people's homes. For example, the Swiss sensory firm Givaudan conducted observational research with Chinese consumers to determine how they cook and consume chicken. The research team followed a volunteer, Mrs. Wu, as she shopped in the local market for the exact chicken she wanted butchered to take home. It then entered her home, observed as she cooked it (until she shooed them out of the kitchen so she could arrange the final dish), and sat with the family as they ate. The researchers noted each ingredient Mrs. Wu used, the exact methods she applied to create the meal, and even how the family disposed of the bones. (For your information, in China, it is considered perfectly acceptable to spit out bones onto the tablecloth.)

As a summary of their report notes, their research confirmed that "consuming chicken in China involves an array of sensory experiences—visual, olfactory, gustatory and tactile—so profoundly different from Western experience that an understanding of chicken flavor cannot be understood without referencing Chinese culture as its source."[23] As we discussed in Chapter 8, similar insights also helped Campbell Soup expand its presence in China.

In most cases, researchers obtain consent from the consumers they are watching and videotaping; in other cases though, they do not. The ethical dilemma for marketing researchers surrounds whether to use observational techniques in which the subjects are not informed that they are being studied, like viewing customers in a mall or a retail store. Observing uninformed consumers very well may lead to important insights that would not otherwise be discovered. But do the results justify the methodology?

By videotaping customers' movements in a store, it can better understand how consumers actually shopped around the various departments to gather products, view signs, and interact with sales associates.

When Kraft considered the launch of its South Beach product line, it created a virtual community of women who wanted to lose weight and health and wellness opinion leaders.

Another creative use of social media for market research involves building online communities for companies. When it considered the launch of its South Beach product line, Kraft hired Communispace to create a virtual community of target consumers: 150 women who wanted to lose weight and 150 health and wellness opinion leaders. The participants openly shared their frustrations and difficulties managing their weight because the community environment prompted them to sense that everyone else on the site struggled with similar issues and concerns. By monitoring the community, Kraft learned that it would need to educate consumers about the South Beach Diet and offer products that could address cravings throughout the day, not just at mealtimes. Six months after the line's introduction, Kraft had earned profits of $100 million.[24]

Noting these various opportunities and market research sources online, many companies—including Ford Motor Co., PepsiCo, Coca-Cola, and Southwest Airlines—have added heads of social media to their management teams. These managers take responsibility for scanning the web for blogs, postings, tweets, or Facebook posts in which customers mention their experience with a brand. By staying abreast of this continuous stream of information, companies can gather the most up-to-date news about their company, products, and services as well as their competitors. These social media searches allow companies to learn about customers' perceptions and resolve customer complaints they may never have heard about through other channels.[25]

The data gathered through the searches also undergo careful analyses: Are customer sentiments generally positive, negative, or neutral? What sort of intensity or interest levels do they imply? How many customers are talking about the firm's products, and how many focus instead on competitors'? This data analysis is understandably challenging, considering the amount of data available online. However, monitoring consumer sentiments has grown easier with the development of social media monitoring platforms.

Salesforce Radian6 is steadily becoming one of the most sought-after firms for monitoring customers using **sentiment mining**. Using social media sites such as Facebook, Twitter, and online blogs, Salesforce Radian6 and other firms collect consumer comments about companies and their products. The data are then analyzed to distill customer attitudes toward and preferences for products and advertising campaigns. Scouring millions of sites by combining automated online search tools with text analysis techniques, sentiment mining yields qualitative data that provide new insight into what consumers really think. Companies plugged into this real-time information can become more nimble, allowing for quick changes in a product roll-out or a new advertising campaign. Some companies take it a step further by joining the online conversation with customers, a process called *social engagement*.[26]

In-Depth Interviews

In an **in-depth interview**, trained researchers ask questions, listen to and record the answers, and then pose additional questions to clarify or expand on a particular issue. For instance, in addition to simply watching teenagers shop for apparel, interviewers might stop them one at a time in the mall to ask them a few questions, such as: "We noticed that you went into and came out of Abercrombie & Fitch very quickly without buying anything. Why was that?" If the subject responds that no one had bothered to wait on her, the interviewer might ask a follow-up question like, "Oh? Has that happened to you before?" or "Do you expect more sales assistance there?"

In-depth interviews provide insights that help managers better understand the nature of their industry as well as important trends and consumer preferences, which can be invaluable for developing marketing strategies. Specifically, they can establish a historical context for the phenomenon of interest, particularly when they include industry experts or experienced consumers. They also can communicate how people really feel about a product or service at the individual level. Finally, marketers can use the results of in-depth interviews to develop surveys.

In-depth interviews are, however, relatively expensive and time consuming. Each interview could cost $200 or more, depending on the length of the interaction and the characteristics of the people included in the sample. If the sample must feature medical doctors, for example, the costs of getting sufficient interviews will be much higher than the costs associated with intercepting teenagers in a mall.

Focus Group Interviews

In **focus group interviews**, a small group of persons (usually 8 to 12) come together for an intensive discussion about a

Although relatively expensive, in-depth interviews can reveal information that would be difficult to obtain with other methods.

Innovative ideas stemming from marketing research and focus groups are not limited to new products though. The U.S. Postal Service also has used them to improve its service offering, as Adding Value 10.2 describes.

The growth of online technology, as well as computer and video capabilities, have provided tremendous benefits for focus group research, which now often takes place online. For example, eFocusGroups offers a secure site as a platform for companies to listen in on focus groups and even interact with consumers, without anyone having to travel. The client company not only saves costs but also gains access to a broader range of potential customers who live in various neighborhoods, states, or even countries. Because eFocusGroups automatically records all the online

particular topic. Using an unstructured method of inquiry, a trained moderator guides the conversation, according to a predetermined, general outline of topics of interest. Researchers usually record the interactions by video- or audiotape so they can carefully comb through the interviews later (or feature them in advertisements, as Domino's did in advertisements designed to reposition their pizza)[27] to catch any patterns of verbal or non-verbal responses. In particular, focus groups gather qualitative data about initial reactions to a new or existing product or service, opinions about different competitive offerings, or reactions to marketing stimuli, like a new ad campaign or point-of-purchase display materials.[28]

To obtain new information to help it continue its innovative success derived from its introduction of low sodium choices, Campbell's Soup conducted extensive focus groups with female shoppers who indicated they would buy ready-to-eat soups. The groups clearly revealed the women's top priorities: a nutritious soup that contained the ingredients they would use if they made soup. They wanted, for example, white meat chicken, fresh vegetables, and sea salt. In addition, focus group participants were equally clear about what they did *not* want, like high fructose corn syrup, MSG, and other stuff whose names they could not even pronounce.[29] The resulting Select Harvest product line showcases the 100 percent natural, flavorful, and healthful ingredients, including vegetables and whole grains. The packaging also reflects the focus groups' preferences, using a simple, clean design that highlights the short list of ingredients. In its first year on the market, the line generated $202 million in sales.[30]

Campbell's Soup learned from focus groups that women want a nutritious soup that contains ingredients they would use if they made it from scratch. This information helped them develop their Select Harvest line.

Adding Value 10.2

The USPS Sample Showcase

Shuttered post offices. No more one-day delivery. The threat of ending Saturday service. The financial struggles of the U.S. Postal Service (USPS), including annual deficits of $8.5 billion,[31] have been widely discussed, and the continued expansion of digital communication suggests that customers are not likely to turn back to traditional mail anytime soon. In addition to its cost-cutting measures, the USPS thus is working to reinvent key aspects of its operations, including enhanced services for manufacturers that want to distribute their product samples.

The USPS has long distributed samples, especially for consumer packaged goods (CPG) companies and retailers.[32] Yet the sample distribution market began to suffer from higher distribution costs, driven by rising postal rates and freight costs. The USPS could no longer rely on its distinctive capability to deliver physical products into consumers' hands; it needed a new source for a sustainable competitive advantage. To develop a new sample distribution concept that would excite both consumers and retailers, the USPS hired Great Lakes Marketing and gave it the task of finding a way to reduce the per unit cost for CPG manufacturers but still make the product samples interesting to potential customers.

In interviews with retailers, other delivery services, and key industry experts, the USPS had learned that single-product distribution would no longer be viable: It was simply too costly to deliver one manufacturer's product to each postal customer. Combining samples from a group of companies into a single delivery batch seemed preferable, in that it would allow manufacturers to share the costs.[33] But would batching appeal to consumers?

In focus groups conducted in Bethesda, Maryland; Seattle, Washington; and Nashville, Tennessee, participants who identified themselves as their households' primary decision makers offered some remarkable input. In addition to reporting their sincere enthusiasm about sampling, these focus group members noted that they considered mailbox delivery far more convenient than in-store

Focus group findings led USPS to offer Sample Showcase—a package containing samples from 12 individual companies.

sample distribution. They would love to receive a mailed, bundled sample offering![34]

The focus group findings were compelling enough that the USPS distributed its first round of the bundled Sample Showcase soon thereafter.[35] Each package contains samples from 12 individual companies, including familiar names such as Secret and Starbucks as well as some less well-known CPG manufacturers, such as Gum Soft-Picks, an oral healthcare company.[36] In addition, the USPS hired an online sample management company to identify 200,000 target households that would opt in to online recruiting and join targeted purchase lists.

Follow-up surveys with consumers have confirmed the focus group attitudes: A month after the first delivery, 25,418 respondents recalled receiving the samples. Of those, 98.4 percent noted that the mix of products appealed to them, and 97.3 percent agreed with the statement that "Sample Showcase is for someone like me."[37] Furthermore, retailers continue to regard sample distributions as a means to distinguish their brands from the clutter in the marketplace. In particular, smaller companies have found that including their products in the same box with high-visibility offerings boosts their own brand recognition.[38]

---

interactions, the company also has a detailed, verbatim transcript of consumers' comments and responses.[39] However, these online focus groups rarely include video feeds, so companies lose some important information that can be gleaned from body language.

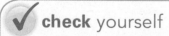

check yourself

1. What are the types of qualitative research?

Survey Research

Arguably the most popular type of quantitative primary collection method is a **survey**—a systematic means of collecting information from people using a questionnaire. A **questionnaire** is a form that features a set of questions designed to gather information

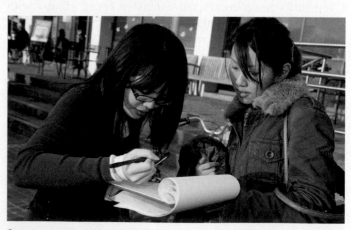

Survey research uses questionnaires to collect primary data. Questions can be either unstructured or structured.

▼ **EXHIBIT 10.6** Structured versus Unstructured Response

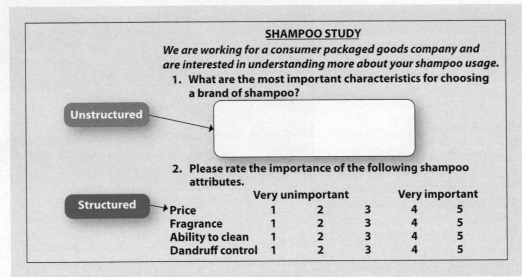

from respondents and thereby accomplish the researchers' objectives. Individual questions on a questionnaire can be either unstructured or structured. **Unstructured questions** are open ended and allow respondents to answer in their own words. An unstructured question like, "What are the most important characteristics for choosing a brand of shampoo?" yields an unstructured response. However, the same question could be posed to respondents in a structured format by providing a fixed set of response categories, such as price, fragrance, ability to clean, or dandruff control, and then asking respondents to rate the importance of each. **Structured questions** thus are closed-ended questions for which a discrete set of response alternatives, or specific answers, is provided for respondents to evaluate (see Exhibit 10.6).

Developing a Questionnaire Is Part Art and Part Science

The questions must be carefully designed to address the specific set of research questions. Moreover, for a questionnaire to produce meaningful results, its questions cannot be misleading in any fashion (e.g., open to multiple interpretations), and they must address only one issue at a time. They also must be worded in vocabulary that will be familiar and comfortable to those being surveyed. The questions should be sequenced appropriately: general questions first, more specific questions next, and demographic questions at the end. Finally, the layout and appearance of the questionnaire must be professional and easy to follow, with appropriate instructions in suitable places. For some tips on what *not* to do when designing a questionnaire, see Exhibit 10.7.[40]

Similar to focus groups, marketing surveys can be conducted either online or offline, but online marketing surveys offer researchers the chance to develop a database quickly with many responses, whereas offline marketing surveys provide a more direct approach that includes interactions with the target

▼ **EXHIBIT 10.7** What Not to Do When Designing a Questionnaire

Issue	Good Question	Bad Question
Avoid questions the respondent cannot easily or accurately answer.	When was the last time you went to the grocery store?	How much money did you spend on groceries last month?
Avoid sensitive questions unless they are absolutely necessary.	Do you take vitamins?	Do you dye your gray hair?
Avoid double-barreled questions, which refer to more than one issue with only one set of responses.	1. Do you like to shop for clothing? 2. Do you like to shop for food?	Do you like to shop for clothing and food?
Avoid leading questions, which steer respondents to a particular response, irrespective of their true beliefs.	Please rate how safe you believe a BMW is on a scale of 1 to 10, with 1 being not safe and 10 being very safe.	BMW is the safest car on the road, right?
Avoid one-sided questions that present only one side of the issue.	To what extent do you believe fast food contributes to adult obesity using a five-point scale? 1: Does not contribute, 5: Main cause	Fast food is responsible for adult obesity: Agree/Disagree

Source: Adapted from A. Parasuraman, Dhruv Grewal, and R. Krishnan, *Marketing Research,* 2nd ed. (Boston: Houghton Mifflin, 2007), Ch. 10.

market. Web surveys have steadily grown as a percentage of all quantitative surveys. Online surveys have a lot to offer marketers with tight deadlines and small budgets.[41]

In particular, the response rates for online surveys are relatively high. Typical response rates run from 1 to 2 percent for mail and 10 to 15 percent for phone surveys. For online surveys, in contrast, the response rate can reach 30 to 35 percent or even higher in business-to-business research. It also is inexpensive. An average 20-minute phone interview can cost $30 to $40, compared with $7 to $10 for an online interview. Costs likely will continue to fall as users become more familiar with the online survey process. Results are processed and received quickly. Reports and summaries can be developed in real time and delivered directly to managers in simple, easy-to-digest reports, complete with color, graphics, and charts. Traditional phone or mail surveys require laborious data collection, tabulation, summary, and distribution before anyone can grasp their results.

Diverse online survey software, such as Qualtrics, Surveymonkey, and Zoomerang, makes it very easy to draft an online survey, using questions from existing survey libraries. A survey link can be sent easily in an e-mail to potential respondents or panelists as well as posted on specific sites that are likely to attract the target audience or people who are willing to perform online work (e.g., Amazon's Mechanical Turk Site).

Panel and Scanner-Based Research

As discussed previously, panel and scanner research can be either secondary or primary. In this section, we consider the use of a panel to collect primary data. Walmart's U.K. subsidiary Asda uses an 18,000-customer panel, which it calls Pulse of the Nation, to help determine which products to carry. Asda sends e-mails to each participant with product images and descriptions

Walmart's U.K. subsidiary Asda uses an 18,000-customer panel, which it calls Pulse of the Nation, to help determine which products to carry.

of potential new products. The customers' responses indicate whether they think each product should be carried in stores. As an incentive to participate, Asda enters respondents automatically in a drawing for free prizes.[42]

Experimental Research

Experimental research (an **experiment**) is a type of quantitative research that systematically manipulates one or more variables to determine which variables have a causal effect on other variables. For example, in our earlier scenario, one thing the hypothetical McDonald's research team was trying to determine was the most profitable price for a new menu combo item (hamburger, fries, and drink). Assume that the fixed cost of developing the item is $300,000 and the variable cost, which is primarily composed of the cost of the food itself, is $2.00. McDonald's puts the item on the menu at four prices in four markets. (See Exhibit 10.8.) In general, the more expensive the item, the less it will sell. But by running this experiment,

> Typical response rates run from 1 to 2 percent for mail and 10 to 15 percent for phone surveys. For online surveys, in contrast, the response rate can reach 30 to 35 percent.

▼ **EXHIBIT 10.8** Hypothetical Pricing Experiment for McDonald's

Market	1 Unit Price	2 Market Demand at Price (in Units)	3 Total Revenue (Col. 1 × Col. 2)	4 Total Cost of Units Sold ($300,000 Fixed Cost + $2.00 Variable Cost)	5 Total Profits (Col. 3 / Col. 4)
1	$4	200,000	$800,000	700,000	$100,000
2	5	150,000	$750,000	600,000	$150,000
3	6	100,000	$600,000	500,000	$100,000
4	7	50,000	$350,000	400,000	($50,000)

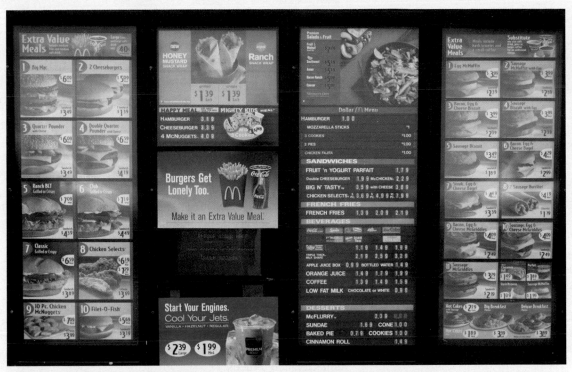

Using an experiment, McDonald's would test the price of new menu items to determine which is the most profitable.

the restaurant chain determines that the most profitable price is the second least expensive ($5.00). These findings suggest some people may have believed the most expensive item ($7.00) was too expensive, so they refused to buy it. The least expensive item ($4.00) sold fairly well, but McDonald's did not make as much money on each item sold. In this experiment, the changes in price likely caused the changes in quantities sold and therefore affected the restaurant's profitability.

LO 10-4 Summarize the differences between secondary data and primary data.

Advantages and Disadvantages of Primary and Secondary Research

Now that we have discussed the various secondary and primary data collection methods, think back over our discussion and ask yourself what seem to be the best applications of each and when you would want to go to secondary sources or use primary collection methods. We can see that both primary data and secondary data have certain inherent and distinct advantages and disadvantages. For a summary of the advantages and disadvantages of each type of research, see Exhibit 10.9.

▼ **EXHIBIT 10.9** Advantages and Disadvantages of Secondary and Primary Data

Type	Examples	Advantages	Disadvantages
Secondary research	❏ Census data ❏ Sales invoices ❏ Internet information ❏ Books ❏ Journal articles ❏ Syndicated data	❏ Saves time in collecting data because they are readily available ❏ Free or inexpensive (except for syndicated data)	❏ May not be precisely relevant to information needs ❏ Information may not be timely ❏ Sources may not be original, and therefore usefulness is an issue ❏ Methodologies for collecting data may not be appropriate ❏ Data sources may be biased
Primary research	❏ Observed consumer behavior ❏ Focus group interviews ❏ Surveys ❏ Experiments	❏ Specific to the immediate data needs and topic at hand ❏ Offers behavioral insights generally not available from secondary research	❏ Costly ❏ Time consuming ❏ Requires more sophisticated training and experience to design study and collect data

> # IT IS PARTICULARLY IMPORTANT FOR MARKETERS TO ADHERE TO ETHICAL PRACTICES WHEN CONDUCTING MARKETING RESEARCH. THE AMERICAN MARKETING ASSOCIATION PROVIDES THREE GUIDELINES.

check yourself

1. What are the types of quantitative research?
2. What are the advantages and disadvantages of primary and secondary research?

LO 10-5 Examine the circumstances in which collecting information on consumers is ethical.

EMERGING TECHNOLOGY AND THE ETHICS OF USING CUSTOMER INFORMATION

As we noted in Chapter 4, upholding strong business ethics requires more than a token nod to ethics in the mission statement. A strong ethical orientation must be an integral part of a firm's marketing strategy and decision making. In Chapter 4, we discussed how marketers have a duty to understand and address the concerns of the various stakeholders in the firm.

It is particularly important for marketers to adhere to ethical practices when conducting marketing research. The American Marketing Association provides three guidelines for conducting marketing research: (1) It prohibits selling or fundraising under the guise of conducting research, (2) it supports maintaining research integrity by avoiding misrepresentation or the omission of pertinent research data, and (3) it encourages fair treatment of clients and suppliers.[43] Numerous codes of conduct written by various marketing research societies all reinforce the duty of researchers to respect the rights of the subjects in the course of their research. The bottom line: Marketing research should be used only to produce unbiased, factual information.

As technology continues to advance, though, the potential threats to consumers' personal information grow in number and intensity. Ethical & Social Dilemma 10.2 discusses an interesting example of how retailers are using mannequins with hidden cameras to monitor shoppers. Marketing researchers must be vigilant to avoid abusing their access to these data. Security breaches at some of the United States' largest retailers, banks, credit-reporting services, and peer-to-peer networks have shown just how easily stored data can be abused.[44] From charitable giving to medical records to Internet tracking, consumers are more anxious than ever about preserving their fundamental right to privacy. They also demand increasing control over the information that has been collected about them.

Many firms therefore voluntarily notify their customers that any information provided to them will be kept confidential and not given or sold to any other firm. Several organizations, including the Center for Democracy & Technology (CDT) and the Electronic Privacy Information Center (EPIC), have emerged as watchdogs over data mining of consumer information. In addition, national and state governments in the United States play a big part in protecting privacy. Companies are legally required to disclose their privacy practices to customers on an annual basis, for example.[45]

But laws have yet to catch up with advances in other areas, including social media, neuromarketing, and facial recognition software. As we noted previously in this chapter, social media have grown into an important resource for marketing researchers because consumers are so willing and likely to share their attitudes and opinions there. In this case, protecting consumers' privacy is mainly up to the consumer.

In contrast, consumers have little control over facial recognition software that allows companies to detect demographic information based on their appearances. For example, digital billboards embedded with such software can identify passersby and then display ads targeted to them, based on their age, gender, and attention level.[46] The resulting communication is precisely targeted, which should make the advertisement more interesting to the consumer walking by—though it also could lead to embarrassing encounters. Imagine, for example, a teenager with skin problems having a billboard loudly broadcast an acne product ad as he walks by!

On Facebook, facial detection software applied to photographs eliminates the need for users to continue to tag the same people multiple times. It also stores all users' biometric data.

Oh, Say, Can You See? The Implications of Mannequins that Capture Shoppers' Demographic Data[47]

The basic elements of a new data-gathering tool development for retailers are not in any real contention. By spending $5,130 to purchase an EyeSee mannequin from a provider called Almax, retailers gain not only a place to display clothing but also a discreet recording tool that indicates the genders, ages, and ethnicities of the customers who walk by the display.

Rather more controversial are the discussions about the implications of this innovation. On one side, consumer privacy advocates complain that the mannequins obtain information about shoppers without their permission. Although Almax asserts that the technology embedded in the displays does not actually record the information, these commentators worry that the mannequins could be used to survey shoppers solely for the benefit of the retailer. Because the mannequins do not look any different from regular mannequins, shoppers have no way of knowing whether someone (or something) is watching them as they walk through the store. Furthermore, consumers have no control over what retailers do with the aggregated data.

On the other side, retailers note that because the mannequins do not record, their use is no different from that of a closed-circuit system. Furthermore, some commentators argue that consumers should have no expectation of privacy in public spaces. Certainly, a staffer could similarly mark down people's ages, races, and genders as they walk through the shop doors. The electronic form simply does this work better and more accurately.

In implementing the new technology, one retailer recognized the predominance of Asian shoppers after about 4:00 p.m., so it hired more Chinese-speaking staffers to put on the floor to assist them. Another retailer realized that a lot of children were walking through its stores, so it added an entirely new children's clothing line to its offerings. Buoyed by its early successes, Almax also plans to add a function that would capture shoppers' conversations as they pass by the mannequins.

Current legislation allows retailers to maintain cameras and record customers for security purposes as long as they post warnings that customers might be recorded. However, the use of the mannequins is clearly for marketing purposes, not security. And most retailers seem to prefer to keep their usage of the new technology under wraps. Almax has not officially released the names of any of its clients—perhaps somewhat ironically, citing their need for privacy.

From your perspective as a consumer, do you believe that mannequins that record your movements, image, and possibly conversations in a store invade your privacy? If so, would you avoid stores that use this technology?

Is it ethical for retailers to monitor shoppers with hidden cameras in mannequins?

biometric data
Digital scanning of the physiological or behavioral characteristics of individuals as a means of identification.

▼ **EXHIBIT 10.10** Findings from Neuromarketing Studies by NeuroFocus

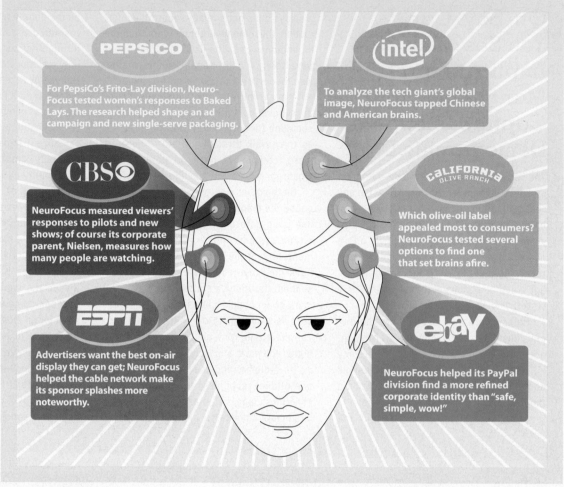

PEPSICO

For PepsiCo's Frito-Lay division, Neuro-Focus tested women's responses to Baked Lays. The research helped shape an ad campaign and new single-serve packaging.

intel

To analyze the tech giant's global image, NeuroFocus tapped Chinese and American brains.

CBS

NeuroFocus measured viewers' responses to pilots and new shows; of course its corporate parent, Nielsen, measures how many people are watching.

CALIFORNIA OLIVE RANCH

Which olive-oil label appealed most to consumers? NeuroFocus tested several options to find one that set brains afire.

ESPN

Advertisers want the best on-air display they can get; NeuroFocus helped the cable network make its sponsor splashes more noteworthy.

ebaY

NeuroFocus helped its PayPal division find a more refined corporate identity than "safe, simple, wow!"

Source: Reprinted with permission of Superexpresso.

Biometric data include one or more physical traits such as facial characteristics, iris scans, or fingerprints. Facebookers can turn off the facial detection function, but their biometric data is still collected. In Germany, with its strict privacy laws, regulators have demanded that Facebook stop collecting any biometric data.

Going even deeper than using biometric data, *neuromarketing* claims the ability to read consumers' minds, using wireless electroencephalogram (EEG) scanners that measure the involuntary brainwaves that occur when they view a product, advertisement, or brand images. Such insights would be invaluable for marketers to discover what truly appeals to consumers. For example, do people love the iPad because of its functionality, or is the true source of its appeal the curves of the tablet, which appeal to a primal preference in humans?[48] But as anyone who has ever seen a science fiction movie can imagine, the potential for abuses of such tools are immense. And a key question

remains: Do any consumers want marketers reading their brain waves and marketing goods and services to them in a manner that bypasses their conscious thoughts? One firm, NeuroFocus, used neuromarketing techniques with several global firms to garner customer information that would be difficult, if not impossible, to obtain using more traditional research methods (see Exhibit 10.10). ■

✓ **check** yourself

1. Under what circumstances is it ethical to use consumer information in marketing research?

2. What challenges do technological advances pose for the ethics of marketing research?

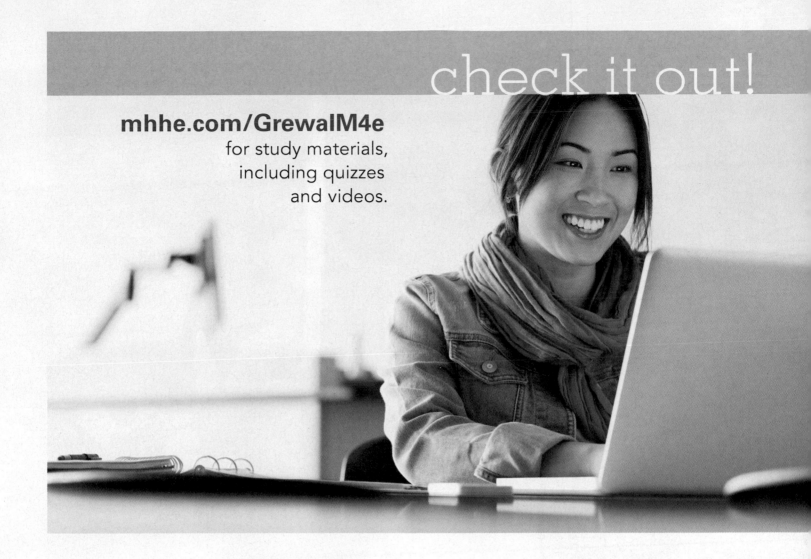

check it out!

mhhe.com/GrewalM4e
for study materials,
including quizzes
and videos.

product, branding, and
packaging decisions

eleven

To convey its brand of unconscious cool and radical adventure, Red Bull embraces daredevil stunts but also seeks to avoid making it look as if it is trying too hard to promote itself in so doing. Thus its branding operations walk a delicate line: Make a name for the brand but without appearing to do so.

Consider the latest example, the Red Bull Stratos project. Over a period of approximately five years, Red Bull bankrolled the experimental development of a flight suit that would enable daredevil and parachuter Felix Baumgartner to free fall from 24 miles up, break the sound barrier, and still survive his jump from space.[1] More than 70 technicians, physicians, and scientists worked for years on the project, ultimately allowing Baumgartner to jump successfully in October 2012.

A camera mounted on his helmet recorded the entire experience, including

LEARNING OBJECTIVES

After reading this chapter, you should be able to:

LO 11-1 Describe the components of a product.

LO 11-2 Identify the types of consumer products.

LO 11-3 Explain the difference between a product mix's breadth and a product line's depth.

LO 11-4 Identify the advantages that brands provide firms and consumers.

LO 11-5 Explain the various components of brand equity.

LO 11-6 Determine the various types of branding strategies used by firms.

LO 11-7 Distinguish between brand extension and line extension.

LO 11-8 Indicate the advantages of a product's packaging and labeling strategy.

the early moments, when he spun out of control in the thin stratosphere, until nearly five minutes later, when he landed. Approximately 8 million people watched the jump live.

continued on p. 234

product Anything that is of value to a consumer and can be offered through a voluntary marketing exchange.

continued from p. 233

Then the video, along with associated footage of the efforts to prepare for the jump, began to enjoy its really massive viral popularity. People wowed at the sight of a man flying through space, literally. They shared links, and mainstream media reported on both the event and the footage.

Despite this popularity, Red Bull purposefully chose not to enter the Stratos marketing communication in any awards competitions for best advertising, noting, "Our approach towards communications is that we don't really talk about ourselves too much. Rather, we focus on what we do—the events we create and produce and the athletes we support—versus who we are. With this guiding principal, we do not submit for awards very often."[2]

Rather, the company has continually sought to reinforce its image as a cutting-edge, danger-seeking, boundary-pushing entity. The data gathered through the Stratos project is being made available to pilots and astronauts who might need to bail out of a disabled aircraft. The newly designed spacesuit also revealed that it could protect the human body against the extreme conditions in the stratosphere. The medical director of the project, who previously was in charge of ensuring the health of NASA's space shuttle crews, noted, "We're pushing the technical envelope" with regard to space jumps.

Pushing the envelope is just what Red Bull wants its brand to be known for doing. By sponsoring events such as the space jump or even its annual Flugtag competition, Red Bull brands itself as fun, a little crazy, and ready for anything. But by letting the events speak largely for themselves, rather than promoting its participation in a traditional sense, it also maintains an image of slightly detached cool. It hopes that consumers who would like to think of themselves the same way will find this branding deeply compelling. ∎

> [When Mars manufactures M&Ms, Snickers, and other confectionary products, or when Trek designs bicycles, each company's core question is, What are customers looking for?]

As a key element of a firm's marketing mix (the four Ps), product strategies are central to the creation of value for the consumer. A **product** is anything that is of value to a consumer and can be offered through a voluntary marketing exchange. In addition to goods, such as soft drinks, or services, such as a stay in a hotel, products might be places (e.g., Six Flags theme parks), ideas (e.g., stop smoking), organizations (e.g., MADD), people (e.g., Oprah Winfrey), or communities (e.g., Facebook) that create value for consumers in their respective competitive marketing arenas.

This chapter begins with a discussion of the complexity and types of products. Next we examine how firms adjust their product lines to meet and respond to changing market conditions. Then we turn our attention to branding—why are brands valuable to the firm, and what are the different branding strategies firms use? We also never want to underestimate the value of a product's package and label. These elements should send a strong message from the shelf: Buy me! The final section of this chapter examines packaging and labeling issues.

LO 11-1 Describe the components of a product.

COMPLEXITY AND TYPES OF PRODUCTS
Complexity of Products

There is more to a product than its physical characteristics or its basic service function. Marketers involved with the development, design, and sale of products think of them in an interrelated fashion, as depicted in Exhibit 11.1. At the center is the **core customer value**, which defines the basic problem-solving benefits that consumers are seeking. When Mars manufactures M&Ms, Snickers, and other confectionary products, or when Trek designs bicycles, each company's core question is, What are customers looking for? With Mars, is it a sweet, great

▼ **EXHIBIT 11.1** Product Complexity

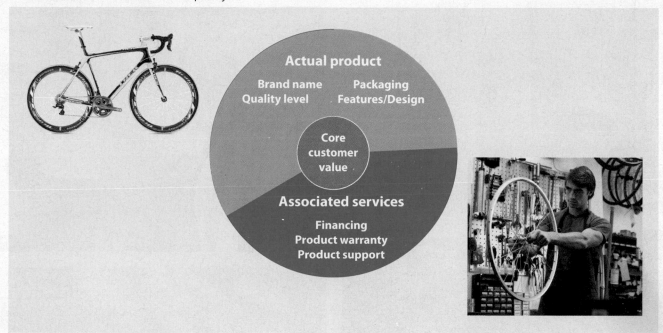

tasting snack, or is it an energy boost? With Trek, is the bike being used for basic green transportation (a cruiser), or is it for speed and excitement (a road, hybrid, or mountain bike)?

Marketers convert core customer value into an **actual product.** Attributes such as the brand name, features/design, quality level, and packaging are important, but the level of their importance varies, depending on the product. The Trek Madone 6 Series, for instance, is positioned as "the most exquisitely engineered bicycle ever made."[3] It features a carbon frame that is light, stiff, and comfortable; an advanced shifting system; and other high-tech features. Not only is it beautiful to look at, but customers can choose from three fits—pro, performance, and touring.

The **associated services** in Exhibit 11.1, also referred to as the **augmented product,** include the nonphysical aspects of the product, such as product warranties, financing, product support, and after-sale service. The amount of associated services also varies with the product. The associated services for a package of M&Ms may include only a customer complaint line, which means they are relatively less important than the associated services for a Trek bicycle. The frame of the Madone 6 Series bicycle is guaranteed for the lifetime of the original owner. Trek only sells its bikes in shops that have the expertise to service them properly. Every possible consumer question is answered on Trek's comprehensive website. Trek even has a financing program that allows customers to purchase a new bike on credit.

When developing or changing a product, marketers start with the core customer value to determine what their potential customers are seeking. Then they make the actual physical product and add associated services to round out the offering.

LO 11-2   Identify the types of consumer products.

Types of Products

Marketers consider the types of products they are designing and selling because these types affect how they will promote, price, and distribute their products. There are two primary categories of products and services that reflect who buys them: consumers or businesses. Chapter 7 discussed products for businesses. Here we discuss consumer products.

Consumer products are products and services used by people for their personal use. Marketers further classify consumer products by the way they are used and how they are purchased.

Specialty Products/Services   **Specialty products/ services** are those for which customers express such a strong preference that they will expend considerable effort to search for the best suppliers. Road bike enthusiasts, like those interested in

shopping products/ services Those for which consumers will spend time comparing alternatives, such as apparel, fragrances, and appliances.

convenience products/services Those for which the consumer is not willing to spend any effort to evaluate prior to purchase.

unsought products/ services Products or services consumers either do not normally think of buying or do not know about.

product mix See *product assortment*. The complete set of all products offered by a firm.

product lines Groups of associated items, such as those that consumers use together or think of as part of a group of similar products.

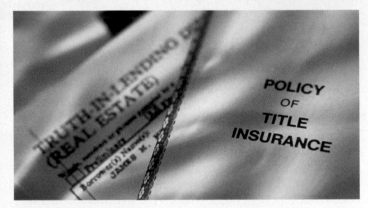

A medical professional is a specialty service. Apparel is a shopping product. Soda is a convenience product. Insurance is an unsought service.

the Trek Madone 6 Series, devote lots of time and effort to selecting just the right one. Other examples might include luxury cars, legal or medical professionals, or designer apparel.

Shopping Products/Services

Shopping products/services are products or services for which consumers will spend a fair amount of time comparing alternatives, such as furniture, apparel, fragrances, appliances, and travel alternatives. When people need new sneakers, for instance, they often go from store to store shopping—trying shoes on, comparing alternatives, and chatting with salespeople.

Convenience Products/Services

Convenience products/services are those products or services for which the consumer is not willing to spend any effort to evaluate prior to purchase. They are frequently purchased commodity items,

usually bought with very little thought, such as common beverages, bread, or soap.

Unsought Products/Services

Unsought products/ services are products consumers either do not normally think of buying or do not know about at all. Because of their very nature, these products require lots of marketing effort and various forms of promotion. When new-to-the-world products, as GPS systems once were, are first introduced, they are unsought products. Do you have cold hands and don't know what to do about it? You must not have heard yet of HeatMax HotHands Hand Warmers, air-activated packets that provide warmth for up to 10 hours. Do you have an internship in a less developed country and your regular insurance cannot give you the coverage you may need in case of an emergency? You now can turn to a Medex insurance policy.

Product Lines			
Ready-to-Eat Cereal	**Toaster Pastries and Wholesome Portable Breakfast Snacks**	**Cookies and Crackers**	**Natural, Organic, and Frozen**
Kellogg's Corn Flakes	Nutri-Grain	Cheez-It	Eggo
All-Bran	Special K	Keebler	Morningstar Farms
Apple Jacks	Kashi	Townhouse	Kashi
Cocoa Krispies	Pop-Tarts	Club	
Frosted Mini-Wheats	Bear Naked	Famous Amos	
Mueslix		Fudge Shoppe	
Kellogg's Raisin Bran		Murray	
Froot Loops			
Kashi			
Special K			
Rice Krispies			

Source: Kellogg's 2010 annual report, http://annualreport2010.kelloggcompany.com/innovation.htm.

check yourself

1. Explain the three components of a product.
2. What are the four types of consumer products?

LO 11-3 Explain the difference between a product mix's breadth and a product line's depth.

PRODUCT MIX AND PRODUCT LINE DECISIONS

The complete set of all products and services offered by a firm is called its **product mix**. An abbreviated version of Kellogg's product mix appears in Exhibit 11.2. The product mix typically consists of various **product lines**, which are groups of associated items that consumers tend to use together or think of as part of a group of similar products or services. Kellogg's product lines include ready-to-eat cereal; toaster pastries and wholesome portable breakfast snacks; cookies and crackers; and natural, organic, and frozen items.

The product mix reflects the breadth and depth of the company's product lines. A firm's product mix **breadth** represents a count of the number of product lines offered by the firm; Kellogg's has four, as indicated by the four columns in Exhibit 11.2. Product line **depth**, in contrast, equals the

number of products within a product line. Within Kellogg's breakfast snack product line, for example, it offers Nutri-Grain, Special K, and Kashi bars as well as Pop-Tarts.

However, adding unlimited numbers of new products can have adverse consequences. Too much breadth in the product mix becomes costly to maintain, and too many brands may weaken the firm's reputation.[4] In the past several years, for example, Revlon undertook a significant restructuring. It introduced a new line, Vital Radiance, aimed at women over the age of 45 years. But this line cut into the sales of its other brands and harmed its reputation among younger consumers, so Revlon eliminated the Vital Radiance line, to refocus on those products and markets that were doing well.[5]

Kellogg's offers four product lines (breadth) and multiple products within each product line (depth).

breadth Number of product lines offered by a firm; also known as variety.

depth The number of categories within a product line.

> ## YET FIRMS OFTEN MUST PRUNE THEIR PRODUCT LINES TO ELIMINATE UNPROFITABLE OR LOW MARGIN ITEMS AND REFOCUS THEIR MARKETING EFFORTS ON THEIR MORE PROFITABLE ITEMS.

▼ **EXHIBIT 11.3** Changes to a Product Mix

Product Line A	Product Line B	Product Line C	Product Line D
MILK			JAM
A1	B1	C1	D1
A2	B2	C2	D2
A3	B3		D3
A4	B4		D4
	B5		
	B6		
Added depth: New product (A4)	**Decreased depth: Dropped B5 & B6**	**Decreased breadth: Dropped product line C (C1 & C2)**	**Added breadth: New line (D1, D2, D3 & D4)**

(see deletion of products B5 and B6 in Exhibit 11.3). The decision is never taken lightly. Generally, substantial investments have been made to develop and manufacture the products. Yet firms often must prune their product lines to eliminate unprofitable or low margin items and refocus their marketing efforts on their more profitable items. Procter & Gamble (P&G) introduced Tide Basic as an extension of its Tide line—probably the best known detergent brand and a product that enjoys a reputation as an innovative, high-end brand. Tide Basic was priced 20 percent cheaper than regular Tide, but P&G deleted the extension less than a year after introducing it, worried that an inexpensive, less effective version simply undermined its brand rather than offering an appealing alternative.[8]

So why do firms change their product mix's breadth or depth?[6]

Increase Depth Firms might add items to address changing consumer preferences or to preempt competitors while boosting sales (see addition of product A4 in Exhibit 11.3). A service provider such as a bank typically offers consumer accounts as one of its product lines. To increase depth in this line, it frequently adds new types of accounts. Bank of America thus added an eChecking account to appeal to online users as an alternative to its traditional high-balance Advantage with Tiered Interest Checking option or its CampusEdge Checking for college students.[7] Social & Mobile Marketing 11.1 describes another extension in a product market, as Axe expands its fragrance product line to create a version for women.

Decrease Depth From time to time, it is also necessary to delete products within a product line to realign the firm's resources

To increase Tide's depth of assortment, P&G introduced Tide Basic, but soon deleted it because it believed it was undermining the Tide brand.

Decrease Breadth Sometimes it is necessary to delete entire product lines to address changing market conditions or meet internal strategic priorities (e.g., deleting product line C in Exhibit 11.3). Thus, the firm drops its line of bread and focuses its attention on its dairy products—milk and cheese (product lines A and B).

Increase Breadth
Firms often add new product lines to capture new or evolving markets and increase sales (e.g., product line D in Exhibit 11.3). The firm adds a whole new line of jam products. Jam is a complementary product to its bread line.

To increase product line breadth, a firm may add a new line of jam products to complement its bread line.

Social & Mobile Marketing
Axe Brand's Anarchy Fragrance and Graphic Novel

Axe body spray already owned 75 percent of the men's fragrance market, so when its owner, Unilever, wanted to grow the brand, it needed to expand its product depth. Thus came Axe Anarchy, a new scent offered in both male and female versions, to exploit the promise of irresistible sexuality that has proven so successful thus far.

In a decade's worth of controversial Axe commercials, average guys drew very attractive women to them simply by spraying themselves with the scent. The Anarchy message is even more edgy. As the name suggests, the product promises the notion of sexual energy that goes slightly out of control. An early commercial depicts a chaotic series of events, including a car pile-up, in which a man and a woman remain oblivious to the havoc but gravitate toward each other until they are just inches apart. "Unleash the chaos," the screen recommends, as the video cuts to shots of the two actors spraying themselves. "New Axe Anarchy for him and for her."[9]

Noting its youthful target market, Unilever also wanted to ensure that the advertising medium for Anarchy fit the brand extension, so the company unleashed an interactive digital campaign in the form of an online graphic novel. The serialized, comic book fantasy about the chaotic exploits of the Anarchy Girls would evolve in real time, in response to viewer input. The author and *X-Men* creator Scott Lobdell was hired to create the narrative in collaboration with any of the 2.3 million fans who registered on YouTube, Facebook, Twitter, and Axe's other social channels to help shape the story.[10]

The marketing subtext was clear: Break the narrative and break through sexually, which seemed to offer a potent message for young women. But some observers remain unconvinced that Axe's bold, crowd-sourced digital venture will help the brand make the cross-over into the women's body spray market. Could graphic novels, with their traditionally young male audience, really connect with young women?[11] Would Axe's explosive brand expansion strategy actually alienate the very audience that built its body spray brand, that is, average-guy male teens trying to attract a special girl? Would advertising to girls make Axe lose credibility among boys?

To promote the Axe Anarchy fragrance to young men and women, Unilever created a comic book fantasy about *Anarchy Girls*, available in real time on You Tube and other social media.

check yourself

1. What is the difference between product mix breadth and product line depth?
2. Why change product mix breadth?
3. Why change product line depth?

BRANDING

A company lives or dies based on brand awareness. Consumers cannot buy products that they don't know exist. Even if the overall brand name is familiar, it won't help sales of individual products unless consumers know what products are available under that name. When an editor at *Mademoiselle,* known for her style, started the Kate Spade brand in 1993, it was quickly a hit as women snapped up the chance to look as if they had just stepped

> " A company lives or dies based on brand awareness. Consumers cannot buy products that they don't know exist. "

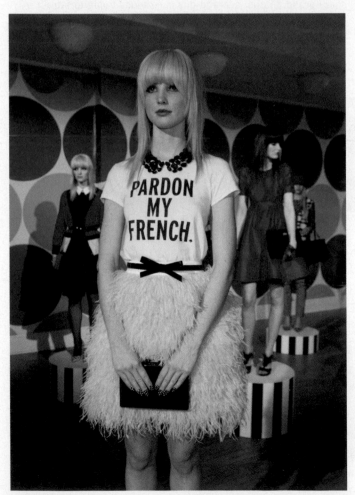
Kate Spade is positioned to appeal to young, fun-loving, urban professionals.

off the pages of a fashion magazine. But after Neiman Marcus bought the company, it failed to maintain the cutting-edge, fashion-forward brand image, and Kate Spade gained an unfortunate reputation for angular bags carried by suburban moms. Fortunately, its name got a boost when Liz Claiborne purchased it from Neiman Marcus and diligently repositioned the purses to appeal to young, fun-loving, urban professionals who appreciate great design, want to appear neat and polished, and enjoy being the most interesting person in the room. Thus Kate Spade is now Liz Claiborne's best performing brand, outpacing such consumer favorites as Juicy Couture, Mexx Europe, and Lucky Brand.[12]

Branding also provides a way for a firm to differentiate its product offerings from those of its competitors. Both Snapple and Tropicana make and sell fruit drinks, yet consumers may choose one over the other because of the associations that the brands invoke. Pioneer televisions use plasma panels manufactured by Panasonic, and yet the brand still enjoys a unique reputation, distinct and perceived by many to be better than Panasonic's.[13] As we discuss in more detail subsequently, brand names, logos, symbols, characters, slogans, jingles, and even distinctive packages constitute the various brand elements firms use,[14] which they usually choose to be easy for consumers to reco gnize and remember. Most consumers know the Nike swoosh and would recognize it even if the word Nike did not appear on the product or in an advertisement. Exhibit 11.4 summarizes some of these brand elements.

LO 11-4 Identify the advantages that brands provide firms and consumers.

Value of Branding for the Customer

Brands add value to merchandise and services, for both consumers and sellers, beyond physical and functional characteristics or the pure act of performing the service.[15] Let's examine some ways in which brands add value for both customers and the firm.

Brands Facilitate Purchases Brands are often easily recognized by consumers, and because they signify a certain quality level and contain familiar attributes, brands help consumers make quick decisions, especially about their purchases.[16] The cola market is a particularly strong example of this benefit. Some people think cola is cola, such that one brand is not too different from another. But branding has made it easy for Pepsi drinkers to find the familiar logo on the store shelf and more likely that they simply buy one of Pepsi's other products, should they decide to switch to a diet soda or a flavored

Brand Element	Description
Brand name	The spoken component of branding, it can describe the product or service/product characteristics and/or be composed of words invented or derived from colloquial or contemporary language. Examples include Comfort Inn (suggests product characteristics), Apple (no association with the product), or Zillow.com (invented term).
URLs (uniform resource locators) or domain names	The location of pages on the Internet, which often substitutes for the firm's name, such as Yahoo! and Amazon.
Logos and symbols	Logos are visual branding elements that stand for corporate names or trademarks. Symbols are logos without words. Examples include the Nike swoosh and the Mercedes star.
Characters	Brand symbols that could be human, animal, or animated. Examples include the Pillsbury Doughboy and the Keebler Elves.
Slogans	Short phrases used to describe the brand or persuade consumers about some characteristics of the brand. Examples include State Farm's "Like A Good Neighbor" and Dunkin' Donuts' "America Runs On Dunkin'."
Jingles/Sounds	Audio messages about the brand that are composed of words or distinctive music. Examples are Intel's four-note sound signature that accompanies the Intel Inside slogan.

Source: Adapted From Kevin Lane Keller, *Strategic Brand Management,* 3rd ed. (Upper Saddle River, NJ: Prentice Hall, 2007).

version. From promotions, past purchases, or information from friends and family, they recognize the offering before they even read any text on the label, and they likely possess a perception of the brand's level of quality, how it tastes, whether it is a good value, and, most important, whether they like it and want to buy it. Brands enable customers to differentiate one firm or product from another. Without branding, how could we easily tell the difference between Coca-Cola and Pepsi before tasting them?

Brands Establish Loyalty
Over time and with continued use, consumers learn to trust certain brands. They know, for example, that they wouldn't consider switching brands and, in some cases, feel a strong affinity to certain brands. Amazon.com has a loyal following because its reputation for service prompts customers to turn to it first. A customer whose $500 Playstation3 was apparently stolen during delivery received another Playstation3, without even having to pay additional shipping costs. Amazon lost $500, plus shipping, on a mistake that was not its fault, but it also gained a reputation for service with this customer, who would not only buy more electronics from Amazon but also tell everyone he could think of about this extraordinary example of customer service and choose Amazon's brand extension into the Kindle offerings before similar options provided by other brands.[17]

Brands Protect from Competition and Price Competition
Strong brands are somewhat protected from competition from other firms and price competition. Because such brands are more established in the market and have a more loyal customer base, neither competitive pressures on price nor retail-level competition is as threatening to the firm. Lacoste is widely known for its golf shirts. Although many similar brands are available and some retailers offer their own brands, Lacoste is perceived to be of superior quality, garners a certain status among its users, and therefore can command a premium price.

Brands Are Assets
For firms, brands are also assets that can be legally protected through trademarks and copyrights and thus constitute a unique form of ownership. Firms sometimes have to fight to ensure their brand names are not being used, directly or indirectly, by others. The term "Footzyroll" is literally different from the brand name Tootsie Roll, but the similarity is enough that the candy company brought suit against the new shoe line. The Footzyroll brand refers to comfortable, ballet-type shoes that women can roll up and stick in their purses to wear instead of heels at the end of the day. But Tootsie Roll claims that the similar-sounding term does more than describe the product; it also creates confusion

Tootsie Roll Industries, makers of Tootsie Roll candies, claims that the Footzyroll brand of shoes is so similar-sounding that it has the potential of significantly diluting its brand.

and implies that the candy company has some association with the shoes—with significant potential for brand dilution.[18]

LO 11-5   Explain the various components of brand equity.

Brands Affect Market Value Having well-known brands can have a direct impact on the company's bottom line. The value of a company is its overall monetary worth, comprising a vast number of assets. The value of the brand, just one of these assets, refers to the earning potential of the brand over the next 12 months.[19] The world's 10 most valuable brands for 2011 appear in Exhibit 11.5; although currently all the brands are U.S.-based firms, that is not the case every year.

Brand Equity for the Owner

The value of a brand translates into **brand equity**, or the set of assets and liabilities linked to a brand that add to or subtract from the value provided by the product or service.[20] Like the physical possessions of a firm, brands are assets a firm can build, manage, and harness over time to increase its revenue, profitability, and overall value. For example, firms spend millions of dollars on promotion, advertising, and other marketing efforts throughout a brand's life cycle. Sometimes this spending comes close to crossing ethical lines, as Ethical & Societal Dilemma 11.1 describes. However, marketing expenditures allocated carefully can result in greater brand recognition, awareness, perceived value, and consumer loyalty for the brand, which all enhance the brand's overall equity.

How do we know how good a brand is, or how much equity it has? Experts look at four aspects of a brand to determine its equity: brand awareness, perceived value, brand associations, and brand loyalty.

Brand Awareness **Brand awareness** measures how many consumers in a market are familiar with the brand and what it stands for and have an opinion about it. The

Coca-Cola is the most valuable brand in the world.

more aware or familiar they are, the easier their decision-making process is, which improves the chances of purchase. Familiarity matters most for products that are bought without much thought, such as soap or chewing gum, but brand awareness is also critical for infrequently purchased items or those the consumer has never purchased before. If the consumer recognizes the brand, it probably has attributes that make it valuable.[21] For those who have never purchased a Toyota, the simple awareness that it exists can help facilitate a purchase. Marketers create brand awareness through repeated exposures of the various brand elements (brand name, logo, symbol, character, packaging, or slogan) in the firm's communications to consumers through advertising, publicity, or other methods (see Chapters 18–20). Certain brands gain such predominance in a particular product market over time that they become synonymous with the product itself; that is, the brand name starts being used as the generic product category. Examples include Kleenex tissue, Clorox bleach, Band-Aid adhesive bandages, and Rollerblade skates. Companies must be vigilant in protecting their brand names because if they are used so generically, over time, the brand itself can lose its trademark status.

Perceived Value The **perceived value** of a brand is the relationship between a product's or service's benefits and its cost. Customers usually determine the offering's value in relationship to that of its close competitors. If they believe a less expensive brand is about the same quality as a premium brand, the

These brands are so strong that they have become synonymous with the product itself.

brand awareness
Measures how many consumers in a market are familiar with the brand and what it stands for; created through repeated exposures of the various brand elements (brand name, logo, symbol, character, packaging, or slogan) in the firm's communications to consumers.

perceived value
The relationship between a product's or service's benefits and its cost.

▼ **EXHIBIT 11.5** The World's Ten Most Valuable Brands

2011 Rank	Brand	Country of Ownership	2011 Brand Value ($ Billions)
1	Coca-Cola	U.S.	71.8
2	IBM	U.S.	69.9
3	Microsoft	U.S.	59.1
4	Google	U.S.	55.3
5	GE	U.S.	42.8
6	McDonald's	U.S.	35.6
7	Intel	U.S.	35.2
8	Apple	U.S.	33.5
9	Disney	U.S.	29.0
10	Hewlett-Packard	U.S.	28.5

Source: Interbrand's Best Global Brands 2013 report is a look at financial performance of the brand, role of brand in the purchase decision process and the brand strength. Go to www.bestglobalbrands.com for more information. Reprinted with permission.

perceived value of that cheaper choice is high. Merchandise sold by Target and Kohl's is not always of the highest quality, nor is the apparel the most fashion-forward. But not every customer needs to show up at school looking like they came from a fashion show runway. At the same time, these retailers hire high-fashion designers to create reasonably priced lines to feature in their stores—as Target did with Isaac Mizrahi and Missoni, to create well-designed pieces at Target-level prices.[22]

ethical & societal dilemma   11.1

Video Girl Barbie Brings Girls to Foursquare

Barbie, the dress-up toy that taught generations of girls what nurses and airline stewardesses look like, has now become a Video Girl with implications for the online generation. As Mattel's gushing, hot-pink YouTube video explains, the new Barbie Video Girl doll "is kind of amazing."[23] She has a tiny video camera in her necklace, an LCD screen on her back, and editing software tucked inside. The new Barbie can record up to 25 minutes of video that "you can download to your computer with a pink USB cable."

And the Video Girl doesn't stop there. She's a celebrity Foursquare user that can stay in touch with fans through the location-based social networking website by uploading clues for the Barbie Video Scavenger Hunt.[24] It's the perfect game for Foursquare, which encourages smartphone users to gather and share information while browsing in restaurants and shops. Now girls who aspire to be like Barbie Video Girls can check in as well and perhaps win the scavenger hunt. But is that what parents want?

Mattel's initiative blurs the line between play and advertising, though such

At New York City's Barbie Fashion Night Out (FNO), a fan scans a QR code of a Barbie wearing Alexis Bittar jewelry. Barbie invited FNO-goers to shop her closet via city-wide scavenger hunt.

confusion is nothing new in an industry that uses children's television shows and movies as marketing vehicles.[25] Spurred by the success of *Transformers: Revenge of the Fallen* and *Hot Wheels: Battle Force 5,* toy companies are investing heavily in content. Hasbro launched a cable channel, The Hub, to target 6–12-year-old viewers.[26] Mattel requires new toy designers to focus on offerings that can be branded simultaneously through a television show, feature film, or game.[27] In 2010, Disney announced that its movie financing would

be prioritized according to toy merchandising potentials.[28]

Groups such as the Coalition for a Commercial-Free Childhood object to this conflation of play and purchasing, especially as the industry reaches into children's lives with everywhere, anytime digital and mobile formats. A recent Federal Trade Commission proposal aims to protect children from unauthorized use of cookies and other online tracking mechanisms. But such limits do nothing to stop Virtual Girl Barbie from moving playtime online.

Brand Associations **Brand associations** reflect the mental and emotional links that consumers make between a brand and its key product attributes, such as a logo and its color, slogan, or famous personality. These brand associations often result from a firm's advertising and promotional efforts. Toyota's hybrid car, the Prius, is known for being economical, a good value, stylish, and good for the environment. But firms also attempt to create specific associations with positive consumer emotions such as fun, friendship, good feelings, family gatherings, and parties. State Farm Insurance thus uses the slogan "like a good neighbor, State Farm is there." Hallmark Cards associates its brand with helping people show they care with quality: "When you care enough to send the very best." Furthermore, the programs on Hallmark television channel are always consistent with the brand's wholesome family image.[29]

Brand Loyalty **Brand loyalty** occurs when a consumer buys the same brand's product or service repeatedly over time rather than buy from multiple suppliers within the same category.[30] Therefore, brand-loyal customers are an important source of value for firms. First, firms such as airlines, hotels, long-distance telephone providers, credit card companies, and retailers reward loyal consumers with loyalty or customer relationship management (CRM) programs, such as points customers can redeem for extra discounts or free services, advance

notice of sale items, and invitations to special events sponsored by the company. Second, the marketing costs of reaching loyal consumers are much lower because the firm does not have to spend money on advertising and promotion campaigns to attract these customers. Loyal consumers simply do not need persuasion or an extra push to buy the firm's brands. Third, loyal customers tend to praise the virtues of their favorite products, retailers, or services to others. This positive word of mouth reaches potential customers and reinforces the perceived value of current customers, all at no cost to the firm. Fourth, a high level of brand loyalty insulates the firm from competition because, as we noted in Chapter 2, brand-loyal customers do not switch to competitors' brands, even when provided with a variety of incentives.

 check yourself

1. How do brands create value for the customer and the firm?
2. What are the components of brand equity?

LO 11-6 Determine the various types of branding strategies used by firms.

BRANDING STRATEGIES

Firms institute a variety of brand-related strategies to create and manage key brand assets, such as the decision to own the brands, establishing a branding policy, extending the brand name to other products and markets, cooperatively using the brand name with that of another firm, and licensing the brand to other firms.

Brand Ownership

Brands can be owned by any firm in the supply chain, whether manufacturers, wholesalers, or retailers. There are two basic brand ownership strategies: manufacturer brands and retailer/store brands, as Exhibit 11.6 shows. Additionally, the brands can be marketed using a common/family name or as individual brands.

Manufacturer Brands **Manufacturer brands**, also known as **national brands**, are owned and managed by the manufacturer. Some famous manufacturer brands are Nike, Coca-Cola, KitchenAid, and Sony. With these brands, the

Companies use color to create different emotional associations to their brands.

Who Owns the Brand?		Manufacturer/National Brand	Retailer/Store Brand
Common Name or Not?	Family Brands	Kellogg's family line	Kroger's line
	Individual Brands	Kellogg's individual brand	Kroger's individual brand

manufacturer develops the merchandise, produces it to ensure consistent quality, and invests in a marketing program to establish an appealing brand image. The majority of the brands marketed in the United States are manufacturer brands, and manufacturing firms spend millions of dollars each year to promote their brands. For example, recently Procter & Gamble spent $3.1 billion on U.S. advertising, more than any other company.[31] By

In the past, sales of store brands were limited. But in recent years, as the size of retail firms has increased through growth and consolidation, more retailers have the scale economies to develop private-label merchandise and use this merchandise to establish a distinctive identity. In addition, manufacturers are more willing to accommodate the needs of retailers and develop co-brands for them. Store brands now account for almost

> "The majority of the brands marketed in the United States are manufacturer brands, and manufacturing firms spend millions of dollars each year to promote their brands."

owning their brands, manufacturers retain more control over their marketing strategy, are able to choose the appropriate market segments and positioning for the brand, and can build the brand and thereby create their own brand equity.

Retailer/Store Brands

Retailer/store brands, also called **private-label brands**, are products developed by retailers. In some cases, retailers manufacture their own products, whereas in other cases they develop the design and specifications for their retailer/store brands and then contract with manufacturers to produce those products. Some national brand manufacturers work with retailers to develop a special version of its standard merchandise offering to be sold exclusively by the retailer.

20 percent of the purchases in North America and close to 30 percent in Europe.[32] Kroger's private label accounts for 27 percent of its sales, and Costco and Trader Joe's both have based their brand identities around their store brands.

Naming Brands and Product Lines

Although there is no simple way to decide how to name a brand or a product line, the more the products vary in their usage or performance, the more likely it is that the firm should use individual brands. For example, General Motors uses several individual brands (Cadillac, Chevrolet, GMC), each catering to very different target markets and meeting different needs. Hyundai, on the other hand, uses only one brand since usage and level of performance are relatively homogeneous.

family brand A firm's own corporate name used to brand its product lines and products.

co-branding The practice of marketing two or more brands together, on the same package or promotion.

individual brands The use of individual brand names for each of a firm's products.

brand extension The use of the same brand name for new products being introduced to the same or new markets.

line extension The use of the same brand name within the same product line and represents an increase in a product line's depth.

brand dilution Occurs when a brand extension adversely affects consumer perceptions about the attributes the core brand is believed to hold.

Kellogg's uses a family branding strategy in which several product lines are sold under one name.

Kellogg's uses its family brand name prominently on its cereal brands (e.g., Kellogg's Special K, Kellogg's Froot Loops, Kellogg's Rice Krispies).

Individual Brands A firm can use **individual brand** names for each of its products. For example, while Kellogg's makes good use of the corporate branding strategy, it also allows other products, such as Morningstar Farms, Famous Amos cookies, Keebler cookies, and Cheez-Its (Exhibit 11.2), to keep individual identities not readily seen as being under the Kellogg's umbrella.[33]

Family Brands

A firm can use its own corporate name to brand all its product lines and products, so Kellogg's incorporates the company name into the brand name of Kellogg's Rice Krispies (refer to Exhibit 11.2). When all products are sold under one **family brand**, the individual brands benefit from the overall brand awareness associated with the family name.

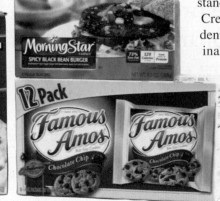

Kellogg's also uses an individual branding strategy since Keebler, Cheez-It, Morningstar, and Famous Amos are all marketed using separate names.

LO 11-7 Distinguish between brand extension and line extension.

Brand and Line Extensions[34]

A **brand extension** refers to the use of the same brand name in a different product line. It is an increase in the product mix's breadth.[35] The dental hygiene market, for instance, is full of brand extensions; Colgate and Crest sell toothpaste, toothbrushes, and other dental hygiene products, even though their original product line was just toothpaste. A **line extension** is the use of the same brand name within the same product line and represents an increase in a product line's depth.

There are several advantages to using the same brand name for new products. First, because the brand name is already well established, the firm can spend less in developing consumer brand awareness and brand associations for the new product.[36] Kellogg's has

> Colgate and Crest sell toothpaste, toothbrushes, and other dental hygiene products, even though their original product line was just toothpaste.

branched out from the cereal company it once was. Its strategy of branding the corporate name into the product name has allowed it to introduce new products quicker and more easily. Kellogg's Eggo Syrup was a natural extension to its product line of breakfast foods.

Second, if either the original brand or the brand extension has strong consumer acceptance, that perception will carry over to the other product. Consumers who had not used the Neutrogena brand before trying the brand extension, Neutrogena Wave power cleanser, might be encouraged to try Neutrogena's core product line of cleansers and moisturizing lotions, especially if their experience with the Wave has been positive.[37]

Third, when brand extensions are used for complementary products, a synergy exists between the two products that can increase overall sales. For example, Frito-Lay markets both chips and dips under its Frito-Lay and Doritos brand names. When people buy the chips, they tend to buy the dips as well.

Not all brand extensions are successful, however. Some can dilute brand equity.[38] **Brand dilution** occurs when the brand extension adversely affects consumer perceptions about the attributes the core brand is believed to hold.[39] Here are some examples of unsuccessful brand extensions:[40]

- Cheetos Lip Balm was based on the idea that if you like Cheetos, you would want to wipe it all over your lips.

- Lifesavers Soda did well in prelaunch taste tests but didn't in subsequent sales.

- Colgate Kitchen Entrees were microwavable frozen dinner entrees that shared the name with the famous toothpaste.

- Bic thought that since people wanted their disposable lighters and razors, they would also want disposable underwear. They were wrong.

> If the fit between the product categories is high, consumers will consider the extension credible, and the brand association will be stronger for the extension.

Lifesavers unsuccessfully attempted a brand extension strategy with its line of soda.

To prevent the potentially negative consequences of brand extensions, firms consider the following:

- Marketers should evaluate the fit between the product class of the core brand and that of the extension.[41] If the fit between the product categories is high, consumers will consider the extension credible, and the brand association will be stronger for the extension. Thus, when Starbucks introduced its line of instant coffee, VIA, it made sense to its customers.

- Firms should evaluate consumer perceptions of the attributes of the core brand and seek out similar attributes for the extension because brand-specific associations are very important for extensions.[42] For example, if HP printers were associated with reliability, performance, and value, consumers would expect the same brand-specific attributes in other products that carried the HP brand name.

- Firms should refrain from extending the brand name to too many products and product categories to avoid diluting the brand and damaging brand equity. Donald Trump has been quite successful lending his name to various property, television lines, and Macy's clothing but was unsuccessful with extending himself to branding steaks.

- Firms should consider whether the brand extension will be distanced from the core brand, especially if the firm wants to use some but not all of the existing brand associations. Marriott has budget, mid-tier, and luxury hotels. Its luxury hotels, including the Ritz-Carlton, Edition, and Renaissance, do not use the name Marriott at all.[43]

Co-branding

Co-branding is the practice of marketing two or more brands together on the same package, promotion, or store. Co-branding can enhance consumers' perceptions of product quality by signaling unobservable product quality through links between the firm's brand and a well-known quality brand. For example, Yum Brands frequently combines two or more of its restaurant chains, including A&W, KFC, Long John Silver's, Pizza Hut, and Taco Bell, into one store space.[44] This co-branding strategy is designed to appeal to diverse market segments and extend the hours in which each restaurant attracts customers. Yet co-branding also creates risks, especially when the customers of each of the brands turn out to be vastly different. For example, the Burger King and Häagen-Dazs co-branding strategy failed because the customer profiles for each brand were too different.[45]

The NBA licenses products like these bobblehead figures of Dallas Mavericks and San Antonio Spurs players to a manufacturer in exchange for a negotiated fee.

Co-branding may also fail when there are disputes or conflicts of interest between the co-brands.

Brand Licensing

Brand licensing is a contractual arrangement between firms whereby one firm allows another to use its brand name, logo, symbols, and/or characters in exchange for a negotiated fee.[46] Brand licensing is common for toys, apparel, accessories, and entertainment products, such as video games. The firm that provides the right to use its brand (licensor) obtains revenues through royalty payments from the firm that has obtained the right to use the brand (licensee). These royalty payments may take the form of an upfront, lump-sum licensing fee or be based on the dollar value of sales of the licensed merchandise.

One very popular form of licensing is the use of characters created in books and other media. Such entertainment licensing has generated tremendous revenues for movie studios. Disney, for instance, flooded retail stores with products based on *The Princess and the Frog* movie. *Star Wars* memorabilia has continued to be successful since the first film was released in the 1970s. A long-standing staple of licensing has been major league sports teams that play in the NBA, NFL, or NHL as well as various collegiate sports teams.

Licensing is an effective form of attracting visibility for the brand and thereby building brand equity while also generating additional revenue. There are, however, some risks associated with it. For the licensor, the major risk is the dilution of its brand equity through overexposure of the brand, especially if the brand name and characters are used inappropriately.[47]

Brand Repositioning

Brand repositioning or **rebranding** refers to a strategy in which marketers change a brand's focus to target new markets or realign the brand's core emphasis with changing market preferences.[48] Although repositioning can improve the brand's fit with its target segment or boost the vitality of old brands, it is not without costs and risks. Firms often need to spend tremendous amounts of money to make tangible changes to the product and packages as well as intangible changes to the brand's image through various forms of promotion. These costs may not be recovered if the repositioned brand and messages are not credible to the consumer or if the firm has mistaken a fad for a long-term market trend.

Yet even when they enjoy the benefits of their well-known name and reputations, brands may find it necessary to reposition, even if that means challenging hundreds of years of tradition. For example, Procter & Gamble's (P&G) Ivory soap brand first appeared in 1879, promoted with an image of purity in white, subdued packaging. The new Ivory comes in brightly colored packages, with cyan, purple, and green splashed across the wrappers and bottles. This new approach nevertheless links to and builds on the brand's well-established position. In humorous televised ads running in select cities with strong markets for the brand, P&G mocks how complicated the use of soap has become today. Unusual soaps made to look like waffles with syrup and sugar contrast against the pure bars that Ivory continues to offer. Yet its repackaging and new advertising push definitely reflect a repositioning. The Ivory brand has long appealed to both men and women, but P&G aims to improve its annual sales of less than $100 million by making a devoted push to appeal to young moms in addition to keeping core customers.[49]

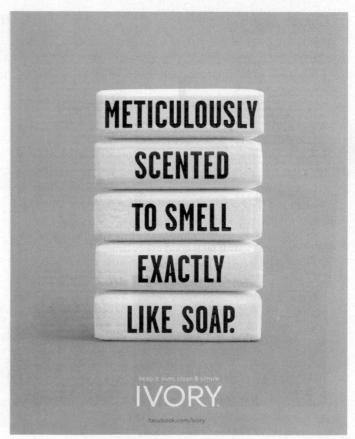

P&G's new ad campaign is positioned to appeal to young moms, in addition to keeping its core customers.

brand licensing
A contractual arrangement between firms, whereby one firm allows another to use its brand name, logo, symbols, or characters in exchange for a negotiated fee.

brand repositioning (rebranding) A strategy in which marketers change a brand's focus to target new markets or realign the brand's core emphasis with changing market preferences.

primary package
The packaging the consumer uses, such as the toothpaste tube, from which he or she typically seeks convenience in terms of storage, use, and consumption.

secondary package
The wrapper or exterior carton that contains the primary package and provides the UPC label used by retail scanners; can contain additional product information that may not be available on the primary package.

 check yourself

1. What are the differences between manufacturer and private-label brands?

2. What is co-branding?

3. What is the difference between brand extension and line extension?

4. What is brand repositioning?

LO 11-8 Indicate the advantages of a product's packaging and labeling strategy.

PACKAGING

Packaging is an important brand element with more tangible or physical benefits than other brand elements. Packages come in different types and offer a variety of benefits to consumers, manufacturers, and retailers. The **primary package** is the one the consumer uses, such as the toothpaste tube. From the primary package, consumers typically seek convenience in terms of storage, use, and consumption.

The **secondary package** is the wrapper or exterior carton that contains the primary package and provides the UPC label used by retail scanners. Consumers can use the secondary package to find additional product information that may not be available on the primary package. Like primary packages, secondary packages add consumer value by facilitating the convenience of carrying, using, and storing the product.

Whether primary or secondary, packaging plays several key roles: It attracts the consumers' attention. It enables products to stand out from their competitors. It offers a promotional tool (e.g., "NEW" and "IMPROVED" promises on labels). Finally, it allows for the same product to appeal to different markets with different sizes, such that convenience stores stock little packages that travelers can buy at the last minute, whereas Costco sells extra large versions of products.

Firms occasionally change or update their packaging as a subtle way of repositioning the product. A change can be used to attract a new target market and/or appear more up to date to its current market. For instance, the Morton Salt umbrella girl has significantly changed since it was first introduced in 1914, but the slogan "when it rains it pours" endures today. Changes also can make consumers feel like they are receiving something

Snapple changed its packages for Snapple iced teas to tout its blend of "better stuff"–healthy and tasty black tea leaves.

ethical & societal dilemma 11.2

Calories 0, Vitamins 0: How Much Information Can Water Labels Provide?

Water, water everywhere. Especially in developed countries, consumers everywhere can simply turn on the tap, and there it is. And yet firms have been successful in packaging this almost free, natural resource, creating some cachet for it, and selling it.

Bottled water enjoyed double-digit growth, year to year, as U.S. consumers doubled the amount they drank from 1997 to 2007, from 13.4 to 29.3 gallons per year. The popularity and growth of the industry has attracted attention, though. Bottled and tap water companies operate under different regulations. Yet many observers and government agencies argue the rules should be the same, with water bottle labeling subject to regulations as detailed as those that the tap water companies experience.

Bottled water, as a food product, currently is regulated by the Food and Drug

Administration, so it lists nutrition information and ingredients on the labels (i.e., 0 percent of most nutrients; contents: water). In contrast, municipal water is controlled by the Environmental Protection Agency, which has more authority to enforce quality standards. The result may be misinformed consumers, many of whom believe bottled water is safer and healthier than tap water. And yet according to the U.S. Government Accounting Office (GAO), the FDA lacks the authority to require water bottlers to use certified water quality tests or report those test results. Also, the existing requirements to ensure safe bottled water, both state and federal, are less comprehensive than the rules about safeguarding tap water.[50]

Even without such regulations, though, consumers may be changing their attitudes. The bottled water industry recently has experienced flat growth. The cause may be the economic downturn, which has forced consumers to cut costs wherever possible. Environmental concerns may be another factor since bottled water creates significant waste.

Perhaps better labeling of products will mean even less ambiguity about the value of bottled versus tap water, which could

Would more comprehensive labels on bottled water change your water consumption behavior?

offer opportunities for differentiation among bottled water brands that adopt different bottling and labeling methods.[51]

Would more comprehensive labels on bottled water change your water consumption behavior? Is bottled water better than tap water? Is buying bottled water an ecologically sound purchase decision?

---

tangible in return for paying higher prices, even when the product itself remains untouched. Whether true or not, consumers see new packaging and tend to think that the "new" product may be worth trying. Dr Pepper Snapple Co. has retooled the packages (with a related ad campaign) for Snapple iced teas to tout its blend of "better stuff"—healthy green and tasty black tea leaves.[52]

Some packaging changes are designed to make the product more ecological, such as PepsiCo.'s response to concerns about the waste associated with bottled water. To reduce the amount of plastic it uses, PepsiCo has decreased the weight of its water bottles by 20 percent. The "Eco-Fina" bottle is nearly 50 percent lighter than the version introduced in 2002, which means less plastic in landfills. In a competitive marketplace, a brand that can associate with less harmful impact on the environment often can gain a significant competitive advantage it can use to induce consumers to purchase in good conscience.[53]

Sometimes packaging changes can backfire, though, such as when Tropicana changed its packaging to feature a picture of a glass of juice, rather than the familiar straw in an orange.

Customers balked, calling the new image "ugly," "stupid," and reminiscent of "a generic bargain brand."[54] The company greatly misjudged its customers' loyalty to its existing brand position, exemplified by its packaging. For example, before the change, the president of Tropicana North America claimed, "The straw and orange have been there for a long time, but people have not necessarily had a huge connection to them." After suffering tremendous backlash and deciding to rescind its repackaging decision, the same executive admitted, "What we didn't get was the passion this very loyal small group of consumers have."[55]

Many consumers experience wrap rage—a great frustration with packaging that makes it seemingly impossible to get at the actual products. So companies are moving away from traditional clamshells, which are the curved plastic package around many electronics goods, because they are so difficult to open. Costco has replaced the clamshells with packaging made of coated paperboard that still requires scissors to open but is flat and therefore can be opened easily.

Retailers' and manufacturers' priorities for secondary packaging often differ from those of its customers. They want

> ## "A product label is much more than just a sticker on the package; it is a communication tool.

convenience in terms of displaying and selling the product. In addition, secondary packages are often packed into larger cartons, pallets, or containers to facilitate shipment and storage from the manufacturer to the retailer. These shipping packages benefit the manufacturer and the retailer, in that they protect the shipment during transit; aid in loading, unloading, and storage; and allow cost efficiencies due to the larger order and shipment sizes.

Packaging can also be used in a far more subtle way, namely, to help suppliers save costs. For routine purchases, consumers rarely engage in actual decision making but rather just grab their familiar jar of peanut butter from the shelf. In so doing, they likely never notice that Skippy peanut butter jars have gone from containing 18 ounces to just 16.3 ounces—same appearance, same diameter and height of the jar, same price, but a bigger indent in the bottom. Approximately 30 percent of packaged goods similarly have lost content recently, and most of the changes have gone unnoticed by consumers. General Mills even has a department devoted to cost cutting through package redesign or clever content reduction ideas, which it calls the "Holistic Margin Management" department. Because 75 percent of a product's cost may be in the packaging, these savings can represent huge overall savings for the company.[56]

Product Labeling

Labels on products and packages provide information the consumer needs for his or her purchase decision and consumption of the product. In that they identify the product and brand, labels are also an important element of branding and can be used for promotion. The information required on them must comply with general and industry-specific laws and regulations, including the constituents or ingredients contained in the product, where the product was made, directions for use, and/or safety precautions.

Many labeling requirements stem from various laws, including the Federal Trade Commission Act of 1914, the Fair Packaging and Labeling Act of 1967, and the Nutrition Labeling Act of 1990. Several federal agencies, industry groups, and consumer watchdogs carefully monitor product labels. The Food and Drug Administration is the primary federal agency that reviews food and package labels and ensures that the claims made by the manufacturer are true. Ethical & Societal Dilemma 11.2 illustrates the problems associated with the different regulations that apply to various edible products as well as some associated labeling concerns.

A product label is much more than just a sticker on the package; it is a communication tool. Many of the elements on the label are required by laws and regulations (i.e., ingredients, fat content, sodium content, serving size, calories), but other elements remain within the control of the manufacturer. How manufacturers use labels to communicate the benefits of their products to consumers varies by the product. Many products highlight specific ingredients, vitamin content or nutrient content (e.g., iron), and country of origin. This focus signals to consumers that the product offers these benefits. The importance of the label as a communication tool should not be underestimated. ■

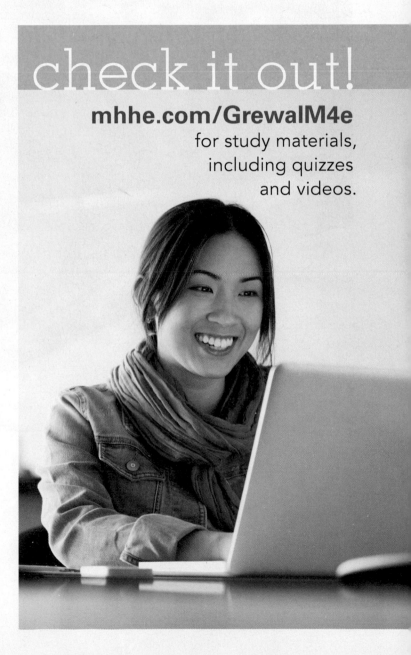

check it out!

mhhe.com/GrewalM4e
for study materials,
including quizzes
and videos.

CHAPTER 11 | Product, Branding, and Packaging Decisions **251**

developing
new products

When LEGOs first arrived in the United States in the early 1960s, the company had devised a set of principles for the design of the molded stud-and-tube bricks:[1]

- Unlimited play potential
- For girls and for boys
- Fun for every age
- Year-round play
- Healthy, quiet play
- Long hours of play
- Development, imagination, creativity
- The more LEGO, the greater the value
- Extra sets available
- Quality in every detail

Over time, the Danish firm grew to become one of the top toy manufacturers in the world, introducing new sets and variations on its basic theme, including an extensive line of *Star Wars* models (as well as lines related to other popular movie franchises), basic robot technology, and superhero-themed collections. Perhaps unintentionally, it appeared that LEGO had come to violate one of its basic principles in that its toys appealed widely to boys but not specifically to girls.

Faced with declining profits in the early 2000s, LEGO had determined that the popularity of video and automated games meant it needed to refocus on these areas. It developed LEGO-branded video games to match its *Star Wars* line of building sets. It pushed its website and interactive opportunities. The My Lego Network social media site encouraged children to build their own

continued on p. 254

After reading this chapter, you should be able to:

LO 12-1 Identify the reasons firms create new products.

LO 12-2 Describe the different groups of adopters articulated by the diffusion of innovation theory.

LO 12-3 Describe the various stages involved in developing a new product or service.

LO 12-4 Explain the product life cycle.

continued from p. 253

web pages, personalized with pictures of their LEGO creations, music, and sticker compositions.[2]

But these changes caused some members of the LEGO team to worry about the effects on its long-standing traditions. Perhaps the predesigned sets were hindering creativity, rather than encouraging it. Maybe telling kids to go online was not really healthy for long-lasting play. And perhaps product lines focused on pirates, science fiction, and robots were not appealing enough to girls and the ways they like to play.

In additional market research involving in-depth observations of children playing—on their own and as they wished, without any direction or guidance from outside—LEGO gained some notable insights.[3] For example, rather than appealing to children by simplifying its toys, LEGO had made its sets too easy to construct, without room for careful thought or creativity. The observational research showed that children wanted a sense of mastery and accomplishment, not just instant gratification. In addition, its research with girls revealed that they were not uninterested in building. They just wanted to tell stories to go along with their construction—an effort that was undermined by the pre-set stories in LEGO video games. As a LEGO vice president summarized, "We heard very clear requests from moms and girls for more details and interior building, a brighter color palette, a more realistic figure, role play opportunities and a story line that they would find interesting."[4]

Thus arrived the LEGO Friends, mini-doll figures whose names, back stories, and adventures are up to girls to develop and include in their own narratives.[5] The friends—Mia, Emma, Stephanie, Olivia, and Andrea—live in treehouses, drive convertibles, run a beauty parlor and a bakery, and play with their dogs. The color schemes for all the sets are heavy in pink and purple. Furthermore, the doll figures are slimmer and curvier than the traditional, blocky LEGO figures.

For some parents, these new products that appeal to a new segment of consumers are problematic: The LEGO Friends do not require children to complete the assembly to begin playing, which seemingly could diminish girls' sense of accomplishment. Others suggest that the offerings of beauty parlor and café sets reinforce gender stereotypes without allowing room for female firefighters or politicians—or space explorers or pirates, for that matter. If the new sets are expressly for girls, does that imply that the old sets were really only for boys?[6]

LEGO insists that it has always tried to appeal to girls through its wide variety of products. And though the final tallies are not in yet on this brand new product, LEGO's legacy suggests it may be on to something big. By focusing on sets, instead of just free-form blocks, LEGO tripled its profits between 2006 and 2010. Three LEGO sets sell every second worldwide.[7] Today, by appealing to girls with an entirely new product, perhaps it can increase that rate to four or five per second. ■

Unlike other LEGO products, LEGO Friends are designed especially for girls.

Few three-letter words are more exciting than "new." It brings forth an image of freshness, adventure, and excitement. Yet "new" also is a complex term when it comes to market offerings because it might mean adding something new to an existing product, introducing a flavor never offered before, or relying on different packaging that provides added value. But

and services on their own. We conclude the chapter with an examination of how new products and services get adopted by the market and how firms can change their marketing mix as the product or service moves through its life cycle.

innovation The process by which ideas are transformed into new products and services that will help firms grow.

> ## Our lives are defined by the many new products and services developed through scientific and technological advances and by the added features included in products that we have always used.

the most exhilarating type of new product is something never seen before. Thousands of patent applications pursue this elusive prize: a successful and truly innovative new product.

Imagine living 200 years ago: You cook meals on a stove fueled by coal or wood; you write out homework by hand (if you are lucky enough to attend school) and by candlelight. To get to school, you hike along unpaved roads to reach a small, cold, basic classroom with just a few classmates who listen to a lecture from a teacher writing on a blackboard.

Today, you finish your homework on a laptop computer with word processing software that appears to have a mind of its own and can correct your spelling automatically. Your climate-controlled room has ample electric light. While you work on your laptop, you also talk with a friend using the hands-free headset of your wireless phone. As you drive to school in your car, you pick up fast food from a convenient drive-through window while browsing and listening to your personal selection of songs playing through your car speakers, connected wirelessly to your iPad. Your friend calls to discuss a slight change to the homework, so you pull over to grab your iPhone, make the necessary change to your assignment, and e-mail it from your smartphone to your professor. When you arrive at school, you sit in a 200-person classroom, where you can plug in your laptop, take notes on your iPad, or digitally record the lecture. The professor adds notes on the day's PowerPoint presentations using her tablet computer. You have already downloaded the PowerPoint presentations and add similar notes through your own laptop. After class, to complete your planning for a last-minute party, you send out a Facebook invitation to your friends and ask for responses to get a headcount. You then text your roommate, telling her to get food and drinks for the right number of people, which she orders through an online grocer that will deliver later in the day.

Our lives are defined by the many new products and services developed through scientific and technological advances and by the added features included in products that we have always used. In this second chapter dealing with the first P in the marketing mix (product), we continue our discussion from the preceding chapter and explore how companies add value to product and service offerings through innovation. We also look at how firms develop new products

LO 12-1   Identify the reasons firms create new products.

WHY DO FIRMS CREATE NEW PRODUCTS?

New market offerings provide value to both firms and customers. But the degree to which they do so depends on how new they really are. When we say a "new product/service," we don't necessarily mean that the market offer has never existed before—kids have long played with LEGOs, but LEGO Friends and James Bond 007 inspired kits are new versions for them. Completely new-to-the-market products represent fewer than 10 percent of all new product introductions each year. It is more useful to think of the degree of newness or innovativeness on a continuum from truly new-to-the-world—as WiFi was a few years ago—to slightly repositioned, such as when Kraft's Capri Sun brand of ready-to-drink beverages were repackaged in a bigger pouch to appeal to teens.

Regardless of where on the continuum a new product lies, firms have to innovate. **Innovation** refers to the process by

LEGO Friends live in treehouses and are designed to appeal to girls.

> WITHOUT INNOVATION AND ITS RESULTING NEW PRODUCTS AND SERVICES, FIRMS WOULD HAVE ONLY TWO CHOICES: CONTINUE TO MARKET CURRENT PRODUCTS TO CURRENT CUSTOMERS OR TAKE THE SAME PRODUCT TO ANOTHER MARKET WITH SIMILAR CUSTOMERS.

which ideas are transformed into new offerings, including products, services, processes, and branding concepts that will help firms grow. Without innovation and its resulting new products and services, firms would have only two choices: continue to market current products to current customers or take the same product to another market with similar customers.

Although innovation strategies may not always work in the short run—some estimates indicate that only about 3 percent of new products actually succeed—various overriding and long-term reasons compel firms to continue introducing new products and services, as the following sections describe.

Changing Customer Needs

When they add products, services, and processes to their offerings, firms can create and deliver value more effectively by satisfying the changing needs of their current and new customers or by keeping customers from getting bored with the current product or service offering. Sometimes, companies can identify

Moving? Rent Frogbox reusable plastic boxes and spare the landfills.

problems and develop products or services that customers never knew they needed. For example, moving can be stressful; among other things, having to buy, build, and dispose of moving boxes is a hassle, expensive, and not very good for the environment. Canadian firm Frogbox rents out reusable plastic moving boxes. It delivers them to the customer and picks them up at the new address when they are finished. The boxes stack neatly inside each other and don't require assembly, eliminating the time-consuming task of building and breaking down boxes. The firm is called Frogbox because it donates 1 percent of sales to frog habitat restoration.[8] Adding to its sustainability efforts, it uses solar energy to power its website and waste-generated biodiesel to fuel its trucks. Adding Value 12.1 examines how Huggies has adapted to consumer needs too.

Market Saturation

The longer a product exists in the marketplace, the more likely it is that the market will become saturated. Without new products or services, the value of the firm will ultimately decline.[9] Imagine, for example, if car companies simply assumed and expected that people would keep their cars until they stopped running. If that were the case, there would be no need to come up with new and innovative models; companies could just stick with the models that sell well. But few consumers actually keep the same car until it stops running. Even those who want to stay with the same make and model often want something new, just to add some variety to their lives. Therefore, car companies revamp their models every year, whether with new features like GPS or a more powerful engine or by redesigning the entire look of the vehicle. The firms sustain their growth by getting consumers excited by the new looks and new features, prompting many car buyers to exchange their old vehicle years before its functional life is over. Adding Value 12.2 notes some other innovations that carmakers are trying.

Saturated markets can also offer opportunities for a company that is willing to adopt a new process or mentality. At one point in time, mass marketers would not even consider entering a market that they believed would not earn at least $50 million. But General Mills is looking to niche markets for its future growth. Whereas only 1 percent of the U.S. population suffers from celiac disease—a condition that damages the digestive system when sufferers ingest gluten—a much higher percentage of U.S. consumers say they want to reduce or eliminate gluten,

Adding Value 12.1

Turning Diaper Changes into Child's Play

Diaper brands face shrinking markets. In most industrialized countries, birth rates are lower than they have been in decades. Furthermore, these fewer parents increasingly note the value of lower cost, store-brand diapers. Then they stick with their choices: 55 percent of diaper purchasers report that they nearly always buy their preferred brand. Facing these tough market dynamics, Huggies, Kimberly-Clark's diaper brand, aimed to introduce a new product to excite, appeal to, and reengage the market of parents of infants.[10]

It knew just where to start—that is, with a consumer study. Huggies quickly recognized that babies around 10 months or so are learning to crawl, starting to walk, and discovering how much fun it is to move around. The parents of these active babies thus had a very particular need: to keep their wild and crazy babies still long enough to get new diapers on them. According to the Huggies study, more than 60 percent of parents reported that their squirmy babies frequently scrambled out of reach, making it tough to complete the diaper change.[11]

Thus Huggies developed a clear-cut concept for its new product. Described as a first of its kind,[12] the Little Movers Slip-On diaper features stretchable material on its sides for a snug fit. Looking a little like regular underwear, the slip-ons with legholes offer the same absorbency and leakage protection as regular Huggies diapers, but they are designed specifically to make life easier for scrambling parents.

In online, print, and in-store ad campaigns, Huggies shows how a diaper change with Little Movers can be fun rather than a battle of wills. Over video of a baby rolling over, a voiceover announces that Huggies' latest product offers parents "a whole new way to change a rolling pin." Then the shot changes to show a series of variations—the acrobutt who bends over and peers through her legs, the streaker who crawls across the screen naked, and the booty scoocher, pushing forward on his backside. No fidgety child, whatever the type, will elude a parent armed with a Little Movers diaper. In addition to showing activity that likely resonates with any parents, Huggies has attempted to engage customers by asking them to upload home video of their babies' own tricky moves onto its YouTube site. More than 2,000 parents responded almost immediately, with funny videos of their Jumping Beans and Kick n' Roller babies.[13]

Although the per-diaper price for a Little Movers slip-on averages about 16 percent higher than the price of competing diapers, Kimberly-Clark hopes that simplifying the diaper change for parents is well worth the savings they offer, in terms of the parents' time and perhaps for saving the furniture from an unfortunate accident by a little wild child.

Huggies Little Movers Slip-On diapers are designed to make life easier for parents.

a wheat protein, from their diet. As awareness increases, those percentages are growing, such that the U.S. market could be worth up to $6.3 billion. General Mills has created more than 300 gluten-free products, including both variations on its regular offerings, like Chex cereals, and brand new concepts, such as gluten-free desserts and pancake mixes.[14]

Managing Risk through Diversity

Through innovation, firms often create a broader portfolio of products, which help them diversify their risk and enhance firm value better than a single product can.[15] If some products in a portfolio perform poorly, others may do well. Firms with multiple products can better withstand external shocks, including changes in consumer preferences or intensive competitive activity. For this reason, firms such as 3M demand that a specific percentage of their sales each year must come from new products introduced within the previous few years. In the cookie aisle, Keebler offers many variations of its basic product, cookies, including Animals, Chips Deluxe, E.L. Fudge, Gripz, Sandies, Vanilla Wafers, and Vienna Fingers. This diversification

diffusion of innovation The process by which the use of an innovation, whether a product or a service, spreads throughout a market group over time and over various categories of adopters.

enables Keebler to enjoy more consistent performance than it would with just one kind of cookie.

Fashion Cycles

In industries that rely on fashion trends and experience short product life cycles—including apparel, arts, books, and software markets—most sales come from new products. For example, a motion picture generates most of its theater, DVD, and cable TV revenues within a year of its release. If the same selection of books were always for sale, with no new titles, there

The Keebler line's risk is lessened by offering many variations of its basic product, cookies.

Adding Value   12.2

Carmakers Look for an Edge, Above and Under the Hood

The competition and new partnerships generated by the global car market have yielded a wealth of new product approaches, both above and below the hood, as automakers strive to meet an international aesthetic while also responding to near-universal demand for more fuel-efficient cars. In particular, U.S. carmakers can no longer simply appeal to American tastes, with tailfins, boxy SUVs, and little concern about fuel economy. Car design must meet the demands of drivers overseas. General Motors recently introduced a new concept car, the Chevrolet Tru 140S, an "affordable exotic" model that gets 40 miles per gallon. Another Chevrolet concept, Code 130R, takes elements from the BMW 1 Series, the 1960s Ford Anglia from Europe, and Japanese subcompact car models.

While crafting new looks, GM also is looking for designs that will survive shifting trends. The Cadillac ATS sedan, which aims to compete with the BMW 3 Series, is not nearly as distinctive as classic Cadillac models from

the past. But its understated style may enable the ATS to age more gracefully and require fewer, less frequent redesigns. Ford hired European designers to come up with many of its most successful recent models, including the Focus and the Fiesta. These small, quick, sporty cars appeal to the worldwide market. Chrysler's new owner Fiat has added Italian elements to make the U.S. brand appear more global in its design.[16]

Automakers also are relying heavily on new engineering to meet global demand. Tighter fuel efficiency standards and shifting buyer preferences are forcing carmakers to develop lighter, smaller-cylinder cars, more electrics and hybrids, and new turbocharged engines that couple with electric motors.[17] Even luxury cars are becoming lighter. Mercedes-Benz has spent seven years developing the aluminum body of its new SL 550, which is 308 pounds lighter than the previous model yet still offers unparalleled torsion resistance.

Smaller engines are getting a second look too: For the first time in 20 years, Cadillac is offering a four-cylinder engine to deliver fuel efficiency in its ATS. The appeal of these smaller, powerful engines is vast. Ford's new Fusion Hybrid couples a new, lighter lithium ion battery with a lighter four-cylinder engine to deliver six more miles per gallon in fuel efficiency. Plug-in hybrids are entering the market, including Ford's Fusion Energi, which competes with the Chevy Volt and models influenced by Toyota's Prius.

While re-designing its cars for more European tastes, Fiat-owned Chrysler has revived some of the engineering that made its Dodge Dart compact so efficient. And GM has used its globally successful small-car platform as the basis for both its Chevrolet Sonic subcompact and the Buick Encore crossover. With design oriented to global tastes and engineering focused on a newer, more efficient bottom line, automakers worldwide are hoping drivers will like what they see.

The Cadillac ATS is less distinctive than earlier models. As a result, its understated style may require fewer redesigns.

Video games like Madden NFL are "fashionable" because consumers demand new versions. Once they have "beat" the game, they want to be challenged with a new experience.

To generate sales, apparel fashion designers produce entirely new product selections a few times per year.

would be no reason to buy more. Consumers of computer software and video games demand new offers because once they have beaten the game, they want to be challenged by another game or experience the most recent version, as the remarkable sales of successive versions of the Madden NFL game exemplify.[18] In the case of apparel, fashion designers produce entirely new product selections a few times per year.

Improving Business Relationships

New products do not always target end consumers; sometimes they function to improve relationships with suppliers. For example, Kraft, the maker of Capri Sun, found that its lemonade flavor was selling poorly. Through a little market research, it realized that the reason was the placement of the packages in pallets. Because it was placed at the bottom of the stack in pallets, lemonade was the last flavor retailers would sell. By changing and innovating its pallet, Kraft offered chimney stacks for each flavor, enabling the retail stockers to reach whichever flavor they needed easily. Sales of Capri Sun's lemonade improved by 162 percent.[19]

Even if they succeed in innovating and creating new products, new-to-the-world products are not adopted by everyone at the same time. Rather, they diffuse or spread through a population in a process known as *diffusion of innovation.*

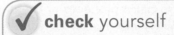

check yourself

1. What are the reasons firms innovate?

LO 12-2   Describe the different groups of adopters articulated by the diffusion of innovation theory.

DIFFUSION OF INNOVATION

The process by which the use of an innovation—whether a product, a service, or a process—spreads throughout a market group, over time and across various categories of adopters, is referred to as **diffusion of innovation**.[20] The theory surrounding diffusion of innovation helps marketers understand the rate at which consumers are likely to adopt a new product or service. It also gives them a means to identify potential markets for their new products or services and predict their potential sales, even before they introduce the innovations.[21]

> "Consumers of computer software and video games demand new offers because once they have beaten the game, they want to be challenged by another game or experience the most recent version."

Apple has released several pioneer products in recent years, including the iPhone.

The Green Mountain Coffee K-Cup Packs are one of the top selling new food and beverage brands.

Truly new product introductions, that is, new-to-the-world products that create new markets, can add tremendous value to firms. These new products, also called **pioneers** or **breakthroughs**, establish a completely new market or radically change both the rules of competition and consumer preferences in a market.[22] The Apple iPod is a pioneer product. Not only did it change the way people listen to music, but it also created an entirely new industry devoted to accessories such as cases, ear buds, docking stations, and speakers. Although Apple offers many of these accessories itself, other companies have jumped on the bandwagon, ensuring that you can strap your iPod to your arm while on the move or insert it into the base of a desk lamp equipped with speakers to get music and light from your desk. And don't forget: The iPod also launched perhaps the most notable other recent pioneer, the iPhone, along with the innovative iTunes service, the iPod Touch, and even the iPad.[23]

Pioneers have the advantage of being **first movers**; as the first to create the market or product category, they become readily recognizable to consumers and thus establish a commanding and early market share lead. Studies also have found that market pioneers can command a greater market share over a longer time period than later entrants can.[24] Some recent new entries that have enjoyed such success appear in Exhibit 12.1.

Yet not all pioneers succeed.[25] In many cases, imitators capitalize on the weaknesses of pioneers and subsequently gain advantage in the market. Because pioneering products and brands face the uphill task of establishing the market alone, they pave the way for followers, who can spend less marketing effort creating demand for the product line and focus directly on creating demand for their specific brand. Also, because the pioneer is the first product in the market, it often has a

less sophisticated design and may be priced relatively higher, leaving room for better and lower-priced competitive products. A majority of new products are failures: As many as 95 percent of all new consumer goods fail, and products across all markets and industries suffer failure rates of 50 to 80 percent.[26]

▼ **EXHIBIT 12.1** Sales of Top Selling New Food and Beverage Brands

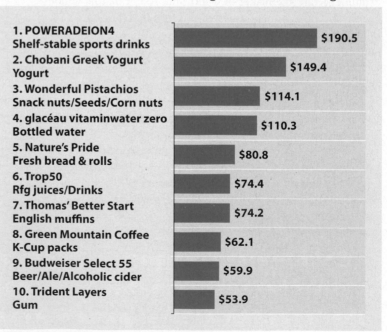

Brand	Sales
1. POWERADEION4 — Shelf-stable sports drinks	$190.5
2. Chobani Greek Yogurt — Yogurt	$149.4
3. Wonderful Pistachios — Snack nuts/Seeds/Corn nuts	$114.1
4. glacéau vitaminwater zero — Bottled water	$110.3
5. Nature's Pride — Fresh bread & rolls	$80.8
6. Trop50 — Rfg juices/Drinks	$74.4
7. Thomas' Better Start — English muffins	$74.2
8. Green Mountain Coffee — K-Cup packs	$62.1
9. Budweiser Select 55 — Beer/Ale/Alcoholic cider	$59.9
10. Trident Layers — Gum	$53.9

Source: Reprinted with permission of Symphony IRI Group.

An important question to ask is, why is the failure rate for new products so high? One of the main reasons is the failure to assess the market properly by neglecting to do appropriate product testing, targeting the wrong segment, and/or poor positioning.[27] Firms may also overextend their abilities or competencies by venturing into products or services that are inconsistent with their brand image and/or value proposition. We discuss some infamous product failures in Exhibit 12.2.

As the diffusion of innovation curve in Exhibit 12.3 shows, the number of users of an innovative product or service spreads through the population over a period of time and generally follows a bell-shaped curve. A few people buy the product or service at first, then more buy, and finally fewer people buy as the degree of the diffusion slows. These purchasers can be divided into five groups according to how soon they buy the product after it has been introduced.

Innovators

Innovators are those buyers who want to be the first on the block to have the new product or service. These buyers enjoy taking risks and are regarded as highly knowledgeable. You probably know someone who is an innovator—or perhaps you are one for a particular product or service category. For example, the person who stood in line overnight to be sure to get a ticket for the very first showing of the latest superhero movie is an innovator in that context. Firms that invest in the latest technology, either to use in their products or services or to make the firm more efficient, also are considered innovators. Typically, innovators keep themselves very well informed about the product category by subscribing to trade and specialty magazines, talking to other experts, visiting product-specific blogs and forums that describe the coolest new products,[28] and attending product-related forums, seminars, and special events. Yet innovators represent only about 2.5 percent of the total market for any new product or service.

These innovators are crucial to the success of any new product or service, though, because they help the product gain market acceptance. Through talking about and spreading positive word of mouth about the new product, they prove instrumental in bringing in the next adopter category, known as early adopters.[29]

Clairol's *Touch of Yogurt Shampoo* failed because consumers didn't like the idea of washing their hair with yogurt.

Early Adopters

The second subgroup that begins to use a product or service innovation is **early adopters**. They generally don't like to take as much risk as innovators do but instead wait and purchase the product after careful review. Thus, this market waits for the first reviews of the latest movie before purchasing a ticket, though they likely still go a week or two after it opens. They do not stand in line to grab the first Samsung LED Thin 3D televisions; only after reading the innovators' complaints and praises do they decide whether the new technology is worth the cost.[30] Most of them go ahead and purchase, though, because early adopters tend to enjoy novelty and often are regarded as the opinion leaders for particular product categories.

This innovator was the first person to purchase an iPad at this Apple store.

pioneers New product introductions that establish a completely new market or radically change both the rules of competition and consumer preferences in a market; also called *breakthroughs*.

breakthroughs See *pioneers*.

first movers Product pioneers that are the first to create a market or product category, making them readily recognizable to consumers and thus establishing a commanding and early market share lead.

innovators Those buyers who want to be the first to have the new product or service.

early adopters The second group of consumers in the diffusion of innovation model, after *innovators,* to use a product or service innovation; generally don't like to take as much risk as innovators but instead wait and purchase the product after careful review.

Product	Concept	Why It Failed
New Coke	In response to growing market pressure, Coca-Cola launched a reformulated version of its classic cola in 1985 that was so hated it was pulled from shelves three months later.	Coke underestimated the consumers affinity to the original formulation and their unwillingness to change.
Sony Betamax	In 1975, Sony bet big on the Betamax, one of the first ever mass-produced home video recording systems.	Unfortunately, the next year, JVC launched the VHS player, ensuring a format-war similar to the Blu-ray and HD-DVD format wars of 2006.
Harley Davidson Perfume	After being successful with lighters and t-shirts bearing the Harley logo, Harley Davidson branched out into its own line of perfumes associated with the motorcyle lifestyle.	Although lighters and t-shirts may resonate with the Harley image, customers were not as attracted to smelling like a motorcycle.
Bic Underwear	Bic is well-known for its disposable products: pens, lighters, and razors. Capitalizing on their ability to cross product categories, Bic began producing underwear.	The concept of buying underwear from a company well-known for disposable pens was confusing and off-putting to consumers.
Bottled Water for Pets	Trying to capitalize on the pet pampering craze, makers of *Thirsty Cat!* and *Thirsty Dog!* launched a line of bottled water for cats and dogs. No longer did owners need to give their pet tap water, instead they could give them a daily pet drink in flavors such as Crispy Beef, Tangy Fish, and Grilled Chicken.	Although people do indeed desire to pamper their pets, the idea of purchasing bottled water for them never caught on. The associations generated by their flavors, such as tangy fish tasting water, probably did not help either.
Frito Lay Lemonade	To Frito Lay, lemonade seemed like a reasonable enough brand extension. After all, the high salt content of corn chips often leads consumers to search out something to quench their thirst.	Associating a salty snack with a supposed thirst quencher did not go over well.
Kellogg's Breakfast Mates	Capitalizing on the convenience market, Kellogg's Breakfast Mates launched a line of cereal products in 1998 that came with cereal, spoon, and milk together.	Sometimes a good idea is poorly executed. The milk was usually warm because it did not require refrigeration and the product was not child-friendly, making its appeal very limited.
Apple Newton	Launched in 1993 with a price tag of more than $700, the Apple Newton was one of the first PDAs, which then led the way for the Palm Pilot, BlackBerry, and iPad.	The Newton concept was ahead of its time. Unfortunately due to its bulky size and ridicule by comedians, the Newton only lasted until 1998.
Colgate Kitchen Entrees	Colgate launched a line of frozen dinners. Apparently the idea was that consumers would enjoy eating a Colgate meal and then using Colgate on their toothbrush afterward.	The association of toothpaste with a chicken stir-fry was something customers did not find appetizing.
Clairol's Touch of Yogurt Shampoo	Shampoo with a touch of yogurt to improve hair quality.	Consumers were not enticed with the idea of washing their hair with yogurt, something Clairol should have known after their Look of Buttermilk failed in test markets a few years earlier.

Source: DailyFinance.com, Top 25 Biggest Product Flops of All Time. http://www.dailyfinance.com/photos/top-25-biggest-product-flops-of-all-time/3662621.

▼ **EXHIBIT 12.3** Diffusion of Innovation Curve

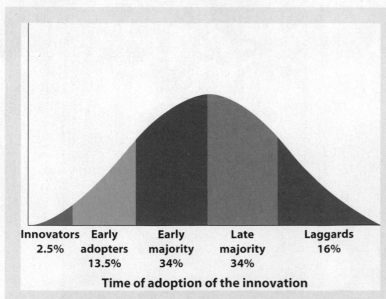

Time of adoption of the innovation

Source: Adapted from Everett M. Rodgers, *Diffusion of Innovation* (New York: The Free Press, 1983).

This group, which represents about 13.5 percent of all buyers in the market, spreads the word. As a result, early adopters are crucial for bringing the other three buyer categories to the market. If the early adopter group is relatively small, the number of people who ultimately adopt the innovation likely will also be small.

Early Majority

The **early majority**, which represents approximately 34 percent of the population, is crucial because few new products and services can be profitable until this large group buys them. If the group never becomes large enough, the product or service typically fails.

The early majority group differs in many ways from buyers in the first two stages. Its members don't like to take as much risk and therefore tend to wait until the bugs are worked out of a particular product or service. This group probably rents the latest *Avengers* movie during the first week it comes out on video. Thus, they

When you go see a movie like The Avengers, *are you an early adopter, early majority, majority, late majority, or laggard viewer?*

experience little risk because all the reviews are in, and their costs are lower because they're renting the movie instead of going to the theater. When early majority customers enter the market, the number of competitors in the marketplace usually also has reached its peak, so these buyers have many price and quality choices.

Late Majority

At 34 percent of the market, the **late majority** is the last group of buyers to enter a new product market. When they do, the product has achieved its full market potential. Perhaps these movie watchers wait until the newest movie is easy to find at the rental store or put it low on their Netflix queue, to be delivered after the other consumers interested in watching it have already seen it. By the time the late majority enters the market, sales tend to level off or may be in decline.

Laggards

Laggards make up roughly 16 percent of the market. These consumers like to avoid change and rely on traditional products

until they are no longer available. In some cases, laggards may never adopt a certain product or service. When *Avengers* eventually shows up on their regular television networks, they are likely to go ahead and watch it.

Using the Diffusion of Innovation Theory

Using the diffusion of innovation theory, firms can predict which types of customers will buy their new product or service immediately after its introduction as well as later as the product is more and more accepted by the market. With this knowledge, the firm can develop effective promotion, pricing, and other marketing strategies to push acceptance among each customer group.

When Amazon first introduced its Kindle e-book reader for around $400, it sold out in less than five hours.[31] The Kindle 2 arrived at an initial price of $359. Within six months, Amazon announced a price level below $300 to acknowledge the inroads made by competitors such as Barnes & Noble, Sony, and Apple.[32] Then as the market continued to grow—to approximately 20 million buyers—and Apple's iPad shifted expectations, Amazon plunged ahead with its iPad competitor, the Kindle Fire, priced at just under $200. The plan seems to have been successful; though Amazon does not publish sales numbers, estimates indicate that it sold approximately 6 million Kindle Fire devices within just a few months of its introduction.[33]

However, because different products diffuse at different rates, marketers must work to understand the diffusion curve for each new product and service as well as the characteristics of the target customers in each stage of the diffusion. For example, the marketing decisions for e-readers are notably different from the parallel decisions for electronic books. When the e-readers first emerged on the market, the price of e-books was a fraction of the price of hardcover versions—a policy that made sense to consumers. But as e-readers have grown increasingly popular and widespread, the price of e-books has become comparable and, in some cases, more expensive than the price of the hardcover versions.[34] Moreover, the speed with which products or services diffuse depends on several characteristics. In the next sections, we'll look at how

> If the early adopter group is relatively small, the number of people who ultimately adopt the innovation likely will also be small.

early majority A group of consumers in the diffusion of innovation model that represents approximately 34 percent of the population; members don't like to take much risk and therefore tend to wait until bugs are worked out of a particular product or service; few new products and services can be profitable until this large group buys them.

late majority The last group of buyers to enter a new product market; when they do, the product has achieved its full market potential.

laggards Consumers who like to avoid change and rely on traditional products until they are no longer available.

> ## THE CHINESE VERSION OF WEB BROWSER FIREFOX HAS DIFFERENT FEATURES THAN ITS WESTERN COUNTERPART BECAUSE RESEARCH INDICATED THAT CHINESE USERS SURF THE INTERNET DIFFERENTLY.

Apple has responded to Amazon's Kindle and the e-reader and tablet market as a whole with its iPad.

Relative Advantage
If a product or service is perceived to be better than substitutes, then the diffusion will be relatively quick. Instead of offering just an e-reader, Apple has developed a multi-purpose tablet device (the iPad). When launched, the iPad had several relative advantages, including a touch screen, a vibrant and large color screen, access to various games and apps, and the ability to watch videos and listen to music.[35]

Compatibility
A diffusion process may be faster or slower, depending on various consumer features, including international cultural differences. For example, the Chinese version of web browser Firefox has different features than its Western counterpart because research indicated that Chinese users surf the Internet differently. The Firefox China Edition has more mouse-based controls, like a double-click to close a tab on the browser, as well as a drop-down button on the toolbar for a calculator, screenshot grabber, and image editor.[36]

Turning from a browser to a tablet, Apple's iPad has been heavily criticized for lack of compatibility. Adobe's Flash, a format that it purports 75 percent of web videos are encoded in, does not work on the iPad. In response to these criticisms, Apple has explained their choice to use HTML5 (over Flash) as being an open-source format, which it considers the future of the Internet.[37]

Observability
When products are easily observed, their benefits or uses are easily communicated to others, which enhances the diffusion process. Consumers seeing their friends using the iPad, seeing the devices on television or on YouTube, or reading about them in the deluge of media coverage surrounding each iPad release may be convinced to purchase one as well. In contrast, since people may not want to talk about their Botox treatments to reduce wrinkles, the use of this product is less easily observed by others and therefore diffused more slowly.

Complexity and Trialability
Products that are relatively less complex are also relatively easy to try. These products will generally diffuse more quickly and lead to greater/faster adoption than those that are not so easy to try. For example, most customers who may be interested in purchasing a new tablet know that they can go to any Apple store and immediately try it there in the store. The options for trying a Kindle are a little more complex. Due to the lack of Amazon stores, consumers may not be aware that they can try one at Best Buy. But even the consumers who go to a Best Buy to try one often run into an availability problem—whereas Apple stores may have dozens of iPads for customers to try, electronics stores typically have just a few floor models.

The diffusion of innovation theory thus comes into play in the immediate and long-term aftermath of a new product or service introduction. But before the introduction, firms must actually develop those new offerings. In the next section, we detail the process by which most firms develop new products and services and how they introduce them into the market.

The Chinese version of Web browser Firefox has different features than its Western counterpart.

 check yourself

1. What are the five groups on the diffusion of innovation curve?
2. What factors enhance the diffusion of a good or service?

Idea generation	Concept testing	Product development	Market testing	Product launch	Evaluation of results
Development of viable new product ideas.	Testing the new product idea among a set of potential customers.	Development of prototypes and/or the product.	Testing the actual products in a few test markets.	Full-scale commercialization of the product.	Analysis of the performance of the new product and making appropriate modifications.

LO 12-3 Describe the various stages involved in developing a new product or service.

HOW FIRMS DEVELOP NEW PRODUCTS

The new product development process begins with the generation of new product ideas and culminates in the launch of a new product and the evaluation of its success. The stages of the new product development process, along with the important objectives of each stage, are summarized in Exhibit 12.4.

Idea Generation

To generate ideas for new products, a firm can use its own internal research and development (R&D) efforts, collaborate with other firms and institutions, license technology from research-intensive firms, brainstorm, research competitors' products and services, and/or conduct consumer research; see Exhibit 12.5. Firms that want to be pioneers rely more extensively on R&D efforts, whereas those that tend to adopt a follower strategy are more likely to scan the market for ideas. Let's look at each of these idea sources.

Internal Research and Development

Many firms have their own R&D departments, in which scientists work to solve complex problems and develop new ideas.[38] Historically, firms such as IBM in the computer industry, Black and Decker in the consumer goods industry, 3M in the industrial goods industry, and Merck and Pfizer in the pharmaceuticals industry have relied on R&D development efforts for their new products. In other industries, such as software, music, and motion pictures, product development efforts also tend to come from internal ideas and R&D financial investments.

The product development costs for these firms are quite high, and the resulting new product or service has a good chance of being a technological or market breakthrough. Firms expect such products to generate enough revenue and profits to make the costs of R&D

worthwhile. R&D investments generally are considered continuous investments, so firms may lose money on a few new products. In the long run, though, these firms are betting that a few extremely successful new products, often known as blockbusters, can generate enough revenues and profits to cover the losses from other introductions that might not fare so well.

Some global firms also are taking an approach called reverse innovation, as we discussed in Chapter 7. They turn to subsidiaries in less developed markets for new product ideas. From its Shanghai research center, Coca-Cola developed Minute Maid Pulpy, a new juice drink that the corporation has moved into 19 countries and is now worth more than $1 billion. Levi's Denizen brand got its start in India and China, where the company worked on ideas for producing more affordable jeans. In the U.S. market, Denizen jeans sell for about half the cost of a pair of regular Levi's and are available exclusively at Target.[39]

R&D Consortia In recent years, more and more firms have been joining consortia, or groups of other firms and institutions, possibly including government and educational institutions, to explore new ideas or obtain solutions for developing

From where do you think the idea for a waterproof tablet from Fujitsu was derived? Internal R&R, R&D consortia, licensing, brainstorming, outsourcing, competitor's products, customer input, or a combination?

had received FDA approval at the time of the deals!

Brainstorming Firms often engage in brainstorming sessions during which a group works together to generate ideas. One of the key characteristics of a brainstorming session is that no idea can be immediately accepted or rejected. The moderator of the session may channel participants' attention to specific product features and attributes, performance expectations, or packaging. Only at the end of the session do the members vote on the best ideas or combinations of ideas. Those ideas that receive the most votes are carried forward to the next stage of the product development process.

Outsourcing In some cases, companies have trouble moving through these steps alone, which prompts them to turn to outside firms such as IDEO, a design firm based in Palo Alto, California. IDEO offers not new products but rather a stellar service that helps clients generate new product and service ideas in industries such as health care, toys, and computers. IDEO employs anthropologists, graphic designers, engineers, and psychologists whose special skills help foster creativity and innovation. As exercise is becoming more and more popular, companies are looking for ways to capitalize on the beginner's market. Balanced Body is a company that makes

new products. Here, the R&D investments come from the group as a whole, and the participating firms and institutions share the results.

In many cases, the consortia involve pharmaceutical or high-tech members, whose research costs can run into the millions—too much for a single company to bear. The National Institutes of Health (NIH) sponsors medical foundations to conduct research to treat rare diseases. The research is then disseminated to the medical community, thus encouraging the development of drugs and therapies more quickly and at a lower cost than would be possible if the research were privately funded. The U.S. cable industry has initiated its CableLabs–Energy Lab consortium to find ways to improve the energy efficiency of cable set-top boxes and develop more advanced cable services, such as better sleep settings, to promote other forms of energy conservation.[40]

Licensing For many other scientific and technological products, firms buy the rights to use the technology or ideas from other research-intensive firms through a licensing agreement. This approach saves the high costs of in-house R&D, but it means that the firm is banking on a solution that already exists but has not been marketed. Some of the largest recent licensing deals in the pharmaceutical industry are for potential weight-loss solutions. In separate deals, one worth $1.4 billion and another worth $1.1 billion, two big pharmaceutical firms licensed the marketing rights for new products developed by small biotechnology firms to combat obesity.[41] Yet neither drug

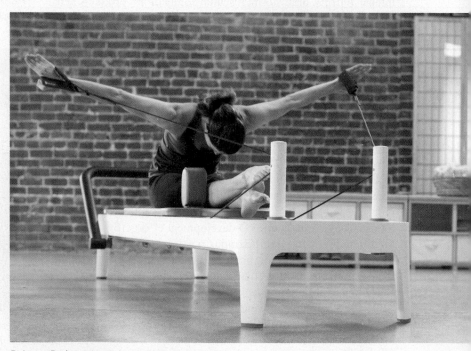

Balance Body partnered with IDEO to develop a less-intimidating, more-user-friendly reformer to be used with Pilates.

and sells reformers to be used with Pilates. A reformer is a device that helps Pilates participants develop good alignment, core strength, and flexibility. When Balanced Body did research and found that people starting Pilates found the reformers that were currently on the market to be too intimidating, it partnered with IDEO to develop a reformer that had better user experience while maintaining the high level of functionality its products engender.[42] In an eight-week period, IDEO created a redesigned model with fewer wheels while improving functionality and adjustability of the product and reducing the cost of the machine.[43]

Competitors' Products

A new product entry by a competitor may trigger a market opportunity for a firm, which can use reverse engineering to understand the competitor's product and then bring an improved version to market. **Reverse engineering** involves taking apart a product, analyzing it, and creating an improved product that does not infringe on the competitor's patents, if any exist. This copycat approach to new product development is widespread and practiced by even the most research-intensive firms. Copycat consumer goods show up in apparel, grocery and drugstore products as well as in technologically more complex products such as automobiles and computers, as Social & Mobile Marketing 12.1 notes.

reverse engineering
Involves taking apart a competitor's product, analyzing it, and creating an improved product that does not infringe on the competitor's patents, if any exist.

Customer Input

Listening to the customer in both B2B and B2C markets is essential for successful idea generation.[44] Because customers for B2B products are relatively few, firms can follow their use of products closely and solicit suggestions and ideas to improve those products either by using a formal approach, such as focus groups, interviews, or surveys, or through more informal discussions. The firm's design and development team then works on these suggestions, sometimes in consultation with the customer. This joint effort between the selling firm and the customer significantly increases the probability that the customer eventually will buy the new product.

Customer input in B2C markets comes from a variety of sources. In some cases, consumers may not expressly demand a new product, though their behavior demonstrates their desire for it. After analyzing its sales data, Walmart realized that the majority of its customers always or often buy store brands

Social & Mobile Marketing 12.1
When Microsoft Plays Catch-Up

Microsoft is one of the most innovative companies of all time. After revolutionizing the home computer industry, it set out to be a leader in the information technology home entertainment fields. It seems like not a year ever goes by without something new from the brainchild of Bill Gates.

But one area in which Microsoft has been behind the curve is the search engine market. Google, with its nearly 80 percent market share and massive name recognition, is in no real danger from competitors, including Bing.com, the newest Microsoft offering. But Bing is challenging Yahoo.com for the remainder of the market. Perhaps most important, it is distinguishing itself by providing more frequent updates and feature additions than the other search engines. Consumers benefit overall because Bing is forcing competitors to improve their offering to keep pace with Microsoft or prevent it from stealing market share from them.

Its efforts have paid off somewhat: Bing now attracts approximately 14 percent of all searches by U.S. users. These gains come mostly at the expense of other competitors such as Yahoo. Google maintains a remarkably high share. And the costs of its copycat efforts meant that the division responsible for Bing lost $2.56 billion in the most recent fiscal year.[45]

To differentiate itself better, Bing is being promoted as a decision engine rather than a search engine. It integrates Foursquare, a

Microsoft's Bing competes with Google in the search engine market.

location-based phone application, into Bing Maps results. Users can focus on a particular area, such as South Boston, which means Bing can act like an integrative day planner and list the best things to do in that area. It is working on developing a desktop application, and Bing links seamlessly with Facebook to show users which search outcome their friends like best.[46] Despite Microsoft's problems developing search engines, Bing suggests it intends to stay aggressive in this market.

Faced with a severe economic downturn, the luxury chocolatier Godiva set out to determine how its customers were changing too. Godiva's premium products generally had been purchased and gifted only on special occasions. But in a members-only online community, called Chocolate Talk, Godiva asked customers for their insights, in the hope of discovering where and when they buy chocolate—Godiva or any other brand.[47]

The results? People buy Godiva for special occasions for others whom they care about or want to impress, especially during the holiday season and for their birthdays. But true chocolate connoisseurs still expressed their preference for premium chocolate, as opposed to lower end brands. Because Godiva sells in mall boutiques, purchasing the chocolates requires a special trip to the mall—acceptable for a special occasion but not for an impulse treat. Therefore, when chocolate lovers wanted to buy a treat for themselves, they bought premium chocolate from the grocery or drug store where they shopped regularly.

Buying chocolate for themselves and eating it all prompted feelings of guilt in a lot of these community members. Thus Godiva realized that people enjoyed sharing chocolate with coworkers. In this setting, the individually wrapped offerings, such as Lindor Truffles and Ghirardelli Squares, were very appealing.

The company put all these insights together to arrive at a new product concept: premium chocolate, available in regular retail channels such as grocery stores, presented as individually

Research with Godiva's online community provided the information necessary to develop its new product concept: premium chocolate available in regular retail channels such as grocery stores.

wrapped treats. In so doing, Godiva also was encouraging a new consumer behavior for its customers: casual purchases of luxury Godiva chocolates.

The new Godiva Gems, stand-up bags of individually wrapped truffles, sell for $4.99 at drug stores and grocery stores. The extensive, technology-enabled market research that Godiva undertook in developing this product led to its widespread and great appeal. It already has surpassed Lindt's market share at CVS with 20 percent of the category. Godiva Gems may still sound luxurious, but they are not just for special occasions, nor just for others. They encourage treats for oneself, on a more frequent basis.

---

rather than national brands. So it developed more varied and appealing versions of its Great Value store brand, including all-natural ice cream in innovative flavors such as cake batter and mocha mud.[48] Staples also observed how customers use its products in their homes. For example, most people open their mail in the kitchen, but then wait to shred it until they get into their home office. Using this information, Staples designed the Mailmate, a stainless steel shredder that looks like a kitchen appliance and sits on the kitchen counter, to help customers shred their mail instantly after opening it.[49]

Companies also realize that their customers are on the web—writing customer reviews on retailers' websites, talking about their experiences on Yelp.com or Twitter. By monitoring feedback

Staples observed how customers opened their mail in the kitchen when it developed the Mailmate shredder to look like a kitchen appliance.

through these online communities, companies can get better ideas about new products or necessary changes to existing ones, as Social & Mobile Marketing 12.2 describes. Many companies also proactively develop their own online communities to focus the conversations around topics in which they are interested.

A particularly successful customer input approach is to analyze **lead users**, those innovative product users who modify existing products according to their own ideas to suit their specific needs.[50] If lead users customize a firm's products, other customers might wish to do so as well. Thus, studying lead users helps the firm understand general market trends that might be just on the horizon. Manufacturers and retailers of fashion products often spot new trends by noticing how innovative trend-setters have altered their clothing and shoes. Designers of high-fashion jeans distress their products in different ways depending on signals they pick up on the street. One season, jeans appear with whiskers, the next season they have holes, the next, paint spots.

At the end of the idea-generation stage, the firm should have several ideas that it can take forward to the next stage: concept testing.

Concept Testing

Ideas with potential are developed further into **concepts**, which in this context refer to brief written descriptions of the product; its technology, working principles, and forms; and what customer needs it would satisfy.[51] A concept might also include visual images of what the product would look like.

Concept testing refers to the process in which a concept statement is presented to potential buyers or users to obtain their reactions. These reactions enable the developer to estimate the sales value of the product or service concept, possibly make changes to enhance its sales value, and determine whether the idea is worth further development.[52] If the concept fails to meet customers' expectations, it is doubtful it would succeed if it were to be produced and marketed. Because concept testing occurs very early in the new product introduction process, even before a real product has been made, it helps the firm avoid the costs of unnecessary product development.

The concept for an electric scooter might be written as follows:

> The product is a lightweight electric scooter that can be easily folded and taken with you inside a building or on public transportation. The scooter weighs 25 pounds. It travels at speeds of up to 15 miles per hour and can go about 12 miles on a single charge. The scooter can be recharged in about two hours from a standard electric outlet. The scooter is easy to ride and has simple controls—just an accelerator button and a brake. It sells for $299.[53]

Concept testing progresses along the research techniques described in Chapter 10. The firm likely starts with exploratory research, such as in-depth interviews or focus groups, to test the concept, after which it can undertake conclusive research through Internet or mall-intercept surveys. Video clips on the Internet might show a virtual prototype and the way it works so that potential customers can evaluate the product or service. In a mall-intercept survey, an interviewer would provide a description of the concept to the respondent and then ask several questions to obtain his or her feedback.

The most important question pertains to the respondent's purchase intentions if the product or service were made available. Marketers also should ask whether the product would satisfy a need that other products currently are not meeting. Depending on the type of product or service, researchers might also ask about the expected frequency of purchase, how much customers would buy, whether they would buy it for themselves or as a gift, when they would buy, and whether the price information (if provided) indicates a good value. In addition, marketers usually collect some information about the customers so they can analyze which consumer segments are likely to be most interested in the product.

Some concepts never make it past concept testing stage, particularly if respondents seem uninterested. Those that do

These innovative consumers are called lead users because they modify existing products according to their own ideas to suit their specific needs.

lead users Innovative product users who modify existing products according to their own ideas to suit their specific needs.

concepts Brief written descriptions of a product or service; its technology, working principles, and forms; and what customer needs it would satisfy.

concept testing The process in which a concept statement that describes a product or a service is presented to potential buyers or users to obtain their reactions.

[If the concept fails to meet customers' expectations, it is doubtful it would succeed if it were to be produced and marketed.]

product development
Also called *product design;* entails a process of balancing various engineering, manufacturing, marketing, and economic considerations to develop a product's form and features or a service's features.

product design
See *product development.*

prototype The first physical form or service description of a new product, still in rough or tentative form, that has the same properties as a new product but is produced through different manufacturing processes, sometimes even crafted individually.

alpha testing
An attempt by the firm to determine whether a product will perform according to its design and whether it satisfies the need for which it was intended; occurs in the firm's research and development (R&D) department.

beta testing
Having potential consumers examine a product prototype in a real-use setting to determine its functionality, performance, potential problems, and other issues specific to its use.

premarket test
Conducted before a product or service is brought to market to determine how many customers will try and then continue to use it.

receive high evaluations from potential consumers, however, move on to the next step, product development.

Product Development

Product development or **product design** entails a process of balancing various engineering, manufacturing, marketing, and economic considerations to develop a product's form and features or a service's features. An engineering team develops a product prototype that is based on research findings from the previous concept testing step as well as their own knowledge about materials and technology. A **prototype** is the first physical form or service description of a new product, still in rough or tentative form, that has the same properties as a new product but is produced through different manufacturing processes—sometimes even crafted individually.[54]

Product prototypes are usually tested through alpha and beta testing. In **alpha testing**, the firm attempts to determine whether the product will perform according to its design and whether it satisfies the need for which it was intended.[55] Rather than use potential consumers, alpha tests occur in the firm's R&D department. For instance, Ben & Jerry's Ice Cream alpha tests all its proposed new flavors on its own (lucky) employees at its corporate headquarters in Vermont.

> " Ben & Jerry's Ice Cream alpha tests all its proposed new flavors on its own (lucky) employees at its corporate headquarters in Vermont. "

Many people, consumer groups, and governmental agencies are concerned when alpha testing involves tests on animals, particularly when it comes to pharmaceuticals and cosmetics. Ethical & Societal Dilemma 12.1 discusses these concerns in the United States and the European Union.

In contrast, **beta testing** uses potential consumers, who examine the product prototype in a real-use setting to determine its functionality, performance, potential problems, and other issues specific to its use. The firm might develop several prototype products that it gives to users, then survey those users to determine whether the product worked as intended and identify any issues that need resolution.

Household products manufacturer Kimberly-Clark uses virtual testing in the beta-testing phase of its product development process. The consumer goods company uses a virtual store aisle that mimics a real-life shopping experience by creating a realistic picture of the interior of the store. A retina-tracking device records the movement of a test customer who shops the virtual aisle of a store and chooses certain products to investigate further in the virtual simulation. Thus, consumer companies can demonstrate the likely success, or failure, of a product without actually having to produce it for a market and, potentially, expose its secrets to competitors.[56]

Ben & Jerry's Ice Cream uses alpha testing with its own employees to make sure its products have the taste and feel they should.

ethical & societal dilemma   12.1

Should Firms Test on Animals?[57]

Product testing on animals has been a primary issue for animal rights activists for years. As public opposition to animal testing increases, so do many companies' declarations that they do not test products on animals. However, such statements can be misleading because even though the whole product may not have been tested on animals, the individual ingredients may have been. To help clarify any confusion, companies can apply to the Coalition for Consumer Information on Cosmetics (CCIC), a national group formed by eight animal welfare group members such as the United States Humane Association and the Doris Day Animal League, and be certified as cruelty free. They then can purchase the trademarked Leaping Bunny Logo from CCIC for use on their labels.

One of the founding principles of The Body Shop, and one that has resonated well with its customers, is that its products are free of animal testing. Another major cosmetics manufacturer, Procter & Gamble, has eliminated animal testing on more than 80 percent of its products. It uses a combination of in vitro testing, computer modeling, and historical data to determine the safety of new products and ingredients. These methods are more expensive than more traditional methods, but P&G claims that the results are better. If performed correctly, new chemicals can either be dropped from consideration or pushed forward in as little as three days compared to the six months previously required for animal testing.

Activists of the People for the Ethical Treatment of Animals (PETA) participate in a protest against animal slaughter near a mall where Hermes—the French luxury goods company—has a store in Jakarta, Indonesia. PETA demanded Hermes stop selling exotic animal skin products and released gruesome videos of reptiles being skinned alive in Indonesia.

However, animal welfare groups continue to push P&G and other firms to stop the use of animal testing altogether. People for the Ethical Treatment of Animals (PETA) publicly cites companies it accuses of engaging in animal testing and other activities considered to be inhumane and praises those that do not. PETA's efforts have caused firms like Hugo Boss, H&M, and Liz Claiborne to stop buying their wool from Australia because some Australian sheep farmers shear their sheep's wool in inhumane ways.

The European Union has passed a ban on animal testing altogether. Beginning in 2009, any cosmetic tested on animals, even in other parts of the world, cannot be sold in the European Union. However, the cosmetics industry is worried that this ban will not only affect their companies' sales but also their customers' ability to find the products

they want. The EU cosmetics industry successfully lobbied for an extension on certain areas of toxicity testing to provide more time to find alternatives. The cosmetics industry believes it will be difficult to find alternative testing methods in time, and if it cannot, it will have fewer ingredients to make the products consumers want.

The issues involved in animal testing are complex. At the broadest level, should firms be allowed to develop products that customers want, even if there is some potential harm to the environment or to those animals that share the environment with humans? More specifically, should firms be allowed to test products on animals, even when those products are not specifically designed to improve the health and well-being of their human users? Does the testing that is performed endanger the lives or health of the animals?

Market Testing

The firm has developed its new product or service and tested the prototypes. Now it must test the market for the new product with a trial batch of products. These tests can take two forms: premarket testing and test marketing.

Premarket Tests Firms conduct **premarket tests** before they actually bring a product or service to market to determine how many customers will try and then continue to use the product or service according to a small group of potential

consumers. One popular proprietary premarket test version is called Nielsen BASES. During the test, potential customers are exposed to the marketing mix variables, such as the advertising, then surveyed and given a sample of the product to try.[58] After some period of time, during which the potential customers try the product, they are surveyed about whether they would buy/use the product again. This second survey provides an estimation of the probability of a consumer's repeat purchase. From these data, the firm generates a sales estimate for the new product that enables it to decide whether to

The new Nano introduced in India costs about $2,000. It weighs less than a Honda Civic, gets 56 miles per gallon, and takes 23 seconds to get to its top speed of 60 miles per hour.

introduce the product, abandon it, redesign it before introduction, or revise the marketing plan. An early evaluation of this sort—that is, before the product is introduced to the whole market—saves marketers the costs of a nationwide launch if the product fails.

Sometimes firms simulate a product or service introduction, in which case potential customers view the advertising of various currently available products or services along with advertising for the new product or service. They receive money to buy the product or service from a simulated environment, such as a mock web page or store, and respond to a survey after they make their purchases. This test thus can determine the effectiveness of a firm's advertising as well as the expected trial rates for the new product.

Test Marketing A method of determining the success potential of a new product, **test marketing** introduces the offering to a limited geographical area (usually a few cities) prior to a national launch. Test marketing is a strong predictor of product success because the firm can study actual purchase behavior, which is more reliable than a simulated test. A test marketing effort uses all the elements of the marketing mix: It includes promotions such as advertising and coupons, just as if the product were being introduced nationally, and the product appears in targeted retail outlets, with appropriate pricing. On the basis of the results

of the test marketing, the firm can estimate demand for the entire market.

Test marketing costs more and takes longer than premarket tests, which may provide an advantage to competitors that could get a similar or better product to market first without test marketing. For this reason, some firms might launch new products without extensive consumer testing and rely instead on intuition, instincts, and guts.[59]

Product Launch

If the market testing returns with positive results, the firm is ready to introduce the product to the entire market. This most critical step in the new product introduction requires tremendous financial resources and extensive coordination of all aspects of the marketing mix. For example, for Tata Motors' Indian launch of its inexpensive (around $2,000), tiny Nano automobile (which we described in Chapter 8), it had to limit its production to just 500,000 cars per year, though it knew the market would be larger. It simply could not afford to bankroll a wider rollout.[60] For any firm, if the new product launch is a failure, it may be difficult for the product—and perhaps the firm—to recover.

So what does a product launch involve? First, on the basis of the research it has gathered on consumer perceptions, the tests it has conducted, and competitive considerations, the firm confirms its target market (or markets) and decides how the product will be positioned. Then the firm finalizes the remaining

> " So what does a product launch involve? "

> ## SOMETIMES MANUFACTURERS PROMOTE NEW PRODUCTS IN ADVANCE OF THE PRODUCT LAUNCH TO CREATE EXCITEMENT WITH POTENTIAL CUSTOMERS AS WELL AS TO MEASURE THE LIKELY DEMAND SO THEY HAVE APPROPRIATE SUPPLY AVAILABLE.

marketing mix variables for the new product, including the marketing budget for the first year.[61]

Promotion The test results help the firm determine an appropriate integrated marketing communications strategy.[62] Promotion for new products is required at each link in the supply chain. If the products are not sold and stocked by retailers, no amount of promotion to consumers will sell the products. **Trade promotions**, which are promotions to wholesalers or retailers to get them to purchase the new products, often combine introductory price promotions, special events, and personal selling. **Introductory price promotions** are limited-duration, lower-than-normal prices designed to provide retailers with an incentive to try the products. Manufacturers may run a special event in the form of a special display in a grocery aisle, an introductory celebration, or a party in conjunction with an interesting event like the Academy Awards.

Another outlet for exposing buyers to new products is a **trade show**, which is a temporary concentration of manufacturers that provides retailers the opportunity to view what is available and new in the marketplace. The fashion world's equivalent to trade shows are fashion weeks in which fashion manufacturers meet with retailers and have elaborate runway shows to introduce their new products. Finally, as in many B2B sales situations, personal selling may be the most efficient way to get retailers to purchase their products.

Manufacturers also use promotion to generate demand for new products with consumers. If manufacturers can create demand for the products among consumers, they will go to retailers asking for it (pull demand; see Chapter 19), thus further inducing retailers to carry the products. These promotions are often coupled with short-term price reductions, coupons, or rebates. Sometimes manufacturers promote new products in advance of the product launch to create excitement with potential customers as well as to measure the likely demand so they have appropriate supply available. Automobile and motorcycle manufacturers, for instance, advertise their new products months before they are available on the dealers' floors.

For products that are somewhat complex or conceptually new, marketers may need to provide for more consumer education about the product's benefits than they would for simpler and more familiar products. The quantum dot technology that is being developed to improve the LCD screens on televisions, computers, and mobile phones is not something that most consumers understand. But marketers can encourage their adoption by highlighting the clearly evident appeal of energy efficiency, longer battery life, and more vibrant color offered by the innovative technology.[63] In addition, technical support staff, such as Apple's Geniuses, often must be trained to answer customer questions that may arise immediately after the launch of a new technical innovation.

Place The manufacturer coordinates the delivery and storage of the new products with its retailers to ensure that it is available for sale when the customer wants it, at the stores the customer is expecting to find it, and in sufficient quantities to meet demand. Manufacturers work with their retailers on decisions such as:

- Should the merchandise be stored at retailers' distribution centers or distributed directly to stores?

- What initial and fill-in quantities should be shipped?

- Should the manufacturer be involved in reordering decisions?

- Should the merchandise be individually packaged so it is easy to display in the stores?

- Should price stickers be affixed on the merchandise at the factory or at the store?

- Should the manufacturer be involved in the maintenance of the merchandise once in the store?

Price Like the promotion of new products, setting prices is a supply chain–wide decision. Manufacturers must decide at what price they would like products to sell to consumers on the basis of the factors to be discussed in Chapter 14. They often encourage retailers to sell at a specified price known as the **manufacturer's suggested retail price (MSRP)**. Although retailers often don't abide by the MSRP, manufacturers can withhold benefits such as paying for all or part of a promotion or even refusing to deliver merchandise to noncomplying retailers. It is sometimes easier to start with a higher MSRP and then over time lower it than it is to introduce the new product at a low price and then try to raise the price.

When setting the MSRP, manufacturers also consider the price at which the new products are sold to the retailers.

slotting allowance
Fees firms pay to retailers simply to get new products into stores or to gain more or better shelf space for their products.

The retailers not only need to make a profit on each sale, but they may also receive a **slotting allowance** from the manufacturer, which is a fee paid simply to get new products into stores or to gain more or better shelf space for their products.

Timing The timing of the launch may be important, depending on the product.[64] Hollywood studios typically release movies targeted toward general audiences (i.e., those rated G or PG) during the summer when children are out of school. New automobile models traditionally are released for sale during September, and fashion products are launched just before the season of the year for which they are intended.

Evaluation of Results

After the product has been launched, marketers must undertake a critical postlaunch review to determine whether the product and its launch were a success or failure and what additional resources or changes to the marketing mix are needed, if any. Many firms use panel data to improve the probability of success during the test marketing phase of a new product introduction. The consumer panel data is collected by panelists scanning in their receipts using a home scanning device. This information is used to measure individual household first-time trials and repeat purchases. Through such data, market demand can be estimated, so the firm can figure out how best to adjust its marketing mix. Some products never make it out of the introduction stage, especially those that seem almost laughable in retrospect. Bottled water for pets? Harley-Davidson perfume?[65]

For those products that do move on though, firms can measure the success of a new product by three interrelated factors: (1) its satisfaction of technical requirements, such as performance; (2) customer acceptance; and (3) its satisfaction of the firm's financial requirements, such as sales and profits.[66] If the product is not performing sufficiently well, poor customer acceptance will result, which in turn leads to poor financial performance.

The new product development process, when followed rationally and sequentially, helps avoid such domino-type failures. Coca-Cola has learned this recommendation well, as Adding Value 12.3 describes. The product life cycle, discussed in the next section, helps marketers manage their products' marketing mix during and after introduction.

 check yourself

1. What are the steps in the new product development process?
2. Identify different sources of new product ideas.

Adding Value   12.3
How Freestyle Works for Everyone[67]

Coca-Cola may never totally outlive its failed New Coke product introduction, but its latest innovation, the Freestyle machine, seems like a good step in that direction. With this introduction, Coke has set out to reinvent the fountain experience and give customers more choice. The result has been a product success for all stakeholders.

For consumers, the Freestyle vending machines offer access to any combination of caffeine, flavor, and calories they prefer. For example, there are 90 caffeine-free options on every machine!

For Coca-Cola, the Freestyle software tracks exactly what was ordered on each machine. It thus not only knows what machines to refill but also learns about which products customers prefer in which markets. It then can target its advertising ever more precisely, based on totally accurate preference information that the consumers provide themselves.

The Coca-Cola vending machine offeres customers any combination of caffeine, flavors, and calories.

▼ **EXHIBIT 12.6** Product Life Cycle

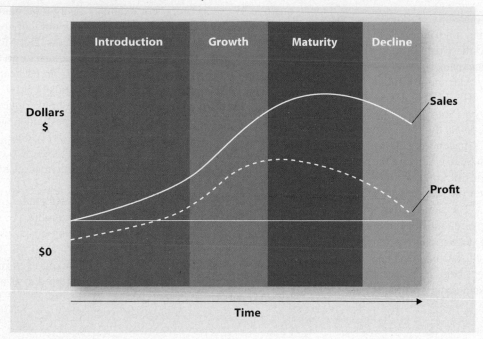

LO 12-4 Explain the product life cycle.

THE PRODUCT LIFE CYCLE

The **product life cycle** defines the stages that products move through as they enter, get established in, and ultimately leave the marketplace. It thereby offers marketers a starting point for their strategy planning. The stages of the life cycle often reflect marketplace trends, such as the healthy lifestyle trend that today places organic and green product categories in their growth stages. Exhibit 12.6 illustrates a typical product life cycle, including the industry sales and profits over time. In their life cycles, products pass through four stages: introduction, growth, maturity, and decline. When the product category first launches, its products initiate the **introduction stage**. In the **growth stage**, the product gains acceptance, demand and sales increase, and more competitors emerge in the product category. In the **maturity stage**, industry sales reach their peak, so firms try to rejuvenate their products by adding new features or repositioning

them. If these efforts succeed, the product achieves new life.[68] If not, it goes into **decline** and eventually exits the market.

Not every product follows the same life cycle curve. Many products, such as home appliances, stay in the maturity stage for a very long time. Manufacturers may add features to dishwashers and washing machines, but the mature product category remains essentially the same and seems unlikely to enter the decline stage unless some innovative, superior solution comes along to replace them.

The product life cycle offers a useful tool for managers to analyze the types of strategies that may be required over the life of their products. Even the strategic emphasis of a firm and its marketing mix (four Ps) strategies can be adapted from insights about the characteristics of each stage of the cycle, as we summarize in Exhibit 12.7.

Let's look at each of these stages in depth.

▼ **EXHIBIT 12.7** Characteristics of Different Stages of the Product Life Cycle

	Introduction	Growth	Maturity	Decline
Sales	Low	Rising	Peak	Declining
Profits	Negative or low	Rapidly rising	Peak to declining	Declining
Typical consumers	Innovators	Early adopters and early majority	Late majority	Laggards
Competitors (number of firms and products)	One or few	Few but increasing	High number of competitors and competitive products	Low number of competitors and products

Introduction Stage

The introduction stage for a new, innovative product or service usually starts with a single firm, and innovators are the ones to try the new offering. Some new-to-the-world products and services that defined their own product category and industry include the telephone (invented by Alexander Graham Bell in 1876), the transistor semiconductor (Bell Laboratories in 1947), the Walkman portable cassette player (Sony in 1979), the Internet browser (Netscape in 1994), personal digital assistant (Palm in 1996), iTunes (Apple in 2001), Facebook (2004), Blu-ray (Sony in 2006) and iPad (Apple in 2010). Sensing the viability and commercialization possibilities of some market-creating new product, other firms soon enter the market with similar or improved products at lower prices. The same pattern holds for less innovative products such as apparel, music, and even a new soft drink flavor. The introduction stage is characterized by initial losses to the firm due to its high start-up costs and low levels of sales revenue as the product begins to take off. If the product is successful, firms may start seeing profits toward the end of this stage.

sales trend and firmly establish the firm's brand, so as not to be outdone by competitors. For example, many food manufacturers are working hard to become the first brand that consumers think of when they consider organic products. Del Monte was the first of the major canned vegetable sellers to go organic, releasing organic versions of its tomatoes, green beans, corn, and sweet peas, along with an organic chicken broth product under its College Inn line. The cans feature bold "organic" banners across the front and promise that no pesticides were used to produce the food items. Even though Del Monte products have been around for over 100 years, in this growth category, the company is a newer entrant in the organic market, so it must work to establish its distinctive appeal.[71]

As firms ride the crest of increasing industry sales, profits in the growth stage also rise because of the economies of scale associated with manufacturing and marketing costs, especially promotion and advertising. At the same time, firms that have not yet established a stronghold in the market, even in narrow segments, may decide to exit in what is referred to as an industry shakeout.

[In the United States, most consumer packaged goods found in grocery and discount stores are already in the maturity stage.]

Growth Stage

The growth stage of the product life cycle is marked by a growing number of product adopters, rapid growth in industry sales, and increases in both the number of competitors and the number of available product versions.[69] The market becomes more segmented and consumer preferences more varied, which increases the potential for new markets or new uses of the product or service.[70]

Also during the growth stage, firms attempt to reach new consumers by studying their preferences and producing different product variations—varied colors, styles, or features—which enable them to segment the market more precisely. The goal of this segmentation is to ride the rising

Does adding crushed diamonds to hair products enhance their value?

Maturity Stage

The maturity stage of the product life cycle is characterized by the adoption of the product by the late majority and intense competition for market share among firms. Marketing costs (e.g., promotion, distribution) increase as these firms vigorously defend their market share against competitors. They also face intense competition on price as the average price of the product falls substantially compared with the shifts during the previous two stages of the life cycle. Lower prices and increased marketing costs begin to erode the profit margins for many firms. In the later phases of the maturity stage, the market has become quite saturated, and practically all potential customers for the product have already adopted the product. Such saturated markets are prevalent in developed countries.

In the United States, most consumer packaged goods found in grocery and discount stores are already in the maturity stage. For example, in the well-established hair care product market, consumer goods companies constantly search for innovations to set themselves apart and extend the time in which they maintain their position in the maturity stage. Nivea added actual, ground up diamonds to its Diamond Gloss line. Women who wash and condition their hair with Diamond Gloss products are promised added brilliance and light reflection, making their hair seem shinier and healthier. The crushed up diamonds do nothing to improve hair health, and the company is careful to avoid making that claim. Rather, it promotes the idea that the diamonds themselves, when applied to hair, will make it shine like a diamond would.[72]

As this example shows, firms pursue various strategies during this stage to increase their customer base and/or defend their market share. Other tactics include entry into new markets and market segments and developing new products.

Entry into New Markets or Market Segments

Because the market is saturated at this point, firms may attempt to enter new geographical markets, including international markets (as we discussed in Chapter 8), that may be less saturated. For example, Whirlpool manufactures washing machines for Brazil, China, and India that it prices lower than those it sells in the United States to attract the large consumer base of lower-income consumers in these countries.[73] In many developing economies, the large and growing proportion of middle-class households is just beginning to buy the home, kitchen, and entertainment appliances that have been fairly standard in U.S. households for several decades. In India alone, roughly 487 million middle-class consumers spend over $100 billion a year on a variety of consumer products.[74]

However, even in mature markets, firms may be able to find new market segments. Laundry may be a mundane chore that most people dislike, but it is also a huge marketing opportunity. New product development tends to focus on the detergent delivery methods. So in the United States, where laundry tablets have never been very popular (Americans prefer to pour their liquid detergent and thus control the amount they add to the wash basket), Dial has developed a laundry sheet, similar to the dryer sheets used as fabric softeners. This 3-in-1 product includes

To generate sales in a mature world, Dial Corporation has developed a laundry sheet that includes detergent, fabric softener, and antistatic agents to appeal to a new market segment that wants a premium product while saving money, without cannibalizing its core customer groups.

laundry detergent, fabric softener, and antistatic agents.[75] It is less expensive than purchasing premium brand versions of the three items. Dial hopes to appeal to a new market segment that wants a premium product and to save money, without cannibalizing its core customer groups.

Development of New Products Despite market saturation, firms continually introduce new products with improved features or find new uses for existing products because they need constant innovation and product proliferation to defend market share from intense competition. Firms such as 3M, P&G, and Hewlett-Packard continually introduce new products. Innovations by such firms ensure that they are able to retain or grow their respective market shares. KFC took its expertise with its existing product line consisting of different types of fried chicken and developed Kentucky Grilled Chicken, a relatively innovative product line in an otherwise mature market.[76] And Hallmark, which has been the hallmark name for greeting cards for a long time, is trying a variety of innovations, as Adding Value 12.4 describes.

Decline Stage

Firms with products in the decline stage either position themselves for a niche segment of diehard consumers or those with special needs or they completely exit the market. The few laggards who have not yet tried the product or service enter the market at this stage. Take vinyl long-playing records (LPs) for example. In an age of Internet-downloaded music files, it may seem surprising that vinyl records are still made and sold. Sales of vinyl LPs had long been declining, but they have enjoyed a resurgence in just the past few years as diehard music lovers demand the unique sound of a vinyl record rather than the digital sound of CDs and music files. Still, the 3.9 million LPs sold in the United States per year pales in comparison with the 1.27 billion digital downloads. The grooves in vinyl records create sound waves that are similar to those of a live performance, though, which means they provide a more authentic sound, which in turn means nightclub DJs, discerning music listeners, and collectors will always prefer them.[77]

Adding Value 12.4

New Options for Opening Up the Greeting Card Market

As more and more consumers just hit the Send button to deliver greetings to their friends and families, Hallmark is looking for ways to reposition itself to facilitate this new type of connection. Fear not: It has no plans to abandon traditional paper cards and envelopes. But Hallmark's new product portfolio includes products that grant consumers creative input, greater convenience, and digital options. For example, customizable greeting cards, plates, and interactive storybooks can be personalized for various recipients, and new greeting applications are available for both iPod and iPad users.[78]

The company is also rethinking the very meaning of "greetings," with the notion that any day can—and should—be special. Research has documented the importance of emotional connectedness for people's physical health and longevity, and marketing studies show that people want to celebrate more of the smaller, often unnoticed moments. As emotion-filled e-mails and text messages seemingly replace more formal ways of saying "I love you," Hallmark needed to meet and resonate with shifting consumer habits and preferences.

The Life is a Special Occasion campaign suggests that every day is a good day to send a greeting. Because the campaign moves beyond the idea that cards are only for holidays or birthdays, it encourages consumers to enjoy the value of connecting with loved ones all the time (and for recipients, the unique pleasure of finding a surprise greeting card in the mailbox). For Hallmark, the campaign also increases the reasons and times when people are likely to make a purchase.

Even with these moves, though, Hallmark faces significant competition on the digital front. Many applications available for the iPhone, iPad, or Android enable users to send customized cards by e-mail or text. A virtual card application from Red Stamp allows consumers to create cards, sent directly from social media sites. Companies such as Sincerely Ink also offer heavy-weight paper printing of customers' personalized, digital cards, to help users mail their greetings the old-fashioned way; even digital natives still like the feel of a physical card.[79] Such nimble product designs may pose the greatest challenge for Hallmark as it moves forward in the digital marketplace.

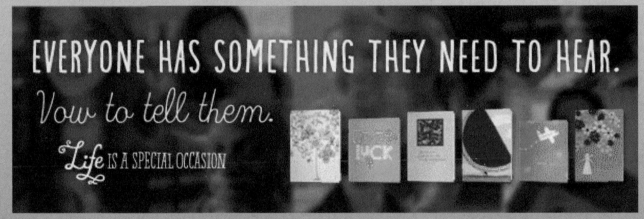

Hallmark's *Life Is a Special Occasion* campaign moves beyond the idea that cards are only for holidays or birthdays. It encourages consumers to connect with loved ones all the time.

Aiding this continued demand is the fact that there are simply too many albums of music from the predigital era that are available only on vinyl. It may take many years, maybe even decades, for all the music from earlier generations to be digitized. Until that time, turntable equipment manufacturers, small record-pressing companies such as Music Connection in Manhattan, and new and emerging record companies, such as Premier Crue Music, continue to have a market that demands their LPs.[80]

The Shape of the Product Life Cycle Curve

In theory, the product life cycle curve is bell shaped with regard to sales and profits. In reality, however, each product or service category has its own individual shape; some move more rapidly through their product life cycles than others, depending on how different the category is from offerings currently in the market and how valuable it is to the consumer. New products and services that consumers accept very quickly have higher consumer adoption rates very early in their product life cycles and move faster across the various stages.

For example, DVD players and DVDs moved much faster than VCRs across the life cycle curve and have already reached the maturity stage, likely because consumers who already owned VCRs were accustomed to recording TV shows and playing prerecorded movies and programs. It also was easy to switch VCR customers to DVD technology because DVDs were more durable and had better resolution than videotapes. Finally, prices for DVDs and DVD players dropped more quickly and drastically than did VCR prices, which made the new technology a better value.

Strategies Based on Product Life Cycle: Some Caveats

Although the product life cycle concept provides a starting point for managers to think about the strategy they want to implement during each stage of the life cycle of a product, this tool must be used with care. The most challenging part of applying the product life cycle concept is that managers do not know exactly what shape each product's life cycle will take, so there is no way to know precisely what stage a product is in. If, for example, a product experiences several seasons of declining sales, a manager may decide that it has moved from the growth stage to decline and stop promoting the product. As a result, of course, sales decline further. The manager then believes he or she made the right decision because the product continues to follow a predetermined life cycle. But what if the original sales decline was due to a poor strategy or increased competition— issues that could have been addressed with positive marketing support? In this case, the product life cycle decision became a self-fulfilling prophecy, and a growth product was doomed to an unnecessary decline.[81]

Fortunately, new research, based on the history of dozens of consumer products, suggests that the product life cycle concept is indeed a valid idea, and new analytical tools now provide rules for detecting the key turning points in the cycle.[82] ■

check yourself

1. What are the stages in the product life cycle?
2. How do sales and profits change during the various stages?

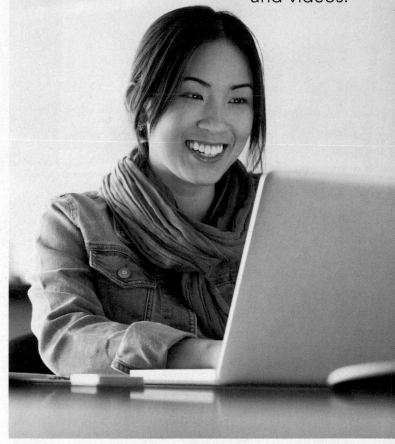

check it out!

mhhe.com/GrewalM4e
for study materials, including quizzes and videos.

thirteen

services: the intangible product

Even when online retailers offer great merchandise, the customer service they offer can be a deciding factor in their success. How well personnel respond to the stream of customer inquiries may determine whether the company thrives or takes a nose dive. But relating to customers also can be highly variable; it depends on individual employees. How do you mobilize an entire company to speak with one voice? How can a service firm ensure that employee–customer interactions consistently meet, or exceed, the company's service standards?

Zappos, the Las Vegas–based online clothing and shoe retailer, seems to have the answers to these questions. Valued at more than $1.6 billion, one year after its acquisition by Amazon,[1] Zappos may sell apparel, but it really

has built its business on its superb service. The company's core values stress that customer satisfaction is more important than cost cutting; that message permeates every single aspect of its operations. The goal is to wow each customer with service that far exceeds expectations.

continued on p. 282

LEARNING OBJECTIVES

After reading this chapter, you should be able to:

LO 13-1 Describe how the marketing of services differs from the marketing of products.

LO 13-2 Discuss the four gaps in the Service Gap Model.

LO 13-3 Examine the five service quality dimensions.

LO 13-4 Explain the zone of tolerance.

LO 13-5 Identify three service recovery strategies.

which lasts up to five weeks, all new employees are required to work in the call center. Anyone who thinks the assignment is beneath them is paid for his or her time and shown the door. Trainees are not given a script or a time limit for calls. Instead, during training and once on the job, workers are urged to solve problems creatively, even if customer satisfaction means doing something a little weird, like buying shoes from a competing retailer for a customer in distress.

That was the solution one worker devised when a woman called, desperate to buy another pair of her favorite Zappos shoes when she discovered, after arriving at her hotel, that she had forgotten to pack them. The shoes were no longer in stock, but the employee located a pair near the woman's hotel and had them hand-delivered—and Zappos paid the bill.[3] The customer was astonished.

That approach was totally consistent with Zappos' core values, which suggest that a little weirdness may be just the right approach if it helps solve a customer problem. And of course, the company doesn't mind the wow stories that such efforts generate for customers to share with all their friends.

Zappos's shopping procedures are also designed to please. Customers are encouraged to order multiple sizes and colors of an item so they can touch, feel, and try on prospective purchases. Returned goods ship free for up to a year. And Zappos likes to impress customers with speedy delivery. So it ships items faster than its website indicates. Good customers often get upgraded to next- or second-day air shipping at no extra cost.[4]

Employees who meet Zappos's unconventional customer service standards are rewarded. Its most common salaried job, fulfillment center process manager, pays more than $47,500 a year, and the company is ranked eleventh among the country's best places to work.[5]

When retail goes online, delivering the product is just half the battle. Distance complicates service, and how that service is delivered, whether online or through a call center, can make or break the customer relationship. Zappos offers a model for delivering service excellence by enlisting workers in the challenge of wowing each and every customer. ■

Zappos provides legendary customer service.

continued from p. 281

Of course, costs are something that every company must address. Therefore, Zappos.com uses automated technology to handle approximately 75 percent of its customer service transactions. But the other 25 percent of calls that go to a human respondent constitute powerful and influential customer service interactions because those human representatives are determined to make the interaction a happy one.[2]

Instilling such values in every worker begins with the interview process. Applicants undergo separate interviews for experience and fit within the company culture. During training,

> ## Services account for 76 percent of the U.S. gross domestic product (GDP), a much higher percentage than they did 50, 20, or even 10 years ago.

Whereas a **service** is any intangible offering that involves a deed, performance, or effort that cannot be physically possessed,[6] **customer service** specifically refers to human or mechanical activities firms undertake to help satisfy their customers' needs and wants. By providing good customer service, firms add value to their products.

Exhibit 13.1 illustrates the continuum from a pure service to a pure good. Most offerings, like those of Zappos, lie somewhere in the middle and include some service and some good (i.e., a hybrid of the two). Even those firms that are engaged primarily in selling a good, such as an apparel store, typically view service as a method to maintain a sustainable competitive advantage. This chapter moves on to take an inclusive view of services as anything from pure service businesses to a business that uses service as a differentiating tool to help it sell physical goods.

Economies of developed countries such as of the United States have become increasingly dependent on services. Services account for 76 percent of the U.S. gross domestic product (GDP), a much higher percentage than they did 50, 20, or even 10 years ago. In turn, the current list of *Fortune* 500 companies contains more service companies and fewer manufacturers than in previous decades.[7] This dependence and the growth of service-oriented economies in developed countries have emerged for several reasons.

First, it is generally less expensive for firms to manufacture their products in less developed countries. Even if the goods are finished in the United States, some of their components likely were produced elsewhere. In turn, the proportion of service production to goods production in the United States, and other similar economies, has steadily increased over time.

Second, people place a high value on convenience and leisure. For instance, household maintenance activities, which many people performed themselves in the past, have become more popular and quite specialized. Food preparation, lawn maintenance, house cleaning, pet grooming, laundry and dry cleaning, hair care, and automobile maintenance are all often performed by specialists.

Third, as the world has become more complicated, people are demanding more specialized services—everything from plumbers to personal trainers, from massage therapists to tax preparation specialists, from lawyers to travel and leisure specialists and even to health care providers. The aging

Specialized services such as personal training are thriving.

▼ **EXHIBIT 13.1** The Service–Product Continuum

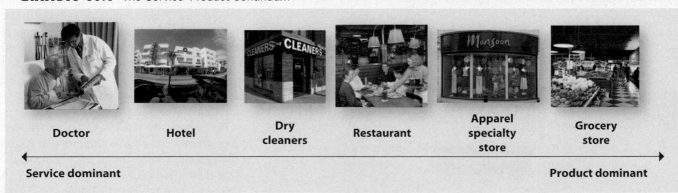

| Doctor | Hotel | Dry cleaners | Restaurant | Apparel specialty store | Grocery store |

Service dominant ←――――――――――――――――――――――――――→ **Product dominant**

population in particular has increased the need for health care specialists, including doctors, nurses, and caregivers in assisted living facilities and nursing homes, and many of those consumers want their specialists to provide personalized, dedicated services.

LO 13-1 Describe how the marketing of services differs from the marketing of products.

SERVICES MARKETING DIFFERS FROM PRODUCT MARKETING

The marketing of services differs from product marketing because of the four fundamental differences involved in services: Services are intangible, inseparable, heterogeneous, and perishable.[8] (See Exhibit 13.2.) This section examines these differences and discusses how they affect marketing strategies.

Intangible

As the title of this chapter implies, the most fundamental difference between a product and a service is that services are **intangible**—they cannot be touched, tasted, or seen like a pure product can. When you get a physical examination, you see and hear the doctor, but the service itself is intangible. This intangibility can prove highly challenging to marketers. For instance, it makes it difficult to convey the benefits of services—try describing whether the experience of visiting your dentist was good or bad and why. Service providers (e.g., physicians, dentists) therefore offer cues to help their customers experience and perceive their service more positively, such as a waiting room stocked with television sets, beverages, and comfortable chairs to create an atmosphere that appeals to the target market.

A service that cannot be shown directly to potential customers also is difficult to promote. Marketers must creatively employ symbols and images to promote and sell services, as Six

Since it is difficult to show a service, marketers like Six Flags evoke images in its advertising of happy families and friends enjoying a ride at one of its amusement parks.

Flags does in using its advertising to evoke images of happy families and friends enjoying a roller coaster ride. Professional medical services provide appropriate images of personnel doing their jobs in white coats surrounded by high-tech equipment. Educational institutions promote the quality of their services by touting their famous faculty and alumni as well as their accreditations. They also often use images of happy students sitting spellbound in front of a fascinating professor or going on to lucrative careers of their own.

Because of the intangibility of services, the images that marketers use must reinforce the benefit or value that a service provides. Professional service providers, such as doctors, lawyers, accountants, and consultants, depend heavily on consumers' perceptions of their integrity and trustworthiness, but they also need to market their offerings using promotional campaigns. At one time, lawyers were prohibited from advertising because such marketing seemingly would undermine the integrity of the profession. The repeal of those laws resulted in much more advertising, some of which may go too far. Critics point to the aggressive promotions some attorneys use to prey on potential clients' vulnerabilities after they have been injured. The lawyers claim instead they are providing a valuable service to society. This ethical debate continues, though the American Bar Association (ABA) has drafted a set of rules that its members must abide by when creating their advertising, such as banning any use of pop-up ads or actors when advertising law services.[9]

For lawyers, the challenge of advertising services creates an ethical dilemma. But some other services have found excellent ways to make their offerings more tangible to their customers, as Adding Value 13.1 notes.

▼ **EXHIBIT 13.2** Core Differences between Services and Goods

Inseparable Production and Consumption

Unlike a pair of jeans that may have been made six months prior to their purchase, halfway around the world, services are produced and consumed at the same time; that is, service and consumption are **inseparable**. When getting a haircut, the customer is not only present but also may participate in the service process. Furthermore, the interaction with the service provider may have an important impact on the customer's perception of the service outcome. If the hair stylist appears to be having fun while cutting hair, it may affect the experience positively.

Because the service is inseparable from its consumption, customers rarely have the opportunity to try the service before they purchase it. And after the service has been performed, it can't be returned. Imagine telling your hair stylist that you want to have the hair around your ears trimmed as a test before doing the entire head. Because the purchase risk in these scenarios can be relatively high, service firms sometimes provide extended warranties and 100 percent

Adding Value 13.1
Carbonite's Secure Online Back-Up

The prospect of losing data haunts virtually every computer user. And for good reason, especially among business users: The Federal Emergency Management Agency says 40–60 percent of small businesses fail to reopen after they suffer a severe data disruption.[10] To address their fears of data loss or contamination, some users rely on external hard drives or disk storage. But that means they have to remember to perform the back-up, and these options do not provide protection against a fire or other emergencies that destroy that hard drive along with the computer.

Online back-ups involve backing up the data on remote servers. This provides a more secure, less user-dependent alternative. Carbonite was one of the first entrants into this market. It provides simple, affordable, unlimited online backup for individual home users as well as small and medium businesses. With these target markets, Carbonite has kept its service, price, and customer support well within the reach of users. The basic yearly rate for a home customer is $59 per computer; a business pays $229 a year to cover all company computers.

Carbonite software runs invisibly on both Macs and PCs,[11] performing back-ups automatically. With customers in more than 100 countries, the company has backed up more than 100 billion files and recovered nearly 10 billion of them in the past few years.[12] For portable, digital access, the company offers free mobile applications for Blackberry, iPad, iPhone, and Android devices.[13]

To live up to its promise of hassle-free service, the company also offers free support by telephone, e-mail, and online live chat. It answers customer inquiries on its Twitter and Facebook sites, which then provide transparent proof of its handling of customer complaints. As for security, Carbonite's system is comparable to the safeguards used by major banks, credit card companies, and online retailers.[14] All files are encrypted with two layers of technology, stored on enterprise-grade servers to protect against mechanical

disk failure, and kept in state-of-the-art data centers guarded 24 hours a day, 365 days a year. Personnel must pass through biometric scans and electronic pin coding to enter.

Carbonite thus has firmly established its market position by delivering a reliable, secure, easy-to-use service, combined with reasonable pricing and easily accessible technical support. As the shift to cloud computing intensifies, the company's main advantage may be its focus on staying abreast of user needs and expectations so it can keep all its customers happy.

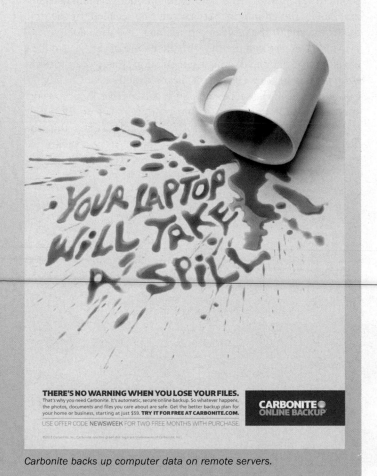

THERE'S NO WARNING WHEN YOU LOSE YOUR FILES.
That's why you need Carbonite. It's automatic, secure online backup. So whatever happens, the photos, documents and files you care about are safe. Get the better backup plan for your home or business, starting at just $59. **TRY IT FOR FREE AT CARBONITE.COM.**
USE OFFER CODE **NEWSWEEK** FOR TWO FREE MONTHS WITH PURCHASE.

CARBONITE
ONLINE BACKUP

Carbonite backs up computer data on remote servers.

> # AN INFERIOR SERVICE CAN'T BE RECALLED;
> # BY THE TIME THE FIRM RECOGNIZES A PROBLEM,
> # THE DAMAGE HAS BEEN DONE.

satisfaction guarantees.[15] The Choice Hotels chain, for instance, states: "We guarantee total guest satisfaction at Comfort Inn, Comfort Suites, Quality, Sleep Inn, Clarion and MainStay Suites hotels. If you are not satisfied with your accommodations or our service, please advise the front desk of a problem right away."[16]

Heterogeneous

The more humans are needed to provide a service, the more likely there is to be **heterogeneity** or variability in the service's quality. A hair stylist may give bad haircuts in the morning because he or she went out the night before. Yet that stylist still may offer a better service than the undertrained stylist working in the next station over. A restaurant, which offers a mixture of services and products, generally can control its food quality but not the variability in food preparation or delivery. If a consumer has a problem with a product, it can be replaced, redone, destroyed, or, if it is already in the supply chain, recalled. In many cases, the problem can even be fixed before the product gets into consumers' hands. But an inferior service can't be recalled; by the time the firm recognizes a problem, the damage has been done.

Marketers also can use the variable nature of services to their advantage. A micromarketing segmentation strategy can customize a service to meet customers' needs exactly (see Chapter 9). For example, a Massachusetts store called Tech Superpowers specializes in helping new Apple customers set up their new toys and enjoy all their functions—basic services that the Geniuses in Apple stores may tend to ignore. At the center of the store is a Lexus IS300, demonstrating how Apple products can be integrated into the vehicle. A 23-inch monitor in the backseat streams content through from a Mac mini. An iPad is mounted in the dashboard. Better than any verbal explanation, this real-world display appeals to customers by promising the great capabilities they gain with Apple products—as well as how clever the Superpowers can be when it comes to anything Apple.[17]

In an alternative approach, some service providers tackle the variability issue by replacing people with machines. For simple transactions such as getting cash, using an ATM is usually quicker and more convenient—and less variable—than waiting in line for a bank teller. Many retailers have installed kiosks with broadband Internet access in their stores. In addition to offering customers the opportunity to order merchandise not available in the store, kiosks can provide routine customer service, freeing employees to deal with more demanding customer requests and problems and reducing service variability. For example, customers can use kiosks to locate merchandise in the store and determine whether specific products, brands, and sizes are available. Kiosks can also be used to automate existing store services, such as gift registry management, rain checks, film drop-off, credit applications, and preordering service for bakeries and delicatessens.

Perishable

Services are **perishable** in that they cannot be stored for use in the future. You can't stockpile your membership at Gold's Gym like you could a six-pack of V-8 juice, for instance. The perishability of services provides both challenges and opportunities to

As hairstylist service can be quite heterogeneous, customers learn the stylist they like and patronize them again and again.

Since services are perishable, service providers such as ski areas offer less expensive tickets at night to stimulate demand.

286 SECTION 4 | Value Creation

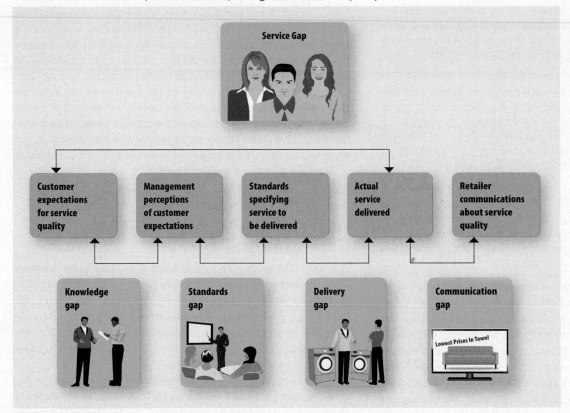

Sources: Adapted from Valarie Zeithaml, A. Parasuraman, and Leonard Berry, *Delivering Quality Customer Service* (New York: The Free Press, 1990); and Valarie Zeithaml, Leonard Berry, and A. Parasuraman, "Communication and Control Processes in the Delivery of Service Quality," *Journal of Marketing* 52, no. 2 (April 1988), pp. 35–48.

heterogeneity
As it refers to the differences between the marketing of products and services, the delivery of services is more variable.

perishable
A characteristic of a service: it cannot be stored for use in the future.

service gap Results when a service fails to meet the expectations that customers have about how it should be delivered.

knowledge gap
A type of *service gap;* reflects the difference between customers' *expectations* and the firm's perception of those expectations.

marketers in terms of the critical task of matching demand and supply. As long as the demand for and supply of the service match closely, there is no problem, but unfortunately, this perfect matching rarely occurs. A ski area, for instance, can be open as long as there is snow, even at night, but demand peaks on weekends and holidays, so ski areas often offer less expensive tickets during off-peak periods to stimulate demand. Airlines, cruise ships, movie theaters, and restaurants confront similar challenges and attack them in similar ways.

Certainly, providing great service is not easy, and it requires a diligent effort to analyze the service process piece by piece. In the next section, we examine what is known as the Gaps Model, which is designed to highlight those areas where customers believe they are getting less or poorer service than they should (the gaps) and how these gaps can be closed.

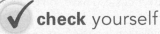 **check** yourself

1. What are the four marketing elements that distinguish services from products?

2. Why can't we separate firms into just service or just product sellers?

LO 13-2   Discuss the four gaps in the Service Gap Model.

PROVIDING GREAT SERVICE: THE GAPS MODEL

Customers have certain expectations about how a service should be delivered. When the delivery of that service fails to meet those expectations, a **service gap** results. The Service Gaps Model (Exhibit 13.3) is designed to encourage the systematic examination of all aspects of the service delivery process and prescribes the steps needed to develop an optimal service strategy.[18]

As Exhibit 13.3 shows, there are four service gaps:

1. The **knowledge gap** reflects the difference between customers' expectations and the firm's perception of those customer expectations. Firms can close this gap by determining what customers really want by doing research using marketing metrics such as service quality and the zone of tolerance.

2. The **standards gap** pertains to the difference between the firm's perceptions of customers' expectations and the service standards it sets. By setting appropriate service standards, training employees to meet and exceed those standards, and measuring service performance, firms can attempt to close this gap.

3. The **delivery gap** is the difference between the firm's service standards and the actual service it provides to customers. This gap can be closed by getting employees to meet or exceed service standards when the service is being delivered by empowering service providers, providing support and incentives, and using technology where appropriate.[19]

4. The **communication gap** refers to the difference between the actual service provided to customers and the service that the firm's promotion program promises. If firms are more realistic about the services they can provide and at the same time manage customer expectations effectively, they generally can close this gap.

As we discuss the four gaps subsequently, we will apply them to the experience that Marcia Kessler had with a motel in Maine. She saw an ad for a package weekend that quoted a very reasonable daily rate and listed the free amenities available at Green Valley Motel: free babysitting services, a piano bar with a nightly singer, a free Continental breakfast, a heated swimming pool, and newly decorated rooms. When she booked the room, Marcia discovered that the price advertised was not available during the weekend, and a three-day minimum stay was required. Because of the nice amenities, however, she went ahead. After checking in with a very unpleasant person at the front desk, Marcia and her

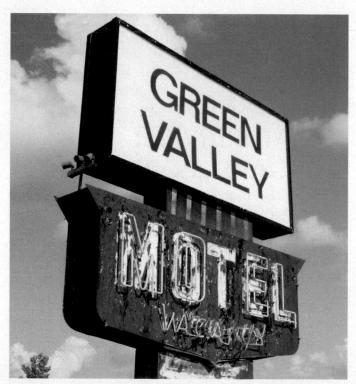

What service gaps did Marcia experience while on vacation at the Green Valley Motel in Maine?

husband found that their room appeared circa-1950 and had not been cleaned. When she complained, all she got was attitude from the assistant manager. Resigned to the fact that they were slated to spend the weekend, she decided to go for a swim. Unfortunately, the water was heated by Booth Bay and stood at around 50 degrees. No one was using the babysitting services because there were few young children at the resort. It turns out the piano bar singer was the second cousin of the owner, and he couldn't carry a tune, let alone play the piano very well. The Continental breakfast must have come all the way from the Continent, because everything was stale and tasteless. Marcia couldn't wait to get home.

The Knowledge Gap: Understanding Customer Expectations

An important early step in providing good service is knowing what the customer wants. It doesn't pay to invest in services that don't improve customer satisfaction.[20] To reduce the knowledge gap, firms must understand customers' expectations. To understand those expectations, firms undertake customer research and increase the interaction and communication between managers and employees.

Customers' expectations are based on their knowledge and experiences.[21] Marcia's expectations were that her room at the motel in Maine would be ready when she got there, the swimming pool would be heated, the singer would be able to sing, and the breakfast would be fresh. Not a lot to expect, but in this extreme example the Green Valley was suffering a severe knowledge gap perhaps based on their assumption that being on the ocean in Maine was enough. If the resort never understood her expectations, it is unlikely it would ever be able to meet them.

Expectations vary according to the type of service. Marcia's expectations might have been higher, for instance, if she were staying at a Ritz-Carlton rather than the Green Valley Motel. At the Ritz, she might expect employees to know her by name, be aware of her dietary preferences, and have placed fresh fruit of her choice and fresh-cut flowers in her room before she arrived. At the Green Valley Motel, she expected easy check-in/checkout, easy access to a major highway, a clean room with a comfortable bed, and a TV, at a bare minimum.

People's expectations also vary depending on the situation. If she had been traveling on business, the Green Valley Motel might have been fine (had the room at least been clean and modern), but if she were celebrating her 10th wedding anniversary, she probably would prefer the Ritz. Thus, the service provider needs to not only know and understand the expectations of the customers in its target market but also have some idea of the occasions of service usage.

To help ensure that JetBlue understands customers' expectations, it surveys at least 35 customers from every flight it operates.[22] The airline brings together top executives to discuss what customers are saying and how it should respond. On the basis of its customer feedback, it has changed the way it deals with customers who face delays and cancellations. It also

standards gap A type of *service gap;* pertains to the difference between the firm's perceptions of customers' expectations and the service standards it sets.

delivery gap A type of *service gap;* the difference between the firm's service standards and the actual service it provides to customers.

communication gap A type of *service gap;* refers to the difference between the actual service provided to customers and the service that the firm's promotion program promises.

service quality Customers' perceptions of how well a service meets or exceeds their expectations.

▼ **EXHIBIT 13.4** Building Blocks of Service Quality

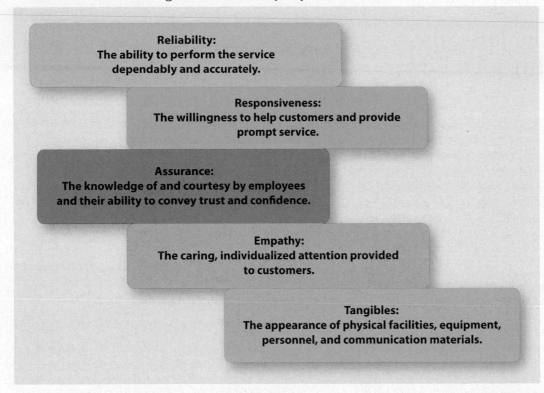

Reliability: The ability to perform the service dependably and accurately.

Responsiveness: The willingness to help customers and provide prompt service.

Assurance: The knowledge of and courtesy by employees and their ability to convey trust and confidence.

Empathy: The caring, individualized attention provided to customers.

Tangibles: The appearance of physical facilities, equipment, personnel, and communication materials.

knows which planes have problems with the entertainment system and which airports have the rudest staff.

LO 12-3 Examine the five service quality dimensions.

Evaluating Service Quality Using Well-Established Marketing Metrics To meet or exceed customers' expectations, marketers must determine what those expectations are. Yet because of their intangibility, the

service quality, or customers' perceptions of how well a service meets or exceeds their expectations, often is difficult for customers to evaluate.[23] Customers generally use five distinct service dimensions to determine overall service quality: reliability, responsiveness, assurance, empathy, and tangibles (see Exhibit 13.4). Adding Value 13.2 describes how the Broadmoor Hotel maintains its five-star rating by focusing on these five service characteristics.

If you were to apply the five service dimensions to your own decision-making process, for instance, when you selected a college—which provides you the service of education—you might find results like those in Exhibit 13.5.

▼ **EXHIBIT 13.5** Collegiate Service Dimensions

	University A	University B
Reliability	Offers sound curriculum with extensive placement services and internships.	Curriculum covers all the basics but important courses are not always available. Career placement is haphazard at best.
Responsiveness	Slow to respond to application. Very structured visitation policy. Rather inflexible with regard to personal inquiries or additional meetings.	Quick response during application process. Open visitation policy. Offers variety of campus resources to help with decision making.
Assurance	Staff seems very confident in reputation and services.	Informal staff who convey enthusiasm for institution.
Empathy	Seems to process student body as a whole rather than according to individual needs or concerns.	Very interested in providing a unique experience for each student.
Tangibles	Very traditional campus with old-world look and feel. Facilities are manicured. Dorm rooms are large, but bathrooms are a little old.	New campus with modern architecture. Campus is less manicured. Dorm rooms are spacious with newer bathrooms.

Adding Value   13.2
The Broadmoor Manages Service Quality for a Five-Star Rating

Established in 1891 as a gambling casino and transformed into a grand resort in 1918, the Broadmoor, in Colorado Springs, Colorado, is one of the world's premier resorts.[24] It has received a record 50 consecutive years of five-star ratings from the *Forbes Travel Guide*. Perry Goodbar, former vice president of marketing for the Broadmoor, emphasizes, "It's the people who truly make this place special. Exceptional service quality begins with exceptional people." Some aspects of its service quality are as follows:

Reliability Every new Broadmoor employee, before ever encountering a customer, attends a two-and-a-half-day orientation session and receives an employee handbook. Making and keeping promises to customers is a central part of this orientation. Employees are trained always to give an estimated time for service, whether it be room service, laundry service, or simply how long it will take to be seated at one of the resort's restaurants. When an employee makes a promise, he or she keeps that promise. Employees are trained to never guess if they don't know the answer to a question. Inaccurate information only frustrates customers. When an employee is unable to answer a question accurately, he or she immediately contacts someone who can.

Assurance The Broadmoor conveys trust by empowering its employees. An example of an employee empowerment policy is the service recovery program. If a guest problem arises, employees are given discretionary resources to rectify the problem or present the customer with something special to help mollify them. For example, if a meal is delivered and there's a mistake in the order or how it was prepared, a waiter can offer the guest a free item such as a dessert or, if the service was well below expectations, simply take care of the bill. Managers then review each situation to understand the nature of the problem and help prevent it from occurring again.

Tangibles One of the greatest challenges for the Broadmoor in recent years has been updating rooms built in the early part of the twentieth century to meet the needs of twenty-first century visitors. To accomplish this, it spent millions in improvements, renovating rooms, and adding a new outdoor pool complex.

Empathy One approach used to demonstrate empathy is personalizing communications. Employees are instructed to always address a guest by name, if possible. To accomplish this, employees are trained to listen and observe carefully to determine a guest's name. Subtle sources for this information include convention name tags, luggage ID tags, credit cards, or checks. In addition, all phones within the Broadmoor display a guest's room number and name on a screen.

Responsiveness Every employee is instructed to follow the HEART model of taking care of problems. First, employees must "Hear what a guest has to say." Second, they must "Empathize with them" and then "Apologize for the situation." Fourth, they must "Respond to the guest's needs" by "Taking action and following up."

The Broadmoor in Colorado Springs, Colorado, is known for exceptional service quality.

If your expectations include an individualized experience at a state-of-the-art institution, perhaps University B is a better alternative for you. But if you are relying heavily on academic performance and career placement from your university experience, then University A might be a better choice in terms of the five service dimensions. If a strong culture and tradition are important to you, University A offers this type of environment. What your expectations are has a lot to do with your perception of how your university falls within these service dimensions.

Marketing research (see Chapter 10) provides a means to better understand consumers' service expectations and their perceptions of service quality. This research can be extensive and expensive, or it can be integrated into a firm's everyday interactions with customers. Today, most service firms have developed voice-of-customer programs and employ ongoing marketing research to assess how well they are meeting their customers' expectations. A systematic **voice-of-customer (VOC) program** collects customer inputs and integrates them into managerial decisions.

LO 13-4   Explain the zone of tolerance.

An important marketing metric to evaluate how well firms perform on the five service quality dimensions (see again Exhibit 13.4) is the **zone of tolerance**, which refers to the area between customers' expectations regarding their desired service and the minimum level of acceptable service—that is, the difference between what the customer really wants and what he or she will accept before going elsewhere.[25] To define the zone of tolerance, firms ask a series of questions

about each service quality dimension that relate to:

- The desired and expected level of service for each dimension, from low to high.

- Customers' perceptions of how well the focal service performs and how well a competitive service performs, from low to high.

- The importance of each service quality dimension.

Exhibit 13.6 illustrates the results of such an analysis for Lou's Local Diner, a family-owned restaurant. The rankings on the left are based on a nine-point scale, on which 1 is low and 9 is high. The length of each box illustrates the zone of tolerance for each service quality dimension. For instance, according to the short length of the reliability box, customers expect a fairly high level of reliability (top of the box) but will accept only a fairly high level of reliability (bottom of the box). On the other end of the scale, customers expect a high level of assurance (top of the box) but will also accept a fairly low level (bottom of the box). This difference is to be expected because the customers also were asked to assign an important score to the five service quality dimensions so that the total equals 100 percent (see bottom of Exhibit 13.6). Looking at the average importance score, we conclude that reliability is relatively important to these customers, but assurance is not.

▼ **EXHIBIT 13.6** Customers' Evaluation of Service Quality

Note: The scale ranges from a 9 indicating very high service quality on a given service quality dimension to a 1 indicating very low service quality.

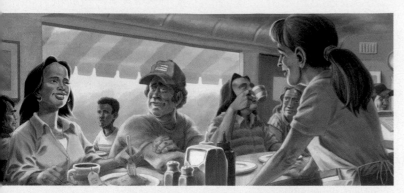

Lou's Local Diner always rates higher than its primary competitor, Well-Known National Chain, on each service quality dimension.

So customers have a fairly narrow zone of tolerance for service dimensions that are fairly important to them and a wider range of tolerance for those service dimensions that are less important. Also note that Lou's Local Diner always rates higher than its primary competitor, Well-Known National Chain, on each dimension.

Further note that Well-Known National Chain scores below the zone of tolerance on the tangibles dimension, meaning that customers are not willing to accept the way the restaurant looks and smells. Lou's Local Diner, in contrast, performs above the zone of tolerance on the responsiveness dimension— maybe even too well. Lou's may wish to conduct further research to verify which responsiveness aspects it is performing so well, and then consider toning those aspects down. For example, being responsive to customers' desires to have a diner that serves breakfast 24 hours a day can be expensive and may not add any further value to Lou's Diner because customers would accept more limited times.

A very straightforward and inexpensive method of collecting consumers' perceptions of service quality is to gather them at the time of the sale. Service providers can ask customers how they liked the service— though customers often are reticent to provide negative feedback directly to the person who provided the service—or distribute a simple questionnaire. Regardless of how information is collected, companies must take care not to lose it, which can happen if there is no effective mechanism for filtering it up to the key decision makers. Furthermore, in some cases, customers cannot effectively evaluate the service until several days or weeks later. Automobile dealers, for instance, often call their customers a week after they perform a service such as an oil change to assess their service quality.[26]

Another excellent method for assessing customers' expectations is making effective use of customer complaint behavior. Even if complaints are handled effectively to solve customers' problems, the essence of the complaint is too often lost on managers. For instance, an airline established a policy that customer service reps could not discuss any issues involving fees to travel agents with customers. So when a customer calls to complain about these fees, the representative just changes the subject, and management therefore never finds out about the complaint.[27]

Even firms with the best formal research mechanisms in place must put managers on the front lines occasionally to interact directly with the customers. The late Sam Walton, founder of Walmart, participated in and advocated this strategy, which is known as, "management by walking around."[28] Unless the managers who make the service quality decisions know what their service providers are facing on a day-to-day basis, and unless they can talk directly to the customers with whom those service providers interact, any customer service program they create will not be as good as it could be.

The Standards Gap: Setting Service Standards

Getting back to the Green Valley Motel in Maine for a moment, suppose because of a number of complaints or because business was falling off it set out to determine customers' service expectations and gained a pretty good idea of them. The next step would be to set its service standards accordingly and develop systems to meet the customers' service expectations. How, for instance, can it make sure that every room is cleaned and ready by an optimum time of day in the eyes of the customers, or that the breakfast is checked for freshness and quality every day? To consistently deliver service that meets customers' expectations, firms must set specific, measurable goals. For instance, for the Green Valley Motel, the most efficient process might have been to start cleaning rooms at 8:00 a.m. and finish by 5:00 p.m. But many guests want to sleep late, and new arrivals want to get into their room as soon as they arrive, often before 5:00. So a customer-oriented standard would mandate that the rooms get cleaned between 10:00 a.m. and 2:00 p.m.

Service providers generally want to do a good job as long as they know what is expected of them.[29] Motel employees should be shown, for instance, exactly how managers expect them to clean a room and what specific tasks they are responsible for performing. In general, more employees will buy into a quality-oriented process if they are involved in setting the goals. For instance, suppose an important employee of the motel objects to disposable plastic cups and suggests actual drinking glasses in the rooms would be classier as well as more ecological. There might be a cost/benefit trade-off to consider here, but if management listens to her and makes the change in this case, it should likely make the employee all the more committed to other tasks involved in cleaning and preparing rooms.

> "In general, more employees will buy into a quality-oriented process if they are involved in setting the goals."

Service providers, like this housekeeper at a hotel, generally want to do a good job, but they need to be trained to know what exactly a good job entails.

The Delivery Gap: Delivering Service Quality

The delivery gap is where the rubber meets the road, where the customer directly interacts with the service provider. Even if there are adequate standards in place, the employees are well-trained, and management is committed to meeting or exceeding customers' service expectations, there can still be delivery gaps. It could very well have been that Marcia experienced several delivery gaps at the Green Valley Motel. It could have been that the unclean room, the assistant manager's attitude, the unheated swimming pool, the poor piano bar singer, or the stale food resulted from unforeseen or unusual circumstances. Although some of these issues such as an unclean room or the attitude Marcia encountered should have been avoided, it is possible that the motel had a power outage resulting in the unheated swimming pool, the regular piano bar singer was ill, and the breakfast was stale because of a missed delivery. The maid could not vacuum the room because of the lack of power, and the assistant manager felt assaulted on all sides by these problems. But the result was a lost customer. Even if there are no other gaps, a delivery gap always results in a service failure.

Delivery gaps can be reduced when employees are empowered to spontaneously act in the customers' and the firm's best interests when problems or crises are experienced. Such empowerment might have saved the day for Marcia and the Green Valley. Empowerment means employees are supported in their efforts to do their jobs effectively.[30] (See Exhibit 13.7.)

Empowering Service Providers In the service context, **empowerment** means allowing employees to make decisions about how service is provided to customers. When frontline employees are authorized to make decisions to help their customers, service quality generally improves. Empowerment becomes more important when the service is more individualized. Nordstrom provides an overall objective—satisfy customer needs—and then encourages employees to do whatever is necessary to achieve the objective. For example, a Nordstrom shoe sales associate decided to break up two pairs of shoes, one a size 10 and the other a size 10½, to sell a hard-to-fit customer.

The employees must be thoroughly trained not only to complete their specific tasks but also how to treat guests, and the manager needs to set an example of high service standards, which will permeate throughout the organization. The kind of attitude Marcia got, for instance, when she registered a complaint with the assistant manager at the Green Valley is not a recipe for generating repeat customers and should not be tolerated. For frontline service employees under stress, however, pleasant interactions with customers do not always come naturally. Although people can be taught specific tasks related to their jobs, this is not easily extended to interpersonal relations. But it is simply not enough to tell employees to be nice or do what customers want. A quality goal should be specific, such as: Greet every customer/guest you encounter with "Good morning/afternoon/evening, Sir or Ma'am." Try to greet customers by name.

In extreme cases, such training becomes even more crucial. From long ticket lines to cancelled flights to lost baggage to safety concerns, customer service incidents are on the rise in the airline industry. (See Social and Mobile Marketing 13.2, later in the chapter, for one such famous incident.) Faced with these mounting complaints, some airlines are attempting to implement better employee training geared toward identifying and defusing potentially explosive situations.

▼ **EXHIBIT 13.7** Methods to Reduce Delivery Gaps

emotional support Concern for others' well-being and support of their decisions in a job setting.

instrumental support Providing the equipment or systems needed to perform a task in a job setting.

Although the other two shoes were unsalable and therefore it made for an unprofitable sale, the customer purchased five other pairs that day and became a loyal Nordstrom customer as a result. Empowering service providers with only a rule like "Use your best judgment" (as Nordstrom does) might cause chaos. At Nordstrom, department managers avoid abuses by coaching and training salespeople to understand what "Use your best judgment" specifically means.

Support and Incentives for Employees

To ensure that service is delivered properly, management needs to support the service providers in several ways and give them incentives. This is basic. A service provider's job can often be difficult, especially when customers are unpleasant or less than reasonable. But the service provider cannot be rude or offensive just because the customer is. The old cliché, "Service with a smile," remains the best approach, but for this to work, employees must feel supported.

physicians to provide great patient care using state-of-the-art procedures and medications, but because they are tied to managed-care systems (health maintenance organizations or HMOs), many doctors must squeeze more people into their office hours and prescribe less optimal, less expensive, courses of treatment. These conflicting goals can be very frustrating to patients.

Finally, a key part of any customer service program is providing rewards to employees for their excellent service. Numerous firms have developed a service reputation by ensuring that their employees are themselves recognized for recognizing the value the firm places on customer service. Travelocity, for example, features employees who champion the customer service experience in a weekly e-mail. Believing that engaged employees are the key to customer satisfaction, it works to create an atmosphere that reinforces the commitment to customers by encouraging employees to nominate colleagues who exemplify its commitment to customers. Through constant feedback about who is serving the customer best, as well as smaller events such as monthly lunches with the CEO for selected employees, Travelocity creates a business environment that recognizes and rewards customer service.[32] The results for Travelocity have been a wealth of awards, such as a top ranking on the Customer

> ## The old cliché, "Service with a smile," remains the best approach, but for this to work, employees must feel supported.

First, managers and coworkers should provide **emotional support** to service providers by demonstrating a concern for their well-being and standing behind their decisions. Because it can be very disconcerting when a waiter is abused by a customer who believes her food was improperly prepared, for instance, restaurant managers must be supportive and help the employee get through his or her emotional reaction to the berating experienced.[31] Such support can extend to empowering the waiter to rectify the situation by giving the customer new food and a free dessert, in which case the manager must understand the waiter's decision, not punish him for giving away too much.

Second, service providers require **instrumental support**—the systems and equipment to deliver the service properly. Many retailers provide state-of-the-art instrumental support for their service providers. In-store kiosks help sales associates provide more detailed and complete product information and enable them to make sales of merchandise that is either not carried in the store or is temporarily out of stock.

Third, the support that managers provide must be consistent and coherent throughout the organization. Patients expect

Online Respect Survey and a designation as the World's Leading Travel Internet Site for several consecutive years.[33]

Use of Technology

Technology can also be employed to reduce delivery gaps. Technology has become an increasingly important facilitator of the delivery of services. Using technology to facilitate service delivery can provide many benefits, such as access to a wider variety of services, a greater degree of control by the customer over the services, and the ability to obtain information. Social & Mobile Marketing 13.1 describes one such option. The use of technology also improves the service provider's efficiency and reduces servicing costs; in some cases, it can lead to a competitive advantage over less service-oriented competitors.[34]

Technological advances that help close the delivery gap are expanding. Salons and cosmetics counters use kiosks to show customers how they would look with different beauty products and various hair colors. Stores enable customers to scan price tags and then have a kiosk recommend complementary items. Touchscreen terminals at tables in Chuck E. Cheese let

Social & Mobile Marketing 13.1
Making Apps Work to Serve[35]

More than 100 million people have smartphones. Approximately half of them make purchases on these devices. Thus nearly 100 percent of companies want to find ways to exploit the potential of this channel. In this huge market, consumers generally are younger and wealthier than others who own older-model mobile phones. For example, more than 50 percent of mobile retail consumers earn at least $75,000 annually.

These statistics also describe the consumers most likely to buy from fashion-oriented companies, whether they sell fashion magazine content, commerce, or brand information. In response, Style.com offers a mobile application for people to access the same content available on the *Style* magazine website, including blogs, reviews, couture shows, and video feeds. Other apps provide a more in-depth look at a particular brand. Louis Vuitton's NOWNESS app combines magazine content with brand promotion. For London's famous Harrods department store, a mobile app helps consumers navigate the extensive geography of the actual store.

With the Stylish Girl app, customers instead can search a variety of stores to compare prices and available assortments while also storing their favorite items from each store in a virtual closet. Pose is a photo-sharing app for style and fashion; Snapette focuses on shoes and bags and aims to help customers find the merchandise they want according to their immediate location.

Even with all of these different types of apps, only a few actually improve the multichannel customer's shopping experience,

Snapette helps customers find shoes and bags according to their immediate location.

such as by helping customers regardless of whether they use their smartphones or visit the stores. Such multichannel services represent the best way forward for mobile applications if they hope to get shoppers, and their vast purchasing power, on board.

---

customers order food and play games from the comfort of their own table.[36] The technological delivery of services can cause problems though. Some customers either do not embrace the idea of replacing a human with a machine for business interactions or have problems using the technology. In other cases, the technology may not perform adequately, such as ATMs that run out of money or are out of order. Supermarket self-checkout devices are too challenging for some customers.

The Communications Gap: Communicating the Service Promise

Poor communication between marketers and their customers can result in a mismatch between an ad campaign's or a salesperson's promises and the service the firm can actually offer. Although firms have difficulty controlling service quality because it can vary from day to day and provider to provider, they have nearly constant control over how they communicate their service package to their customers. This control involves a significant responsibility, as Ethical & Societal Dilemma 13.1 notes.

If a firm promises more than it can deliver, customers' expectations won't be met. An advertisement may lure a customer into a service situation once, but if the service doesn't deliver on the promise, the customer will never return. Dissatisfied customers also are likely to tell others about the underperforming service, using word of mouth or, increasingly, the Internet, which has become an important channel for dissatisfied customers to vent their frustrations.

The communications gap can be reduced by managing customer expectations and by promising only what you can deliver, or possibly even a little less.[37] Suppose you need an operation, and the surgeon explains, "You'll be out of the hospital in five days and back to your normal routine in a month." You have the surgery and feel well enough to leave the hospital three days later. Two weeks after that, you're playing tennis again. Clearly, you will tend to think your surgeon is a genius. However, regardless of the operation's success, if you had to stay in the hospital for 10 days and it took you two months to recover, you would undoubtedly be upset.

A relatively easy way to manage customer expectations is to coordinate how the expectation is created and the way the

Which store has better customer service: the one with self-checkout (left), or the store offering a face-to-face interaction with the customer? It depends on whom you ask.

ethical & societal dilemma 13.1

Fake Reviews[38]

Yelp, TripAdvisor, and Amazon have all made user ratings and reviews a familiar—and even essential—part of the online toolbox for shoppers and other consumers. From the consumer's perspective, what better preparation could there be for a major purchase than to see what other, objective customers have to say about the product or service under consideration?

For retailers and service professionals, online reviews offer a huge benefit too. For some companies, especially small service providers that cannot afford much marketing, online reviews function as a low-cost form of advertising. A business seeking to meet or exceed customer expectations receives valuable, candid feedback from customers, which it can use to measure how well it is meeting customer expectations. Some firms even use this feedback in their formal voice-of-customer programs to improve company operations.

But who benefits from fake consumer reviews? Seemingly the company might, assuming it does not get caught But federal regulators are taking action to ensure that such deceptive advertising does not pay, and recent events suggest that companies that fake their reviews often get caught.

VIP Deals, an online retailer that sells leather cases for digital tablets on Amazon, invited its customers to post reviews—and promised that if those reviews were positive, the customer would receive a complete refund. Within weeks, nearly all of the company's 355 online reviews gave the VIP Deals leather case four or five stars. But Amazon guidelines prohibit compensation for customer reviews, and the VIP Deals page soon disappeared.

A leather case for your iPad is one thing. Accurate, truthful information takes on paramount importance for a service like plastic surgery. But Lifestyle Lift seemed to disregard customers' expectations that they

could receive truthful information. When unhappy customers started posting too many negative comments on its website, the company launched a coverup, rather than investigating the complaints to help its physicians and staff address the problems. On bogus websites, fictitious posters gave high praise to the company, while also asserting that previously posted complaints had been phony. The state of New York soon filed suit and prompted a $300,000 settlement from Lifestyle Lift.

Crowd-sourced online opinions of consumers have become a major source of information about products and services (recall our discussion of crowd-sourcing in Chapter 11). When that information is authentic, it serves consumers and companies both. But when companies manipulate online reviews, it seems as if all of society is harmed. What—if anything—should be done about it?

EXHIBIT 13.8 Top Ten Retailers for Customer Service

Ranking	2010	2011
1.	Zappos	Amazon.com
2.	Amazon.com	L.L.Bean
3.	L.L. Bean	Zappos
4.	Overstock.com	Overstock.com
5.	Lands' End	QVC
6.	JCPenney	Kohl's
7.	Kohl's	Lands' End
8.	QVC	JCPenney
9.	Nordstrom	Newegg
10.	Newegg	Nordstrom

Source: NRF Foundation/American Express, "Consumer Choice Awards," http://www.nrffoundation.com. Reprinted with permission of NRF Foundation.

service is provided. Expectations typically are created through promotions, advertising, or personal selling. Delivery is another function altogether. If a salesperson promises a client that an order can be delivered in one day, and that delivery actually takes a week, the client will be disappointed. However, if the salesperson coordinates the order with those responsible for the service delivery, the client's expectations likely will be met. As we noted in this chapter's opener, Zappos regularly provides better than promised delivery dates to help delight their customers.

Customer expectations can be managed when the service is delivered. Recorded messages tell customers who have phoned a company with a query how many minutes they will have to wait before the next operator is available. Sellers automatically inform online customers of any items that are out of stock. Whether online or in a store, retailers can warn their customers to shop early during a sale because supplies of the sale item are limited. People are generally reasonable when they are warned that some aspect of the service may be below their expectations. They just don't like surprises!

Service Quality and Customer Satisfaction and Loyalty

Good service quality leads to satisfied and loyal customers. As we discussed in Chapter 6, customers inevitably wind up their purchase decision process by undertaking a postpurchase evaluation. This evaluation after the purchase may produce three outcomes: satisfaction, dissonance, and loyalty (see again Exhibit 6.3 in Chapter 6). Dissonance may just be a passing emotion that is overcome; we will discuss recovery from an actual service failure in the next section. Satisfaction, on the other hand, often leads to loyalty.

Assuming that none of the service gaps that we have discussed above occur, or at least are not too wide, customers should be more or less satisfied. Surveys of customers that ask them to identify the retailer that provides the best customer service thus often show some consistency. A service provider that does a good job one year is likely to keep customers satisfied the next year too, as Exhibit 13.8 shows.

 check yourself

1. Explain the four service gaps identified by the Gaps Model.
2. List at least two ways to overcome each of the four service gaps.

LO 13-5 Identify three service recovery strategies.

SERVICE RECOVERY

Despite a firm's best efforts, sometimes service providers fail to meet customer expectations. When this happens, the best course of action is to attempt to make amends with the customer and learn from the experience. Of course, it is best to avoid a service

> It is best to avoid a service failure altogether, but when a failure does occur, the firm has a unique opportunity to demonstrate its customer commitment.

failure altogether, but when a failure does occur, the firm has a unique opportunity to demonstrate its customer commitment.[39] Effective service recovery efforts can significantly increase customer satisfaction, purchase intentions, and positive word of mouth, though customers' post-recovery satisfaction levels usually fall lower than their satisfaction level prior to the service failure.[40]

Social & Mobile Marketing 13.2 articulates how social media such as YouTube have provided customers with an enormous stage on which to air their dissatisfaction with a product or service. No longer are dissatisfied customers only able to vent their frustrations with a few friends. Today, word of mouth, especially in electronic form, can spread to millions of recipients.

Social & Mobile Marketing
The 4-Minute and 37-Second Complaint Heard by Millions

13.2

Thanks to the Internet, customer service has gone viral. According to an old adage, when customers have a good experience, they tell one person. Those who have a bad experience tell four. But the rise of blogs, Twitter, YouTube, and similar sites has changed the very meaning of word of mouth. Whereas once, to spread word of mouth, a sender had to know the recipient, today millions of people can learn about service problems that strangers experience, all in a matter of hours.

United Airlines learned this lesson the hard way. A member of the band Sons of Maxwell watched from a plane window as baggage handlers tossed luggage with little regard for the value or fragility of the instruments in the cargo.[41] Musician Dave Carroll complained immediately to flight attendants, but to no avail. After arriving at his destination, Carroll discovered his $3,500 acoustic guitar was broken. He made it through his performances using alternative guitars and then, on his return flight a week later, complained again about the damaged instrument. Over the next weeks and months, he contacted the airline repeatedly about the problem while also shelling out $1,200 to get his guitar fixed. When Carroll did finally hear from the airline regarding compensation, he was informed that his claim was denied because he hadn't filed it appropriately.

He responded with a 4-minute and 37-second complaint in the form of songs and videos posted to the Internet. The first tune, called "United Breaks Guitars," suggests that flying a different airline or driving would have been preferable to flying United. The video scored 5 million hits in a matter of weeks, with more than 11.5 million views to date.[42] A month later, the band released another song that poked fun at one of United's customer service employees and the airline's policies for handling baggage complaints. The third tune acknowledged United's attempts to improve but also cautioned that customers would switch to other carriers without lasting improvements. Even though bloggers were not uniformly impressed by the music, many offered their own horror stories of United's customer service, creating a maelstrom of bad public relations for the airline.

United responded with an admission of guilt on Twitter, a $3,000 donation to a musical charity, and an ad campaign indicating it took complaints about luggage handling seriously. The company also saw an opportunity to turn a single customer service problem into a training opportunity: With Carroll's permission, they use the video to improve passenger service worldwide.[43] But United Airlines still lost $180 million, or 10 percent of its stock price, due to this incident.[44]

Warning to United Airlines: Don't mess with Dave Carroll or his guitar. If you do, he will write a song about you and post it on the Internet.

Remember the Green Valley Motel in Maine? It could have made amends with Marcia Kessler after its service failures if it had taken some relatively simple, immediate steps: The assistant manager could have apologized for his bad behavior and quickly upgraded her to a suite and/or given her a free night's lodging for a future stay. The motel could also have given her a free lunch or dinner to make up for the bad breakfast. Alternatively, the assistant manager could have asked Marcia how he could resolve the situation and worked with her to come up with an equitable solution. None of these actions would have cost the motel much money.

Had it used the customer lifetime value approach we described in Chapter 10, the motel would have realized that by not taking action, it lost Marcia as a customer forever. Over the next few years, she could have been responsible for several thousand dollars in sales. Instead, Marcia is now likely to spread negative word of mouth about the motel to her friends, family, and through social media such as Yelp.com because of its failure to recover. Effective service recovery thus demands (1) listening to the customers and involving them in the service recovery, (2) providing a fair solution, and (3) resolving the problem quickly.[45]

Listening to the Customers and Involving Them in the Service Recovery

Firms often don't find out about service failures until a customer complains. Whether the firm has a formal complaint department or the complaint is offered directly to the service provider, the customer must have the opportunity to air the complaint completely, and the firm must listen carefully to what he or she is saying.

Customers can become very emotional about a service failure, whether the failure is serious (a botched surgical operation) or minor (the wrong change at a restaurant). In many cases, the customer may just want to be heard, and the service provider should give the customer all the time he or she needs to get it out. The very process of describing a perceived wrong to a sympathetic listener is therapeutic in and of itself. Service providers therefore should welcome the opportunity to be that sympathetic ear, listen carefully, and appear (and actually be) anxious to rectify the situation to ensure it doesn't happen again.[46]

When the company and the customer work together, the outcome is often better than either could achieve on their own. This co-creation logic applies especially well to service recovery. A service failure is a negative experience, but when customers participate in its resolution, it results in a more positive outcome than simply listening to their complaint and providing a preapproved set of potential solutions that may satisfy them.

Suppose, for instance, that when you arrived at the airport in San Francisco, your flight had been overbooked, and you were bumped. Of course, good customer service required the ticket agent to listen to your frustration and help provide a fair solution. But the most obvious potential solution from the airline's perspective might not have been the best solution for you. It might have been inclined to put you on the next available flight, which would be a red-eye that left at midnight and got you to New York at 6:30 a.m. But if you don't sleep well on planes and you have an important business meeting the next afternoon, the best solution from your perspective would be to have the airline put you up in an airport hotel so you can get a good night's sleep and then put you on an early morning flight that would get you to New York in time for your meeting, well-rested and ready to go. Thus, by working closely with you to understand your needs, the ticket agent would be able to co-create a great solution to the service failure.

Finding a Fair Solution

Most people realize that mistakes happen. But when they happen, customers want to be treated fairly, whether that means *distributive* or *procedural* fairness.[47] Their perception of what "fair" means is based on their previous experience with other firms, how they have seen other customers treated, material they have read, and stories recounted by their friends.

Distributive Fairness
Distributive fairness pertains to a customer's perception of the benefits he or she received compared with the costs (inconvenience or loss). Customers want to be compensated a fair amount for a perceived loss that resulted from a service failure. If, for instance, a person arrives at the airport gate and finds her flight is overbooked, she may believe that taking the next flight that day and receiving a travel voucher is adequate compensation for the inconvenience. But if no flights are available until the next day, the traveler may require additional compensation, such as overnight accommodations, meals, and a round-trip ticket to be used at a later date.[48]

The key to distributive fairness, of course, is listening carefully to the customer. One customer, traveling on vacation, may be satisfied with a travel voucher, whereas another

distributive fairness
Pertains to a customer's perception of the benefits he or she received compared with the costs (inconvenience or loss) that resulted from a service failure.

"
REGARDLESS OF HOW THE PROBLEM IS SOLVED, CUSTOMERS TYPICALLY WANT TANGIBLE RESTITUTION—IN THIS CASE, TO GET TO THEIR DESTINATION—NOT JUST AN APOLOGY."

may need to get to the destination on time because of a business appointment. Regardless of how the problem is solved, customers typically want tangible restitution—in this case, to get to their destination—not just an apology. If providing tangible restitution isn't possible, the next best thing is to assure the customer that steps are being taken to prevent the failure from recurring.

Procedural Fairness With regard to complaints, **procedural fairness** refers to the perceived fairness of the process used to resolve them. Customers want efficient complaint procedures over whose outcomes they have some influence. Customers tend to believe they have been treated fairly if the service providers follow specific company guidelines. Nevertheless, rigid adherence to rules can have deleterious effects. Have you ever returned an item to a store, even a very inexpensive item, that needed a manager's approval? The process can take several minutes and irritate everyone in the checkout line. Furthermore, most managers' cursory inspection of the item or the situation would not catch a fraudulent return. In a case like this, the procedure the company uses to handle a return probably overshadows any potential positive outcomes. Therefore, as we noted previously, service providers should be empowered with some procedural flexibility to solve customer complaints.

A no-questions-asked return policy has been offered as a customer service by many retailers such as L.L. Bean. But because of its high cost as a result of customers abusing the policy, many retailers such as Bean's competitor, REI, have modified their return policies.[49] Some large retailers now limit their returns to 90 days, considered a reasonable amount of time for customers to return an item. Others will only grant a store credit based on the lowest selling price for the item if the customer doesn't have a receipt. In addition, for some consumer electronics products that have been opened, customers must pay a 15 percent restocking fee.

Resolving Problems Quickly

The longer it takes to resolve a service failure, the more irritated the customer will become and the more people he or she is likely to tell about the problem. To resolve service failures quickly, firms need clear policies, adequate training for their employees, and empowered employees. Health insurance companies, for instance, have made a concerted effort in recent years to avoid service failures that occur because customers' insurance claims have not been handled quickly or to the customers' satisfaction.

In the age of social media, companies can respond and resolve customer issues even faster. For example, Time Warner Cable, the second largest cable provider in the United States, actively monitors and responds to tweets via @TWCableHelp. If the employee listening cannot resolve the issue, it is automatically escalated to the technical support team, which then reaches out to the customer by phone or online. ∎

 check yourself

1. Why is service recovery so important to companies?
2. What can companies do to recover from a service failure?

L.L. Bean's satisfaction guarantee has helped it become a consistent leader in customer service.

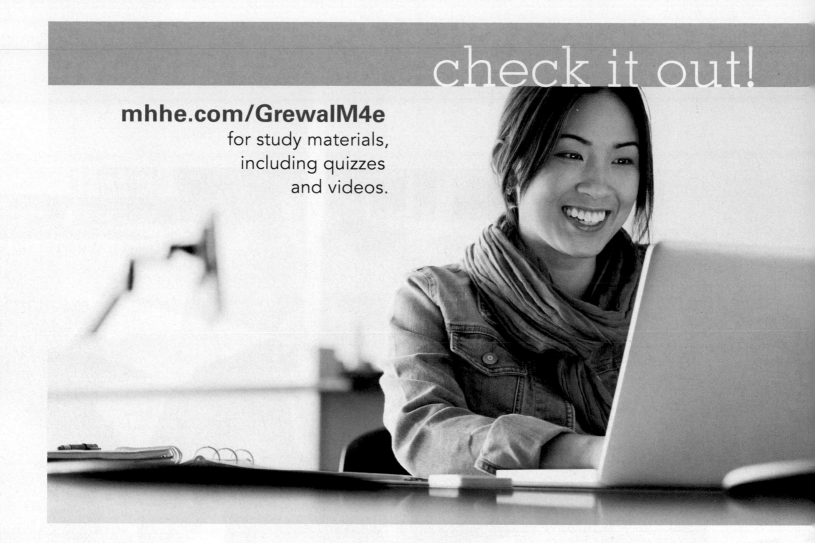

check it out!

mhhe.com/GrewalM4e
for study materials,
including quizzes
and videos.

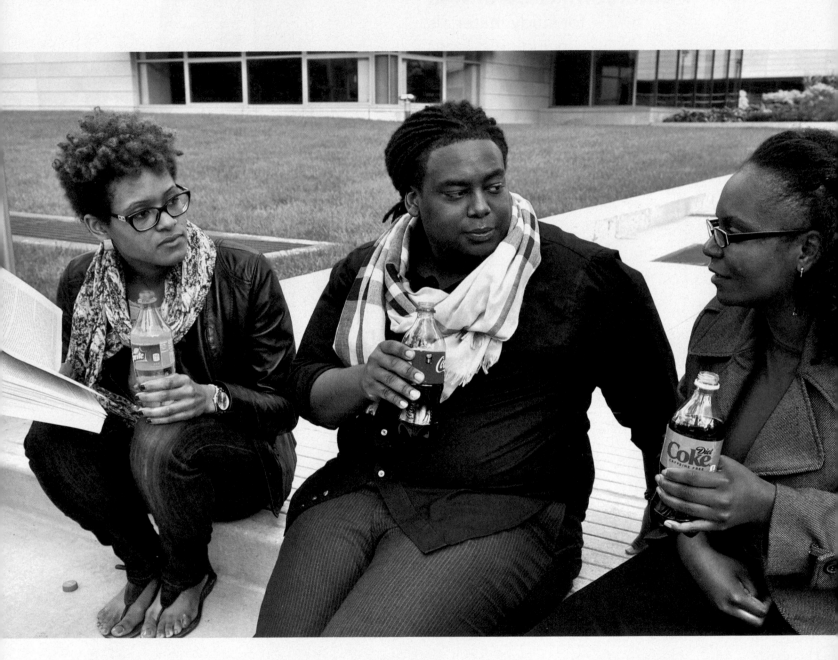

chapter fourteen

pricing concepts for establishing value

Pricing is a key part of the value proposition for any purchase. After all, value reflects the relationship between benefits and costs. And when the economy sours, and consumer income drops, no sticker price escapes sharp scrutiny, especially in the supermarket. Shoppers on a tight budget may still need to buy that gallon of milk every week; but demand is far more elastic for items like candy or soft drinks. For such nonessential products, the challenge comes down to pricing strategy: How do you lure customers back when they're desperate to spend less?

Even corporate giant Coca-Cola has had to grapple with this question. The soda that became shorthand worldwide for a quick, ice-cold drink started out in 1886 as a headache cure called Coca-Cola. By the end of World War II, the popular American brand controlled more than 60 percent of the soft drink market worldwide. Over the years, that dominance gave way to an intense

LEARNING OBJECTIVES

After reading this chapter, you should be able to:

LO 14-1 List the four pricing orientations.

LO 14-2 Explain the relationship between price and quantity sold.

LO 14-3 Explain price elasticity.

LO 14-4 Describe how to calculate a product's break-even point.

LO 14-5 Indicate the four types of price competitive levels.

LO 14-6 Describe the difference between an everyday low price strategy (EDLP) and a high/low strategy.

LO 14-7 Explain the difference between a price skimming and a market penetration pricing strategy.

LO 14-8 List pricing practices that have the potential to deceive customers.

rivalry with Pepsi-Cola; today each company controls about a third of the $75 billion U.S. retail soda market, the other key player being Dr Pepper Snapple Group.[1]

But recent market changes have transformed the soda industry. Health-conscious consumers have abandoned high-sugar sodas, and new alternative

continued on p. 304

Manufacturing costs are up about $700 million a year to cover higher prices for plastic, high-fructose syrup, and fruit.[5]

So Coke's new pricing approach had to reconcile two diverging trends: rising costs and the demand for lower prices. Fortunately, the company had already confronted this problem in Mexico, the world's largest per-capita consumer of Coke. When economic crisis hit and the peso dropped in 1994, Coca-Cola started offering smaller, lower-priced packages to get customers to buy again. Today, Coke fans there have more than 30 package options, from 6.75 ounce containers to three-liter bottles.[6]

In the U.S., Coke traditionally has offered three sizes—20-ounce bottles, two-liter bottles, and cases of 12-ounce cans. Now it has added three smaller package options for consumers looking to spend less. Under this increasingly segmented price-packaging strategy, Coke now comes in a 12.5-ounce bottle for 89 cents and a new 99-cent 16-ounce bottle. The company also cut the price on its eight-pack of 7.5-ounce mini-cans, hoping that the smaller can originally designed for weight-conscious consumers will also appeal to those on a budget.

Can Coca-Cola boost U.S. revenue and profits while offering reduced-volume options? That seems like a paradox, but the company may have found a strategic sweet spot. Smaller containers cost less, but consumers pay more per ounce. Those who still want larger bottles and cans will face higher prices. Coca-Cola is hoping that its selection of sizes and prices will ensure that for every fan, Coke is still the real thing. ∎

continued from p. 303

beverages—iced teas, bottled waters, and vitamin drinks—now compete for shelf space. U.S. soda consumption has declined, as a result, for six years in a row,[2] and over the past decade, Coke and its rivals have lost well over a third of their sales.[3] Overseas business now generates the bulk of Coca-Cola's revenue growth, much of it coming from Russia and China.[4]

In the search for a pricing strategy to jumpstart flagging U.S. revenues, Coca-Cola has also confronted another problem.

> # Coke's new pricing approach had to reconcile two diverging trends: rising costs and the demand for lower prices.

Although knowing how consumers arrive at their perceptions of value is critical to developing successful pricing strategies, sellers also must consider other factors—which is why developing a good pricing strategy is such a formidable challenge to all firms. Do it right, and the rewards to the firm will be substantial. Do it wrong, and failure will be swift and severe. But even if a pricing strategy is implemented well, consumers, economic conditions, markets,

competitors, government regulations, and even a firm's own products change constantly—and that means that a good pricing strategy today may not remain an effective pricing strategy tomorrow.

Imagine that a consumer realizes that to save money on a particular item, she will have to drive an additional 20 miles. She may determine that her time and travel costs are not worth the savings, so even though the price tag is higher at a nearby

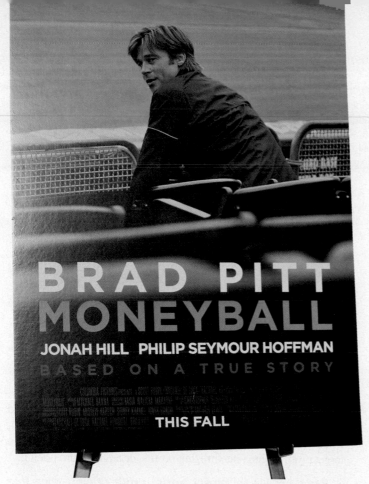

Demonstrating that price is often used to judge quality, in the movie Moneyball, *Jonah Hill explains to Brad Pitt's character that baseball teams often overpay for young, untested talent or big name players because they don't know how else to gauge an appropriate salary.*

store, she judges the overall cost of buying the product there to be lower. To include aspects of price such as this, we may define **price** as the overall sacrifice a consumer is willing to make to acquire a specific product or service. This sacrifice necessarily includes the money that must be paid to the seller to acquire the item, but it also may involve other sacrifices, whether nonmonetary, like the value of the time necessary to acquire the product or service, or monetary, like travel costs, taxes, shipping costs, and so forth, all of which the buyer must give up to take possession of the product.[7] It's useful to think of overall price like this to see how the narrower sense of purchase price fits in.

Because price is the only element of the marketing mix that does not generate costs, but instead generates revenue, it is important in its own right. Every other element in the marketing mix may be perfect, but with the wrong price, sales and thus revenue will not accrue. Research has consistently shown that consumers usually rank price as

Since people use price to judge quality or performance of a product, when a group of people paid less for an energy drink, they were able to solve fewer puzzles than those who paid more.

one of the most important factors in their purchase decisions.[8]

Knowing that price is so critical to success, why don't managers put greater emphasis on it as a strategic decision variable? Price is the most challenging of the four Ps to manage, partly because it is often the least understood. Historically, managers have treated price as an afterthought to their marketing strategy, setting prices according to what competitors were charging or, worse yet, adding up their costs and tacking a desired profit on to set the sales price. Prices rarely changed except in response to radical shifts in market conditions. Even today, pricing decisions are often relegated to standard rules of thumb that fail to reflect our current understanding of the role of price in the marketing mix.

Price is a particularly powerful indicator of quality when consumers are less knowledgeable about the product category—a lesson brought home by the movie (based on the book of the same name) *Moneyball*. As the character played by Jonah Hill argues convincingly to Brad Pitt's character, baseball teams often overpay for young, untested talent or big name players because they don't know how else to set an accurate price.[9]

In summary, marketers should view pricing decisions as a strategic opportunity to create value rather than as an afterthought to the rest of the marketing mix. Let us now turn to the five basic components of pricing strategies.

THE FIVE CS OF PRICING

Successful pricing strategies are built around the five critical components (the five Cs) of pricing found in Exhibit 14.1.

We examine these components in some detail because each makes a significant contribution to formulating good pricing policies.[10] To start, the first step is to develop the company's pricing objectives.

Company Objectives

By now, you know that different firms embrace very different goals. These goals should spill down to the pricing strategy, such that the pricing of a company's products and services should support and allow the firm to reach its overall goals. For example, a firm with a primary goal of very high sales growth will likely have a different pricing strategy than a firm with the goal of being a quality leader.

Each firm then embraces objectives that seem to fit with where management thinks the firm needs to go to be successful, in whatever way it defines success. These specific objectives usually reflect

profit orientation
A company objective that can be implemented by focusing on *target profit pricing, maximizing profits,* or *target return pricing.*

target profit pricing A pricing strategy implemented by firms when they have a particular profit goal as their overriding concern; uses price to stimulate a certain level of sales at a certain profit per unit.

maximizing profits A profit strategy that relies primarily on economic theory. If a firm can accurately specify a mathematical model that captures all the factors required to explain and predict sales and profits, it should be able to identify the price at which its profits are maximized.

target return pricing A pricing strategy implemented by firms less concerned with the absolute level of profits and more interested in the rate at which their profits are generated relative to their investments; designed to produce a specific return on investment, usually expressed as a percentage of sales.

sales orientation A company objective based on the belief that increasing sales will help the firm more than will increasing profits.

▼ **EXHIBIT 14.1** The 5 Cs of Pricing

how the firm intends to grow. Do managers want it to grow by increasing profits, increasing sales, decreasing competition, or building customer satisfaction?

Company objectives are not as simple as they might first appear. They often can be expressed in slightly different forms that mean very different things. Exhibit 14.2 introduces some common company objectives and corresponding examples of their implications for pricing strategies. These objectives are not always mutually exclusive because a firm may embrace two or more noncompeting objectives.

LO 14-1   List the four pricing orientations.

Profit Orientation   Even though all company methods and objectives may ultimately be oriented toward making a profit, firms implement a **profit orientation** specifically by focusing on target profit pricing, maximizing profits, or target return pricing.

· Firms usually implement **target profit pricing** when they have a particular profit goal as their overriding concern. To meet this targeted profit objective, firms use price to stimulate a certain level of sales at a certain profit per unit.

· The **maximizing profits** strategy relies primarily on economic theory. If a firm can accurately specify a mathematical model that captures all the factors required to explain and predict sales and profits, it should be able to identify the price at which its profits are maximized. Of course, the

> ## "Do managers want to grow by increasing profits, increasing sales, decreasing competition, or building customer satisfaction?"

▼ **EXHIBIT 14.2** Company Objectives and Pricing Strategy Implications

Company Objective	Examples of Pricing Strategy Implications
Profit-oriented	Institute a companywide policy that all products must provide for at least an 18 percent profit margin to reach a particular profit goal for the firm.
Sales-oriented	Set prices very low to generate new sales and take sales away from competitors, even if profits suffer.
Competitor-oriented	To discourage more competitors from entering the market, set prices very low.
Customer-oriented	Target a market segment of consumers who highly value a particular product benefit and set prices relatively high (referred to as premium pricing).

problem with this approach is that actually gathering the data on all these relevant factors and somehow coming up with an accurate mathematical model is an extremely difficult undertaking.

· Other firms are less concerned with the absolute level of profits and more interested in the rate at which their profits are generated relative to their investments. These firms typically turn to **target return pricing** and employ pricing strategies designed to produce a specific return on their investment, usually expressed as a percentage of sales.

Sales Orientation   Firms using a **sales orientation** to set prices believe that increasing sales will help the firm more than will increasing profits. Coca-Cola might adopt such an

Philadelphia brand cream cheese dominates its market and is a premium-priced brand.

orientation selectively, when it introduces new products that it wants to establish in the market. A new health club might focus on unit sales, dollar sales, or market share and therefore be willing to set a lower membership fee and accept less profit at first to focus on and generate more unit sales. In contrast, a high-end jewelry store might focus on dollar sales and maintain higher prices. The jewelry store relies on its prestige image, as well as the image of its suppliers, to provoke sales. Even though it sells fewer units, it can still generate high dollar sales levels.

Some firms may be more concerned about their overall market share than about dollar sales per se (though these often go hand in hand) because they believe that market share better reflects their success relative to the market conditions than do sales alone. A firm may set low prices to discourage new firms from entering the market, encourage current firms to leave the market, and/or take market share away from competitors—all to gain overall market share. For example, though Apple has sold more than 10 billion songs since the introduction of its iTunes service, it wants to keep increasing its market share, especially as competitors such as Amazon.com make inroads in this arena. Therefore, instead of 99 cents per song—the fixed pricing structure it previously maintained—Apple sets three price tiers (69 cents, 99 cents, and $1.29) for its songs, according to their popularity and recency. The songs that are the most popular cost the most, but by charging less for less popular songs, Apple aims to increase its sales per customer.[11]

Yet adopting a market share objective does not always imply setting low prices. Rarely is the lowest-price offering the dominant brand in a given market. Heinz ketchup, Philadelphia brand cream cheese, Crest toothpaste, and Nike athletic shoes have all dominated their markets, yet all are premium-priced brands. On the services side, IBM claims market dominance in human resource outsourcing, but again, it is certainly not the lowest price competitor.[12] **Premium pricing** means the firm deliberately prices a product above the prices set for competing products to capture those customers who always shop for the best or for whom price does not matter. Thus, companies can gain market share by offering a high-quality product at a price that is perceived to be fair by its target market as long as they use effective communication and distribution methods to generate high value perceptions among consumers. Although the concept of value is not overtly expressed in sales-oriented strategies, it is at least implicit because, for sales to increase, consumers must see greater value.

Competitor Orientation When firms take a **competitor orientation**, they strategize according to the premise that they should measure themselves primarily against their competition. Some firms focus on **competitive parity**, which means they set prices that are similar to those of their major competitors. Another competitor-oriented strategy, **status quo pricing**,

> **SOME FIRMS MAY BE MORE CONCERNED ABOUT THEIR OVERALL MARKET SHARE THAN ABOUT DOLLAR SALES PER SE (THOUGH THESE OFTEN GO HAND IN HAND) BECAUSE THEY BELIEVE THAT MARKET SHARE BETTER REFLECTS THEIR SUCCESS RELATIVE TO THE MARKET CONDITIONS THAN DO SALES ALONE.**

changes prices only to meet those of the competition. For example, when Delta increases its average fares, American Airlines and United often follow with similar increases; if Delta rescinds that increase, its competitors tend to drop their fares too.[13] Value is only implicitly considered in competitor-oriented strategies, but in the sense that competitors may be using value as part of their pricing strategies, copying their strategy might provide value.

Customer Orientation A **customer orientation** is when a firm sets its pricing strategy based on how it can add value to its products or services. When CarMax promises a no-haggle pricing structure, it exhibits a customer orientation because it provides additional value to potential used-car buyers by making the process simple and easy.[14]

Firms may offer very high-priced, state-of-the-art products or services in full anticipation of limited sales. These offerings are

Can you tell the difference between the $8,500 and the $320 speakers?

designed to enhance the company's reputation and image and thereby increase the company's value in the minds of consumers. Paradigm, a Canadian speaker manufacturer, produces what many audiophiles consider a high-value product, yet offers speakers priced as low as $320 per pair. However, Paradigm also offers a very high-end speaker for $8,500 per pair. Although few people will spend $8,500 on a pair of speakers, this statement speaker communicates what the company is capable of and can increase the image of the firm and the rest of its products—even that $320 pair of speakers. Setting prices with a close eye to how consumers develop their perceptions of value can often be the most effective pricing strategy, especially if it is supported by consistent advertising and distribution strategies.

After a company has a good grasp on its overall objectives, it must implement pricing strategies that enable it to achieve those objectives. As the second step in this process, the firm should look toward consumer demand to lay the foundation for its pricing strategy.

Adding Value   14.1

Lower Apple Prices in the Premium Price Segment[15]

For years, Apple had a strong reputation for offering high quality at high prices. The first iPhone cost nearly $500—way more than most other phones, but well worth it for Apple aficionados. Mac computers also cost more, but they offered great quality, advanced technology, and better protection from viruses and malware.

Today, though, Apple actually undercuts many of its competitors. Although Apple products still appear in the premium price category and continue to offer significant quality, the iPad (at $499) costs less than a comparable Xoom tablet from Motorola ($800). The 11-inch MacBook Air is $999; Samsung's entry into the ultrathin notebook category, the Series 9, instead runs $1,049. Obviously, there are cheaper computers available. But when it comes to matching offerings, Apple is often the least expensive entrant in the premium market.

It is able to do so largely because of its increasing popularity. As more and more consumers adopt Apple products, its increasing scale has enabled the company to buy more supplies for less. For example, it had the resources to enter into a five-year, $1.25 billion deal that gave Apple first dibs on flash memory chips, which are

critical for iPods and similar devices. With the supply going first to Apple, its competitors have had to scramble to find and bid for the remaining chips on the market, which has pushed their costs higher. But rather than increase the prices of its consumer products, Apple has chosen to pass on its supply chain efficiencies to customers in the form of lower prices. With this customer-oriented strategy, it should increase its market share even further, leading to a virtuous cycle that may be hard for any competitors to break.

Although Apple products are considered to be in the premium price category, it continues to price below competition.

Customers

When firms have developed their company objectives, they turn to understanding consumers' reactions to different prices. The second C of the five Cs of pricing focuses on the customers. Customers want value, and as you likely recall, price is half of the value equation.

To determine how firms account for consumers' preferences when they develop pricing strategies, we must first lay a foundation of traditional economic theory that helps explain how prices are related to demand (consumers' desire for products) and how managers can incorporate this knowledge into their pricing strategies.[16] But first read through Adding Value 14.1, which considers how Apple has leveraged consumers' love for its offerings into a sophisticated pricing strategy.

LO 14-2 Explain the relationship between price and quantity sold.

Demand Curves and Pricing A **demand curve**

shows how many units of a product or service consumers will demand during a specific period of time at different prices. Although we call them curves, demand curves can be either straight or curved, as Exhibit 14.3 shows. Of course, any demand curve relating demand to price assumes that everything else remains unchanged. For the sake of experiment, marketers creating a demand curve assume that the firm will not increase its expenditures on advertising and that the economy will not change in any significant way.

Exhibit 14.3 illustrates a classic downward-sloping demand curve for teeth whitening kits. As price increases, demand for the product or service decreases. In this case, consumers will buy more as the price decreases. As we noted in Adding Value 14.1, Apple expects increasing purchases with lower prices. We can expect a demand curve similar to this one for many, if not most, products and services.

▼ **EXHIBIT 14.3** Demand Curve for Teeth Whitening Kits

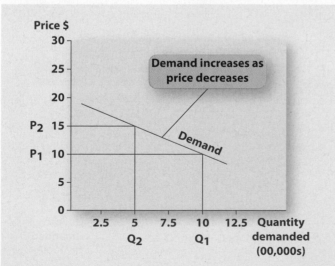

The horizontal axis in Exhibit 14.3 measures the quantity demanded for the teeth whitening kits in units and plots it against the various price possibilities indicated on the vertical axis. Each point on the demand curve then represents the quantity demanded at a specific price. So, in this instance, if the price of a kit is $10 per unit ($P_1$), the demand is 1,000,000 units (Q_1), but if the price were set at $15 ($P_2$), the demand would only be 500,000 units (Q_2). The firm will sell far more teeth whitening kits at $10 each than at $15 each. Why? Because of the greater value this price point offers.

Knowing the demand curve for a product or service enables a firm to examine different prices in terms of the resulting demand and relative to its overall objective. In our preceding example, the retailer will generate a total of $10,000,000 in sales at the $10 price ($10 × 1,000,000 units) and $7,500,000 in sales at the $15 price ($15 × 500,000 units). In this case,

Based on Exhibit 14.3, what is the best price for White Light?

> "When customers value the increase in prestige more than the price differential between the prestige product and other products, the prestige product attains the greater value overall."

given only the two choices of $10 or $15, the $10 price is preferable as long as the firm wants to maximize its sales in terms of dollars and units. But what about a firm that is more interested in profit? To calculate profit, it must consider its costs, which we cover in the next section.

Not all products or services follow the downward-sloping demand curve for all levels of price depicted in Exhibit 14.3 though. Consider **prestige products or services**, which consumers purchase for their status rather than their functionality. The higher the price, the greater the status associated with it and the greater the exclusivity because fewer people can afford to purchase it. Faberge, the French jeweler known for making jeweled eggs for the Russian Tsar Alexander III, among other exotic items, considers itself so prestigious that it doesn't even have a physical store. It offers its latest jewelry line on its website (www.faberge.com), with prices ranging from $40,000 to $7 million per item. According to Mark Dunhill, Faberge's CEO, "Our customers won't need to appear outside of a store between 10 in the morning and 6 in the evening. They can log on anytime, while sitting on their yacht, their chalet or their country home."[17] But don't expect to go surfing their site: You need to register and make an appointment, and then Faberge will contact you.

With prestige products or services, a higher price may lead to a greater quantity sold, but only up to a certain point. The price demonstrates just how rare, exclusive, and prestigious the product is. When customers value the increase in prestige more than the price differential between the prestige product and other products, the prestige product attains the greater value overall.

However, prestige products can also run into pricing difficulties. The Fender Telecaster and Stratocaster guitars are absolute necessities for any self-respecting guitar hero, but for students just learning or hobbyists, the price of owning a Fender axe was simply too much. In response, Fender introduced a separate, budget-priced line of similar guitars under a different brand name, so as not to dilute the prestige of the Fender name. The Squier line, made in Japan with automated manufacturing and less expensive parts, offers a look similar to the famous Fender guitars and performance just a notch below

With prestige products like this expensive Faberge egg, the higher the price, the higher the status associated with it, and possibly, the more it will sell.

the originals. Today, an American-made Vintage Hot Rod '62 Fender Stratocaster lists for $2,400, more than 10 times as much as a Squire Bullet Strat model that retails for around $200.[18]

Exhibit 14.4 illustrates a demand curve for another hypothetical prestige service, a Caribbean cruise. As the graph indicates, when the price increases from $1,000 ($P_1$) to $5,000 ($P_2$), the quantity demanded actually increases from 200,000 (Q_1) to 500,000 (Q_2) units. However, when the price increases to $8,000 ($P_3$), the demand then decreases to 300,000 (Q_3) units.

Although the firm likely will earn more profit selling 300,000 cruises at $8,000 each than 500,000 cruises at $5,000 each, we do not know for sure until we bring costs into the picture. However, we do know that more consumers are willing to book the cruise as the price increases initially from $1,000 to $5,000 and that more consumers will choose an alternative vacation as the price increases further from $5,000 to $8,000.

We must consider this notion of consumers' sensitivity to price changes in greater depth.

▼ **EXHIBIT 14.4** Demand Curve for Caribbean Cruise

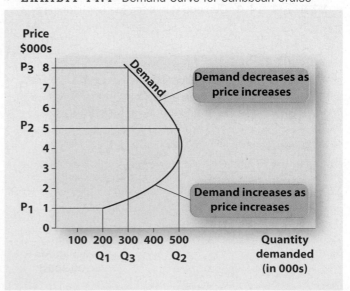

> **310 SECTION 5** | Value Capture

Singer Avril Lavigne uses a Fender guitar.

or brand so they can determine whether it makes sense for them to raise or lower prices.

Price elasticity of demand measures how changes in a price affect the quantity of the product demanded. Specifically, it is the ratio of the percentage change in quantity demanded to the percentage change in price.

We can calculate it with the following formula:

$$\text{Price elasticity of demand} = \frac{\%\ \text{Change in quantity demanded}}{\%\ \text{Change in price}}$$

The demand curve provides the information we need to calculate the price elasticity of demand. For instance, what is the

Consumers are less sensitive to the price of milk than to steak. When the price of milk goes up, demand does not fall significantly because people still need to buy milk. However, if the price of steak rises beyond a certain point, people will buy less because they can turn to many substitutes for steak.

LO 14-3 Explain price elasticity.

Price Elasticity of Demand

Although we now know something about how consumers react to different price levels, we still need to determine how consumers respond to actual changes in price. These responses vary depending on the product or service. For example, consumers are generally less sensitive to price increases for necessary items, like milk, because they have to purchase the items even if the price climbs. When the price of milk goes up, demand does not fall significantly because people still need to buy milk. However, if the price of T-bone steaks rises beyond a certain point, people will buy less because they can turn to the many substitutes for this cut of meat. Marketers need to know how consumers will respond to a price increase (or decrease) for a specific product

ethical & societal dilemma   14.1

The Incredible Shrinking Package[19]

When the costs of raw materials increase, producers have to increase prices or lose profits. But raising prices, especially in the tough economic environment that prompted the higher costs, is a risky proposition. Consumers are struggling too, and finding higher prices for the staples they need to feed their families can cause a lot of anger and frustration. To avoid such a confrontation, manufacturers are turning to a more subtle strategy: Keep prices the same but reduce package sizes a bit.

Thus cans of corn, once sold in 16 ounce sizes, are now 14.5 ounces. Virtually every product on grocery store shelves shows similar shrinking trends: cereal, crackers, orange juice, diapers, pasta, canned tuna, candy, ketchup . . . the list goes on and on. In some cases, the manufacturers tout the smaller sizes as an added value, such as when smaller package sizes for cookies or ice cream are sold as healthy portions, at a higher price per unit than the larger package sizes.

When customers notice the difference, their reaction is often just what the manufacturers had hoped to avoid— anger and frustration, plus a sense of being tricked or cheated. But the producers are counting on a well-known marketing rule: People tend to be more sensitive to price changes than to quantity changes. Thus if the firm can make the change subtle—such as by leaving the package the same size but filling it less—it knows that few consumers are likely to look closely at the contents. In many cases, they won't even notice, until they start cooking and realize that they don't have enough in the pot to feed everyone around the dinner table.

Coca-Cola has smaller bottles so it can charge more per ounce.

---

price elasticity of demand if we increase the price of our teeth whitening kit from $10 to $15?

$$\frac{\% \text{ Change in}}{\text{quantity demanded}} = \frac{(1,000,000 - 500,000)}{1,000,000} = 50\%, \text{ and}$$

$$\% \text{ Change in price} = \frac{(\$10 - \$15)}{10} = -50\%, \text{ so}$$

$$\frac{\text{Price elasticity}}{\text{of demand}} = \frac{50\%}{-50\%} = -1.$$

Thus, the price elasticity of demand for our teeth whitening kit is −1.

In general, the market for a product or service is price sensitive (or **elastic**) when the price elasticity is less than −1, that is, when a 1 percent decrease in price produces more than a 1 percent increase in the quantity sold. In an elastic scenario, relatively small changes in price will generate fairly large changes in the quantity demanded, so if a firm is trying to increase its sales, it can do so by lowering prices. However, raising prices can be problematic in this context because doing so will lower sales. To refer back to our grocery examples, a retailer can significantly increase its sales of filet mignon by lowering its price because filets are elastic.

The market for a product is generally viewed as price insensitive (or **inelastic**) when its price elasticity is greater than −1, that is, when a 1 percent decrease in price results in less than a 1 percent increase in quantity sold. Generally, if a firm must raise prices, it is helpful to do so with inelastic products or services because in such a market, fewer customers will stop buying or reduce their purchases. However, if the products are inelastic, lowering prices will not appreciably increase demand; customers just don't notice or care about the lower price.

Consumers are generally more sensitive to price increases than to price decreases.[20] That is, it is easier to lose current customers with a price increase than it is to gain new customers with a price decrease. Also, the price elasticity of demand usually changes at different points in the demand curve unless the curve is actually a straight line, as in Exhibit 14.3. For instance, a prestige product or service, like our Caribbean cruise example in Exhibit 14.4, enjoys a highly inelastic demand curve up to a certain point, so price increases do not affect sales significantly. But when the price reaches that certain point, consumers start turning to other alternatives because the value of the cruise has finally been reduced by the extremely high price.

When companies believe they cannot raise prices without invoking negative consumer responses, they can turn to different strategies to increase prices without changing the numbers on the price tag. Ethical & Societal Dilemma 14.1 describes one such method that some consumers question.

elastic Refers to a market for a product or service that is price sensitive; that is, relatively small changes in price will generate fairly large changes in the quantity demanded.

inelastic Refers to a market for a product or service that is price insensitive; that is, relatively small changes in price will not generate large changes in the quantity demanded.

income effect Refers to the change in the quantity of a product demanded by consumers due to a change in their income.

substitution effect Refers to consumers' ability to substitute other products for the focal brand, thus increasing the price elasticity of demand for the focal brand.

cross-price elasticity The percentage change in demand for product A that occurs in response to a percentage change in price of product B; see *complementary products*.

Factors Influencing Price Elasticity of Demand

We have illustrated how price elasticity of demand varies across different products and at different points along a demand curve as well as how it can change over time. What causes these differences in the price elasticity of demand? We discuss a few of the more important factors next.

Income Effect. The **income effect** refers to the change in the quantity of a product demanded by consumers due to a change in their income. Generally, as people's income increases, their spending behavior changes: They tend to shift their demand from lower-priced products to higher-priced alternatives. That is, consumers buy hamburger when they're stretching their money but steak when they're flush. Similarly, they may increase the quantity they purchase and splurge on a five-star hotel during their six-day Las Vegas trip rather than three-star lodging over a weekend visit. In turn, when the economy is good and consumers' incomes are rising overall, the price elasticity of steak or hotel rooms may actually drop, even though the price remains constant. Conversely, when incomes drop, consumers turn to less expensive alternatives or purchase less.

Substitution Effect. The **substitution effect** refers to consumers' ability to substitute other products for the focal brand. The greater the availability of substitute products, the higher the price elasticity of demand for any given product will be. For example, there are many close substitutes for the various brands of orange juice. If Tropicana raises its prices, many consumers will turn to Minute Maid, Florida's Natural, or the store brand, because they are more sensitive to price increases when they can easily find lower-priced substitutes. Extremely brand-loyal consumers, however, are willing to pay a higher price, up to a point, because in their minds, Tropicana still offers a better value than the competing brands, and they believe the other brands are not adequate substitutes.

Keep in mind that marketing plays a critical role in making consumers brand loyal. And because of this brand loyalty and the lack of what consumers judge to be adequate substitutes, the price elasticity of demand for some brands is very low. For example, Polo/Ralph Lauren sells millions of its classic polo shirts at $85, while shirts of equal quality but without the polo player logo sell for much less. Getting consumers to believe that a particular brand is unique, different, or extraordinary in some way makes other brands seem less substitutable, which in turn increases brand loyalty and decreases the price elasticity of demand.

Cross-Price Elasticity. **Cross-price elasticity** is the percentage change in the quantity of Product A demanded compared with the percentage change in price in Product B. If Product A's price increased, Product B could either increase or decrease, depending on the situation and whether the producs are complementary or substitutes. We refer to products such as Blu-ray discs and Blu-ray players as **complementary products**, which are products whose demands are positively related, such that they rise or fall together. In other words, a percentage increase in the quantity demanded for Product A results in a percentage increase in the quantity demanded for Product B.[21] However, when the price for Blu-ray players

complementary products Products whose demand curves are positively related, such that they rise or fall together; a percentage increase in demand for one results in a percentage increase in demand for the other.

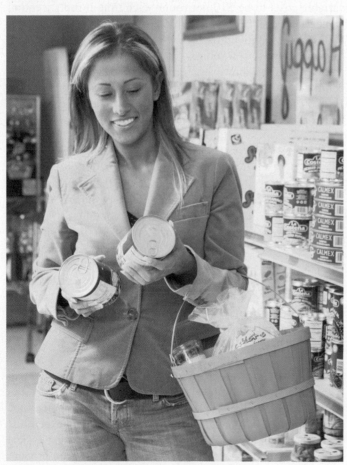

If there are many close substitutes for a product, customers will be sensitive to small price changes, and the product will be highly elastic. If, for instance, Campbell's soup raises its price, many customers will switch to another brand.

substitute products Products for which changes in demand are negatively related; that is, a percentage increase in the quantity demanded for product A results in a percentage decrease in the quantity demanded for product B.

variable costs Those costs, primarily labor and materials, that vary with production volume.

fixed costs Those costs that remain essentially at the same level, regardless of any changes in the volume of production.

total cost The sum of the *variable* and *fixed costs*.

dropped, the demand for DVD players went down, so DVD players and Blu-ray players are **substitute products** because changes in their demand are negatively related. That is, a percentage increase in the quantity demanded for Product A results in a percentage decrease in the quantity demanded for Product B.[22] In addition, on the Internet, shopping bots like TheFind.com and Bizrate.com have made it much easier for people to shop for substitutable products such as consumer electronics, which likely has affected the price elasticity of demand for such products.[23]

The way a product or service is marketed to customers can have a profound effect on its price elasticity. Prior to this point, we have focused on how changes in prices affect how much customers buy. Clearly, knowing how prices affect sales is important, but it cannot give us the whole picture. To know how profitable a pricing strategy will be, we must also consider the third C, costs.

Costs

To make effective pricing decisions, firms must understand their cost structures so they can determine the degree to which their products or services will be profitable at different prices. In general, prices should *not* be based on costs because consumers make purchase decisions based on their perceived value; they care little about the firm's costs to produce and sell a product or deliver a service. For example, Bank of America (BOA) announced it would charge a monthly fee to some customers to use their debit cards, ostensibly to cover increasing costs. Recognizing they had many choices for banking services and that BOA was no longer providing sufficient value, a significant number took their business elsewhere. Within weeks, BOA rescinded the new fee.[24] Consumers use just the price they must pay and the benefits they may receive to judge value; they will not pay a higher price for an inferior product simply because the firm cannot be as cost efficient as its competitors or because events out of their control drive the cost of raw materials or labor higher.

Bank of America may have had trouble passing its costs on to consumers, but other companies can do so with few negative repercussions. For example, even though deodorant sales have been stagnant for years, revenues shot up recently as a result of a price hike. The clinical formula of Secret deodorant costs $8.50 per tube, more than twice as much as the regular version. The reason consumers likely accept this price increase is the value that deodorant offers in the form of peace of mind. To avoid the social embarrassment associated with sweat-stained clothing, consumers overlook the higher price.[25]

Although companies incur many types of costs as a natural part of doing business, there are two primary cost categories: variable and fixed.

Variable Costs **Variable costs** are those costs, primarily labor and materials, that vary with production volume. As a firm produces more or less of a good or service, the total variable costs increase or decrease at the same time. Because each unit of the product produced incurs the same cost, marketers generally express variable costs on a per-unit basis. Consider a bakery such as Entenmann's: The majority of the variable costs are the cost of the ingredients, primarily flour. Each time Entenmann's makes a loaf of bread, it incurs the cost of the ingredients.

In the service industry, variable costs are far more complex. A hotel, for instance, incurs certain variable costs each time it rents a room, including the costs associated with the labor and supplies necessary to clean and restock the room. Note that the hotel does not incur these costs if the room is not booked. Suppose that a particular hotel calculates its total variable costs to be $10 per room; each time it rents a room, it incurs another $10 in variable costs. If the hotel rents out 100 rooms on a given night, the total variable cost is $1,000 ($10 per room × 100 rooms).

In either case, however, variable costs tend to change depending on the quantity produced. If Entenmann's makes 100,000 loaves of bread in a month, it would have to pay a higher price for ingredients on a per pound basis than if it were producing a million loaves. Similarly, a very large hotel will be able to get a lower per unit price on most, if not all, the supplies it needs to service the room because it purchases such a large volume. However, as the hotel company continues to grow, it may be forced to add more benefits for its employees or increase wages to attract and keep long-term employees. Such changes will increase its overall variable labor costs and affect the total variable cost of cleaning a room. Thus, though not always the case, variable costs per unit may go up or down (for all units) with significant changes in volume.

> In the service industry, variable costs are far more complex.

Fixed Costs **Fixed costs** are those costs that remain essentially at the same level, regardless of any changes in the volume of production. Typically, these costs include items such as rent, utilities, insurance, administrative salaries (for executives and higher-level managers), and the depreciation of the physical plant and equipment. Across reasonable fluctuations in production volume, these costs remain stable; whether Entenmann's makes 100,000 loaves or a million, the rent it pays for the bakery remains unchanged.

Total Cost Finally, the **total cost** is simply the sum of the variable and fixed costs. For example, in one year, our hypothetical hotel incurred $100,000 in fixed costs. We also know that because the hotel booked 10,000 room nights, its total variable cost is $100,000 (10,000 room nights × $10 per room). Thus, its total cost is $200,000.

Next, we illustrate how to use these costs in simple analyses that can inform managerial decision making about setting prices.

LO 14-4   Describe how to calculate a product's break-even point.

Break-Even Analysis and Decision Making

A useful technique that enables managers to examine the relationships among cost, price, revenue, and profit over different levels of production and sales is called **break-even analysis**. Central to this analysis is the determination of the **break-even point**, or the point at which the number of units sold generates just enough revenue to equal the total costs. At this point, profits are zero. Although profit, which represents the difference

break-even analysis
Technique used to examine the relationships among cost, price, revenue, and profit over different levels of production and sales to determine the *break-even point*.

break-even point
The point at which the number of units sold generates just enough revenue to equal the total costs; at this point, profits are zero.

The total cost curve starts where the fixed cost curve intersects the vertical axis at $100,000. When volume is equal to zero (no units are produced or sold), the fixed costs of operating the business remain and cannot be avoided. Thus, the lowest point the total costs can ever reach is equal to the total fixed costs. Beyond that point, the total cost curve increases by the amount of variable costs for each additional unit, which we calculate by multiplying the variable cost per unit by the number of units, or quantity.

Finally, the total revenue curve increases by the price of each additional unit sold. To calculate it, we multiply the price per unit by the number of units sold. The formulas for these calculations are as follows:

$$\text{Total variable cost} = \text{Variable cost per unit} \times \text{Quantity}$$

$$\text{Total cost} = \text{Fixed cost} + \text{Total variable cost}$$

$$\text{Total revenue} = \text{Price} \times \text{Quantity}$$

> ## The break-even point at which the number of units sold generates just enough revenue to equal the total costs, and profits are zero.

between the total cost and the total revenue (total revenue or sales = selling price of each unit sold × number of units sold), can indicate how much money the firm is making or losing at a single period of time, it cannot tell managers how many units a firm must produce and sell before it stops losing money and at least breaks even, which is what the break-even point does.

How do we determine the break-even point? Exhibit 14.5 presents the various cost and revenue information we have discussed in a graphic format. The graph contains three curves (recall that even though they are straight, we still call them curves): fixed costs, total costs, and total revenue. The vertical axis measures the revenue or costs in dollars, and the horizontal axis measures the quantity of units sold. The fixed cost curve will always appear as a horizontal line straight across the graph because fixed costs do not change over different levels of volume.

▼ **EXHIBIT 14.5** Break-Even Analysis

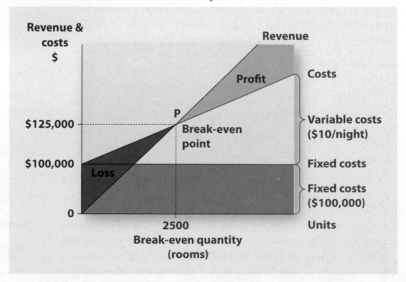

> ## A BREAK-EVEN ANALYSIS CANNOT INDICATE FOR SURE HOW MANY UNITS WILL SELL AT A GIVEN PRICE. IT ONLY TELLS THE FIRM WHAT ITS COSTS, REVENUES, AND PROFITABILITY WILL BE GIVEN A SET PRICE AND AN ASSUMED QUANTITY.

We again use the hotel example to illustrate these relationships. Recall that the fixed costs are $100,000 and the variable costs are $10/room rented. If the rooms rent for $50 per night, how many rooms must the hotel rent over the course of a year to break even? If we study the graph carefully, we find the break-even point at 2,500, which means that the hotel must rent 2,500 rooms before its revenues equal its costs. If it rents fewer rooms, it loses money (the red area); if it rents more, it makes a profit (the green area). To determine the break-even point in units mathematically, we must introduce one more variable, the **contribution per unit**, which is the price less the variable cost per unit.

In this case,

Contribution per unit = $50 − $10 = $40

Therefore, the break-even point becomes

$$\text{Break-even point (units)} = \frac{\text{Fixed costs}}{\text{Contributions per unit}}$$

That is,

$$\text{Break-even point (units)} = \frac{\$100,000}{\$40} = 2,500 \text{ room nights}$$

When the hotel has crossed the break-even point of 2,500 rooms, it will start earning profit at the same rate of the contribution per unit. So if the hotel rents 4,000 rooms—1,500 rooms more than the break-even point—its profit will be $60,000 (1,500 rooms × $40 contribution per unit).

Profit = (Contribution per unit × Quantity) − Fixed Cost

Profit = ($40 × 4,000) − $100,000 = $60,000

Or an alternative formula would be:

Profit = (Price × Quantity) − (Fixed Cost + (Variable Cost × Quantity))

Profit = ($50 × 4,000) − ($100,000 + ($10 × 4,000))

Profit = $200,000 − ($100,000 + $40,000) = $60,000

Let's extend this simple break-even analysis to show how many units a firm must produce and sell to achieve a target profit. Say the hotel wanted to make $200,000 in profit each year. How many rooms would it have to rent at the current price? In this instance, we need only add the targeted profit to the fixed costs to determine that number:

$$\text{Break-even point (units)} = \frac{(\text{Fixed costs} + \text{Target profit})}{\text{Contributions per unit}}$$

or

$$7,500 \text{ rooms} = \frac{(\$100,000 + \$200,000)}{\$40}$$

Although a break-even analysis cannot actually help managers set prices, it does help them assess their pricing strategies because it clarifies the conditions in which different prices may make a product or service profitable. It becomes an even more powerful tool when performed on a range of possible prices for comparative purposes. For example, the hotel management could analyze various prices, not just $50, to determine how many hotel rooms it would have to rent at what price to make a $200,000 profit.

Naturally, however, there are limitations to a break-even analysis. First, it is unlikely that a hotel has one specific price that it charges for each and every room, so the price it would use in its break-even analysis probably represents an average price that attempts to account for these variances. Second, prices often get reduced as quantity increases because the costs decrease, so firms must perform several break-even analyses at different quantities. Third, a break-even analysis cannot indicate for sure how many rooms will be rented or, in the case of products, how many units will sell at a given price. It only tells the firm what its costs, revenues, and profitability will be given a set price and an assumed quantity. To determine how many units the firm actually will sell, it must bring in the demand estimates we discussed previously.

Mark-Up and Target Return Pricing

In many situations, the manufacturer may want to achieve a standard markup—let's say 10 percent of cost. In our example of the teeth whitening kit, let's assume:

Variable costs per unit are:	$8.00
Fixed costs are:	$1,000,000
Expected sales are:	1,000,000 units

contribution per unit Equals the price less the variable cost per unit. Variable used to determine the break-even point in units.

monopoly One firm provides the product or service in a particular industry.

In this example, this would result in the firm charging $9.90.

$$\text{Target return price} = (\$8 + (\$1,000,000 \div 1,000,000)) \times (1 + 0.10)$$

$$\text{Target return price} = \$9.00 \times 1.1 = \$9.90$$

LO 14-5 Indicate the four types of price competitive levels.

In a hotel, the cost of the physical structure, including the lobby, is fixed—
i̶t̶ ̶m̶u̶s̶t̶ ̶b̶e̶ ̶p̶a̶i̶n̶t̶e̶d̶. The costs of washing the ̶s̶h̶e̶e̶t̶s̶ ̶f̶o̶r̶ ̶t̶h̶e̶ rooms that are rented, the ̶.̶.̶.̶

...manufacturer would like to calculate ...would make a 10 percent mark-up. The ...ting a target return price based on a mark-up

$$\begin{aligned}\text{return} \\ \text{price}\end{aligned} = \begin{aligned}(\text{Variable cost} + (\text{Fixed cost} \div \text{Expected} \\ \text{unit sales})) \times (1 + \text{Target return \%} \\ [\text{expressed as a decimal}])\end{aligned}$$

Competition

Because the fourth C, competition, has a profound impact on pricing strategies,[26] we use this section to focus on its effect as well as on how competitors react to certain pricing strategies. There are four levels of competition—monopoly, oligopolistic competition, monopolistic competition, and pure competition—and each has its own set of pricing challenges and opportunities (see Exhibit 14.6).

In a **monopoly**, one firm provides the product or service in a particular industry, which results in less price competition.

▼ **EXHIBIT 14.6** Four Levels of Competition: Can you match each photo to its respective type of competition?

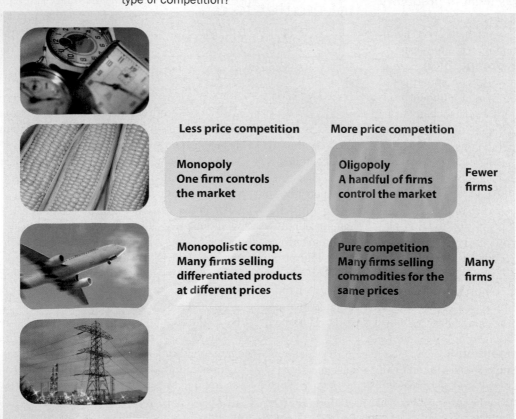

Less price competition	More price competition	
Monopoly One firm controls the market	**Oligopoly** A handful of firms control the market	**Fewer firms**
Monopolistic comp. Many firms selling differentiated products at different prices	**Pure competition** Many firms selling commodities for the same prices	**Many firms**

For example, there is often only one provider of power in each region of the country: Florida Power and Light in most of Florida, NStar in most of Massachusetts, and so forth. Power companies operate more efficiently when there is one service provider, so the government regulates the pricing of utility monopolies to prevent them from raising prices uncontrollably. A monopoly that restricts competition by controlling an industry can be deemed illegal and broken apart by the government.

When a market is characterized by **oligopolistic competition**, only a few firms dominate. Firms typically change their prices in reaction to competition to avoid upsetting an otherwise stable competitive environment. Examples of oligopolistic markets include the soft drink market and commercial airline travel. Sometimes reactions to prices in oligopolistic markets can result in a **price war**, which occurs when two or more firms compete primarily by lowering their prices. Firm A lowers its prices; Firm B responds by meeting or beating Firm A's new price. Firm A then responds with another new price, and so on. In some cases, though, these tactics result in **predatory pricing**, when a firm sets a very low price for one or more of its products with the intent to drive its competition out of business.

Monopolistic competition occurs when there are many firms competing for customers in a given market but their products are differentiated. When so many firms compete, product differentiation rather than strict price competition tends to appeal to consumers. This is the most common form of competition. Hundreds of firms make wristwatches, and thus the market is highly differentiated. Timex sells a durable watch that tells time, has a stop watch, and a sporty design. Swatch watches have more style than a Timex, but if you are really looking for a lot of style, fashion designers such as Armani have their own wrist watches. Timepiece aficionados may opt for the high quality workmanship of a Patek Philippe or a Vacheron Constantin. Depending on the features, style and quality, companies compete in very different markets for the same product. Thus, by differentiating their products using various attributes, prices, brands, etc., they have created unique value propositions in the minds of their customers.

With **pure competition**, there is a large number of sellers of standardized products or commodities that consumers perceive as substitutable, such as grains, gold, meat, spices, or minerals. In such markets, price usually is set according to the laws of supply and demand. For example, wheat is wheat, so it does not matter to a commercial bakery whose wheat it buys. However, the secret to pricing success in a pure competition market is not necessarily to offer the lowest price, because doing so might create a price war and erode profits.

Instead, some firms have brilliantly decommoditized their products. For example, most people feel that all chickens purchased in a grocery are the same. But companies like Tyson's have branded their chickens to move into a monopolistically competitive market.

When a commodity can be differentiated somehow, even if simply by a sticker or logo, there is an opportunity for consumers to identify it as distinct from the rest, and in this case, firms can at least partially extricate their product from a pure competitive market.

> "Wheat is wheat, so it does not matter to a commercial bakery whose wheat it buys."

Channel Members

Channel members—manufacturers, wholesalers, and retailers—can have different perspectives when it comes to pricing strategies. Consider a manufacturer that is focused on increasing the image and reputation of its brand but working with a retailer that is primarily concerned with increasing its sales. The manufacturer may desire to keep prices higher to convey a better image, whereas the retailer wants lower prices and will accept lower profits to move the product, regardless of consumers' impressions of the brand. Unless channel members carefully communicate their pricing goals and select channel partners that agree with them, conflict will surely arise.

Channels can be very difficult to manage, and distribution outside normal channels does occur. A **gray market** employs irregular but not necessarily illegal methods; generally, it legally circumvents authorized channels of distribution to sell goods at prices lower than those intended by the manufacturer.[27] Many manufacturers of consumer electronics therefore require retailers to sign an agreement that demands certain activities (and prohibits others) before they may become authorized dealers. But if a retailer has too many high-definition TVs in stock, it may sell them at just above its own cost to an unauthorized discount dealer. This move places the merchandise in the market at prices far below what authorized dealers can charge, and in the long term, it may tarnish the image of the manufacturer if the discount dealer fails to provide sufficient return policies, support, service, and so forth.

To discourage this type of gray market distribution, some manufacturers, such as Fujitsu, have resorted to large disclaimers on their websites, packaging, and other communications to warn consumers that the manufacturer's product warranty becomes null and void unless the item has been purchased from an authorized dealer.[28]

LO 14-6   Describe the difference between an everyday low price strategy (EDLP) and a high/low strategy.

PRICING STRATEGIES

In this section, we discuss a number of commonly used price strategies: everyday low pricing, high/low pricing, and new product strategies.[29]

Everyday Low Pricing (EDLP)

With an **everyday low pricing (EDLP)** strategy, companies stress the continuity of their retail prices at a level somewhere between the regular, nonsale price and the deep-discount sale prices their competitors may offer.[30] By reducing consumers' search costs, EDLP adds value; consumers can spend less of their valuable time comparing prices, including sale prices, at different stores. With its EDLP strategy, Walmart communicates to consumers that, for any given group of often-purchased items, its prices will tend to be lower than those of any other company in that market. This claim does not necessarily mean that every item that consumers may purchase will be priced lower at Walmart than anywhere else—in fact, some competitive retailers will offer lower prices on some items. However, for an average purchase, Walmart's prices tend to be lower overall. Social & Mobile Marketing 14.1 reinforces the advantages of offering everyday low prices.

The bottom line is that if sellers want to imply EDLP, odd prices may be appropriate. However, odd prices also can suggest lower quality.[31] Some consumers may perceive higher value because of the low price (especially if quality is less important to them than price), whereas others may infer lower value on the basis of the low-quality image the odd price suggests (especially if price is less important to them than quality).

High/Low Pricing

An alternative to EDLP is a **high/low pricing** strategy, which relies on the promotion of sales, during which prices are temporarily reduced to encourage purchases. A high/low strategy is attractive because it attracts two distinct market segments: those who are not price sensitive and are willing to pay the high price and more price-sensitive customers who wait for the low sale price. High/low sellers can also create excitement and attract customers through the "get them while they last" atmosphere that occurs during a sale.

everyday low pricing (EDLP) A strategy companies use to emphasize the continuity of their retail prices at a level somewhere between the regular, nonsale price and the deep-discount sale prices their competitors may offer.

high/low pricing A *pricing* strategy that relies on the promotion of sales, during which prices are temporarily reduced to encourage purchases.

Odd prices signal to consumers that the price is low.

Walmart uses an everyday low pricing (EDLP) strategy.

Sellers using a high/low pricing strategy often communicate their strategy through the creative use of a **reference price**, which is the price against which buyers compare the actual selling price of the product and that facilitates their evaluation process. The seller labels the reference price as the regular price or an original price. When consumers view the sale price and compare it with the provided reference price, their perceptions of the value of the deal will likely increase.[32]

In the advertisement on this page, Sears has provided a reference price, in smaller print and labeled "Reg.," to indicate that $24.99 is the regular price of Lee jeans. In addition, the advertisement highlights the current "sale" price of $19.99 for the khakis and $21.99 for the jeans. Thus, the reference price suggests to consumers that they are getting a good deal and will save money.

Sears ad with reference price.

Social & Mobile Marketing 14.1
Price Check on Aisle . . . Anywhere[33]

Most marketers assume that a Gen X guy and his mom would shop in very different ways. But the benefits offered by the latest mobile phone software are blending those shopping methods by helping consumers of all types shop smarter.

Eric Olson wanted a Blu-ray version of *Heat,* but at Best Buy, where he was shopping before Christmas, the disc cost $26, which seemed high to the 33-year-old consumer. Therefore, while still in Best Buy, he scanned the UPC barcode using his Android smartphone and went on the mobile application ShopSavvy to check the price of the disc at nearby stores. Walmart.com was charging only $19. Eric's mom Carrie Olson also regularly uses a RedLaser application to scan the bar codes of books and DVDs.

Amazon wants both Eric and Carrie to shop its site instead, for everything they need, so its price checking application is not only free to customers, but at times, it even offers them money to use it. In the preholiday shopping season, Amazon promised customers a $5 discount on their order if they scanned a barcode on an item in a competitor's store, then bought that same item from Amazon.[34]

It is nothing new to check on prices online. It is the mobility of these checks

Using a smartphone with the ShopSavvy app, consumers can find out which nearby stores carry the desired product at the lowest prices as well as which stores are closest to them.

that is really advancing the practice—and making some sellers really nervous. Anyone with a smartphone can use ShopSavvy to find out which nearby stores carry the desired product at the lowest price as well as which stores are closest to the consumer. Amazon's version only compares prices with the items available on its site, but as the site continues to grow, that includes a lot of items.

ShopSavvy's database instead includes tens of thousands of retailers and millions of store locations, such as Walmart, Target, American Eagle, Best Buy, The Gap, and online-only retailers. Because these technologies rely on the retailers' websites or databases for pricing information, sometimes the details provided are a little out of date, especially if the retailer decides to change the price at the last minute. But 20 million people have downloaded the application, and 10 million of them use it with some frequency—about 20 percent of the total population of smartphone users in the United States.

For Eric and Carrie Olson, the options are nearly endless. But for retailers, especially those that cannot compete very well on price, the options seem to be shrinking fast. If everyone can instantly perform price research, what is a higher priced seller to do?

New Product Pricing Strategies

Developing pricing strategies for new products is one of the most challenging tasks a manager can undertake. When the new product is similar to what already appears on the market, this job is somewhat easier because the product's approximate value has already been established and the value-based methods described earlier in this chapter can be employed. But when the new product is truly innovative, or what we call new to the world, determining consumers' perceptions of its value and pricing it accordingly become far more difficult.

Two distinct new product pricing strategies are discussed next: market penetration pricing and price skimming.

MARKET PENETRATION PRICING

Firms using a **market penetration strategy** set the initial price low for the introduction of the new product or service. Their objective is to build sales, market share, and profits quickly. The low market penetration price is an incentive to purchase the product immediately. Vendors of security software often adopt such a tactic: By adding their products, such as Microsoft's antivirus package, to a computer software bundle at no extra charge, providers can increase their market share. They also increase the likelihood that customers will pay to obtain updates of software that is already implanted into their computer. Firms using a market penetration strategy expect the unit cost to drop significantly as the accumulated volume sold increases, an effect known as the **experience curve effect**. With this effect, as sales continue to grow, the costs continue to drop.

In addition to offering the potential to build sales, market share, and profits, penetration pricing discourages competitors from entering the market because the profit margin is relatively low. Furthermore, if the costs to produce the product drop because of the accumulated volume, competitors that enter the market later will face higher unit costs, at least until their volume catches up with the early entrant.

A penetration strategy has its drawbacks. First, the firm must have the capacity to satisfy a rapid rise in demand—or at least be able to add that capacity quickly. Second, low price does not signal high quality. Of course, a price below their expectations decreases the risk for consumers to purchase the product and test its quality for themselves. Third, firms should avoid a penetration pricing strategy if some segments of the market are willing to pay more for the product; otherwise, the firm is just leaving money on the table.

Price Skimming

In many markets, and particularly for new and innovative products or services, innovators and early adopters (see Chapter 12) are willing to pay a higher price to obtain the new product or service. This strategy, known as **price skimming**, appeals to these segments of consumers who are willing to pay the premium price to have the innovation first. This tactic is particularly common in technology markets, where sellers know that fans of *Call of Duty* will wait in line for hours, desperate to be the first to own the newest version. These innovators are willing to pay the very highest prices to obtain brand-new examples of technology advances with exciting product enhancements. However, after this high-price market segment becomes saturated and sales begin to slow down, companies generally lower the price to capture (or skim) the next most price sensitive market segment, which is willing to pay a somewhat lower price. For most companies, the price dropping process can continue until the demand for the product has been satisfied, even at the lowest price points.

The spread of new media for movies illustrates a price skimming strategy. As with VCRs in the 1970s and DVD players in the 1990s, consumers were slow to embrace the new, more

Price skimming is often used for high demand video games like Call of Duty *because fans will pay a higher price to be one of the first to own the newest version.*

market penetration strategy A growth strategy that employs the existing marketing mix and focuses the firm's efforts on existing customers.

experience curve effect Refers to the drop in unit cost as the accumulated volume sold increases; as sales continue to grow, the costs continue to drop, allowing even further reductions in the price.

price skimming A strategy of selling a new product or service at a high price that *innovators* and *early adopters* are willing to pay in order to obtain it; after the high-price market segment becomes saturated and sales begin to slow down, the firm generally lowers the price to capture (or skim) the next most price sensitive segment.

expensive Blu-ray discs. But enough early adopters purchased the Blu-ray discs that manufacturers continued to refine Blu-ray players to penetrate wider target markets. Consumers are buying the devices at a faster pace than the earlier movie-playing devices. One obvious reason for this sales growth is that prices for high-quality Blu-ray players have dropped below $80, a steep drop from the $300-plus that retailers charged for debut models.[35]

> **check** yourself
>
> 1. Explain the difference between EDLP and high/low pricing,
> 2. What pricing strategies should be considered when introducing a new product?

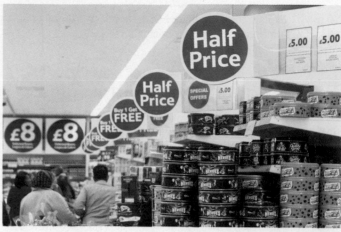

U.K.-based Tesco wasn't allowed to make the claim that it is Britains's Biggest Discounter because it was considered misleading. Such a claim would probably be considered puffery in the U.S. and therefore allowed.

LO 14-8 List pricing practices that have the potential to deceive customers.

LEGAL AND ETHICAL ASPECTS OF PRICING

With so many pricing strategies and tactics, it is no wonder that unscrupulous firms find ample opportunity to engage in pricing practices that can hurt consumers. We now take a look at some of the legal and ethical implications of pricing.

Chapter 19).[36] But price advertisements should never deceive consumers to the point of causing harm. For example, a local car dealer's advertising that it had the best deals in town would likely be considered puffery. In contrast, advertising the lowest prices, guaranteed makes a very specific claim and, if not true, can be considered deceptive. The European Union takes a more stringent view of puffery than the United States. For example, when U.K.-based Tesco advertised that it was Britain's Biggest Discounter, the U.K. Advertising Standards Authority forced it to end the campaign. Because differences in the items purchased made it difficult to determine whether Tesco really was less expensive than its competitors, such as

> [A host of laws and regulations at both the federal and state levels attempt to prevent unfair pricing practices, but some are poorly enforced, and others are difficult to prove.]

Prices tend to fluctuate naturally and respond to varying market conditions. Thus, though we rarely see firms attempting to control the market in terms of product quality or advertising, they often engage in pricing practices that can unfairly reduce competition or harm consumers directly through fraud and deception. A host of laws and regulations at both the federal and state levels attempt to prevent unfair pricing practices, but some are poorly enforced, and others are difficult to prove.

Deceptive or Illegal Price Advertising

Although it is always illegal and unethical to lie in advertising, a certain amount of puffery is typically allowed (see

Aldi or Asda, the Authority ruled that the claim was inherently misleading.[37]

Deceptive Reference Prices Previously, we introduced reference prices, which create reference points for the buyer against which to compare the selling price. If the reference price is bona fide, the advertisement is informative. If the reference price has been inflated or is just plain fictitious, however, the advertisement is deceptive and may cause harm to consumers. But it is not easy to determine whether a reference price is bona fide. What standard should be used? If an advertisement specifies a regular price, just what qualifies as regular? How many units must the store sell at this price for it to be a bona fide regular price—half the stock? A few? Just one? Finally, what if the store offers the item for sale at the

Is this a legitimate sale, or is the retailer using deceptive reference prices?

regular price but customers do not buy any? Can it still be considered a regular price? In general, if a seller is going to label a price as a regular price, the Better Business Bureau suggests that at least 50 percent of the sales have occurred at that price.[38]

Loss Leader Pricing

Leader pricing is a legitimate attempt to build store traffic by pricing a regularly purchased item aggressively, but still above the store's cost. **Loss leader pricing** takes this tactic one step further by lowering the price *below* the store's cost. No doubt you have seen buy one, get one free offers at grocery and discount stores. Unless the markup for

model (the switch) by disparaging the low-priced item, comparing it unfavorably with the higher-priced model, or professing an inadequate supply of the lower-priced item. Again, the laws against bait-and-switch practices are difficult to enforce because salespeople, simply as a function of their jobs, are always trying to get customers to trade up to a higher-priced model without necessarily deliberately baiting them. The key to proving deception centers on the intent of the seller, which is also difficult to prove.

Predatory Pricing

When a firm sets a very low price for one or more of its products with the intent to drive its competition out of business, it is using predatory pricing. Predatory pricing is illegal under both the Sherman Antitrust Act and the Federal Trade Commission Act because it constrains free trade and represents a form of unfair competition. It also tends to promote a concentrated market with a few dominant firms (an oligopoly).

But again, predation is difficult to prove. First, one must demonstrate intent, that is, that the firm intended to drive out its

> ## If a seller is going to label a price as a regular price, the Better Business Bureau suggests that at least 50 percent of the sales have occurred at that price.

the item is 100 percent of the cost, these sales obviously do not generate enough revenue from the sale of one unit to cover the store's cost for both units, which means it has essentially priced the total for both items below cost, unless the manufacturer is absorbing the cost of the promotion to generate volume. In some states, this form of pricing is illegal and considered a form of bait and switch.

Bait and Switch

Another form of deceptive price advertising occurs when sellers advertise items for a very low price without the intent to really sell any. This **bait-and-switch** tactic is a deceptive practice because the store lures customers in with a very low price on an item (the bait), only to aggressively pressure these customers into purchasing a higher-priced

competition or prevent competitors from entering the market. Second, the complainant must prove that the firm charged prices lower than its average cost, an equally difficult task. The American Booksellers Association, which represents independent booksellers, has asked the U.S. Department of Justice to investigate the practice of selling hardcover best-seller books for approximately $9, about $25 less than the suggested retail price.[39] The issue to be resolved by the Justice Department is whether the intent of large stores is to put small stores out of business or whether they are being highly price competitive on books to bring customers into their stores to buy other, more profitable merchandise.

Another challenging case involves Google's dominance in the search engine market. Advertisers on Google bid on

Is this a legitimate sale, or is the retailer using deceptive reference prices?

loss leader pricing
Loss leader pricing takes the tactic of *leader pricing* one step further by lowering the price below the store's cost.

bait-and-switch
A deceptive practice of luring customers into the store with a very low advertised price on an item (the bait), only to aggressively pressure them into purchasing a higher-priced model (the switch) by disparaging the low-priced item, comparing it unfavorably with the higher-priced model, or professing an inadequate supply of the lower-priced item.

model (the switch) by disparaging the low-priced item, comparing it unfavorably with the higher-priced model, or professing an inadequate supply of the lower-priced item. Again, the laws against bait-and-switch practices are difficult to enforce because salespeople, simply as a function of their jobs, are always trying to get customers to trade up to a higher-priced model without necessarily deliberately baiting them. The key to proving deception centers on the intent of the seller, which is also difficult to prove.

Predatory Pricing

When a firm sets a very low price for one or more of its products with the intent to drive its competition out of business, it is using predatory pricing. Predatory pricing is illegal under both the Sherman Antitrust Act and the Federal Trade Commission Act because it constrains free trade and represents a form of unfair competition. It also tends to promote a concentrated market with a few dominant firms (an oligopoly).

But again, predation is difficult to prove. First, one must demonstrate intent, that is, that the firm intended to drive out its

regular price but customers do not buy any? Can it still be considered a regular price? In general, if a seller is going to label a price as a regular price, the Better Business Bureau suggests that at least 50 percent of the sales have occurred at that price.[38]

Loss Leader Pricing Leader pricing is a legitimate attempt to build store traffic by pricing a regularly purchased item aggressively, but still above the store's cost. **Loss leader pricing** takes this tactic one step further by lowering the price *below* the store's cost. No doubt you have seen buy one, get one free offers at grocery and discount stores. Unless the markup for

> ## If a seller is going to label a price as a regular price, the Better Business Bureau suggests that at least 50 percent of the sales have occurred at that price.

the item is 100 percent of the cost, these sales obviously do not generate enough revenue from the sale of one unit to cover the store's cost for both units, which means it has essentially priced the total for both items below cost, unless the manufacturer is absorbing the cost of the promotion to generate volume. In some states, this form of pricing is illegal and considered a form of bait and switch.

Bait and Switch Another form of deceptive price advertising occurs when sellers advertise items for a very low price without the intent to really sell any. This **bait-and-switch** tactic is a deceptive practice because the store lures customers in with a very low price on an item (the bait), only to aggressively pressure these customers into purchasing a higher-priced

competition or prevent competitors from entering the market. Second, the complainant must prove that the firm charged prices lower than its average cost, an equally difficult task. The American Booksellers Association, which represents independent booksellers, has asked the U.S. Department of Justice to investigate the practice of selling hardcover best-seller books for approximately $9, about $25 less than the suggested retail price.[39] The issue to be resolved by the Justice Department is whether the intent of large stores is to put small stores out of business or whether they are being highly price competitive on books to bring customers into their stores to buy other, more profitable merchandise.

Another challenging case involves Google's dominance in the search engine market. Advertisers on Google bid on

> BECAUSE OF GOOGLE'S DOM[I]
> SEARCH ENGINE MARKET, WITH ITS RES[U]
> TO CONTROL PRICES, WOULD ITS PRACTICE
> MORE FOR ITS QUALITY HANDICAP BE

specific keywords; if they win the auction, their product appears first in the paid results section on the search engine. However, Google also includes a quality handicap and charges poor quality advertisers more. It claims this tactic ensures that users are more likely to find high quality results from their searches. The algorithm it uses to define quality is confidential, though, so some observers allege that Google can manipulate the paid search results in such a way that it undermines competitors' offerings while promoting its own.[40] The unresolved question is: because of Google's dominance in the search engine market, with its resulting ability to control prices, would its practice of charging more for its quality handicap be predatory?

Price Discrimination

There are many forms of price discrimination, but only some of them are considered illegal under the Clayton Act and the Robinson-Patman Act. When firms sell the same product to different resellers (wholesalers, distributors, or retailers) at different prices, it can be considered **price discrimination**; usually, larger firms receive lower prices.

The legality of quantity discounts, a legitimate method of charging different prices to different customers on the basis of the quantity they purchase, stems from the assumption that it costs less to sell and service 1,000 units to one customer than 100 units to 10 customers. But quantity discounts must be available to all customers and not be structured in such a way that they consistently and obviously favor one or a few buyers over others.

The Robinson-Patman Act does not apply to sales to end consumers, at which point many forms of price discrimination occur. For example, students and seniors often receive discounts on food and movie tickets, which is perfectly acceptable under federal law. Those engaged in online auctions like eBay are also practicing a legal form of price discrimination because sellers are selling the same item to different buyers at various prices. In addition, to deal ethically with the rising costs of health care, some hospitals offer a sliding scale based on income such that lower-income patients receive discounts or even free medical care, especially for children.[41]

Price Fixing

Price fixing is the practice of colluding with other firms to control prices. Price fixing might be either horizontal or

Is this price discrimination illegal?

vertical. Whereas horizontal pr[ice] under the Sherman Antitrust Ac[t] into a gray area.[42]

Horizontal price fixing oc[curs] produce and sell competing prod[ucts] work together, to control prices, e[ven] the decision process for consu[mers] reduces competition and is illega[l] were accused of colluding to hike within the country during the Wo[rld] companies also have been accu[sed] prices of cigarettes worldwide.[44] competing firms should refrain terms and conditions of sale with know competitors' prices, they c[an] vertisements, its websites, or its

Vertical price fixing occu[rs] levels of the same marketing c[hannel] and retailers) agree to control t[he] sumers. Manufacturers often enc[ourage] merchandise at a specific price, **er's suggested retail price** MSRP prices to reduce retail pri[ce] ers, stimulate retailers to provi[de] and support the manufacturer's enforce MSRPs by withholding advertising or even refusing to complying retailers. The Sup[reme] ability of a manufacturer to re[quire] dise at MSRP should be deci[ded] pending on the individual circ[um]

As these legal issues clearl[y] involve many ethical consider[ations] pricing strategies and their always balance their goal o[f]

Is this a legitimate sale, or is the retailer using deceptive reference prices?

model (the switch) by disparaging the low-priced item, comparing it unfavorably with the higher-priced model, or professing an inadequate supply of the lower-priced item. Again, the laws against bait-and-switch practices are difficult to enforce because salespeople, simply as a function of their jobs, are always trying to get customers to trade up to a higher-priced model without necessarily deliberately baiting them. The key to proving deception centers on the intent of the seller, which is also difficult to prove.

Predatory Pricing

When a firm sets a very low price for one or more of its products with the intent to drive its competition out of business, it is using predatory pricing. Predatory pricing is illegal under both the Sherman Antitrust Act and the Federal Trade Commission Act because it constrains free trade and represents a form of unfair competition. It also tends to promote a concentrated market with a few dominant firms (an oligopoly).

But again, predation is difficult to prove. First, one must demonstrate intent, that is, that the firm intended to drive out its

regular price but customers do not buy any? Can it still be considered a regular price? In general, if a seller is going to label a price as a regular price, the Better Business Bureau suggests that at least 50 percent of the sales have occurred at that price.[38]

Loss Leader Pricing
Leader pricing is a legitimate attempt to build store traffic by pricing a regularly purchased item aggressively, but still above the store's cost. **Loss leader pricing** takes this tactic one step further by lowering the price *below* the store's cost. No doubt you have seen buy one, get one free offers at grocery and discount stores. Unless the markup for

the item is 100 percent of the cost, these sales obviously do not generate enough revenue from the sale of one unit to cover the store's cost for both units, which means it has essentially priced the total for both items below cost, unless the manufacturer is absorbing the cost of the promotion to generate volume. In some states, this form of pricing is illegal and considered a form of bait and switch.

Bait and Switch
Another form of deceptive price advertising occurs when sellers advertise items for a very low price without the intent to really sell any. This **bait-and-switch** tactic is a deceptive practice because the store lures customers in with a very low price on an item (the bait), only to aggressively pressure these customers into purchasing a higher-priced

> **If a seller is going to label a price as a regular price, the Better Business Bureau suggests that at least 50 percent of the sales have occurred at that price.**

competition or prevent competitors from entering the market. Second, the complainant must prove that the firm charged prices lower than its average cost, an equally difficult task. The American Booksellers Association, which represents independent booksellers, has asked the U.S. Department of Justice to investigate the practice of selling hardcover best-seller books for approximately $9, about $25 less than the suggested retail price.[39] The issue to be resolved by the Justice Department is whether the intent of large stores is to put small stores out of business or whether they are being highly price competitive on books to bring customers into their stores to buy other, more profitable merchandise.

Another challenging case involves Google's dominance in the search engine market. Advertisers on Google bid on

> # BECAUSE OF GOOGLE'S DOMINANCE IN THE SEARCH ENGINE MARKET, WITH ITS RESULTING ABILITY TO CONTROL PRICES, WOULD ITS PRACTICE OF CHARGING MORE FOR ITS QUALITY HANDICAP BE PREDATORY?

specific keywords; if they win the auction, their product appears first in the paid results section on the search engine. However, Google also includes a quality handicap and charges poor quality advertisers more. It claims this tactic ensures that users are more likely to find high quality results from their searches. The algorithm it uses to define quality is confidential, though, so some observers allege that Google can manipulate the paid search results in such a way that it undermines competitors' offerings while promoting its own.[40] The unresolved question is: because of Google's dominance in the search engine market, with its resulting ability to control prices, would its practice of charging more for its quality handicap be predatory?

Price Discrimination

There are many forms of price discrimination, but only some of them are considered illegal under the Clayton Act and the Robinson-Patman Act. When firms sell the same product to different resellers (wholesalers, distributors, or retailers) at different prices, it can be considered **price discrimination**; usually, larger firms receive lower prices.

The legality of quantity discounts, a legitimate method of charging different prices to different customers on the basis of the quantity they purchase, stems from the assumption that it costs less to sell and service 1,000 units to one customer than 100 units to 10 customers. But quantity discounts must be available to all customers and not be structured in such a way that they consistently and obviously favor one or a few buyers over others.

The Robinson-Patman Act does not apply to sales to end consumers, at which point many forms of price discrimination occur. For example, students and seniors often receive discounts on food and movie tickets, which is perfectly acceptable under federal law. Those engaged in online auctions like eBay are also practicing a legal form of price discrimination because sellers are selling the same item to different buyers at various prices. In addition, to deal ethically with the rising costs of health care, some hospitals offer a sliding scale based on income such that lower-income patients receive discounts or even free medical care, especially for children.[41]

Price Fixing

Price fixing is the practice of colluding with other firms to control prices. Price fixing might be either horizontal or

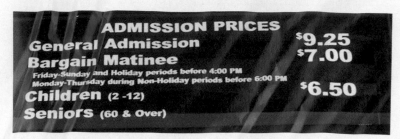

Is this price discrimination illegal?

vertical. Whereas horizontal price fixing is clearly illegal under the Sherman Antitrust Act, vertical price fixing falls into a gray area.[42]

Horizontal price fixing occurs when competitors that produce and sell competing products or services collude, or work together, to control prices, effectively taking price out of the decision process for consumers. This practice clearly reduces competition and is illegal. Six South African airlines were accused of colluding to hike the price of fares for flights within the country during the World Cup.[43] The major tobacco companies also have been accused of colluding to fix the prices of cigarettes worldwide.[44] As a general rule of thumb, competing firms should refrain from discussing prices or terms and conditions of sale with competitors. If firms want to know competitors' prices, they can look at a competitor's advertisements, its websites, or its stores.

Vertical price fixing occurs when parties at different levels of the same marketing channel (e.g., manufacturers and retailers) agree to control the prices passed on to consumers. Manufacturers often encourage retailers to sell their merchandise at a specific price, known as the **manufacturer's suggested retail price (MSRP)**. Manufacturers set MSRP prices to reduce retail price competition among retailers, stimulate retailers to provide complementary services, and support the manufacturer's merchandise. Manufacturers enforce MSRPs by withholding benefits such as cooperative advertising or even refusing to deliver merchandise to noncomplying retailers. The Supreme Court has ruled that the ability of a manufacturer to require retailers to sell merchandise at MSRP should be decided on a case-by-case basis, depending on the individual circumstances.[45]

As these legal issues clearly demonstrate, pricing decisions involve many ethical considerations. In determining both their pricing strategies and their pricing tactics, marketers must always balance their goal of inducing customers, through price, to find value and the need to deal honestly and fairly with those same customers. Whether another business or an individual consumer, buyers can be influenced by a variety of pricing methods. It is up to marketers to determine which of these methods works best for the seller, the buyer, and the community. ■

 check yourself

1. What common pricing practices are considered to be illegal or unethical?

check it out!

mhhe.com/GrewalM4e
for study materials, including quizzes and videos.

supply chain and channel management

When a company saves a dollar by increasing the efficiency of its distribution system, the overall benefits are worth much more than that single dollar. So for example, if a retailer can get its goods to its stores quickly, in the right quantities, and when its customers want them, customers are happy, which ultimately increases sales and profits. At the same time, the retailer can reduce one of its costliest expenses, namely its distribution costs. Also, because of these distribution systems, manufacturers that sell products in its stores have a good sense of how much they need to make and when, which reduces their inventory costs. Thus profits rise, and everyone is happy.

That claim is perhaps too simplistic, but when we consider Walmart, the largest retailer in the world, it seems about right. Most of Walmart's power—in terms of setting prices, growing rapidly, and pleasing customers—stems directly from its notable innovations in marketing

LEARNING OBJECTIVES

After reading this chapter, you should be able to:

LO 15-1 Understand the importance of marketing channels and supply chain management.

LO 15-2 Understand the difference between direct and indirect marketing channels.

LO 15-3 Describe how marketing channels are managed.

LO 15-4 Describe the flow of information and merchandise in the marketing channel.

channel and supply chain management. Its influence has also spread to its vendors, altering the way they manufacture and deliver merchandise.

Walmart's cooperation with the consumer goods giant Procter & Gamble (P&G) is unusual in its scope. Software links the two corporations closely, such that the moment Walmart's distribution centers run out of a certain brand or size of a P&G product, P&G initiates a shipment to replenish it. Such cooperation helps P&G plan its production, but it

continued on p. 328

By picking up goods directly from manufacturers, Walmart is able to keep its trucks full more often.

Even w___
cesses, W___
so it cons___
new effici___
pany has s___
trucks full ___
to make ret___
many of the___
trailers now___
facturers rat___
forth from stor___
they still make___
sult, its travel___

continued from p. 327

also enables Walmart to track arrivals at its distribution centers and thus coordinate shipments to stores more effectively.

Other innovations (many of which have been copied throughout the retail industry) by Walmart include extensive information systems to transmit the millions of point-of-sale transactions that take place in its stores every day; cross-docking to ensure that approximately half the goods that arrive at a distribution center move out to stores within 24 hours; the widespread adoption of bar codes and radio frequency identification tags for keeping track of inventory; and consolidated global sourcing to purchase directly from suppliers rather than relying on third-party procurement services.[1]

miles relative to the past year___
trips and avoiding trucks on the m___

In all these cases, Walmart's ___
supply chain management has e___
higher levels of customer service___
tion and transportation costs, ar___
retail space. Fundamentally, Wal___
suppliers, distribution centers, re___
tomers, regardless of their locatic___
achieved by both Walmart and its___
lines. Even more, when those co___
they benefit customers in the forr___
other reason for them to shop the___

But even if firms execute these activities flawlessly, ur___ secure the placement of products in appropriate outlet___ quantities exactly when customers want them, they ar___

In this chapter, we discuss the third P, *place*, which includes all activities required to get the right product to the right customer when that customer wants it.[3] Specifically, as we noted in Chapter 1, **marketing channel management**, which also has been called **supply chain management**, refers to a set of approaches and techniques firms employ to efficiently and effectively integrate their suppliers, manufacturers, warehouses, stores, and transportation intermediaries into a seamless operation in

which merchandise is produced___
tities, to the right locations, an___
minimize systemwide costs v___
their customers require.[4] Stude___
underestimate the importance ___
ply because it happens behind ___
management adds value, say fo___
gets the products to them effici___

supply chain and channel management

When a company saves a dollar by increasing the efficiency of its distribution system, the overall benefits are worth much more than that single dollar. So for example, if a retailer can get its goods to its stores quickly, in the right quantities, and when its customers want them, customers are happy, which ultimately increases sales and profits. At the same time, the retailer can reduce one of its costliest expenses, namely its distribution costs. Also, because of these distribution systems, manufacturers that sell products in its stores have a good sense of how much they need to make and when, which reduces their inventory costs. Thus profits rise, and everyone is happy.

That claim is perhaps too simplistic, but when we consider Walmart, the largest retailer in the world, it seems about right. Most of Walmart's power—in terms of setting prices, growing rapidly, and pleasing customers—stems directly from its notable innovations in marketing

LEARNING OBJECTIVES

After reading this chapter, you should be able to:

LO 15-1 Understand the importance of marketing channels and supply chain management.

LO 15-2 Understand the difference between direct and indirect marketing channels.

LO 15-3 Describe how marketing channels are managed.

LO 15-4 Describe the flow of information and merchandise in the marketing channel.

channel and supply chain management. Its influence has also spread to its vendors, altering the way they manufacture and deliver merchandise.

Walmart's cooperation with the consumer goods giant Procter & Gamble (P&G) is unusual in its scope. Software links the two corporations closely, such that the moment Walmart's distribution centers run out of a certain brand or size of a P&G product, P&G initiates a shipment to replenish it. Such cooperation helps P&G plan its production, but it

continued on p. 328

By picking up goods directly from manufacturers, Walmart is able to keep its trucks full more often.

Even with its remarkable supply chain successes, Walmart is hesitant to rest on its laurels, so it constantly reviews its supply chain to find new efficiencies. In a recent move, the company has sought out ways to keep its delivery trucks full more often, instead of allowing them to make return trips with empty trailers. Thus, many of the retailer's 6,500 trucks and 55,000 trailers now pick up goods directly from manufacturers rather than just traveling back and forth from stores to a distribution center (though they still make these trips, of course). As a result, its travel miles have fallen by 100 million miles relative to the past year—simply by reducing the number of trips and avoiding trucks on the move with empty trailers.[2]

continued from p. 327

also enables Walmart to track arrivals at its distribution centers and thus coordinate shipments to stores more effectively.

Other innovations (many of which have been copied throughout the retail industry) by Walmart include extensive information systems to transmit the millions of point-of-sale transactions that take place in its stores every day; cross-docking to ensure that approximately half the goods that arrive at a distribution center move out to stores within 24 hours; the widespread adoption of bar codes and radio frequency identification tags for keeping track of inventory; and consolidated global sourcing to purchase directly from suppliers rather than relying on third-party procurement services.[1]

In all these cases, Walmart's superior marketing channel and supply chain management has enabled it to reap the rewards of higher levels of customer service and satisfaction, lower production and transportation costs, and mo re productive uses of its retail space. Fundamentally, Walmart has a unique ability to link suppliers, distribution centers, retail outlets, and, ultimately, customers, regardless of their location. As a result, the cost savings achieved by both Walmart and its suppliers benefit their bottom lines. Even more, when those cost savings are passed through, they benefit customers in the form of lower prices, which is another reason for them to shop the world's largest retailer. ∎

> But even if firms execute these activities flawlessly, unless they can secure the placement of products in appropriate outlets in sufficient quantities exactly when customers want them, they are likely to fail.

In this chapter, we discuss the third P, *place*, which includes all activities required to get the right product to the right customer when that customer wants it.[3] Specifically, as we noted in Chapter 1, **marketing channel management**, which also has been called **supply chain management**, refers to a set of approaches and techniques firms employ to efficiently and effectively integrate their suppliers, manufacturers, warehouses, stores, and transportation intermediaries into a seamless operation in which merchandise is produced and distributed in the right quantities, to the right locations, and at the right time, as well as to minimize systemwide costs while satisfying the service levels their customers require.[4] Students of marketing often overlook or underestimate the importance of place in the marketing mix, simply because it happens behind the scenes. Yet marketing channel management adds value, say for customers at Walmart, because it gets the products to them efficiently, quickly, and at low cost.

THE IMPORTANCE OF MARKETING CHANNEL/SUPPLY CHAIN MANAGEMENT

So far in this book, we have reviewed the methods companies use to conduct in-depth market research, gain insights into consumer and business behaviors, segment markets, select the best target markets, develop new products and services, and set prices that provide good value. But even if firms execute these activities flawlessly, unless they can secure the placement of products in appropriate outlets in sufficient quantities exactly when customers want them, they are likely to fail. Adding Value 15.1 examines how Goya Foods recognized it needed

marketing channel management Also called supply chain management, refers to a set of approaches and techniques firms employ to efficiently and effectively integrate their suppliers.

wholesalers Those firms engaged in buying, taking title to, often storing, and physically handling goods in large quantities, then reselling the goods (usually in smaller quantities) to retailers or industrial or business users.

supply chain management Refers to a set of approaches and techniques firms employ to efficiently and effectively integrate their suppliers, manufacturers, warehouses, stores, and transportation intermediaries into a seamless value chain in which merchandise is produced and distributed in the right quantities, to the right locations, and at the right time, as well as to minimize systemwide costs while satisfying the service levels their customers require.

to do a better job at getting products into stores to satisfy customers' demand and what it did about it.

Convincing wholesalers and retailers to carry new products can be more difficult than you might think. **Wholesalers** are firms that buy products from manufacturers and resell them to

Adding Value 15.1

The Beans May Be Slow Cooked, but the Delivery Is Quick[5]

As Goya Foods celebrated its 75th year in business, its top managers were dealing with some very serious growing pains. Selling a wide variety of Hispanic and Latin foods, the company had achieved a dominant market share, was the largest Hispanic-owned company in the United States, and had annual sales of around $1 billion. In specific local and regional markets, demand for its products was substantial—a great success that also came with a notable challenge.

That is, many of the markets that loved Goya products had slightly different preferences, reflecting the diversity of Hispanic consumers in the United States. People of Cuban heritage wanted items made somewhat differently than consumers whose families originated in Mexico, and so on. Thus, the number of unique inventory items or stockkeeping units (SKUs) that Goya provided reached over 1,600. The supply chain network grew more complex. And in all the confusion, service levels, as measured by its in-stock availability, dropped. Quite simply, with all the complexity, buyers were spending too much time manually calculating and determining shipments and inventory levels, leaving them insufficient time or energy to think strategically. Making decisions

To simplify its supply chain, Goya automated the transportation and inventory planning processes that enabled it to keep track of demand, order fulfillment, and replenishment.

without sophisticated analytics was not something that Goya could sustain anymore.

For Goya, the solution was to automate the transportation and inventory planning processes, using software that enabled it to keep track of demand, order fulfillment, and replenishment with minimal effort. By automating its ordering processes, Goya's buyers could work smarter. For example, making sure delivery trucks were more efficiently used resulted in millions of dollars in transportation savings. The new system also improved its in-stock availability to 98 percent, which resulted in a proportional increase in sales.

retailers; retailers sell products directly to consumers. For example, PenAgain, a small California-based manufacturer of ergonomic pens and other writing instruments, wanted to put its offerings in Walmart stores, but first it had to get Walmart to buy what it was selling.[6] After a tough selling session, Walmart agreed to give PenAgain a one-month trial in 500 stores, but only if it lowered its costs. PenAgain thus moved production overseas. Walmart provided no marketing support though, and PenAgain was too small to afford traditional print or television advertising, so it developed a viral marketing program and produced displays to use in the stores. To keep track of sales, it relied on Walmart's Internet-based Retail Link system, though it also hired a firm that sends representatives into stores to check out display placement and customer traffic. Finally, PenAgain agreed to adhere to strict packaging, labeling, and shipping requirements. And remember, for all this effort, its entry in stores was only a test, and a very expensive gamble! But if it could succeed in Walmart stores, PenAgain would be well on its way to prosperity.

In the simplified supply chain in Exhibit 15.1, manufacturers make products and sell them to retailers or wholesalers. The exhibit would be much more complicated if we had included the suppliers of materials to manufacturers and all the manufacturers, wholesalers, and stores in a typical marketing channel.

Exhibit 15.1 represents a typical flow of manufactured goods: Manufacturers ship to a wholesaler or to a retailer's distribution center (e.g., Manufacturer 1 and Manufacturer 3) or directly to stores (Manufacturer 2). In addition, many variations on this supply chain exist. Some retail chains, such as Home Depot or Costco, function as both retailers and wholesalers. They act as retailers when they sell to consumers directly and as wholesalers when they sell to other businesses such as building contractors or restaurant owners. When manufacturers such as Avon sell directly to consumers, they perform both production and retailing activities. When Dell sells computers to a university or business, it becomes a business-to-business (B2B) transaction, but when it sells to students or employees individually, it is a B2C (business-to-consumer) operation.

▼ **EXHIBIT 15.1** Simplified Supply Chain

Marketing Channels Add Value

Why do manufacturers use wholesalers or retailers? Don't these added channel members just cut into their profits? Wouldn't it be cheaper for consumers to buy directly from manufacturers? In a simple agrarian economy, the best supply chain likely does follow a direct route from manufacturer to consumer: The consumer goes to the farm and buys food directly from the farmer. Modern eat-local environmental campaigns suggest just such a process. But before the consumer can eat a fresh steak procured from a local farm, she needs to cook it. Assuming the consumer doesn't know how to make a stove and lacks the materials to do so, she must rely on a stove maker. The stove maker, which has the necessary knowledge, must buy raw materials and components from various suppliers, make the stove, and then make it available to the consumer. If the stove maker isn't located near the consumer, the stove must be transported to where the consumer has access to it. To make matters even more complicated, the consumer may want to view a choice of stoves, hear about all their features, and have the stove delivered and installed.

Each participant in the channel adds value.[7] The components manufacturer helps the stove manufacturer by supplying parts and materials. The stove maker turns the components into the stove. The transportation company gets the stove to the retailer. The retailer stores the stove until the customer wants it, educates the customer about product features, and delivers and installs the stove. At each step, the stove becomes more costly but also more valuable to the consumer.

Marketing Channel Management Affects Other Aspects of Marketing

Every marketing decision is affected by and has an effect on marketing channels. When products are designed and manufactured, how and when the critical components reach the factory must be coordinated with production. The sales department must coordinate its delivery promises with the factory or distribution centers. A **distribution center**, a facility for the

How many companies are involved in making and getting a stove to your kitchen?

receipt, storage, and redistribution of goods to company stores or customers, may be operated by retailers, manufacturers, or distribution specialists.[8] Furthermore, advertising and promotion must be coordinated with those departments that control inventory and transportation. There is no faster way to lose credibility with customers than to promise deliveries or run a promotion and then not have the merchandise when the customer expects it.

LO 15-2 Understand the difference between direct and indirect marketing channels.

DESIGNING MARKETING CHANNELS

When a firm is just starting out or entering a new market, it doesn't typically have the option of designing the best marketing channel structure—that is, choosing from whom it buys or to whom it sells. A new sporting goods retailer may not have the option of carrying all the manufacturer lines it wants because other competing retailers in its market area might carry the same products. On the other side, a small specialty sporting goods apparel manufacturer may not be able to place its products in major stores like Sports Authority because its line is unproven, and the products might duplicate lines that the retailer already carries. Chapter 16 discusses how manufacturers choose their retailer partners in more depth.

Although there are thus various constraints on marketing channel partners with regard to the design of the best channel structure, all marketing channels take the form of a direct channel, an indirect channel, or some combination thereof.

Direct Marketing Channel

As shown in Exhibit 15.2, there are no intermediaries between the buyer and seller in a **direct marketing channel**. Typically, the seller is a manufacturer, such as when a carpentry business sells bookcases through its own store and online to individual consumers. The seller also can be an individual, such as when a knitter sells blankets and scarves

indirect marketing channels When one or more intermediaries work with manufacturers to provide goods and services to customers.

vertical channel conflict A type of channel conflict in which members of the same marketing channel, for example, manufacturers, wholesalers, and retailers, are in disagreement or discord.

horizontal channel conflict A type of channel conflict in which members at the same level of a marketing channel, for example, two competing retailers or two competing manufacturers, are in disagreement or discord, such as when they are in a price war.

▼ **EXHIBIT 15.2** Channel Strategies

at craft fairs, on Craigslist, or through eBay. (Recall our discussion of consumer-to-consumer [C2C] transactions in Chapter 1.) When the buyer is another business, such as when Boeing sells planes to JetBlue, the marketing channel still is direct, but in this case, the transaction is a business-to-business one (see Chapter 7).

Indirect Marketing Channel

In **indirect marketing channels**, one or more intermediaries work with manufacturers to provide goods and services to customers. In some cases, only be one intermediary might be involved. Automobile manufacturers such as Ford and General Motors often use indirect distribution, such that dealers act as retailers, as shown in Exhibit 15.2 (middle). As shown in Exhibit 15.2 (right), wholesalers are more common when the company does not buy in sufficient quantities to make it cost-effective for the manufacturer to deal directly with them—independent book sellers, wine merchants, or independent drug stores. Wholesalers are also prevalent in less-developed economies where large retailers are rare.

LO 15-3 Describe how marketing channels are managed.

MANAGING THE MARKETING CHANNEL AND SUPPLY CHAIN

Marketing channels and supply chains comprise various buying entities, such as retailers and wholesalers; sellers, such as manufacturers or wholesalers; and facilitators of the exchange, such as transportation companies. Similar to interpersonal interactions, their relationships can range from close working partnerships to one-time arrangements. In almost all cases, though, interactions occur because the parties want something from each other: Home Depot wants hammers from Stanley Tool Company; Stanley wants an opportunity to sell its tools to the general public; both companies want UPS to deliver the merchandise.

Each member of the marketing channel also performs a specialized role. If one member believes that another has failed to do its job correctly or efficiently, it can replace that member. So, if Stanley isn't getting good service from UPS, it can switch to FedEx. If Home Depot believes its customers do not perceive Stanley tools as a good value, it may buy from another tool company. Home Depot even could decide to make its own tools or use its own trucks to pick up tools from Stanley. However,

332 SECTION 6 | Value Delivery: Designing the Channel and Supply Chain

The Home Depot and Stanley Tool Company have a mutually beneficial partnership. The Home Depot buys tools from Stanley because its customers find value in Stanley products. Stanley sells tools to Home Depot because it has established an excellent market for its products.

any time a marketing channel member is replaced, the function it has performed remains, so someone needs to complete it.[9]

If a marketing channel is to run efficiently, the participating members must cooperate. Often, however, supply chain members have conflicting goals, and this may result in channel conflict (Exhibit 15.3). For instance, Stanley wants Home Depot to carry all its tools but not those of its competitors so that Stanley can maximize its sales. But Home Depot carries a mix of tool brands so it can maximize the sales in its tool category. When supply chain members that buy and sell to one another are not in agreement about their goals, roles, or rewards, **vertical channel conflict** or discord results.

Horizontal channel conflict can also occur when there is disagreement or discord among members at the same level of marketing channel, such as two competing retailers or two competing manufacturers. For instance, if Home Depot and Lowe's engage in a price war on Stanley tools, all three parties are affected. Home Depot and Lowe's make less money because they are both offering lower prices. Stanley tools may experience increased pressure from Home Depot and Lowe's to recover some of its lost profits by pressuring it to lower its prices to them. Also, other retailers may stop buying Stanley tools because they cannot afford to get involved in the price war between Home Depot and Lowe's.

Avoiding vertical channel conflicts demands open, honest communication. Buyers and vendors all must understand what drives the other party's business, their roles in the relationship, each firm's strategies, and any problems that might arise over the course of the relationship. As we mentioned in the opening vignette for this chapter, Walmart and Procter & Gamble (P&G) recognize that it is in their common interest to remain profitable business partners. Walmart's customers demand and expect to find P&G products in stores; P&G needs the sales generated through the

▼ **EXHIBIT 15.3** Vertical versus Horizontal Channel Conflict

Vertical conflict

Manufacturer

Retailer 1 | Retailer 2 | Retailer 3

Horizontal conflict

world's largest retailer. Walmart cannot demand prices so low that P&G cannot make money, and P&G must be flexible enough to accommodate the needs of its biggest customer. With a common goal, both firms then have the incentive to cooperate

Walmart and Procter & Gamble (P&G) recognize that it is in their common interest to remain profitable business partners.

because they know that by doing so, each will boost its sales.

Common goals also help sustain the relationship when expected benefits fail to arise. If one P&G shipment fails to reach a Walmart store on time, due to an uncontrollable event such as a misrouting by the trucking firm, Walmart does not suddenly call off the whole arrangement. Instead, it recognizes the incident as a simple, isolated mistake and maintains the good working relationship, because Walmart knows that both it and P&G are committed to the same goals in the long run.

In this sense, their partnership exhibits both of the non–mutually exclusive ways that exist to manage a marketing channel or supply chain: Coordinate the channel using a vertical marketing system and develop strong relationships with marketing channel partners—topics we now examine.

Managing the Marketing Channel and Supply Chain through Vertical Marketing Systems

Although conflict is likely in any marketing channel, it is generally more pronounced when the channel members are independent entities. Marketing channels that are more closely aligned, whether by contract or ownership, share common goals and therefore are less prone to conflict.

In an **independent** or **conventional marketing channel**, several independent members—a manufacturer, a wholesaler, and a retailer—each attempts to satisfy its own objectives and maximize its profits, often at the expense of the other members, as we portray in Exhibit 15.4 (left). None of the participants has any control over the others. Using our previous example, the first time Walmart purchases pens from PenAgain, both parties likely try to extract as much profit from the deal as possible. After the deal is consummated, neither party feels any responsibility to the other.

Over time, though, Walmart and PenAgain might develop a relationship marked by routinized, automatic transactions, such

▼ **EXHIBIT 15.4** Independent versus Vertical Marketing Channels

that Walmart's customers come to expect PenAgain products in stores, and PenAgain depends on Walmart to buy a good portion of its output. This scenario represents the first phase of a **vertical marketing system**, a marketing channel in which the members act as a unified system, as in Exhibit 15.4 (right). Three types of vertical marketing systems—administered, contractual, and corporate—reflect increasing phases of formalization and control. The more formal the vertical marketing system, the less likely conflict will ensue.

Administered Vertical Marketing System The Walmart/PenAgain marketing channel relationship offers an example of an **administered vertical marketing system**: There is no common ownership or contractual relationships, but the dominant channel member controls or holds the balance of power. Because of its size and relative power, Walmart imposes controls on PenAgain. **Power** in a marketing channel exists when one firm has the means or ability to dictate the actions of another member at a different level of distribution (Exhibit 15.5). A retailer like Walmart exercises its power over suppliers in several ways. With its **reward power**, Walmart offers rewards, often a monetary incentive, if PenAgain will do what Walmart wants it to do. **Coercive power** arises when Walmart threatens to punish or punishes the other channel member for

expertise power
When a channel member uses its expertise as leverage to influence the actions of another channel member.

information power
A type of marketing channel power that occurs if the channel member exerting the power has information that the other channel member wants or needs and can therefore get them to do what they want.

legitimate power
A type of marketing channel power that occurs if the channel member exerting the power has a contractual agreement with the other channel member that requires the other channel member to behave in a certain way. This type of power occurs in an administered vertical marketing system.

contractual vertical marketing systems
A system in which independent firms at different levels of the supply chain join together through contracts to obtain economies of scale and coordination and to reduce conflict.

franchising
A contractual agreement between a *franchisor* and a *franchisee* that allows the franchisee to operate a business using a name and format developed and supported by the franchisor.

▼ **EXHIBIT 15.5** Bases of Power

not undertaking certain tasks, such as if it were to delay payment to PenAgain for a late delivery. Walmart may also have **referent power** over PenAgain if the supplier desperately wants to be associated with Walmart, because being known as an important Walmart supplier enables PenAgain to attract other retailers' business. If Walmart exerts **expertise power** over PenAgain, it relies on its expertise with marketing of pens. Because Walmart has vast information about the office supply and back-to-school markets, it can exert **information power** over PenAgain by providing or withholding such important market information. Finally, **legitimate power** is based on getting a channel member, such as PenAgain, to behave in a certain way because of a contractual agreement between the two firms. As Walmart deals with PenAgain and its other suppliers, it likely exerts multiple types of power to influence their behaviors. If either party dislikes the way the relationship is going, though, it can simply walk away.

Contractual Vertical Marketing System Over time, Walmart and PenAgain may formalize their relationship by entering into contracts that dictate various terms, such as how much Walmart will buy each month and at what price as well as the penalties for late deliveries. In **contractual vertical marketing systems** like this, independent firms at different levels of the marketing channel join through contracts to obtain economies of scale and coordination and to reduce conflict.[10]

Franchising is the most common type of contractual vertical marketing system. **Franchising** is a contractual agreement between a franchisor and a franchisee that allows the franchisee to operate a retail outlet using a name and format developed and supported by the franchisor. Exhibit 15.6 lists the

United States' top franchise opportunities. These rankings, determined by *Entrepreneur* magazine, are created using a number of objective measures such as financial strength, stability, growth rate, and size of the franchise system.[11]

In a franchise contract, the franchisee pays a lump sum plus a royalty on all sales in return for the right to operate a business in a specific location. The franchisee also agrees to operate the outlet in accordance with the procedures prescribed by the franchisor. The franchisor typically provides assistance in locating and building the business, developing the products or services sold, management training, and advertising. To maintain the franchisee's reputation, the franchisor also makes sure that all outlets provide the same quality of services and products.

Hampton Hotels are ranked the number one franchise by Entrepreneur *magazine in 2012.*

▼ **EXHIBIT 15.6** Top 10 Franchises for 2012

Rank	Franchise Name	Number of US Outlets	Number of Non-US Outlets	Startup Costs
1	Hampton Hotels **Midprice hotels**	1,775	58	$3.75M–13.11M
2	Subway **Submarine sandwiches and salads**	24,899	11,454	$84.8K–258.8K
3	7-Eleven Inc. **Convenience store**	6,723	32,880	$30.8K–611.1K
4	Servpro **Insurance/disaster restoration and cleaning**	1,580	1	$132.05K–180.45K
5	Days Inn **Midprice hotels**	1,662	203	$202.17K–6.76M
6	McDonald's **Hamburgers, chicken, salads**	12,546	14,532	$1.07M–1.89M
7	Denny's Inc. **24/7 lowprice restaurant**	1,386	92	$1.13M–2.4M
8	H & R Block **Tax preparation and electronic filing**	4,317	558	$35.51K–136.2K
9	Pizza Hut Inc. **Pizza, sandwiches, pasta**	7,083	4,570	$295K–2.15M
10	Dunkin' Donuts **Coffee shop**	6,900	3,120	$368.9K–1.74M

Source: From Entrepreneur's 2012 Franchise 500, www.entrepreneur.com with permission of Entrepreneur Media, Inc. © 2012 by Entrepreneur Media, Inc. All rights reserved.

A franchise system combines the entrepreneurial advantages of owning a business with the efficiencies of vertical marketing systems that function under single ownership (i.e., a corporate system, as we discuss next). Franchisees are motivated to make their stores successful because they receive the profits after they pay the royalty to the franchisor. The franchisor is motivated to develop new products, services, and systems and to promote the franchise because it receives royalties on all sales. Advertising, product development, and system development are all done efficiently by the franchisor, with costs shared by all franchisees.

Corporate Vertical Marketing System

In a **corporate vertical marketing system**, the parent company has complete control and can dictate the priorities and objectives of the marketing channel because it owns multiple segments of the channel, such as manufacturing plants, warehouse facilities, and retail outlets. By virtue of its ownership and resulting control, potential conflict among segments of the channel is lessened.

American Apparel, a clothing manufacturer based in Los Angeles, California, represents a corporate vertical marketing system because it manufacturers its own products rather than having contractual relationships with other firms, and it operates its own retail stores selling T-shirts and other men's and women's sportswear. With this corporate ownership structure, it is able to bring fashion-sensitive items from the idea stage to market in a very short time.

American Apparel represents a corporate vertical marketing system because it manufacturers its own products and operates its own retail stores.

> # IN A CONVENTIONAL MARKETING CHANNEL, RELATIONSHIPS BETWEEN MEMBERS OFTEN ARE BASED ON THE ARGUMENT OVER THE SPLIT OF THE PROFIT PIE—IF ONE PARTY GETS AHEAD, THE OTHER PARTY FALLS BEHIND.

Managing Marketing Channels and Supply Chains through Strategic Relationships

There is more to managing marketing channels and supply chains than simply exercising power over other members in an administered system or establishing a contractual or corporate vertical marketing system. There is also a human side.

In a conventional marketing channel, relationships between members often are based on the argument over the split of the profit pie—if one party gets ahead, the other party falls behind. Sometimes this type of transaction is acceptable if the parties have no interest in a long-term relationship. For instance, if Walmart believes that the PenAgain's ergonomic pens are just a short-term fad, it may only be interested in purchasing once. In that case, it might seek to get the best one-time price, even if it means that PenAgain will make very little money and therefore might not want to sell to Walmart again.

More often than not, however, firms seek a **strategic relationship**, also called a **partnering relationship**, in which the marketing channel members are committed to maintaining the relationship over the long term and investing in opportunities that are mutually beneficial. In a conventional or administered marketing channel, there are significant incentives to establishing a strategic relationship, even without contracts or ownership relationships. Both parties benefit because the size of the profit pie has increased, so both the buyer and the seller increase their sales and profits. These strategic relationships are created explicitly to uncover and exploit joint opportunities, so members depend on and trust each other heavily; share goals and agree on how to accomplish those goals; and are willing to take risks, share confidential information, and make significant investments for the sake of the relationship. Successful strategic relationships require mutual trust, open communication, common goals, interdependence, and credible commitments.

Mutual Trust Mutual trust holds a strategic relationship together. Trust is the belief that a partner is honest (i.e., reliable, stands by its word, sincere, fulfills obligations) and benevolent (i.e., concerned about the other party's welfare). When vendors and buyers trust each other, they are more willing to share

relevant ideas, clarify goals and problems, and communicate efficiently. Information shared between the parties, such as inventory positions in stores, thus becomes increasingly comprehensive, accurate, and timely.

With trust, there's also less need for the supply chain members to constantly monitor and check up on each other's actions because each believes the other won't take advantage, even if given the opportunity. Although it is important in all relationships, monitoring supply chain members becomes particularly pertinent when suppliers are located in less-developed countries, where issues such as the use of child labor, poor working conditions, and below-subsistence wages have become a shared responsibility. Ethical & Societal Dilemma 15.1 highlights how Apple has both stumbled in this responsibility and changed its practices to improve its dedication to ethical choices.

Open Communication To share information, develop sales forecasts together, and coordinate deliveries, Walmart and its suppliers maintain open and honest communication. This maintenance may sound easy in principle, but some businesses don't tend to share information with their business partners. But open, honest communication is a key to developing successful relationships because supply chain members need to understand what is driving each other's business, their roles in the relationship, each firm's strategies, and any problems that arise over the course of the relationship.

Common Goals Supply chain members must have common goals for a successful relationship to develop. Shared goals give both members of the relationship an incentive to pool their strengths and abilities and exploit potential opportunities together. Such commonality also offers an assurance that the other partner won't do anything to hinder the achievement of those goals within the relationship.

Walmart and its suppliers recognize that it is in their common interest to be strategic partners. Walmart needs its suppliers to satisfy its customers, and those manufacturers recognize that if they can keep Walmart happy, they will have more than enough business for years to come. With common goals, both firms have an incentive to cooperate because they know that by doing so, both can boost sales. If Walmart needs a special

ethical & societal dilemma 15.1

Do Customers Care More about the Newest iPhone or about Working Conditions in China?[12]

An iPad user reading a recent issue of *The New York Times* on his or her tablet might have suffered a strange sense of guilt. The newspaper published reports of labor abuses that seemingly run rampant in the Chinese factories responsible for producing Apple's most popular products. These in-depth reports catalogued a long list of fail-ures: the presence of child workers, more than 12-hour shifts, regular work weeks of longer than 60 hours, workers housed in tiny dormitories with approximately 20 peo-ple limited to three rooms, allegations of suicides, and lax safety standards that have led to fatal explosions.

The reports focus mostly on a Foxconn factory in Chengdu, in southwestern China, that manufactures iPhones and iPads. An explosion caused by insufficient ventilation of aluminum dust (created when the cases for the gadgets are polished) in May 2011 killed four workers. A similar explosion fol-lowed six months later at another factory. The ensuing investigations by *The New York Times* revealed multiple other viola-tions of the code of conduct that Apple has established for its suppliers.

With this code of conduct, as well as the frequent audits it performs, Apple asserts that it is doing the best that it can to ensure its suppliers live up to reasonable standards and fair labor practices. An anonymous for-mer Apple executive asserts, "There is a genuine, companywide commitment to the code of conduct." Yet abuses continue, as Apple's own corporate responsibility reports reveal. Audits show that several supply com-panies continue to engage in labor practices that violate the code, with few punishments or changes to the supply chain.

Part of the reason stems from Apple's need for secrecy—once it finds a supply partner that can manufacturer its high-tech gadgets, it wants to maintain that relationship to avoid any leakage of innovation informa-tion. So even if a supplier violates the code again and again, Apple is unlikely to switch.

Furthermore, Apple's focus on innova-tion means that it must work constantly to come up with new ideas and products, which it needs to produce quickly and in sufficient quantities to keep customers happy. This demanding supply chain leaves little room for flexibility. When Apple says it needs 1 million products, say, then its sup-plier is going to do whatever it takes to get those products ready in time. The code of conduct might ask that factory workers be limited to 60-hour work weeks, but in truth, Apple is asking the factories to keep run-ning all day, every day, to make the order.

To keep its costs low, Apple also offers very slim profit margins to suppliers. In turn, these factories aim to reduce their own costs. Another Apple supplier thus began using a toxic chemical, instead of rubbing alcohol, to polish the screens of iPhones, because the chemical dries faster. But it ex-poses workers to the threat of paralysis and nerve damage.

The primary reason for these labor abuses may come only at the end of the supply chain—the consumer. A survey of Apple consumers showed that only 2 per-cent of them recognized labor issues as a concern. In a remarkably succinct sum-mary of the challenge, another anonymous Apple executive asserted, "You can either manufacture in comfortable, worker-friendly factories, or you can reinvent the product every year, and make it better and faster and cheaper, which requires facto-ries that seem harsh by American stan-dards. And right now, customers care more about a new iPhone than working condi-tions in China."

Although Apple attempts to monitor its channel partners' behavior with regard to labor issues, sometimes abuses fall through the cracks.

production run of pens to meet demand for back-to-school buy-ers, PenAgain will work to meet the challenge. If PenAgain has difficulty financing its inventory, it is in Walmart's best interest to help it because they are committed to the same goals in the long run.

Interdependence When supply chain members view their goals and ultimate success as intricately linked, they develop deeper long-term relationships. Interdependence between supply chain members that is based on mutual benefits is key to devel-oping and sustaining the relationship.[13] Walmart's suppliers recognize that without Walmart, their sales would be significantly less. Although certainly the more powerful member of the supply chain, Walmart also recognizes that it can depend on these suppliers to be a dependable source of supply, thus enabling it to have a very efficient marketing channel.

Credible Commitments Successful relationships develop because both parties make credible commitments to, or tangible investments in, the relationship. These commitments go beyond just making the hollow statement, "I want to be your partner"; they involve spending money to improve the products or services provided to the customer and on information technology to improve supply chain efficiency.[14] Walmart works closely with its suppliers to streamline the entire marketing channel. In an early endeavor, it collaborated with P&G to link its distribution centers with the giant consumer packaged goods manufacturer. When a Walmart store sold a particular P&G item, the information flowed directly to P&G's planning and control systems. When the inventory level of P&G's products at Walmart's distribution center got to the point where it needed to reorder, the system automatically alerted P&G to ship more products. This information helped P&G plan its production. Walmart was also able to track when a P&G shipment arrived at one of its distribution warehouses, which enabled it to coordinate its own outbound shipments to stores. Both Walmart and P&G realized savings from the better inventory management and order processing, savings that in turn were passed on to Walmart's consumers through its everyday low prices.

Just like many other elements of marketing, managing the marketing channel can seem like an easy task at first glance: Put the right merchandise in the right place at the right time. But the various elements and actors involved in a marketing channel create its unique and compelling complexities and require firms to work carefully to ensure they are achieving the most efficient and effective chain possible. We now turn our attention to how information and merchandise flows through marketing channels.

> ✓ **check** yourself
>
> 1. What is the difference between an indirect and a direct marketing channel?
> 2. What are the differences among the three types of vertical marketing systems?
> 3. How do firms develop strong strategic partnerships with their marketing channel partners?

LO 15-4 Describe the flow of information and merchandise in the marketing channel.

MAKING INFORMATION FLOW THROUGH MARKETING CHANNELS

Information flows from the customer to stores, to and from distribution centers, possibly to and from wholesalers, to and from product manufacturers, and then on to the producers of any components and the suppliers of raw materials. To simplify our discussion and because information flows are similar in other marketing channel links and B2B channels, we shorten the supply chain in this section to exclude wholesalers as well as the link from suppliers to manufacturers. Exhibit 15.7 illustrates the flow of information that starts

▼ **EXHIBIT 15.7** Information Flows

CHAPTER 15 | Supply Chain and Channel Management **339**

when a customer buys a Sony HDTV at Best Buy. The flow follows these steps:

Flow 1 (Customer to Store): The sales associate at Best Buy scans the **Universal Product Code (UPC)** tag on the HDTV packaging, and the customer receives a receipt. The UPC tag is the black-and-white bar code found on most merchandise. It contains a 13-digit code that indicates the manufacturer of the item, a description of the item, information about special packaging, and special promotions.[15] In the future, RFID tags, discussed at the end of this chapter, may replace UPC tags.

Flow 2 (Store to Buyer): The point-of-sale (POS) terminal records the purchase information and electronically sends it to the buyer at Best Buy's corporate office. The sales information is incorporated into an inventory management system and used to monitor and analyze sales and decide to reorder more HDTVs, change a price, or plan a promotion. Buyers also send information to stores about overall sales for the chain, ways to display the merchandise, upcoming promotions, and so on.

Flow 3 (Buyer to Manufacturer): The purchase information from each Best Buy store is typically aggregated by the retailer as a whole, which creates an order for new merchandise and sends it to Sony. The buyer at Best Buy may also communicate directly with Sony to get information and negotiate prices, shipping dates, promotional events, or other merchandise-related issues. Adding Value 15.2 examines how Neiman Marcus works with its suppliers to expedite a key issue in this flow: U.S. Customs import processes.

Flow 4 (Store to Manufacturer): In some situations, the sales transaction data are sent directly from the store to the manufacturer, and the manufacturer decides when to ship more merchandise to the distribution centers and the stores. In other situations, especially when merchandise is reordered frequently, the ordering process is done automatically, bypassing the buyers. By working together, the retailer and manufacturer can better satisfy customer needs.[16]

Flow 5 (Store to Distribution Center): Stores also communicate with the Best Buy distribution center to coordinate deliveries and check inventory status. When the store inventory drops to a specified level, more HDTVs are shipped to the store, and the shipment information is sent to the Best Buy computer system.

Flow 6 (Manufacturer to Distribution Center and Buyer): When the manufacturer ships the HDTVs to the Best Buy distribution center, it sends an advanced shipping notice to the distribution centers. An **advanced shipping notice (ASN)** is an electronic document that the supplier sends the retailer in advance of a shipment to tell the retailer exactly what to expect in the shipment. The center then makes appointments for trucks to make the delivery at a specific time, date, and loading dock. When the

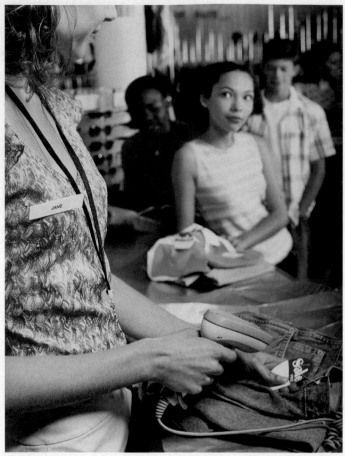

The flow of information starts when the UPC tag is scanned at the point-of-purchase.

shipment is received at the distribution center, the buyer is notified and authorizes payment to the vendor.

Data Warehouse

Purchase data collected at the point of sale (information flow 2 in Exhibit 15.7) goes into a huge database known as a data warehouse. Using the data warehouse, the CEO might be interested in how the corporation is generally doing and could look at the data aggregated by quarter for a merchandise division, a region of the country, or the total corporation. A buyer may be more interested in a particular manufacturer in a certain store on a particular day. Analysts from various levels of the retail operation extract information from the data warehouse to make a plethora of marketing decisions about developing and replenishing merchandise assortments.

In some cases, manufacturers also have access to this data warehouse. They communicate with retailers by using electronic data interchange (EDI) and use supply chain systems known as vendor-managed inventory.

In information flows 3, 4, and 6 in Exhibit 15.7, the retailer and manufacturer exchange business documents through EDI. **Electronic data interchange (EDI)** is the computer-to-computer exchange of business documents from a retailer to a vendor and

Adding Value 15.2

Neiman Marcus Expedites Shipments through Customs

Neiman Marcus receives most of its apparel, accessories, jewelry, and home products from other countries. Because it deals with fashions that have short product life cycles, good communication with its suppliers is essential.[17]

A major impediment to getting deliveries in a timely manner was the delay caused by U.S. Customs and Border Protection agencies, which demand comprehensive and complicated paperwork before they will allow shipments into the United States. With so much paperwork, incomplete information and errors are common, which kept Neiman Marcus' shipments from arriving on time. The company therefore instituted an Internet-based system that remains in contact with every business partner that touches a shipment, to ensure that the documents are prepared properly for U.S. Customs. Trust is one thing, but this system guarantees that the work is done correctly. Any missing paperwork prompts an automatic alert to the appropriate business partner, which can then send the required paperwork to U.S. Customs while the shipment is still en route rather than wait to be notified by Customs after it has arrived. Missing or incorrect documents found by Customs once the shipment has arrived can delay the process even more. This initiative eliminated a full two days from the shipping cycle.

As an added bonus, Neiman Marcus uses the system to comply more closely with import regulations. The duty/tariff laws of different countries vary and can change quickly. To keep up to date with these changes in the more than 60 countries with which it does business, Neiman Marcus requires vendors to guarantee that they will update any tariff changes on the Internet-based system within 24 hours of the country's rule change. Shipments then receive an HTSUS (harmonized tariff schedule of the United States), making it easier for U.S. Customs to identify the import shipments and move them through the clearance process. As a result, Neiman Marcus shipments have a low risk rating and move through Customs much faster than those of many of its competitors.

Changes like these demonstrate the symbiotic nature of relationships along the marketing channel. Retailers with sufficient strength in the marketplace can insist that their vendors adhere to new processes, even if they demand new investments by the vendor. In a recent initiative to address shrinking profits, for example, Neiman Marcus asked its vendors to create designer merchandise at a lower price point.[18] The replicas, produced in the same style and same factory as more expensive models, still sport a designer's name but are made from less costly materials. Some suppliers found the request too challenging, but others embraced it, recognizing an opportunity to protect future sales and expand their offerings. As news about these lower-cost designer items spreads across the Internet, Neiman Marcus will learn quickly whether this approach buoys its flagging sales or sends customers to other stores that have retained their luxury brand image.

To facilitate getting merchandise through U.S. Customs, it uses an Internet-based system that remains in contact with every business partner that touches a shipment.

back. In addition to sales data, purchase orders, invoices, and data about returned merchandise can be transmitted back and forth. EDI enables vendors to transmit information about on-hand inventory status, vendor promotions, and cost changes to the retailer as well as information about purchase order changes, order status, retail prices, and transportation routings. EDI enables channel members to communicate more quickly and with fewer errors than in the past. This enables merchandise to move from vendors to retailers more quickly.

Vendor-managed inventory (VMI) is an approach for improving marketing channel efficiency in which the manufacturer is responsible for maintaining the retailer's inventory levels in each of its stores.[19] By sharing the data in the retailer's data warehouse and communicating that information via EDI, the manufacturer automatically sends merchandise to the retailer's store or distribution center when the inventory at the store reaches a pre-specified level.[20]

In ideal conditions, the manufacturer replenishes inventories in quantities that meet the retailer's immediate demand, reducing stockouts with minimal inventory. In addition to better match retail demand to supply, VMI can reduce the vendor's and the retailer's costs. Manufacturer sales people no longer need to spend time generating orders on items that are already in the stores, and their role shifts to selling new items and maintaining relationships. Retail buyers and planners no longer need to monitor inventory levels and place orders.

> " Push strategies are efficient for merchandise that has steady, predictable demand, such as milk and eggs, basic men's underwear, and bath towels. "

Push versus Pull Marketing Channels

As illustrated in Exhibit 15.8, the way information is transferred from one party to another in a marketing channel is generally classified as either a pull or a push strategy. In a **push marketing strategy** merchandise is allocated to stores based on previous sales forecasts. Once a forecast is developed, specified quantities of merchandise are shipped (pushed) to distribution centers and stores at predetermined time intervals. The manufacturer works with wholesalers and retailers to get the products on the shelf by providing incentives such as slotting allowances, contests for salespeople, and other promotional support at all levels of the marketing channel. The goal is to increase demand for the product by providing incentives and focusing one's efforts on wholesalers, retailers, or their sales people. These campaigns attempt to motivate the seller to highlight the product, rather than those of competitors, and thereby *push* the product to consumers.

With a **pull marketing strategy**, the amount of merchandise sent to the store is determined based on sales data captured by POS terminals. In essence, customers *pull* the product into the marketing channel by demanding it. Marketers create customer pull-based demand by designing integrative marketing campaigns to create awareness and ultimately demand for the product.

With a pull marketing strategy, there is less likelihood of being overstocked or out of stock because the store orders merchandise as needed on the basis of consumer demand. As a result, a pull strategy increases inventory turnover and is more responsive to changes in customer demand.

Although generally more desirable, a pull approach is not the most effective in all situations. First, a pull approach is more costly.

▼ **EXHIBIT 15.8** Push versus Pull Marketing Strategies

Second, for some merchandise, retailers do not have the flexibility to adjust inventory levels on the basis of demand. For example, commitments must be made months in advance for fashion and private-label apparel. Because these commitments cannot be easily changed, the merchandise has to be pre-allocated to the stores at the time the orders are formulated. Third, push strategies are efficient for merchandise that has steady, predictable demand, such as milk and eggs, basic men's underwear, and bath towels. Because both pull and push marketing strategies have their advantages, most channel partners use a combination of these approaches.

 check yourself

1. What are the marketing channel links associated with each information flow?

2. How do marketing channel members use data warehouses to make decisions?

3. What is EDI and how is it used?

4. Why do some marketing channels use VMI, while others do not?

5. What is the difference between a push and a pull marketing channel?

MAKING MERCHANDISE FLOW THROUGH MARKETING CHANNELS

Exhibit 15.9 illustrates different types of merchandise flows:

1. Sony to Best Buy's distribution centers, or

2. Sony directly to stores.

3. If the merchandise goes through distribution centers, it is then shipped to stores

4. and then to the customer.

Making merchandise flow involves first deciding whether the merchandise will go from the manufacturer to a retailer's distribution center or directly on to stores. Once in a distribution center, multiple activities take place before it is shipped on to a store.

Distribution Centers versus Direct Store Delivery

As indicated in Exhibit 15.9, manufacturers can ship merchandise directly to a

retailer's stores—direct store delivery (flow 2)—or to their distribution centers (flow 1). Although manufacturers and retailers may collaborate, the ultimate decision is usually up to the retailer and depends on the characteristics of the merchandise and the nature of demand. To determine which distribution system—distribution centers or direct store delivery—is better, retailers consider the total cost associated with each alternative and the customer service criterion of having the right merchandise at the store when the customer wants to buy it.

There are several advantages to using a distribution center:

- More accurate sales forecasts are possible when retailers combine forecasts for many stores serviced by one distribution center rather than doing a forecast for each store. Consider a set of 50 Target stores, serviced by a single distribution center that each carries Michael Graves toasters. Each store normally stocks 5 units for a total of 250 units in the system. By carrying the item at each store, the retailer must develop individual forecasts, each with the possibility of errors that could result in either too much or too little merchandise. Alternatively, by delivering most of the inventory to a distribution center and feeding the stores merchandise as they need it, the effects of forecast errors for the individual stores are minimized, and less backup inventory is needed to prevent stockouts.

- Distribution centers enable the retailer to carry less merchandise in the individual stores, which results in lower inventory

▼ **EXHIBIT 15.9** Merchandise Flows

investments systemwide. If the stores get frequent deliveries from the distribution center, they need to carry relatively less extra merchandise as backup stock.

- It is easier to avoid running out of stock or having too much stock in any particular store because merchandise is ordered from the distribution center as needed.

- Retail store space is typically much more expensive than space at a distribution center, and distribution centers are better equipped than stores to prepare merchandise for sale. As a result, many retailers find it cost-effective to store merchandise and get it ready for sale at a distribution center rather than in individual stores.

But distribution centers aren't appropriate for all retailers. If a retailer has only a few outlets, the expense of a distribution center is probably unwarranted. Also, if many outlets are concentrated in metropolitan areas, merchandise can be consolidated and delivered by the vendor directly to all the stores in one area economically. Direct store delivery gets merchandise to the stores faster and thus is used for perishable goods (meat and produce), items that help create the retailer's image of being the first to sell the latest product (e.g., video games), or fads. Finally, some manufacturers provide direct store delivery for retailers to ensure that their products are on the store's shelves, properly displayed, and fresh. For example, employees delivering Frito-Lay snacks directly to supermarkets replace products that have been on the shelf too long and are stale, replenish products that have been sold, and arrange products so they are neatly displayed.

buyer also specifies how the merchandise should be placed on pallets for easy unloading.

The truck must arrive within the specified time because the distribution center has all of its 100 receiving docks allocated throughout the day, and much of the merchandise on this particular truck is going to be shipped to stores that evening. Unfortunately, the truck was delayed in a snowstorm. The dispatcher—the person who coordinates deliveries to the distribution center—reassigns the truck delivering the HDTVs to a Wednesday morning delivery slot and charges the firm several hundred dollars for missing its delivery time. Although many manufacturers pay transportation expenses, some retailers negotiate with their vendors to absorb this expense. These retailers believe they can lower their net merchandise cost and better control merchandise flow if they negotiate directly with trucking companies and consolidate shipments from many vendors.

Receiving and Checking Using UPC Receiving is the process of recording the receipt of merchandise as it arrives at a distribution center. Checking is the process of going through the goods upon receipt to make sure they arrived undamaged and that the merchandise ordered was the merchandise received.

In the past, checking merchandise was a very labor-intensive and time-consuming process. Today, however, many distribution systems using EDI are designed to minimize, if not eliminate, these processes. The advance shipping notice (ASN) tells the distribution center what should be in each carton. A UPC

[Some manufacturers provide direct store delivery for retailers to ensure that their products are on the store's shelves, properly displayed, and fresh.]

The Distribution Center

The distribution center performs the following activities: coordinating inbound transportation; receiving, checking, storing, and cross-docking; getting merchandise floor ready; and coordinating outbound transportation. To illustrate these activities being undertaken in a distribution center, we'll continue our example of Sony HDTVs being shipped to a Best Buy distribution center.

Management of Inbound Transportation Traditionally, buyers focused their efforts, when working with vendors, on developing merchandise assortments, negotiating prices, and arranging joint promotions. Now, buyers and planners are much more involved in coordinating the physical flow of merchandise to the stores. **Planners** are employees responsible for the financial planning and analysis of merchandise and its allocation to stores. The TV buyer has arranged for a truckload of HDTVs to be delivered to its Houston, Texas, distribution center on Monday between 1:00 and 3:00 p.m. The

label or radio frequency identification (RFID) tag on the shipping carton that identifies the carton's contents is scanned and automatically counted as it is being received and checked. **Radio frequency identification (RFID) tags** are tiny computer chips that automatically transmit to a special scanner all the information about a container's contents or individual products. Approximately as large as a pinhead, these RFID tags consist of an antenna and a chip that contains an electronic product code that stores far more information about a product than bar (UPC) codes can. The tags also act as passive tracking devices, signaling their presence over a radio frequency when they pass within a few yards of a special scanner. The tags have long been used in high-cost applications, such as automated highway toll systems and security identification badges.

Storing and Cross-Docking After the merchandise is received and checked, it is either stored or cross-docked. When merchandise is stored, the cartons are transported by a conveyor

Walmart speeds merchandise from its distribution centers to stores.

system and forklift trucks to racks that go from the distribution center's floor to its ceiling. Then, when the merchandise is needed in the stores, a forklift driver goes to the rack, picks up the carton, and places it on a conveyor system that routes the carton to the loading dock of a truck going to the store.

Merchandise cartons that are cross-docked are prepackaged by the vendor for a specific store. The UPC labels on the carton indicate the store to which it is to be sent. The vendor also may affix price tags to each item in the carton. Because the merchandise is ready for sale, it is placed on a conveyor system that routes it from the unloading dock at which it was received to the loading dock for the truck going to the specific store—thus, the name *cross-docked*. The cartons are routed on the conveyor system automatically by sensors that read the UPC label on the cartons. Cross-docked merchandise is in the distribution center only for a few hours before it is shipped to the stores.

Merchandise sales rate and degree of perishability or fashionability typically determine whether cartons are cross-docked or stored. For instance, because Sony's HDTVs sell so quickly, it is in Best Buy's interest not to store them in a distribution center. Similarly, cross-docking is preferable for fashion apparel or perishable meat or produce.

Getting Merchandise Floor-Ready

For some merchandise, additional tasks are undertaken in the distribution center to make the merchandise floor-ready. Floor-ready merchandise is merchandise that is ready to be placed on the selling floor. Getting merchandise floor-ready entails ticketing, marking, and, in the case of some apparel, placing garments on hangers (or maybe attaching RFID chips). At U.K. based grocery chain, Tesco, it is essential that products ship in ready-to-sell units so that it has little manipulation or sorting to do at the distribution center or in the stores. To move the store-ready merchandise it receives from suppliers quickly into the store, Tesco demands that products sit on roll cages rather than pallets. Then, store employees can easily wheel them onto the retail floor. The stores' backrooms only have two or three days' worth of backup inventory, and it is important to keep inventory levels low and receive lots of small, accurate deliveries from its suppliers—which also helps cut costs.[21]

Ticketing and marking refers to affixing price and identification labels to the merchandise. It is more efficient for a retailer to perform these activities at a distribution center than in its stores. In a distribution center, an area can be set aside and a process implemented to efficiently add labels and put apparel on hangers. Conversely, getting merchandise floor-ready in stores can block aisles and divert sales people's attention from their customers. An even better approach from the retailer's perspective is to get vendors to ship floor-ready merchandise, thus totally eliminating the expensive, time-consuming ticketing and marking process.

Preparing to Ship Merchandise to a Store

At the beginning of the day, the computer system in the distribution center generates a list of items to be shipped to each

Tesco makes sure its merchandise is floor-ready before it is shipped to its stores.

To reduce lead time, UPS works with adidas by providing it with special labeling, garments on hangers, and advanced shipping notices.

store on that day. For each item, a pick ticket and shipping label is generated. The **pick ticket** is a document or display on a screen in a forklift truck indicating how much of each item to get from specific storage areas. The forklift driver goes to the storage area, picks up the number of cartons indicated on the pick ticket, places UPC shipping labels on the cartons that indicate the stores to which the items are to be shipped, and puts the cartons on the conveyor system, where they are automatically routed to the loading dock for the truck going to the stores.

straints to develop the most efficient routes possible. As a result, stores are provided with an accurate estimated time of arrival, and vehicle usage is maximized.

Inventory Management through Just-In-Time Inventory Systems

Marketing channel management offers the 21st century's answer to a host of distribution problems faced by firms. As recently as the early 1990s, even the most innovative firms needed 15 to 30 days—or even more—to fulfill an order from the warehouse to the customer. The typical order-to-delivery process

> "As recently as the early 1990s, even the most innovative firms needed 15 to 30 days—or even more—to fulfill an order from the warehouse to the customer."

Shipping Merchandise to Stores Shipping merchandise to stores from a distribution center has become increasingly complex. Most distribution centers run 50–100 outbound truck routes in one day. To handle this complex transportation problem, the centers use sophisticated routing and scheduling computer systems that consider the locations of the stores, road conditions, and transportation operating con-

had several steps: order creation, usually using a telephone, fax, or mail; order processing, using a manual system for credit authorization and assignment to a warehouse; and physical delivery. Things could, and often did, go wrong. Ordered goods were not available. Orders were lost or misplaced. Shipments were misdirected. These mistakes lengthened the time it took to get merchandise to customers and potentially made the entire process more expensive. As Neiman Marcus, profiled in Adding Value 15.2, realized, the traditional ways of doing things were not necessarily the best ways.

Faced with such predicaments, firms began stockpiling inventory at each level of the supply chain (retailers, wholesalers, and manufacturers), but keeping inventory where it is not needed becomes a huge and wasteful expense. If a manufacturer has a huge stock of items stuck in a warehouse, it not only is not earning profits by selling those items but also must pay to maintain and guard that warehouse.

Therefore, more recently, many firms, such as American Apparel, Zara, Mango, and Forever 21, have adopted a practice developed by Toyota in the 1950s (see the Zara case study at the end of this chapter). **Just-in-time inventory systems**, also known as **quick response** (QR) systems in retailing, are inventory management systems that deliver less merchandise on a more frequent basis than traditional inventory systems. The firm gets the merchandise just-in-time for it to be used in the manufacture of another product or for sale when the customer wants it. The benefits of a JIT system include reduced lead time (the amount of time between the recognition that an order needs to be placed and the arrival of the needed merchandise at the seller's store), increased product availability, and lower inventory investment.[22]

✔ **check** yourself

1. How does merchandise flow through a typical marketing channel?

2. Why have just-in-time inventory systems become so popular?

check it out!

mhhe.com/GrewalM4e
for study materials,
including quizzes
and videos.

retailing and multichannel marketing

Begun as a local cable channel in 1982, Home Shopping Network (HSN) offered consumers a central location from which to buy through their televisions.[1] The format for home shopping networks like HSN and QVC has remained the same for years: products loaded with kitsch, hawked by energetic salespeople who promise an incredible deal. As competition in this field increased, HSN tailored its communication strategy to reach more shoppers. For example, HSN.com was one of the top 10 most visited e-commerce sites, and its Facebook, Twitter, and YouTube presence fill out HSN's marketing mix. Today, it carries higher-end brands to appeal to the nearly 90 million households that watch shopping networks.[2]

The television broadcasts are only the first step. The HSN channel simulcasts all its shows on its website, and customers have constant access to related YouTube footage. Across these

LEARNING OBJECTIVES

After reading this chapter, you should be able to:

LO 16-1 Discuss the four factors manufacturers should consider as they develop their strategy for working with retailers.

LO 16-2 Outline the considerations associated with choosing retail partners.

LO 16-3 List the three levels of distribution intensity.

LO 16-4 Describe the various types of retailers.

LO 16-5 Describe the components of a retail strategy.

LO 16-6 Identify the benefits of stores.

LO 16-7 Identify the benefits of multichannel retailing.

LO 16-8 Detail the challenges of multichannel retailing.

media, the shopping networks have developed a somewhat lower key sales approach, such that they use a talk show, lifestyle-oriented atmosphere to promise exclusive, branded products, including HSN's exclusive fragrance

continued on p. 350

Jennifer Lopez and her Mom promote her Love & Light fragrance on HSN.

continued from p. 349

with Mary J. Blige, *ELLE* magazine–endorsed fashion products, and Emeril Lagasse and Wolfgang Puck lines of kitchenware. Jennifer Lopez recently promoted her Love & Light fragrance.

The reinvention of television shopping makes such retail channels relevant to customers because they sell lifestyles as well as the products to attain those lifestyles. An average customer of HSN earns a household income of more than $75,000; for QVC, this average is $200,000! Thus, a viewer who loves reality television and keeps up with the Kardashians can easily tune in to QVC to enjoy the K-Dash line, then visit the pop-up store that QVC set up in Rockefeller Center during Fashion Night Out (the kickoff of fashion week).

Although both HSN and QVC are much more than television channels, television is still their core delivery medium. Even in this forum, though, the communication has evolved—from pitching products to providing an entertaining, multipronged selling machine. A cooking show demonstrates how viewers can make a featured recipe, offers some helpful hints, and then highlights all the pots and kitchenware for sale (which are also available on the website, of course). In a not-so-subtle form of product placement, Jamie Oliver, the chef and show host, makes a pasta dish using Barilla pasta, with the brand displayed on screen. Oliver mentions that the pasta is multigrain and a great source of protein, fiber, and omega 3 that also tastes great. In exchange, HSN receives advertising revenue from Barilla.[3]

On YouTube, visitors are affluent and of the age range most appealing to retailers.[4] By reaching 40–50 percent of the company's target market, YouTube gives HSN a way to interact differently with its customers and further increase its share of wallet from its current customers. In addition, these videos show up in Google searches, so it offers an appealing vehicle for retailers. The video format humanizes the connection and provides additional information about products. For example, HSN has a dedicated channel on YouTube that enables it to control the content and look of its page.[5] The site's tracking capabilities also facilitate a deeper understanding of HSN customers,[6] including which other videos and programs attract their attention.

For consumers, YouTube offers a seamless multichannel experience. Products promoted on HSN, such as Tori Spelling's jewelry line,[7] are available on YouTube almost immediately after they appear on television. Then HSN marketers can use the information gathered from YouTube to target direct mail campaigns. For example, HSN should send jewelry promotions to households that viewed the YouTube video clip for a necklace from the Tori Spelling Collection. Consumer responses are monitored 24/7 and measured against hourly sales goals. There's never a dull moment—it's like the CNN of shopping! ■

▼ **EXHIBIT 16.1** Factors for Establishing a Relationship with Retailers

| 1. Choosing retailing partners | → | 2. Identifying types of retailers | → | 3. Developing a retail strategy | → | 4. Managing a multichannel strategy |

retailing The set of business activities that add value to products and services sold to consumers for their personal or family use; includes products bought at stores, through catalogs, and over the Internet, as well as services like fast-food restaurants, airlines, and hotels.

Retailing sits at the end of the supply chain, where marketing meets the consumer. But there is far more to retailing than just manufacturing a product and making it available to its customers. It is primarily the retailer's responsibility to make sure that these customers' expectations are fulfilled.

Retailing is defined as the set of business activities that add value to products and services sold to consumers for their personal or family use. Our definition includes products bought at stores, through catalogs, and over the Internet as well as services such as fast-food restaurants, airlines, and hotels. Some retailers claim they sell at wholesale prices, but if they sell to customers for their personal use, they are still retailers, regardless of their prices. Wholesalers (see Chapter 15) buy products from manufacturers and resell them to retailers or industrial or business users.

Retailing today is changing, both in the United States and around the world. Manufacturers no longer rule many supply chains, as they once did. Retailers such as Walmart, Carrefour (a French hypermarket), Metro (a German retail conglomerate), Tesco, Schwarz (another German conglomerate), Kroger, Costco, Aldi, Home Depot, and Target[8]—the largest retailers in the world—dictate to their suppliers what should be made, how it should be configured, when it should be delivered, and, to some extent, what it should cost. These retailers are clearly in the driver's seat.

This chapter extends Chapter 15's discussion of supply chain management by examining why and how manufacturers use retailers. The manufacturer's strategy depends on its overall

market power and how consistent a new product or product line is with current offerings. Consider the following scenarios:

- Scenario 1: Cosmetics conglomerate Estée Lauder's subsidiary brand M·A·C is introducing a new line of mascara.

- Scenario 2: Coach, well-known for its women's handbags, has introduced a line of men's leather goods, apparel, gifts, shoes, and other accessories—products not previously in its assortment.

- Scenario 3: Eva, a young entrepreneur, is launching a new line of environmentally friendly (green) cosmetics.

Each of these scenarios is different and requires the manufacturer to consider alternatives for reaching its target markets through retailers.

LO 16-1 Discuss the four factors manufacturers should consider as they develop their strategy for working with retailers.

Exhibit 16.1 illustrates four factors manufacturers consider to establish their strategy for working with retailers.[9] In choosing retail partners, the first factor, manufacturers assess how likely it is for certain retailers to carry their products. Manufacturers also consider where their target customers expect to find the products because those are exactly the stores in which they want to place their products. The overall size and level of sophistication of the manufacturer will determine how many of the marketing channel functions it performs and how many it will hand off to other channel members. Finally, the type and availability of the product and the image the manufacturer wishes to portray will determine how many retailers within a geographic region will carry the products.

For the second factor, manufacturers identify the types of retailers that would be appropriate to carry their products. Although the choice is often obvious—such as a supermarket for fresh produce—manufacturers may have a choice of retailer types for some products.

As we discussed in Chapter 15, a hallmark of a strong marketing channel is one in which manufacturers and retailers coordinate their efforts. In the third factor, manufacturers and retailers therefore develop their strategy by implementing the four Ps.

M·A·C will use different criteria for placing products in retail stores than either Coach for Men or Eva's green cosmetics.

Finally, many retailers and some manufacturers use a **multichannel strategy**, which involves selling in more than one channel (e.g., store, catalog, and Internet). The fourth factor therefore consists of examining the circumstances in which sellers may prefer to adopt a particular strategy. Although these factors are listed consecutively, manufacturers may consider them all simultaneously or in a different order.

Coach partners with retailers to help conveniently deliver its products to satisfied customers.

LO 16-2 Outline the considerations associated with choosing retail partners.

CHOOSING RETAILING PARTNERS

Imagine, as a consumer, trying to buy a new leather jacket without being able to visit a retailer or buy online. You would have to figure out exactly what size, color, and style of jacket you wanted. Then you would need to contact various manufacturers, whether in person, by phone, or over the Internet, and order the jacket. If the jacket fit you reasonably well but not perfectly, you still might need to take it to a tailor to have the sleeves shortened. You wouldn't find this approach to shopping very convenient.

Manufacturers like Coach use retailers such as Macy's to undertake partnerships that create value by pulling together all the actions necessary for the greatest possible customer convenience and satisfaction. The store offers a broad selection of

find the products, channel member characteristics, and distribution intensity.

Channel Structure

The level of difficulty a manufacturer experiences in getting retailers to purchase its products is determined by the degree to which the channel is vertically integrated, as described in Chapter 15; the degree to which the manufacturer has a strong brand or is otherwise desirable in the market; and the relative power of the manufacturer and retailer.

Scenario 1 represents a corporate vertical marketing system. Because M-A-C is made by Estée Lauder and operates its own stores, when the new mascara line is introduced, the stores receive the new line automatically with no decision on the part of the retailer. In contrast, Revlon would have a much more difficult time getting CVS to buy a new mascara line because these supply chain partners are not vertically integrated.

When an established firm such as Coach enters a new market with men's leather goods, apparel, gifts, shoes, and other

> The level of difficulty a manufacturer experiences in getting retailers to purchase its products is determined by the degree to which the channel is vertically integrated.

purses, leather jackets, scarves, and other accessories that its buyers have carefully chosen in advance. Customers can see, touch, feel, and try on any item while in the store. They can buy one scarf or leather jacket at a time or buy an outfit that works together. Finally, the store provides a salesperson to help customers coordinate their outfits and a tailor to make the whole thing fit perfectly.

When choosing retail partners, manufacturers look at the basic channel structure, where their target customers expect to

accessories, as is the case in Scenario 2, it cannot place the products with any retailer. It must determine where its customers would expect to find these products and then use its established relationships with women's handbag buyers, the power of its brand, and its overall reputation to leverage its position in this new product area.

Eva (Scenario 3) would have an even more difficult time convincing a retailer to buy and sell her green cosmetics line because she lacks power in the marketplace—she is small, and her brand is unknown. She would have trouble getting buyers to see her, let alone consider her line. She might face relatively high slotting allowances just to get space on retailers' shelves. But like Coach in Scenario 2, Eva should consider where the end customer expects to find her products as well as some important retailer characteristics.

Most consumer packaged goods companies, such as Pepsi (left), strive for intensive distribution—they want to be everywhere. But cosmetics firms such as Estee Lauder (right) use an exclusive distribution strategy by limiting their distribution to a few select higher-end retailers in each region.

Customer Expectations

Retailers should also know customer preferences regarding manufacturers. Manufacturers, in contrast, need to know where their target market customers expect to find their products and those of their competitors. As we see in the hypothetical example in Exhibit 16.2, Coach currently sells handbags at stores such as Dillard's, Neiman Marcus, and Marshall's as well as in its own stores (orange arrows). Its competitor Cole Haan sells at Dillard's and Neiman Marcus (green arrows). A survey of male Coach customers shows that they would expect to find its products at Saks Fifth Avenue, Dillard's, Neiman Marcus, and its own stores (blue box). On the basis of this information, Coach decides to try selling at Saks Fifth Avenue but to stop selling at Marshall's to meet customers' expectations better.

Customers generally expect to find certain products at some stores but not at others. For example, Estée Lauder would not choose to sell to CVS or Dollar General because its customers would not expect to shop at those stores for high-end cosmetics such as Estée Lauder's. Instead, CVS might carry less expensive cosmetic brands, such as Revlon and Maybelline, and bargain closeouts probably appear at Dollar General. But male

Coach customers definitely expect to find the brand's clothing offerings at major department stores and at Coach stores.

Channel Member Characteristics

Several factors pertaining to the channel members themselves help determine the channel structure. Generally, the larger and more sophisticated the channel member, the less likely that it will use supply chain intermediaries. Eva will probably use a group of independent salespeople to help sell her line of green cosmetics, whereas a large manufacturer such as Estée Lauder will use its own sales force that already has existing relationships in the industry. In the same way, an independent grocery store might buy merchandise from a wholesaler, but Walmart, the world's largest grocer, only buys directly from the manufacturer. Larger firms often find that by performing the channel functions themselves, they can gain more control, be more efficient, and save money.

LO 16-3 List the three levels of distribution intensity.

Distribution Intensity

When setting up distribution for the first time, as is the case with Eva's green cosmetics (Scenario 3), or introducing a new product line, as is the case with Coach for men (Scenario 2), firms decide the appropriate level of **distribution intensity**—the number of channel members to use at each level of the marketing channel. Distribution intensity commonly is divided into three levels: intensive, exclusive, and selective.

Intensive Distribution An **intensive distribution** strategy is designed to place products in as many outlets as possible. Most consumer packaged goods companies, such as Pepsi, Procter & Gamble, Kraft, and other nationally branded products found in grocery and discount stores, strive for and often achieve intensive distribution. Pepsi wants its product available

▼ **EXHIBIT 16.2** Coach and Cole Haan Distribution

exclusive distribution Strategy in which only selected retailers can sell a manufacturer's brand.

selective distribution Lies between the intensive and exclusive distribution strategies; uses a few selected customers in a territory.

everywhere—grocery stores, convenience stores, restaurants, and vending machines. The more exposure the products get, the more they sell.

Exclusive Distribution

Manufacturers also might use an **exclusive distribution** policy by granting exclusive geographic territories to one or very few retail customers so no other retailers in the territory can sell a particular brand. Exclusive distribution can benefit manufacturers by assuring them that the most appropriate retailers represent their products. Luxury goods firms such as Coach limit distribution to a few select, higher-end retailers in each region. The company believes that selling its products to full-line discount stores or off-price retailers would weaken its image.

When supply is limited or a firm is just starting out, providing an exclusive territory to one retailer or retail chain helps ensure enough inventory to provide the buying public an adequate selection. By granting exclusive territories, Eva

consumer electronics. Retailers still have a strong incentive to sell the products but not to the same extent as if they had an exclusive territory.

As we noted in Chapter 15, like any large complicated system, a marketing channel is difficult to manage. Whether the balance of power rests with large retailers such as Walmart or with large manufacturers such as Procter & Gamble, channel members benefit by working together to develop and implement their channel strategy. In the next section, we explore the different types of retailers with an eye toward which would be most appropriate for each of our scenarios: M-A-C Cosmetics, Coach's products for men, and Eva's new line of environmentally friendly cosmetics.

 check yourself

1. What issues should manufacturers consider when choosing retail partners?
2. What are the differences among intensive, exclusive, and selective levels of distribution intensity?

> ## Like exclusive distribution, selective distribution helps a seller maintain a particular image and control the flow of merchandise into an area.

guarantees her retailers will have an adequate supply of her green cosmetics. This guarantee gives these retailers a strong incentive to market her products. The retailers that Eva uses know there will be no competing retailers to cut prices, so their profit margins are protected. This knowledge gives them an incentive to carry more inventory and use extra advertising, personal selling, and sales promotions.

Selective Distribution Between the intensive and exclusive distribution strategies lies **selective distribution**, which relies on a few selected retail customers in a territory to sell products. Like exclusive distribution, selective distribution helps a seller maintain a particular image and control the flow of merchandise into an area. These advantages make this approach attractive to many shopping goods manufacturers. Recall that shopping goods are those products for which consumers are willing to spend time comparing alternatives, such as most apparel items, home items like branded pots and pans or sheets and towels, branded hardware and tools, and

LO 16-4   Describe the various types of retailers.

IDENTIFY TYPES OF RETAILERS

At first glance, identifying the types of retailers that Coach and Eva may wish to pursue when attempting to place their new lines seems straightforward. But the choice is not always easy. Manufacturers need to understand the general characteristics of different types of retailers to determine the best channels for their product. The characteristics of a retailer that are important to a food manufacturer may be quite different from those considered valuable by a cosmetics manufacturer. In the next few sections, we examine the various types of retailers, identify some major players, and discuss some of the issues facing each type (Exhibit 16.3).

▼ **EXHIBIT 16.3** Types of Retailers

Food Retailers

The food retailing landscape is changing dramatically. Twenty years ago, consumers primarily purchased food at conventional supermarkets. Now conventional supermarkets account for slightly more than half of food sales (not including restaurants). Bankruptcies have closed the doors of many supermarket chains and independent franchises.[10] The fastest growing sectors of the food retail market are supercenters, warehouse clubs, convenience stores, and extreme value food retailers.[11] While full-line discount stores like Walmart and warehouse clubs like Costco are offering more food items, traditional supermarkets are carrying more nonfood items. Many supermarkets offer pharmacies, health care clinics, photo processing centers, banks, and cafés.

The world's largest food retailer, Walmart, has more than $310 billion in sales of supermarket-type merchandise, followed by Carrefour (France), Metro Group (Germany), Tesco (U.K.), Schwartz Group (Germany), and Kroger (U.S.).[12]

Supermarkets
A **conventional supermarket** is a self-service retail food store offering groceries, meat, and produce with limited sales of nonfood items such as health and beauty aids and general merchandise.[13] Perishables including meat, produce, baked goods, and dairy account for approximately 50 percent of supermarket sales and typically have higher margins than packaged goods.[14]

Conventional supermarkets carry about 30,000 individual items or **stock keeping units (SKUs)**. An SKU represents a unique inventory item. **Limited assortment supermarkets** or **extreme value food retailers** such as Save-A-Lot and

ALDI stock only 2,000 SKUs.[15] Rather than carry 20 brands of laundry detergent, limited assortment stores offer one or two brands and sizes, one of which is a store brand. By trimming costs, limited assortment supermarkets can offer merchandise at 40 percent lower prices than conventional supermarkets.[16]

Conventional supermarkets thus are under substantial competitive pressure from other types of food retailers, full-line discount chains, supercenters, warehouse clubs, extreme value retailers, convenience stores, online grocers, and restaurants.

Thus to compete successfully against intrusions by other food retailing formats, conventional supermarkets have begun to differentiate their offerings by (1) emphasizing fresh, locally sourced perishables; (2) targeting health-conscious and ethnic consumers with new lines of natural, organic, or culture-specific items; (3) offering more private-label brands; and (4) providing a better in-store experience with a better overall atmosphere, demonstrations, and fun, as Adding Value 16.1 describes.

Supercenters
Supercenters are large stores (185,000 square feet) that combine a supermarket with a full-line discount store. Walmart operates more than 3,000 supercenters in the United States,[17] accounting for the vast majority of total supercenter sales—far outpacing its competitors Meijer, Super-Target (Target), Fred Meyer (Kroger Co.), and Super Kmart Center (Sears Holding). By offering broad assortments of grocery and general merchandise products under one roof, supercenters provide a one-stop shopping convenience to customers.

Warehouse Clubs
Warehouse clubs are large retailers (100,000–150,000 square feet) that offer a limited and

irregular assortment of food and general merchandise, little service, and low prices to the general public and small businesses. The largest warehouse club chains are Costco, Sam's Club (Walmart), and BJ's Wholesale Club (operating only on the east coast of the United States). Customers are attracted to these stores because they can stock up on large packs of basics like paper towels, mega-sized packaged groceries such as a quart of ketchup, best-selling books and CDs, fresh meat and produce, and an unpredictable assortment of upscale merchandise and services (e.g., jewelry, electronics, home décor) at lower prices than are available at other retail stores. Typically, members pay an annual fee of around $50, which amounts to significant additional income for the chains.

Although both Coach for Men and Eva's products could be sold in warehouse clubs, these retailers probably are not the best choices. Both product lines will have an upscale image, which is inconsistent with any warehouse club. If, however, either firm has overstock merchandise as a result of overestimating demand or underestimating returned merchandise from retailers, warehouse clubs are a potential outlet.

Convenience Stores
Convenience stores provide a limited variety and assortment of merchandise at a convenient location in 3,000–5,000 square foot stores with speedy checkout. They are the modern version of the neighborhood mom-and-pop grocery/general store. Convenience stores enable consumers to make purchases quickly without having to search through a large store and wait in a lengthy checkout line. Convenience store assortments are limited in terms of depth and breadth, and they charge higher prices than supermarkets. Milk, eggs, and bread once represented the majority of their sales, but now most sales come from gasoline and cigarettes.

Convenience stores also face increased competition from other retail formats. In response to these competitive pressures,

Warehouse clubs have expanded their assortment of the electronics category, and are known for great prices.

In addition to convenience, Seven-Eleven is a trendy place for young consumers in Indonesia to hang out.

convenience stores are taking steps to decrease their dependency on gasoline sales by offering fresh food and healthy fast food, tailoring assortments to local markets, and making their stores even more convenient to shop. Finally, convenience stores are adding new services, such as financial service kiosks that give customers the opportunity to cash checks, pay bills, and buy prepaid telephone minutes, theater tickets, and gift cards.

General Merchandise Retailers

The major types of general merchandise retailers are department stores, full-line discount stores, specialty stores, category specialists, home improvement centers, off-price retailers, and extreme value retailers.

Department Stores **Department stores** are retailers that carry a broad variety and deep assortment, offer customer services, and organize their stores into distinct departments for displaying merchandise. The largest department store chains in the United States include Sears, Macy's, Kohl's, JCPenney, and Nordstrom.[19] Department stores would be an excellent retail channel for Coach for Men and Eva's new lines.

To compete and gain better traction among younger consumers, who generally favor smaller specialty stores,[20] many department stores are increasing the amount of exclusive and private-label merchandise they sell. For example, Macy's has introduced exclusive apparel and home lines from celebrities Donald Trump, Jessica Simpson and Martha Stewart.[21] In addition, department stores are becoming true multichannel retailers: At Macy's and Nordstrom, customers can buy or reserve products online, then pick them up in the store.

Full-Line Discount Stores **Full-line discount stores** are retailers that offer a broad variety of merchandise, limited service, and low prices. The largest full-line discount store chains are Walmart, Target, and Kmart (Sears Holding).

Although full-line discount stores typically might carry men's leather goods, accessories, and cosmetics, they are not good options for Coach for Men or Eva's new green cosmetics line. Customers do not expect higher-end products in full-line discount stores. Rather, they are looking for value prices on these items and are willing to compromise on quality or cachet.

Walmart accounts for approximately two-thirds of full-line discount store retail sales in the United States.[22] Target has experienced considerable growth because its stores offer fashionable merchandise at low prices in a pleasant shopping environment. The retailer has developed an image of cheap chic by offering limited-edition exclusive apparel and cosmetic lines.

Specialty Stores **Specialty stores** concentrate on a limited number of complementary merchandise categories targeted toward very specific market segments by offering deep but narrow assortments and sales associate expertise.

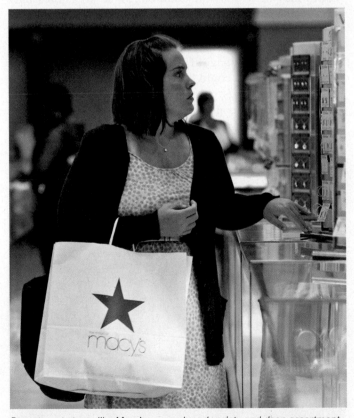

Department stores like Macy's carry a broad variety and deep assortment, offer customer services, and organize its stores into distinct departments for displaying merchandise.

Although such shops are familiar in brick-and-mortar forms, more retailers also are expanding their online specialty profile as well.

Estée Lauder's M-A-C line of cosmetics sells in the company's own retail specialty stores as well as in some department stores. Certain specialty stores would be excellent outlets for the new lines by Coach for Men and Eva. Customers likely expect to find Coach for Men leather goods and accessories in men's apparel or leather stores. Eva's line of green cosmetics would fit nicely in a cosmetics specialty store such as Sephora.

Drugstores

Drugstores are specialty stores that concentrate on pharmaceuticals and health and personal grooming merchandise. Prescription pharmaceuticals represent almost 70 percent of drugstore sales. The largest drugstore chains in the United States are CVS, Walgreens, and Rite Aid—three chains that account for about 38 percent of U.S. drugstore revenue.[23] In this concentrated industry, the top 50 chains also account for 70 percent of revenues.[24]

Although Estée Lauder's new line would not be consistent with the merchandise found in drugstores, Eva's green cosmetics may be a welcome addition. Some drugstores have recognized consumer demand for green products, even though Eva's cosmetics may be priced higher than its competitors. Eva must decide whether her high-end products will suffer a tarnished image if she sells them in drugstores or whether drugstores could be a good channel for increasing her brand awareness.

Drugstores face competition from pharmacies in discount stores and pressure to reduce health care costs. Drugstores also are expanding their role as a fill-in trip destination by carrying products typically found in convenience and grocery stores, including fresh produce. The jury is still out, however, regarding how successful this initiative will be because drugstore prices on these items are at par with convenience stores—about 25 percent higher than grocery stores.[25]

> "Prescription pharmaceuticals represent almost 70 percent of drugstore sales."

Category Specialists

Category specialists are **big box retailers** or **category killers** that offer a narrow but deep assortment of merchandise. Most category specialists use a predominantly self-service approach, but they offer assistance to customers in some areas of the stores. For example, the office supply store Staples has a warehouse atmosphere with cartons of copy paper stacked on pallets, plus equipment in boxes on shelves. But in some departments, such as computers or electronics and other high-tech products, salespeople staff the display area to answer questions and make suggestions.

By offering a complete assortment in a category at somewhat lower prices than their competition, category specialists can kill a category of merchandise for other retailers, which is why they are frequently called category killers. Using their category dominance, these retailers exploit their buying power to negotiate low prices.

Extreme Value Retailers

Extreme value retailers are small, full-line discount stores that offer a limited merchandise assortment at very low prices. The largest extreme value retailers are Dollar General and Family Dollar Stores.

Like limited assortment food retailers, extreme value retailers reduce costs and maintain low prices by buying opportunistically from manufacturers with excess merchandise,

Estee Lauder's M-A-C cosmetic lines sell in specialty stores such as Sephora.

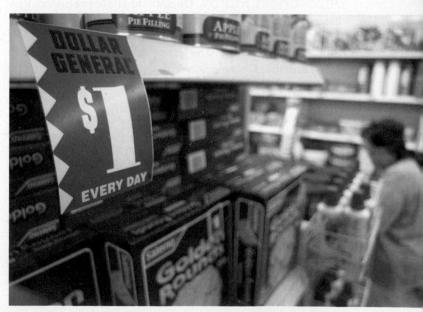

Dollar General is one of the United States' largest extreme value retailers. It has small full-line discount stores that offer a limited assortment at very low prices.

offering a limited assortment, and operating in low-rent locations. They offer a broad but shallow assortment of household goods, health and beauty aids, and groceries.

Many value retailers target low-income consumers, whose shopping behavior differs from that of typical discount store or warehouse club customers. Although these consumers might demand well-known national brands, they often cannot afford to buy large-sized packages. So vendors such as Procter & Gamble often create special, smaller packages for extreme value retailers, often using the reverse innovation approaches we discussed in Chapter 8. Also, higher-income consumers are increasingly patronizing these stores for the thrill of the hunt. Some shoppers regard the extreme value retailers as an opportunity to find some hidden treasure among the household staples.

Extreme value retailers would not be an obvious consumer choice for Coach for Men or Eva's new lines because these stores are not consistent with the brands' image. But if these manufacturers find themselves in an overstock situation, they could use these retailers to reduce inventory. For the same reason, they might use off-price retailers.

Off-Price Retailers

Off-price retailers offer an inconsistent assortment of brand name merchandise at a significant discount from the manufacturer's suggested retail price (MSRP). In today's market, these off-price retailers may be brick-and-mortar stores, online outlets, or a combination of both. America's largest off-price retail chains are TJX Companies (which operates TJMaxx, Marshalls, Winners [Canada], HomeGoods, AJWright, and HomeSense [Canada]), Ross Stores, Burlington Coat Factory, Big Lots Inc., Overstock.com, and Bluefly.com.

To be able to sell at prices 20–60 percent lower than the MSRP,[26] most merchandise is bought opportunistically from manufacturers or other retailers with excess inventory at the end of the season. Therefore, customers cannot be confident that the same merchandise or even type of merchandise will be available each time they visit a store or website. The discounts off-price retailers receive from manufacturers reflect what they do not do as well: They do not ask suppliers to help them pay for advertising, make them take back unsold merchandise, charge them for markdowns, or ask them to delay payments.

Services Retailers

The retail firms discussed in the previous sections sell products to consumers.[27] However, **services retailers**, or firms that primarily sell services rather than merchandise, are a large and growing part of the retail industry. Consider a typical Saturday: After a bagel and cup of coffee at a nearby Peet's Coffee and Tea, you go to the laundromat to wash and dry your clothes, drop a suit off at a dry cleaner, have a prescription filled at a CVS drugstore, and make your way to Jiffy Lube to have your car's oil changed. In a hurry, you drive through a Burger King so you can eat lunch quickly and be on time for your haircut at Supercuts. By midafternoon, you're ready for a workout at your health club. After stopping at home for a change of clothes, you're off to dinner, a movie, and dancing with a friend. Finally, you end your day with a café latte at Starbucks, having interacted with 10 services retailers during the day.

There are a wide variety of services retailers, along with some national companies that provide these services. These companies are retailers because they sell goods and services to consumers. However, some are not just retailers. For example, airlines, banks, hotels, and insurance and express mail companies sell their services to businesses as well as consumers. Adding Value 16.2 highlights how restaurateurs are selling exciting food offerings out of trucks.

The outlet mall in San Marco, Texas, has tenants such as Neiman Marcus Last Call, Zegna, Escada, and Salvatore Ferragamo.

drugstores A specialty store that concentrates on health and personal grooming merchandise, though pharmaceuticals may represent more than 60 percent of its sales.

category specialists A retailer that offers a narrow variety but a deep assortment of merchandise.

big box retailers Discount stores that offer a narrow but deep assortment of merchandise; see category killer.

category killers A specialist that offers an extensive assortment in a particular category, so overwhelming the category that other retailers have difficulty competing.

extreme value retailers A general merchandise discount store found in lower-income urban or rural areas.

off-price retailers A type of retailer that offers an inconsistent assortment of merchandise at relatively low prices.

services retailers A firm that primarily sells services rather than merchandise.

Organizations such as banks, hospitals, health spas, legal clinics, entertainment firms, and universities that offer services to consumers traditionally have not considered themselves retailers. Yet due to increased competition, these organizations are adopting retailing principles to attract customers and satisfy their needs.

Several trends suggest considerable future growth in services retailing. For example, the aging population will increase demand for health care services. Younger people are also spending more time and money on health and fitness. Busy parents in two-income families are willing to pay to have their homes cleaned, lawns maintained, clothes washed and pressed, and meals prepared so they can spend more time with their families.

Now that we've explored the types of stores, we can examine how manufacturers and retailers coordinate their retail strategy using the four Ps.

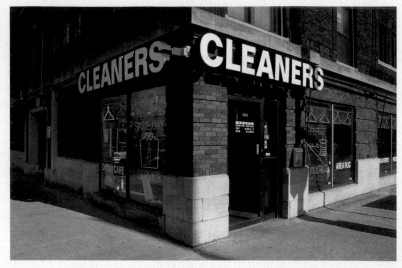

Dry cleaners are retailers that provide services instead of products.

Adding Value 16.2

Giving New Meaning to Going Mobile: Restaurateurs Move from Storefronts to Trucks

The success of fast food in the United States resulted from the growth of the car culture—people in cars loved to grab a burger, some fries, and a shake and then keep on driving down the road. But several restaurants are flipping this traditional model, in which customers drove to the restaurant, by taking their food to customers in food trucks.

The explosive popularity of food trucks has created multiple effects, especially in urban locations and on campuses that now host food truck rallies but also engage in vigorous debates about where the trucks can locate. For food retailers, these new options also create a new form of competition. Why would college students undergo the chore of driving to a restaurant if a food truck is parked right next to their dorm, for example? As a representative of the National Restaurant Association noted, "When you think of consumer needs for convenience, food trucks are a natural evolution of the growth of the off-premises market."[28]

Accordingly, chains such as White Castle have begun experimenting with expanding into this mobile supply channel. Beginning with just a couple of trucks, White Castle will make its mobile food supply available for events and weddings.[29] As it tests various locations, the long-standing chain will add more CraveMobiles, which it plans to keep open 24/7.

In addition to making it easier to access its products (and eliminating the type of quest made infamous by Harold and Kumar), the food trucks give White Castle and other chains—including Wendy's, Taco Bell, and Applebee's, among others—an optimal environment for testing out new recipes and menu additions prior to adding them to their brick-and-mortar stores throughout the country.

This added sales channel is not limited to fast food or quick service restaurants either. Consumer packaged goods companies such as Stouffer's are jumping on the bandwagon too. Several branded food trucks have already begun rolling through the United States, handing out samples of its macaroni and cheese. Although this food truck version has clear marketing benefits, it also seeks to benefit communities. The Stouffer's trucks mainly will locate at or near charitable events, whether during benefit concerts or in locations where people could use a little comfort food. In the aftermath of Hurricane Sandy, the Mac 'n Cheese truck provided victims in New York with a welcome sight and a warm meal.[30]

> IT IS DIFFICULT FOR RETAILERS TO DISTINGUISH THEMSELVES FROM THEIR COMPETITORS THROUGH THE MERCHANDISE THEY CARRY BECAUSE COMPETITORS CAN PURCHASE AND SELL MANY OF THE SAME POPULAR BRANDS.

check yourself

1. What strategies distinguish the different types of food retailers?
2. What strategies distinguish the different types of general merchandise retailers?
3. Are organizations that provide services to consumers retailers?

LO 16-5 Describe the components of a retail strategy.

DEVELOPING A RETAIL STRATEGY USING THE FOUR PS

Like other marketers, retailers perform important functions that increase the value of the products and services they sell to consumers. We now examine these functions, classified into the four Ps: product, price, promotion, and place.

Product

A typical grocery store carries 30,000 to 40,000 items; a regional department store might carry as many as 100,000. Providing the right mix of merchandise and services that satisfies the needs of the target market is one of retailers' most fundamental activities. Offering assortments gives customers a choice. To reduce transportation costs and handling, manufacturers typically ship cases of merchandise, such as cartons of mascara or boxes of leather jackets, to retailers. Because customers generally do not want or need to buy more than one of the same item, retailers

Material Girl is a Macy's exclusive co-brand developed by Madonna and her daughter Lourdes.

break up the cases and sell customers the smaller quantities they desire.

Manufacturers don't like to store inventory because their factories and warehouses are typically not available or attractive shopping venues. Consumers don't want to purchase more than they need because storage consumes space. Neither group likes keeping inventory that isn't being used because doing so ties up money that could be used for something else. Retailers thus provide, in addition to other values to both manufacturers and customers, a storage function, although many retailers are beginning to push their suppliers to hold the inventory until they need it. (Recall our discussion of JIT inventory systems in Chapter 15.)

It is difficult for retailers to distinguish themselves from their competitors through the merchandise they carry because competitors can purchase and sell many of the same popular brands. Thus, many retailers have developed private-label brands (also called store brands), which are products developed and marketed by a retailer and available only from that retailer. For example, if you want a Giani Bernini leather hand bag, you have to go to Macy's.

Retailers often work together with their suppliers to develop an exclusive co-brand. An **exclusive co-brand** is a brand that is developed by a national brand vendor, often in conjunction with a retailer, and is sold exclusively by the retailer. So, for example, Karl Lagerfeld, the internationally famous designer known for working with luxury fashion houses such as Chanel and Fendi, is collaborating with Macy's to design a line aimed at 18- to 30-year-olds who want to move beyond the fast fashion offered by Zara, H&M, Mango, and Forever 21 but cannot quite afford the prices that most designers charge.[31] The Lagerfeld collection at Macy's includes around 45 items that are similar to his more expensive designs but produced with less expensive fabrics and fewer details.

Exclusive co-brands offer a double benefit: They are available at only one retailer, and they provide name recognition similar to that of a national brand. The disadvantage of exclusive

Given the price of a Coach bag, would you expect to find it in Saks Fifth Avenue or JCPenney?

co-brands, from the manufacturer's perspective, is that they can be sold by only one retailer, and therefore, the manufacturer's market is limited. From the retailer's perspective, the disadvantage is that it has to share its profits with the national brand manufacturer, whereas with a private-label brand, it does not.

Price

Price helps define the value of both the merchandise and the service, and the general price range of a particular store helps define its image. Although both Saks Fifth Avenue and JCPenney are department stores, their images could not be more different. Thus, when Coach considers which of these firms is most appropriate for its new line for men, it must keep customers' perceived images of these retailers' price–quality relationship in mind. The company does not, for instance, want to attempt to sell its new line at JCPenney if it is positioning the line with a relatively high price.

Price must always be aligned with the other elements of a retailer's strategy: product, promotion, and place. A customer would not expect to pay $600 for a Coach for Men briefcase at a JCPenney store, but she might question the briefcase's quality if its price is significantly less than $600 at Neiman Marcus. As we discovered in Chapters 14 and 15, there is much more to pricing than simply adding a markup onto a product's cost. Manufacturers must consider at what price they will sell the product to retailers so that both the manufacturer and the retailer can make a reasonable profit. At the same time, both the manufacturer and the retailer are concerned about what the customer is willing and expecting to pay.

Promotion

Retailers and manufacturers know that good promotion, both within the retail environments and in the media, can mean the difference between flat sales and a growing consumer base. Advertising in traditional media such as newspapers, magazines, and television continues to be important to get customers into stores. Increasingly, electronic communications are being used for promotions as well. Some traditional approaches, such as direct mail, are being reevaluated by retailers, but many are still finding value in sending catalogs to customers and selected mailing lists. Companies also offer real-time promotions on their websites. For example, CVS.com contains in-store and online coupons that customers can use immediately on the website or print to use in the store. Coupons.com similarly offers an array of promotions for many grocery store items. Customers can even follow this vendor on Twitter@Coupons to find even more savings opportunities.

Technology is thus expanding the ways in which retailers can reach customers with their promotional message. For example, customers can access a retailer's Internet site using a variety of devices, ranging from a computer to a mobile phone. Due to the rapid growth of domestic and international broadband access through mobile devices, retailers are investing in **mobile commerce (M-commerce)**—product and service purchases through mobile devices. However, the typical retailer's website is not designed to accommodate a mobile device's small screen and slower download speeds. Various firms, including HSN, therefore have developed special sites for users to access through mobile devices. In addition, retailers have created specialized applications that enable mobile device users to shop or obtain more merchandise information. Technology innovations will continue to provide growing opportunities for new forms of promotion. Social & Mobile Marketing 16.1 describes the value of mobile applications for customers.

A coordinated effort between the manufacturer and retailer helps guarantee that the customer receives a cohesive message and that both entities maintain their image. For example, Coach for Men might work with its most important retailers to develop advertising and point-of-sale signs. It may even help defray the costs of advertising by paying all or a portion of the advertising's production and media costs, an agreement called **cooperative (co-op) advertising**.

Store credit cards and gift cards are more subtle forms of promotion that also facilitate shopping. Retailers might offer pricing promotions—such as coupons, rebates, in-store or online discounts, or perhaps buy-one-get-one-free offers—to attract consumers and stimulate sales. These promotions play a very important role in driving traffic to retail locations, increasing average purchase size, and creating opportunities for repeat purchases. But retail promotions also are valuable to customers; they inform customers about what is new and available and how much it costs.

Consumers can access retailers' coupons from their mobile devices.

Another type of promotion occurs inside the store, where retailers use displays and signs, placed at the point of purchase (POP) or in strategic areas such as the end of aisles, to inform customers and stimulate purchases of the featured products.

In addition to traditional forms of promotion, many retailers are devoting more resources to their overall retail environment as a means to promote and showcase what the store has to offer. These promotions may take the form of recognizable approaches, such as in-store and window displays, or they may be entirely new experiences designed to help retailers draw customers and add value to the shopping experience. Bass Pro Shops Outdoor World in Lawrenceville, Georgia, offers a 30,000-gallon aquarium stocked with fish for casting demonstrations, an indoor archery range, and a 43-foot climbing wall. These features enhance customers' visual experiences, provide them with educational information, and enhance the store's sales potential by enabling customers to try before they buy. In addition to adding fun to the shopping experience, these

mobile commerce (M-commerce) Communicating with or selling to consumers through wireless handheld devices such as cellular phones.

cooperative (co-op) advertising An agreement between a manufacturer and retailer in which the manufacturer agrees to defray some advertising costs.

Social & Mobile Marketing 16.1
Mobile Apps Meet the Physical World[32]

Mobile applications that drive customers into the stores have great value for retailers. But simple gimmicks cannot hold consumers' attention for long—and may even annoy them—such that their retention rate is poor, regardless of the number of downloads. Instead, customers like using applications that are fun, convenient, and helpful in terms of making their tasks easier.

Walgreens' successful mobile application has a simple primary goal: improve convenience for customers. Before customers even get in their cars to go to the store, they can order a prescription refill. The application also includes a feature called Refill by Scan that lets customers scan their medication's bar code with their smartphone camera to order their refill. Customers then can change their store pickup locations if needed and select the pickup date and time that is convenient for them. When the prescription is filled, the store sends the customer a text alert. Thus the application drives traffic to the stores by helping them get through the stores more efficiently. More than 1 million people already have opted in for such alerts.

Other retailers turn to Shopkick, a location-based application that partners with the retailers to encourage customers to check in at the stores by rewarding them with points and coupons. Unlike Foursquare or other location-based applications, which estimate your location within 1000 feet, Shopkick communicates with a specific sensor in each store, ensuring you are actually in the store. Customers automatically receive points or kickbucks when they enter the store, and retailers know exactly where the customer is. To encourage customers to browse, various location hotspots grant them additional kickbucks when they enter the target area, whether the electronics department or housewares.

The Shopkick app encourages customers to check in at stores by rewarding them with points and coupons.

Some of the biggest names in retailing—including Target, Best Buy, Macy's, Crate & Barrel, and American Eagle—thus pay Shopkick a fee for each customer the application gets inside their doors. Some of that fee goes back to the customer: They earn 75 kickbucks just by entering and can earn more if they purchase products in the store (875 kickbucks are equivalent to a $25 gift certificate). Then they can instantly redeem their kickbucks by downloading the rewards to their smartphones and presenting the downloaded information at the register.

Walgreens' phone app, Refill by Scan, lets customers scan their prescription bar code with their smartphone camera to order their refill.

activities help offset the current drop in brick-and-mortar customers engendered by online shopping.

A variety of factors influence whether customers will actually buy once they are in the store. Some of these factors are quite subtle. Consumers' perceptions of value and their subsequent patronage are heavily influenced by their perceptions of the store's look and feel. Music, color, scent, aisle size, lighting, the availability of seating, and crowding can also significantly affect the overall shopping experience.[33] Therefore, the extent to which stores offer a more pleasant shopping experience fosters a better mood, resulting in greater spending.

Consider the funky C. Wonder emporium for example. This 72,000-square-foot megastore is divided into various nooks, each with its own personality or feel, including English Town House, Vail Cabin, Palm Springs Modern, and Hollywood Regency. The separate sectors help customers navigate through the vast amount of merchandise available. To grant them control over their experience, C. Wonder's fitting rooms also come equipped with control panels, such that people trying on items can adjust the type and volume of music played, as well as the lighting, to suit their preferences.[34]

Bass Pro Shops Outdoor World in Lawrenceville, Georgia, uses its 43-foot climbing wall as a way to promote its store.

In some retail firms, salesperson and customer service functions are being augmented, or even replaced, by technology in the form of in-store kiosks, the Internet, or self-checkout lanes. At C. Wonder, microchips embedded in the sales tags of every item help the sales staff keep track of where the merchandise is in the store. They also can check out customers anywhere in the store, using handheld registers, which eliminates the need for customers to head to the checkout counter before they leave.[35]

Traditionally, retailers treated all their customers the same. Today, the most successful retailers concentrate on providing more value to their best customers. The knowledge retailers gain from their store personnel, the Internet browsing and buying activities of customers, and the data they collect on customer shopping habits can be used in customer relationship management (CRM). Using this information, retailers may modify product, price, and/or promotion to attempt to increase their **share of wallet**—the percentage of the customer's purchases made from that particular retailer. For instance, multichannel retailers use consumer information collected from the customers' Internet browsing and buying behavior to send

> Traditionally, retailers treated all their customers the same. Today, the most successful retailers concentrate on providing more value to their best customers.

Personal selling and customer service representatives are also part of the overall promotional package. Retailers must provide services that make it easier to buy and use products, and retail associates—whether in the store, on the phone, or on the Internet—provide customers with information about product characteristics and availability. These individuals can also facilitate the sale of products or services that consumers perceive as complicated, risky, or expensive, such as an air conditioning unit, a computer, or a diamond ring. Manufacturers can play an important role in preparing retail sales and service associates to sell their products. Eva thus could conduct seminars or webinars about how to use and sell her new line of green cosmetics and supply printed educational materials to sales associates. Last but not least, sales reps handle the sales transactions.

dedicated e-mails to customers promoting specific products or services. Retailers also may offer special discounts to good customers to help them become even more loyal.

Place

Retailers already have realized that convenience is a key ingredient to success, and an important aspect of this success is convenient locations.[36] As the old cliché claims, the three most important things in retailing are location, location, location. Many customers choose stores on the basis of where they are located, which makes great locations a competitive advantage that few rivals can duplicate. For instance, once Starbucks saturates a market by opening in the best locations, Peet's will have difficulty breaking into that same market—where would it put its stores?

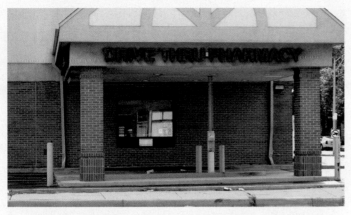

To make their locations more convenient, Walgreens has some free-standing stores, not connected to other retailers, so the stores can offer a drive-up window for customers to pick up their prescriptions.

In pursuit of better and better locations, retailers are experimenting with different options to reach their target markets. Walgreens has free-standing stores, unconnected to other retailers, so the stores can offer a drive-up window for customers to pick up their prescriptions. Other stores, like Brookstone, have opened stores where they have a captive market—airports. Walmart, Staples, and others are opening smaller stores in urban locations to serve those markets better.

LO 16-6   Identify the benefits of stores.

BENEFITS OF STORES FOR CONSUMERS

In this section, we explore the relative advantages of the most traditional retail channels, the bricks-and-mortar store, from consumers' perspective. In the following section, we examine how the addition of the Internet channel has added value to retailers' ability to satisfy their customers' needs.

Browsing   Shoppers often have only a general sense of what they want (e.g., a sweater, something for dinner, a gift) but don't know the specific item they want. They go to a store to see what is available before making their final decision about what to buy. Although some consumers surf the web and look through catalogs for ideas, many still prefer browsing in stores. Some also employ both approaches, getting a sense of what's available through catalogs or the Internet and then going to the store to try on apparel or view the actual object.

Touching and Feeling Products   Perhaps the greatest benefit offered by stores is the opportunity for customers to use all five of their senses—touch, smell, taste, vision, and hearing—to examine products.

share of wallet The percentage of the customer's purchases made from a particular retailer.

Personal Service   Sales associates have the capability to provide meaningful, personalized information. Salespeople can be particularly helpful when purchasing a complicated product, like consumer electronics, or something the customer doesn't know much about, like raw Japanese selvedge denim jeans.

Cash and Credit Payment   Stores are the only channel that accepts cash payments. Some customers prefer to pay with cash because it is easy, resolves the transaction immediately, and does not result in potential interest payments. And, of course, some people don't have a credit card. Some customers also prefer to use their credit card or debit card in person rather than send the payment information electronically via the Internet.

Entertainment and Social Experience   In-store shopping can be a stimulating experience for some people, providing a break in their daily routine and enabling them to interact with friends.

Immediate Gratification   Stores have the advantage of allowing customers to get the merchandise immediately after paying for it.

At LegoLand in Minneapolis' Mall of America, customers can browse, touch, and feel the product, enjoy personal service, be entertained, and interact with others.

online chats Instant messaging or voice conversation with an online sales representative.

Risk Reduction When customers purchase merchandise in stores, the physical presence of the store reduces their perceived risk of buying and increases their confidence that any problems with the merchandise will be corrected.

LO 16-7 Identify the benefits of multichannel retailing.

BENEFITS OF THE INTERNET AND MULTICHANNEL RETAILING

In the previous section, we detailed the relative benefits of stores from the consumers' perspective. In this section, we examine how the addition of the Internet channel to traditional store-based retailers has improved their ability to serve their customers and build a competitive advantage in several ways.

First, the addition of an Internet channel has the potential to offer a greater selection of products. Second, an Internet channel enables retailers to provide customers with more personalized information about products and services. Third, it offers sellers the unique opportunity to collect information about consumer shopping behavior—information that they can use to improve the shopping experience across all channels. Fourth, the Internet channel allows sellers to enter new markets economically.

Deeper and Broader Selection

One benefit of adding the Internet channel is the vast number of alternatives retailers can make available to consumers without crowding their aisles or increasing their square footage. Stores and catalogs are limited by their size. By shopping on the Internet, consumers can easily visit and select merchandise from a broader array of retailers. Individual retailers' websites typically offer deeper assortments of merchandise (more colors, brands, and sizes) than are available in stores or catalogs. This expanded offering enables them to satisfy consumer demand for less popular styles, colors, or sizes. Many retailers also offer a broader assortment (more categories) on their websites. Staples.com, for instance, offers soft drinks and cleaning supplies, which are not available in stores, so that its business customers will view it as a one-stop shop.

Personalization

Another benefit of adding the Internet channel is the ability to personalize promotions and services economically, including heightened service or individualized offerings.

Personalized Customer Service Traditional Internet channel approaches for responding to customer questions—such

At Bluefly.com, customers can have an instant messaging, e-mail, or voice conversation with a customer service representative.

as FAQ (frequently asked questions) pages and offering an 800 number or e-mail address to ask questions—often do not provide the timely information customers are seeking. To improve customer service from an electronic channel, many firms offer live **online chats**, so that customers can click a button at any time and participate in an instant messaging conversation with a customer service representative. This technology also enables firms to send a proactive chat invitation automatically to customers on the site. At Bluefly.com, for example, if a visitor searches for more than three items in five minutes, thereby demonstrating more than a passing interest, Bluefly will display a pop-up window with a friendly face offering help.[37]

Personalized Offering The interactive nature of the Internet also provides an opportunity for retailers to personalize their offerings for each of their customers, based on customers' behavior. Just as a well-trained salesperson would make recommendations to customers prior to checkout, an interactive webpage can make suggestions to the shopper about items that he or she might like to see based on previous purchases, what other customers who purchased the same item purchased, or common web viewing behavior.

Some multichannel retailers are able to personalize promotions and Internet homepages on the basis of several attributes tied to the shopper's current or previous web sessions, such as the time of day, time zone as determined by a computer's Internet address, and assumed gender.[38] However, some consumers worry about this ability to collect information about purchase histories, personal information, and search behavior on the Internet. How will this information be used in the future? Will it be sold to other firms, or will the consumer receive unwanted promotional materials online or in the mail?

Expand Market Presence

The market for customers who shop in stores is typically limited to consumers living in proximity to those stores. The market for catalogs is limited by the high cost of printing and mailing them and increasing consumer interest in environmentally friendly practices. By adding the Internet channel, retailers can expand their market without having to build new stores or incur the high cost of additional catalogs. Adding an Internet channel is particularly attractive to retailers with strong brand names but limited locations and distribution. For example, retailers such as Nordstrom, REI, IKEA, and L.L. Bean are widely known for offering unique, high-quality merchandise. If these retailers only had a store, customers would have to travel vast distances to buy the merchandise they carry.

LO 16-8 Detail the challenges of multichannel retailing.

EFFECTIVE MULTICHANNEL RETAILING

Consumers desire a seamless experience when interacting with multichannel retailers. They want to be recognized by a retailer, whether they interact with a sales associate, the retailer's website, or the retailer's call center by telephone. Customers want to buy a product through the retailer's Internet or catalog channels and pick it up or return it to a local store; find out if a product offered on the Internet channel is available at a local store; and, when unable to find a product in a store, determine if it is available for home delivery through the retailer's Internet channel.

However, providing this seamless experience for customers is not easy for retailers. Because each of the channels is somewhat different, a critical decision facing multichannel retailers is the degree to which they should or are able to integrate the operations of the channels. To determine how much integration is best, each retailer must address issues such as integrated CRM, brand image, pricing, and the supply chain.[39]

Integrated CRM

Effective multichannel operations require an integrated CRM (customer relationship management) system with a centralized customer data warehouse that houses a complete history of each customer's interaction with the retailer, regardless of whether the sale occurred in a store, on the Internet, or on the telephone.[40] Adding Value 16.3 provides an interesting example of how one well-known chain has done so. This information

---

Adding Value 16.3

Personalization in the Warehouse[41]

Walmart and its wholesale club, Sam's Club, are known best for their mass marketing approaches. They offer something for everyone. But when customers purchase a membership in Sam's Club's eValues program, they also receive customized, targeted offers from the retailer. These smart discounts are more appealing than generic promotional campaigns because they pertain specifically to items the customer already has expressed interest in through past purchases.

Sam's Club relies on sophisticated data mining techniques to collect information from every transaction. This information not only enables it to target customers better but also supports complex evaluations of the best products to carry and which to eliminate.

In turn, Sam's Club develops predictive analytics that estimate what any particular customer will buy in the future. As a simple example, imagine a household that buys newborn baby diapers. During that shopping trip, these customers might receive a coupon for wipes to encourage immediate purchases. Then later, the family might receive a coupon for the next larger diaper size to encourage future purchase. Each customer's offers are loaded onto his or her member card, so there is no need to remember to bring discount coupons on the shopping trip.

Sam's Club uses sophisticated data mining techniques to analyze every purchase transaction.

Sam's Club designates its offers into three categories and ensures that customers receive promotions in each: rewards, incentives for products the customer normally purchases, and cross-category offers for items the customer has never bought. The response rates for the targeted items are impressive. Whereas mass marketing offers usually yield a 1–2 percent response rate and segmented offers increase that rate to 5–6 percent, Sam's Club has achieved a 20–30 percent response rate with its predictive analytics.

With the power of analytics, Sam's Club thus is offering tremendous value to its customers.

Multichannel retailers like Patagonia sell on the Internet (left), in catalogs (right), and in stores (bottom).

storehouse allows retailers to efficiently handle complaints, expedite returns, target future promotions, and provide a seamless experience for customers when they interact with the retailer through multiple channels.

Brand Image

Retailers need to provide a consistent brand image across all channels. For example, Patagonia reinforces its image of selling high-quality, environmentally friendly sports equipment in its stores, catalogs, and website. Each of these channels emphasizes function, not fashion, in the descriptions of Patagonia's products. Patagonia's position about taking care of the environment is communicated by carefully lighting its

stores and using recycled polyester and organic, rather than pesticide-intensive cotton, in many of its clothes.

Pricing

Pricing represents another difficult decision for a multichannel retailer. Customers expect pricing consistency for the same SKU across channels (excluding shipping charges and sales tax). However, in some cases, retailers need to adjust their pricing strategy because of the competition they face in different channels. For example, Barnes & Noble offers lower prices through its Internet channel (www.bn.com) than in its stores to compete effectively against Amazon.com.

Retailers with stores in multiple markets often set different prices for the same merchandise to compete better with local stores. Customers generally are not aware of these price differences because they are only exposed to the prices in their local markets. However, multichannel retailers may have difficulties sustaining these regional price differences when customers can easily check prices on the Internet.

Supply Chain

Multichannel retailers struggle to provide an integrated shopping experience across all their channels because unique skills and resources are needed to manage each channel.[42] For example, store-based retail chains operate and manage many stores, each requiring the management of inventory and people. With Internet and catalog operations, inventory and telephone salespeople instead are typically centralized in one or two locations. Also, retail distribution centers (DCs) supporting a store channel are designed to ship many cartons of merchandise to stores. In contrast, the DCs supporting a catalog and Internet channel are designed to ship a few items to individual customers. The difference in shipping orientation for the two types of operations requires a completely different type of distribution center.

Due to these operational differences, many store-based retailers have a separate organization to manage their Internet and catalog operations. But as the multichannel operation matures, retailers tend to integrate all operations under one organization. Both Walmart and JCPenney initially had separate organizations for their Internet channel but subsequently integrated them with stores and catalogs. ■

 check yourself

1. What are the components of a retail strategy?

2. What are the advantages of traditional stores versus Internet-only stores?

3. What challenges do retailers face when marketing their products through multiple channels?

check it out!

mhhe.com/GrewalM4e
for study materials,
including quizzes
and videos.

chapter seventeen

integrated marketing communications

The incredible expansion of the Internet and online tools has radically changed advertising. More and more, companies spread their messages over all sorts of media—television, print, radio, e-mail, Internet, and so on. To really stand out then, a company may need to go further than ever.

To achieve success in a market, companies invariably must communicate the value of their offerings in diverse, well-rounded ways. When companies promote their brands through multiple channels, they stand a better chance of reaching their customers. Coordination across these platforms is the key to effective multichannel marketing communications. But it is difficult to ensure brand consistency when their radio, television, and print ads each require different types of elements, unique voices, and varying styles. In addition, firms need to integrate their marketing communications even further by incorporating new opportunities to reach customers through social media sites, such as Facebook and Twitter.

A great example of such communications integration appeared during Super Bowl XLVI, when the marketing giant Coca-Cola introduced its integrated marketing event through televised advertising that also drove consumers to its social media marketing channels. As the New York Giants beat the New England Patriots, the well-known polar

continued on p. 372

LEARNING OBJECTIVES

After reading this chapter, you should be able to:

LO 17-1 Identify the components of the communication process.

LO 17-2 Explain the four steps in the AIDA model.

LO 17-3 Describe the various integrative communication channels.

LO 17-4 Explain the methods used to allocate the integrated marketing communications (IMC) budget.

LO 17-5 Identify marketing metrics used to measure IMC success.

continued from p. 371

bears that serve as Coca-Cola's spokescharacters appeared in a series of commercials featuring updated, live-animation techniques.[1] The bears first appeared in Coke's 1993 Super Bowl commercials. This time around, the technologically remarkable animation showed the bears reacting to actual events during the game. The televised spots also invited viewers to plug into Coke's live-stream YouTube feed to watch the bears react to the game in real time, not just during the commercial breaks.[2]

In addition to nearly half a million views of "Catch," Coca-Cola's halftime commercial, in which a rotund bear gracefully stumbles on the ice to catch a precious bottle of Coke, YouTube registered more than 33,000 views of bears doing a fourth-quarter touchdown dance.[3] Thus Coca-Cola was named the Super Bowl's brand winner, and three of its ads were rated among the 10 most effective spots for this contest[4]—as ever, the Super Bowl is the world's largest stage for advertisers.[5]

By reaching through the television screen to connect with the approximately 100 million Super Bowl viewers, Coca-Cola integrated its traditional commercials with its live-stream YouTube feed as well as Twitter and Facebook. The integrated marketing event thus offered consumers multiple ways to interact with the bears. For example, viewers could exchange their Super Bowl reactions with the bears through Twitter. In a post-game extension, Coke also offered fans of the winning and losing teams a choice of Facebook apps to share video of either a delighted or a dismayed bear, along with a coupon for a free Coke, of course.

The costs were substantial, though. Coca-Cola spent more than $10 million just to buy Super Bowl airtime, without even calculating the production costs.[6] Why? A pregame announcement suggests one answer: Coca-Cola produced the multimedia experience for viewers to remind them that popping open an ice-cold Coke is one way to Open Happiness, a phrase that also serves as the name of the overall campaign.[7]

Furthermore, Coca-Cola's integrated Super Bowl campaign gave it a great way to connect with consumers through their computers, smartphones, and tablet devices. As the boundaries of advertising shift to include digital and social media, the integration of multiple marketing channels is crucial for catching customers wherever they are: in front of the television, typing on their home computer, or on the go. The challenge persists, even for a marketing giant like Coca-Cola. ∎

> [Coca-Cola spent more than $10 million just to buy Super Bowl airtime, without even calculating the production costs.]

As the description of Coke's innovative campaign attests, each element of an integrated marketing communication (IMC) strategy must have a well-defined purpose and support and extend the message delivered by all the other elements. (For a description of how another soft drink has used some notably similar elements to create its latest integrated campaign, see the discussion of Tropicana in the next chapter.)

Throughout this book, we have focused our attention on how firms create value by developing products and services. However, consumers are not likely to come flocking to new products and services unless they are aware of them. Therefore, marketers must consider how to communicate the value of a product and/or service—or more specifically, the value proposition—to the target market. A firm must develop a communication strategy to demonstrate the value of its product. We begin our consideration by examining what IMC is, how it has developed, and how it contributes to value creation.

Integrated marketing communications (IMC) represents the Promotion P of the four Ps. It encompasses a variety of communication disciplines—advertising, personal selling, sales promotion, public relations, direct marketing, and online marketing including social media—in combination to provide

Noise from the environment

Sender (Firm) → Transmitter encodes message → Communications channel (Media) → Receiver (Consumer) decodes message

Feedback

integrated marketing communications (IMC) Represents the promotion dimension of the four Ps; encompasses a variety of communication disciplines—general advertising, personal selling, sales promotion, public relations, direct marketing, and electronic media—in combination to provide clarity, consistency, and maximum communicative impact.

sender The firm from which an IMC message originates; the sender must be clearly identified to the intended audience.

clarity, consistency, and maximum communicative impact.[8] Instead of consisting of separated marketing communication elements with no unified control, IMC programs regard each of the firm's marketing communications elements as part of a whole, each of which offers a different means to connect with the target audience. This integration of elements provides the firm with the best means to reach the target audience with the desired message, and it enhances the value story by offering a clear and consistent message.

There are three elements in any IMC strategy: the consumer, the channels through which the message is communicated, and the evaluation of the results of the communication. This chapter is organized around these three elements. In the first section, the focus is on consumers, so we examine how consumers receive communications, whether via media or other methods, as well as how the delivery of that communication affects a message's form and contents. The second section examines the various communication channels that make up the components of IMC and how each is used in an overall IMC strategy. The third section considers how the level of complexity in IMC strategies leads marketers to design new ways to measure the results of IMC campaigns.

COMMUNICATING WITH CONSUMERS

As the number of communication media has increased, the task of understanding how best to reach target consumers has become far more complex. In this section, we examine a model that describes how communications go from the firm to the consumer and the factors that affect the way the consumer perceives the message. Then we look at how marketing communications influence consumers—from making them aware that a product or service exists to moving them to buy.

LO 17-1 Identify the components of the communication process.

The Communication Process

Exhibit 17.1 illustrates the communication process. Let's first define each component and then discuss how they interact.

The Sender The message originates from the **sender**, who must be clearly identified to the intended audience. Recall the case study in Chapter 9, which described how Coca-Cola has introduced new options, including its Freestyle vending machines. To make customers aware of this option, Coke works with retailers and other outlets that host Freestyle, such as Burger King, Kroger, Five Guys Burgers, or Kmart, to send messages about its new machines.

To make customers aware of Coke's Freestyle vending machines, it works with retailers such as Dairy Queen to send messages.

> " Feedback can take many forms: a customer's purchase of the item, a complaint or compliment, the redemption of a coupon or rebate, a tweet about the product on Twitter. "

The Transmitter The sender works with a creative department, whether in-house or from a marketing (or advertising) agency, to develop marketing communications to highlight the new beverage. With the assistance of its marketing department, Coca-Cola and its partners might develop flyers, in-store displays, and window banners. The marketing department or external agency receives the information and transforms it for use in its role as the **transmitter**.

Encoding **Encoding** means converting the sender's ideas into a message, which could be verbal, visual, or both. A television commercial could show consumers pouring a new beverage from a Freestyle machine. Billboards showcasing the well-designed machines might highlight their pictures with a message asking, "Have You Tried It Yet?" Although a picture can be worth a thousand words, the most important facet of encoding is not what is sent but rather what is received. Consumers must receive information that makes them want to try the new machine and to continue to buy from it for the innovation to be successful.

The Communication Channel The **communication channel** is the medium—print, broadcast, the Internet, and so forth—that carries the message. Coca-Cola could transmit through television, radio, and various print advertisements, but it also realizes that the media chosen must be appropriate to connect itself (the sender) with its desired recipients. If the company believes its target market is broad, Coca-Cola might advertise on popular television shows such as *The Big Bang Theory* (see Adding Value 17.1) and *The Voice*. As the opening vignette suggested, Coke is also likely to rely on social media channels to encourage fans to consider this alternative source for some of their favorite beverage flavors.

The Receiver The **receiver** is the person who reads, hears, or sees and processes the information contained in the message and/or advertisement. The sender, of course, hopes that the person receiving it will be the one for whom it was

originally intended. Coca-Cola wants its message received and decoded properly by a broad population, including teens, young adults, and families who often visit fast food restaurants. **Decoding** refers to the process by which the receiver interprets the sender's message.

The intended receivers of a Coca-Cola Zero ad are male.

Noise **Noise** is any interference that stems from competing messages, a lack of clarity in the message, or a flaw in the medium. It poses a problem for all communication channels. Coca-Cola may choose to advertise in newspapers that its target market doesn't read, which means the rate at which the message is received by those to whom it has relevance has been slowed considerably. As we have already defined, encoding is what the sender intends to say, and decoding is what the receiver hears. If there is a difference between them, it is probably due to noise.

Feedback Loop The **feedback loop** allows the receiver to communicate with the sender and thereby informs the sender whether the message was received and decoded properly. Feedback can take many forms: a customer's purchase of the item, a complaint or compliment, the redemption of a coupon or rebate,

Adding Value   17.1

The Appeal of Scripted Nerds[9]

For several years, television critics have suggested that the success of *American Idol* would change the face of the medium forever: We would no longer find scripted shows, as networks continued to rely on less expensive, highly appealing contests, as well as their cousins, the ubiquitous reality shows. But a recent trend suggests there is still some value to be found, for viewers, networks, and their advertisers, in more traditional forms of entertainment.

The Big Bang Theory has been on the air since 2007. But its popularity has never been greater. For a few weeks, it even beat *American Idol* in viewing numbers in their head-to-head competition. Social media tracking for the most recent season also showed that the number of comments about the show, its characters, and their scripted quotes nearly quadrupled compared with the previous year.

Yet *American Idol* still attracts far more social media comments overall. Whereas the 12,000 comments from social media users represented a huge jump for *The Big Bang Theory*, they still paled in comparison with *Idol*'s 110,000 comments per episode. The difference reflects the basic appeals of the varying types of shows and the integrated marketing they comprise. Inherently, reality and contest shows rely on social media connections, because viewers already are online to vote for their favorites. Adding comments in another channel thus is simple.

But fans of *The Big Bang Theory* have plenty to say as well. They claim to feel smarter just from watching a show featuring theoretical physicists, and they enjoy repeated references to Sheldon's Rock, Paper, Scissors, Lizard, Spock game. The implications for advertisers are appealing. Even when a show seems to involve only one media channel, it still can attract attention in other realms. In addition, advertisers can communicate with significant numbers of young, hip viewers by buying airtime during various types of shows. Such promise may be particularly appealing for firms whose products do not fit very well with reality shows—and maybe especially those that target a nerd-friendly audience.

Firms can communicate with hip viewers of The Big Bang Theory *through various communication channels.*

Consumers will perceive this giant billboard differently depending on their level of knowledge and attitude toward the brand.

a tweet about the product on Twitter, and so forth. Social & Mobile 17.1 describes another kind of feedback that Mars used in a successful IMC campaign for its M&Ms brand. More simply, though, if Coca-Cola observes an increase in sales, its managers know that the intended audience received the message.

How Consumers Perceive Communication

The actual communication process is not as simple as the model in Exhibit 17.1 implies. Each receiver may interpret the sender's message differently, and senders often adjust their

Social & Mobile Marketing 17.1
Hiring the Newest Chief Chocolate Officer, with Consumers' Help[10]

In the opening vignette, we described one of the great ad campaigns of the 2012 Super Bowl—an event for which the ad rates reached $3.5 million for 30 seconds of airtime. But 111 million people watched Super Bowl XLV, so this massive audience remains appealing for marketers, including Mars, the makers of M&M's. It grabbed the opportunity to respond to consumers' frequent question: "Of all the candy spokescharacters—grumpy Red, innocent Yellow, sexy Green—why was there no Brown?"

In an earlier contest that asked consumers to vote for their favorite character, many responded by asking why they could not vote for brown M&M's. After several years of skipping the Super

Bowl, Mars chose to introduce Ms. Brown, the Chief Chocolate Officer, on this grand stage.

This strategic use of the feedback loop paid off well for Mars. The Just My Shell ad that introduced Ms. Brown won YouTube's Ad Blitz, a contest in which users vote for their favorite commercials. That earned it prime position on YouTube's homepage. Furthermore, approximately one-third of the votes in the Ad Blitz contest came from tablet devices, which gave Mars significant information about how, when, and where consumers were viewing its ads. That is, even as they watched the ad on their television screens during game time, people were logging on to sites using portable devices, which gave advertisers an additional channel through which to reach them.

message according to the medium used and the receivers' level of knowledge about the product or service.

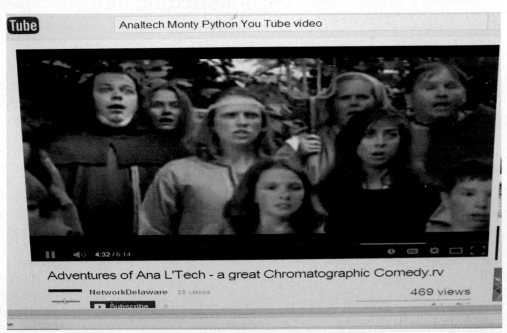

Receivers Decode Messages Differently Each receiver decodes a message in his or her own way, which is not necessarily the way the sender intended. Different people shown the same message will often take radically different meanings from it. For example, what does the image above convey to you?

Online grocery retailer Peapod adjusted its communication medium and message to attract more customers.

If you are a user of this brand, it may convey satisfaction. If you recently went on a diet and gave up your soda, it may convey dismay or a sense of loss. If you have chosen to be a nonuser, it may convey some disgust. If you are a recently terminated employee, it may convey anger. The sender has little, if any, control over what meaning any individual receiver will take from the message.

Senders Adjust Messages According to the Medium and Receivers' Traits Different media communicate in very ways, so marketers make adjustments to their messages and media depending on whether they want to communicate with suppliers, shareholders, customers, or the general public as well as the specific segments of those groups.[11]

For example, the high-technology firm Analtech sells thin layer chromatography plates to companies that need equipment to determine the ingredients of samples of virtually anything. It is not a particularly easy product to explain and sell to laypeople, even though some purchasers might not have a science degree. Therefore, in addition to traditional marketing through trade shows and scientific conferences, Analtech developed a Monty Python–inspired YouTube video (http://www.ichromatography.com/adventuresofana.html) in which a witch overcomes threats to drown her by proving that the ink in the king's decree is actually from the sheriff's pen. It also highlights points in *CSI* episodes when the television detectives rely on its products. With these more broadly popular appeals, Analtech ensures its messages reach and can be received accurately by a wider audience, with less noise than might occur through more scientific appeals.

LO 17-2 Explain the four steps in the AIDA model.

The AIDA Model

Clearly, IMC is not a straightforward process. After being exposed to a marketing communication, consumers go through several steps before actually buying or taking some other action. There is not always a direct link between a particular marketing communication and a consumer's purchase.

Analtech's products are so difficult to understand by non-scientists that it developed a Monty Python-inspired YouTube video in which a witch overcomes threats to drown her by proving that the ink in the king's decree is actually from the sheriff's pen.

To create effective IMC programs, marketers must understand how marketing communications work. Generally, marketing communications move consumers stepwise through a series of mental stages, for which there are several models. The most common is the **AIDA model** (Exhibit 17.2),[12] which suggests that **A**wareness leads to **I**nterest, which leads to **D**esire, which leads to **A**ction. At each stage, the consumer makes judgments about whether to take the next step in the process. Customers actually have three types of responses, so the AIDA model is also known as the think, feel, do model. In making a purchase decision, consumers go through each of the AIDA steps to some degree, but the steps may not always follow the AIDA order. For instance, during an impulse purchase, a consumer may feel and do before he or she thinks.

Awareness Even the best marketing communication can be wasted if the sender doesn't gain the attention of the consumer first. **Brand awareness**

> **Harley-Davidson has top-of-mind awareness if a consumer responds "Harley" when asked about American-made motorcycles.**

refers to a potential customer's ability to recognize or recall that the brand name is a particular type of retailer or product/service. Thus, brand awareness is the strength of the link between the brand name and the type of merchandise or service in the minds of customers.

Coca-Cola already has excellent brand awareness and thus might not have to focus as much effort on this step when it wants to introduce a new flavor or its Free-style machines. Social & Mobile 17.2 highlights how Google used these Freestyle machines to allow customers to send a Coke across the world.

There are several awareness metrics, including aided recall and top-of-mind awareness. **Aided recall** is when consumers indicate they know the brand when the name is presented to them. **Top-of-mind awareness**, the highest level of awareness, occurs when consumers mention a specific brand name first when they are asked about a product or service. For example, Harley-Davidson has top-of-mind awareness if a consumer responds "Harley" when asked about American-made motorcycles. High top-of-mind awareness means that the brand probably enters the evoked set of brands (see Chapter 6) when customers decide to shop for that particular product or service. Manufacturers, retailers, and service providers build top-of-mind awareness by having memorable names; repeatedly exposing their name to customers through advertising, locations, and sponsorships; and using memorable symbols.

As an excellent example of the last method, imagine two smaller circles, sitting on opposite sides atop a larger circle. Did you see Mickey Mouse ears? Did you think of Disney? In addition, the company has moved on to images brighter than circles to ensure that its name comes easily to the front of young consumers' minds. Whether individual acts such as Miley Cyrus, Selena Gomez, or Demi Lovato or groups such as the KSM, Lemonade Mouth, and Allstar Weekend, Disney starts off its stars with Disney Channel shows, records them on the Disney-owned Hollywood Record label, plays the songs in heavy rotation on Radio Disney and Disney movie soundtracks, organizes concert tours with Disney-owned Buena Vista Concerts, and sells tie-in merchandise throughout Disney stores. Each of these marketing elements reminds the various segments of the target market about both the brand (e.g., Hannah Montana, Jonas Brothers) and its owner, Disney. With this multichannel approach, Disney gets the same product into more markets than would be possible with a more conservative approach—further building top-of-mind awareness for both Disney and its stars.[13]

▼ **EXHIBIT 17.2** The AIDA Model

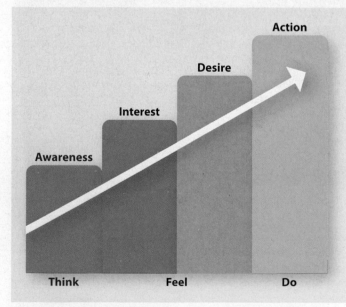

Interest Once the consumer is aware that the company or product exists, communication must work to increase his or her interest level. It isn't enough to let people know that the product exists; consumers must be persuaded that it is a product worth investigating. Marketers do so by ensuring that the ad's message includes attributes that are of interest to the target audience. Disney increases interest in an upcoming tour or record by including a mention, whether casual or not, in the stars' television shows. Because the primary target market for the tour is also probably watching the show, the message is received by the correct recipient.

Desire After the firm has piqued the interest of its target market, the goal of subsequent IMC messages should move the consumer from "I like it" to "I want it." If Allstar Weekend appears on *Good Morning America* (on ABC, which is owned

Social & Mobile Marketing 17.2
Making the Old New by Turning a Classic Campaign into a Mobile Event

I'd like to teach the world to sing
In perfect harmony.
I'd like to buy the world a Coke
And keep it company.

Even if you weren't alive in 1971, when Coca-Cola's famous Hilltop ad premiered, you likely can sing along to its theme song. This enduring familiarity reflects the success of the original ad campaign, which is a significant part of the reason that Google is remixing the notion, both literally and figuratively, in its latest marketing communications.

The utopian ideal behind the Hilltop advertisement and song was that everyone across the world could get along, if only given the chance to share a Coke. Google's new advertising seeks to put that theory to the test by establishing a mobile app that allows people to buy a drink for someone on the other side of the Earth. A user in New York purchases the Coke, and then a specially designed vending machine in Buenos Aires, Argentina, or Cape Town, South Africa, distributes the can to a surprised buyer. In addition, the machine records the recipient's reaction and allows him or her to send a thank-you note, if he or she chooses. After receiving the video of the reaction, the Coke-sender has an option to post it to social media sites to demonstrate the connection made.

Although the program might seem to be advertising for Coca-Cola (and certainly it creates communication about Coke), it is actually a campaign by and for Google, "to show what our technology was capable of, not talk about it," as Google's product marketing manager put it.[14]

The campaign, which Google calls Project Re:Brief, also is not limited to Coke. Google also has put a modern spin on Alka-Seltzer's

Google integrates this classic ad for a classic product into its campaign to highlight its technological capabilities.

classic 1972 "I can't believe I ate the whole thing" advertisement as well as two ads from the 1960s: Volvo's "Drive it like you hate it" and Avis car rental's "We try harder." In the revised Volvo commercial, Google links the car's driver to Google Maps, showing where he has gone as his car approaches 3 million miles on its odometer. The Alka-Seltzer update shows videos of the overeater throughout the day, using links to Google's YouTube service.[15]

The Re:Brief ads thus marry nostalgia with modern conveniences—a combination that Google would love to exploit in all its communications.

When young consumers read the Jonas Brothers' blog, they might beg their parents to buy a concert ticket. The marketing communication drives the customer to take action.

by Disney) and talks about its upcoming activity and how great it is going to be, the viewing audience is all the more likely to demand access—in this case, probably parents who hope to score points with their adolescent children by buying the latest album or reserving seats to an upcoming tour.

Action The ultimate goal of any marketing communication is to drive the receiver to action. If the message has caught consumers' attention and made them interested enough to consider the product as a means to satisfy a specific desire of theirs, they likely will act on that interest by either searching for the product or making a purchase. If young consumers read the Jonas Brothers' blog, they might in turn beg their parents to make an actual purchase of a concert ticket or album related to this favorite Disney Channel show.

The Lagged Effect. Sometimes consumers don't act immediately after receiving a marketing communication because of the **lagged effect**—a delayed response to a marketing communication campaign. It generally takes several exposures to an ad before a consumer fully processes its message.[16] In turn, measuring the effect of a current campaign becomes more difficult because of the possible lagged response to a previous one.[17] For example, Toyota's Prius Goes Plural campaign promotes its addition of a family-sized (Prius v) and urban version (Prius c) of its popular hybrid car model. The campaign demands consumer participation by challenging the viewing public to come up with a plural form of the word *Prius* (e.g., Prii, Prien, Priuses), as touted in online banner and television ads, virtual polling booths, and videos. But the Prius v was not slated for release until six months after the campaign started, and the lag time for the Prius c was even longer. Thus the company might never know for sure whether exposure to this marketing communication actually led consumers to check out or purchase the new vehicles.[18]

Now that we've examined various aspects of the communication process, let's look at how specific media are used in an IMC program.

 check yourself

1. What are the different steps in the communication process?
2. What is the AIDA model?

prius goes plural

Toyota's Prius Goes Plural campaign promotes its addition of a family-sized (Prius v) and urban version (Prius c) of its popular hybrid car model.

ELEMENTS OF AN INTEGRATED MARKETING COMMUNICATION STRATEGY

For any communications campaign to succeed, the firm must deliver the right message to the right audience through the right media, with the ultimate goal of profiting from long-term customer relationships rather than just short-term transactions. Reaching the right audience is becoming more difficult, however, as the media environment grows more complicated.[19]

No single channel is necessarily better than another channel; the goal of IMC is to use them in conjunction so that the sum exceeds the total of the individual channels. However, advances in technology have led to a variety of new and traditional media options for consumers, all of which vie for consumers' attention. Print media have also grown and become more specialized. This proliferation of media has led many firms to shift their promotional dollars from advertising to direct marketing, website development, product placements, and other forms of promotion in search of the best way to deliver messages to their target audiences.

lagged effect A delayed response to a marketing communication campaign.

advertising A paid form of communication from an identifiable source, delivered through a communication channel, and designed to persuade the receiver to take some action, now or in the future.

public relations The organizational function that manages the firm's communications to achieve a variety of objectives, including building and maintaining a positive image, handling or heading off unfavorable stories or events, and maintaining positive relationships with the media.

sales promotions Special incentives or excitement-building programs that encourage the purchase of a product or service, such as coupons, rebates, contests, free samples, and point-of-purchase displays.

LO 17-3 Describe the various integrative communication channels.

We now examine the individual elements of IMC and the way each contributes to a successful IMC campaign (see Exhibit 17.3). The elements can be viewed on two axes: passive and interactive (from the consumer's perspective) and offline and online. Some elements (e.g., advertising, sales promotion, public relations, personal selling, direct and online marketing) are discussed in far more detail in subsequent chapters, so we discuss them only briefly here.

Note that as the marketer's repertoire of IMC elements has expanded, so too have the ways in which marketers can communicate with their customers. So, for instance, direct marketing appears in all four boxes. Firms have expanded their use of these traditional media (e.g., advertising, public relations, and sales promotions) from pure offline approaches to a combination of offline and online.

▼ **EXHIBIT 17.3** Elements of an IMC Strategy

Advertising

Perhaps the most visible of the IMC components, **advertising**, entails the placement of announcements and persuasive messages in time or space purchased in any of the mass media by business firms, nonprofit organizations, government agencies, and individuals who seek to inform and/or persuade members of a particular target market or audience about their products, services, organizations, or ideas.[20] In Chapter 18, we discuss the purpose of advertising and its various types, but for now, we note that advertising is extremely effective for creating awareness of a product or service and generating interest. Mass advertising can entice consumers into a conversation with marketers, though it does not necessarily require much action by consumers, which places it on the passive end of the spectrum. Traditionally, advertising has been passive and offline (e.g., television, magazines, newspapers; see Exhibit 17.3), though recently there has been a growth in online advertising and interactive features. Advertising thus must break through the clutter of other messages to reach its intended audience. To do so, many advertisers rely on certain images; Ethical & Societal Dilemma 17.1 notes the conflict when advertisers use underweight, skinny models in ads they aim at teenaged consumers.

Public Relations (PR)

Public relations is the organizational function that manages the firm's communications to achieve a variety of objectives, including building and maintaining a positive image, handling or heading off unfavorable stories or events, and maintaining positive relationships with the media. Like advertising, this tactic is relatively passive in that customers do not have to take any action to receive it. Public relations activities support the other promotional efforts by the firm by generating free media attention, as we discuss further in Chapter 18.

Sales Promotions

Sales promotions are special incentives or excitement-building programs that encourage the purchase of a product or service, such as coupons, rebates, contests, free samples, and point-of-purchase

Too Skinny

The objective of an integrated marketing communications (IMC) campaign is to build profits by encouraging consumers to purchase more products. But what happens if the campaign leads to harmful behaviors? Companies could claim that shoppers have a choice about the goods they purchase or assert that marketing only influences brand decisions. But sometimes marketing directed at younger consumers complicates that reasoning, because few children or teens can separate unhealthy body images from the popular fashion looks that surround them.

Advertising models have always tended to be thin. But they have become increasingly so in the past decade or so. The tragic deaths of Ana Carolina Reston and Isabelle Caro—two very thin models suffering from anorexia—led some fashion industry leaders to call for a change. That was nearly a decade ago, and still underage and dangerously thin young girls continue to find work as fashion advertising models. The designers and clothing companies continue to hire girls as young as 14 years of age to walk the runway—a clear child-labor law violation according to critics.[21] Even worse, it continues to reinforce the notion that to be beautiful, women and girls need to starve themselves.

These concerns apply not only to the teenaged girls targeted by such ads but also to the models themselves—young girls who are working long hours, subjected to harsh criticisms and widespread rejection. Most child development research suggests that children younger than 16 years are ill-prepared to deal with such scenarios.

In the United Kingdom, the Advertising Standards Authority (ASA) thus has banned some ads outright for being "socially irresponsible." An ad run by Drop Dead, a British clothing line, prompted the watchdog agency to condemn the brand's image: a shockingly thin model who sends dangerously inappropriate style signals to teenage girls. In its statement, the ASA complained that the young model's "hip, rib and collar bones were highly visible" and noted that she had visible (and unnatural) "hollows in her thighs."[22] Under such pressures, some U.K. companies have begun to respond. The fashion brand Topshop removed an ad from its website after advocates complained that the featured model was dangerously gaunt and thus a negative influence on young shoppers.[23]

In the United States, the Council of Fashion Designers of America (CFDA) also has denounced the hiring of underage models, yet violations continue. Recently, it called on designers and modeling agencies to require identification from models, showing that they were at least 16 years old. It also began educating industry members to recognize early signs of eating disorders, called for the provision of healthy snacks backstage, and banned the use of models under 18 years at fittings or photo shows held after midnight. Despite widespread skepticism that the industry can regulate itself, the National Eating Disorders Association has applauded the CFDA guidelines.

Change thus appears to be coming, but slowly still. Designers such as Tommy Hilfiger and Tory Burch complain that the models who apply with them continue to appear young and thin. "I still see some girls coming in who are really emaciated," Burch said. "It's still a problem." Those concerned about the ultra-thin style promoted by fashion advertising for young girls will be watching, but changing the tone of this communication is more challenging than just checking IDs and offering up a snack.

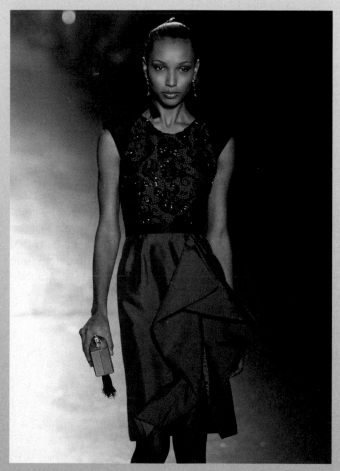

Promoting products using ultra-thin models sends dangerously inappropriate style signals to teenage girls.

displays. Marketers typically design these incentives for use in conjunction with other advertising or personal selling programs. Many sales promotions, such as free samples or point-of-purchase displays, are designed to build short-term sales. Others, such as contests and sweepstakes, have become integral components of firms' CRM programs as a means to build customer loyalty. We discuss such sales promotions in more detail in Chapter 18.

Personal Selling

Personal selling is the two-way flow of communication between a buyer and a seller that is designed to influence the buyer's purchase decision. Personal selling can take place in various settings: face-to-face, video teleconferencing, on the telephone, or over the Internet. Although consumers don't often interact with professional sales people, personal selling represents an important component of many IMC programs, especially in business-to-business (B2B) settings.

The cost of communicating directly with a potential customer is quite high compared with other forms of promotion, but it is simply the best and most efficient way to sell certain products and services. Customers can buy many products and services without the help of a salesperson, but salespeople simplify the buying process by providing information and services that save customers time and effort. In many cases, sales representatives add significant value, which makes the added expense of employing them worthwhile. We devote Chapter 19 to personal selling and sales management.

Direct Marketing

The component of IMC that has received the greatest increase in aggregate spending recently is **direct marketing**, or marketing that communicates directly with target customers to generate a response or transaction.[24] Direct marketing contains a variety of traditional and new forms of marketing communication initiatives. Traditional direct marketing includes mail and catalogs sent through the mail; direct marketing also includes e-mail and mobile marketing.

Internet-based technologies have had a profound effect on direct marketing initiatives. E-mail, for instance, can be directed to a specific consumer. Firms use e-mail to inform customers of new merchandise and special promotions, confirm the receipt of an order, and indicate when an order has been shipped. Currently available technologies also mean handheld devices can function as a payment medium: Just tap your cell phone, and the transaction occurs in much the same way it occurs with a credit card.[25]

The increased use of customer databases has enabled marketers to identify and track consumers over time and across purchase situations, which has contributed to the rapid growth of direct marketing. Marketers have been able to build these databases, thanks to consumers' increased use of credit and debit cards, store-specific credit and loyalty cards, and online shopping, all of which require the buyer to give the seller personal information that becomes part of its database. Because firms understand customers' purchases better when they possess such information, they can more easily focus their direct marketing efforts appropriately. Ethical & Societal Dilemma 17.2 details how companies are targeting consumers with promotions based on their purchasing behavior and how the government has reacted to curb potential abuse.

personal selling
The two-way flow of communication between a buyer and a seller that is designed to influence the buyer's purchase decision.

direct marketing
Sales and promotional techniques that deliver promotional materials individually.

ethical & societal dilemma   17.2

The Consumer Privacy Bill of Rights

Whereas once companies bought ads on websites related to the product being promoted (e.g., a healthy drink on the GNC website), more targeted advertising now pursues a particular customer rather than all visitors to a particular site.[26] Based on web browsing activity and past purchases, a firm such as Target can, for instance, determine with some degree of accuracy who among its customers is pregnant.[27] It can then entice those women or their husbands to visit Target or Target.com and buy baby-related products, using promotions and coupons geared directly to them. But how would these customers react if they were to receive these promotions knowing that Target should have no idea that they were pregnant? Even worse, what would be the

reaction if a targeted promotion was sent to the home of an unwed teenage mother whose father was unaware of the pregnancy?

Because of the changing ways in which firms are using data collected from their customers, the Consumer Privacy Bill of Rights was passed, so that consumers can more easily choose not to be tracked. In particular, consumers now have the following rights:[28]

- **Individual Control** Consumers can control what personal data companies collect and how it is used.
- **Transparency** Consumers should be able to easily find and understand the privacy practices of companies.
- **Context** Companies that collect and use personal data will do so in ways consistent with how consumers provided the data.
- **Security** The use of personal data will not put consumers at risk.

- **Access and Accuracy** Companies should make efforts to make sure that personal data is accurate and provide access to consumers to correct data that is inaccurate.
- **Focused Collection** The collection of consumers' personal data will be limited and restricted by the context of how it was supplied in the first place.
- **Accountability** Companies are responsible to establish systems, train employees, and limit the access of third parties to consumers' personal data. They are responsible both to consumers and enforcement authorities to ensure that this takes place.

Are consumers' personal privacy rights being unjustly invaded by firms that provide them with targeted promotions based on their browsing habits? Or are the marketing firms engaged in these activities just providing them with helpful information that may make their buying decisions more pleasant and efficient?

Companies	Campaign
Dr Pepper HTML5 animation	Using its mobile app, and drawing on its animated television commercials, Dr Pepper presents customers with banner pop-ups of an animated boy enlisting their help in finding his cartoon friends. By using HTML5 animation, Dr Pepper has found a way to keep customers engaged with its ad longer than they normally would.
Herbal Essences Microsoft tags	Herbal Essences launched a mobile campaign to help customers determine the optimal product for their own personal type of hair. In more than 53,000 stores, customers can scan a Microsoft tag with their smart-phones that will bring them to a customized site featuring in-depth information on Herbal Essences, including recommendations for hair types and styling tips.
Volkswagen Augmented reality	Volkswagen has put a new twist on an old print campaign concept. Customers could use their Apple devices to take a virtual test drive of the Passat. By placing their iPhone over the print ad, an animated Passat appears on the road. If customers drive too close to the edges of the road, the iPhone vibrates, simulating the Lane Assist feature. In Adaptive Lights mode, the animated car's headlights follow the edge of the road.
Kimberly Clark Pull-Ups iPad magazine	Although print media are declining, interest in tablet-oriented magazines is increasing. Pull-ups designed multimedia ads for the iPad version of *Parents* magazine to promote its Go Potty application, in which users can color a picture of a mother and child doing The Potty Dance.
Westin Hotels and Resorts Geo-targeted ads	Customers in cold climates using The Weather Channel app see a small banner ad inviting them to "Tap here to warm up," after which they are invited to "wipe away the frost" from their screens. This brings them to images of Westin Hotels in warm areas as well as an opportunity to reserve a room or view their reservations at Westin Hotels.

Source: Adapted from Gisele Tsirulnik, "Top 10 Mobile Advertising Campaigns in Q1," *Mobile Marketer*, April 20, 2011, http://www.mobilemarketer.com/cms/news/advertising/9747.html.

Direct marketing retailers try to target their customers carefully so they will be more receptive to their messages. Omaha Steaks, for example, sends e-mail coupons for items that customers have purchased previously, mails slick pictures of gourmet steaks and meal packages to addresses that have received orders in the past, and calls customers personally during likely gift-giving occasions, such as the holidays, to offer to repeat a previous gift order. These different forms of direct marketing demonstrate how this IMC format can vary on both the interactivity and online/offline dimensions of the matrix.

Mobile marketing is marketing through wireless handheld devices, such as cellular telephones.[29]

Smartphones have become far more than tools to place calls; they offer a kind of mobile computer with the ability to obtain sports scores, weather, music, videos, and text messages as well as purchase merchandise. Marketing success rests on integrating marketing communications with fun, useful apps that are consistent with these consumer attitudes toward mobile devices. In response, firms are steadily improving customers' potential experience with their mobile interface. Exhibit 17.4 highlights five successful mobile marketing campaigns; the Westin mobile campaign is discussed in more detail in Social & Mobile Marketing 17.3.

Online Marketing

We now examine in greater depth several electronic media vehicles: websites, blogs, and social media.

Social & Mobile Marketing 17.3
Getting Tourists to Tap into Hotel Bookings[30]

It was a rough winter. People living in colder climates suffered through snowstorm after snowstorm, broken up only by freezing temperatures and icy winds. Recognizing that a large group of travelers was likely ready to take a break, Westin Hotels offered an easily accessible, aptly targeted campaign that held out the promise of sunshine.

When miserable cold-weather sufferers opened their Weather Channel app on their mobile devices, to see how long the latest cold snap would last, a banner appeared on their screens. "Tap here to warm up," it invites, nearly irresistibly. When their shivering fingers do so, users find the screens on their phones covered by the image of a layer of frost. Wiping it away (virtually) leads them to a carousel of glamorous images of pools, palm trees, and beaches that sit right outside Westin hotels in places like Maui, Scottsdale, Cancun, Fort Lauderdale, Puerto Vallarta, and Palm Springs.

The app is appealing: Users get to play a little when wiping away the frost, and the narrative keeps them entertained, as do the pretty pictures. If they are entranced enough, it also allows them to move directly to the Westin reservation page, of course. Furthermore, the precise targeting—the banner ad only appears to people who have actively chosen to check the weather in cold geographies—and opt-in nature of the app mean that the visitors are already interested in the promise of a warm vacation.

Websites Firms have increased their emphasis on communicating with customers through their websites. They use their websites to build their brand image and educate customers about their products or services as well as where they can be purchased. Retailers and some manufacturers sell merchandise directly to consumers over the Internet. For example, in addition to selling merchandise, Office Depot's website hosts a Business Resource Center for its business customers that provides advice, product knowledge, and connections to networking contacts in other businesses. It also provides forms that businesses can use to comply with Occupational Safety and Health Act (OSHA) requirements, check job applicant records, estimate cash flow, and develop a sexual harassment policy; posts workshops for running a business; and summarizes local and national business news. By providing this information, Office Depot reinforces its image as an essential source of products, services, and information for small businesses.

the quality of the reviews. Research has shown that these online product reviews increase customer loyalty and provide a competitive advantage for sites that offer them.[31]

Blogs A **blog (weblog)** contains periodic posts on a common webpage. A well-received blog can communicate trends, announce special events, create positive word of mouth, connect customers by forming a community, allow the company to respond directly to customers' comments, and develop a long-term relationship with the company. By its very nature, a blog is

> "By its very nature, a blog is supposed to be transparent and contain authors' honest observations, which can help customers determine their trust and loyalty levels."

Many firms operate websites devoted to community building. These sites offer an opportunity for customers with similar interests to learn about products and services that support their hobbies and share information with others. Visitors can also post questions seeking information and/or comments about issues, products, and services. For example, at www.theknot.com, a community site targeting couples planning their weddings, a bride-to-be might ask how to handle an overly zealous bachelor party being planned by the best man. Others who have experienced this problem then can post their advice.

Many firms, especially retailers, encourage customers to post reviews of products they have bought or used and even have visitors to their websites rate

supposed to be transparent and contain authors' honest observations, which can help customers determine their trust and loyalty levels.

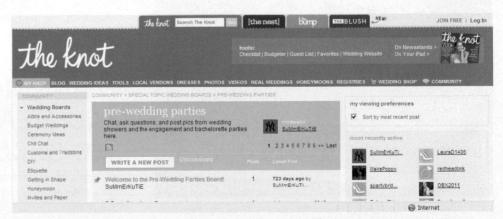

Theknot.com builds a community by allowing brides-to-be to post questions and/or comments about issues such as what to do about an overly zealous bachelor party being planned by the best man.

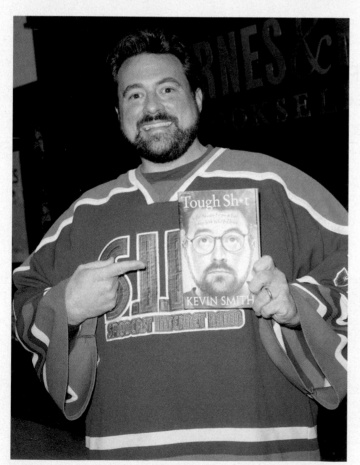

Southwest Airlines' blog, "Nuts about Southwest," is used primarily to connect customers with the company's employees.

Nowadays, blogs are becoming more interactive as the communication between bloggers and customers has increased. Southwest Airlines' blog, "Nuts about Southwest," is used primarily to connect customers with the company's employees, letting them in on the culture and operations. The corporate

When Kevin Smith was removed from a Southwest Airlines flight because his large size required him to purchase two seats, he tweeted to his 1.6 million Twitter followers.

contributors include everyone from mechanics to executives to pilots. The blog is also used to announce new product launches and collect information on which to base corporate decisions.[32]

In addition, blogs can be linked to other social media such as microblog Twitter. Consider the situation in which Kevin Smith, the popular director of films such as *Clerks* and *Dogma* (and the actor who played Silent Bob in several of his movies), was removed from a Southwest flight because his large size required him to purchase two seats. Smith immediately tweeted about the situation to his more than 1.6 million Twitter followers. Then when he got onto another flight, he followed up with a picture of himself, proclaiming "SouthwestAir! Look how fat I am on your plane! Quick! Throw me off!"[33] Southwest quickly responded on its blog, citing its long-standing rules and concern for other passengers. Consumers' responses were about equally split in support of the airline and Smith.[34]

Social Media **Social media** is media content distributed through social interactions (see Chapter 3). The three most popular facilitators of social media are YouTube, Facebook, and Twitter. In these online sites, consumers review, communicate about, and aggregate information about products, prices, and promotions. These social media also allow users to interact among themselves (e.g., form a community) as well as provide other like-minded consumers (i.e., members of their community) and marketers their thoughts and evaluations about a firm's products or services. Thus, social media help facilitate the consumer decision process (Chapter 6) by encouraging need recognition, information search, alternative evaluation, purchase, and postpurchase reviews.

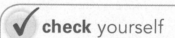

✓ **check** yourself

1. What are the different elements of an IMC program?

PLANNING FOR AND MEASURING IMC SUCCESS

We begin by examining how marketers set strategic goals before implementing any IMC campaign. After they have established those goals, marketers can set the budget for the campaign and choose marketing metrics they will use to evaluate whether it has achieved its strategic objectives.

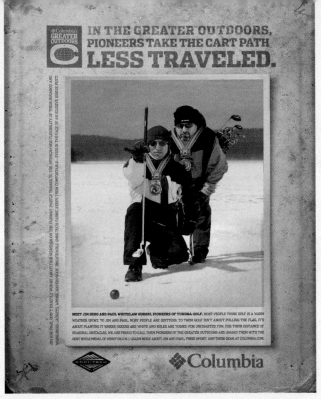

Southwest Airlines' *Grab Your Bag. It's On* campaign's goal is to encourage travelers to fly despite tough economic conditions.

Columbia Sportswear Company's *Greater Outdoors* campaign's goal is to showcase Columbia's technical innovation ability and overcome perceptions of inferior products.

Goals

As with any strategic undertaking, firms need to understand the outcome they hope to achieve before they begin. These goals can be short-term, such as generating inquiries, increasing awareness, and prompting trial. Or they can be long-term in nature, such as increasing sales, market share, and customer loyalty. Selling beverages is always the primary and long-term goal of Coca-Cola, but in the short term, its polar bear advertising campaign (as described in the opening vignette) aimed to establish brand awareness and purchase intentions. Some other goals are outlined in Exhibit 17.5.

Such goals, both short- and long-term, should be explicitly defined and measured. Regardless of their measure or changes, though, goals constitute part of the overall promotional plan, which is usually a subsection of the firm's marketing plan. Another part of the promotional plan is the budget.

▼ **EXHIBIT 17.5** Illustrative Marketing Goals and Related Campaigns

Company and Campaign	Goals	Target Market	Media Used	Outcome
ASICS **Sound Mind, Sound Body**	Branch out beyond serious runner market segment and target casual runners.	Even split males and females, age 30–49	Television and print ads, online advertising	12% increase in market share
Columbia Sportswear Company **Greater Outdoors**	Showcase Columbia's technical innovation ability and overcome perceptions of inferior products.	60% males, age 20–59	Print ads, mobile media, social media, videos, online advertising	1% increase in sales, and +2 point brand awareness increase compared with previous year
GAP **Ready for Holiday Cheer**	Capture consumers' attention and get them to shop in the store during the holiday season.	Even split males and females, age 20–39	Print inserts, television ads, special website, social media, customizable videos	Kelly Awards Best Inset Winner, sales turned from a 12% decline in the previous year to a 1% increase
Southwest Airlines **Grab Your Bag. It's On!**	Encourages travelers to fly despite tough economic conditions.	Even split males and females, all ages	Television, radio, print, and in-airport ads	Contributed $99 million in profits
BMW **Diesel Reinvented**	Overcome the negative image of diesel that most consumers have.	Three segments: idea class, enthusiasts, and environmentally conscious	Print ads, videos	+1,463% year-to-year sales increase

Source: http://www.magazine.org/advertising/case_studies/.

BECAUSE ALL THE METHODS OF SETTING
A PROMOTIONAL BUDGET HAVE BOTH ADVANTAGES
AND DISADVANTAGES, NO ONE METHOD SHOULD BE
USED IN ISOLATION.

LO 17-4 Explain the methods used to allocate the integrated
marketing communications (IMC) budget.

Setting and Allocating
the IMC Budget

Firms use a variety of methods to plan their marketing communications budgets. Because all the methods of setting a promotional budget have both advantages and disadvantages, no one
method should be used in isolation.[35]

The **objective-and-task method** determines the budget
required to undertake specific tasks to accomplish communication objectives. To use this method, marketers first establish a
set of communication objectives, then determine which media
best reach the target market and how much it will cost to run the
number and types of communications necessary to achieve the
objectives. This process—set objectives, choose media, and determine costs—must be repeated for each product or service.
The sum of all the individual communication plan budgets becomes the firm's total marketing communications budget. In addition to the objective-and-task method, various **rule-of-thumb
methods** can be used to set budgets (see Exhibit 17.6).

These rule-of-thumb methods use prior sales and communication activities to determine the present communication budget. Although they are easy to implement, they have various
limitations, as noted in Exhibit 17.6. Clearly, budgeting is not a

simple process. It may take several rounds of negotiations
among the various managers, who are each competing for resources for their own areas of responsibility, to devise a final
IMC budget.

LO 17-5 Identify marketing metrics used to measure IMC
success.

Measuring Success
Using Marketing Metrics

Once a firm has decided how to set its budget for marketing
communications and its campaigns have been developed and
implemented, it reaches the point that it must measure the success of the campaigns, using various marketing metrics.[36] Each
step in the IMC process can be measured to determine how effective it has been in motivating consumers to move to the next
step in the buying process. However, recall that the lagged effect influences and complicates marketers' evaluations of a promotion's effectiveness as well as the best way to allocate
marketing communications budgets. Because of the cumulative
effect of marketing communications, it may take several exposures before consumers are moved to buy, so firms cannot expect too much too soon. They must invest in the marketing
communications campaign with the idea that it may not reach
its full potential for some time. In the same way, if firms cut

▼ **EXHIBIT 17.6** Rule-of-Thumb Methods

Method	Definition	Limitations
Competitive parity	The communication budget is set so that the firm's share of communication expenses equals its share of the market.	Does not allow firms to exploit the unique opportunities or problems they confront in a market. If all competitors use this method to set communication budgets, their market shares will stay approximately the same over time.
Percentage-of-sales	The communication budget is a fixed percentage of forecasted sales.	Assumes the same percentage used in the past, or by competitors, is still appropriate for the firm. Does not take into account new plans (e.g., to introduce a new line of products in the current year).
Available budget	Marketers forecast their sales and expenses, excluding communication, during the budgeting period. The difference between the forecast sales and expenses plus desired profit is reserved for the communication budget. That is, the communication budget is the money available after operating costs and profits have been budgeted.	Assumes communication expenses do not stimulate sales and profit.

When calculating the gross rating points (GRP) of America's Next Top Model, *the advertiser would multiply the reach times the frequency.*

objective-and-task method An IMC budgeting method that determines the cost required to undertake specific tasks to accomplish communication objectives; process entails setting objectives, choosing media, and determining costs.

rule-of-thumb methods Budgeting methods that base the IMC budget on either the firm's share of the market in relation to competition, a fixed percentage of forecasted sales, or what is left after other operating costs and forecasted sales have been budgeted.

frequency Measure of how often the audience is exposed to a communication within a specified period of time.

reach Measure of consumers' exposure to marketing communications; the percentage of the target population exposed to a specific marketing communication, such as an advertisement, at least once.

gross rating points (GRP) Measure used for various media advertising—print, radio, or television; GRP = reach × frequency.

marketing communications expenditures, it may take time before they experience a decrease in sales.

Traditional Media

When measuring IMC success, the firm should examine when and how often consumers have been exposed to various marketing communications. Specifically, they use measures of frequency and reach to gauge consumers' exposure to marketing communications. For most products and situations, a single exposure to a communication is hardly enough to generate the desired response. Therefore, marketers measure the **frequency** of exposure—how often the audience is exposed to a communication within a specified period of time. The other measure used to measure consumers' exposure to marketing communications is **reach**, which describes the percentage of the target population exposed to a specific marketing communication, such as an advertisement, at least once.[37] Marketing communications managers usually state their media objectives in terms of **gross rating points (GRP)**, which represents reach multiplied by frequency (GRP = reach × frequency).

This GRP measure can refer to print, radio, or television, but any comparisons require a single medium. Suppose that Kenneth Cole places seven advertisements in *Vogue* magazine, which reaches 50 percent of the fashion-forward target segment. The total GRP generated by these seven magazine advertisements is 50 reach × 7 advertisements = 350 GRP. Now suppose Kenneth Cole includes 15 television ads as part of the same campaign, run during the program *America's Next Top Model,* which has a rating (reach) of 9.2. The total GRP generated by these 15 advertisements is 138 (9.2 × 15 = 138). However, advertisements typically appear in more than one television program. So, if Kenneth Cole also advertises 12 times during *The Voice,* which earns a rating of 1.8, its GRP would be 1.8 × 12 = 21.6, and the total GRP for both programs would be 138 + 21.6 = 159.6.

Web-Based Media

Firms are spending over $26 billion dollars annually on online advertising, which includes paid search, display ads, e-mail, and sponsorships.[38] Although GRP is an adequate measure for television and radio advertisements, assessing the effectiveness of any web-based communication efforts in an IMC campaign generally requires web tracking software to measure how much time viewers spend on particular webpages, the number of pages they view, how many times users click banner ads, which website they came from, and so on. All these performance metrics can be easily measured and assessed using a variety of software, including Google Analytics.

Facebook also helps companies to see who has been visiting their fan pages, what those people are doing on the fan pages, and who is clicking their advertisements.[39] By keeping track of who is visiting their fan pages, marketers can better customize the material on their pages by getting to know the people visiting.

Planning, Implementing, and Evaluating IMC Programs—An Illustration of Google Advertising

Imagine a hypothetical upscale sneaker store in New York City, called Transit, that is modeled after vintage New York City subway trains. Transit's target market is young, well-educated, hip men and women aged 17–34 years. The owner's experience indicates the importance of personal selling for this market because they (1) make large purchases, and (2) seek considerable information before making a decision. Thus, Jay Oliver, the owner, spends part of his communication budget on training his sales associates.

Advertisers pay Google to show up in the Sponsored Link section in the right-hand column of this screen grab based on the keywords customers use in their searches.

Oliver has realized his communication budget is considerably less than that of other sneaker stores in the area. He has therefore decided to concentrate his limited budget on a specific segment and use electronic media exclusively in his IMC program.

The IMC program Oliver has developed emphasizes his store's distinctive image and uses his website, social shopping, and some interesting community building techniques. For instance, he has an extensive customer database as part of his CRM system from which he draws information for matching new merchandise with his customers' past purchase behaviors and little personal nuggets of information that he or other sales associates have collected on the customers. He then e-mails specific customers information about new products that he believes they will be interested in. He also encourages customers to use blogs hosted on his website. Customers chat about the hot new sneakers, club events, and races. He does everything with a strong sense of style.

To reach new customers, he is using **search engine marketing (SEM)**. In particular, he is using Google AdWords, a search engine marketing tool offered by Google that allows

advertisers to show up in the Sponsored Links section of the search results page based on the keywords potential customers use (see the sponsored link section in the right-hand column of the preceding Google screen grab).

Oliver must determine the best keywords to use for his sponsored link advertising program. Some potential customers might search using the key words, "sneakers," "sneakers in New York City," "athletic shoes," or other such versions. Using Google AdWords, Oliver can assess the effectiveness of his advertising expenditures by measuring the reach, relevance, and return on investment for each of the keywords that potential customers used during their Internet searches.

To estimate reach, Oliver uses the number of **impressions** (the number of times the ad appears in front of the user) and the **click-through rate (CTR)**. To calculate CTR, he divides the number of times a user clicks an ad by the number of impressions.[40] For example, if a sponsored link was delivered 100 times and 10 people clicked on it, then the number of impressions is 100, the number of clicks is 10, and the CTR would be 10 percent.

The **relevance** of the ad describes how useful an ad message is to the consumer doing the search. Google provides a measure of relevance through its AdWords system using a quality score. The quality score looks at a variety of factors to measure how relevant a keyword is to an ad's text and to a user's search query. In general, a high quality score means that a keyword will trigger ads in a higher position and at a lower cost-per click.[41] In a search for "sneaker store," the Transit ad showed up fourth, suggesting high relevance.

▼ **EXHIBIT 17.7** ROI Assessment

(1) Keyword	(2) Clicks	(3) Cost	(4) Sales	(5) Sales Revenue (Col. 4) — Cost (Col. 3)	(6) ROI = (Col. 5/Col. 3) × 100
Sneaker store	110	$10/day	$35/day	$25	250%
New York City sneakers	40	$25/day	$40/day	$15	60%

Communication Objective	Questions	Before Campaign	6 Months After	One Year After
Awareness (% mentioning store)	What stores sell sneakers?	38%	46%	52%
Knowledge (% giving outstanding rating for sales assistance)	Which stores would you rate outstanding on the following characteristics?	9	17	24
Attitude (% first choice)	On your next shopping trip for sneakers, which store would you visit first?	13	15	19
Visit (% visited store)	Which of the following stores have you been to?	8	15	19

Using the following formula, Oliver also can determine an ad's **return on investment (ROI)**:

$$ROI = \frac{\text{Sales revenue} - \text{Advertising cost}}{\text{Advertising cost}}$$

For the two keyword searches in Exhibit 17.7, Oliver finds how much the advertising cost him (Column 3), the sales produced as a result (Column 4), and the ROI (Column 6). For "sneaker store," the Transit website had a lot more clicks (110) than the clicks received from "New York City sneakers" (40) (see Column 2, Exhibit 17.7). Even though the sales were lower for the keywords "sneaker store" at $35/day, versus $40/day for the keywords "New York City sneakers," the ROI was much greater for the "sneaker store" keyword combination. In the future, Oliver should continue this keyword combination, in addition to producing others that are similar to it, in the hope that he will attain an even greater return on investment.

To evaluate his IMC program, Oliver compares the results of the program with his objectives (Exhibit 17.8). To measure his program's effectiveness, he conducted an inexpensive online survey using the questions in Exhibit 17.8, which shows the survey results for one year.

The results show a steady increase in awareness, knowledge of the store, and choice of the store as a primary source of sneakers. This research provides evidence that the IMC program was conveying the intended message to the target audience. ■

check it out!

mhhe.com/GrewalM4e
for study materials, including quizzes and videos.

 check yourself

1. Why is the objective-and-task method of setting an IMC budget better than the rule-of-thumb methods?

2. How do firms use GRP to evaluate the effectiveness of traditional media?

3. How would a firm evaluate the effectiveness of its Google advertising?

advertising, public relations, and sales promotions

f it ain't broke, don't fix it! This conventional wisdom seems so obvious, and so conventional, that it is the rare company that would go against it. And yet when it comes to their advertising, it seems that more and more companies are going after campaigns that already work well, in an attempt to make them even more successful.

In particular, when competition gets heavy between two dominant players in a market, the result is often new, more aggressive advertising. In the orange juice wars for example, the top-selling brand is PepsiCo's Tropicana, which dominates the domestic orange juice market with approximately $1 billion in annual sales.[1] Despite its existing advantage, though, Tropicana wanted to consolidate its lead over Coca-Cola's Simply Orange. Therefore, the brand unleashed a new wave of advertising, with costs of $500–$600 million, in a vigorous attempt to gain even more market share.[2]

LEARNING OBJECTIVES

After reading this chapter, you should be able to:

LO 18-1 Describe the steps in designing and executing an advertising campaign.

LO 18-2 Identify three objectives of advertising.

LO 18-3 Describe the different ways that advertisers appeal to consumers.

LO 18-4 Identify the various types of media.

LO 18-5 Identify agencies that regulate advertising.

LO 18-6 Describe the elements of a public relations toolkit.

LO 18-7 Identify the various types of sales promotions.

For example, Tropicana's Awake to Alive campaign in the United Kingdom suggests its juice as a gentle, natural way to start the day, with the tagline, Tap Into Nature. A family wakens slowly as the soothing voice of an older, British man proffers morning greetings that

continued on p. 394

This Tropicana art installation in London provided three hours of additional "sunlight" and promoted Tropicana orange juice.

continued from p. 393

parallel the phrasing from the beloved children's book, *Goodnight Moon*. "Good morning, morning," he murmurs, against shots of a city asleep, then "Good morning, sideways world," as a man peers from the sheets at his knocked-over digital alarm clock. "Good morning, ruffled hair," he adds, as a woman rises, rubbing her hair, and "Good morning, sleepyheads, everywhere," he says to the child emerging from blankets. As these sleepy actors begin their days with glasses of juice, the reassuring voice promises, "The Tropicana oranges have been gently picked and squeezed. It's time to wake up."

The commercial suggests that the world wakes up to a brighter morning with Tropicana. The wider campaign added an innovative promotional event in London's Trafalgar Square to reinforce the concept. An enormous, orange-sheathed globe resembling a small sun, lit from within, hung in mid-air in the famous site, glowing from just before dawn until early evening on a dreary January day.[3] The January launch was purposeful: "At a really dark and slightly miserable time of year," said Peter Charles, Tropicana's U.K. marketing director, "we wanted to bring us a slice of brightness and really make people feel alive."[4]

Indeed, the art installation provided mid-winter London with three hours of additional "daylight."[5] The whimsical structure, with no mention of orange groves, pulp, fruit growers, or any other such links, was suspended from a cable connected to the famous Nelson's Column (which honors Admiral Horatio Nelson, a Napoleonic War hero). Weighing 2.5 tons and emitting 210,000 watts of light,[6] it did look a little like an enormous orange.

A video of the installation's first public unveiling showed a public enchanted by the warm glow arising from Trafalgar Square.[7] For those who live outside the city or could not make it to the Square that day, Tropicana posted two videos of the day-long spectacle (see www.facebook.com/tropicanajuices). Furthermore, PepsiCo gave away free cartons of Tropicana through a link on its Facebook page.

Tropicana's New York City campaign had a very different tone and style—though the advertising concept was similarly emotional, location-driven, and public, as part of people's daily routines. However, these edgy ads, posted in Penn Station and

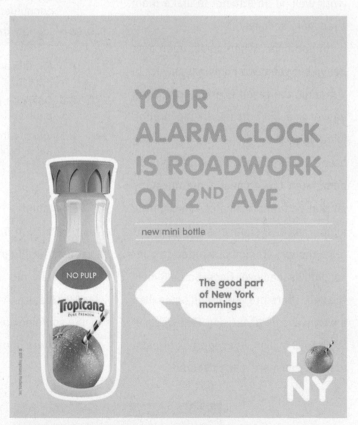

Tropicana's New York City ad campaign reflects the private reality of its inhabitants.

several other well-traveled subway locations, spoke uniquely to Manhattanites.[8]

With a focus on the new mini-carafe container, the ads maintained a simple image, but the copy varied for each panel. The nearly two dozen versions, each just a few words, represented excerpts of the private reality of New Yorkers, always in a hurry ("You woke up 30 minutes early and got to work 30 minutes late") and rarely able to get a good night's sleep in the city ("Your alarm clock is roadwork outside your window"). The copy also empathized with the irritations that beset transit riders, like getting stuck on the platform ("Mariachi band only knows one song") or inadvertently hopping on the wrong train ("You could've sworn you read downtown").[9] Still other ads, in a clear nod to the city's singles community, commented on the occasional embarrassments of Manhattan's dating life ("City of 8 million and you run into that guy" or "One train two ex-boyfriends").

Across these varying, cryptic thought-bites, the consistent refrain was a reminder—pointing to the new mini-carafe—that Tropicana's juice is "the good part of New York mornings." This amusing, rather intimate tone knowingly teased New Yorkers about their morning complaints. Thus the campaign deftly suggested that Tropicana orange juice really understands, and even is a part of, life in the Big Apple. If a company can take the edge off a wintry, dreary day or make an annoying commute a little entertaining, how can it go wrong? ■

> **advertising** A paid form of communication from an identifiable source, delivered through a communication channel, and designed to persuade the receiver to take some action, now or in the future.

> ## "If a company can take the edge off a wintry, dreary day or make an annoying commute a little entertaining, how can it go wrong?"

Advertising is a paid form of communication, delivered through media from an identifiable source, about an organization, product, service, or idea, designed to persuade the receiver to take some action, now or in the future.[10] This definition provides some important distinctions between advertising and other forms of promotion, which we discussed in the previous chapter. First, advertising is not free; someone has paid, with money, trade, or other means, to get the message shown. Second, advertising must be carried by some medium—television, radio, print, the web, T-shirts, sidewalks, and so on. Third, legally, the source of the message must be known or knowable. Fourth, advertising represents a persuasive form of communication, designed to get the consumer to take some action. That desired action can range from "Don't drink and drive" to "Buy a new Mercedes."

Advertising encompasses an enormous industry and clearly is the most visible form of marketing communications—so much so that many people think of marketing and advertising as synonymous. Global advertising expenditures are almost $500 billion, and almost half that amount is spent in the United States. Although expenditures dropped somewhat during the global downturn, advertising remains virtually everywhere, and predictions are that it will continue to grow.[11]

Yet how many of the advertisements you were exposed to yesterday do you remember today? Probably not more than three or four. As you learned in Chapter 6, perception is a highly selective process. Consumers simply screen out messages that are not relevant to them. When you notice an advertisement, you may not react to it. Even if you react to it, you may not remember it later. Even if you remember the ad, you may not remember the brand or sponsor—or worse yet from the advertiser's point of view, you may remember it as an advertisement for another brand.[12]

To get you to remember their ad and the brand, advertisers must first get your attention. As we discussed in Chapter 16, the increasing number of communication channels and changes in consumers' media usage have made the job of advertisers far more difficult.[13] As our opening example about Tropicana's constant efforts, despite its market leadership, demonstrated, advertisers continually endeavor to use creativity and various media to reach their target markets.

As a consumer, you are exposed only to the end product—the finished advertisement. But many actions must take place before you actually get to see an ad, as the Toolkit available online for this chapter will show you. In this chapter, we examine the ingredients of a successful advertising campaign from identifying a target audience to creating the actual ad to assessing performance. Although our discussion is generally confined to advertising, much of the process for developing an advertising campaign is applicable to the IMC media vehicles discussed in Chapter 18. We conclude with some regulatory and ethical

Step 1	Step 2	Step 3	Step 4	Step 5	Step 6	Step 7
Identify target audience	Set advertising objectives	Determine the advertising budget	Convey the message	Evaluate and select media	Create advertisements	Assess impact

issues for advertising, then move on to public relations, sales promotions, and their use.

LO 18-1 Describe the steps in designing and executing an advertising campaign.

Designing and carrying out a successful advertising program requires much planning and effort. Exhibit 18.1 shows the key steps in the process, each of which helps ensure that the intended message reaches the right audience and has the desired effect. Let's examine each of these steps.

STEP 1: IDENTIFY TARGET AUDIENCE

The success of an advertising program depends on how well the advertiser can identify its target audience. Firms conduct research to identify their target audience, then use the information they gain to set the tone for the advertising program and help them select the media they will use to deliver the message to that audience.

During this research, firms must keep in mind that their target audience may or may not be the same as current users of the product. For example, adidas knows that NBA fans likely are at least familiar with its offerings, even if they do not currently purchase sports gear from adidas. Thus some advertisements feature Chicago Bulls guard, Derrick Rose, to encourage them to buy more of the brand's products. But teenaged pop music fans might be less likely to pay attention to sporting goods. So in its marketing, adidas also features Selena Gomez.[14] Another example of marketing and advertising toward different segments (e.g., consumer vs. business users) is illustrated by Visa and MasterCard, which have different ads and offerings aimed at these segments.

STEP 2: SET ADVERTISING OBJECTIVES

Advertising campaign objectives are derived from the overall objectives of the marketing program and clarify the specific goals that the ads are designed to accomplish. Generally, these objectives appear in the **advertising plan**, a subsection of the firm's overall marketing plan that explicitly analyzes the marketing and advertising situation, identifies the objectives of the advertising campaign, clarifies a specific strategy for accomplishing those objectives, and indicates how the firm can determine whether the campaign was successful.[15] An advertising plan is crucial because it will later serve as the yardstick against which advertising success or failure is measured.

Generally, in advertising to consumers, the objective is a **pull strategy** in which the goal is to get consumers to pull the

To target multiple audiences, adidas uses ads featuring both Derrick Rose (left) and Selena Gomez (right).

product into the marketing channel by demanding it. **Push strategies** also exist and are designed to increase demand by focusing on wholesalers, retailers, or salespeople. These campaigns attempt to motivate the seller to highlight the product, rather than the products of competitors, and thereby push the product to consumers. In this chapter, we will focus on pull strategies. Push strategies are examined in Chapters 15, 16, and 19.

All advertising campaigns aim to achieve certain objectives: to inform, persuade, and remind customers. Another way of looking at advertising objectives is to examine an ad's focus. Is the ad designed to stimulate demand for a particular product or service or more broadly for the institution in general? Also, ads

advertising plan
A section of the firm's overall marketing plan that explicitly outlines the objectives of the advertising campaign, how the campaign might accomplish those objectives, and how the firm can determine whether the campaign was successful.

pull strategy
Designed to get consumers to pull the product into the supply chain by demanding it.

push strategy
Designed to increase demand by motivating sellers—wholesalers, distributors, or salespeople—to highlight the product, rather than the products of competitors, and thereby push the product onto consumers.

can be used to stimulate demand for a product category or an entire industry, or for a specific brand, firm, or item. Fiat's U.S. ads suggest its efforts to stimulate demand for specific models, with relevant messages in each case, as Adding Value 18.1 shows. We first look at the broad overall objectives: to inform,

Adding Value 18.1

Jenny from the Block, or Charlie on House Arrest[16]

As Fiat, the Italian car company that purchased Chrysler, increases its presence in the United States, it wants car buyers to recognize its overall brand name. But it also needs to get people excited about each of the models it will be putting on dealers' floors.

The ad campaign began with Jennifer Lopez, who drove her Fiat 500 through Bronx-related scenery, in line with her well-known claim to be "Jenny from the block." But the ads were more sweet than anything, and Fiat realized that it had faltered by making the car look too girly.

Although its next ad featured a woman as well, there was nothing sweet about it. Premiering during the Super Bowl, the Seduction ad for Fiat's Abarth model—the bad boy in its lineup—allowed a nervous-looking fellow to dream of a connection with a striking, tall model, whose scorpion tattoo matched the brand logo. In this campaign, Fiat aimed to capture the spirit of the Abarth, which the firm's chief marketing officer calls "the 'small but wicked' personality of the Fiat." That is, the Jennifer Lopez ad might have helped increase brand awareness, but the Abarth ads offered a different kind of messaging. The Seduction spot originally was not intended for television, but positive feedback on the sexy ad shown online (it received more than 8 million YouTube hits) led Fiat to tap it for the Super Bowl.

The Super Bowl slot was available because the planned ad was not ready. Now that it has emerged, the latest House Arrest ad takes the bad boy image even further by featuring perhaps the most notorious modern celebrity bad boy: Charlie Sheen. His well-publicized, erratic behavior, which prompted his firing from a hit sitcom, has gained him a notable reputation for breaking the rules. But Fiat upends the moral lesson: Sheen races a black Abarth model throughout a mansion before screeching to a stop and emerging from the

car to show off his ankle monitor and claim, "I love being under house arrest." (Notably, the model whom Sheen embraces as he drops his line is the same scorpion-tattooed woman, Catrinel Menghia from the Seduction campaign.)

Pleased with its ability to develop specific and unique images of the models, Fiat plans to persist in its advertising plans for the Fiat 500 and the Abarth separately. The need for consumers to ask for these models has been heightened by failures in other elements of Fiat's marketing campaign, including delayed dealer rollouts and supply chain disruptions. In the meantime, the focus remains on building more awareness of the brand.

Fiat has separate advertising plans for its Fiat 500 and its souped-up, sexy Abarth.

> # IF YOU DECIDE TO BUY TISSUE PAPER, DO YOU CAREFULLY CONSIDER ALL THE OPTIONS, COMPARING THEIR SIZES, PRICES, AND PERFORMANCE, OR DO YOU JUST GRAB THE FIRST THING YOU SEE ON THE SHELF?

persuade, and remind. Then we examine advertising objectives based on the focus of the ad: product versus institutional.

LO 18-2   Identify three objectives of advertising.

Informative Advertising

Informative advertising is a communication used to create and build brand awareness, with the ultimate goal of moving the consumer through the buying cycle to a purchase. Such advertising helps determine some important early stages of a product's life cycle (see Chapter 12), particularly when consumers have little information about the specific product or type of product. Retailers often use informative advertising to tell their customers about an upcoming sales event or the arrival of new merchandise.

Persuasive Advertising

When a product has gained a certain level of brand awareness, firms use **persuasive advertising** to motivate consumers to take action. Persuasive advertising generally occurs in the growth and early maturity stages of the product life cycle, when competition is most intense, and attempts to accelerate the market's acceptance of the product. In later stages of the product life cycle, persuasive advertising may be used to reposition an established brand by persuading consumers to change their existing perceptions of the advertised product. Firms such as Cover Girl often use persuasive advertising to convince consumers to take action—switch brands,[17] try a new product, or even continue to buy the advertised product.

Reminder Advertising

Finally, **reminder advertising** is a communication used to remind or prompt repurchases, especially for products that have gained market acceptance and are in the maturity stage of their life cycle. Such advertising

certainly appears in traditional media, such as television or print commercials, but it also encompasses other forms of advertising. For example, if you decide to buy tissue paper, do you carefully consider all the options, comparing their sizes, prices, and performance, or do you just grab the first thing you see on the shelf? When your grocery store places a display of Kleenex on the end of the paper products aisle, it relies on your top-of-the-mind awareness of Kleenex, which the manufacturer has achieved through advertising. That is, Kleenex tissue paper maintains a prominent place in people's memories and triggers their response, without them having to put any thought into it. The advertising and the end cap display thus prompt you, and many other consumers, to respond by buying a package, just the response Kleenex hoped to attain.

Focus of Advertisements

An ad campaign's objectives determine each specific ad's focus. The ad can be product-focused, might have an institutional focus, or could have a public service focus. **Product-focused advertisements** inform, persuade, or remind consumers

Cover Girl's persuasive ads attempt to motivate consumers to take action: try the product, switch brands, or continue to buy the product.

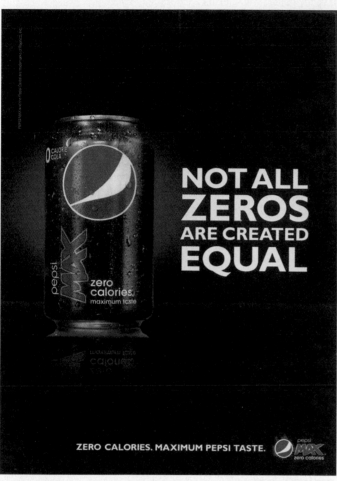

This product-focused advertisement is designed to inform, persuade, or remind consumers about Pepsi Max.

A recent campaign, as exemplified in the ad with Rebecca Romjin and her babies, even promises that drinking milk helps families stay together.[19]

A specific category of institutional advertising is **public service advertising (PSA)**. PSAs focus on public welfare; generally they are sponsored by nonprofit institutions, civic groups, religious organizations, trade associations, or political groups.[20] Like product and institutionally focused advertising, PSAs also inform, persuade, or remind consumers, but the focus is for the betterment of society. As such, PSAs represent a form of **social marketing**, defined about a specific product or service. The Pepsi Max ad shown here is designed to generate sales for Pepsi Max.

Institutional advertisements inform, persuade, or remind consumers about issues related to places, politics, or an industry. Perhaps the best-known institutional advertising campaign is the long-running Got Milk? campaign to encourage milk consumption by appealing to consumers' needs to affiliate with the milk-mustached celebrities shown in the ads.[18] The ads highlight the beneficial properties of milk for building strong bones, which involves a more informative appeal, combined with a mild emotional fear appeal in its assertion that failing to drink milk can lead to medical problems. Its Spanish-language ad campaign, Toma Leche, similarly touts milk as a wonder tonic that fights cavities, sleeplessness, and bone loss.

Now that it's over, there's only one thing I want to do. Repeat. But next season, every other team will be chasing us. So I fuel up to play 60 with the protein in milk. This morning and every morning. That's worth repeating, too.

got milk?
facebook.com/MilkMustache

The Got Milk institutional advertising campaign is used to encourage milk consumption by appealing to consumers' needs to affiliate with milk-mustached celebrities like the Baltimore Ravens' Ray Rice.

ethical & societal dilemma   18.1

Getting to the Truth[21]

Smoking is the single biggest preventable cause of death in the world; someone dies from tobacco use every eight seconds.[22] Smoking causes cancers of the lung, throat, and mouth; it also leads to high blood pressure, heart problems, and lung diseases other than cancer. Yet worldwide, one in five teens between the ages of 13 and 15 years smokes, and many of those smokers will reach for their cigarettes for another 15 to 20 years. What can marketers do to help people avoid or quit this hazardous habit?

As part of the historic tobacco settlement between various states' attorneys general and the tobacco industry, The American Legacy Foundation receives over a billion dollars to educate the public about the dangers of smoking. The Foundation uses this money to fund the truth® campaign, the largest national young antismoking campaign and the only campaign not controlled by the tobacco industry. The campaign's goal is to tell the truth about the tobacco industry, including health effects, marketing strategies, and manufacturing practices. Focused primarily on youths between the ages of 12 and 17 years, the campaign presents facts and allows teens to make their own decisions rather than telling them what they should or should not do.

The campaign had a direct impact on smoking, accelerating the decline in teen smoking during its first two years. Seven years after truth® was launched, research showed that teens exposed to the campaign had a more accurate perception of the number of their peers who smoke. Considering how much most teens want to fit in with their peers, changing perceptions can help reduce the number of young people who pick up a cigarette.

To reach them, truth® uses videos online and in cinemas as well as social media, website games, television integration, radio advertising, and live tours. It has employed scare tactics, such as a pile of body bags piled up in front of Philip Morris headquarters.[23] But it also relies on humor, animation, murals at the SXSW music festival, and Broadway-style song and dance routines to communicate the message.

But is humor the right way to communicate about a subject that kills millions of people each year? Is a pile of body bags an effective way to reach young smokers, who don't believe nicotine-related diseases will happen to them? Is this kind of messaging, which tobacco companies claim is abusive to them and their employees, appropriate or fair? How would you feel if you worked for a tobacco company? How would you feel about tobacco advertising if someone in your family had emphysema from smoking?

---

as the application of marketing principles to a social issue to bring about attitudinal and behavioral change among the general public or a specific population segment.

Although the Got Milk campaign is actually sponsored by sellers of milk, it can claim some PSA elements, in that it touts the improvement of people's health through milk consumption. Another recent PSA campaign is sponsored by Yum Brands, the corporation that owns Pizza Hut, Taco Bell, and KFC. To promote hunger relief efforts, Yum has created World Hunger Relief, with a focus on "fighting hunger, not marketing products."[24] The related PSAs, featuring Christina Aguilera, describe ways to help combat hunger, with no mention of purchasing from the fast-food giants. To expand the reach of the PSA campaign, the CEO of Yum Brands, David Novak, appeared in a separate campaign targeted at the business community. PSAs can also be targeted to decrease consumption. For instance, the Indoor Tanning Is Out campaign is designed to raise awareness of the increased risk of melanoma, the deadliest form of skin cancer, and decrease usage of tanning salons.[25]

Because PSAs are a special class of advertising, under Federal Communications Commission (FCC) rules, broadcasters must devote a specific amount of free airtime to them.

> **For a brand awareness campaign, the objective might be to increase brand awareness among the target market by 50 percent within six months.**

Also, since they often are designed by top advertising agencies for nonprofit clients, PSAs usually are quite creative and stylistically appealing. For example, what is your reaction to the truth public service antismoking campaign summarized in Ethical & Societal Dilemma 18.1?

Regardless of whether the advertising campaign's objective is to inform, persuade, or remind, with a focus on a particular product or the institution in general, each campaign's objectives must be specific and measurable. For a brand awareness campaign, for example, the objective might be to increase brand awareness among the target market by 50 percent within six months. Another campaign's goal may be to persuade 10 percent of a competitor's customers to switch to the advertised brand. Once the advertising campaign's objectives are set, the firm sets the advertising budget.

STEP 3: DETERMINE THE ADVERTISING BUDGET

The various budgeting methods for marketing communication (Chapter 17) also apply to budgeting for advertising. First, firms must consider the role that advertising plays in their attempt to meet their overall promotional objectives. Second, advertising expenditures vary over the course of the product life cycle. Third, the nature of the market and the product influence the size of advertising budgets. The nature of the market also determines the amount of money spent on advertising. For instance, less money is spent on advertising in B2B (business-to-business) marketing contexts than in B2C (business-to-consumer) markets. Personal selling, as we discuss in Chapter 19, likely is more important in B2B markets.

STEP 4: CONVEY THE MESSAGE

In this step, marketers determine what they want to convey about the product or service. First, the firm determines the key message it wants to communicate to the target audience. Second, the firm decides what appeal would most effectively convey the message. We present these decisions sequentially, but in reality, they must be considered simultaneously.

The Message

The message provides the target audience with reasons to respond in the desired way. A logical starting point for deciding on the advertising message is to tout the key benefits of the product or service. The message should communicate its problem-solving ability clearly and in a compelling fashion. In this context, advertisers must remember that products and services solve

TNT . . . We Know Drama

Kellogg's Corn Flakes® Is The Original and Best™ Cereal

The New York Times . . . All The News That's Fit to Print

Trek . . . We Believe in Bikes

Vail . . . Like Nothing On Earth

The selling proposition communicated by the advertising must be not only unique to the brand but also meaningful to the consumer. It furthermore must be sustainable over time, even with repetition.

LO 18-3 Describe the different ways that advertisers appeal to consumers.

The Appeal

According to early theories of rhetoric (the study of the principles and rules of composition), there are three main types of appeals that an argument may use: logos (logical), ethos (ethical), and pathos (emotional). Advertisers similarly use different appeals to portray their product or service and persuade consumers to purchase them, though advertising tends to combine the types of appeals into two categories: informational and emotional.

[People are not looking for 1/4-inch drill bits; they are looking for 1/4-inch holes to hang a picture on the wall.]

problems, whether real or perceived. That is, people are not looking for 1/4-inch drill bits; they are looking for 1/4-inch holes to hang a picture on the wall.[26] Because there are many ways to make a 1/4-inch hole, a firm like Black & Decker must convey to consumers that its drill bit is the best way to get that hole.

Another common strategy differentiates a product by establishing its unique benefits. This distinction forms the basis for the **unique selling proposition (USP)** or the value proposition (as discussed in Chapter 9), which is often the common theme or slogan in an advertising campaign. A good USP communicates the unique attributes of the product and thereby becomes a snapshot of the entire campaign. Some of the most famous USPs include the following:

Red Bull . . . Gives You Wings

Ford . . . Built Tough

Oreo . . . Milk's Favorite Cookie

Chrysler's new USP is "Imported from Detroit."

▼ **EXHIBIT 18.2** Emotional Appeals in Advertising

Emotional Appeal	Company	Example
Fear/Safety	ADT Security	"Breaking into Your Apartment Is Easier than You Think"
Humor	Best Buy	"Game On, Santa"
Happiness	Tropicana	"Awake to Alive"
Love/sex	Axe Body Spray	"Unleash the Chaos"
Comfort	Kleenex	"Softness Worth Sharing"
Nostalgia	Chevrolet	"Chevy Runs Deep"

Informational Appeals

Informational appeals help consumers make purchase decisions by offering factual information that encourages consumers to evaluate the brand favorably on the basis of the key benefits it provides.[27] Thus Exxon Mobil attempts to explain technical aspects of its products, such as lithium ion batteries, hydrogen technology, biofuels, and CO_2-capture technologies, in an attempt to convince consumers that the company is environmentally friendly, efficient, innovative and responsible.[28] This appeal is well suited to this type of product: By informing consumers about a potential source of its competitive advantage, including tangible features and images of science, the advertising copy directly delivers an informational, persuasive message.

Emotional Appeals

An **emotional appeal** aims to satisfy consumers' emotional desires rather than their utilitarian needs. These appeals therefore focus on feelings about the self.[29] Although the term *emotion* often conveys the image of tears, many other effective appeals are used in advertising. The key to a successful emotional appeal is the use of emotion to create a bond between the consumer and the brand. Exhibit 18.2 shows firms and examples of the most common types of emotional appeals: fear, safety, humor, happiness, love (or sex),[30] comfort, and nostalgia.[31]

Chevrolet is providing information to prospective consumers by favorably comparing its Equinox FWD to the Toyota Rav4 4 × 2.

STEP 5: EVALUATE AND SELECT MEDIA

The content of an advertisement is tied closely to the characteristics of the media that firms select to carry the message and vice versa. **Media planning** refers to the process of evaluating and selecting the **media mix**—the combination of the media used and the frequency of advertising in each medium—that will deliver a clear, consistent, compelling message to the intended audience.[32] For example, Macy's may determine that a heavy dose of television, radio, print, and billboards is appropriate for the holiday selling season between Thanksgiving and the end of the year.

Because the **media buy**, the actual purchase of airtime or print pages, is generally the largest expense in the advertising budget, marketers must make their decisions carefully. Television advertising is by far the most expensive. Total U.S. advertising expenditures per medium have remained roughly constant for some time, though some shifts are currently taking place. For example, whereas television advertising is consistent at approximately 45 percent, digital advertising continues to grow and now accounts for 21 percent of spending. Spanish-language media also are growing, but newspaper advertising is rapidly

losing share.[33] To characterize these various types of media, we use a dichotomy: mass and niche media.

LO 18-4 Identify the various types of media.

Mass and Niche Media

Mass media channels include national newspapers, magazines, radio, and television and are ideal for reaching large numbers of anonymous audience members. **Niche media** channels are more focused and generally used to reach narrower segments, often with unique demographic characteristics or interests. Specialty television channels (e.g., Home and Garden TV) and specialty magazines such as *Skateboarder* or *Cosmo Girl* all provide examples of niche media. The Internet provides an opportunity to appeal to the masses through ads on the home page of Internet sites such as www.comcast.net or www.yahoo.com or more niched opportunities such as an American Express business card on *The Wall Street Journal* site (www.wsj.com). In a similar fashion, a billboard advertising McDonald's displays on a major highway would target the masses, but a McDonald's billboard in a specific community would target a more focused niche market.

Choosing the Right Medium

For each class of media, each alternative has specific characteristics that make it suitable for meeting specific objectives (see Exhibit 18.3).[34] For example, consumers use different media

The emotional appeal of Halle Berry's new perfume is love.

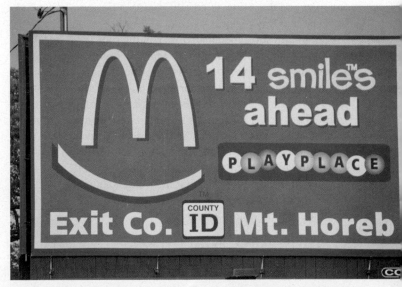

A McDonald's billboard in a specific community, like Mt. Horeb, targets a focused niche market.

advertising schedule
The specification of the timing and duration of advertising.

continuous schedule
Runs steadily throughout the year and therefore is suited to products and services that are consumed continually at relatively steady rates and that require a steady level of persuasive or reminder advertising.

flighting An advertising schedule implemented in spurts, with periods of heavy advertising followed by periods of no advertising.

pulsing Combines the continuous and flighting schedules by maintaining a base level of advertising but increasing advertising intensity during certain periods.

▼ **EXHIBIT 18.3** Types of Media Available for Advertising

Medium	Advantages	Disadvantages
Television	Wide reach. Incorporates sound and video.	High cost. A lot of channel and program options. May increase awareness of competitors' products.
Radio	Relatively inexpensive. Can be selectively targeted. Wide reach.	No video, which limits presentation. Consumers give less focused attention than TV. Exposure periods are short.
Magazines	Very targeted. Subscribers pass along to others.	Relatively inflexible. Takes some time for the magazine to be available.
Newspapers	Flexible. Timely. Able to localize.	Can be expensive in some markets. Advertisements have short life span.
Internet	Can be linked to detailed content. Highly flexible and interactive. Allows for specific targeting.	Becoming cluttered. The ad may be blocked by software on the computer.
Outdoors	Relatively inexpensive. Offers opportunities for repeat exposure.	Is not easily targeted. Has placement problems in some markets. Exposure time is very short.
Direct Marketing	Is highly targeted. Allows for personalization.	Cost can vary depending on type of direct marketing used. Traditional media, like mail, will be more expensive than newer media.

" Airlines, hotels, and car rental companies might continuously advertise to ensure brand awareness but might increase the advertising in spikes during certain low demand periods. "

for different purposes, to which advertisers should match their messages. Television is used primarily for escapism and entertainment, so most television advertising relies on a mix of visual and auditory techniques.

Communication media also vary in their ability to reach the desired audience. For instance, radio is a good medium for products such as grocery purchases or fast food because many consumers decide what to purchase either on the way to the store or while in the store. Because many people listen to the radio in their cars, it becomes a highly effective means to reach consumers at a crucial point in their decision process. As we discussed in Chapter 17, each medium also varies in its reach and frequency. Advertisers can determine how effective their media mix has been in reaching their target audience by calculating the total GRP (reach × frequency) of the advertising schedule, which we discuss next.

Determining the Advertising Schedule

Another important decision for the media planner is the **advertising schedule**, which specifies the timing and duration of advertising. There are three types of schedules, as Exhibit 18.4 displays:[35]

- A **continuous schedule** runs steadily throughout the year and therefore is suited to products and services that are consumed continually at relatively steady rates and that require a steady level of persuasive and/or reminder advertising. For example, Procter & Gamble advertises its Tide brand of laundry detergent continuously.

- **Flighting** refers to an advertising schedule implemented in spurts, with periods of heavy advertising followed by periods of no advertising. This pattern generally functions for products whose demand fluctuates, such as suntan lotion, which manufacturers may advertise heavily in the months leading up to and during the summer.

- **Pulsing** combines the continuous and flighting schedules by maintaining a base level of advertising but increasing advertising intensity during certain periods. For example, airlines, hotels, and car rental companies might continuously advertise to ensure brand awareness but might increase the advertising in spikes during certain low demand periods.

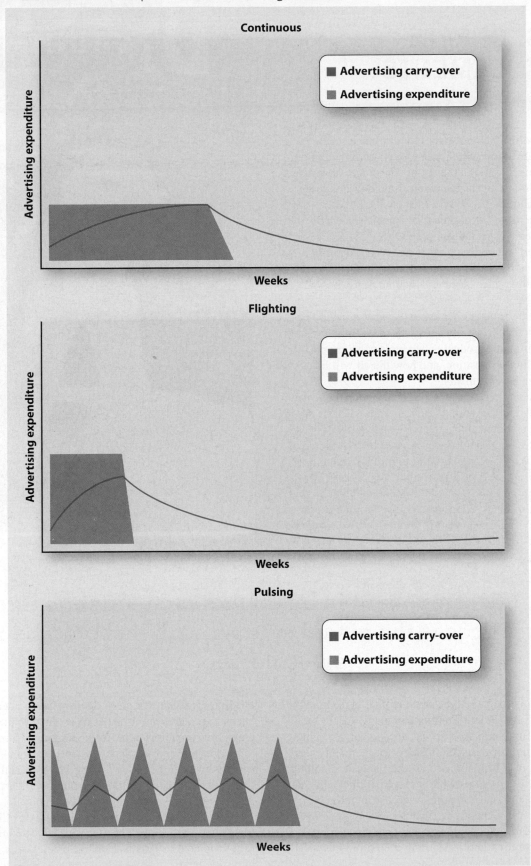

Source: Reprinted with permission from Brand Science Network, http://www.brandsciencenetwork.com/pages/tv_flighting_pattern_works_best.htm.

STEP 6: CREATE ADVERTISEMENTS

After the advertiser has decided on the message, type of ad, and appeal, its attention shifts to the actual creation of the advertisement. During this step, the message and appeal are translated creatively into words, pictures, colors, and/or music. Often, the execution style for the ad will dictate the type of medium used to deliver the message. To demonstrate an image, advertisers can use television and magazines. To promote price, they can use newspapers and radio. To appeal to specific target markets, they can use some of the electronic media vehicles described in Chapter 17. When using multiple media to deliver the same message, however, they must maintain consistency across the execution styles—that is, integrated marketing—so that the different executions deliver a consistent and compelling message to the target audience.

How do advertisers go about creating advertisements? They simultaneously consider the objectives of the ad, the targeted customer segment(s), the product or service's value proposition or the unique selling proposition, and how the ad will be coordinated with other IMC elements.

They then go about creating an ad or the ad campaign. Using the print ad for Duluth Trading Company shown here as an example, the first component that the reader generally notices is the visual, and as such it should be eye-catching. The picture of the shipyard welder denotes tough masculinity. Although it is not always possible to meet all possible objectives with the visual, other important purposes are to identify the subject of the ad, show the product being used and its unique features, create a favorable impression of the product or advertiser, and arouse the readers' interest in the headline, which is generally noticed second.[36]

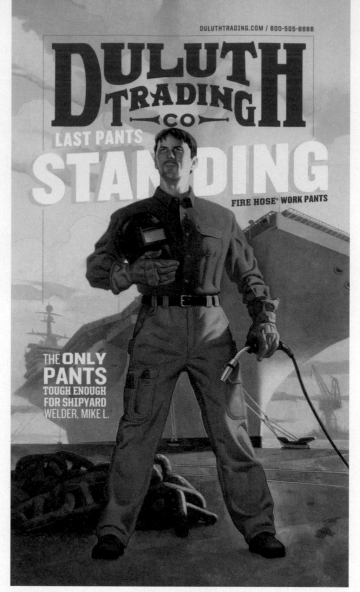

Duluth Trading Company creates powerful ads through simple yet powerful visuals and text.

[The first component in an ad that the reader generally notices is the visual, and as such it should be eye-catching.]

The **headline** is the large type in an ad that is designed to draw attention. In the Duluth Trading Company ad, the headline, Last Pants Standing, works with the visual to connote toughness and durability. But the **subhead**, a smaller headline, provides more information about the pants it is selling; specifically, it is the fire hose workpants. Headlines and subheads should be short and use simple words; include the primary product or service benefits, the name of the brand, and an interest-provoking idea. It should ideally contain an action verb and give enough information for learning even if only the headline is read.

The **body copy** represents the main text portion of the ad. It is used to build on the interest generated by the visual and

headlines, explains in more depth what the headline and subheads introduced, arouses desire for the product, and provides enough information to move the target consumer to action. In this case, the body copy, "The only pants tough enough for shipyard welder, Mike L," is short but powerful.

Finally, the ad typically has a number of **brand elements** that identify the sponsor of the ad, typically through a logo (Duluth Trading Company) and a unique selling proposition (not found in this ad). The advertiser must convey its message using compelling visuals, headlines, body copy, and identifying brand elements.

Although creativity plays a major role in the execution stage, advertisers must remain careful not to let their creativity

Although the Chevy Malibu offers a fuel-efficient hybrid model, it is positioned as a family sedan.

Ads for the new Ford Fusion emphasize fuel economy as well as interesting technology that it hopes will appeal to young consumers.

overshadow the message. Whatever the execution style, the advertisement must be able to attract the audience's attention, provide a reason for the audience to spend its time viewing the advertisement, and accomplish what it set out to do. In the end, the execution style must match the medium and objectives.

Automobile manufacturers and dealers are among the most active advertisers and use very different messages in their advertising campaigns. Consider, for instance, two well-known car companies that recently introduced new four-door sedan models, each with very different advertising campaigns.

- **Chevrolet Malibu.** Another entry into the hybrid market, the Malibu employs a battery pack and offers good gas mileage. It is also positioned as a family sedan, though the most recent revamping reduced the size of the backseat. Likely advertising outlets include family-oriented magazines and television spots.

- **Ford Fusion.** With a focus on fuel economy, ads for the new Fusion promise its availability with both a hybrid and a conventional engine. Furthermore, it emphasizes Ford's SYNC technology which uses voice recognition to make phone calls, find and play music, and get directions. With these appeals, Ford is focusing largely on social media to get young consumers, who tend to care about technology and environmental concerns, attached to the new model.[37]

At times, though, even when advertisers think they have done their best to appeal to consumers, their actions can backfire, as Ethical & Societal Dilemma 18.2 describes.

STEP 7: ASSESS IMPACT USING MARKETING METRICS

The effectiveness of an advertising campaign must be assessed before, during, and after the campaign has run. **Pretesting** refers to assessments performed before an ad campaign is implemented to ensure that the various elements are working in an integrated fashion and doing what they are intended to do.[38] **Tracking** includes monitoring key indicators, such as daily or weekly sales volume, while the advertisement is running to shed light on any problems with the message or the medium. **Posttesting** is the evaluation of the campaign's impact after it is has been implemented. At this last stage, advertisers assess the sales and/or communication impact of the advertisement or campaign.

Measuring sales impact can be especially challenging because of the many influences other than advertising on consumers'

> "The effectiveness of an advertising campaign must be assessed before, during, and after the campaign has run."

lift Additional sales caused by advertising.

choices, purchase behavior, and attitudes. These influences include the level of competitors' advertising, economic conditions in the target market, sociocultural changes, in-store merchandise availability and even the weather, all of which can influence consumer purchasing behavior. For instance, the sales resulting from even the best ads can be foiled by a lack of merchandise in the stores or a blizzard. Advertisers must try to identify these influences and isolate those of the particular advertising campaign.

For frequently purchased consumer goods in the maturity stage of the product life cycle such as soda, sales volume offers a good indicator of advertising effectiveness. Because their sales are relatively stable, and if we assume that the other elements of the marketing mix and the environment have not changed, we

Sales volume is a good indicator of advertising effectiveness for frequently purchased consumer goods in the maturity stage of the product life cycle, such as Red Bull energy drink.

can attribute changes in sales volume to changes in advertising. Exhibit 18.5 illustrates a hypothetical sales history for Red Bull in a grocery store chain. Using a statistical technique called

time-series analysis, sales data from the past is used to forecast the future. The data in Exhibit 18.5 can be decomposed into its basic trend (green), the seasonal influences (red), and the **lift** or additional sales caused by the advertising (orange). In this case, the lift caused by the advertising campaign is substantial.

For other types of goods in other stages of the product life cycle, sales data offer but one of the many indicators that marketers need to examine to determine advertising effectiveness. For instance, in high-growth markets, sales growth alone can be misleading because the market as a whole is growing. In such a situation, marketers measure sales relative to those of competitors to determine their relative market share. Firms find creative ways to identify advertising effectiveness. For example, digital cable allows them to present a specific advertisement to certain neighborhoods and then track sales by local or regional retailers.

✓ check yourself

1. What are the steps involved in planning an ad campaign?
2. What is the difference between informational, persuasive, and reminder advertising?
3. What are the pros and cons of the different media types?
4. How can the effectiveness of advertising be evaluated?

ethical & societal dilemma 18.2

When Makeup Companies Really Do Make Up Models' Faces

Is Julia Roberts really that good looking? Of course, she's beautiful, but the portrayal of her face in advertising has, more likely than not, been given a Photoshop fix. Airbrushing may be as old as advertising, but improved technology makes the changes nearly imperceptible—can you tell the difference between the normal thickness of an eyelash and the version that Taylor Swift sported in a CoverGirl NatureLeuxe Mousse Mascara ad? Ultimately, the National Advertising Division of the Council of Better Business Bureaus ruled the ad was misleading,[39] prompting the brand to pull the ad.

But in other cases, cosmetics and fashion companies claim that fixing elements of appearance is both ubiquitous and expected by

When selling cosmetics, is it ethical to touch up photos of models and celebrities like Julia Roberts to make them even more beautiful?

consumers. They assert they are not misleading anyone but rather creating a perfect image for their brand. So is it wrong for cosmetic companies to retouch ads, brushing away wrinkles and skin imperfections digitally?[40]

The U.K. Advertising Standards Agency considers touching up photos in ads to be wrong. That oversight agency banned two ads by L'Oreal recently, charging that they were misleading. One ad featured Julia Roberts promoting Teint Miracle, a new Lancome skin product that, according to the company, provides "luminosity to the skin." The other featured the model Christy Turlington, promoting a cosmetic concealer called Eraser that promises to hide wrinkles and skin discoloration. Although the company protested that the ads did not exaggerate their product effectiveness, the U.K. Advertising Standards Agency was not convinced.[41]

Do consumers want realistic images and measured promises, or do they accept and even prefer exaggerated claims and unrealistic images of beauty?

▼ **EXHIBIT 18.5** Sales History for Red Bull in a Grocery Store Chain

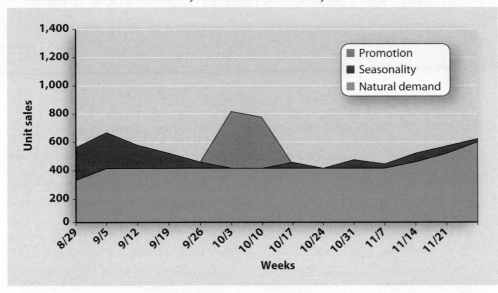

- ■ Promotion
- ■ Seasonality
- ■ Natural demand

LO 18-5   Identify agencies that regulate advertising.

REGULATORY AND ETHICAL ISSUES IN ADVERTISING

In the United States, the regulation of advertising involves a complex mix of formal laws and informal restrictions designed to protect consumers from deceptive practices.[42] Many federal and state laws, as well as a wide range of self-regulatory agencies and agreements, affect advertising (Exhibit 18.6). The primary federal agencies that regulate advertising activities are the Federal Trade Commission (FTC), Federal Communications Commission (FCC), and Food and Drug Administration (FDA). In addition to these agencies, others, such as the Bureau of Alcohol, Tobacco, and Firearms and the U.S. Postal Service, regulate advertising to some degree.

The FTC is the primary enforcement agency for most mass media advertising. Occasionally, it cooperates with other agencies to investigate and enforce regulations on particular advertising practices. For example, when the Smart Choices program logo, which was designed to indicate healthier foods, somehow appeared on boxes of Fruit Loops, the FTC relied on the FDA. The confusion and apparent lack of regulation, along with consumer complaints, led the FDA to issue warning letters that asked manufacturers to review their nutrition labels and claims for accuracy. The program also was suspended while the FDA reviewed the claims that the logos implied.[43]

Many product categories fall under self-regulatory restrictions or guidelines. For example, advertising to children is regulated primarily through self-regulatory mechanisms designed by the National Association of Broadcasters and the

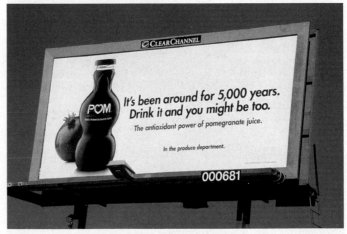

Is this ad an example of puffery or deception?

▼ **EXHIBIT 18.6** Federal Agencies That Regulate Advertising

Federal Agency	General Purpose	Specific Jurisdiction
Federal Trade Commission (FTC) (established 1914)	Enforces federal consumer protection laws.	Enforces truth in advertising laws; defines deceptive and unfair advertising practices.
Federal Communications Commission (FCC) (1934)	Regulates interstate and international communications by radio, television, wire, satellite, and cable.	Enforces restrictions on broadcasting material that promotes lotteries (with some exceptions); cigarettes, little cigars, or smokeless tobacco products; or that perpetuates a fraud. Also enforces laws that prohibit or limit obscene, indecent, or profane language.
Food and Drug Administration (1930)	Regulates food, dietary supplements, drugs, cosmetics, medical devices (including radiation-emitting devices such as cell phones), biologics (biological issues), and blood products.	Regulates package labeling and inserts, definition of terms such as *light* and *organic,* and required disclosure statements (warning labels, dosage requirements, etc.).

"EVENTS SUCH AS THE OSCARS, WITH ITS 35 MILLION ANNUAL VIEWERS, PROVIDE AN UNPARALLELED OPPORTUNITY TO SHOWCASE THE EMOTIONAL BENEFITS OF THE BRAND AND MAKE OTHERS WANT TO BE A PART OF IT."

Better Business Bureau's Children's Advertising Review Unit. The only formal regulation of children's advertising appears in the Children's Television Act of 1990, which limits the amount of advertising broadcast during children's viewing hours.[44]

Recently, to make matters even more complicated for advertisers, state attorneys general's offices have begun to inquire into various advertising practices and assert their authority to regulate advertising in their states. The EU also has increased its regulation of advertising for EU member nations. Many of these state and European regulations are more restrictive than existing U.S. federal requirements.

When Fergie arrived at the 52nd Annual Grammy Awards, she generated positive PR for the designer clothing, shoes, and bag she was wearing.

The line between what is legal and illegal is more difficult to discern when it comes to **puffery**, which is the legal exaggeration of praise, stopping just short of deception, lavished on a product. When Match.com claims that it leads to Better First Dates, it's puffery, because *better* is a subjective measure. But if it claims it produces More Second Dates, it must be able to back up its numerical, quantitative assertion. Even cartoon bears must follow the rules: Charmin's animated spokescharacters need to be drawn with a few pieces of toilet paper on their rears, instead of none, to ensure that Charmin's claims only extend to leaving less toilet paper behind than other brands (puffery), not eliminating the problem altogether (deception).[45]

How do the courts determine what makes an ad deceptive, rather than simply puffery? The FTC's position is that it "will not pursue cases involving obviously exaggerated or puffing representations, i.e., those that ordinary consumers do not take seriously."[46] In general, the less specific the claim, the less likely it is considered to be deceptive. In the end, puffery is acceptable as long as consumers know that the firm is stretching the truth through exaggeration.[47]

PUBLIC RELATIONS

As you may recall from Chapter 17, **public relations (PR)** involves managing communications and relationships to achieve various objectives, such as building and maintaining a positive image of the firm, handling or heading off unfavorable stories or events, and maintaining positive relationships with the media. In many cases, public relations activities support other promotional efforts by generating free media attention and general goodwill.

Designers, for example, vie to have celebrities, especially those nominated for awards, wear their fashions on the red carpet. Their brands offer intangible benefits, not just functional benefits. Events such as the Oscars, with its 35 million annual viewers, provide an unparalleled opportunity to showcase the emotional benefits of the brand and make others want to be a part of it. Thus, the celebrities that designers pursue and offer their items are those that will sell the most or provide the best iconic images. When Fergie wore an Emilio Pucci dress to the Grammys, paired with a Judith Leiber clutch, both brands sent out press releases to make sure everyone knew.[48] The placement of designer apparel at media events benefits both the designer and the celebrity. And neither happens by accident. Public relations people on both

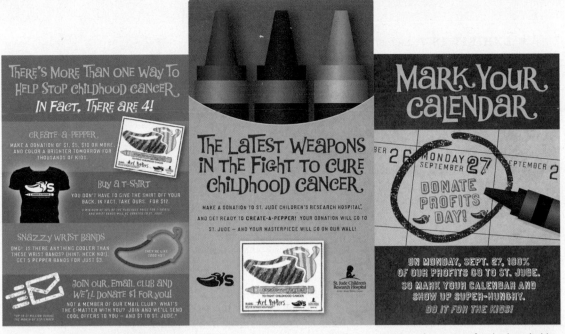

Chili's partners with St. Jude's Research Hospital in a cause-related marketing program to raise money for the hospital by donating its profits on the last Monday of September.

sides help orchestrate the events to get the maximum benefit for both parties.

Good PR has always been an important success factor. Yet in recent years, the importance of PR has grown as the cost of other forms of marketing communications has increased. At the same time, the influence of PR has become more powerful as consumers have become increasingly skeptical of marketing claims made in other media.[49] In many instances, consumers view media coverage generated through PR as more credible and objective than any other aspects of an IMC program because the firm does not buy the space in print media or time on radio or television.

Certainly the Chili's restaurant chain conducts plenty of media buys in traditional advertising spaces. But it also has partnered, since 2004, with St. Jude's Research Hospital in one of the most successful examples of **cause-related marketing** (i.e., commercial activity in which businesses and charities form a partnership to market an image, product, or service for their mutual benefit)[50] in history. For several years, the restaurant has offered customers the opportunity to purchase a paper icon, in the shape of a chili, natch, that they may color and hang on restaurant walls. The cause marketing campaign runs in September, which is also National Childhood Cancer Awareness Month. On the last Monday of the month, the restaurant puts its money where its mouth is and donates all its profits on sales during the day to St. Jude. In addition to the relatively common Create-a-Chili paper icons, employees of the restaurants make and sell customized T-shirts and wristbands. Chili's also hosts a dedicated website, www.createapepper.com, where civic-minded consumers can purchase or donate more as well as buy St. Jude–branded Chili's gift cards.[51]

Another very popular PR tool is event sponsorship. **Event sponsorship** occurs when corporations support various activities (financially or otherwise), usually in the cultural or sports and entertainment sectors. Red Bull is a frequent sponsor of various kinds of sports events, such as Red Bull Air Race and numerous extreme sports events (e.g., cliff diving). Some of them are big name events; the titles of most college football playoff games now include the name of their sponsors (e.g., the Allstate Sugar Bowl). Others are slightly less famous; for example, Rollerblade USA, the maker

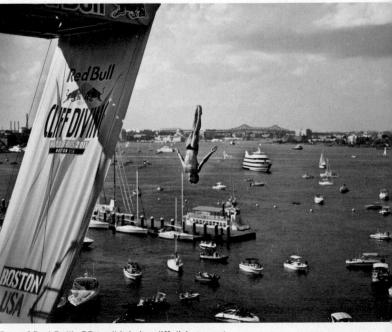

Part of Red Bull's PR toolkit is its cliff diving event.

EXHIBIT 18.7 Elements of a Public Relations Toolkit

PR Element	Function
Publications: Brochures, special-purpose single-issue publications such as books	Inform various constituencies about the activities of the organization and highlight specific areas of expertise.
Video and audio: Programs, public service announcements	Highlight the organization or support cause-related marketing efforts.
Annual reports	Give required financial performance data and inform investors and others about the unique activities of the organization.
Media relations: Press kits, news releases, speeches, event sponsorships	Generate news coverage of the organization's activities or products/services.
Electronic media: Websites, e-mail campaigns	Websites can contain all the previously mentioned toolbox elements while e-mail directs PR efforts to specific target groups.

sales promotions Special incentives or excitement-building programs that encourage the purchase of a product or service, such as coupons, rebates, contests, free samples, and point-of-purchase displays.

coupons Provides a stated discount to consumers on the final selling price of a specific item; the retailer handles the discount.

deal A type of short-term price reduction that can take several forms, such as a "featured price," a price lower than the regular price; a "buy one, get one free" offer; or a certain percentage "more free" offer contained in larger packaging; can involve a special financing arrangement, such as reduced percentage interest rates or extended repayment terms.

premium An item offered for free or at a bargain price to reward some type of behavior, such as buying, sampling, or testing.

of Rollerblade in-line skates, sponsors Skate-In-School, a program it developed with the National Association for Sport and Physical Education (NAPSE) to promote the inclusion of rollerblading in physical education curricula.

LO 18-6 Describe the elements of a public relations toolkit.

Firms often distribute a PR toolkit to communicate with various audiences. Some toolkit elements are designed to inform specific groups directly, whereas others are created to generate media attention and disseminate information. We depict the various elements of a PR toolkit in Exhibit 18.7.

check yourself

1. Why do companies use public relations as part of their IMC strategy?
2. What are the elements of a public relations toolkit?

LO 18-7 Identify the various types of sales promotions.

SALES PROMOTION

Advertising rarely provides the only means to communicate with target customers. As we discussed in Chapter 17, a natural link appears between advertising and sales promotion. **Sales promotions** are special incentives or excitement-building programs that encourage consumers to purchase a particular product or service, typically used in conjunction with other advertising or personal selling programs. Many sales promotions, like free samples or point-of-purchase (POP) displays, attempt to build short-term sales, whereas others, such as loyalty programs, contests, and sweepstakes, have become integral components of firms' long-term customer relationship management (CRM) programs, which they use to build customer loyalty.

We present these sales promotions tools next. The tools of any sales promotion can be focused on any channel member—wholesalers, retailers, or end-user consumers. Just as we delineated for advertising, when sales promotions are targeted at channel members, the marketer is employing a push strategy; when it targets consumers themselves, it is using a pull strategy. Some sales promotion tools can be used with either a push or pull strategy. We now consider each of the tools and how they are used.

Types of Sales Promotion

Coupons **Coupons** offer a discount on the price of specific items when they're purchased. Coupons are issued by manufacturers and retailers in newspapers, on products, on the shelf, at the cash register, over the Internet, and through the mail to stimulate demand. Some retailers have linked their coupons directly to their loyalty programs. The drugstore chain CVS tracks customers' purchases when they use their Extra Care loyalty card and gives them coupons that are tailored just for them and their unique needs.[52] If a customer typically spends a small amount during each shopping trip, he or she might receive coupons to encourage larger purchases, such as buy one, get one free.

Internet sites also provide customers with instant coupons of their choosing. Imagine a customer who visits her local Walmart and finds a Hot Wheels video game for $29.99. By scanning the bar code, using her cell phone, she connects to ShopSavvy.com and finds that same item, at a Target store a mile away, is only $19.99. Another scan and a connection to MyCoupons.com provides her with a $10 coupon—which means she's saved $20 in a matter of minutes and just a few clicks.

This sales promotion deal for Payless ShoeSource is a short-term price promotion that encourages customers to buy a second pair of shoes at one-half off.

The Old Spice Guy campaign attracted consumer attention, and sales of Old Spice jumped. But the company offered so many buy one, get one free deals at the same time that the potential profit impact of the great ads was essentially eliminated by the costs of the deals.

> "The Old Spice company offered so many buy one, get one free deals at the same time that the potential profit impact of the great ads was essentially eliminated by the costs of the deals."

Some coupons, whether printed from the Internet or sent to mobile phones, also contain information about the customer who uses it.[53] The bar code may identify the customer, his or her Internet address, Facebook page information, and even the search terms the customer used to find the coupon in the first place. These new breeds of coupons may look standard, but they offer up a startling amount of data, which promises benefits for advertisers who want to target their marketing more closely. Traditionally, coupons had low redemption rates and were therefore a relatively inexpensive sales promotion tool, but firms like Groupon have resulted in higher redemption rates, increasing their expense.

Deals A **deal** refers generally to a type of short-term price reduction that can take several forms, such as a featured price, a price lower than the regular price; a buy one, get one free offer; or a certain percentage more free offer contained in larger packaging. Another form of a deal involves a special financing arrangement, such as reduced percentage interest rates or extended repayment terms. Deals encourage customers to try a product because they lower the risk for consumers by reducing the cost of the good.

But deals can also alter perceptions of value—a short-term price reduction may signal a different price/quality relationship than would be ideal from the manufacturer's perspective. In addition, as Old Spice learned, offering too many deals can offset likely gains. Its popular Old Spice Guy campaign attracted consumer attention through funny television commercials and interactive online campaigns, and sales of Old Spice jumped. But the company offered so many buy one, get one free deals at the same time that the potential profit impact of the great ads was essentially eliminated by the costs of the deals.[54]

Premiums A **premium** offers an item for free or at a bargain price to reward some type of behavior, such as buying, sampling, or testing. These rewards build goodwill among consumers, who often perceive high value in them. Premiums can be distributed in a variety of ways: They can be included in the product packaging, such as the toys inside cereal boxes; placed visibly on the package, such as a coupon for free milk on a box of Cheerios; handed out in the store; or delivered in the mail, such as the free perfume offers Victoria's Secret mails to customers. Furthermore, premiums can be very effective if they are consistent with the brand's message and image and highly desirable to the target market. However, finding a premium that meets these criteria at a reasonable cost can be a serious challenge.

Contests A **contest** refers to a brand-sponsored competition that requires some form of skill or effort. ESPN's website hosts a page devoted just to sports-related contests: Get me to the World Cup sponsored by Sony or Player of the month presented by Kia.[55] For the Get Me to the World Cup contest, each participant must create and upload a short video demonstrating why he or she should be the one picked to attend the international event. For those who need some help sparking their creativity, ESPN provides some sample videos—including one by Kobe Bryant. Similarly, Nivea held a contest to win tickets to see Rihanna in concert. Since contests require consumer involvement, they can create a lot of excitement or buzz around a product or service.

Sweepstakes A form of sales promotion that offers prizes based on a chance drawing of entrants' names, **sweepstakes**

[Retailers have long recognized that the most valuable real estate in the store is at the POP (point of purchase) since they increase product visibility and encourage trial.]

Nivea uses contests, such as a chance to win tickets to see Rihanna, to promote their products.

do not require the entrant to complete a task other than buying a ticket or filling out a form. For example, fans who purchased movie tickets to see *Dolphin Tale* from the Fandango website were automatically entered into a sweepstakes for a family vacation to St. Petersburg, Florida, where the movie's star Winter—a dolphin fitted with a prosthetic tail—lives. Often the key benefit of sweepstakes is that they encourage current consumers to consume more if the sweepstakes form appears inside the packaging or with the product. Many states, however, specify that no purchase can be required to enter sweepstakes.

Samples **Sampling** offers potential customers the opportunity to try a product or service before they make a buying decision. Distributing samples is one of the most costly sales promotion tools but also one of the most effective. Quick service restaurants and grocery stores frequently use sampling. For instance, Starbucks provides samples of new products to customers. Costco uses so many samples that customers

Axeman, the new personalized gaming experience from AXE, lets users play their own music while earning points to redeem more than 1.2 million dollars in real rewards from Planet AXE.

can have an entire meal. Sometimes trial-size samples come in the mail or are distributed in stores.

Loyalty Programs

Loyalty Programs As part of a sales promotion program, **loyalty programs** are specifically designed to retain customers by offering premiums or other incentives to customers who make multiple purchases over time. Well-designed loyalty programs encourage consumers to increase their engagement and purchases from a given firm. Such sales promotions are growing increasingly popular and are tied to long-term CRM systems. (Loyalty programs are examined in Chapters 2 and 3.) These programs need to be carefully managed because they can be quite costly.

Point-of-Purchase Displays

Point-of-Purchase Displays **Point-of-purchase (POP) displays** are merchandise displays located at the point of purchase, such as at the checkout counter in a supermarket. Retailers have long recognized that the most valuable real estate in the store is at the POP (point of purchase) since they increase product visibility and encourage trial. Customers see products such as a magazine or a candy bar while they are waiting to pay for their purchases and impulsively purchase them. In the Internet version of a point-of-purchase display, shoppers are stimulated by special merchandise, price reductions, or complementary products that Internet retailers feature on the checkout screen.

Rebates **Rebates** are a particular type of price reduction in which a portion of the purchase price is returned by the seller to the buyer in the form of cash. Many products, such as consumer electronics, offer significant mail-in rebates that may lower the price of the item significantly. Some companies enjoy the added exposure when they appear on consumer websites like PriceGrabber.com and Nextag.com, where products are sorted by the price, with links to the retailer's website. Firms offer such generous rebates because the likelihood that consumers will actually apply for the rebate is low. The firms garner considerable value from rebates because they attract consumers and therefore stimulate sales, but they may not have to pay off all the rebates offered.

Product Placement When marketers use **product placement**, they pay to have their product included in nontraditional situations, such as in a scene in a movie or television program.[56] By doing so, they increase the visibility of their products. Product placement may be subtly placed, such as when American Idol judges are seen drinking Coca-Cola. On CBS's *The Big Bang Theory*, not only do scenes regularly show the characters working and eating there, but Sheldon also asserts his need to get "access to the Cheesecake Factory walk-in freezer."

A new Bollywood film is taking the approach further, though. In the popular roadtrip film *Zindagi Na Milegi Dobara* (*You Only Live Once*), the lead characters are inspired by a Spanish flamenco dancer and proceed through a series of adventures in Seville, Costa Brava, Pamplona, and other locations in Spain. The selection of these locales was made not by the film's writers or its director, but by Turespana, Spain's tourism agency, which helped turn the film into a kind of feature-length tourism guide. The agency also helped promote the film, spending more than $660,000 on television ads. And its investment worked: Indian tourism to Spain increased 65 percent after the film's release.[57] Although other countries have worked with Bollywood, too, offering tax breaks or subsidies, no other site has gained so much influence over the production, plot, and promotion of a major Indian film.

The hard part is determining which movies will be successes. For Apple, the challenge is a little less stringent, because U.S. film directors seem to love its sleek white laptops, ear-budded iPods, and ubiquitous iPhones. Thus more than one-third of all top grossing films at the U.S. box office—129 of 374 movies—have included Apple-branded products in the past decade. Recent appearances include both hits and Oscar-nominated offerings, such as *Green Lantern, Transformers: Dark of the Moon, Rise of the Planet of the Apes, Bridesmaids, The Girl with the Dragon Tattoo,* and *Diary of a Wimpy Kid.*[58] Matt Damon's *We Bought a Zoo* even featured an extended

rebates A consumer discount in which a portion of the purchase price is returned to the buyer in cash; the manufacturer, not the retailer, issues the refund.

product placement Inclusion of a product in nontraditional situations, such as in a scene in a movie or television program.

scene showing how to use the iPhoto app. Apple is also unique in that it claims it does not pay for product placement, nor does it comment on film appearances. An analytics firm that estimates the dollar value of product placements has reported that Apple's five-minute screen time in *Mission Impossible* alone was worth more than $23 million.[59] Apple seemingly can earn those returns without paying for the placements, but not all companies are so lucky.

Using Sales Promotion Tools

Marketers must be careful in their use of sales promotions, especially those that focus on lowering prices. Depending on the item, consumers may stock up when items are offered at a lower price, which simply shifts sales from the future to now and thereby leads to short-run benefits at the expense of long-term sales stability. For instance, using sales promotions such as coupons to stimulate sales of household cleaning supplies may cause consumers to stockpile the products and decrease demand for those products in the future. But a similar promotion used with a perishable product such as Dannon yogurt should increase its demand at the expense of competitors like Yoplait.

Many firms are also realizing the value of **cross-promoting**, when two or more firms join to reach a specific target market. To achieve a successful cross-promotion, the two products must appeal to the same target market and together create value for consumers. J. Crew has teamed up with several famous brands, including Belstaff, Levi's, Barbour, Timex, and Sperry Top-Sider, to offer exclusive products in the J. Crew stores and website.[60]

The goal of any sales promotion is to create value for both the consumers and the firm. By understanding the needs of its customers, as well as how best to entice them to purchase or consume a particular product or service, a firm can develop promotional messages and events that are of interest to and achieve the desired response from those customers. Traditionally, the role of sales promotion has been to generate short-term results, whereas the goal of advertising was to generate long-term results. As this chapter demonstrates, though, both sales promotion and advertising can generate both long- and short-term effects. The effective combination of both types of activities leads to impressive results for the firm and the consumers. ■

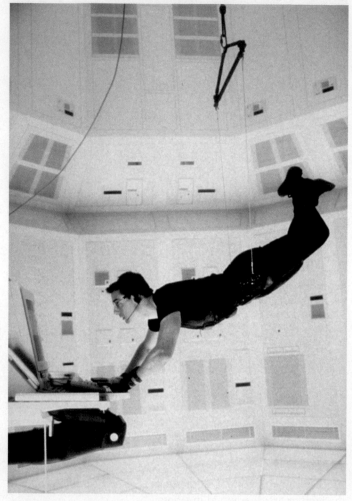

Product placement can be profitable. Apple's computer placement in the original *Mission Impossible* movie was estimated to be worth $23 million.

 check yourself

1. What are various forms of sales promotions?
2. What factors should a firm consider when evaluating a sales promotion?

> " MORE THAN ONE-THIRD OF ALL TOP GROSSING FILMS AT THE U.S. BOX OFFICE—129 OF 374 MOVIES—HAVE INCLUDED APPLE-BRANDED PRODUCTS IN THE PAST DECADE. "

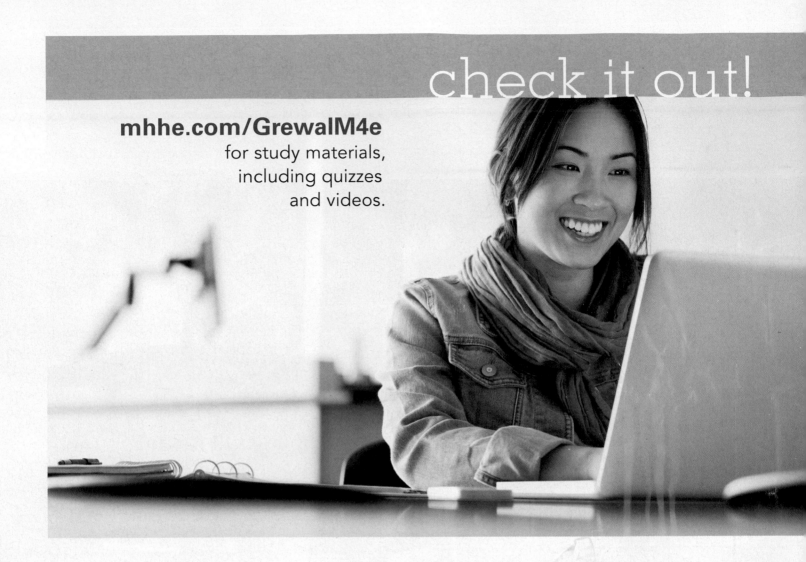

check it out!

mhhe.com/GrewalM4e
for study materials,
including quizzes
and videos.

nineteen

personal selling and
sales management

When she was just 31 years of age, Lauren Crampsie landed a top job at Ogilvy & Mather, one of the largest marketing communications companies in the world.[1] In her new position, worldwide chief marketing officer for global operations, Crampsie is responsible for developing the business strategy that will engage clients with Ogilvy & Mather's full range of marketing services, even as she continues to lead the company's North American business development efforts.

Despite her meteoric rise in the eight years since she entered the job force, Crampsie's original career aspirations had nothing to do with marketing. After graduating from Lehigh University, she deferred an acceptance to law school to work as an assistant in broadcast television. Two years later, she joined Ogilvy as a new business coordinator. And then just six years after that, she was the agency's youngest new business director and then the youngest director of business development for all of North America.[2]

The secret to her success? According to her supervisors, the key is Crampsie's track record of bringing new clients—such as IKEA, UPS, and Intercontinental Hotels Group—into the Ogilvy & Mather portfolio.[3] She achieves these integrations largely through her stellar understanding of how to use both new and

continued on p. 420

LEARNING OBJECTIVES

After reading this chapter, you should be able to:

LO 19-1 Describe the value added of personal selling.

LO 19-2 Define the steps in the personal selling process.

LO 19-3 Describe the key functions involved in managing a sales force.

LO 19-4 Describe the ethical and legal issues in personal selling.

continued from p. 419

established marketing channels to give clients the results they want. Furthermore, Crampsie works tirelessly to build relationships with everyone she meets, whether they are CEOs, junior staffers, or just an interesting contact in a social setting. Anyone has the potential to provide her with insight into the culture and business goals of a potential new client. Armed with this knowledge, she carefully considers the unique challenges and needs of prospective clients, then demonstrates how her agency can surmount those obstacles using a combination of creativity and strategic insights.

To build client trust and overcome resistance put up by business prospects, Crampsie uses high-tech tools, including social media, digital strategies, and other marketing innovations. But she never ignores her old-fashioned social and conversational skills either. Her client and staff interactions run the gamut from check-ins on Foursquare to text messages to morning jogs with her staff to face-to-face briefings over coffee to formal cocktail receptions.[4] Combining all these attributes is critical to making a great salesperson—along with trustworthiness, a relentless passion for the company's product or service, and a personality that attracts others, including customers.[5]

Crampsie's approach may seem closely linked to her youth and hipness, but her sales arsenal isn't all that different from that of another successful saleswoman and 68-year-old grandmother, Holly Chen. Chen heads a 300,000-member sales force for Amway that earns the former first-grade teacher an estimated $10 million annually.[6] The keys to success,

according to Chen, are an ability to use emotion to motivate action and a knack for making friends and forming connections. She agrees that potential relationships are everywhere: standing next to you in line at Starbucks, seated at an adjoining table in a restaurant, embedded in the social networks of people you have already met. Anyone who crosses Chen's path, whether on the street or in cyberspace, is a possible recruit to her legendary sales force. Once recruited, new salespeople reach out to their friends and acquaintances to make a sale, encourage them to join the team, or simply spread the word.

Modern marketing companies like Amway use an arsenal of social media tools to give them a competitive edge much greater than the face-to-face sales interactions of the past. Today, companies that lag in their use of developing direct connections with potential customers through Google, Twitter, Yelp, and so on are overlooking remarkable resources. Not only do these networks offer information that can influence, but they also offer a key path to savvy customers and closed deals.[7] Well-informed customers, who find a wealth of information in their myriad web interactions, usually have both factual and emotional data about a product or service long before they contact a salesperson. If sellers understand how to use all their interactions while applying and updating the conventional wisdom about how to ensure successful sales, they will be the ones—like Lauren Crampsie and Holly Chen—who achieve success for their customers, their companies, and themselves. ■

> "Companies that lag in their use of developing direct connections with potential customers through Google, Twitter, Yelp, and so on are overlooking remarkable resources."

Just like advertising, which we discussed in Chapter 18, personal selling is so important to integrated marketing communications that it deserves its own chapter. Almost everyone is engaged in some form of selling. On a personal level, you sell your ideas or opinions to your friends, family, employers, and professors. Even if you have no interest in personal selling as a career, a strong grounding in the topic will help you in numerous career choices. Consider, for instance, Harry Turk, a very successful labor attorney. He worked his way through college selling sweaters to fraternities across the country. Although he loved his part-time job, Harry decided to become an attorney. When asked whether he misses selling, he said, "I use my selling skills every day. I have to sell new clients on the idea that I'm the best attorney for the job. I have to sell my partners on my legal point of view. I even use selling skills when I'm talking to a judge or jury."

LO 19-1   Describe the value added of personal selling.

THE SCOPE AND NATURE OF PERSONAL SELLING

Personal selling is the two-way flow of communication between a buyer or buyers and a seller, designed to influence the buyer's purchase decision. Personal selling can take place in various situations: face-to-face, via video teleconferencing, on the telephone, or over the Internet, for example. More than 15 million people are employed in sales positions in the United States,[8] including those involved in business-to-business (B2B) transactions—like manufacturers' representatives selling to retailers or other businesses—and those completing business-to-consumer (B2C) transactions, such as retail salespeople, real estate agents, and insurance agents. Salespeople are referred to in many ways: sales representatives or reps, account executives, agents. And as Harry Turk found, most professions rely on personal selling to some degree.

work with their managers and other colleagues, salespeople tend to be responsible for planning their own day. This flexibility translates into an easier balance between work and family than many office-bound jobs can offer. Many salespeople now can rely on virtual offices, which enable them to communicate from anywhere and at any time with their colleagues and customers. Because salespeople are evaluated primarily on the results they produce, as long as they meet and exceed their goals, they experience little day-to-day supervision. You thus might find a salesperson at the gym in the middle of the day, when few other people are there, because no one keeps track of the length of his or her lunch break.

Second, the variety of the job often attracts people to sales. Every day is different, bringing different clients and customers, often in a variety of places. Their issues and problems and the solutions to those problems all differ and require creativity.[10] For example, when Lauren Crampsie signed The Gap as an account with Ogilvy, she worked with the company's CEO in a boardroom meeting, but she also got a chance to chat with some junior designers from the firm about trends they'd all noticed in nightclubs. Such diversity is a regular feature of personal selling. Especially for outgoing, vivacious personalities, the broad range of client relations can be professionally rewarding, as well as fun.

Third, professional selling and sales management can be a very lucrative career. Sales is among the highest-paying careers for college graduates, and compensation often includes perks,

> **personal selling**
> The two-way flow of communication between a buyer and a seller that is designed to influence the buyer's purchase decision.

[**More than 15 million people are employed in sales positions in the United States.**]

Salespeople don't always get the best coverage in popular media. In Arthur Miller's famous play *Death of a Salesman,* the main character Willie Loman leads a pathetic existence and suffers from the loneliness inherent in being a traveling salesman.[9] The characters in David Mamet's play *Glengarry Glen Ross* portray salespeople as crude, ruthless, and of questionable character. Unfortunately, these powerful Pulitzer Prize–winning pieces of literature weigh heavily on our collective consciousness and often overshadow the millions of hardworking professional salespeople who have fulfilling and rewarding careers and who add value to their firm and provide value for their customers.

Personal Selling as a Career

Personal or professional selling can be a satisfying career for several reasons. First, many people love the lifestyle. Salespeople are typically out on their own. Although they occasionally

such as the use of a company car or bonuses for high performance. A top performer can have a total compensation package of over $150,000; even lower-level salespeople can make well over $50,000. Although the monetary compensation can be significant, the satisfaction of being involved in interesting, challenging, and creative work is rewarding in and of itself.

Fourth, because salespeople are the frontline emissaries for their firm, they are very visible to management. Furthermore, their performance is fairly straightforward to measure, which means that high-performing salespeople who aspire to management positions are in a good position to be promoted.

The Value Added by Personal Selling

The benefits for salespeople mean that they are expensive for firms. Experts estimate that the average cost of a single B2B sales call is about $400.[11] So why include them in the marketing channel at all? In response to this question, some firms have turned to the Internet and technology to lower the costs of personal selling. (See Social & Mobile Marketing 19.1.) Other firms, especially some retailers, have made the decision not to use a sales force and thus require customers to perform the sales function on their own. But the firms that continue to use personal selling as part of their integrated marketing communications program recognize the value that it adds to their product or service mix. That is, personal selling is worth more than it costs. Personal selling adds value by educating customers and providing advice, saving the customer time, making things easier for customers, and building long-term strategic relationships with customers.[12]

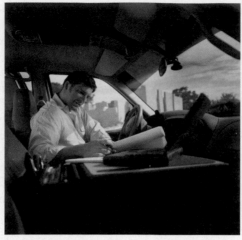

Many salespeople now can rely on virtual offices, which enable them to communicate via the Internet with colleagues and customers.

Salespeople Provide Information and Advice

Imagine how difficult it would be to buy a custom suit, a house, or a car without the help of a salesperson. UPS wouldn't dream of investing in a new fleet of airplanes without the benefit of Boeing's selling team. Boeing's sales team can provide UPS with the technical aspects of the aircraft as well as the economic justification for the purchase. If you need formalwear for your friend's upcoming wedding or a school dance, you might find it helpful to solicit the input of a retail sales associate, who can tell you what colors are hot this season, how to tie a bowtie, how each garment tends to fit, what the latest fashions are in formalwear, and how long your dress should be for a function that starts at 6:00 p.m. Certainly you could figure out most of this information on your own, but most customers find value in and are willing to pay for the education and advice that salespeople provide.

Salespeople Save Time and Simplify Buying

Time is money! Customers perceive value in time and labor savings. In many grocery and drugstore chains, salespeople employed by the vendor supplying merchandise straighten stock, set up displays, assess inventory levels, and write orders. In some cases, such as bakeries or soft drink sales, salespeople and truck drivers even bring in the merchandise and stock the shelves. These are all tasks that retail employees would otherwise have to do. To appeal to end customers, manufacturers might send salespeople into stores to provide cooking demonstrations or free samples in the case of grocery stores, or trunk or made-to-measure shows in the case of apparel or shoe retailers. In this case, the vendor increases convenience for both its immediate customer (the retailer) and the end consumer.

Sometimes however, turning over too many tasks to suppliers' salespeople can cause problems. Imagine a grocery store that has turned its inventory management function over to a supplier, like the consumer packaged goods firm Kraft. The

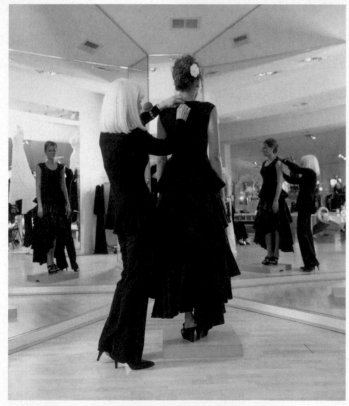

Salespeople provide information and advice.

A salesperson's product knowledge and ability to facilitate the sale can make buying a car easy and possibly even enjoyable.

Rising fuel costs, increasing staff productivity, cutbacks in airline service, minimizing carbon footprints, reducing corporate expenditure—these are just some of the reasons for meetings to go virtual. Foremost among them is that the technology has matured to the point that conversing in cyberspace frequently makes more sense than meeting in the same room.[13]

The most advanced of these technologies, telepresence, includes three screens that display life-size images of conference attendees, plus an additional screen for shared work. Resolution on the screens exceeds that of high-definition televisions. Images can be magnified, allowing attendees to view minute product details from across the globe. These systems, which also feature custom lighting and acoustics, cost as much as $350,000. For corporations such as Cisco, which has more than 200 telepresence rooms, the investment still represents a savings over travel costs. It isn't alone: The management consulting and technology service firm Accenture estimates its teleconferencing rooms save millions of dollars each year as well as saving its staff the wear and tear of travel.

Other collaborative technologies involve less financial outlay. Web-meeting services, for example, allow companies to conduct online training, edit documents collaboratively, demonstrate applications, give training or sales presentations, poll attendees, chat online, conduct question and answer sessions, and provide technical support.[14] As long as you have a computer with a web browser and an Internet connection, you can use collaborative tools such as wikis or VoIP technology such as Skype.

This technology also helps small companies go global. Lisa Kirschner, president of a Chicago-based marketing and graphic design firm, had a hot lead in Italy.[15] But she lacked the resources to meet in person and felt brainstorming via e-mail would be too cumbersome. Taking the risk of investing in web conferencing, which was unheard of in her industry, she secured clients in Italy, Japan, and Britain. The technology has earned her $100,000—one-eighth of her total annual revenue.

Reduced business travel means a slump in the conference business.[16] Increasingly, companies are relying on technology for virtual conferences. One product, Expos2, digitizes the conference. Attendees begin with a screen showing the convention center layout and follow links to exhibits, programs, and live presentations that have interactive functionality. Digital meeting technology isn't intended to replace face-to-face meetings or travel but rather to provide an alternative for companies hoping to optimize their travel budgets. Closing a deal is more likely during an in-person meeting, and business travel to other countries provides important insights into communities and cultures. All transactions benefit from a personal touch. Nevertheless, web-based and conventional videoconferencing technology will have a profound impact on the way companies do business in the coming years.

Salespeople no longer have to meet face to face with their customers to make the sale.

> WHETHER YOU ARE SELLING YOURSELF AS A JOB CANDIDATE, A PRODUCT PRODUCED BY YOUR COMPANY, OR A CONCEPT TO A CLIENT, YOUR SALE IS NOT SUCCESSFUL IF IT LEADS TO JUST A ONE-TIME TRANSACTION. "

supplier might place competitors' products in disadvantageous shelf positions. Unless the relationship involves significant trust or the grocery has precautionary measures in place, the Kraft sales representative might place plenty of Kraft Thousand Island dressing on the shelf but leave little room for its competitors' products, designating a suboptimal amount of shelf space to Wishbone's Thousand Island offering. Although this relationship benefits Kraft, it may not help the grocer, especially if that retailer earns better margins on the competitors' products. Salespeople certainly can help facilitate a buying situation, but they should never be allowed to take it over.

The same might be said of your own personal shopping. When you go to buy a new car, the salesperson likely will work hard to convince you that you should purchase a specific make or model. Although an automotive salesperson has a significant amount of knowledge about the products and therefore can simplify the car buying process, the final decision must remain up to you, the consumer.

Salespeople Build Relationships

As we discussed in Chapter 15, building strong marketing channel relationships is a critical success factor. Who in the organization is better equipped to manage this relationship than the salesperson, the frontline emissary for the firm? The most successful salespeople are those who build strong relationships with their customers—a rule that holds across all sorts of sales. That is, whether you are selling yourself as a job candidate, a product produced by your company, or a concept to a client, your sale is not successful if it leads to just a one-time transaction. Instead, good salespeople of all stripes consistently take a long-term perspective.

Building on the relationship concept introduced in Chapter 15, **relationship selling** refers to a sales philosophy and process that emphasizes a commitment to maintaining the relationship over the long term and investing in opportunities that are mutually beneficial to all parties.[17] Relationship-oriented salespeople work with their customers to find mutually beneficial solutions to their wants and needs. As we described in Chapter 7, colleges often negotiate long-term agreements with apparel companies to supply their sports teams. Similarly, a Lenovo sales team might be working with your university to provide you with the computer support and security you need for all four years you spend working on the school's network or in its computer labs.

LO 19-2 Define the steps in the personal selling process.

THE PERSONAL SELLING PROCESS

Although selling may appear a rather straightforward process, successful salespeople must follow several steps. Depending on the sales situation and the buyer's readiness to purchase, the salesperson may not use every step, and the time required for each step varies with the situation. For example, if a customer goes into The Gap already prepared to purchase some chinos, the selling process will be fairly quick. But if IBM is attempting to sell personal computers for the first time to your university, the process may take several months. With this in mind, let's examine each step of the selling process (Exhibit 19.1).

▼ **EXHIBIT 19.1** The Personal Selling Process

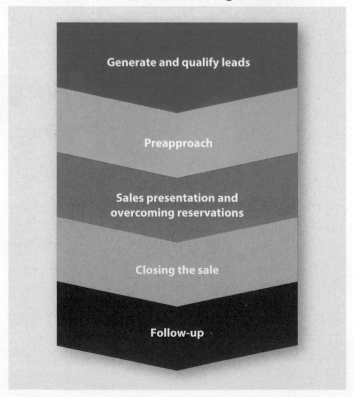

Generate and qualify leads

Preapproach

Sales presentation and overcoming reservations

Closing the sale

Follow-up

relationship selling
A sales philosophy and process that emphasizes a commitment to maintaining the relationship over the long term and investing in opportunities that are mutually beneficial to all parties.

leads
A list of potential customers.

qualify The process of assessing the potential of sales leads.

trade shows
Major events attended by buyers who choose to be exposed to products and services offered by potential suppliers in an industry.

cold calls
A method of prospecting in which salespeople telephone or go to see potential customers without appointments.

telemarketing
A method of prospecting in which salespeople telephone potential customers.

Step 1: Generate and Qualify Leads

The first step in the selling process is to generate a list of potential customers (**leads**) and assess their potential (**qualify**). Salespeople who already have an established relationship with a customer will skip this step, and it is not used extensively in retail settings. In B2B situations, however, it is important to work continually to find new and potentially profitable customers.

Salespeople can generate and qualify leads in a variety of ways.[18] They might discover potential leads by talking to current customers, doing research on the Internet, or networking at events such as trade shows, industry conferences, or chamber of commerce meetings. Salespeople can also generate leads through cold calls.

The Internet has been a boon for generating and qualifying leads. Prior to its explosion, it was cumbersome to perform research on products, customers, or competitors. Salespeople would rely on a research staff for this information, and it could take weeks for the research to be completed and sent through the mail.

Trade shows also offer an excellent forum for finding leads. These major events are attended by buyers who choose to be exposed to products and services offered by potential suppliers in an industry. Consumer electronics buyers always make sure that they attend the annual International Consumer Electronics Show (CES) in Las Vegas, the world's largest trade show for consumer technology (www.cesweb.org). The most recent show was attended by 153,000 people (including more than 34,000 international attendees), such as vendors, developers, and suppliers of consumer-technology hardware, content, technology delivery systems, and related products and services. Nearly 3,100 vendor exhibits took up 1.861 million net square feet of exhibit space, showcasing the very latest products and services. Vendors often use CES to introduce new products, including the first camcorder (1981), high-definition television (HDTV, 1998), and Internet protocol television (IP TV, 2005). More than 20,000 new products were launched at the 2012 conference alone.[19] In addition to providing an opportunity for retail buyers to see the latest products, the CES conference program features prominent speakers from the technology sector.[20]

Cold calls are a method of prospecting in which salespeople telephone or go to see potential customers without appointments.[21] **Telemarketing** is similar to a cold call, but it always occurs over the telephone. Sometimes professional telemarketing firms, rather than the firm's salespeople, make such calls. Adding Value 19.1 examines how colleges use it to boost attendance at sports events.

However, cold calls and telemarketing have become less popular over time, primarily because their success rate is fairly low. During cold calls, the salesperson is not able to establish the potential customer's specific needs ahead of time.

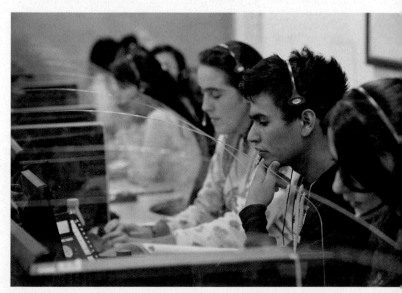

Trade shows, like the International Consumer Eletronics Show in Las Vegas, are an excellent way to generate and qualify leads.

Telemarketing is a type of cold call in which salespeople generate or qualify leads on the telephone.

Adding Value 19.1

College Athletics Turn to the Pros for Sales Help

Not that long ago, a few billboards and word of mouth were enough to sell out tickets for a college game. Demand for tickets to college basketball and football games was so high that many schools added seats as fast as they could and still had to turn fans away. But a dip in the economy, increased demands on leisure time, rising gas prices, and better television technology have combined to diminish ticket sales, leaving colleges with empty seats and a diminishing revenue stream, even as they face other budget constraints.[22] In response, some athletic programs are outsourcing ticket sales to commission-driven experts, in the hopes of bringing fans back to the bleachers.[23]

Ticket marketing companies catering to colleges use the model adopted by professional sports organizations: Sales staff work for commissions and make as many as 100 calls a day to students, alumni, faculty, and anyone else connected to the university. As these callers chat about the team, the school, or college athletics, they listen for clues to customers' personalities and needs, then adjust their sales strategy accordingly. The commission structure ensures the strong motivation of the sales force, which benefits the schools because every ticket sold promises additional potential income in the form of concessions. Furthermore, filled stadiums significantly improve the public perception of the team, team spirit, and the likelihood of national publicity.

Some ticketing companies also provide related services to help generate revenue. Callers versed in the specifics of the college's athletics program might request donations for athletic scholarships or sport-related programming. Sport marketers with contacts in the world of professional athletics can help schools pull together appropriate fundraising events. They provide research and insights, coordinate print production for programs and signage, assist with challenging media situations, help build sales of apparel and merchandise, and even rent seat cushions for homecoming games.[24] Sophisticated software programs link ticketing, fundraising, and marketing functions to help track interactions, increase ticket sales, and improve the college's brand.[25]

Other athletic departments prefer to hire and manage their own ticket sales staff. This approach gives the school greater control over its brand. It also avoids privacy concerns about sharing university databases with an external seller, which may be too aggressive for the school's educational environment, or running afoul of complex NCAA rules. However, internal sales might not be as effective, considering the competing priorities that confront the athletic department, the limited experience of the sales staff, the prohibitions on commission-based incentives for university employees, and ineffective channels of communication.

More than 100 million fans are available to attend college athletic events. Thus universities want the pros on their team, selling tickets to their events.

Accordingly, these methods can be very expensive. Second, both federal and state governments are regulating the activities of telemarketers. Federal rules prohibit telemarketing to consumers whose names appear on the national Do-Not-Call list, which is maintained by the Federal Trade Commission. Even for those consumers whose names are not on the list, the rules prohibit calling before 8:00 a.m. or after 9:00 p.m. (in the consumer's time zone) or after the consumer has told the telemarketer not to call. Federal rules also prohibit unsolicited fax messages and unsolicited telephone calls as well as e-mail messages to cell phones.

consider, for example, whether the potential customer's needs pertain to a product or a service. They should assess whether the lead has the financial resources to pay for the product or service.[26] Clients looking to sell multi-million dollar properties want real estate agents to qualify potential buyers first. Therefore, the sales agents might create a password-protected website that features floor plans and inside views for the shopping convenience of interested buyers. But to obtain the password, the customer must be prequalified as someone who could actually afford to buy the property. Such qualifications save both the agent and the seller the trouble of showing

> [Retail salespeople should never judge a book by its cover and assume that a person in the store doesn't fit the store's image or cannot afford to purchase there.]

After salespeople generate leads, they must qualify those leads by determining whether it is worthwhile to pursue them and attempt to turn them into customers. In B2B settings, the costs of preparing and making a presentation are so substantial that the seller must assess a lead's potential. Salespeople

properties to curious people who could never actually afford to buy.

In a retail setting, though, qualifying potential customers is both dangerous and potentially illegal. Retail salespeople should never judge a book by its cover and assume that a person in the store doesn't fit the store's image or cannot afford to purchase there. Imagine going to an upscale jewelry store to purchase an engagement ring, only to be snubbed because you are dressed in your everyday, casual school clothes.

Step 2: Preapproach and the Use of CRM Systems

The **preapproach** occurs prior to meeting the customer for the first time and extends the qualification of leads procedure described in Step 1. Although the salesperson has learned about the customer during the qualification stage, in this step, he or she must conduct additional research and develop plans for meeting with the customer. Suppose, for example, a management consulting firm wants to sell a bank a new system for finding checking account errors. The consulting firm's salesperson should first find out everything possible about the bank: How many checks does it process? What system is the bank using now? What are the benefits of the consultant's proposed system compared with the competition? The answers to these questions provide the basis for establishing value for the customer.

In the past, this customer information, if it was available at all, was typically included in a manual system that each individual salesperson kept, using a notebook or a series of cards. Today, salespeople often can access all this information immediately and conveniently from their firm's CRM system.

In most cases, these CRM systems have several components. There is a customer database or data warehouse. Whether the salesperson is working for a retail store or manages a selling team for an aerospace contractor, he or she can record transaction information, customer contact information, customer preferences, and market segment information about the customer. Once the data have been analyzed and CRM programs developed, salespeople can help implement the programs.

Having done the additional research, the salesperson establishes goals for meeting with the customer. It is important that he or she knows ahead of time exactly what should be accomplished. For instance, the consulting firm's salesperson cannot expect to get a purchase commitment from the bank after just the first visit. But a demonstration of the system and a short presentation about how the system would benefit the customer would be appropriate. It is often a good idea to practice the presentation prior to the meeting, using a technique known as **role playing**, in which the salesperson acts out a simulated buying situation while a colleague or manager acts as the buyer. Afterward, the practice sales presentation can be critiqued and adjustments can be made.

Step 3: Sales Presentation and Overcoming Reservations

The Presentation Once all the background information has been obtained and the objectives for the meeting are set, the salesperson is ready for a person-to-person meeting. Let's continue with our bank example. During the first part of the meeting, the salesperson needs to get to know the customer, get his or her attention, and create interest in the presentation to follow. The beginning of the presentation may be the most important part of the entire selling process because it is when the salesperson establishes exactly where the customer is in his or her buying process (Exhibit 19.2). (For a refresher on the B2B buying process, see Chapter 7.)

Suppose, for instance, that the bank is in the first stage of the buying process: need recognition. It would not be prudent for the salesperson to discuss the pros and cons of different potential suppliers because doing so would assume that the customer already had reached Step 4 (of the B2B buying process), proposal analysis and customer selection. By asking a series of questions, though, the salesperson can assess the bank's need for the product or service and adapt or customize the presentation to match the customer's need and stage in the decision process.[27]

Salespeople input customer information into their tablets to develop a customer database for CRM systems.

These salespeople are role playing. The woman standing at the easel is acting out a simulated buying situation while her colleagues act as the buying group. Afterward, they will critique her presentation.

Some salespeople, particularly inexperienced ones, believe that to be in control, they must do all the talking. Yet it is impossible to really understand where the customer stands without listening carefully.

"

▼ **EXHIBIT 19.2** Aligning the Personal Selling Process with the B2B Buying Process

Personal selling process	B2B buying process
Generate and qualify leads	Need recognition
Preapproach	Product specification
Sales presentation and overcoming reservations	RFP process
Closing the sale	Proposal analysis and supplier selection
Follow-up	Order specification
	Performance assessment

Asking questions is only half the battle; carefully listening to the answers is equally important. Some salespeople, particularly inexperienced ones, believe that to be in control, they must do all the talking. Yet it is impossible to really understand where the customer stands without listening carefully. What if the COO says, "It seems kind of expensive"? If the salesperson isn't listening carefully, he or she won't pick up on the subtle nuances of what the customer is really thinking. In this case, it probably means the COO doesn't see the value in the offering.

When the salesperson has gotten a good feel for where the customer stands, he or she can apply that knowledge to help the customer solve its problem or satisfy its need. The salesperson might begin by explaining the features or characteristics of the system that will reduce checking account errors. It may not be obvious, solely on the basis of these features, however, that the system adds value beyond the bank's current practices. Using the answers to some of the questions the salesperson posed earlier in the meeting, he or she can clarify the product's advantages over current or past practices as well as the overall benefits of adopting the new system. The salesperson might explain, for instance, that the bank can expect a 20 percent improvement in checking account errors and that, because of the size of the bank and number of checks it processes per year, this improvement would represent $2 million in annual savings. Because the system

costs $150,000 per year and will take only three weeks to integrate into the current system, it will add significant and almost immediate value.

Handling Reservations An integral part of the sales presentation is handling reservations or objections that the buyer might have about the product or service. Although reservations can arise during each stage of the selling process, they are very likely to occur during the sales presentation. Customers may raise reservations pertaining to a variety of issues, but they usually relate in some way to value, such as that the price is too high for the level of quality or service.

Good salespeople know the types of reservations buyers are likely to raise. They may know, for instance, that their service is slower than competitors' or that their selection is limited. Although not all reservations can be forestalled, effective salespeople can anticipate and handle some. For example, when the bank COO said the check service seemed expensive, the salesperson was ready with information about how quickly the investment would be recouped.

As in other aspects of the selling process, the best way to handle reservations is to relax and listen, then ask questions to

An integral part of the sales presentation is handling reservations or objections that the buyer might have about the product or service.

clarify any reservations.[28] For example, the salesperson could respond to the COO's reservation by asking, "How much do you think the bank is losing through checking account errors?" Her answer might open up a conversation about the positive trends in a cost–benefit analysis. Such questions are usually more effective than trying to prove the customer's reservation is not valid, because the latter approach implies the salesperson isn't really listening and could lead to an argument—the last thing a customer usually wants.

Step 4: Closing the Sale

Closing the sale means obtaining a commitment from the customer to make a purchase. Without a successful close, the salesperson goes away empty handed, so many salespeople find this part of the sales process very stressful. Although losing a sale is never pleasant, salespeople who are involved in a relationship with their customers must view any specific sales presentation as part of the progression toward

to solidify the customer relationship through great service quality. Let's apply the five service quality dimensions we discussed in Chapter 13 to the follow-up:[30]

- **Reliability.** The salesperson and the supporting organization must deliver the right product or service on time.
- **Responsiveness.** The salesperson and support group must be ready to deal quickly with any issue, question, or problem that may arise.
- **Assurance.** Customers must be assured through adequate guarantees that their purchase will perform as expected.
- **Empathy.** The salesperson and support group must have a good understanding of the problems and issues faced by their customers. Otherwise, they cannot give them what they want.

[**The attitudes customers develop after the sale become the basis for how they purchase in the future.**]

ultimately making the sale or building the relationship. An unsuccessful close on one day may just be a means of laying the groundwork for a successful close during the next meeting.

Although we have presented the selling process as a series of steps, closing the sale rarely follows so neatly. However, good salespeople listen carefully to what potential customers say and pay attention to their body language. By reading these signals, they can achieve an earlier close. Suppose that our hypothetical bank, instead of being in the first step of the buying process, were in the final step of negotiation and selection. An astute salesperson would pick up on these signals and ask for the sale.

Step 5: Follow-Up

"It ain't over till it's over."
—Yogi Berra[29]

With relationship selling, it is never really over, even after the sale. The attitudes customers develop after the sale become the basis for how they purchase in the future. The follow-up therefore offers a prime opportunity for a salesperson

A postsale follow-up letter, call, or e-mail is the first step in initiating a new order and sustaining the relationship.

- **Tangibles.** Because tangibles reflect the physical characteristics of the seller's business, such as its website, marketing communications, and delivery materials, their influence is more subtle than that of the other four service quality dimensions. That doesn't mean it is any less important. Retail customers are generally more pleased with a purchase if it is carefully wrapped in nice paper instead of being haphazardly thrown into a crumpled plastic bag. The tangibles offer a signal that the product is of high quality, even though the packaging has nothing to do with the product's actual performance.

When customers' expectations are not met, they often complain—about deliveries, the billing amount or process, the product's performance, or after-sale services such as installation or training (recall the Gaps Model from Chapter 13). Effectively handling complaints is critical to the future of the relationship. As we noted in Chapter 13, the best way to handle complaints is to listen to the customer, provide a fair solution to the problem, and resolve the problem quickly.

The best way to nip a postsale problem in the bud is to check with the

sales management
Involves the planning, direction, and control of personal selling activities, including recruiting, selecting, training, motivating, compensating, and evaluating, as they apply to the sales force.

company sales force Comprised of people who are employees of the selling company and are engaged in the selling process.

independent agents Salespeople who sell a manufacturer's products on an extended contract basis but are not employees of the manufacturer; also known as *manufacturer's representatives* or *reps*.

manufacturer's representative See *independent agents*.

reps See *independent agents*.

order getter A salesperson whose primary responsibilities are identifying potential customers and engaging those customers in discussions to attempt to make a sale.

customer right after he or she takes possession of the product or immediately after the service has been completed. This speed demonstrates responsiveness and empathy. It also shows the customer that the salesperson and the firm care about customer satisfaction. Finally, a postsale follow-up call, e-mail, or letter takes the salesperson back to the first step in the sales process for initiating a new order and sustaining the relationship.

---

 check yourself

1. Why is personal selling important to an IMC strategy?
2. What are the steps in the personal selling process?

Sales Force Structure

Imagine the daunting task of putting together a sales force from scratch. Will you hire your own salespeople, or should they be manufacturer's representatives? What will each salesperson's primary duties be: order takers, order getters, sales support? Finally, will they work together in teams? In this section, we examine each of these issues.

Company Sales Force or Manufacturer's Representative

A **company sales force** comprises people who are employees of the selling company. **Independent agents**, also known as **manufacturer's representatives**, or **reps**, are salespeople who sell a manufacturer's products on an extended contract basis but are not employees

> **Good sales representatives have many established contacts and can sell multiple products from noncompeting manufacturers during the same sales call.**

LO 19-3   Describe the key functions involved in managing a sales force.

MANAGING THE SALES FORCE

Like any business activity involving people, the sales force requires management. **Sales management** involves the planning, direction, and control of personal selling activities, including recruiting, selecting, training, motivating, compensating, and evaluating, as they apply to the sales force.

Managing a sales force is a rewarding yet complicated undertaking. In this section, we examine how sales forces can be structured, some of the most important issues in recruiting and selecting salespeople, sales training issues, ways to compensate salespeople, and finally how to supervise and evaluate salespeople.

of the manufacturer. They are compensated by commissions and do not take ownership or physical possession of the merchandise.

Manufacturer's representatives are useful for smaller firms or firms expanding into new markets because such companies can achieve instant and extensive sales coverage without having to pay full-time personnel. Good sales representatives have many established contacts and can sell multiple products from noncompeting manufacturers during the same sales call. Also, the use of manufacturer's representatives facilitates flexibility; it is much easier to replace a rep than an employee and much easier to expand or contract coverage in a market with a sales rep than with a company sales force.

Company sales forces are more typically used for established product lines. Because the salespeople are company employees, the manufacturer has more control over what they do. If, for example, the manufacturer's strategy is to provide extensive customer service, the sales manager can specify exactly what actions a company sales force must take. In contrast, because manufacturer's representatives are paid on a commission basis, it is difficult to persuade them to take any action that doesn't directly lead to sales.

Salesperson Duties

Although the life of a professional salesperson is highly varied, salespeople generally play three important roles: order getting, order taking, and sales support.

Order Getting. An **order getter** is a salesperson whose primary responsibilities are identifying potential customers and engaging those customers in discussions to attempt to make a sale. An order getter is also responsible for following up with the customer to ensure that the customer is satisfied and to build the relationship. In B2B settings, order getters are primarily involved in new buy and modified new buy situations (see Chapter 7). As a result, they require extensive sales and product knowledge training. The Coca-Cola salesperson who goes to Safeway's headquarters to sell a special promotion of Vanilla Coke is an order getter.

Order Taking. An **order taker** is a salesperson whose primary responsibility is to process routine orders, reorders, or rebuys for products. Colgate employs order takers around the globe who go into stores and distribution centers that already carry Colgate products to check inventory, set up displays, write new orders, and make sure everything is going smoothly.

Sales Support. **Sales support personnel** enhance and help with the overall selling effort. For example, if a Best Buy customer begins to experience computer problems, the company has a Geek Squad door-to-door service as well as support in the store. Those employees who respond to the customer's technical questions and repair the computer serve to support the overall sales process.

Combination Duties. Although some salespeople's primary function may be order getting, order taking, or sales support, others fill a combination of roles, as the creative approach in Social & Mobile Marketing 19.2 suggests. For instance, a computer salesperson at Staples may spend an hour with a customer educating him or her about the pros and cons of various systems and then make the sale. The next customer might simply need a specific printer cartridge. A third customer might bring in a computer and seek advice about an operating system problem. The salesperson was

Order takers process routine orders, reorders, or rebuys for products.

first an order getter, next an order taker, and finally a sales support person.

Some firms use **selling teams** that combine sales specialists whose primary duties are order getting, order taking, or sales support but who work together to service important accounts. As companies become larger and products more complicated, it is nearly impossible for one person to perform all the necessary sales functions.

Recruiting and Selecting Salespeople

When the firm has determined how the sales force will be structured, it must find and hire salespeople. Although superficially this task may sound as easy as posting the job opening on the Internet or running an ad in a newspaper, it must be performed carefully because firms don't want to hire the wrong person. Salespeople are very expensive to train. Recall our discussion of Zappos in Chapter 13, a company that considers finding the right people so important that it will pay them to leave after a few weeks if they are not a good fit.

The most important activity in the recruiting process is to determine exactly what the salesperson will be doing and what personal traits and abilities a person should have to do the job well. For instance, the Coca-Cola order getter who goes to Safeway to pitch a new product will typically need significant sales experience, coupled with great communication and analytical skills. Coke's order takers need to be reliable and able to get along with lots of different types of people in the stores, from managers to customers.

Many firms give candidates personality tests, but they stress different personality attributes, depending on the requisite traits for the position and the personality characteristics of their most successful salespeople.[31] For instance, impatience is often a positive characteristic for sales because it creates a sense of urgency to close the sale. But for very large, complicated sales targeting large institutions, like the bank in our

> " Zappos considers finding the right people so important that it will pay them to leave after a few weeks if they are not a good fit. "

Social media have revolutionized buying, such that consumers can learn lots about products and services from sources such as Facebook, Google+, Twitter, Yelp, and LinkedIn. Salespeople therefore have begun exploring creative ways to use social media in their various roles, with the ultimate goal of building sales.

On Broadway, pop star Ricky Martin played in a revival of *Evita*. He was not a traditional salesperson, yet for his more than 3 million Facebook fans and 5 million Twitter followers, he functioned as an order getter.[32] Five days before show tickets went on sale to the public, Martin created a video that showed his Twitter followers how to buy tickets early. These fans snatched up about a half million dollars' worth of tickets.

Real estate agents may not be quite as fabulous as the singer of "Livin' La Vida Loca," but they are crazy about social media, which offer a great way to stay in touch with current and past clients, offer support after the sale, maintain an image of relevance in a changing marketplace, and build a referral network for new business.[33]

A survey of 1,000 sales professionals in the United States, United Kingdom, Brazil, and China revealed that nearly half of them viewed social media as important to their success.[34] Some traditionalists may be hesitant to use social networking sites, which offer no guarantee of control over a brand image as consumers use them to spread their own opinions about a particular company. But by embracing social marketing, as the *Evita* producers did, sellers can turn it into a valuable additional marketing channel. The sites can be used to provide shoppers with the information they crave, including factual advice, expert opinions, and information about special offers. They can be mined for information about consumers' behavior, needs, and stages in the buying process as well as for finding sales leads and then following up with previous buyers.

Ricky Martin stars as Che in a Broadway production of Evita.

previous example, an impatient salesperson may irritate the decision makers and kill the deal.

When recruiting salespeople, is it better to look for candidates with innate sales ability, or can a good training program make anyone a successful salesperson? In other words, are good salespeople born, or are they made?[35] By a margin of seven to one in a survey of sales and marketing executives, respondents believed that training and supervision are more critical determinants of selling success than the salesperson's inherent personal characteristics.[36] Yet some of those same respondents noted that they knew born salespeople and that personal traits are important for successful sales careers. So, it appears that while training is critical, it also helps to possess certain personal traits.

What are those personal traits? Managers and sales experts have identified the following:[37]

- *Personality.* Good salespeople are friendly, sociable, and, in general, like being around people. Customers won't buy from someone they don't like.

- *Optimism.* Good salespeople tend to look at the bright side of things. Optimism also may help them be resilient—the third trait.

- *Resilience.* Good salespeople don't easily take no for an answer. They keep coming back until they get a yes.

- *Self-motivation.* As we have already mentioned, salespeople have lots of freedom to spend their days the way they believe will be most productive. But if the salespeople are not self-motivated to get the job done, it probably won't get done.

- *Empathy.* Empathy is one of the five dimensions of service quality discussed previously in this chapter and in Chapter 13. Good salespeople must care about their customers, their issues, and their problems.

Sales Training

Even people who possess all these personal traits need training. All salespeople benefit from training about selling and negotiation techniques, product and service knowledge, technologies used in the selling process, time and territory management, and company policies and procedures.

Firms use varied delivery methods to train their salespeople, depending on the topic of the training, what type of salesperson is being trained, and the cost versus the value of the training. For instance, an on-the-job training program is excellent for communicating selling and negotiation skills because managers can observe the sales trainees in real selling situations and provide instant feedback. They can also engage in role-playing exercises in which the salesperson acts out a simulated buying situation and the manager critiques the salesperson's performance.

A much less expensive, but for some purposes equally valuable, training method is the Internet. Online training programs have revolutionized the way training happens in many firms. Firms can provide new product and service knowledge, spread the word about changes in company policies and procedures, and share selling tips in a user-friendly environment that salespeople can access anytime and anywhere. Distance learning sales training programs through teleconferencing enable a group of salespeople to participate with their instructor or

Is P90X creator Tony Horton a born salesperson or was he made into one?

manager in a virtual classroom. And testing can occur online as well. Online sales training may never replace the one-on-one interaction of on-the-job training for advanced selling skills, but it is quite effective and efficient for many other aspects of the sales training task.

Motivating and Compensating Salespeople

An important goal for any effective sales manager is to get to know his or her salespeople and determine what motivates them to be effective. Some salespeople prize their freedom and like to be left alone; others want attention and are more productive when they receive accolades for a job well done. Still others are motivated primarily by monetary compensation. Great sales managers determine how best to motivate each of their salespeople according to what is most important to each individual. Although sales managers can emphasize different motivating factors, except in the smallest companies, the methods used to compensate salespeople must be fairly standardized and can be divided into two categories: financial and nonfinancial.

Technology has changed the lives of salespeople and sales training. Companies can conduct distance learning and training through videoconferencing.

Financial Rewards
Salespeople's compensation usually has several components. Most salespeople receive at least part of their compensation as a **salary**, a fixed sum of money paid at regular intervals. Another common financial incentive is a **commission**, which is money paid as a percentage of the sales volume or profitability. A **bonus** is a payment made at management's discretion when the salesperson attains certain

for not only selling advice but also companywide recognition of individual salespeople's accomplishments.[38]

Nonfinancial rewards should have high symbolic value, as plaques, pens, or rings do. Free trips or days off are also effective rewards. More important than what the reward is, however, is the way it is operationalized. For instance, an award should be given at a sales meeting and publicized in the company newsletter. It should also be done in good taste, because if the award is perceived as tacky, no one will take it seriously.[39] Mary Kay recognizes salespeople's success with unusually large rewards that have both high symbolic and high material value. More than 100,000 independent beauty consultants and sales directors have earned the use of one of the famous pink Cadillacs, but it is also possible to gain rewards and recognition such as a set of faux pearl earrings within the first week of becoming a consultant.

Evaluating Salespeople by Using Marketing Metrics
Salespeople's evaluation process must be tied to their reward structure. If salespeople do well, they should receive their rewards in the same way that if you do well on your

> **If salespeople do well, they should receive their rewards in the same way that if you do well on your exams and assignments in a class, you should earn a good grade.**

goals. Bonuses usually are given only periodically, such as at the end of the year. A **sales contest** is a short-term incentive designed to elicit a specific response from the sales force. Prizes might be cash or other types of financial incentives. For instance, Volkswagen may give a free trip to Germany for the salesperson who sells the most Touaregs.

The bulk of any compensation package is made up of salary, commission, or a combination of the two. The advantage of a salary plan is that salespeople know exactly what they will be paid, and sales managers have more control. Salaried salespeople can be directed to spend a certain percentage of their time handling customer service issues. Under a commission system, however, salespeople have only one objective—make the sale! Thus, a commission system provides the most incentive for the sales force to sell.

Nonfinancial Rewards
As we have noted, good salespeople are self-motivated. They want to do a good job and make the sale because it makes them feel good. But this good feeling also can be accentuated by recognition from peers and management. For instance, the internal monthly magazine at the cosmetics firm Mary Kay provides an outlet

Sales contests are a type of financial reward that provides prizes like these or other types of financial incentives.

Mary Kay gives high-performing salespeople an award that has both high symbolic value and material value—a pink Cadillac.

as much potential as salesperson A's. Knowing this, we might suppose that salesperson A has actually done a better job. For this reason, firms use ratios such as profit per customer, orders per call, sales per hour, or expenses compared to sales as their objective measures.

Whereas objective measures are quantitative, subjective measures seek to assess salespeople's behavior: what they do and how well they do it. By their very nature, subjective measures reflect one person's opinion about another's performance. Thus, subjective evaluations can be biased and should be used cautiously and only in conjunction with multiple objective measures.

exams and assignments in a class, you should earn a good grade. However, salespeople should be evaluated and rewarded for only those activities and outcomes that fall under their control. If Macy's makes a unilateral decision to put Diesel jeans in all its stores, after a negotiation with Diesel's corporate headquarters in Italy, the Diesel sales representatives responsible for individual Macy's stores should not receive credit for making the sale, nor should they get all the windfall commission that would ensue from the added sales.

Considering this guiding principle—evaluate and reward salespeople for what they do and not for what they don't do—how should sales managers evaluate salespeople? The answer is never easy because measures must be tied to performance, and

 check yourself

1. What do sales managers need to do to manage their sales force successfully?
2. What is the difference between monetary and nonmonetary incentives?

> [Evaluate and reward salespeople for what they do and not for what they don't do.]

there are many ways to measure performance in a complex job such as selling. For example, evaluating performance on the basis of monthly sales alone fails to consider how profitable the sales were, whether any progress was made to build new business that will be realized sometime in the future, or the level of customer service the salesperson provided. Because the sales job is multifaceted with many contributing success factors, sales managers should use multiple measures.[40]

Evaluation measures can be objective or subjective. Sales, profits, and the number of orders represent examples of objective measures. Although each is somewhat useful to managers, such measures do not provide an adequate perspective for a thorough evaluation because there is no means of comparison with other salespeople. For instance, suppose salesperson A generated $1 million last year, but salesperson B generated $1.5 million. Should salesperson B automatically receive a significantly higher evaluation? Now consider that salesperson B's territory has twice

LO 19-4 Describe the ethical and legal issues in personal selling.

ETHICAL AND LEGAL ISSUES IN PERSONAL SELLING

Although ethical and legal issues permeate all aspects of marketing, they are particularly important for personal selling. Unlike advertising and other communications with customers, which are planned and executed on a corporate level, personal selling involves a one-to-one, and often face-to-face, encounter with the customer. Thus, sellers' actions are not only highly

ethical & societal dilemma

19.1

When Realtors Become Reality Stars[41]

Reality television has spread to nearly every facet of life, and real estate is no exception. On shows such as *Million Dollar Listing, House Hunters, Property Virgins, Selling New York,* and *Designed to Sell,* viewers can watch as homeowners try to sell their properties and potential buyers search for their perfect home. Helping them every step of the way are real estate professionals, some of whom have gained notoriety as reality television stars themselves.

The *Million Dollar Listing* series, with versions in New York and Los Angeles, has made household names out of agents such as Ryan Serhant and Josh Altman. The handsome, young realtors not only broker massive real estate deals but also share stories about their personal lives and allow cameras to catch them in the shower, in at least one memorable episode. As Altman recognized, "Nobody wants to see the guy who just sells houses every week. They want to see that drama between the realtors." As a result, some of the featured realtors have developed such an extensive fan base that they have hired publicists, managers, and drivers as well as assistants whose sole job is to respond to contacts from fans.

The depictions of real estate transactions clearly make for great television. Consumers enjoy the voyeuristic glimpse into other people's financial affairs and living conditions, especially when those conditions include multimillion dollar homes. The *Million Dollar Listing* episodes each average around 1.25 million viewers, leading networks such as Bravo and HGTV to keep adding new versions and twists to their line-ups of real estate reality television shows.

But according to some observers, the shows create a destructive and potentially dangerous impression of what real estate transactions involve and what the responsibilities of professional realtors are. The agents often are presented in less than flattering light, which could be damaging for their reputation. For example, one cast member on *The Real Housewives of Orange County* left the show mainly because she believed that participating in bickering and being subjected to wine thrown on her ultimately would be too professionally embarrassing to be healthy for her business.

Agencies that prohibit their brokers from appearing on such shows also note that discretion and clients' privacy are central goals for realtors—aspects that rarely are prioritized on reality television. Furthermore, if the agent becomes the star, the broker might come to overshadow the agency's brand as well as the sale itself.

The shows also present a condensed, highly edited version of the real estate process, naturally. Sales of big properties (and even smaller ones) take months to complete, and much of the activity involves paperwork, e-mailing, and research. None of these elements are particularly compelling in video, so the shows tend to exclude them and focus more on loud negotiations, flashy open houses, or snarky interactions.

Yet for many of the star realtors, these potentially negative effects fade away in the face of the massive marketing bump they receive from their notoriety. Bravo asserts that every broker who has appeared on one of its shows has enjoyed increased business through the association. The well-known agents agree: One indicated that his business had jumped by 20 percent, and another noted that he moved from selling midrange condos to dealing in luxury estates, which earned him $200 million in commissions in a single recent year.

---

visible to customers but also to other stakeholders, such as the communities in which they work.

Ethical and legal issues arise in three main areas. First, there is the relationship between the sales manager and the sales force. Second, in some situations, an inconsistency might exist between corporate policy and the salesperson's ethical comfort zone. Third, both ethical and legal issues can arise when the salesperson interacts with the customer, especially if that salesperson or the selling firm collects significant information about the customer. To maintain trustworthy customer relationships, companies must take care that they respect customer privacy and respect the information comfort zone—that is, the amount of information a customer feels comfortable providing.[42]

The Sales Manager and the Sales Force

Like any manager, a sales manager must treat people fairly and equally in everything he or she does. With regard to the sales force, this fairness must include hiring, promotion, supervision, training, assigning duties and quotas, compensation and

incentives, and firing.[43] Federal laws cover many of these issues. For instance, equal employment opportunity laws make it unlawful to discriminate against a person in hiring, promotion, or firing because of race, religion, nationality, sex, or age.

The Sales Force and Corporate Policy

Sometimes salespeople face a conflict between what they believe represents ethical selling and what their company asks them to do to make a sale. Suppose an insurance agent, whose compensation is based on commission, sells a homeowner's policy to a family that has just moved to New Orleans, an area prone to flooding as a result of hurricanes. Even though the policy covers hurricane damage, it does not cover water damage from hurricanes. If the salesperson discloses the inadequate coverage, the sale might be lost because additional flood insurance is very expensive. What should the salesperson do? Salespeople must live within their own ethical comfort zone. If this, or any other situation, is morally repugnant to the salesperson, he or she must question the choice to be associated with such a company.[44]

436 SECTION 7 | Value Communication

Salespeople must live within their own ethical comfort zone. Should insurance salespeople disclose inadequate hurricane coverage and risk not making the sale?

Salespeople also can be held accountable for illegal actions sanctioned by the employer. If the homeowner asks if the home is above the floodplain or whether water damage from flooding is covered by the policy, and it is company policy to intentionally mislead potential customers, both the salesperson and the insurance dealership could be susceptible to legal action.

The Salesperson and the Customer

As the frontline emissaries for a firm, salespeople have a duty to be ethically and legally correct in all their dealings with their customers. Not only is it the right thing to do, it simply means good business. Long-term relationships can deteriorate quickly if customers believe that they have not been treated in an ethically proper manner. Unfortunately, salespeople sometimes get mixed signals from their managers or simply do not know when their behaviors might be considered unethical or illegal. Formal guidelines can help, but it is also important to integrate these guidelines into training programs in which salespeople can discuss various issues that arise in the field with their peers and managers.[45] Most important, however, is for sales managers to lead by example. If managers are known to cut ethical corners in their dealings with customers, it shouldn't surprise them when their salespeople do the same. Ethical & Societal Dilemma 19.1 considers the ethical issues that realtors face. ▪

✓ **check** yourself

1. What are three areas of personal selling in which ethical and legal issues are more likely to arise?

check it out!

mhhe.com/GrewalM4e
for study materials,
including quizzes
and videos.

endnotes

CHAPTER 1

1. "Ice Cream and Frozen Desserts in the U.S.: Markets and Opportunities in Retail and Foodservice, 6th ed., *Packaged Facts,* (January 2010).

2. http://www.unileverusa.com/brands/foodbrands/benandjerrys/.

3. http://www.redmangousa.com/red-mango/.

4. http://www.redmangousa.com/menu/.

5. "Menu_Nutrition," http://tcby.com/menu-nutrition/soft-serve/.

6. Jaime Levy Pessin, "Yogurt Chains Give Power to the People," *The Wall Street Journal,* August 22, 2011.

7. Packaged Facts, op. cit., p. 135.

8. The American Marketing Association, http://www.marketingpower .com/AboutAMA/Pages/DefinitionofMarketing.aspx. Word in italics was added by the authors. Discussions of the latest revision of the AMA's marketing definition are widespread. See Gregory T. Gundlach and William L. Wilkie, "AMA's New Definition of Marketing: Perspective and Commentary on the 2007 Revision," *Journal of Public Policy & Marketing* 28, no. 2 (2008), pp. 259–64; see also *Journal of Public Policy & Marketing* 26, no. 2 (Fall, 2007), which contains eight perspectives on the new definition.

9. Mike Esterl, "Coke Tailors Its Soda Sizes," *The Wall Street Journal,* September 19, 2011, http://online.wsj.com/article /SB10001424053111903374004576578980270401662 .html; Natalie Zmuda, "Diet Coke Blasts Past Pepsi," *Advertising Age,* March 17, 2011, http://adage.com/article/news/diet-coke-blasts-past-pepsi/149453/; Natalie Zmuda, "Can Pepsi's Big Marketing Shake-Up Bring Back Fizz to Its Beverage Brands?" *Advertising Age,* June 20, 2011, http://adage.com /article/news/pepsi-s-marketing-reorg-bring-back-fizz-beverages/228292/.

10. http://www.lexus.com/models/LSh/index.html.

11. The idea of the four Ps was conceptualized by E. Jerome McCarthy, *Basic Marketing: A Managerial Approach* (Homewood, IL: Richard D. Irwin, 1960). Also see Walter van Watershoot and Christophe Van den Bulte, "The 4P Classification of the Marketing Mix Revisited," *Journal of Marketing* 56 (October 1992), pp. 83–93.

12. Raphael Thomadsen, "Seeking an Expanding Competitor: How Product Line Expansion Can Increase All Firms' Profits," *Journal of Marketing Research* 49 (2012), pp. 349–60.

13. http://www.nitrodessertstation.com/.

14. Wolfgang Ulaga and Werner Reinartz, "Hybrid Offerings: How Manufacturing Firms Combine Goods and Services Successfully," *Journal of Marketing* 75 (November 2011), pp. 5–23.

15. Anja Lambrecht and Catherine Tucker, "Paying with Money or Effort: Pricing When Customers Anticipate Hassle," *Journal of Marketing Research* 49 (2012), pp. 66–82.

16. Jaime Levy Pessin, "Yogurt Chains Give Power to the People," *The Wall Street Journal,* August 22, 2011, http://online.wsj.com /article/SB10001424405270230336580457643206365832 3394.html.

17. Pew Internet and American Life Project, "Social Networking Sites and Our Lives," June 16, 2011, http://pewinternet.org /~/media//Files/Reports/2011/PIP%20-%20Social% 20networking%20sites%20and%20our%20lives.pdf; "Statistics," http://www.facebook.com/press/info.php? statistics; Mike Elgan, "Click 'Like' if You Like 'Like'," *Bloomberg Businessweek,* May 4, 2011; David Goldman, "Get Ready for Some Big Facebook Changes," CNNMoney.com, April 21, 2010; Venture Capital Dispatch, "Giving Credits Where Credits Are Due: Facebook to Aid Developers," *The Wall Street Journal,* April 22, 2010; Liz Gannes, "Facebook: The Entire Web Will Be Social," Gigaom.com, April 21, 2010; Jessica Vascellaro, "Facebook Wants to Know More Than Just Who Your Friends Are," *The Wall Street Journal,* April 22, 2010; Samuel Axon, "Facebook's Open Graph Personalizes the Web," Mashable.com, April 21, 2010; Harry McCracken, "Microsoft Melds Office with Facebook," Technologizer.com, April 21, 2010.

18. George S. Day, "Aligning the Organization with the Market," *Marketing Science Institute* 5, no. 3 (2005), pp. 3–20.

19. Kimmy Wa Chan, Chi Kin (Bennett) Yim, and Simon S. K. Lam, "Is Customer Participation in Value Creation a Double-Edged Sword? Evidence from Professional Financial Services across Cultures," *Journal of Marketing* 74, no. 3 (May 2010); Dhruv Grewal, Kent B. Monroe, and R. Krishnan, "The Effects of Price Comparison Advertising on Buyers' Perceptions of Acquisition Value and Transaction Value," Journal of Marketing 62 (April 1998), pp. 46–60.

20. Anne L. Roggeveen, Michael Tsiros and Dhruv Grewal, "Understanding the Co-Creation Effect: When Does Collaborating with Customers Provide a Lift to Service Recovery?" *Journal of the Academy of Marketing Science,* 40, no. 6 (2012), pp. 771–790.; Sigurd Troye and Magne Supphellen, "Consumer Participation in Coproduction: 'I Made It Myself' Effects on Consumers' Sensory Perceptions and Evaluations of Outcome and Input Product," Journal of Marketing, 76, no. 2 (2012), pp. 33–46; Neeli Bendapudi and Robert P. Leone, "Psychological Implications of Customer Participation in Co-Production," Journal of Marketing 67 (January 2003), pp. 14–28.

21. Alvaris Falcon, "20 Gadgets That Make Your Smartphone Even Smarter," Hongkiat.com, http://www.hongkiat.com/blog /innovative-smartphone-gadgets/.

22. David Pogue, "2 Wristbands Keep Tabs on Fitness," *The New York Times,* November 14, 2012, http://www.nytimes.com /2012/11/15/technology/personaltech/a-review-of-new-activity-tracking-bands-from-nike-and-jawbone.html.

23. Falcon, op. cit.

24. Clare Cain Miller, "New Apps Arrive on Google Glass," *The New York Times,* May 16, 2013, http://bits.blogs.nytimes.com/2013 /05/16/new-apps-arrive-on-google-glass/.

25. Daniel J. Simons and Christopher F. Chabris, "Is Google Glass Dangerous?" *The New York Times,* May 24, 2013, http://www .nytimes.com/2013/05/26/opinion/sunday/google-glass-may-be-hands-free-but-not-brain-free.html.

26. V. Kumar and Denish Shah., "Can Marketing Lift Stock Prices?" *Sloan Management Review* 52, no. 4 (2011), pp. 24–26; V. Kumar, Eli Jones, Rajkumar Venkatesan, and Robert P. Leone, "Is Market Orientation a Source of Sustainable Competitive Advantage or Simply the Cost of Competing?" *Journal of Marketing* 75 (January 2011), pp. 16–30; Stephen A. Samaha, Robert W. Palmatier, and Rajiv P Dant, "Poisoning Relationships: Perceived Unfairness in Channels of Distribution," *Journal of*

Marketing 75 (May 2011), pp. 99–117; Alexander Krasnikov, Satish Jayachandran, and V. Kumar, "The Impact of CRM Implementation on Cost and Profit Efficiencies: Evidence from US Commercial Banking Industry," *Journal of Marketing* 73 (November 2009), pp. 61–76.

27. Krasnikov, Jayachandran, and Kumar, op. cit.; V. Kumar, Denish Shah, and Rajkumar Venkatesan, "Managing Retailer Profitability—One Customer at a Time!" *Journal of Retailing* 82, no. 4 (2006), pp. 277–94.

28. Randy Schrum, "Social Media 2010, The Fastest Growth Ever," mycorporatemedia.com, January 30, 2011; http://www .onlinemarketing-trends.com/2011/03/50-of-us-users-will-be-facebook-in-2013.html; Jonah Berger and Katherine L. Milkman, "What Makes Online Content Viral?" *Journal of Marketing Research* 49, no. 2 (2012), pp. 192–205.

29. http://mobithinking.com/stats-corner/global-mobile-statis-tics-2011-all-quality-mobile-marketing-research-mobile-web-stats-su.

30. http://thenextweb.com/socialmedia/2011/01/20/could-facebook-reach-one-billion-users-in-2011/

31. Geoffrey A. Fowler, "Facebook Tops Billion-User Mark," *The Wall Street Journal,* October 4, 2012; "Statistics," http://www.facebook .com/press/info.php?statistics; "Twitter Statistics: Updated Stats for 2011," July 7, 2011, http://www.marketinggum.com /twitter-statistics-2011-updated-stats/; "About Us," http://press .linkedin.com/about; Amy Lee, "YouTube Shares Surprising Statistics on 6th Birthday," *The Huffington Post,* May 25, 2011, http://www.huffingtonpost.com/2011/05/25/youtube-statistics-birthday_n_866707.html.

32. Julie Weed, "Hotels Turn to Social Media to Connect with Travelers," *The New York Times,* April 18, 2011.

33. Elizabeth Olson, "Restaurants Reach Out to Customers with Social Media," *The New York Times,* January 19, 2011.

34. Ibid.

35. Raji Srinivasan, Gary L. Lilien, and Shrihari Sridhar, "Should Firms Spend More on Research and Development and Advertising during Recessions?" *Journal of Marketing* 75 (May 2011), pp. 49–65.

36. http://www.ahold.com.

37. Philip Kotler, "Reinventing Marketing to Manage the Environmental Imperative," *Journal of Marketing* 75 (July 2011), pp. 132–35; Katherine White, Rhiannon MacDonnell, and John H. Ellard, "Belief in a Just World: Consumer Intentions and Behaviors toward Ethical Products," *Journal of Marketing* 76 (January 2012), pp. 103–118.

38. http://dictionary.reference.com/browse/Entrepreneurship?s=t.

39. Tina Rosenberg, "A Scorecard for Companies with a Conscience," *The New York Times,* April 11, 2011, http://opinionator.blogs .nytimes.com/2011/04/11/a-scorecard-for-companies-with-a-conscience/.

40. Ibid.

41. "P&G Professional's Green Guarantee," http://www .greenguarantee.com/faqs.htm.

42. "Commitment to Everyday Life," 2011 Sustainability Overview, http://www.pg.com/en_US/downloads/sustainability/reports /PG_2011_Sustainability_Overview.pdf.

43. Jonathan Bardeline, "P&G Scorecard Puts Supply Chain on Notice," *Greenbiz.com,* April 7, 2011, http://www.greenbiz.com /news/2011/04/07/procter-gamble-scorecard-puts-supply-chain-notice.

44. "Commitment to Everyday Life," op. cit.

45. http://www.oprah.com; "Oprah Winfrey," http://en.wikipedia.org /wiki/Oprah_Winfrey.

CHAPTER 2

1. "About Nike Inc.," http://nikeinc.com/pages/about-nike-inc.

2. Bob Young, "No NBA? Let the Shoe Wars Begin," *The Arizona Republic,* October 16, 2011, http://www.azcentral.com/sports /suns/articles/2011/10/16/20111016heat-index-nba-lockout-shoe-wars.html.

3. Nike, 10-K report, July 20, 2010.

4. "Sneaker Wars: adidas Puts a Chainsaw to Kobe Bryant's Nikes," http://balljunkie.com/2011/05/27/sneaker-wars-adidas-puts-a-chainshaw-to-kobe-bryants-nikes/.

5. "Nike + iPod," http://www.apple.com/ipod/nike/run.html.

6. "Nike vs. Adidas," http://recomparison.com/comparisons /100305/nike-vs-adidas/.

7. Georgios Dogiamis and Narain Vijayshanker, "adidas: Sprinting Ahead of Nike," White paper, Winter 2009.

8. "Nike Crushes adidas on the Track in Olympic Shoe Wars," http://www.tracktownusa.com/track.item.79/Nike-Crushes-Adidas-on-the-Track-in-Olympic-Shoe-Wars.html.

9. Michael Treacy and Fred Wiersema, *The Disciplines of Market Leaders* (Reading, MA: Addison Wesley, 1995). Treacy and Weirsema suggest the first three strategies. We suggest the fourth—locational excellence.

10. J. Andrew Petersen, Leigh McAlister, David J. Reibstein, Russell S. Winer, V. Kumar, and Geoff Atkinson, "Choosing the Right Metrics to Maximize Profitability and Shareholder Value," *Journal of Retailing* 85, no. 1 (2009), pp. 95–111.

11. Andrew Petersen et al., "Choosing the Right Metrics to Maximize Profitability and Shareholder Value"; V. Kumar, "Tough Times Call for CLV," *The Economist,* March 29, 2009; V. Kumar, *Managing Customers for Profit: Strategies to Increase Profits and Build Loyalty* (Philadelphia: Wharton School Publishing, 2008).

12. Valarie A. Zeithaml, Mary Jo Bitner, and Dwayne D. Gremler, *Services Marketing: Integrating Customer Focus across the Firm,* 5th ed. (Burr Ridge, IL: McGraw-Irwin, 2009).

13. James R. Stock, Stefanie L. Boyer, and Tracy Harmon, "Research Opportunities in Supply Chain Management," *Journal of the Academy of Marketing Science* 38, no. 1 (2010), pp. 32–41. Also see articles in special issue edited by John T. Mentzer and Greg Gundlach, "Exploring the Relationship between Marketing and Supply Chain Management: Introduction to the Special Issue," *Journal of the Academy of Marketing Science* 38, no. 1 (2010), pp. 1–4.

14. http://www.interbrand.com/en/best-global-brands/Best-Global-Brands-2011.aspx.

15. http://www.marketingpower.com/_layouts/Dictionary. aspx?dLetter=M.

16. Donald Lehman and Russell Winer, *Analysis for Marketing Planning,* 7th ed. (Burr Ridge, IL: McGraw-Hill/Irwin, 2008).

17. Andrew Campbell, "Mission Statements," *Long Range Planning,* 30 (1997), pp. 931–933.

18. Alfred Rappaport, *Creating Shareholder Value: The New Standard for Business Performance* (New York: Wiley, 1988).

19. http://help-us.nike.com/app/answers/detail/a_id/113/~ /what-is-nike's-mission-statement%3F.

20. http://adidas-group.corporate-publications.com/2010/gb/en/group-management-report-our-group/corporate-mission-statement.html.

21. http://www.teachforamerica.org/mission/mission_and_approach.htm.

22. Michael McCarthy, "NBA Lockout Not Good for the Shoes," *USA Today*, November 1, 2011, http://www.usatoday.com/sports/basketball/nba/story/2011-10-30/NBA-lockout-not-good-for-the-shoes/51007210/1.

23. Matt Townsend, "As Nike Scoffs, Toning Shoes Gain Traction," *Bloomberg Businessweek*, June 7–13, 2010, pp. 22–24.

24. Eric Siemers, "Nike Takes New Marketing Tack," *Portland Business Journal*, September 12, 2010, http://www.bizjournals.com/portland/stories/2010/09/13/story9.html.

25. Nike 10-K report, July 20, 2010.

26. Russel Parsons, "Nike Beating Official Sponsor adidas in World Cup Stakes," *Marketing Week*, June 24, 2010, p. 7.

27. Eric Siemans, "New Balance TV Spots Target Nike," *Portland Business Journal*, March 7, 2011, http://www.bizjournals.com/portland/blog/2011/03/new-balance-tv-spots-target-nike.html?page=2.

28. Nike 10-K report, July 20, 2010.

29. http://www.hertz.com/rentacar/vehicleguide/index.jsp?targetPage=vehicleGuideHomeView.jsp&countryCode=US&category=Car/Sedan.

30. https://images.hertz.com/pdfs/VMVWeb.pdf; http://www.adweek.com/aw/content_display/creative/new-campaigns/e3i21cea1586dd4edf5d50f9a17e7f18bf3.

31. Ian Chant, "Sign of the End Times: Pizza Hut Allows You To Order Pizza Without Letting Go of Xbox Controller," *GeekSystem*, April 23, 2013; Peter Johnston, "Share of the Mobile Pie," *Stores*, October 2011.

32. Andy Potts, "The Emporium Strikes Back," *The Economist*, July 13, 2013, http://www.economist.com/news/briefing/2158155-retailers-rich-world-are-suffering-people-buy-more-things-onlinethey-are-finding.

33. Rick Moss, "What Whole Foods Gained from Its LivingSocial Deal," *Forbes*, September 15, 2011, http://www.forbes.com/sites/retailwire/2011/09/15/what-whole-foods-gained-from-its-livingsocial-deal/.

34. Sandy Smith, "Category Killing, Korea Style," *Stores*, October 2011.

35. Tesco, "Tesco HomePlus Expands Number of Virtual Stores," new release, February 7, 2012, http://www.tescoplc.com/index.asp?pageid=17&newsid=593.

36. Andy Potts, "The Emporium Strikes Back," *The Economist*, July 13, 2013, http://www.economist.com/news/briefing/2158155-retailers-rich-world-are-suffering-people-buy-more-things-online-they-are-finding.

37. Kevin Chung, Timothy Derdenger, and Kannan Srinivasan, "Economic Value of Celebrity Endorsement: Tiger Woods' Impact on Sales of Nike Golf Balls," Working paper, Carnegie Mellon University, December 2, 2010, http://www.andrew.cmu.edu/user/derdenge/TWExecutiveSummary.pdf.

38. Chung, Derdenger, and Srinivasan, op cit.

39. "More Driven: Goodyear 2010 Annual Report," http://www.goodyear.com/investor/pdf/ar/2010ar.pdf.

40. This discussion is adapted from Roger A. Kerin, Steven W. Hartley, and William Rudelius, *Marketing*, 10th ed. (Burr Ridge, IL: McGraw-Hill/Irwin, 2011).

41. Paul W. Farris, Neil T. Bendle, Phillip E. Pfeifer, and David J. Reibstein, *Marketing Metrics: 50+ Metrics Every Executive Should Master* (Upper Saddle River, NJ: Pearson Education, Inc., 2006), p. 17.

42. Natasha Singer and Peter Lattman, "Is the Seller to Blame? Workout Supplement Challenged after Death of Soldier," *The New York Times*, March 15, 2013.

43. Monster Energy Drink Maker Sued for 14-Year-Old's Death, *CMSNews.com*, October 22, 2012, http://www.cbsnews.com/8301-204_162-57537545/monster-energy-drink-maker-sued-for-14-year-olds-death/.

44. "Monster Energy Drink Linked to Another Teen's Death; Lawsuit Filed," *CBSNews.com*, June 26, 2013, http://www.cbsnews.com/8301-204_162-57591097/monster-energy-drink-linked-to-another-teens-death-lawsuit-filed/.

45. Barry Meier, "Suit Claims Energy Drink Maker Markets to Children," *The New York Times*, May 6, 2013, http://www.nytimes.com/2013/05/07/business/suit-claims-monster-beverage-markets-to-children.html.

46. Singer and Lattman, op. cit.

47. Barry Meier, "In a New Aisle, Energy Drinks Sidestep Some Rules," *The New York Times*, March 19, 2013, http://www.nytimes.com/2013/03/20/business/in-a-new-aisle-energy-drinks-sidestep-rules.html?pagewanted=all&_r=0.

48. Relative market share = brand's market share ÷ largest competitor's market share. If, for instance, there are only two products in a market, A and B, and product B has 90 percent market share, then A's relative market share is 10 ÷ 90 = 11.1 percent. If, on the other hand, B only has 50 percent market share, then A's relative market share is 10 ÷ 50 = 20 percent. Farris et al., *Marketing Metrics*, p. 19.

49. Apple Inc., "Form 10-K 2011 Annual Report," http://files.shareholder.com/downloads/AAPL/1710549824x0x512287/5a5d7b14-9542-4640-841d-e047ec28bb96/AAPL_10K_FY11_10.26.11.pdf.

50. "Strategy Analytics: Apple Becomes World's Largest Smartphone Vendor in Q4 2011," *Business Wire*, January 26, 2012, http://www.businesswire.com/news/home/20120126006752/en/Strategy-Analytics-Apple-Worlds-Largest-Smartphone-Vendor

51. Sherilynn Macale, "Apple Has Sold 300M iPods, Currently Holds 78% of the Music Player Market," *The Next Web*, October 4, 2011, http://thenextweb.com/apple/2011/10/04/apple-has-sold-300m-ipods-currently-holds-78-of-the-music-player-market/; Chris Smith, "iPad Tablet Market Share Down to 57 Percent," Techradar.com, February 16, 2012, http://www.techradar.com/news/mobile-computing/tablets/ipad-tablet-market-share-down-to-57-per-cent-1064010.

52. Joe Wilcox, "iPad Market Share Plunged 20 Percent in Q4 2010," *BetaNews*, February 2011, http://betanews.com/2011/03/10/ipad-market-share-plunged-20-percent-in-q4-2010/; Mohit Agrawal, "Tablets OS Market Share," *Telecom Circle*, October 7, 2011, http://www.telecomcircle.com/2011/10/tablets-os-market-share/

53. Roger Kerin, Vijay Mahajan, and P. Rajan Varadarajan, *Contemporary Perspectives on Strategic Market Planning* (Boston: Allyn & Bacon, 1991), chapter 6; Susan Mudambi, "A Topology of Strategic Choice in Marketing," *International Journal of Market & Distribution Management* (1994), pp. 22–25.

54. http://www.gamestop.com/xbox-360/movies-tv/yoostar-on-mtv/91616.

55. http://www.mtv.com/shows/teen_mom/season_3/series.jhtml.

56. http://www.viacom.com/ourbrands/globalreach/Pages/default.aspx.

57. http://www.stayteen.org/; http://www.mtv.com/mobile/.

58. A. A. Thompson, Margaret A. Peteraf, John E. Gamble, and A. J. Strickland, *Crafting and Executing Strategy,* 18th ed. (New York, NY: McGraw-Hill Irwin, 2012).

59. http://www.mtv.com/shows/made/series.jhtml; Tim Arango, "Make Room, Cynics: MTV Wants to Do Some Good," *The New York Times,* April 18, 2009; Robert Seidman, "MTV Continues to Diversify Slate with New Scripted Comedies: 'The Hard Times of RJ Berger' and 'Warren the Ape,'" tvbythenumbers.com, January 15, 2010.

CHAPTER 3

1. Adam Ostrow, "Inside Gatorade's Social Media Control Center," *Mashable.com,* June 15, 2010, http://mashable.com/2010/06/15/gatorade-social-media-mission-control/?utm_source=feedburner&utm_medium=feed&utm_campaign=Feed%3A+Mashable+%28Mashable%29.

2. PepsiCo, "Gatorade Mission Control," YouTube, https://www.youtube.com/watch?v=InrOvEE2v38&feature=player_embedded.

3. Sarah McNew, "Social Media Breakdown: A Look at Gatorade's Social Media Marketing Efforts," *Social Toaster,* May 6, 2013, http://www.socialtoaster.com/blog-entry/social-media-breakdown-look-gatorades-social-media-marketing-efforts.

4. "Gatorade's Social Media Command Center?" *Hive Health Media,* May 17, 2013, http://www.hivehealthmedia.com/gatorades-social-media-command-center/.

5. Lisa Joy Rosner, "Gatorade Generates the Buzz, Pocari Sweat Heats Up in Love; NetBase Brand Passion Index Measures Social Data on Sports Drinks," *The Wall Street Journal,* July 10, 2013, http://online.wsj.com/article/PR-CO-20130710-906433.html.

6. Samantha Murphy, "Viral Dove Campaign Becomes Most Watched Ad Ever," *Mashable.com,* May 20, 2013, http://mashable.com/2013/05/20/dove-ad-most-watche/.

7. Tanzina Vega, "Ad about Women's Self Image Creates a Sensation," *The New York Times,* April 18, 2013, http://www.nytimes.com/2013/04/19/business/media/dove-ad-on-womens-self-image-creates-an-online-sensation.html.

8. Avi Dan, "Dove's New Video Is a Beauty, But Is It a Bit Skin Deep?" *Forbes,* April 21, 2013, http://www.forbes.com/sites/avidan/2013/04/21/doves-new-video-is-a-beauty-but-is-it-a-bit-skin-deep/.

9. Jazz Brice, "Little Drops," http://jazzylittledrops.tumblr.com/post/48118645174/why-doves-real-beauty-sketches-video-makes-me.

10. "Dove's 'Real Beauty Sketches' Wins Ogilvy Brazil the Titanium Gran Prix," *AdWeek,* June 22, 2013, http://www.adweek.com/news/advertising-branding/doves-real-beauty-skieches-earns-ogilvy-brazil-titanium-grand-prix-150587.

11. HubSpot company website, http://www.hubspot.com/internet-marketing-company/; Canadian Mountain Holidays website, http://www.canadiananmountainholidays.com/heli-skiing/trips; http://www.hubspot.com/customer-case-studies/bid/31288/Travel-and-Leisure-Industry-Sucess-Story-CMH-Heli-Skiing-Summer-Adventures.

12. Nikon, press release, August 22, 2007, http://press.nikonusa.com/post/2007/08/22/nikons-new-digital-learning-center-on-flickr-provides-a-first-of-its-kind-interactive-experience-that-assists-everyday-people-in-taking-better-photos/.

13. Chris Barry, Rob Markey, Eric Almquist, and Chris Brahm (2011), "Putting Social Media to Work," Bain & Co.

14. Coca-Cola Retailing Research Council and the Integer Group, "Social Networking Personas: A Look at Consumer and Shopper Mind Sets," in Untangling the Social Web: Insights for Users, Brands, and Retailers, March 2012, http://www.cokesolutions.com/BusinessSolutions/Studies/Untangling%20the%20Social%20Web_Part%203.pdf.

15. Forever 21 Facebook Fan Page, http://www.facebook.com/#!/Forever21?ref=ts.

16. Ibid.

17. Andrew LaVallee, "Burger King Cancels Facebook Ad Campaign," *The Wall Street Journal,* January 15, 2009.

18. Ann-Christine Diaz, "Facebook 101: Is Your Brand Worth a Like?" Ad Age Digital, January 30, 2012.

19. Pam Dyer, "Facebook Advertising Case Study: Clorox Green Works," http://www.pamorama.net/2011/02/26/facebook-advertising-case-study-clorox-green-works/.

20. "LinkedIn Announces Fourth Quarter and 2011 Fiscal Year Financial Results," LinkedIn, February 9, 2012, http://press.linkedin.com/node/1104.

21. Guy Kawaski, "Ten Ways for Small Businesses to Use LinkedIn," LinkedIn Blog, April 12, 2010, http://blog.linkedin.com/2010/04/12/linkedin-small-business-tips/.

22. Catherine Smith, "Google + Adds Games: Angry Birds, Zynga Poker, and Bejeweled," *Huffington Post,* August 11, 2011.

23. Ibid.

24. "Instagram," Wikipedia, August 2, 2013, http://en.wikipedia.org/wiki/Instagram.

25. Somini Sengupta, Nicole Perlroth, and Jenna Wortham, "Behind Instagram's Success, Networking the Old Way," *The New York Times,* April 12, 2012, http://www.nytimes.com/2012/04/14/technology/instagram-founders-were-helped-by-bay-area-connections.html?pagewanted=all&_r=2.

26. Shayndi Raice and Spencer E. Ante, "Insta-Rich: $1 Billion for Instagram," *The Wall Street Journal,* April 10, 2012, http://online.wsj.com/article/SB100014240527023038154045733840377381670.html.

27. Finlo Rohrer, "Vine: Six Things People Have Learned about Six-Second Video in a Week," http://www.bbc.co.uk/news/magazine-21267741.

28. "In The Know," *YouTube,* Fall 2009, http://www.gstatic.com/youtube/engagement/platform/autoplay/advertise/downloads/YouTube_InTheKnow.pdf.

29. "Brand Channels," *YouTube,* http://www.gstatic.com/youtube/engagement/platform/autoplay/advertise/downloads/YouTube_BrandChannels.pdf.

30. M. P. Mueller, "Small Businesses That Understand Social Media," *The New York Times,* July 11, 2011, http://boss.blogs.nytimes.com/2011/07/11/small-businesses-that-understand-social-media/.

31. Mueller, op. cit.

32. David H. Freedman, "Debating the Merits of Facebook and Google+," *The New York Times,* February 7, 2012, http://boss

.blogs.nytimes.com/2012/02/07/debating-the-merits-of-facebook-and-google/.

33. Ross Blum, "Where Have All the Customers Gone?" p. 8

34. Leah Shafer, "Re-Branding the Dynasty: Tori Spelling's HSN Clips on YouTube," March 25, 2010, http://mediacommons .futureofthebook.org/imr/2010/03/24/re-branding-dynasty-tori-spellings-hsn-clips-youtube.

35. "Brands on Flickr," Supercollider, July 12, 2008, http: //geoffnorthcott.com/blog/2008/07/brands-on-flickr/.

36. Leah Shafer, "Re-Branding the Dynasty: Tori Spelling's HSN Clips on YouTube," March 25, 2010, http://mediacommons .futureofthebook.org/imr/2010/03/24/re-branding-dynasty-tori-spellings-hsn-clips-youtube.

37. "So How Many Blogs Are There Anyways?" Hat Trick Associates, February 1, 2012. http://www.hattrickassociates.com/tag /how-many-blogs-exist/.

38. Mark W. Schaefer, "The 10 Best Corporate Blogs in the World," BusinessGrow.com, January 1, 2011, http://www .businessesgrow.com/2011/01/05/the-10-best-corporate-blogs-in-the-world/.

39. "Top 10 Most Influential Mommy Blogs," Cision Navigator, May 5, 2011, http://navigator.cision.com/Top-10-Most-Influential-Mommy-Bloggers.aspx.

40. Elizabeth Holmes, "Tweeting without Fear," *The Wall Street Journal,* December 9, 2011.

41. Ibid.

42. Ganesh Babu, "Justin Bieber's Social Media Fame [Infographic]," AXLERATION, http://www.axleration.com/justin-biebers-social-media-fame-infographic/.

43. Famecount, "Justin Bieber Facebook Statistics," www.famebook .com/facebook/justin-bieber.

44. Eric Goldstein, "Justin Bieber: A Social Media Case Study," *Social Media Today,* June 12, 2011, http://socialmediatoday.com /eric-goldstein/305692/justin-bieber-social-media-case-study.

45. Babu, op. cit.

46. Ibid.

47. Goldstein, op. cit.

48. Babu, op. cit.

49. Goldstein, op. cit.

50. Goldstein, op. cit.

51. Coca-Cola Retailing Research Council and the Integer Group, "Assessing the Social Networking Landscape," in Untangling the Social Web: Insights for Users, Brands, and Retailers, January 2012.

52. Brad Tuttle, "Use Amazon's Price Check App and Save $15 This Saturday," http://moneyland.time.com/2011/12/08 /use-amazons-price-check-app-and-save-15-this-saturday/.

53. "Local Bookstores Ask Customers to Boycott Amazon over New Price Check App Offer," http://www.commondreams.org /headline/2011/12/12-3.

54. Brad Tuttle, "How Smartphones, Price-Check Apps, and Daily Deals Are Changing Black Friday—and the Entire Holiday Season," *Time Magazine Moneyland Blog,* November 25, 2011, http://moneyland.time.com/2011/11/25/how-smartphones-price-check-apps-and-daily-deals-are-changing-black-friday-and-the-entire-holiday-shopping-season/.

55. Tom Ryan, "Target Looks to Battle Pricing App, *Retail Wire,* January 24, 2012.

56. Marguerite Darlington, "The History and Future of Mobile's Role in Fashion," FashionablyMarketing.me, November 22, 2011.

57. Katie Van Domelin, "Social Media Monitoring Tools–How to Pick the Right One," July 7, 2010, http://www.convinceandconvert .com/social-media-monitoring/social-media-monitoring-tools-how-to-pick-the-right-one/.

58. "New Radian6 Features Help to Scale 'Social' Across the Enterprise," Radian6 website, November 12, 2011, http: //www.radian6.com/wp-content/uploads/2010/12 /NovemberRelease.pdf.

59. Radian6 website, http://www.radian6.com/2011.

60. Let's Get Ready website, http://www.letsgetready.org/About /MissionAndVision.

61. Laura S. Quinn and Kyle Andrei, "A Few Good Web Analytics Tools," May 19, 2011, http://www.techsoup.org/learningcenter /internet/page6760.cfm.

62. Christina Warren, "How to Measure Social Media ROI," Ocotber 27, 2009, http://mashable.com/2009/10/27 /social-media-roi/.

63. "iNoobs: What Is Google Analytics?" http://inspiredm.com /what-is-google-analytics/; http://www.google.com/analytics /features/index.html; http://www.advanced-web-metrics.com /docs/web-data-sources.pdf; http://mobile.tutsplus.com /articles/marketing/7-solutions-for-tracking-mobile-analytics/; http://www.practicalecommerce.com/articles/3062-10-Web-Analytics-Solutions-for-Ecommerce-Merchants.

64. Amy Porterfield, "3 Steps to an Effective Social Media Strategy," *Social Media Examiner,* March 1, 2012, http://www .socialmediaexaminer.com/3-steps-to-an-effective-social-media-strategy/.

65. Sarah Mahoney, "Macy's Gets Face(book) Lift, Expands 'Ecosystem'," *Marketing Daily,* February 29, 2012.

66. Andy Shaw, "How to Create a Facebook Ad Campaign," Social Media Tips, September 23, 2011, http://exploringsocialmedia .com/how-to-create-a-facebook-ad-campaign/.

67. Karen Kroll, "Localizing the Message," *Stores News,* September 2011.

68. "Should Social Media Listening Replace Your Asking Consumer Research?" April 6, 2012, http://socialmediatoday.com /neilglassman/485074/should-social-media-listening-replace-your-asking-consumer-research-convo.

69. "What Is the Best Alternative to Klout?" http://www.quora .com/What-is-the-best-alternative-to-Klout.

70. Mark W. Schaefer, "Google and Bing Reveal that Social Influence Bumps Search Engine Results," December 2, 2010, http://www.businessesgrow.com/2010/12/02/google-and-bing-reveal-that-social-influence-bumpdrives-search-engine-results/.

71. Erin Griffith, "Getting Your Klout Out," *AdWeek,* May 17, 2011, http://www.adweek.com/news/advertising-branding/getting-your-klout-out-131629.

72. Landman, "Are You a V.I.P.? Check Your Klout Score," *The New York Times,* November 18, 2011.

73. "Social Media Career Advice from Leading Marketers," http: //www.onwardsearch.com/Social-Media-Career-Advice/; Griffith, op. cit.

74. James Tomerson, "Looking for Job Opportunities in Social Media?" http://www.jobdiagnosis.com/myblog/social-media-jobs.htm.

75. Shan Li, "Employers Are Liking—and Hiring—Social Media Workers," *Los Angeles Times,* September 28, 2011, http://articles.latimes.com/2011/sep/28/business/la-fi-social-media-jobs-20110929.

76. "The Klout Score," http://klout.com/understand/score.

77. Seth Stevenson, "What Your Klout Score Really Means," *Wired,* April 24, 2012, http://www.wired.com/epicenter/2012/04/ff_klout/.

78. Schaefer, op. cit.

79. Kashmir Hill, "Facebook Can Tell You If a Person Is Worth Hiring," *Forbes,* March 5, 2012, http://www.forbes.com/sites/kashmirhill/2012/03/05/facebook-can-tell-you-if-a-person-is-worth-hiring/?partner=yahoo.

80. Barry Murphy, "The Next Governance Frontier: Social Media," *Forbes,* http://www.forbes.com/sites/barrymurphy/2012/02/28/the-next-governance-frontier-social-media/.

CHAPTER 4

1. National Geographic, "Overfishing: Plenty of Fish in the Sea? Not Always," http://ocean.nationalgeographic.com/.

2. Jennifer L. Jacquet and Daniel Pauly, "Trade Secrets: Renaming and Mislabeling of Seafood," *Marine Policy* 32 (2008), pp. 309–18.

3. Stephen Nolgren and Terry Tomalin, "You Order Grouper; What Do You Get?" *St. Petersburg Times,* August 6, 2006, http://www.sptimes.com/.

4. "On the Menu, But Not on Your Plate," *Boston Globe,* October 23, 2011, http://www.boston.com/business/articles/2011/10/23/on_the_menu_but_not_on_your_plate/?cbResetParam=1/; Chris Reidy, "Consumer Reports 'Mystery Fish' Story Finds Similar Results to Globe's Investigation into Seafood Mislabeling," *Business Updates,* October 28, 2011, http://www.boston.com. See also "Fish Fraud Exposé in *Boston Globe* Sparks Conversation," http://jacquelinechurch.com.

5. Theodore Levitt, *Marketing Imagination* (Detroit, MI: The Free Press, 1983).

6. Kevin Peachy, "EU Toy Safety Rules to Be Stricter," *BBC News,* July 7, 2011, http://www.bbc.co.uk.

7. "Mattel Apologizes to China for Recall," *The New York Times,* September 21, 2007, http://www.nytimes.com; "Plenty of Blame to Go Around," *The Economist,* September 29, 2007.

8. Andrew Martin, "Toy Makers Fight for Exemption from Rules," *The New York Times,* September 28, 2010, http://www.nytimes.com.

9. For a detailed compilation of articles that are involved with ethical and societal issues, see Gregory T. Gundlach, Lauren G. Block, and William W. Wilkie, *Explorations of Marketing in Society* (Mason, OH: Thompson Higher Education, 2007); G. Svensson and G. Wood, "A Model of Business Ethics," *Journal of Business Ethics* 77, no. 3 (2007), pp. 303–22.

10. Christy Ashley and Hillary A. Leonard, "Betrayed by the Buzz? Covert Content and Consumer–Brand Relationships," *Journal of Public Policy & Marketing* 28, no. 2 (2009), pp. 212–20.

11. Elizabeth S. Moore and Victoria J. Rideout, "The Online Marketing of Food to Children: Is it Just Fun and Games?" *Journal of Public Policy & Marketing* 26, no. 2 (2007), pp. 202–20; Elizabeth S. Moore, "Perspectives on Food Marketing and Childhood Obesity: Introduction to the Special Section," *Journal of Public Policy & Marketing* 26, no. 2, (2007), pp. 157–161; Elizabeth S. Moore (2007), "Food Marketing Goes Online: A Content Analysis of Websites for Children," in *Obesity in America: Development and Prevention,* vol. 2, Hiram E. Fitzgerald and Vasiliki Mousouli (eds.) (Westport, CT: Praeger, 2007) pp. 93–115. William L. Wilkie and Elizabeth S. Moore, "Marketing's Contributions to Society," *Journal of Marketing,* 63 (Special Issue, 1999), pp. 198–219.

12. Jeffrey M. Jones, "Nurses Top Honesty and Ethics List for 11th Year," Gallup, December 3, 2010, http://www.gallup.com.

13. http://www.workingvalues.com.

14. http://www.jnj.com.

15. Vanessa O'Connell and Shirley Wang, "J&J Acts Fast on Tylenol," *The Wall Street Journal,* July 9, 2009.

16. Erin Cavusgil, "Merck and Vioxx: An Examination of an Ethical Decision-Making Model," *Journal of Business Ethics* 76 (2007), pp. 451–61.

17. Jeanne Whalen, "AstraZeneca Sharpens Focus on Ethics," *The Wall Street Journal,* December 3, 2009, http://online.wsj.com; "AstraZeneca Weighs Response to UK Body on Ethics Code Breach," *The Wall Street Journal,* March 9, 2010, http://online.wsj.com.

18. For an interesting discussion of why pharmaceutical companies seem to have lost their ethical luster, see Matthew Herper, "Big Pharma: What Went Wrong?" http://www.forbes.com.

19. "In Brief: Retailers Sever Ties over Child Labor," *The Spokesman-Review,* October 31, 2009; George Anderson, "Walmart Says 'No' to Uzbek Cotton over Child Labor," *Retail Wire,* October 1, 2008; Dan McDougall, "Child Sweatshop Shame Threatens Gap's Ethical Image," *The Observer,* October 28, 2007.

20. http://www.limitedbrands.com; http://www.greenamericatoday.org/.

21. "Walmart Launches Major Initiative to Make Food Healthier and Healthier Food More Affordable," http://walmartstores.com; Stephanie Rosenbloom, "At Walmart, Labeling to Reflect Green Intent," *The New York Times,* July 16, 2009; Stephanie Rosenbloom, "Wal-Mart to Toughen Standards," *The New York Times,* October 22, 2008; Adam Aston, "Walmart: Making Its Suppliers Go Green," *Bloomberg Businessweek,* May 18, 2009.

22. http://www.marketingpower.com/AboutAMA/Pages/Statement%20of%20Ethics.aspx.

23. http://www.cmomagazine.com. This survey was conducted in 2006; more recent reports suggest that 49 percent of respondents to a 2009 survey reported having seen ethical misconduct overall. See Ethics Resource Center, "2009 National Business Ethics Survey," http://www.ethics.org.

24. Alexander Dahlsrud lists 37 definitions! See "How Corporate Social Responsibility Is Defined," *Corporate Social Responsibility and Environmental Management* 15, no. 1 (January/February 2008), pp. 1–13.

25. "Social Responsibility," *AMA Dictionary of Marketing Terms,* http://www.marketingpower.com/_layouts/Dictionary.aspx?dLetter=S.

26. Christopher Marquis, Pooja Shah, Amanda Tolleson, and Bobbi Thomason, "The Dannon Company: Marketing and Corporate Social Responsibility," Harvard Business School Case 9-410-121, April 1, 2010.

27. "Restoring the Economy," BP, http://www.bp.com.

28. Michael Connor, "Survey: U.S. Consumers Willing to Pay for Corporate Responsibility," *Business Ethics,* March 29, 2010, http://business-ethics.com.

29. Richard Stengel, "Doing Well by Doing Good," *Time Magazine,* September 10, 2009, http://www.time.com.

30. http://www.toms.com/our-movement; http://www.toms.com /corporate-info/; http://www.insightargentina.org; Christina Binkley, "Charity Gives Shoe Brand Extra Shine," *The Wall Street Journal,* April 1, 2010, http://online.wsj.com.

31. "2011 World's Most Ethical Companies," *Ethisphere,* http: //ethisphere.com/2011-worlds-most-ethical-companies.

32. http://www.burtsbees.com.

33. General Electric, "Sustainable Growth: GE 2010 Citizenship Report," http://www.gecitizenship.com; General Electric, "The Spirit and the Letter," http://integrity.ge.com.

34. Interviews with Nell Newman and Peter Meehan, co-founders of Newman's Own Organic, 2007.

35. Suzanne Vranica, "Tweeting to Sell Cars," *The Wall Street Journal,* November 14, 2010; http://business.ftc.gov; Gary Hoffman, "Selling Cars on Twitter," AOL Autos, August 10, 2010.

36. Andrew J. Blumberg and Peter Eckerdsly, "On Locational Privacy, and How to Avoid Losing It Forever," Electronic Frontier Foundation White Paper, August 2009, http://www.eff.org.

37. Sustainability Scorecard, http://www.aboutmcdonalds.com.

38. The most famous proponent of this view was Milton Friedman. See, for example, *Capitalism and Freedom* (Chicago: University of Chicago Press, 2002) or *Free to Choose: A Personal Statement* (Orlando, FL: Harcourt, 1990).

39. Dan Amos, "Aflac's Ethics in Action: Pay for Performance— Keep Stakeholders Informed," January 12, 2009, http: //ethisphere.com.

40. James Townsend, "Smart Choice Program Set to Begin," *Functional Ingredients,* June 23, 2009.

41. Frito-Lay, "Straight Talk on Snacking," http://www.fritolay.com; Mike Esterl, "Can This Chip Be Saved?" *The Wall Street Journal,* March 24, 2011, http://online.wsj.com.

42. http://www.ge.com/news/our_viewpoints/energy_and_ climate.html; "GE Launches New Ecomagination Healthcare Products, Opens Renewable Energy HQ," February 2, 2010, http://www.greenbiz.com.

43. D. B. Bielak, S. Bonini, and J. M. Oppenheim, "CEOs on Strategy and Social Issues," *McKinsey Quarterly,* 2007, http://www .mckinseyquarterly.com.

CHAPTER 5

1. http://www.thecoolhunter.net/architecture, November 3, 2011.

2. http://www.thecoolhunter.net/lifestyle, September 7, 2011.

3. http://www.trendhunter.com/join.

4. Michael Hines, "Smelly Billboards," http://www.trendhunter.com.

5. Alex Scott, "Guerilla Socialvertising," http://www.trendhunter .com.

6. Katherine Vong, "Guerilla Asphalt Garden," http://www .trendhunter.com.

7. Peter F. Drucker, *The Essential Drucker* (New York: Harper Collins, 2001).

8. Linda Doell, "In Razor vs. Razor, Neither Gillette nor Schick Gains Edge with Ad Watchdog," March 17, 2011, http://www .dailyfinance.com.

9. http://www.nau.com; Chris Dannen, "Wanted: The Light, Recycled Trench," Fast Company, November 19, 2010, http:

//www.fastcompany.com; Polly Labarre, "Leap of Faith," Fast Company, June 2007.

10. http://www.coolhunting.com.

11. Del I. Hawkins, David L. Mothersbaugh, *Consumer Behavior: Building Marketing Strategy,* 11e (Burr Ridge, IL: McGraw-Hill /Irwin, 2009); Philip Cateora and John Graham, *International Marketing,* 13e (Burr Ridge, IL: McGraw-Hill/Irwin, 2006).

12. http://popvssoda.com/.

13. http://www.drpepper.com.

14. "Corporate Responsibility," http://info.cvscaremark.com.

15. Geoffrey E. Meredith, Charles D. Schewe, and Janice Karlovich, *Defining Markets, Defining Moments: America's 7 Generational Cohorts, Their Shared Experiences, and Why Businesses Should Care* (New York: Wiley, 2002).

16. "Consumers of Tomorrow: Insights and Observations about Generation Z," *Grail Research,* June 2010.

17. Suzy Menkes, "Marketing to the Millennials," *The New York Times,* March 2, 2010; Pamela Paul, "Getting Inside Gen Y," *American Demographics* 23, no. 9; Sharon Jayson, "A Detailed Look at the Millennials," *USA Today,* February 23, 2010.

18. Wendy Wang and Paul Taylor, "For Millennials, Parenthood Trumps Marriage," March 9, 2011, http://www.pewsocial-trends.org.

19. Brenda Wells, "Truly Understanding Millennials," September 2011, http://www.irmi.com.

20. Julia B. Isaacs, "Economic Mobility of Families Across Generations," http://www.economicmobility.org.

21. "Baby Boomers, Gen X and Gen Y (Consumer Patterns, Behaviors, Lifestyles and Demographics): How Generations Are Changing the Face of Consumer Goods Market," March 10, 2009, http://www.smartbrief.com.

22. Brian Braiker, "The Next Great American Consumer," *Adweek,* September 26, 2011, http://www.adweek.com.

23. Dan Hardy, "To Balance Budgets, Schools Allow Ads," October 16, 2011, http://articles.philly.com; Tonyaa Wethersby, "Ad on School Buses a Tacky Idea," October 5, 2011, http://jacksonville .com.

24. "That Facebook Friend Might be 10 Years Old, and Other Troubling News," *Consumer Reports,* June 2011, http://www. consumerreports.org; Matt Richtel and Miguel Helft, "Facebook Users Who Are Underage Raise Concerns," *The New York Times,* March 12, 2011, http://www.nytimes.com.

25. Emily Bazelon, "Why Facebook Is After Your Kids," *The New York Times,* October 12, 2011, http://www.nytimes.com.

26. Yale Rudd Center for Food Policy and Obesity, "Sugary Drink Facts," report, October 2011.

27. Ibid.

28. Meredith et al., *Defining Markets, Defining Moments.*

29. Robert Brown and Ruth Washton, "Healthy 50+ Americans: Trends and Opportunities in the Emerging Wellness Market," April 2011, Rockville, MD: Packaged Facts.

30. Rieva Lesonsky, "Small Retailers: Don't Ignore Senior Consumers," *Retail Trends,* October 26, 2011.

31. http://www.familiesusa.org; http://www.bls.gov; U.S. Bureau of the Census, "Income, Poverty, and Health Insurance Coverage in the United States, 2010," http://www.census .gov.

32. Dave Gilson and Carolyn Perot, "It's the Inequality, Stupid," *Mother Jones* (March/April 2011), http://motherjones.com; OECD,

"Growing Unequal? Income Distribution and Poverty in OECD Countries," 2008, http://www.oecd.org.

33. http://www.Hammacher.com.

34. http://www.census.gov; http://www.infoplease.com.

35. Bureau of Labor Statistics, "Education Pays," May 4, 2011, http://www.bls.gov.

36. http://inside.nike.com/blogs/nikerunning_events-en_US/?tags=nike_womens_marathon_2010.

37. Tom Pirovano, "U.S. Demographics Are Changing . . . Are Your Marketing Plans Ready?" *NielsenWire,* March 10, 2010, http://blog.nielsen.com; "Cents and Sensibility: Why Marketing to Multicultural Consumers Requires a Subtle Touch," *Knowledge@Wharton,* March 10, 2010, http://www.wharton.universia.net; "Ethnic Consumers Hold $282 Billion in Purchasing Power," February 24, 2009, http://news.newamericamedia.org.

38. Jeffrey S. Passel and D'Vera Cohn, "U.S. Population Projections: 2005–2050," Pew Research Center, http://pewhispanic.org.

39. Joel Kotkin, "The Changing Demographics of America," *Smithsonian Magazine* (August 2010), http://www.smithsonianmag.com.

40. Julie Jargon, "Pizza Chain Seeks Slice of Bicultural Pie," *WSJ.com,* December 30, 2010.

41. Richard Westlund, "Finding the Gold in Hispanic Marketing," *Adweek,* July 27, 2010, http://www.adweek.com.

42. Todd Wasserman, "Report: Shifting African American Population," *Adweek,* January 12, 2010, http://www.adweek.com; U.S. Bureau of the Census, "Annual Social and Economic Supplement to the Current Population Survey," http://www.census.gov.

43. "The State of the African-American Consumer," *Nielsen,* September 2011, p. 5.

44. Leah Ingram, "Suddenly Frugal," http://www.suddenlyfrugal.com/; Brad Tuttle, "Cash Crunch: Why Extreme Thriftiness Stunts Are the Rage," *Time,* April 5, 2010, http://www.time.com.

45. Stephanie Clifford and Andrew Martin, "In Time of Scrimping, Fun Stuff Is Still Selling," The New York Times, September 23, 2011, http://www.nytimes.com.html?_r=1&ref=consumerbehavior. Brad Tuttle. "Smart Spending: Consumer Phrase of the Day: 'Lipstick Effect'," Time, April 19, 2011, http://moneyland.time.com

46. Laura T. Coffey, "Extreme Couponing! How to Get $1,100 of Merchandise for $40," Today.com, April 6, 2011, http://today.msnbc.msn.com.

47. Extreme Couponing, http://tlc.discovery.com/videos/extreme-couponing/; Jon Caramanica, "Miles of Aisles, Endless Opportunities to Save," The New York Times, April 5, 2011. http://tv.nytimes.com.

48. EJ Schultz, "Retailers Start to Suffer Super-Couponer Fatigue," Advertising Age, July 11, 2011.

49. Seth Fiegerman, "Deal Burnout: Too Many Discounts?" The Street, August 8, 2011.

50. Centers for Disease Control and Prevention, "National Diabetes Fact Sheet, 2011," http://www.cdc.gov.

51. "Guidelines for Marketing Food to Kids Proposed," CSPI Press Release, January 5, 2005.

52. Yoga Buzz, "Yoga Biz Thrives Despite Economy," October 24, 2011, http://blogs.yogajournal.com.

53. Catherine Clifford, "Yoga: The Booming Business of Zen," CNNMoney, October 18, 2011, http://money.cnn.com.

54. This definition of green marketing draws on work by Jacquelyn A. Ottman, Green Marketing: Opportunity for Innovation (Chicago: NTC Publishing, 1997).

55. http://www.sunchips.com/healthier_planet.shtml.

56. Emily Steel, "Nestlé Takes a Beating on Social-Media Sites," *The Wall Street Journal,* March 29, 2010.

57. Jerry Lynch, "Achieving a Sustainable Palm Oil Commitment," *Taste of General Mills,* December 7, 2012, http://www.blog.generalmills.com.

58. "Haagen-Dazs and General Mills to Help Smallholder Vanilla Farmers Increase Yields and Improve Sustainability Practices in Madagascar," *MarketWatch,* press release, February 20, 2013.

59. "General Mills Joins U.S. Food Waste Challenge as Founding Partner," *The Wall Street Journal,* press release, June 4, 2013, http://online.wsj.com.

60. "General Mills Reports Progress on Global Responsibility Efforts," *The New York Times,* press release, April 30, 2013, http://markets.on.nytimes.com.

61. Matt Liebowitz, "2011 Set to Be Worst Year Ever for Security Breaches," *Security News Daily,* June 9, 2011, http://www.securitynewsdaily.com.

62. http://www.ftc.gov/opa/2008/04/dncfyi.shtm; http://www.ftc.gov/os/2010/12/101206dncdatabook.pdf.

63. Bureau of Labor Statistics, "American Time Use Survey Summary," http://www.bls.gov; Martin Peers, "Buddy, Can You Spare Some Time?" *The Wall Street Journal,* January 26, 2004, pp. B1, B3; additional statistics from Harris Interactive.

64. http://www.bravotv.com; https://secure.shopbybravo.com.

65. http://www.safeway.com; "Safeway CEO Steve Burd Says Fresh, Prepared Food Sales at $100 Million Annually," February 25, 2010, http://freshneasybuzz.blogspot.com.

66. Doug Sovern, "Walgreens Opens First 'Fresh Food Oasis' in Underserved San Francisco Neighborhood," July 8, 2011, http://sanfrancisco.cbslocal.com; http://news.walgreens.com.

67. http://news.walgreens.com/article_display.cfm?article_id=5515.

68. "What Is Foursquare?" https://foursquare.com. Membership data as of April 2011.

69. Mark Didas, "Market Your Regional Product or Service with Foursquare," http://www.wavespawn.com/market-regional-product-service-foursquare.

70. "About Foursquare," https://foursquare.com; "Facebook Introduces Check-in Feature," CNN.com, August 18, 2010.

71. Marianne Wilson, "Growing Power of Mobile," *Chain Store Age,* December 2010; Deena M. Amato-McCoy, "Focus on: The Mobile Channel," *Chain Store Age,* March 2011.

72. William L. Watts and Lisa Twaronite, "Dollar Sags as Bernanke Cites Growth Risks," *MarketWatch,* July 15, 2008.

73. Catherine Rampell, "The Euro Zone Crisis and the U.S.: A Primer," *The New York Times,* November 14, 2011, http://economix.blogs.nytimes.com.

74. Brendan Greeley, "Providing Internet Access to the Poor," *Bloomberg Businessweek,* November 17, 2011, http://www.businessweek.com.

75. Ashley Lutz, "Lululemon Envy Has Retailers from Gap to Nordstrom Chasing Yoga Devotees," *Bloomberg Businessweek,* September 9, 2011; Ian Austin, "Lululemon Athletica Combines Ayn Rand and Yoga," *The New York Times,* November 27, 2011, http://www.nytimes.com.

CHAPTER 6

1. Natasha Singer, "On Campus, It's One Big Commercial," *The New York Times*, September 10, 2011.

2. Paul Vlasic, "Via Zipcar, Ford Seeks Young Fans," *The New York Times*, August 31, 2011.

3. James R. Healey, "Ford and Zipcar Court College Kids with High-Tech Focus," *USA Today*, August 31, 2011.

4. J. Jeffrey Inman, Russell S. Winer, and Rosella Ferraro, "The Interplay among Category Characteristics, Customer Characteristics, and Customer Activities on In-Store Decision Making," *Journal of Marketing* 73, no. 5 (September 2009), pp. 19–29.

5. For example, when trying on a dress, Katie might be influenced by the way that same dress looks on a salesperson in the store. See Darren W. Dahl, Jennifer J. Argo, and Andrea C. Morales, "Social Information in the Retail Environment: The Importance of Consumption Alignment, Referent Identity, and Self-Esteem," *Journal of Consumer Research 38*, no. 5 (February 2012), pp. 860–871.

6. For a detailed discussion of customer behavior, see J. Paul Peter and Jerry C. Olson, *Consumer Behavior and Marketing Strategy*, 9th ed. (New York: McGraw-Hill, 2009).

7. Martin R. Lautman and Koen Pauwels, "Metrics That Matter: Identifying the Importance of Consumer Wants and Needs," *Journal of Advertising Research* 49, no. 3 (2009), 339–59.

8. Liz C. Wang, Julie Baker, Judy A. Wagner, and Kirk Wakefield, "Can a Retail Web Site Be Social?" *Journal of Marketing* 71, no. 3 (2007), pp. 143–57; Barry Babin, William Darden, and Mitch Griffin, "Work and/or Fun: Measuring Hedonic and Utilitarian Shopping Value," *Journal of Consumer Research* 20 (March 1994), pp. 644–56.

9. Jing Xu and Norbert Schwarz, "Do We Really Need a Reason to Indulge?" *Journal of Marketing Research* 46, no. 1 (February 2009), pp. 25–36.

10. "Christian Louboutin Styles for the Uptown Girl," http://www.newshoefashion.com/; "Celebrities Who Love Christian Louboutin Shoes," http://fashion.telegraph.co.uk/; Cindy Clark, "Christian Louboutin's Red-Soled Shoes Are Red-Hot," *USA Today*, http://www.usatoday.com.

11. Peng Huang, Nicholas H. Lurie, and Sabyasachi Mitra, "Searching for Experience on the Web: An Empirical Examination of Consumer Behavior for Search and Experience Goods," *Journal of Marketing* 73, no. 2 (March 2009), pp. 55–69.

12. http://store.cwtv.com.

13. http://www.lnaclothing.com.

14. http://www.mytruefit.com.

15. Ruth La Ferla, "The Campus as Runway," *The New York Times*, October 12, 2011.

16. http://www.signature9.com.

17. http://www.collegefashion.net.

18. "Quiz: Which Celebrity Is Your Style Icon?" http://www.collegefashion.net/inspiration/quiz-which-celebrity-is-your-style-icon/.

19. Ibid.

20. http://www.signature9.com.

21. Ying Zhang, Jing Xu, Zixi Jiang, and Szu-chi Huang, "Been There, Done That: The Impact of Effort Investment on Goal Value and Consumer Motivation," *Journal of Consumer Research* 38, no. 1 (June 2011), pp. 78–93.

22. Debabrata Talukdar, "Cost of Being Poor: Retail Price and Consumer Price Search Differences across Inner-City and Suburban Neighborhoods," *Journal of Consumer Research* 35, no. 3 (October 2008), pp. 457–71.

23. Bianca Banova, "The Future of Mobile Technology in Medicine: Innovative Medical Apps," *MedCity News*, April 24, 2013, http://medcitynews.com; William Cook, "Is That Little Mole a Big Problem?" *Daily Mail*, October 3, 2012, http://www.dailymail.co.uk; "mySugr App, Award-Winning iPhone App That Gamifies Blood Sugar Monitoring for People with Diabetes, Launches in US," *The Wall Street Journal*, June 6, 2013, press release, http://online.wsj.com; Mike H, "'Diabetes Monster' App Actually Motivates!" *Diabetes Mine*, June 19, 2013, http://www.diabetesmine.com.

24. David Dubois, Derek D. Rucker, and Adam D. Galinsky, "Super Size Me: Product Size as a Signal of Status," *Journal of Consumer Research 38*, no. 6, April 2012, pp. 1047–1062.

25. Diane M. Gibson, "Food Stamps and Obesity," *The New York Times*, September 27, 2011, http://www.nytimes.com.

26. Jane E. Brody, "Attacking the Obesity Epidemic by First Figuring Out Its Cause," *The New York Times*, September 12, 2011, http://www.nytimes.com.

27. Ibid.

28. "Burger King Joins McDonald's in Charging for Kids' Meal Toys to Comply with San Francisco Ban," *Washington Post*, December 1, 2011, http://www.washingtonpost.com.

29. Benjamin Scheibehenne, Rainer Greifeneder, and Peter M. Todd, "Can There Ever Be Too Many Options? A Meta-Analytic Review of Choice Overload," *Journal of Consumer Research* 37, no. 3 (October 2010), pp. 409–45.

30. The term *determinance* was first coined by James Myers and Mark Alpert nearly three decades ago; http://www.sawtooth-software.com.

31. http://www.sawtoothsoftware.com.

32. Julie R. Irwin and Rebecca Walker Naylor, "Ethical Decisions and Response Mode Compatibility: Weighting of Ethical Attributes in Consideration Sets Formed by Excluding Versus Including Product Alternatives," *Journal of Marketing Research* 46, no. 2 (April 2009), pp. 234–46; Richard Lutz, "Changing Brand Attitudes through Modification of Cognitive Structure," *Journal of Consumer Research* 1, no. 1 (1975), pp. 125–36.

33. 2011 U.S. Organic Industry Overview, Organic Trade Association, http://www.ota.com.

34. Ashby Jones, "Is Your Dinner 'All Natural'?" *The Wall Street Journal*, September 20, 2011; "Diet and Nutrition Report," *Consumer Reports*, February 2009, http://www.consumerreports.org.

35. Rachel Gross, "Farmers Seek to Raise Standards for Berries," *The New York Times*, September 23, 2011, http://www.nytimes.com.

36. Mayo Clinic Staff, "Organic Foods: Are They Safer? More Nutritious?" http://www.mayoclinic.com.

37. Gross, op. cit.

38. Natural and Organic Foods Backgrounder, Food Marketing Institute, http://www.fmi.org.

39. Stacey R. Finkelstein and Ayelet Fishbach, "When Healthy Food Makes You Hungry," *Journal of Consumer Research* 37, no. 3 (October 2010), pp. 357–67.

40. Caroline Goukens, Siegfried Dewitte, and Luk Warlop, "Me, Myself, and My Choices: The Influence of Private Self-Awareness

on Choice," *Journal of Marketing Research* 46, no. 5 (October 2009), pp. 682–92.

41. Ruby Roy Dholakia and Miao Zhao, "Retail Web Site Interactivity: How Does It Influence Customer Satisfaction and Behavioral Intentions?" *International Journal of Retail & Distribution Management* 37 (2009), pp. 821–38.

42. "30 Under 30 2011: Where Are They Now?" http://www.inc.com; http://www.renttherunway.com.

43. Brooks Barnes, "A Bid to Get Film Lovers Not to Rent," *The New York Times*, November 11, 2011, http://www.nytimes.com.

44. Claire Cain Miller, "Closing the Deal at the Virtual Checkout Counter," *New York Times,* October 12, 2009.

45. "Beware of Dissatisfied Consumers: They Like to Blab," *Knowledge@Wharton,* March, 8, 2006, based on the "Retail Customer Dissatisfaction Study 2006" conducted by the Jay H. Baker Retailing Initiative at Wharton and The Verde Group.

46. Goutam Challagalla, R. Venkatesh, and Ajay K. Kohli, "Proactive Postsales Service: When and Why Does It Pay Off?" *Journal of Marketing* 73, no. 2 (March 2009), pp. 70–87.

47. Randall Stross, "Consumer Complaints Made Easy. Maybe Too Easy," *The New York Times,* May 28, 2011, http://www.nytimes.com.

48. For a more extensive discussion on these factors, see Banwari Mittal, *Consumer Behavior* (Cincinnati, OH: Open Mentis, 2008); Peter and Olson, *Consumer Behavior and Marketing.*

49. A. H. Maslow, *Motivation and Personality* (New York: Harper & Row, 1970).

50. Kelly D. Martin and Ronald Paul Hill, "Life Satisfaction, Self-Determination, and Consumption Adequacy at the Bottom of the Pyramid," *Journal of Consumer Research 38,* no. 6 April 2012, pp. 1155–1168; Hazel Rose Markus and Barry Schwartz, "Does Choice Mean Freedom and Well-Being?" *Journal of Consumer Research* 37, no. 2 (August 2010), pp. 344–55.

51. Stacy Wood, "The Comfort Food Fallacy: Avoiding Old Favorites in Times of Change," *Journal of Consumer Research* 36, no. 6 (April 2010), pp. 950–63; Stacey Finkelstein and Ayelet Fishbach, "When Healthy Food Makes You Hungry," *Journal of Consumer Research* 37, no. 3 (October 2010), pp. 357–67.

52. Lee, Leonard, On Amir, and Dan Ariely. "In search of homo economicus: cognitive noise and the role of emotion in preference consistency." *Journal of Consumer Research,* 36, no. 2 (2009), pp. 173–187. Anish Nagpal and Parthasarathy Krishnamurthy, "Attribute Conflict in Consumer Decision Making: The Role of Task Compatibility," *Journal of Consumer Research* 34, no. 5 (February 2008), pp. 696–705.

53. http://www.bostonbackbay.com/.

54. For more discussion on these factors, see: Mittal, *Consumer Behavior;* Peter and Olson, *Consumer Behavior and Marketing Strategy;* Michael Levy and Barton A. Weitz, *Retailing Management,* 7th ed. (Burr Ridge IL: Irwin/McGraw-Hill, 2009), chapter 4.

55. Juliano Laran, "Goal Management in Sequential Choices: Consumer Choices for Others Are More Indulgent than Personal Choices," *Journal of Consumer Research* 37, no. 2 (August 2010), pp. 304–14.

56. "Retailers Must Understand Modern Family Buying Decisions," http://www.articlesnatch.com.

57. "The Power of the Grandparent Economy," http://www.grandparents.com.

58. Todd Hale, "Mining the U.S. Generation Gaps," *Nielsen Wire,* March 4, 2010, http://blog.nielsen.com

59. Morgan K. Ward and Susan Bronziarczyk, "It's Not Me, It's You: How Gift Giving Creates Giver Identity Threat as a Function of Social Closeness," *Journal of Consumer Research* 38, no. 1 (June 2011), pp. 164–81.

60. Dahl et al., "Social Information in the Retail Environment," op. cit.

61. For a greater discussion on these factors, see Mittal, *Consumer Behavior;* Peter and Olson, *Consumer Behavior and Marketing Strategy.*

62. The concept of atmospherics was introduced by Philip Kotler, "Atmosphere as a Marketing Tool," *Journal of Retailing,* 49 (Winter 1973), pp. 48–64.

63. Sylvie Morin, Laurette Dubé, and Jean-Charles Chebat, "The Role of Pleasant Music in Servicescapes: A Test of the Dual Model of Environmental Perception," *Journal of Retailing,* 83, no. 1 (2007), pp. 115–30.

64. www.wegmans.com; http://wholefoodsmarket.com/stores/cooking-classes/; Tracy Turner, "New Hangout Supermarket," *Columbus Dispatch,* March 20, 2011.

65. Alexander Chernev and Ryan Hamilton, "Assortment Size and Option Attractiveness in Consumer Choice among Retailers," *Journal of Marketing Research* 46, no. 3 (June 2009), pp. 410–20; Marc-Andre Kamel, Nick Greenspan, and Rudolf Pritzl, "Standardization Is Efficient but Localization Helps Shops to Stand Out," *The Wall Street Journal,* January 21, 2009.

66. Christine Birkner, "Thinking Outside of the Box," *Marketing News,* March 30, 2011.

67. Jeffrey Trachtenberg, "Publishers Bundle E-Books to Boost Sales, Promote Authors," *The Wall Street Journal,* February 11, 2011.

68. Pierre Chandon, J. Wesley Hutchinson, Eric T. Bradlow, and Scott H. Young, "Does In-Store Marketing Work? Effects of the Number and Position of Shelf Facings on Brand Attention and Evaluation at the Point of Purchase," *Journal of Marketing* 73, no. 6 (November 2009), pp. 1–17.

69. Dan King and Chris Janiszewski, "Affect-Gating," *Journal of Consumer Research* 38, no. 4 (December 2011), pp. 697–711.

70. Mittal, *Consumer Behavior;* Peter and Olson, *Consumer Behavior and Marketing Strategy.*

71. Karen M. Stilley, J. Jeffrey Inman, and Kirk L. Wakefield, "Planning to Make Unplanned Purchases? The Role of In-Store Slack in Budget Deviation," *Journal of Consumer Research* 37, no. 2 (2010), pp. 264–278, DOI: 10.1086/651567.

CHAPTER 7

1. Leslie Kaufman, "Stone Washed Blue Jeans (Minus the Wash)," *The New York Times,* November 1, 2011, http://www.nytimes.com.

2. Ibid.

3. Ibid.

4. "Cotton/Raw Materials," http://www.levistrauss.com.

5. "Worker Rights," http://www.levistrauss.com.

6. Christina Binkley, "How Green Are Your Jeans?" *The Wall Street Journal,* Classroom Edition, October 2010, http://wsjclassroom.com.

7. Arun Sharma, R. Krishnan, and Dhruv Grewal, "Value Creation in Markets: A Critical Area of Focus for Business-to-Business Markets," *Industrial Marketing Management* 30, no. 4 (2001), pp. 391–402.

8. http://www.intel.com.

9. http://www.usa.siemens.com.

10. http://www.volkswagenag.com; Martin Hofmann, Emily-Sue Sloane, and Elena Malykhina, "VW Revs Its B2B Engine," *Optimize,* March 2004, pp. 22–26.

11. http://www.vwgroupsupply.com.

12. Stephanie Reitz, "Many US Schools Adding iPads, Trimming Textbooks," *Yahoo Finance,* September 3, 2011, http://finance.yahoo.com.

13. "Do iPads in Schools Change Behavior?" February 22, 2011, http://www.ipadinschools.com.

14. Nick Wingfield, "Once Wary, Apple Warms Up to Business Market," *The New York Times,* November 15, 2011, http://www.nytimes.com.

15. Rachel King, "Apple Woos Businesses Despite Security Worries," *Bloomberg Businessweek,* July 7, 2010, http://www.msnbc.msn.com.

16. Ibid.; Reitz, op. cit., "Do iPads in Schools Change Behavior," op. cit.; Wingfield, op.cit.

17. Dawn Kawamoto, "iPad 2 Launch Adds Muscle to Apple's Invasion of Corporate America," *Daily Finance,* March 10, 2011, http://www.dailyfinance.com; Leander Kahney, "iPad May Replace Computers and Textbooks in Schools, Experts Predict," *Cult of Mac,* http://www.cultofmac.com.

18. "Budget of the United States Government: Fiscal Year 2014," Executive Office of the United States: Office of Management and Budget.

19. Ibid.

20. http://www.hoovers.com.

21. "The Social Media RFP: How to Get the Best Results," January 18, 2010, http://hashtagsocialmedia.com.

22. David Whitford, "Hired Guns on the Cheap," *Fortune Small Business,* January 3, 2008.

23. These definitions are provided by www.marketingpower.com (the American Marketing Association's website). We have bolded key terms.

24. Sean Silverthorne, "Business Ethics: Pay the Bribe?" *CBS Money Watch,* http://www.cbsnews.com.

25. Stephen H. Unger, "Ethical Aspects of Bribing People in Other Countries," http://www1.cs.columbia.edu.

26. Transparency International, "Bribe Payers Index 2011," http://bpi.transparency.org/; "International Back Scratching," *The Economist,* November 2, 2011, http://www.economist.com.

27. Ernst and Young, "European Fraud Survey 2011: Recovery, Regulation and Integrity," http://www.ey.com.

28. http://www.goer.state.ny.us.

29. Kimberly Maul, "More B-to-B Companies Find That Social Media is an Essential Business Platform," PRweekus.com, June 2009; Ellis Booker, "B-to-B Marketers Apply Analytics to Social Media," *BtoB,* April 12, 2010; Elisabeth A. Sullivan, "A Long Slog," *Marketing News,* February 28, 2009.

30. http://www.hootsuite.com.

31. Daniel B. Honigman, "Make a Statement," *Marketing News,* May 1, 2008.

32. LinkedIn Press Center, "About Us," http://press.linkedin.com.

33. Heidi Cohen, "5 LinkedIn Business Goals," March 25, 2011, http://heidicohen.com.

34. Maria Tabaka, "How to Launch a LinkedIn Company Page," *Inc.,* April 17, 2011, http://www.inc.com.

35. Michael Krause, "How Does Oregon Football Keep Winning? Is It the Uniforms?" *Grantland,* August 30, 2011, http://www.grantland.com.

36. Barton A. Weitz, Stephen B. Castleberry, and John F. Tanner, *Selling Building Partnerships,* 6th ed. (Burr Ridge, IL: McGraw-Hill/Irwin, 2005), p. 93.

37. http://www.hubspot.com.

38. http://www.hubspot.com/customer-case-studies/.

39. Maggie Hira, "How Does a Fashion Buyer Spend a Workday?" http://www.ehow.com; U.S. Department of Labor, http://www.bls.gov; Amanda Fortini, "How the Runway Took Off: A Brief History of the Fashion Show," *Slate Magazine,* February 8, 2006.

CHAPTER 8

1. "McDonald's Sees Strong Revenue on Global Demand," *Associated Press,* December 8, 2011, http://www.msnbc.msn.com; Annie Gasparro, "Yum Splits India into Separate Division, Names New International CEO," *The Wall Street Journal,* November 23, 2011, http://online.wsj.com.

2. "McDonald's China Plans to Open a New Store Every Day in Four Years," *Huffington Post,* September 28, 2011, http://www.huffingtonpost.com.

3. "McDonald's Best Practices," http://bestpractices.mcdonalds.com; Gasparro, op. cit.

4. Julie Jargon, "For Food Delivery, China Calls McDonald's," *The Wall Street Journal,* December 12, 2011, http://online.wsj.com.

5. "McDonald's Sees Strong Revenue," op. cit.; Ravi Krishnani, "McDonald's in Russia: Defeated Communism with a 'Happy' Meal," *Business Today,* http://www.businesstoday-eg.com; Press Brief, http://www.mcdpressoffice.eu/downloads/pr/2010/Factsheet_Russia_20yr_Anniversary.pdf.

6. Andrew E. Kramer, "Russia's Evolution, Seen through Golden Arches," *The New York Times,* February 2, 2010, http://www.nytimes.com.

7. Pierre-Richard Agenor, *Does Globalization Hurt the Poor?* (Washington, DC: World Bank, 2002); "Globalization: Threat or Opportunity," International Monetary Fund, http://www.imf.org.

8. For example, the deficit for the month of October 2011 was $43.5 billion. See http://www.census.gov.

9. http://www.acdi-cida.gc.ca.

10. http://siteresources.worldbank.org/DATASTATISTICS/Resources/GNIPC.pdf; Arthur O'Sullivan, Steven Sheffrin, and Steve Perez, *Macroeconomics: Principles and Tools Activebook,* 5th ed. (Upper Saddle River, NJ: Prentice Hall, 2007).

11. The Economist, "Currency Comparisons, To Go," July 28, 2011, http://www.economist.com.

12. Justin Dove, "Taking Advantage of Dollar Weakness," *Investor U,* July 28, 2011, http://www.investmentu.com.

13. Jack Neff, "Emerging-Market Growth War Pits Global Brand Giants against Scrappy Local Rivals," *Ad Age,* June 13, 2011, http://adage.com.

14. Jeremiah McWilliams, "Pepsi, Coke in Race to Conquer China," *Atlanta Journal-Constitution,* May 28, 2010.

15. Chris Gaylord, "World's Cheapest Car, Tata Nano, Revs toward US," *The Christian Science Monitor,* January 15, 2011, http://www.csmonitor.com; Nandini Lakshman, "Indian Car Buyers Snap Up the Nano," May 6, 2009, http://www.time.com. Jyoti

Thottam and Niljanjana Bhowmick, "Nano Power," *Time,* April 13, 2009.

16. "Coca-Cola Tackles Rural Indian Market," (video) *The Wall Street Journal,* May 3, 2010.

17. Neff, op. cit.

18. David L. Scott, *Wall Street Words: An A to Z Guide to Investment Terms for Today's Investor* (Boston: Houghton Mifflin, 2003).

19. Leslie Josephs, "U.S. Increases Sugar Quota for Second Time," *Wall Street Journal,* June 23, 2011.

20. "Exchange Rate," http://en.wikipedia.org/wiki/Exchange_rate.

21. http://ucatlas.ucsc.edu.

22. http://www.unescap.org.

23. http://en.wikipedia.org/wiki/European_Union; http://www .nationsonline.org/oneworld/europe_map.htm.

24. Johny Johansson, *Global Marketing,* 5th ed. (New York: McGraw-Hill/Irwin, 2008).

25. Philip R. Cateora, Mary C. Gilly, and John L. Graham, *International Marketing,* 15th ed. (New York: McGraw-Hill, 2011); Danielle Medina Walker and Thomas Walker, *Doing Business Internationally: The Guide to Cross-Cultural Success,* 2nd ed. (Princeton, NJ: Trade Management Corporation, 2003).

26. Devorah Lauter, "IKEA Fined for Sunday Opening in France," *Forbes,* April 6, 2008.

27. Stefania Summermatter, "Can Sunday Shopping Help Beat the Crisis," Swissinfo.ch, August 1, 2009.

28. For a website dedicated to Hofstede's research, see http://www .geert-hofstede.com/. Some of his more influential publications include Geert Hofstede and Gert Jan Hofstede, *Cultures and Organizations: Software of the Mind* (New York: McGraw-Hill/ Irwin, 2004); Geert Hofstede, "Management Scientists Are Human," *Management Science,* 40 (January 1994), pp. 4–13; Geert Hofstede and Michael H. Bond, "The Confucius Connection from Cultural Roots to Economic Growth," *Organizational Dynamics,* 16 (Spring 1988), pp. 4–21. See also Masaaki Kotabe and Kristiaan Helsen, *Global Marketing Management,* 3rd ed. (Hoboken, NJ: John Wiley & Sons, 2004).

29. http://geert-hofstede.com/countries.html.

30. James W. Carey, *Communication as Culture,* rev, edition (New York: Routledge, 2009); Tian Feng and Julian Lowe, "The Influence of National and Organizational Culture on Absorptive Capacity of Chinese Companies," *International Journal of Knowledge, Culture, and Change Management* 7, no. 10 (2007), pp. 9–16.

31. Colgate Palmolive 2010 Annual Report, "Colgate: Global Strategies, Local Strength."

32. "Brazil," U.S. Department of State, November 30, 2011, http: //www.state.gov.

33. "Russia," U.S. Department of State, November 2, 2011, http: //www.state.gov.

34. "India," U.S. Department of State, November 8, 2011, http: //www.state.gov.

35. Megha Bahree, "India Unlocks Door for Global Retailers," *Wall Street Journal*, November 25, 2011.

36. Gary Locke, "U.S. Trade with China," U.S. Department of State, November 29, 2011, http://www.state.gov.

37. "China," U.S. Department of State, September 6, 2011, http: //www.state.gov.

38. Jason Kincaid, "Mark Zuckerberg on Facebook's Strategy for China (and His Wardrobe)," *Tech Crunch,* October 16, 2010, http://techcrunch.com.

39. Normandy Madden, "What Will Facebook Find If It Ventures into China?" *Ad Age Global,* June 13, 2011, http://adage.com.

40. Chloe Albanesius, "Human Rights Group Slams Facebook over China Strategy," PCMag.com, June 3, 2011, http://www.pcmag .com.

41. Lance Eliot Brouthers, George Nakos, John Hadjimarcou, and Keith D. Brouthers, "Key Factors for Successful Export Performance for Small Firms," *Journal of International Marketing* 17, no. 3 (2009), pp. 21–38; "Selling Overseas," November 12, 2009, http://www.entrepreneur.com.

42. http://www.sonyericsson.com/cws/corporate/press /pressreleases/pressreleasedetails/ericssonsshare- 20111027.

43. Andy Pasztor, "Virgin Galactic Spacecraft Test Rocket in Flight," *The Wall Street Journal,* April 29, 2013, http://online.wsj.com; Kenneth Chang, "Privately Financed Spacecraft Roars Closer to space," *The New York Times,* April 29, 2013, http://www .nytimes.com; "Press Releases," The Spaceship Company, http://www.thespaceshipcompany.com; Kriss MacDonald, "First Space Tourist Flights from Christmas Day with Virgin Galactic. Will My Kids Be Space Tourists in the Future?" *Over There to Here,* May 16, 2013, http://over theretohere.com.

44. Philip R. Cateora, Mary C. Gilly, and John L. Graham, *International Marketing,* 14th ed. (New York: McGraw-Hill, 2009); Bruce D. Keillor, Michael D'Amico, and Veronica Horton, "Global Consumer Tendencies," *Psychology & Marketing* 18, no. 1 (2001), pp. 1–20.

45. "Top 10 Best-Selling Cars November 2011," http://blogs.cars .com.

46. "Figo Drives New Sales Records for Ford in India," April 1, 2010, http://media.ford.com; "Figo Chassis Designed for the Global Market—Tailored for Indian Roads," March 9, 2010, http://www.india.ford.com.

47. "Ford India Delivers 100,000th Figo: Vehicle Sales up 53 Percent for the Year," July 1, 2011, http://media.ford.com.

48. Michael J. Ureel, "Ford Looks to Improve Market Share, Sales in Emerging Indian Economy," http://media.ford.com.

49. Jack Neff, "Yahoo Ramps Up Global Study of Moms and Technology," *Ad Age,* November 17, 2011, http://adage.com.

50. http://www.pgeverydaysolutions.ca/thankyoumom/helping- moms.jsp.

51. Charles W. L. Hill, *Global Business Today,* 7e, New York, McGraw-Hill/Irwin, 2011.

52. Lidia Kelly and Maya Dyakina, "Analysis: Russia's Wealth Gap Wounds Putin," *Reuters,* December 20, 2011, http://www .reuters.com; Transparency International, http://www.transpar- ency.org.

53. Julie Jargon, "Can M'm, M'm Good Translate?" *The Wall Street Journal,* July 9, 2007, p. A16; Brad Dorfman and Martinne Geller, "Campbell Soup in Joint Venture to Expand in China," *Reuters,* January 12, 2011, http://www.reuters.com; Julie Jargon, "Campbell Soup to Exit Russia," *The Wall Street Journal,* June 29, 2011, http://online.wsj.com.

54. http://www.pringles.it/.

55. Natalie Zmuda, "P&G, Levi's, GE Innovate by Thinking in Reverse," *Ad Age,* June 13, 2011, http://adage.com.

56. Silvia Fabiana, Claire Loupias, Fernando Martins, and Roberto Sabbatini (eds.), *Pricing Decisions in the Euro Era: How Firms Set Prices and Why* (Oxford: Oxford University Press, 2007); Gilly et al., *International Marketing.*

57. Fabiana et al., *Pricing Decisions;* Amanda J. Broderick, Gordon E. Greenley, and Rene Dentiste Mueller, "The Behavioural Homogeneity Evaluation Framework: Multi-level Evaluations of Consumer Involvement in International Segmentation," *Journal of International Business Studics,* 38 (2007), pp. 746–763; Terry Clark, Masaaki Kotabe, and Dan Rajaratnam, "Exchange Rate Pass-Through and International Pricing Strategy: A Conceptual Framework and Research Propositions," *Journal of International Business Studies* 30, no. 2 (1999), pp. 249–68.

58. David Kiley, "One World, One Car, One Name," *Bloomberg Businessweek,* March 13, 2008, http://www.businessweek .com; "2012 Ford Fiesta Review," November 2, 2011, http:// usnews.rankingsandreviews.com.

59. Sarah Morris, "How Zara Clothes Turned Galacia into a Retail Hotspot," *Reuters,* October 31, 2011, http://www.reuters.com.

60. "India: Creating Rural Entrepreneurs," http://www.unilever.com.

61. https://www.cia.gov/library/publications/the-world-factbook /fields/2103.html.

62. Jess Halliday, "Industry Prepares to Fight Junk Food Ad Watershed," Food and Drink Europe.com, January 3, 2008, http://www.foodanddrinkeurope.com.

63. Michael Wines, "Picking Brand Names in Asia Is a Business Itself," *Ad Age,* November 11, 2011, http://www.nytimes.com; Brand Channel, http://www.brandchannel.com.

64. Simon Owens, "The Secrets of Lady Gaga's Social Media Success," *TNW Media,* March 15, 2011; "Undressing Lady Gaga's Social Strategy," http://www.houseblogger.com.

65. Caitlin Burns, "Lady Gaga and Social Media," http://thesocialrobot .com.

66. Joan Voight, "How to Customize Your U.S. Branding Effort to Work around the World," *Adweek,* September 3, 2008.

CHAPTER 9

1. LimitedBrands, http://limited.com.

2. "The Designer Collection," http://www.victoriassecret.com; Elizabeth Holmes, "Victoria's Secret Shifts Focus to Lower-Price Items," *The Wall Street Journal,* August 20, 2009, http://online .wsj.com.

3. "Multi-Way Bras," http://www.victoriassecret.com.

4. http://www.buec.udel.edu/antil/BUAD%20301/BUAD%20 301%20Fall%20%2708/Victoria%27s%20Secret%20Pink.pdf.

5. Tim Feran, "How to Insult the Whole State of Michigan," *The Columbus Dispatch,* November 22, 2011, http://www.dispatch .com.

6. http://www.victoriassecret.com/pink/nfl-shop-by-team; "Victoria's Secret PINK and Major League Baseball Properties Announce New Co-Branded Collection," Forbes.com, March 15, 2010, http: //www.forbes.com.

7. "With Wings and Little Else: Behind Victoria's Secret Fashion Show," *The New York Times,* http://www.nytimes.com; Christine Whitney, "Where Angels Learn to Tread," *The New York Times Magazine,* November 10, 2011, http://tmagazine.blogs .nytimes.com.

8. James Agarwal, Naresh K. Malhotra, and Ruth N. Bolton, "A Cross-National and Cross-Cultural Approach to Global Market Segmentation: An Application Using Consumers' Perceived Service Quality," *Journal of International Marketing* 18, no. 3 (September 2010), pp. 18–40.

9. Alex Sood, "The Lost Boys Found: Marketing to Men through Games," *Fast Company,* March 10, 2011, http://www.fastcom-

10. Bill Carter and Tanzina Vega, "In Shift, Ads Try to Entice Over 55 Set," *The New York Times,* May 13, 2011, http://www.nytimes .com.

11. Augusta Christensen, "No, Skechers, Shape-Ups Are Nothing Like the First Lady's Let's Move Campaign," *The Huffington Post,* May 13, 2011, http://www.huffingtonpost.com.

12. "Mark Cuban 'Buys Into' Skechers," January 10, 2012, http: //skx.com.

13. Banwari, Mittal, *Consumer Behavior* (Cincinnati, OH: Open Mentis, 2008); J. Paul Peter and Jerry C. Olson, *Consumer Behavior and Marketing Strategy,* 8th ed. (New York: McGraw-Hill, 2008); Michael R. Solomon, *Consumer Behavior: Buying, Having, and Being,* 7th ed. (Upper Saddle River, NJ: Prentice Hall, 2006); Jagdish Sheth, Banwari Mittal, and Bruce I. Newman, *Customer Behavior: Consumer Behavior and Beyond* (Fort Worth, TX: The Dryden Press, 1999).

14. Chi Kin (Bennett) Yim, Kimmy Wa Chan, and Kineta Hung, "Multiple Reference Effects in Service Evaluations: Role of Alternative Attractiveness and Self-Image Congruity," *Journal of Retailing* 83, no. 1 (2007), pp. 147–57; Tamara Mangleburg, M. Joseph Sirgy, Dhruv Grewal, Danny Axsom, Maria Hatzios, C. B. Claiborne, and Trina Bogle, "The Moderating Effect of Prior Experience in Consumers' Use of User-Image Based versus Utilitarian Cues in Brand Attitude," *Journal of Business & Psychology* 13 (Fall 1998), pp. 101–13; M. Joseph Sirgy, D. Grewal, T. F. Mangleburg, J. Park, K. Chon, C. C. Claiborne, J. S. Johar, H. Berkman, "Direct versus Indirect Measures of Self-Image Congruence," *Journal of the Academy of Marketing Science* 25, no. 3 (1997), pp. 229–41.

15. Mittal, *Consumer Behavior;* Peter and Olson, *Consumer Behavior and Marketing Strategy;* Solomon, *Consumer Behavior: Buying, Having, and Being;* Sheth, Mittal, and Newman, *Customer Behavior: Consumer Behavior and Beyond.*

16. James M. Hagerty, "Harley, with Macho Intact, Tries to Court More Women," *The Wall Street Journal,* October 31, 2011, http://online.wsj.com; Harley-Davidson, "Global Customer Focus," http://investor.harley-davidson.com.

17. Harley-Davidson, "Women Riders," http://www.harley-davidson .com.

18. http://www.strategicbusinessinsights.com/vals/store /USconsumers/intro.shtml.

19. http://www.strategicbusinessinsights.com/vals/applications /apps-pos.shtml.

20. "Segmentation and Targeting," http://www.kellogg.northwest-ern.edu; Michael D. Lam, "Psychographic Demonstration: Segmentation Studies Prepare to Prove Their Worth," *Pharmaceutical Executive,* January 2004.

21. For an interesting take on this issue, see Joseph Jaffe, *Flip the Funnel* (Hoboken, NJ: John Wiley & Sons, 2010).

22. Irit Nitzan and Barak Libai, "Social Effects on Customer Retention," *Journal of Marketing* 75, no. 6 (November 2011), pp. 24–38; Yuping Liu, "The Long-Term Impact of Loyalty Programs on Consumer Purchase Behavior and Loyalty," *Journal of Marketing* 71, no. 4 (October 2007), pp. 19–35; V. Kumar and Denish Shah, "Building and Sustaining Profitable Customer Loyalty for the 21st Century," *Journal of Retailing* 80, no. 4 (2004), pp. 317–30.

23. http://www.united.com.

24. Bryan Alexander, "Up in the Air Fantasies: What Does 10 Million Miles Get You?" *Time*, December 22, 2009.

25. John Melloy, "Heinz Facebook Gaffe: 'Where's My Balsamic Ketchup?'" *Fast Money*, November 14, 2011, http://www.cnbc.com; Andrew Adam Newman, "Ketchup Moves Upmarket, with a Balsamic Tinge," *The New York Times*, October 25, 2011, http://www.nytimes.com; Brian Steinberg, "Recognition Factor," *Boston Globe*, March 25, 2009; Mary H. J. Farrell, "New Heinz Balsamic Ketchup Available Only on Facebook," *Consumer Reports*, November 16, 2011, http://news.consumerreports.org.

26. Dhruv Grewal, "Marketing Is All About Creating Value: 8 Key Rules," in *Inside the Mind of Textbook Marketing* (Boston, MA: Aspatore Inc., 2003), pp. 79–96.

27. Ben Sisario, "You've Got a Fan Club? Network and Mobilize It," *The New York Times*, March 2, 2011, http://www.nytimes.com; Ben Sisario, "Online Tools Help Bands Do Business," *The New York Times*, October 2, 2011, http://www.nytimes.com; Ian Rogers, "Getting Practical: A Step-by-Step Guide to Building an Online Marketing Plan that Works," Topspin.com, February 17, 2011, http://www.topspinmedia.com.

28. Thorsten Blecker, *Mass Customization: Challenges and Solutions* (New York: Springer, 2006); B. Joseph Pine, *Mass Customization: The New Frontier in Business Competition* (Cambridge, MA: Harvard Business School Publishing, 1999); James H. Gilmore and B. Joseph Pine, eds., *Markets of One: Creating Customer-Unique Value through Mass Customization* (Cambridge, MA: Harvard Business School Publishing, 2000).

29. G. R. Iyer, A. D. Miyazaki, D. Grewal, and M. Giordano, "Linking Web-Based Segmentation to Pricing Tactics," *Journal of Product & Brand Management* 11, no. 5 (2002), pp. 288–302; B. Jaworski and K. Jocz, "Rediscovering the Consumer," *Marketing Management* (September/October 2002), pp. 22–27; L. Rosencrance, "Customers Balk at Variable DVD Pricing," *Computer World* (September 11, 2000), p. 4; M. Stephanek, "None of Your Business: Customer Data Were Once Gold to E-Commerce. Now, Companies Are Paying a Price for Privacy Jitters," *BusinessWeek* (June 26, 2000), p. 78; D. Wessel, "How Technology Tailors Price Tags," *The Wall Street Journal*, June 23, 2001, p. A1.

30. C. Page Moreau, Leff Bonney, and Kelly B. Herd, "It's the Thought (and the Effort) That Counts: How Customizing for Others Differs from Customizing for Oneself," *Journal of Marketing* 75, no. 5 (September 2011), pp. 120–33.

31. This circular depiction of value proposition is based on work by John Bers (Vanderbilt University) and adaptation and development of circles of success by Ronald Goodstein (Georgetown University).

32. http://www.gatorade.com/frequently_asked_questions/default.aspx.

33. http://www.drpeppersnapplegroup.com/brands/7up/.

34. Allen Adamson, "Pitch Your Luxury Offering as an 'Investment Brand'," *Forbes*, May 4, 2010, http://www.forbes.com.

35. Stuart Schwartzapfel, "Volvo S80: Playing It Too Safe?" *BusinessWeek*, July 23, 2007; Jean Halliday, "Maloney Wants Volvo Viewed as Both Safe and Luxurious," *Advertising Age* 75, no. 12 (2004), p. 22.

36. Kris Hudson, "Hotelier Gets Face-Lift to Draw Young Travelers," *The Wall Street Journal*, November 14, 2011, http://online.wsj.com.

CHAPTER 10

1. In-Store Marketing Institute, "Shaping Retail: The Use of Virtual Store Simulations in Marketing Research and Beyond," http://kelley.iu.edu.

2. Alliston Ackerman, "P&G Shapes the Store," *Consumer Goods Technology*, November 16, 2011, http://consumergoods.edgl.com.

3. Accenture, "Accenture and Procter & Gamble Partner in Delivering Virtual Solutions BPO Services," http://www.accenture.com.

4. Michael Letchford, "Pioneering Virtual Stores with Procter and Gamble," *Insights in Retail*, http://www.insightsinretail.com.

5. Michael Letchford, "Virtual Shelf–Next Generation Visual Merchandising?" *Insights in Retail*, http://www.insightsinretail.com.

6. A. Parasuraman, Dhruv Grewal, and R. Krishnan, *Marketing Research*, 2nd ed. (Boston: Houghton Mifflin, 2007), p. 9.

7. Jack Honomichl, "The Honomichl Global Top 25 Report," *Marketing News*, August 30, 2011.

8. Detailed illustrations of scales are provided in two books: Gordon C. Bruner, *Marketing Scales Handbook: A Compilation of Multi-Item Measures*, vol. v (Carbondale, IL: GCBII Productions, 2009); William O. Bearden and Richard G. Netemeyer, *Handbook of Marketing Scales: Multi-Item Measures for Marketing and Consumer Behavior Research* (Thousand Oaks, CA: Sage Publications, 1999). Sources for the scales used in the exhibit are: Dhruv Grewal, Gopalkrishnan Iyer, Jerry Gotlieb, and Michael Levy, "Developing a Deeper Understanding of Post-Purchase Perceived Risk and Repeat Purchase Behavioral Intentions in a Service Setting," *Journal of the Academy of Marketing Science* 35, no. 2 (2007), pp. 250–58; Anthony Miyazaki, Dhruv Grewal, and Ronald C. Goodstein, "The Effect of Multiple Extrinsic Cues on Quality Perceptions: A Matter of Consistency," *Journal of Consumer Research* 32 (June 2005), pp. 146–53.

9. For a more thorough discussion of effective written reports, see Parasuraman, Grewal, and Krishnan, *Marketing Research*, chapter 16.

10. John Cloud, "McDonald's Chef: The Most Influential Cook in America?" *Time Magazine*, February 22, 2010, http://www.time.com.

11. Kristen McQueary, "A Revolution in Canvassing among Voters," *The New York Times*, November 19, 2011, http://www.nytimes.com.

12. "About," http://symphonyiri.com.

13. "Who We Are," http://iridev.blueboltlive.com.

14. SymphonyIRI, "Special Report: Retail Private Label Brands in Europe—Current and Emerging Trends," December 15, 2011, http://www.symphonyiri.com.

15. SymphonyIRI, "The CPG Basket: Fostering Growth in a Time of Conservation," December 14, 2011, http://www.symphonyiri.com.

16. Thomas Davenport, "Realizing the Potential of Retail Analytics," *Babson Executive Education*, August 2008; Marc-Andre Kamel, Nick Greenspan, and Rudolf Pritzl, "Standardization Is Efficient but Localization Helps Shops to Stand Out," *The Wall Street Journal*, January 21, 2009.

17. Jennifer Reingold, "Can P&G Make Money in a Place Where People Earn $2 Per Day?" *CNN Money*, January 6, 2011, http://features.blogs.fortune.cnn.com.

18. Elisabeth A. Sullivan, "Be Sociable," *Marketing News,* January 15, 2008.

19. Harry McCracken, "The Best Blogs of 2011," *Time,* June 6, 2011, http://www.time.com.

20. http://www.thetruthaboutcars.com/.

21. Andrew Adam Nieman, "Bloggers Don't Follow the Script, to ConAgra's Chagrin," *The New York Times,* September 6, 2011, http://www.nytimes.com.

22. "History: The Science of Shopping," http://www.envirosell.com.

23. Michael P. Cook and Hy Mariampolski, "How Culture Helps Marketers Understand Sensory Experiences," *Quirk's Marketing Research Review,* November 2009, p. 26.

24. "Client Story: Kraft," http://www.communispace.com.

25. Sarah Needleman, "For Companies, a Tweet in Time Can Avert PR Mess," *The Wall Street Journal,* August 3, 2009.

26. Rachael King, "Sentiment Analysis Gives Companies Insight into Consumer Opinion," *Bloomberg BusinessWeek,* March 1, 2011, http://www.businessweek.com.

27. Ashley Heher, "Our Pizza Didn't Taste Good, Domino's Says in New Ads," *Boston Globe,* January 12, 2010.

28. Richard A. Krueger and Mary Anne Casey, *Focus Groups: A Practical Guide for Applied Research* (Thousand Oaks, CA: Sage Publications, 2009).

29. "Campbell's Select Harvest Soups Top 2009 IRI New Product Pacesetters List: Second Time in Three Years That Campbell's Soups Top List," *MarketWatch,* March 23, 2010, http://www.marketwatch.com.

30. http://www.campbellsoup.com.

31. Amanda Green, "Smaller Companies Embrace USPS Sampling," *Direct Marketing News,* May 1, 2011, http://www.dmnews.com.

32. Emily Goon, "How Research Helped Develop the USPS's Sample Showcase Program," *Quirk's Marketing Research Review* (December 2011).

33. Ibid.

34. Ibid.

35. "Sample Showcase," http://www.startsampling.com.

36. Green, op. cit.

37. United States Postal Service, "Getting the Most Out of Sampling," *Promotion Marketing Association, Inc.,* April 2011, http://www.pmalink.org.

38. Green, op. cit.

39. http://www.e-focusgroups.com.

40. Adapted from A. Parasuraman, Dhruv Grewal, and R. Krishnan, *Marketing Research,* 2nd ed. (Boston: Houghton Mifflin, 2007), Ch. 10.

41. Floyd J. Fowler, *Survey Research Methods* (Thousand Oaks, CA: Sage Publications, 2009); Don A. Dillman, Glenn Phelps, Robert Tortora, Karen Swift, Julie Kohrell, Jodi Berck, and Benjamin L. Messer, "Response Rate and Measurement Differences in Mixed-Mode Surveys Using Mail, Telephone, Interactive Voice Response (IVR) and the Internet," *Social Science Research* 38 (March 2009), pp. 1–18.

42. https://pulse.asda.com; Joel Warady, "Asda Takes the 'Pulse of the Nation'," *Retail Wire,* July 16, 2009.

43. http://www.marketingpower.com/AboutAMA/Pages/Statement%20of%20Ethics.aspx; http://www.helleniccomserve.com.

44. Federal Trade Commission, "Widespread Data Breaches Uncovered by FTC Probe: FTC Warns of Improper Release of Sensitive Consumer Data on P2P File-Sharing Networks," February 22, 2010, http://www.ftc.gov.

45. Cecilia Kang, "Library of Congress Plan for Twitter: A Big, Permanent Retweet," *Washington Post,* April 16, 2010; www.cdt.org; Mark Penn, "Did Google Violate Privacy Laws?" www.politicallyillustrated.com, April 2, 2010; Lona M. Farr, "Whose Files Are They Anyway? Privacy Issues for the Fundraising Profession," *International Journal of Nonprofit and Voluntary Sector Marketing* 7, no. 4 (November 2002), p. 361.

46. Natasha Singer, "Face Recognition Makes the Leap from Sci-Fi," *The New York Times,* November 12, 2011.

47. Andrew Roberts, "In Some Stores, the Mannequins Are Watching You," *Bloomberg BusinessWeek,* December 6, 2012, http://www.businessweek.com; Amar Toor, "EyeSee Mannequin Silently Collects Customer Data for Overzealous Retailers," *The Verge,* November 20, 2012, http://www.theverge.com; Joanna Stern, "Department Store Mannequins Are Watching You. No, Really," *ABC News,* November 26, 2012, http://abcnews.go.com.

48. Adam Penenberg, "NeuroFocus Uses Neuromarketing to Hack Your Brain," *Fast Company,* August 8, 2011, http://www.fastcompany.com.

CHAPTER 11

1. John Tierney, "24 Miles, 4 Minutes, and 834 M.P.H., All in One Jump," *The New York Times,* October 14, 2012, http://www.nytimes.com.

2. Ann-Christine Diaz, "Notably Missing at Cannes? Red Bull 'Stratos'," *Creativity,* June 25, 2013, http://creativity-online.com.

3. http://www.trekbikes.com.

4. Sharon Ng, "Cultural Orientation and Brand Dilution: Impact of Motivation Level and Extension Typicality," *Journal of Marketing Research* 47, no. 1 (February 2010), pp. 186–98; Paraskevas C. Argouslidis and George Baltas, "Structure in Product Line Management: The Role of Formalization in Service Elimination Decisions," *Journal of the Academy of Marketing Science,* 35, no. 4 (2007), pp. 475–91; John A. Quelch and David Kenny, "Extend Profits, Not Product Lines," *Harvard Business Review,* September–October 1994, pp. 153–60.

5. Simon Pittman, "Revlon Switches CEO as Pressure Mounts over Performance," Cosmeticsdesign.com, September 19, 2006.

6. Michael A. Wiles, Neil A. Morgan, and Lopo L. Rego, "The Effect of Brand Acquisition and Disposal on Stock Returns," *Journal of Marketing* 76, no. 1 (2012), pp. 38–58.

7. "Compare Checking Accounts," https://www.bankofamerica.com.

8. Ellen Byron, "Tide Turns 'Basic' for P&G in Slump," *The Wall Street Journal,* August 6, 2009; Barry Silverstein, "P&G Scrubs Out Tide Basic," *BrandChannel,* June 6, 2010, http://www.brandchannel.com.

9. Andrew Adam Newman, "Axe Adds Fragrance for Women to Its Lineup," *The New York Times,* January 8, 2012, http://www.nytimes.com.

10. Dianna Dilworth, "Axe Campaign Has Fans Collaboratively Write Graphic Novel Online," *Direct Marketing News,* January 10, 2012, http://www.dmnews.com.

11. Todd Wasserman, "Axe Launches Fragrance with a Graphic Novel on YouTube," *Mashable Business,* January 10, 2012, http://mashable.com.

12. Cotton Timberlake, "Kate Spade's Got a Brand New Bag," *Bloomberg BusinessWeek,* February 24, 2011.

13. *Consumer Reports,* "TV Buying Guide: Brands," http://www.consumerreports.org.

14. Kevin Lane Keller, *Strategic Brand Management: Building, Measuring, and Managing Brand Equity,* 3rd ed. (Upper Saddle River, NJ: Prentice Hall, 2007).

15. This discussion of the advantages of strong brands is adapted from Keller, *Strategic Brand Management,* pp. 104–112; Elizabeth S. Moore, William L. Wilkie, and Richard J. Lutz, "Passing the Torch: Intergenerational Influences as a Source of Brand Equity," *Journal of Marketing* 66, no. 2 (2002), p. 17. See also Kevin Lane Keller and Donald R. Lehmann, "Brands and Branding: Research Findings and Future Priorities," *Marketing Science* 25 (November 2006), pp. 740–59.

16. Kevin Lane Keller and Donald R. Lehmann, "Assessing Long-Term Brand Potential," *Journal of Brand Management* 17 (2009), pp. 6–17.

17. Evan Carmichael, "Obsess Over Your Customers—Jeff Bezos," www.youngentrepreneur.com, April 7, 2009; http://www.amazon.com/New-Rules-Marketing-PR-Podcasting/dp/0470113456.

18. Parija Kavilanz, "Tootsie Roll to Footzyroll: See Ya in Court!" *CNN Money,* November 18, 2011, http://money.cnn.com.

19. http://www.interbrand.com. The net present value of the earnings over the next 12 months is used to calculate the value.

20. David Aaker, *Brand Portfolio Strategy: Creating Relevance, Differentiation, Energy, Leverage, and Clarity* (New York: Free Press, 2004); David A. Aaker, *Managing Brand Equity* (New York: Free Press, 1991).

21. Lopo L. Rego, Matthew T. Billett, and Neil A. Morgan, "Consumer-Based Brand Equity and Firm Risk," *Harvard Business Review* 73, no. 6, November 2009, pp. 47–60; Natalie Mizik and Robert Jacobson, "Valuing Branded Businesses," *Harvard Business Review* 73, no. 6, November 2009, p. 137–53; Shuba Srinivasan and Seenu Srinivasan, *Brand Equity: Measuring, Analyzing, and Predicting* (Boston: Harvard Business Press, May 8, 2006); David Aaker, *Building Strong Brands* (New York: Simon & Schuster, 2002); David A. Aaker, "Measuring Brand Equity Across Products and Markets," *California Management Review* 38 (1996), pp. 102–20.

22. Stephanie Clifford, "Demand at Target for Fashion Line Crashes Web Site," *The New York Times,* September 13, 2011, http://www.nytimes.com/2011/09/14/business/demand-at-target-for-fashion-line-crashes-web-site.html; Kara G. Morrison, "Chic on the Cheap," *The Detroit News,* February 15, 2008; http://www.fxmagazine.co.uk/story.asp?storyCode51632.

23. Jennifer Van Grove, "Barbie Joins Foursquare," *Mashable Business,* July 15, 2010, http://mashable.com.

24. "Video Girl Scavenger Hunt: Lights! Barbie! Action!" http://alldolldup.typepad.com.

25. Campaign for a Commercial-Free Childhood, "The Commercialization of Childhood," http://www.commercialfreechildhood.org.

26. T. L. Stanley, "Mattel, Hasbro Transform Themselves," *BrandWeek,* June 2010, http://login.vnuemedia.com.

27. Claude Brodesser-Akner, "Thanks to a Big Mattel Move, Toys and Movies Come One Step Closer to Being the Exact Same Thing," *New York Magazine,* March 24, 2010, http://nymag.com.

28. Claude Brodesser-Akner, "Disney to Hollywood: If It Can't Sell Toys, It Had Better Be Cheap," February 17, 2010, http://nymag.com.

29. www.hallmarkchannel.com.

30. http://www.marketingpower.com/_layouts/Dictionary.aspx?dLetter=B.

31. "Kantar Media Reports U.S. Advertising Expenditures Increased 6.5 Percent in 2010," March 17, 2011, http://kantarmediana.com.

32. Lien Lamey, Barbara Deleersnyder, Marnik G. Dekimpe, and Jan-Benedict E.M. Steenkamp, "How Business Cycles Contribute to Private-Label Success: Evidence from the United States and Europe," *Journal of Marketing* 71 (January 2007), pp. 1–15; PLMA (2009), http://www.plmainternational.com.

33. Kellogg's 2010 annual report, http://annualreport2010.kelloggcompany.com.

34. The distinction between brand and line extensions is clarified in Barry Silverstein, "Brand Extensions: Risks and Rewards," Brandchannel.com, January 5, 2009.

35. See Thorsen Hennig-Thurau, Mark B. Houson, and Torsten Heitjans, "Conceptualizing and Measuring the Monetary Value of Brand Extensions: The Case of Motion Pictures," *Journal of Marketing* 73, no. 6 (November 2009), pp. 167–83; Rohini Ahluwalia, "How Far Can a Brand Stretch? Understanding the Role of Self-Construal," *Journal of Marketing Research* 45, no. 3 (2008); Byung Chul Shine, Jongwon Park, and Robert S. Wyer, "Brand Synergy Effects in Multiple Brand Extensions," *Journal of Marketing Research* 44, no. 4 (2007), pp. 663–70; Gochen Wu and Yung-Ghien Yen, "How the Strength of Parent Brand Associations Influences the Interaction Effects of Brand Breadth and Product Similarity with Brand Extension Evaluations," *Journal of Product & Brand Management* 16, no. 4–5 (2007), pp. 334–41; Franziska Volckner and Henrik Sattler, "Drivers of Brand Extension Success," *Journal of Marketing* 70, no. 2 (2006), pp. 18–34; Subramanian Balachander and Sanjoy Ghose, "Reciprocal Spillover Effects: A Strategic Benefit of Brand Extensions," *Journal of Marketing* 67, no. 1 (2003), pp. 4–13; Kalpesh Kaushik Desai and Kevin Lane Keller, "The Effects of Ingredient Branding Strategies on Host Brand Extendibility," *Journal of Marketing* 66, no. 1 (2002), pp. 73–93; Tom Meyvis and Chris Janiszewski, "When Are Broader Brands Stronger Brands? An Accessibility Perspective on the Success of Brand Extensions," *Journal of Consumer Research* 31, no. 2 (2004), pp. 346–57.

36. David Aaker, "Brand Extensions: The Good, the Bad, and the Ugly," *Sloan Management Review* 31 (Summer 1990), pp. 47–56.

37. www.neutrogena.com; Vanitha Swaminathan, Richard J. Fox, and Srinivas K. Reddy, "The Impact of Brand Extension Introduction on Choice," *Journal of Marketing* 65, no. 3 (2001), pp. 1–15.

38. Devon DelVecchio and Daniel C. Smith, "Brand-Extension Price Premiums: The Effects of Perceived Fit and Extension Product Category Risk," *Journal of the Academy of Marketing Science* 33, no. 2 (2005), pp. 184–96; Jennifer Aaker, Susan Fournier, and S. Adam Brasel, "When Good Brands Do Bad," *Journal of Consumer Research* 31, no. 1 (2004), pp. 1–16.

39. Costas Hadjicharalambous, "A Typology of Brand Extensions: Positioning Cobranding as a Sub-Case of Brand Extensions," *Journal of American Academy of Business* 10, no. 1 (2006), pp. 372–77; H. Sjodin and F. Torn, "When Communication Challenges Brand Associations: A Framework for Understanding Consumer Responses to Brand Image Incongruity," *Journal of Consumer Behaviour* 5, no. 1 (2006), pp. 32–42; C. H. Chen and S. K. Chen, "Brand Dilution Effect of Extension Failure–A Taiwan Study," *Journal of Product and Brand Management* 9, no. 4 (2000), pp. 243–54.

40. Mario Marsicano, "Cheetos Lip Balm & More Bizarre Brand Extensions," *The Wall Street Journal,* July 15, 2009.

41. David A. Aaker and Kevin Lane Keller, "Consumer Evaluations of Brand Extensions," *Journal of Marketing* 54, no. 1 (1990), pp. 27–41.

42. Guoqun Fu, Jiali Ding, and Riliang Qu, "Ownership Effects in Consumers' Brand Extension Evaluations," *Journal of Brand Management* 16 (2009), pp. 221–233; Christoph Burmann, Sabrina Zeplin, and Nicola Riley, "Key Determinants of Internal Brand Management Success: An Exploratory Empirical Analysis," *Journal of Brand Management* 16 (2009), pp. 264–84; Raisa Yakimova and Michael Beverland, "The Brand-Supportive Firm: An Exploration of Organisational Drivers of Brand Updating," *Journal of Brand Management* 12, no. 6 (2005), pp. 445–60.

43. http://www.marriott.com/corporateinfo/glance.mi.

44. Cathy Enz, "Multibranding Strategy: The Case of Yum! Brands," *Cornell Hotel & Restaurant Administration Quarterly*, February 2005.

45. T. Kippenberger, "Co-Branding as a Competitive Weapon," *Strategic Direction* 18, no. 10 (2002), pp. 31–33.

46. Keller, *Strategic Brand Management: Building, Measuring, and Managing Brand Equity*.

47. Keller, *Strategic Brand Management: Building, Measuring, and Managing Brand Equity*.

48. Laurent Muzellec, and Mary Lambkin, "Corporate Rebranding and the Implications for Brand Architecture Management: The Case of Guinness (Diageo) Ireland," *Journal of Strategic Marketing* 16, no. 4. (2008), pp. 283–99; W. Lomax and M. Mador, "Corporate Re-Branding: from Normative Models to Knowledge Management," *Journal of Brand Management* 14, no. 1/2, (2006), pp. 82–95; B. Merrilees and D. Miller, "Principles of Corporate Rebranding," *European Journal of Marketing* 42, no. 5/6, (2008) pp. 537–552; L. Muzellec and M. Lambkin, "Corporate Rebranding: Destroying, Transferring or Creating Brand Equity?" *European Journal of Marketing* 40, no. 7/8 (2006), pp. 803–24; Yakimova and Beverland, "The Brand-Supportive Firm"; Stephen Brown, Robert V. Kozinets, and John F. Sherry Jr., "Teaching Old Brands New Tricks: Retro Branding and the Revival of Brand Meaning," *Journal of Marketing* 67, no. 2 (2003), p. 19.

49. Jane Levere, "Ivory Soap Refreshes Its Ads and Its Look, But Is Resolutely Simple," *The New York Times*, November 7, 2011.

50. U.S. Government Accounting Office, "Bottled Water: FDA Safety and Consumer Protections Are Often Less Stringent Than Comparable EPA Protections for Tap Water," July 8, 2009.

51. Associated Press, "Stricter Labeling Urged for Bottled Water," *The Wall Street Journal*, July 8, 2008.

52. Brian Steinberg, "Recognition Factor," *Boston Globe*, March 25, 2009.

53. Valerie Bauerlein, "Pepsi to Pare Plastic for Bottled Water," *The Wall Street Journal*, March 25, 2009.

54. Steve Inskeep, "Consumers Reject New Tropicana Carton," *Morning Edition*, February 23, 2009.

55. Stuart Elliot, "Tropicana Discovers Some Buyers Are Passionate about Packaging," *The New York Times*, February 22, 2009.

56. Chris Serres, "It's True: Food Packages Shrunk Last Year," *Minneapolis Star Tribune* December 31, 2008.

CHAPTER 12

1. "LEGO History Timeline," http://aboutus.lego.com.

2. http://mln.lego.com/en-us/network/status.aspx?icmp=COUS CreateShareSL100MLN.

3. Brad Wieners, "Lego Is for Girls," *BusinessWeek*, December 14, 2011.

4. Shari Roan, "A New Lego Line for Girls Is Offensive, Critics Say," *Los Angeles Times*, January 23, 2012, http://www.latimes.com/.

5. http://friends.lego.com/en-us/Products/Default.aspx.

6. Carrie Goldman, "Legos for Girls: Let's Focus the Discussion on the Right Issues," *Portrait of an Adoption*, January 30, 2012, http://www.chicagonow.com; Ruth Davis Konigsberg, "Lego Friends for Girls: Have They Stooped to Stereotype?" *Time Magazine*, January 2, 2012, http://ideas.time.com; "Whether Pink Legos Are Just Building Stereotypes," *NPR*, January 24, 2012, http://www.npr.org.

7. Scott Stinson and Hollie Shaw, "Gender Games," *National Post*, January 21, 2012, http://www.nationalpost.com.

8. "Doing the Right Thing," www.frogbox.com/therightthing.php.

9. Koen Pauwels, Jorge Silva-Risso, Shuba Srinivasan, and Dominique M. Hanssens, "New Products, Sales Promotions, and Firm Value: The Case of the Automobile Industry," *Journal of Marketing* 68, no. 4 (2008), p. 142.

10. Andrew Adam Newman, "Making the Diaper Change Easier for the Changer," *The New York Times*, July 28, 2011, http://www.nytimes.com.

11. "Huggies Brand Announces a Whole New Way to Change Diapers," July 13, 2011, http://investor.kimberly-clark.com.

12. Ibid.

13. "The Huggies Brand Encourages Parents to Showcase Their Active Babies," *The New York Times*, January 19, 2012, http://markets.on.nytimes.com.

14. Keith O'Brien, "Should We All Go Gluten-Free?" *The New York Times*, November 25, 2011, http://www.nytimes.com.

15. Kalpesh Kaushik Desai and Kevin Lane Keller, "The Effects of Ingredient Branding Strategies on Host Brand Extendibility," *Journal of Marketing* 66, no. 1 (2002), pp. 73–93.

16. Phil Patton, "Out of the Melting Pot and Into a Global Market," January 13, 2012, *The New York Times*, http://www.nytimes.com.

17. Paul Stenquist, "A Buffet of Canny Tweaks in Hot Pursuit of Mileage," January 13, 2012, *The New York Times*, http://www.nytimes.com.

18. Don Reisinger, "Madden Sales Up 10 Percent Over Last Year," cnet.com, September 8, 2011, http://news.cnet.com.

19. http://www.ideo.com/work/featured/kraft.

20. http://www.marketingpower.com/_layouts/Dictionary.aspx?dLetter=D.

21. Barak Libai, Eitan Muller, and Renana Peres, "The Diffusion of Services," *Journal of Marketing Research* 46 (April 2009), pp. 163–75; Yvonne van Everdingen, Dennis Fok, and Stefan Stemersch, "Modeling Global Spillover of New Product Takeoff," *Journal of Marketing Research* 46 (October 2009), pp. 637–52.

22. Rosabeth Moss Kanter, *SuperCorp: How Vanguard Companies Create Innovation, Profits, Growth, and Social Good* (New York: Crown Business, 2009); Rajesh K. Chandy, Jaideep C. Prabhu, and Kersi D. Antia, "What Will the Future Bring? Dominance, Technology Expectations, and Radical Innovation," *Journal of Marketing* 67, no. 3 (2003), pp. 1–18; Harald J. van Heerde, Carl F. Mela, and Puneet Manchanda, "The Dynamic Effect of Innovation on Market Structure," *Journal of Marketing Research* 41, no. 2 (2004), pp. 166–83.

23. http://www.apple.com; Clayton M. Christensen and Michael E. Raynor, *The Innovator's Solution* (Boston: Harvard Business School Press, 2003).

24. James L. Oakley, Adam Duhachek, Subramanian Balachander, and S. Sriram, "Order of Entry and the Moderating Role of Comparison Brands in Brand Extension Evaluation," *Journal of Consumer Research* 34, no. 5 (2008), pp. 706–12; Fernando F. Suarez and Gianvito Lanzolla, "Considerations for a Stronger First Mover Advantage Theory," *Academy of Management Review* 33, no. 1 (2008), pp. 269–70; Ralitza Nikolaeva, "The Dynamic Nature of Survival Determinants in E-commerce," *Journal of the Academy of Marketing Science* 35, no. 4 (2007), pp. 560–71.

25. Matt Haig, *Brand Failures* (London: Kogan Page, 2005); Raji Srinivasan, Gary L. Lilien, and Arvind Rangaswamy, "First in, First out? The Effects of Network Externalities on Pioneer Survival," *Journal of Marketing* 68, no. 1 (2004), p. 41.

26. K. Tyagi, "New Product Introductions and Failures under Uncertainty," *International Journal of Research in Marketing* 23, no. 2 (2006), pp. 199–213; Lori Dahm, "Secrets of Success: The Strategies Driving New Product Development at Kraft," *Stagnito's New Products Magazine* 2 (January 2002), p. 18ff; *BusinessWeek*, "Flops," August 16, 1993, p. 76ff.

27. "Top 10 Reasons for New Product Failure," *The Marketing Fray*, January 7, 2010 (http://www.marketingfray.com).

28. http://smashinghub.com/10-coolest-upcoming-gadgets-of-2011.htm.

29. Jacob Goldenberg, Sangman Han, Donald R. Lehmann, and Jae Weon Hong, "The Role of Hubs in the Adoption Process," *Journal of Marketing* 73 (March 2009), pp. 1–13.

30. "25 Most Promising Products for 2011," http://www.business-pundit.com.

31. Erica Ogg, "ZOMG: Amazon.com Drops Kindle Price 10 Percent," *CNET News*, May 27, 2008.

32. Dylan F. Tweney, "Large-Screen Kindle Won't Mean Squat If Apple Tablet Arrives," *Wired*, May 4, 2009.

33. David Streitfeld, "Will the Kindle Fire Kill E-Readers," *The New York Times*, January 10, 2012, http://bits.blogs.nytimes.com; Julie Bosman, "Table and E-Reader Sales Soar," *The New York Times*, January 22, 2012, http://mediadecoder.blogs.nytimes.com.

34. Jeffrey A. Trachtenberg, "E-Book Readers Face Sticker Shock," *The Wall Street Journal*, December 15, 2011.

35. "Kindle vs. the iPad," Go4Expert.com, November 3rd, 2010 (http://www.go4expert.com).

36. Sarah Perez, "Firefox China Edition: Everything a Local Browser Should Be," ReadWriteWeb.com, November 24, 2008.

37. Steve Jobs, "Thoughts on Flash," Apple.com (http://www.apple.com).

38. L. M. De Luca and K. Atuahene-Gima, "Market Knowledge Dimensions and Cross-Functional Collaboration: Examining the Different Routes to Product Innovation Performance," *Journal of Marketing* 71 (2007), pp. 95–112; Subin Im and John P. Workman Jr., "Market Orientation, Creativity, and New Product Performance in High-Technology Firms," *Journal of Marketing*, 68, no. 2 (2004), p. 114.

39. Natalie Zmuda, "P&G, Levi's, GE Innovate by Thinking in Reverse," *Ad Age*, June 13, 2011, http://adage.com "Minute Maid Pulpy Joins Growing List of Billion Dollar Brands for the Coca-Cola Company," press release, February 1, 2011, http://www.thecoca-colacompany.com.

40. Rajani Baburajan, "U.S. Cable Industry Launches CableLabs—Energy Lab within its R&D Consortium," *Green Technology World*, November 21, 2011, http://green.tmcnet.com.

41. Stefan Stremersch and Walter Van Dyck, "Marketing of the Life Sciences: A New Framework and Research Agenda for a Nascent Field," *Journal of Marketing* 73 (July 2009), pp. 4–30; Brady Huggett, John Hodgson, and Riku Lähteenmäki, "Public Biotech 2010–The Numbers," *Nature Biotechnology* 29 (2011), pp. 585–91, http://www.nature.com.

42. "Pilates Allegra 2 Reformer for Balanced Body," IDEO Case Study, 2011.

43. Ibid.

44. Pilar Carbonell, Ana I. Rodríguez-Escudero, Devashish Pujari, "Customer Involvement in New Service Development: An Examination of Antecedents and Outcomes," *Journal of Product Innovation Management* 26 (September 2009), pp. 536–50; Glen L. Urban and John R. Hauser, "'Listening In' to Find and Explore New Combinations of Customer Needs," *Journal of Marketing* 68, no. 2 (2004), p. 72.

45. Steve Lohr, "Can Microsoft Make You 'Bing'?" *The New York Times*, July 30, 2011, http://www.nytimes.com.

46. Renay San Miguel, "Bing's New Bells and Whistles Could Leave Searchers' Heads Ringing," *TechNewsWorld*, March 29, 2010; Jared Newman, "How Microsoft Plans to Beat Google with Bing," *PCWorld*, August 1, 2011, http://www.pcworld.com.

47. "Godiva Gems and Communispace for B2C Listening," *Communispace*, 2010.

48. Associated Press, "Wal-Mart Adds Products as Store Brands Boom," *Boston Globe*, March 17, 2009; Matthew Boyle, "Wal-Mart Gives Its Store Brand a Makeover," *BusinessWeek*, March 16, 2009.

49. Interview with Jevin Eagle, Executive Vice President of Merchandising and Marketing at Staples, June 18, 2009.

50. Jim Highsmith, *Agile Product Management: Creating Innovative Products* (Boston, Addison-Wesley, 2009); http://www.betterproductdesign.net; Eric von Hippel, *The Sources of Innovation* (New York: Oxford University Press, 1988); Eric von Hippel, "Successful Industrial Products from Consumers' Ideas," *Journal of Marketing* 42, no. 1 (1978), pp. 39–49.

51. Karl T. Ulrich and Steven D. Eppinger, *Product Design and Development*, 4th ed. (Boston: Irwin-McGraw-Hill, 2008).

52. http://www.marketingpower.com.

53. Ulrich and Eppinger, *Product Design and Development*.

54. Min Zhao, Steven Hoeffler, and Darren W. Dahl, "The Role of Imagination-Focused Visualization on New Product Evaluation," *Journal of Marketing Research* 46 (February 2009), pp. 46–55; http://www.marketingpower.com.

55. Ulrich and Eppinger, *Product Design and Development*.

56. Ellen Byron, "A Virtual View of the Store Aisle," *The Wall Street Journal*, October 3, 2007.

57. The Humane Society, "Cosmetic and Product Testing," http://www.humanesociety.org; The Body Shop, "Saying No to Animal Testing," http://www.thebodyshop.com; Proctor & Gamble, "Animal Welfare and Alternatives," http://www.pg.com; http://www.peta.org.

58. http://en-us.nielsen.com/tab/product_families/nielsen_bases.

59. Gernot H. Gessinger, *Materials and Innovative Product Development: From Concept to Market* (Oxford: Elsevier, 2009).

60. Jyoti Thottam Pune and Niljanjana Bhowmick, "Nano Power," *Time*, April 13, 2009.

61. Product Development Management Association, *The PDMA Handbook of New Product Development*, 2nd ed., Kenneth K. Kahn, ed. (New York: John Wiley & Sons, 2004).

62. Christian Homburg, Jan Wieske, and Torsten Bornemann, "Implementing the Marketing Concept at the Employee–Customer Interface: The Role of Customer Need Knowledge," *Journal of Marketing* 73 (July 2009), pp. 64–81; Torsten Bornemann Ashwin W. Joshi and Sanjay Sharma, "Customer Knowledge Development: Antecedents and Impact on New Product Performance," *Journal of Marketing* 68, no. 4 (2004), p. 47.

63. Katherine Bourzac, "Colorful Quantum Dot Displays Coming to Market," *Technology Review*, http://www.technologyreview.com.

64. Yuhong Wu, Sridhar Balasubramanian, and Vijay Mahajan, "When Is a Preannounced New Product Likely to Be Delayed?" *Journal of Marketing* 68, no. 2 (2004), p. 101.

65. http://www.walletpop.com/specials/top-25-biggest-product-flops-of-all-time.

66. http://www.pdma.org/.

67. "Coca-Cola Freestyle, Best Global Brands 2011," *Interbrand,* 2011.

68. Theodore Levitt, *Marketing Imagination* (New York: The Free Press, 1986).

69. Donald R. Lehmann and Russell S. Winer, *Analysis for Marketing Planning,* 7th ed. (Burr Ridge Il.: McGraw-Hill/Irwin, 2008).

70. Ibid.; Glen L. Urban and John R. Hauser, *Design and Marketing of New Products,* 2nd ed. (Upper Saddle River, NJ: Prentice Hall, 1993), pp. 120–21.

71. http://www.organicearthday.org/DelMonteFoods.htm; http://www.delmonte.com/Products/.

72. http://www.beiersdorf.com/Brands_Innovations/Innovations.html?TG=Brands_Sustainability; http://www.nivea.com/high-lights/int_product/show/nhc_diamond_gloss/.

73. "Whirlpool Washing Machines," http://www.scribd.com; Miriam Jordan and Jonathan Karp, "Machines for the Masses; Whirlpool Aims Cheap Washer at Brazil, India and China; Making Do with Slower Spin," *The Wall Street Journal,* December 9, 2003, p. A19.

74. "The New Global Middle Class: Potentially Profitable—But also Unpredictable," *Knowledge@Wharton*, July 9, 2008; Eric D. Beinhocker, Diana Farrell, and Adil S. Zainulbhai, "Tracking the Growth of India's Middle Class," *McKinsey Quarterly* (August 2007).

75. Ellen Byron, "Purex Tackles Tough Market, Using New Spin," *The Wall Street Journal,* April 28, 2009.

76. Noreen O'Leary, "KFC's Grilled Chicken Tops Most-Recalled '09 Launches," *Brandweek*, December 12, 2009; "BrandIndex: Big Spenders on Advertising Get the Most Buzz," *Advertising Age*; Lisa Respers France, "Oprah Coupon Craze Leaves KFC Customers Hungry for More," CNN.com, May 8, 2009.

77. Yvonne Zipp, "As Vinyl Records Get Back in the Groove, Kalamazoo Record Stores See Sales Climb," *MLive*, January 15, 2012, http://www.mlive.com.

78. Natalie Zmuda and Jennifer Rooney, "Hallmark Breaks Out of Special Occasion Mold," *Advertising Age*, July 6, 2011, http://adage.com.

79. Claire Cain Miller, "Smartphone Apps Send Holiday Greetings," *The New York Times*, November 23, 2011, http://www.nytimes.com.

80. Steven Levenstein, "Sony's New USB Turntable Sparks Vinyl Revival," www.inventospot.com, March 14, 2008; http://www.electronichouse.com; Roy Bragg, "LP Vinyl Records Are Making a Comeback in Audiophile Circles," *Knight Ridder Tribune Business News*, January 3, 2004 (ProQuest Document ID: 521358371); Susan Adams, "You, the Record Mogul," *Forbes,* October 27, 2003, p. 256ff.

81. Goutam Challagalla, R. Venkatesh, and Ajay Kohli, "Proactive Postsales Service: When and Why Does It Pay Off?" *Journal of Marketing* 73 (March 2009), pp. 70–87; Kevin J. Clancy and Peter C. Krieg, "Product Life Cycle: A Dangerous Idea," *Brandweek,* March 1, 2004, p. 26; Nariman K. Dhalla and Sonia Yuseph, "Forget the Product Life-Cycle Concept," *Harvard Business Review* (January–February 1976), p. 102ff.

82. Peter Golder and Gerard Tellis, "Cascades, Diffusion, and Turning Points in the Product Life Cycle," MSI Report No. 03-120, 2003.

CHAPTER 13

1. Aida Ahmed, "Zappos Ranks No. 11 on List of Best Companies to Work For," *VegasInc,* January 19, 2012, http://www.vegasinc.com.

2. Doug Stephens, "The Declining Need for and Escalating Value of Human Service," Retail Prophet, September 26, 2011.

3. Armando Roggio, "The Zappos Effect: 5 Great Customer Service Ideas for Smaller Businesses," *Practical Ecommerce,* http://www.practicalecommerce.com.

4. Janine Popick, "Zappos: A Great Example of Exceeding Expectations," *Vertical Response,* http://blog.verticalresponse.com.

5. Ahmed, op. cit.

6. Valarie A. Zeithaml, Mary Jo Bitner, and Dwayne D. Gremler, *Services Marketing: Integrating Customer Focus across the Firm,* 5th ed. (Burr Ridge, IL: McGraw-Irwin, 2009).

7. Bureau of Economic Analysis, news release, January 27, 2012, http://www.bea.gov; "Fortune 500," *CNNMoney,* May 23, 2011, http://money.cnn.com.

8. Zeithaml, Bitner, and Gremler, *Services Marketing*.

9. "Center for Professional Responsibility," http://www.abanet.org.

10. Ramon Ray, "Carbonite Offers Data Peace of Mind: A Solid Solution for Small Biz," *Business Insider,* January 24, 2012, http://www.businessinsider.com.

11. David Huber, "Carbonite Inc. (CARB) Online Backup Service," IRA.com, January 26, 2011, http://www.ira.com.

12. http://www.carbonite.com.

13. Eric A. Taub, "Storing Your Files inside the Cloud," *The New York Times,* March 2, 2011, http://www.nytimes.com.

14. http://www.carbonite.com.

15. Dhruv Grewal, Michael Levy, Gopal Iyer, and Jerry Gotlieb, "Developing a Deeper Understanding of Post-Purchase Perceived Risk and Repeat Purchase Behavioral Intentions in a Service Setting," *Journal of the Academy of Marketing Science* 35, no. 2 (2007), pp. 250–58; Jerry Gotlieb, Dhruv Grewal, Michael Levy, and Joan Lindsey-Mullikin, "An Examination of Moderators of the Effects of Customers' Evaluation of Employee Courtesy on Attitude toward the Service Firm," *Journal of Applied Social Psychology* 34 (April 2004), pp. 825–47.

16. Choice Hotels, "Special Guest Policies," http://www.choice-hotels.com.

17. Jesse Serwer, "I.T. with a Personal Touch," *SCT,* September 2011.

18. The discussion of the Gaps Model and its implications draws heavily from Michael Levy and Barton A. Weitz, *Retailing Management,* 7th ed. (Burr Ridge, IL: Irwin/McGraw-Hill, 2009); it is also based on Deon Nel and Leyland Pitt, "Service Quality in a Retail Environment: Closing the Gaps," *Journal of General*

Management 18 (Spring 1993), pp. 37–57; Zeithaml, Parasuraman, and Berry, *Delivering Quality Service;* Valerie Zeithaml, Leonard Berry, and A. Parasuraman, "Communication and Control Processes in the Delivery of Service Quality," *Journal of Marketing* 52, no. 2 (April 1988), pp. 35–48.

19. Zhen Zhu, Cheryl Nakata, K. Sivakumar, and Dhruv Grewal, "Self-Service Technology Effectiveness: The Roles of Interactivity, Comparative Information, and Individual Differences on Perceived Control and Interface Evaluation," *Journal of the Academy of Marketing Science* 35, no. 4 (2007), pp. 492–506; Zhen Zhu, Cheryl Nakata, K. Sivakumar, and Dhruv Grewal, "Fix It Or Leave it? Customer Recovery from Self-Service Technology Failures," working paper, 2012, Babson College; Peter C. Verhoef, Katherine N. Lemon, A. Parasuraman, Anne Roggeveen, Michael Tsiros, and Leonard A. Schlesinger, "Customer Experience Creation: Determinants, Dynamics and Management Strategies," *Journal of Retailing* 85, no. 1 (2009), pp. 31–41.

20. Adam Braff and John C. DeVine, "Maintaining the Customer Experience," *The McKinsey Quarterly,* December 2008.

21. J. Aspara and H. Tikkanen, "Interactions of Individuals' Company-Related Attitudes and Their Buying of Companies' Stocks and Products," *Journal of Behavioral Finance* 9 (2008), pp. 85–94; Caroline Goukens, Siegfried Dewitte, and Luk Warlop, "Me, Myself, and My Choices: The Influence of Private Self-Awareness on Choice," *Journal of Marketing Research* 46 (October 2009), pp. 703–14.

22. Kemba J. Dunham, "Beyond Satisfaction," *The Wall Street Journal,* October 30, 2006, p. R4.

23. Zeithaml, Bitner, and Gremler, op. cit.

24. http://www.forbestravelguide.com/five-star-spas.htm; Allison Scott, "New Renovations Add to the Guest and Meeting Experience," www.release-news.com; http://www.broadmoor.com.

25. Stephen L. Vargo, Kaori Nagao, Yi He, and Fred W. Morgan, "Satisfiers, Dissatisfiers, Criticals, and Neutrals: A Review of Their Relative Effects on Customer (Dis)Satisfaction," *Academy of Marketing Science Review* (January 2007), p. 1.

26. Goutam Challagalla, R. Venkatesh, and Ajay K. Kohli, "Proactive Postsales Service: When and Why Does It Pay Off?" *Journal of Marketing* 73 (March 2009), pp. 70–87.

27. Janelle Barlow, "A Complaint Is a Gift Corner," http://www.tmius.com.

28. Michael Bergdahl, *The Retail Revolution: How Wal-Mart Created a Brave New World of Business* (New York: Metropolitan Books, 2009); and Michael Bergdahl, *The 10 Rules of Sam Walton: Success Secrets for Remarkable Results* (Hoboken, NJ: John Wiley & Sons, 2006).

29. Hazel-Anne Johnson and Paul Spector, "Service with a Smile: Do Emotional Intelligence, Gender, and Autonomy Moderate the Emotional Labor Process?" *Journal of Occupational Health Psychology,* October 2007, pp. 319–33; Merran Toerien and Celia Kitzinger, "Emotional Labour in Action: Navigating Multiple Involvements in the Beauty Salon," *Sociology,* August 2007, pp. 645–62.

30. Michael T. Manion and Joseph Cherian, "Do Services Marketers' Success Measures Match Their Strategies?" *Journal of Services Marketing* 23, no. 7 (2009), pp. 476–86; Alison M. Dean and Al Rainnie, "Frontline Employees' Views on Organizational Factors that Affect the Delivery of Service Quality in Call Centers," *Journal of Services Marketing* 23, no. 5 (2009), pp. 326–37.

31. Jason Colquitt, Jeffery LePine, and Michael Wesson, *Organizational Behavior: Improving Performance and Commitment in the Workplace,* 2nd ed. (Burr Ridge, IL: McGraw-Hill, 2010); Felicitas M. Morhart, Walter Herzog, and Torsten Tomczak, "Brand-Specific Leadership: Turning Employees into Brand Champions," *Journal of Marketing* 73 (September 2009), pp. 122–42.

32. Marguerite Darlington, "The History and Future of Mobile's Role in Fashion," *FashionablyMarketing.me,* November 22, 2011.

33. "Travelocity," http://www.sabre-holdings.com/ourBrands/travelocity.html; "Awards," http://svc.travelocity.com.

34. Suzanne C. Makarem, Susan M. Mudambi, and Jeffrey S. Podoshen, "Satisfaction in Technology-Enabled Service Encounters," *Journal of Services Marketing* 23, no. 1 (2009).

35. Carmine Gallo, "Bringing Passion to Starbucks, Travelocity," *BusinessWeek,* January 9, 2008.

36. Anne Eisenberg, "Thinking of Going Blond? Consult the Kiosk First," *The New York Times,* March 29, 2009; Marianne Wilson, "Digital Dining," *Chain Store Age,* September 2008.

37. Anita Whiting and Naveen Donthu (2009), "Closing the Gap between Perceived and Actual Waiting Times in a Call Center: Results from a Field Study," *Journal of Services Marketing* 23, no. 5 (2009), pp. 279–328.

38. David Streitfeld, "For $2 a Star, an Online Retailer Gets 5-Star Product Reviews," *The New York Times,* January 26, 2012, http://www.nytimes.com; David Streitfeld, "Faking It to Make It: A Beautiful Try," *The New York Times,* January 27, 2012, http://bits.blogs.nytimes.com.

39. Christopher Reynolds, "Smashed Guitar, YouTube Song—United is Listening Now," *Los Angeles Times,* July 7, 2009.

40. http://www.youtube.com/watch?v=5YGc4zOqozo; Steve Keenan, "United Broke My Guitar: Song 2," *Times Online,* August 19, 2009.

41. Alison Bonaquro, "United Broke His Guitar and Learned a Lesson," July 10, 2009, http://blog.cmt.com.

42. Dhruv Grewal, Anne L. Roggeveen, and Michael Tsiros, "The Effect of Compensation on Repurchase Intentions in Service Recovery," *Journal of Retailing* 84, no. 4 (2008), pp. 424–34.

43. http://www.economist.com.

44. Dhruv Grewal, Anne Roggeveen, and Michael Tsiros, "Compensation as a Service Recovery Strategy: When Does it Work?" *Journal of Retailing* 84, no. 4 (2008), pp. 424–34.

45. Peter C. Verhoef, Katherine N. Lemon, A. Parasuraman, Anne Roggeveen, Michael Tsiros, and Leonard A. Schlesinger, "Customer Experience Creation: Determinants, Dynamics and Management Strategies," *Journal of Retailing* 85, no. 1 (2009), pp. 31–41; Beibei Dong, Kenneth R. Evans, and Shaoming Zou, "The Effects of Customer Participation in Co-Created Service Recovery," *Journal of the Academy of Marketing Science* 36 (Spring 2008), pp. 123–37; Dhruv Grewal, Anne Roggeveen, and Michael Tsiros, "Compensation as a Service Recovery Strategy: When Does it Work?" *Journal of Retailing* 84, no. 4 (2008), pp. 424–34.

46. Dhruv Grewal, Anne L. Roggeveen, and Michael Tsiros, "The Effect of Compensation on Repurchase Intentions in Service Recovery," *Journal of Retailing* 84, no. 4 (2008), pp. 424–34.

47. Yany Grégoire, Thomas M. Tripp, and Renaud Legoux, "When Customer Love Turns into Lasting Hate: The Effects of Relationship Strength and Time on Customer Revenge and Avoidance," *Journal of Marketing* 73 (November 2009), pp. 18–32.

48. Anne L. Roggeveen, Michael Tsiros, and Dhruv Grewal, "Understanding the Co-Creation Effect: When Does Collaborating

with Customers Provide a Lift to Service Recovery?" *Journal of the Academy of Marketing Science* 40, no. 6 (2012), pp. 771–90; B. Dong, K. R. Evans, and S. Zou, "The Effects of Customer Participation in Co-created Service Recovery," *Journal of the Academy of Marketing Science* 36, no. 1, (2008), pp. 123–37. Grewal, Roggeveen, and Tsiros, "The Effect of Compensation on Repurchase Intentions"; Amy K. Smith, Ruth N. Bolton, and Janet Wagner, "A Model of Customer Satisfaction with Service Encounters Involving Failure and Recovery," *Journal of Marketing Research* 36 (August 1999), pp. 356–72; Scott R. Swanson and Scott W. Kelley, "Attributions and Outcomes of the Service Recovery Process," *Journal of Marketing: Theory and Practice* 9 (Fall 2001), pp. 50–65.

49. Jayne O'Donnell, "Some Retailers Tighten Return Policies," *USA Today,* February 1, 2008.

CHAPTER 14

1. Mike Esterl, "Coke Tailors Its Soda Sizes," *Wall Street Journal,* http://online.wsj.com, September 19, 2011.

2. Ibid.

3. Douglas A. McIntyre, "The Sodas America No Longer Drinks," 247wallst.com (online), http://247wallst.com, November 18, 2011.

4. Reuters, "Coca-Cola's Results Are Lifted by Overseas Business," *The New York Times,* http://www.nytimes.com, July 19, 2011.

5. Ibid, Reuters.

6. Ibid, Esterl.

7. Hooman Estelami, Dhruv Grewal, and Anne L. Roggeveen, "The Effect of Policy Restrictions on Consumer Reactions to Price-Matching Guarantees," *Journal of the Academy of Marketing Science,* 35, no. 2 (2007), pp. 208–219; Monika Kukar-Kinney and Dhruv Grewal, "Comparison of Consumer Reactions to Price-Matching Guarantees in Internet and Bricks-and-Mortar Retail Environments," *Journal of the Academy of Marketing Science,* 35, no. 2 (2007), pp. 197–207; Sujay Dutta, Abhijit Biswas, and Dhruv Grewal, "Low Price Signal Default: An Empirical Investigation with Low-Price Guarantees," *Journal of the Academy of Marketing Science,* 35, no. 1 (2007), pp. 76–88; Kent B. Monroe, *Pricing: Making Profitable Decisions,* 3rd ed. (New York: McGraw-Hill, 2003); Dhruv Grewal, Kent B. Monroe, and R. Krishnan, "The Effects of Price Comparison Advertising on Buyers' Perceptions of Acquisition Value and Transaction Value," *Journal of Marketing,* 62 (April 1998), pp. 46–60.

8. Jennifer Frighetto, "U.S. Consumers Place More Importance on Price and Value," ACNielsen, October 28, 2008; Laura Wood, "It's Not Easy Being Green, Part 2," *Research and Markets*, October 6, 2009; Food Marketing Institute (2003), "American Shoppers Economize, Show Greater Interest in Nutrition and Awareness of Food Safety Issues, According to Trends in the United States: Consumer Attitudes and the Supermarket 2003"; "The New Value Equation," *Supermarket News,* 50 (June 10, 2002), p. 12.

9. *Moneyball,* directed by Bennett Miller (2011; Sony Pictures). See also Michael Lewis, *Moneyball* (New York: W.W. Norton, 2004).

10. Bang-Ning Hwang, Jack Tsai, Hsiao-Cheng Yu, and Shih-Chi Chang, "An Effective Pricing Framework in a Competitive Industry: Management Processes and Implementation Guidelines," *Journal of Revenue and Pricing Management* (November 2009); Oliver Roll, "Pricing Trends from a Management Perspective," *Journal of Revenue and Pricing Management* 8 (July 2009), pp. 396–98; Robert J. Dolan,

"Note on Marketing Strategy," Harvard Business School (November 2000), pp. 1–17; Dhruv Grewal and Larry D. Compeau, "Pricing and Public Policy: An Overview and a Research Agenda," *Journal of Public Policy & Marketing,* 18 (Spring 1999), pp. 3–11.

11. Ethan Smith and Yukari Iwatani Kane, "Apples Changes Tune on Music Pricing," *The Wall Street Journal,* January 7, 2009.

12. "IBM Market Share Leader in Human Resources (HR) Business Transformation Outsourcing, Enterprise Sector," press release.

13. Rebecca Heslin, "Virgin America Joins Airline Fare Sale Stampede," *USA Today,* January 6, 2010; "Delta Rescinds Fare Increase on Some of Its U.S. Routes," *Salt Lake City News,* September 11, 2007 (accessed electronically January 3, 2010).

14. http://www.carmax.com.

15. Monroe, *Pricing: Making Profitable Decisions.*

16. Nick Wingfield, "Apple's Lower Prices Are All Part of the Plan," *The New York Times*, October 24, 2011, http://www.nytimes.com.

17. William Lee Adams, "Would You Buy this $320,000 Brooch Online?" *Time,* November 9, 2009.

18. Fender Electric Guitars, http://www.fender.com.

19. Stephanie Clifford and Catherine Rampell, "Food Inflation Kept Hidden in Tinier Bags," *The New York Times,* March 29, 2011, http://www.nytimes.com.

20. Monroe, *Pricing: Making Profitable Decisions.* See also Richard B. McKenzie, *Why Popcorn Costs So Much at the Movies: And Other Pricing Puzzles* (New York: Springer, 2008).

21. http://www.marketingpower.com/_layouts/Dictionary. aspx?dLetter=C.

22. http://www.marketingpower.com/_layouts/Dictionary. aspx?dLetter=S.

23. Joan Lindsey-Mullikin and Dhruv Grewal, "Market Price Variation: The Availability of Internet Market Information," *Journal of the Academy of Marketing Science*, 34, no. 2 (2006), pp. 236–243.

24. Chris Morran, "Bank Of America Debit Card Fiasco Resulted In 20% Jump In Closed Accounts," *The Consumerist,* January 23, 2012.

25. Andrew Adam Newman, "If You're Nervous, Deodorant Makers Have a Product for You," *The New York Times,* February 17, 2009.

26. Cenk Koça and Jonathan D. Bohlmann, "Segmented Switchers and Retailer Pricing Strategies," *Journal of Marketing,* 72, no. 3 (2008), pp. 124–142; Ruth N. Bolton and Venkatesh Shankar, "An Empirically Derived Taxonomy of Retailer Pricing and Promotion Strategies," *Journal of Retailing,* 79, no. 4 (2003), pp. 213–224; Rajiv Lal and Ram Rao, "Supermarket Competition: The Case of Every Day Low Pricing," *Marketing Science,* 16, no. 1 (1997), pp. 60–80.

27. *Merriam-Webster's Dictionary of Law,* 1996.

28. http://www.plasmavision.com/warranty.htm.

29. Kristina Shampanier, Nina Mazar, and Dan Ariely, "Zero as a Special Price: The True Value of Free Products," *Marketing Science* 26, no. 6 (2007), pp. 742–57; Sucharita Chandran and Vicki G. Morvitz, "The Price of 'Free'-dom: Consumer Sensitivity to Promotions with Negative Contextual Influences," *Journal of Consumer Research* 33, no. 4 (2006), pp. 384–92; E. Shafir and R. H. Thaler, "Invest Now, Drink Later, Spend Never: On the Mental Accounting of Delayed Consumption," *Journal of Economic Psychology* 27 (2006), pp. 694–712; Lisa E. Bolton, Luk Warlop, and Joseph W. Alba, "Consumer Perceptions of

Price (Un)Fairness," *Journal of Consumer Research* 29 (March 2003), pp. 474–91; Peter R. Darke and Darren W. Dahl, "Fairness and Discounts: The Subjective Value of a Bargain," *Journal of Consumer Psychology* 13, no. 3 (2003), pp. 328–38; Margaret C. Campbell, "Perceptions of Price Unfairness: Antecedents and Consequences," *Journal of Marketing Research* 36 (May 1999), pp. 187–99; Sarah Maxwell, "What Makes a Price Increase Seem 'Fair'?" *Pricing Strategy & Practice* 3, no. 4 (1995), pp. 21–27.

30. Michael Levy and Barton A. Weitz, *Retailing Management,* 8th ed. (Burr Ridge, IL: Irwin/McGraw-Hill, 2012).

31. Brad Tuttle, "Use Amazon's Price Check App and Save $15," *Time,* December 8, 2011, http://moneyland.time.com; Susan Payton, "Amazon Price Check App: Small Business Threat or Sign of the Times?" *Small Business Trends,* December 15, 2011, http://smallbiztrends.com.

32. Dhruv Grewal, Kent B. Monroe, and R. Krishnan, "The Effects of Price Comparison Advertising on Buyers' Perceptions of Acquisition Value and Transaction Value," *Journal of Marketing,* 62, April 1998, pp. 46–60.

33. Geoffrey A. Fowler and Yukari Iwatani Kane, "New Mobile Applications Use Bar-Code Scanners," *The Wall Street Journal,* December 16, 2009; http://shopsavvy.mobi/.

34. Brad Tuttle, "Use Amazon's Price Check App and Save $15," *Time,* December 8, 2011, http://moneyland.time.com; Susan Payton, "Amazon Price Check App: Small Business Threat or Sign of the Times?" *Small Business Trends*, December 15, 2011, http://smallbiztrends.com.

35. Eric A. Staub, "As Prices Fall, Blu-ray Players Are Invited Home," *The New York Times*, December 13, 2009.

36. Alison Jing Xu and Robert S. Wyer, Jr., "Puffery in Advertisements: The Effects of Media Context, Communication Norms and Consumer Knowledge," *Journal of Consumer Research,* August 2010.

37. "Tesco Rapped Over 'Misleading' Price Claims," *Sky News*, July 29, 2009; www.asa.org.uk/.

38. Joan Lindsey-Mullikin and Ross D. Petty, "Marketing Tactics Discouraging Price Search: Deception and Competition," *Journal of Business Research* 64, no. 1 (2011), pp. 67-73, DOI: 10.1016/j.jbusres.2009.10.003.

39. Maria Sciullo, "Will Price War Hurt Independent Bookstores?" *Pittsburgh Post-Gazette*, October 27, 2009.

40. FairSearch, "Google's Transformation from Gateway to Gatekeeper," white paper, http://www.fairsearch.org.

41. Uwe E. Reinhardt, "Ending Hospital Price Discrimination against the Uninsured," *The New York Times*, January 8, 2010.

42. Daniel M. Garrett, Michelle Burtis, and Vandy Howell, "Economics of Antitrust: An Economic Analysis of Resale Price Maintenance," www.GlobalCompetitionReview.com, 2008; Stephen Labaton, "Century-Old Ban Lifted on Minimum Retail Pricing," *The New York Times,* June 29, 2007.

43. "South African Airlines to Be Investigated for Alleged World Cup Price-Fixing, Report DialAFlight," *Business Wire*, February 1, 2010.

44. Tom Bawden, "Bloody Nose for OFT in Row over Tobacco Price-Fixing," *The Independent (London)*, December 13, 2011, http://www.independent.co.uk; "The Marlboro Cartel," http://www.smokingate.com.

45. Daniel M. Garrett, Michelle Burtis, and Vandy Howell, "Economics of Antitrust; Stephen Labaton, "Century-Old Ban Lifted on Minimum Retail Pricing."

CHAPTER 15

1. William B. Cassidy, "Wal-Mart Tightens the Chain," *Journal of Commerce,* January 18, 2010.

2. Chris Burritt, Carol Wolf, and Matthew Boyle, "Wal-Mart Asks Suppliers to Cede Control of Deliveries (Update2)," *Bloomberg Businessweek,* June 1, 2010.

3. This chapter draws from Michael Levy and Barton A. Weitz, *Retailing Management,* 8th ed. (Burr Ridge, IL: McGraw-Hill/Irwin, 2012).

4. Ibid.

5. SCDigest, "Supply Chain News: Goya Foods Shows Path to Success for Mid-Market Companies from New Supply Chain Planning Tools," July 13, 2011, http://www.scdigest.com.

6. Based on Barton A. Weitz, "PenAgain Sells to Walmart," in Michael Levy and Barton A. Weitz, *Retailing Management,* 8th ed. (Burr Ridge, IL: McGraw-Hill/Irwin, 2012), pp. 564–565; http://www.Penagain.com; Gwendolyn Bounds, "The Long Road to Walmart," *The Wall Street Journal,* September 19, 2005, p. R1; Gwendolyn Bounds, "One Mount to Make It," *The Wall Street Journal,* May 30, 2006, p. B1.

7. Terry L. Esper, Alexander Ellinger, Theodore Stank, Daniel Flint, Mark Moon, "Demand and Supply Integration: A Conceptual Framework of Value Creation through Knowledge Management," *Journal of the Academy of Marketing Science* 38, no. 1 (2010), pp. 5–18.

8. See http://www.marketingpower.com/_layouts/Dictionary.aspx.

9. George E. Stigler, "The Division of Labor Is Limited by the Extent of the Market," *Journal of Political Economy* 59, no. 3 (1951), pp. 185–93.

10. http://www.marketingpower.com/live/mg-dictionary.

11. "Entrepreneur's 2012 Franchise 500," http://www.entrepreneur.com.

12. Charles Duhigg and David Barbosa, "In China, Human Costs Are Built into an iPad," *The New York Times,* January 25, 2012, http://www.nytimes.com/; Melissa J. Anderson, "The Supply Chain Enters the Spotlight," *Evolved Employer,* February 14, 2012, http://www.evolvedemployer.com/.

13. Lisa Scheer, Fred Miao, and Jason Garrett, "The Effects of Supplier Capabilities on Industrial Customers' Loyalty: The Role of Dependence," *Journal of the Academy of Marketing Science* 38, no. 1 (2010), pp. 90–104; Robert W. Palmatier, Rajiv Dant, and Dhruv Grewal, "A Longitudinal Analysis of Theoretical Perspectives of Interorganizational Relationship Performance," *Journal of Marketing* 71 (October 2007), pp. 172–94; Robert W. Palmatier, Rajiv Dant, Dhruv Grewal, and Kenneth Evans, "A Meta-Analysis on the Antecedents and Consequences of Relationship Marketing Mediators: Insight into Key Moderators," *Journal of Marketing* 70 (October 2006), pp. 136–53.

14. Donna Davis and Susan Golicic, "Gaining Comparative Advantage in Supply Chain Relationships: The Mediating Role of Market-Oriented IT Competence," *Journal of the Academy of Marketing Science* 38, no. 1 (2010), pp. 56–70; Beth Davis-Sramek, Richard Germain, and Karthik Iyer, "Supply Chain Technology: The Role of Environment in Predicting Performance," *Journal of the Academy of Marketing Science* 38, no. 1 (2010), pp. 42–55; Erin Anderson and Barton Weitz, "The Use of Pledges to Build and Sustain Commitment in Distribution Channels," *Journal of Marketing Research* 29 (February 1992), pp. 18–34.

15. http://www.marketingpower.com/_layouts/Dictionary.aspx.

16. Vanessa O'Connell and Peter Latman, "Neiman Enlists Designers in Cost-Cutting Plan," *The Wall Street Journal,* December 10, 2009.

17. Jean Thilmany, "Neiman Marcus Sails through Customs," *Apparel Magazine* 49, no. 2 (2007).

18. Matthew Waller, Brent Williams, Andrea Tangari, and Scot Burton, "Marketing at the Retail Shelf: An Examination of Moderating Effects of Logistics on SKU Market Share," *Journal of the Academy of Marketing Science* 38, no. 1 (2010), pp. 105–17.

19. http:// http://www.vendormanagedinventory.com.

20. G. P. Kiesmüller and R. A. C. M. Broekmeulen, "The Benefit of VMI Strategies in a Stochastic Multi-Product Serial Two Echelon System," *Computers and Operations Research* 37, no. 2 (2010), pp. 406–16; Dong-Ping Song and John Dinwoodie, "Quantifying the Effectiveness of VMI and Integrated Inventory Management in a Supply Chain with Uncertain Lead-Times and Uncertain Demands," *Production Planning & Control* 19, no. 6 (2008), pp. 590–600; S. P. Nachiappan, A. Gunasekaran, and N. Jawahar, "Knowledge Management System for Operating Parameters in Two-Echelon VMI Supply Chains," *International Journal of Production Research* 45, no. 11 (2007), pp. 2479–2505; Andres Angulo, Heather Nachtmann, and Matthew A. Waller, "Supply Chain Information Sharing in a Vendor Managed Inventory Partnership," *Journal of Business Logistics* 25 (2004), pp. 101–120.

21. Kevin Scarpati, "Tesco Big Price Drop Helped by Supply Chain Management," *Supply Chain Digital,* September 23, 2011, http://www.supplychaindigital.com; Michael Garry, "Supply Chain Systems Seen Boosting Tesco's U.S. Stores," *Supermarket News,* 55, no. 43 (2007).

22. André Luís Shiguemoto, and Vinícius Amaral Armentano, "A Tabu Search Procedure for Coordinating Production, Inventory and Distribution Routing Problems," *International Transactions in Operational Research* 17, no. 2 (2009), pp. 179–95; Ayse Akbalik, Sekoun Kebe, Bernard Penz, and Najiba Sbihi, "Exact Methods and a Heuristic for the Optimization of an Integrated Replenishment-Storage Planning Problem," *International Transactions in Operational Research* 15, no. 2 (March 2008), pp. 195–214.

CHAPTER 16

1. Wikipedia, http://en.wikipedia.org/wiki/Home_Shopping_Network;

2. Barbara Thau, "HSN, QVC Makeover: Tacky Baubles Out, Couture In," CNBC, August 18, 2010.

3. Suzanne Vranica, "HSN Starts Mixing Ads into Its Usual Sales Pitches," *The Wall Street Journal,* September 28, 2009.

4. "In The Know," YouTube, Fall 2009, http://www.gstatic.com; http://www.youtube.com/t/advertising_audience_targeting.

5. "Brand Channels," YouTube, Fall 2009, http://www.gstatic.com; http://www.youtube.com/t/advertising_brand_channels.

6. "YouTube Insight," YouTube, Fall 2009, http://www.gstatic.com; http://www.youtube.com/t/advertising_insight.

7. Leah Shafer, "Re-Branding the Dynasty: Tori Spelling's HSN Clips on YouTube," http://mediacommons.futureofthebook.org, March 25, 2010.

8. "Top 10 Global Retailers," http://www.cnbc.com.

9. This chapter draws heavily from Michael Levy and Barton A. Weitz, *Retailing Management,* 8th ed. (Burr Ridge, IL: McGraw-Hill /Irwin, 2012).

10. Patricia Marx, "A Bushel and a Peck," *The New Yorker,* January 16, 2012, pp. 32–36.

11. Industry Outlook: Food Channel (Columbus, OH: Retail Forward, July 2008); Industry Outlook: Food Channel (Columbus, OH: Retail Forward, April 2007).

12. Mary Holz-Clause and Malinda Geisler, "Grocery Industry," February 2012, http://www.agmrc.org; "Top 25 Global Retailers 2011, http://supermarketnews.com.

13. http://www.fmi.org/glossary/?search=Yes&letter=C.

14. "Supermarket Sales by Department," October 2011, http://www.fmi.org.

15. http://www.tmcnet.com/usubmit/2007/10/13/3012485.htm.

16. http://www.tmcnet.com/usubmit/2007/10/13/3012485.htm.

17. "Walmart Supercenters," http://walmartstores.com.

18. "Supermarket Social Scenes," *Retail Wire,* March 22, 2011.

19. https://www.deloitte.com/assets/Dcom-Global/Local%20Assets/Documents/Consumer%20Business/dtt_CBT_GPRetailing2012.pdf.

20. Karen Talley, "Department Stores Are in Good Position after 1Q Resurgence," *Dow Jones Newswires,* May 16, 2011.

21. http://www.walletpop.com/blog/2009/05/14/love-amidst-the-layoffs-macys-parades-its-new-fashion-label/.

22. http://walmartstores.com/sites/annualreport/2011/financials/Walmart_2011_Annual_Report.pdf; Sandra M. Jones, "Wal-Mart Making Little Plans," *Chicago Tribune,* May 14, 2011.

23. Russell Redman, "Industry Outlook: Drug Chains Lifted by Improved Economy," *Chain Drug Review,* May 2, 2011, http://www.chaindrugreview.com.

24. Hoover's, "Drug Stores," http://www.hoovers.com.

25. George Anderson, "Are Drugstores Priced Too High to Compete in Grocery?" *Retailwire,* October 7, 2011.

26. http://www.wikinvest.com/industry/Off-price_Retail.

27. This section draws from Michael Levy and Barton A. Weitz, *Retailing Management,* 9e, (Burr Ridge II: McGraw-Hill/Irwin, 2015), Chapter 2.

28. Cary Stemle, "Has the Food Truck Bubble Burst?" *QSR News,* May 1, 2013, http://www.qsrweb.com.

29. Venessa Wong, "White Castle Slides into Food-Truck Trend," *Bloomberg Businessweek,* June 12, 2013, http://www.businessweek.com.

30. Dale Buss, "White Castle Joins CPG, QSR Brands on Food Truck Bandwagon," *BrandChannel,* June 21, 2013, http://www.brandchannel.com.

31. Lydia Dishman, "Why Karl Lagerfeld's Collection for Macy's Is the Retailer's Ticket to Profits," *Fortune.com,* July 21, 2011.

32. Sandhya Raman, "Shopkick's CEO Talks Entrepreneurship, Mobile Marketing and the Future," Fiercemobilecontent.com, May 10, 2011; Adam Ostrow, "How Accurate Is Your Smartphone's GPS? [MAP]," *Mashable,* March 9, 2011; Rimma Kats, "Walgreens: Mobile is Key Component of Multichannel Loyalty Strategy," Mobilecommercedaily.com, March 4, 2011; Jennifer Van Grove, "242 Target Stores Start Offering Shopkick Checkin Rewards," *Mashable,* November 16, 2010.

33. Nancy M. Pucinelli, Dhruv Grewal, Susan Andrzejewski, Ereni Markos, and Tracy Noga, "The Value of Knowing What Customers Really Want: Interpersonal Accuracy as an Environmental Cue," working paper (2012); Nancy Puccinelli, Ronald C. Goodstein, Dhruv Grewal, Rob Price, Priya Raghubir, and David Stewart, "Customer Experience Management in Retailing: Understanding the Buying Process," *Journal of Retailing* 85 (2009), pp. 15–30.

34. Patricia Marx, "C. Wonder," *The New Yorker,* November 21, 2011, p. 34.

35. Ibid.

36. Kathleen Seiders, Glenn B. Voss, Andrea L. Godfrey, and Dhruv Grewal, "SERVCON: A Multidimensional Scale for Measuring Perceptions of Service Convenience," *Journal of the Academy of Marketing Science* 35, no. 1 (2007), pp. 144–56; Leonard Berry, Kathleen Seiders, and Dhruv Grewal, "Understanding Service Convenience," *Journal of Marketing* 66, no. 3 (July 2002).

37. Kenneth Hein, "Study: Web Research Nets In-Store Sales," *Brandweek,* May 7, 2007.

38. "Sponsored Supplement: Expanding the Reach of Personalization," *Internet Retailer,* March 2010.

39. Jill Avery, Thomas J. Steenburgh, John Deighton, and Mary Caravella, "Adding Bricks to Clicks: The Contingencies Driving Cannibalization and Complementarity in Multichannel Retailing," *SSRN working paper* (2009), http:\\ssrn.com.

40. J. C. Williams Group, "Organizing for Cross-Channel Retailing," white paper, Toronto, January 2008; IBM Global Business Services, "Customer Centricity Drives Retail's Multichannel Imperative," white paper, Armonk, NY, 2008.

41. Susan Reda, "The Personal Touch," *Stores,* January 2011.

42. Jie Zhang, Paul Farris, John Irvin, Tarun Kushwaha, Thomas Steenburgh, and Barton Weitz, "Crafting Integrated Multichannel Retailing Strategies," *Journal of Interactive Marketing,* 2010.

CHAPTER 17

1. Coca-Cola Company, "Treasure Hunt for the 1922 Coca-Cola Polar Bear Ad," October 28, 2011, http://www.coca-colaconversations.com.

2. Coca-Cola Company, "Live from the Arctic: Coca-Cola Animated Polar Bears to 'Catch' the Big Game on Feb. 5,"pPress release, January 26, 2012, http://www.thecoca-colacompany.com.

3. Coca-Cola Company, "The Coca-Cola Polar Bowl–Game Day Moments," http://www.youtube.com.

4. Ace Metrix, "Doritos Crashes the Super Bowl Once Again and So Does M&Ms," press release, https://www.acemetrix.com.

5. Ibid.

6. Alan Parker, "Coca-Cola and the Polar Bears," *Toronto Star,* December 1, 2011, http://blogs.canoe.ca.

7. Coca-Cola Company, "Live from the Arctic," op. cit.

8. Terence A. Shimp, *Advertising Promotion and Other Aspects of Integrated Marketing Communication,* 8th ed. (Mason, OH: South-Western College Publishers, 2008); T. Duncan and C. Caywood, "The Concept, Process, and Evolution of Integrated Marketing Communication," in *Integrated Communication: Synergy of Persuasive Voices,* eds. E. Thorson and J. Moore (Mahwah, NJ: Lawrence Erlbaum Associates, 1996); see also various issues of the *Journal of Integrated Marketing Communications,* http://jimc.medill.northwestern.edu.

9. Simon Dumenco, "The Show That Beats American Idol: Exploring the Popularity of *The Big Bang Theory,*" *Ad Age,* February 24, 2012, http://adage.com.

10. Stuart Elliott, "M&M's to Unveil New Speaking Role at Super Bowl," *The New York Times,* January 16, 2012; Tim Nudd, "M&M's Wins YouTube's Super Bowl Ad Blitz Contest," *Ad Week,* February 20, 2012, http://www.adweek.com.

11. Terence A. Shimp, *Advertising Promotion and Other Aspects of Integrated Marketing Communication;* Deborah J. MacInnis, Christine Moorman, and Bernard J. Jaworski, "Enhancing and Measuring Consumers' Motivation, Opportunity," *Journal of Marketing* 55, no. 4 (October 1991), pp. 32–53; Joan Meyers-Levy, "Elaborating on Elaboration: The Distinction between Relational and Item-Specific Elaboration," *Journal of Consumer Research,* 18 (December 1991), pp. 358–367.

12. E. K. Strong, *The Psychology of Selling* (New York: McGraw Hill, 1925).

13. Disney, "Music Stars," http://disney.go.com; Belinda Luscombe, "How Disney Builds Stars," *Time,* November 2, 2009.

14. Todd Wasserman, "How Coke Spread Happiness (and Cokes) via Mobile," *Mashable.com,* August 7, 2012, http://mashable.com.

15. Stuart Elliot, "Google Remixes Old Campaigns, Adding Dash of Digital Tools," *The New York Times,* March 8, 2012, http://www.nytimes.com.

16. John Philip Jones, "What Makes Advertising Work?" *The Economic Times,* July 24, 2002.

17. http://www.legamedia.net/lx/result/match/0591dfc9787c111b1b24dde6d61e43c5/index.php.

18. http://popsop.com/wp-content/uploads/toyota_prius_plural_02.jpg; http://www.youtube.com/watch?v=nUor4gdFoyg&feature=player_embedded#!; http://www.saatchi.com/news/archive/prius_goes_plural_through_new_integrated_campaign.

19. Chris Barrows, "Unauthorized Verses," *Journal of Integrated Marketing Communications* (Evanston: Northwestern University, 2009).

20. American Marketing Association, *Dictionary of Marketing Terms* (Chicago: American Marketing Association, 2008).

21. Eric Wilson, "Checking Models' IDs at the Door," *The New York Times,* February 8, 2012, http://www.nytimes.com.

22. Ellie Krupnick, "Drop Dead Ads Banned by ASA for Too-Skinny Model," *The Huffington Post,* November 10. 2011, http://www.huffingtonpost.com.

23. David Gianastasio, "Fashion Site Nixes Photo of Freakishly Thin-Looking Model," *AdWeek,* July 13, 2011, http://www.adweek.com.

24. Teri Evans, "Firms Hold Fast to Snail Mail Marketing," *The Wall Street Journal,* January 12, 2010, http://online.wsj.com; George E. Belch and Michael A. Belch, *Advertising and Promotion: An Integrated Marketing Communications Perspective* (New York: McGraw-Hill, 2007).

25. Rebecca Lieb, "Q&A: Cindy Krum Cuts through the Mobile Marketing Alphabet Soup of NFC and RFID," http://econsultancy.com, March 16, 2010.

26. Emily Steel, "How Marketers Hone Their Aim Online," *The Wall Street Journal,* June 19, 2007.

27. Charles Duhigg, "How Companies Learn Your Secrets," *New York Times,* February 16, 2012.

28. George Anderson, "White House, Web Giants Address Consumer Privacy Online," *Retail Wire,* February 24, 2012.

29. Akihisa Fujita, "Mobile Marketing in Japan: The Acceleration of Integrated Marketing Communications," *Journal of Integrated*

Marketing Communications (2008), pp. 41–46; Mobile update: http://www.businessinsider.com; http://www.informationweek .com; http://www.nearbynow.com, accessed May 26, 2010.

30. Tanya Irwin, "Weston Invites Customers to 'Warm Up'," *Marketing Daily*, March 13, 2011, http://www.mediapost.com; Rimma Kats, "Westin Hotels & Resorts Aiming for Increased Bookings via Geo-Targeted Mobile Ad," *Mobile Commerce Daily*, March 9, 2011, http://www.mobilecommercedaily.com; Rimma Kats, "Westin Hotels & Resorts Bolsters Mobile Bookings via TWC iPad Sponsorship," *Mobile Commerce Daily*, October 24, 2011, http://www.mobilecommercedaily.com.

31. Yubo Chen, Scott Fay, and Qi Wang, "The Role of Marketing in Social Media: How Online Consumer Reviews Evolve," *Journal of Interactive Marketing* 25, no. 2 (May 2011), pp. 85–94; Bonnie Rochman, "Sweet Spot," *Time*, November 2009.

32. www.blogsouthwest.com.

33. Chris Lee, "Kevin Smith's Southwest Incident Sets Web All A-Twitter," *Los Angeles Times*, February 16, 2010, http://articles .latimes.com.

34. Christi Day, "Not So Silent Bob," February 14, 2010, http://www .blogsouthwest.com.

35. This section draws from Michael Levy and Barton A. Weitz, *Retailing Management*, 8th ed. (Burr Ridge, IL: McGraw-Hill /Irwin, 2012).

36. Megan Halscheid, Micheline Sabatté, and Sejal Sura, "Beyond the Last Click: Measuring ROI and Consumer Engagement with Clickstream Analysis," *Journal of Integrated Marketing Communications* (2009), pp. 43–50; Vikram Mahidhar and Christine Cutten, "Navigating the Marketing Measurement Maze," *Journal of Integrated Marketing Communications* (2007), pp. 41–46.

37. http://www.riger.com.

38. "IAB Reports Full-Year Internet Ad Revenues for 2010 Increase 15% to $26 Billion, a New Record," April 13, 2011, http://www .iab.net.

39. "Facebook Pages: Insights for your Facebook Page," http://www .facebook.com.

40. "Marketing and Advertising Using Google," Google 2007.

41. http://publishing2.com.

CHAPTER 18

1. Natalie Zmuda, "Tropicana Goes Back to Nature in New Global Pitch," *Ad Age Global*, February 20, 2012, http://adage.com.

2. Stuart Elliott, "Marketing Budgets Rise for Some Giants," *The New York Times*, February 21, 2012, http://www.nytimes .com.

3. Shirley Brady, "Here Comes the Sun: Tropicana Wakes Up London," brandchannel.com, January 24, 2012, http://www.brandchannel .com.

4. Ibid.

5. Greyworld, "Trafalgar Sun 2012," http://greyworld.org.

6. Ibid.

7. Brady, op. cit.

8. Jeff Greenhouse, "Tropicana Playfully Squeezes the Big Apple with New Ad Campaign," August 4, 2011, http://www.jeffgreenhouse .com.

9. Jeff Greenhouse, "DDB Squeezes New York for Another Round of Great Tropicana Ads," February 2, 2010, http://www .jeffgreenhouse.com.

10. George E. Belch and Michael A. Belch, *Advertising and Promotion: An Integrated Marketing Communications Perspective* (New York: McGraw-Hill, 2007); Jef I. Richards and Catherine M. Curran, "Oracles on 'Advertising': Searching for a Definition," *Journal of Advertising* 31, no. 2 (Summer 2002), pp. 63–77.

11. Alexandra Bruell, "ZenithOptimedia Forecasts Slow, Steady Growth in Global Ad Spend," *Ad Age*, March 12, 2012, http: //adage.com.

12. Dan Zigmond, Sundar Dorai-Raj, Yannet Interian, and Igor Naverniouk, "Measuring Advertising Quality on Television: Deriving Meaningful Metrics from Audience Retention Data," *Journal of Advertising Research* 49, no. 4 (December 2009), pp. 419–28; Robert G. Heath, Agnes C. Nairn, and Paul A. Bottomley, "How Effective is Creativity? Emotive Content in TV Advertising Does Not Increase Attention," *Journal of Advertising Research* 49, no. 4 (December 2009), pp. 450–63; Raymond R. Burke and Thomas K. Srull, "Competitive Interference and Consumer Memory for Advertising," *Journal of Consumer Research*, 15 (June 1988), pp. 55–68; Kevin Lane Keller, "Memory Factors in Advertising: The Effect of Advertising Retrieval Cues on Brand Evaluation," *Journal of Consumer Research*, 14 (December 1987), pp. 316–33.

13. Markus Pfeiffer and Markus Zinnbauer, "Can Old Media Enhance New Media? How Traditional Advertising Pays Off for an Online Social Network," *Journal of Advertising Research* 50, no. 1 (2010), pp. 42–49; Terry Daugherty, Matthew Eastin, and Laura Bright, "Exploring Consumer Motivations for Creating User-Generated Content," *Journal of Interactive Advertising* 8, no. 2 (2008); Anthony Bianco, "The Vanishing Mass Market," *BusinessWeek*, July 12, 2004, pp. 61–68.

14. David Griner, "Adidas Fires Up Its Largest Ad Campaign Ever," *AdWeek*, March 16, 2011.

15. William F. Arens, Michael F. Weigold, and Christian Arens, *Contemporary Advertising*, 12th ed. (New York: McGraw-Hill, 2008).

16. Stephen Williams, "Fiat Enlists Ultimate Bad Boy for Ads: Charlie Sheen," *Ad Age*, March 1, 2012, http://adage.com.

17. Tulin Erdem, Michael Keane, and Baohong Sun, "The Impact of Advertising on Consumer Price Sensitivity in Experience Goods Markets," *Quantitative Marketing and Economics* 6 (June 2008), pp. 139–76; Xiaojing Yang and Robert E. Smith, "Beyond Attention Effects: Modeling the Persuasive and Emotional Effects of Advertising Creativity," *Marketing Science* 28 (September/October 2009), pp. 935–49; Matthew Shum, "Does Advertising Overcome Brand Loyalty? Evidence from the Breakfast Cereal Market," *Journal of Economics and Management Strategy* 13, no. 2 (2004), pp. 77–85.

18. "Got Milk?" http://www.gotmilk.com.

19. Elaine Wong, "Rebecca Romjin Makes Milk Run," *Brandweek*, January 13, 2010.

20. http://www.marketingpower.com/_layouts/Dictionary.aspx? dLetter=P

21. http://www.thetruth.com.

22. truth, "Facts," http://www.thetruth.com/facts/.

23. Alina Tugend, "Cigarette Makers Take Anti-Smoking Ads Personally," *The New York Times*, October 27, 2002.

24. Jonathan Blum, "Why Yum Brands Fights Hunger," *Ad Age*, November 1, 2011, http://adage.com.

25. "Jaime's Story," http://www.aad.org.

26. Theodore Leavitt, *The Marketing Imagination* (New York: The Free Press, 1986).

27. Belch and Belch, *Advertising and Promotion: An Integrated Marketing Communications Perspective.*

28. Exxon Mobil, http://www.exxonmobil.com.

29. Katherine White and John Peloza, "Self-Benefit Versus Other-Benefit Marketing Appeals: Their Effectiveness in Generating Charitable Support," *Journal of Marketing* 73 (July 2009), pp. 109–24.

30. Darren W. Dahl, Jaideep Sengupta, and Kathleen D. Vohs, "Sex in Advertising: Gender Differences and the Role of Relationship Commitment," *Journal of Consumer Research* 36, no. 2 (2009), pp. 215–31; Jaideep Sengupta and Darren W. Dahl, "Gender-Related Reactions to Gratuitous Sex Appeals in Advertising," *Journal of Consumer Psychology* 18, no. 1 (2008), pp. 62–78.

31. Jack Loftus, "ADT Ad Campaign Scares Homeowners into Buying ADT Security," *Gizmodo,* http://gizmodo.com; Jack Neff, "What the Stylish Garbage Can Is Wearing," *Ad Age,* November 3, 2011, http://adage.com; Natalie Zmuda, "Best Buy Ups Holiday Spending, Introduces 'Game On, Santa' Campaign," *Ad Age,* November 17, 2011, http://adage.com; Andrew Adam Newman, "Axe Adds Fragrance for Women to Its Lineup," *The New York Times,* January 8, 2012, http://www.nytimes.com.

32. AMA Dictionary, http://www.marketingpower.com/_layouts/Dictionary.aspx?dLetter=M.

33. Anthony Crupy, "Cable Sports Take a Bite Out of Broadcast Ad Sales," *Adweek,* September 13, 2011, http://www.adweek.com; John Tejada, "Marketers Flock to Digital Media," *Adweek,* November 30, 2011, http://www.adweek.com.

34. Some illustrative articles look at the effectiveness of given media: Robert Heath, "Emotional Engagement: How Television Builds Big Brands at Low Attention," *Journal of Advertising Research* 49, no. 1 (March 2009), pp. 62–73; Lex van Meurs and Mandy Aristoff, "Split-Second Recognition: What Makes Outdoor Advertising Work?" *Journal of Advertising Research* 49, no. 1 (March 2009), pp. 82–92.

35. Arens, Weigold, and Arens, *Contemporary Advertising.*

36. William F. Arens, David H. Schaefer, Michael F. Weigold, *Advertising, M-Series* (Burr Ridge: Irwin/McGraw-Hill, 2012).

37. Stephen Williams, "New Sedans Aim to Break Out of the Pack," *AdAge,* February 20, 2012, http://adage.com.

38. Dean M. Krugman, Leonard N. Reid, S. Watson Dunn, and Arnold M. Barban, *Advertising: Its Role in Modern Marketing* (New York: The Dryden Press, 1994), pp. 221–26.

39. David Kiefaber, "Taylor Swift's CoverGirl Ad Is Pulled Over Bogus Eyelashes," *Adweek,* December 23, 2011, http://www.adweek.com.

40. David Gianastasio, "Turlington Ads: So Photoshopped They're Misleading?" *Adweek,* July 28, 2011, http://www.adweek.com.

41. Tanzina Vega, "British Authority Bans Two Ads by L'Oreal," *The New York Times,* July 27, 2011, http://mediadecoder.blogs.nytimes.com.

42. Herbert Jack Rotfeld and Charles R. Taylor, "The Need for Interdisciplinary Research of Advertising Regulation: A Roadmap for Avoiding Confusion and Errors," *Journal of Advertising* (Winter 2009).

43. Andrea Thompson, "Misleading Food Labels to Get Makeover," MSNBC.com, March 15, 2010, http://www.msnbc.msn.com.

44. Debra Harker, Michael Harker, and Robert Burns, "Tackling Obesity: Developing a Research Agenda for Advertising Researchers," *Journal of Current Issues & Research in Advertising* 29, no. 2 (2007), pp. 39–51; N. Kapoor and D. P. S. Verma, "Children's Understanding of TV Advertisements: Influence of Age, Sex and Parents," *Vision* 9, no. 1 (2005), pp. 21–36; Catharine M. Curran and Jef I. Richards, "The Regulation of Children's Advertising in the U.S.," *International Journal of Advertising and Marketing to Children* 2, no. 2 (2002).

45. Irina Slutsky, "Nine Things You Can't Do in Advertising if You Want to Stay on the Right Side of the Law," *AdAge,* March 7, 2011, http://adage.com.

46. Bob Hunt, "Truth in Your Advertising: Avoid Puffery?" *Realty Times,* June 20, 2007.

47. Ibid.

48. Christina Binkley, "Which Stars Sell Fashion?" *The Wall Street Journal,* February 4, 2010.

49. Diego Rinallo and Suman Basuroy, "Does Advertising Spending Influence Media Coverage of the Advertiser?" *Journal of Marketing* 73 (November 2009), pp. 33–46; Carl Obermiller and Eric R. Spangenberg, "On the Origin and Distinctness of Skepticism toward Advertising," *Marketing Letters* 11, no. 4 (2000), p. 311.

50. Jackie Huba, "A Just Cause Creating Emotional Connections with Customers," http://www.inc.com.

51. http://www.createapepper.com; http://causerelatedmarketing.blogspot.com/2008/03/how-chilis-used-cause-related-marketing.html.

52. Personal communication with Rob Price, VP of Retail Marketing, CVS, June 16, 2009; Carol Angrisani, "CVS Moves to Personalization," *SN: Supermarket News* 56, no. 2 (March 24, 2008), p. 29.

53. Stephanie Clifford, "Web Coupons Know Lots about You, and They Tell," *The New York Times,* April 16, 2010.

54. Jack Neff, "Old Spice Is Killing It on YouTube Again, But Sales Are Down Double-Digits," *AdAge,* August 4, 2011, http://adage.com.

55. http://sports.espn.go.com/espn/contests/index.

56. Eva A. van Reijmersdal, Peter C. Neijens, and Edith G. Smit, "A New Branch of Advertising: Reviewing Factors That Influence Reactions to Product Placement," *Journal of Advertisng Research* 49, no. 4 (December 2009), pp. 429–49; Pamela Mills Homer, "Product Placement: The Impact of Placement Type and Repetition on Attitude," *Journal of Advertising* (Fall 2009); Elizabeth Cowley and Chris Barron, "When Product Placement Goes Wrong: The Effects of Program Liking and Placement Prominence," *Journal of Advertising* (Spring 2008).

57. Neil Munshi, "Spain's Starring Role in Bollywood Movie a Boon to Tourism," *AdAge,* February 6, 2012, http://adage.com.

58. Abe Sauer, "Announcing the 2012 Brandcameo Product Placement Award Winners," brandchannel.com, February 13, 2012, http://www.brandchannel.com.

59. Ibid.

60. www.jcrew.com.

CHAPTER 19

1. "Lauren Crampsie Named Worldwide Chief Marketing Officer, Ogilvy & Mather," press release, January 4, 2012, http://www.ogilvy.com-Crampsie-to-be-new-Ogilvy-Mather-Worldwide-Chief-Marketing-Officer.aspx.

2. Rupal Parekh, "Women to Watch: Lauren Crampsie, Ogilvy," *Ad Age,* May 30, 2011, http://adage.com.

3. "New Appointments Drive Growth and Multi-Channel Ideas for Ogilvy," press release, June 7, 2010, http://www.ogilvy.com.

4. "A Day in the Life of *Adweek,*" http://advertising.yahoo.com.

5. Brian Fetherstonhaugh, "The Future of Selling," http://www.slideshare.net.

6. "Inside the Amway Selling Machine," February 14, 2012, http://infoseekchina.blogspot.com.

7. Brian Fetherstonhaugh, "The Future of Selling: It's Social," Forbes.com, December 3, 2010, http://www.forbes.com.

8. Bureau of Labor Statistics, "Employed and Unemployed Persons by Occupation," March 9, 2012, http://www.bls.gov.

9. This section draws from Mark W. Johnston and Greg W. Marshall, *Relationship Selling,* 3rd ed. (Burr Ridge, IL: Irwin/McGraw-Hill, 2009); Mark W. Johnston and Greg W. Marshall, *Relationship Selling and Sales Management,* 2nd ed. (Burr Ridge, IL: Irwin/McGraw-Hill, 2007).

10. Geoffrey James, "Selling Gets Complex," *Strategy+Business,* August 27, 2009; Dale Carnegie, *How to Win Friends and Influence People* (New York: Pocket, 1990); Neil Rackham, *SPIN Selling* (New York: McGraw-Hill, 1988).

11. John Fox, "What Is the Real Cost of a B2B Sales Call?" http://www.marketing-playbook.com.

12. Bill Stinnett, *Think Like Your Customer* (Burr Ridge, IL: McGraw-Hill, 2004).

13. Al Jury, "The Golden Ratio of Virtual Meetings to Face-to-Face," June 19, 2011, http://virtualteamsblog.com.

14. Brad Grimes, "Have Web, Don't Travel," http://pcworld.about.com.

15. "Brainstorming Online," *BusinessWeek,* Fall 2005, http://www.businessweek.com.

16. Joe Sharkey, "On the Road—New Meetings Industry Arises after Boom and Bust," *The New York Times,* February 1, 2010.

17. Pam Baker, "Best Sales Practices: Build Lasting Relationships," *CRM Buyer,* January 27, 2009.

18. Mark W. Johnston and Greg W. Marshall, *Relationship Selling,* 2nd ed. (Burr Ridge, IL: Irwin/McGraw-Hill, 2008).

19. Paciolan, http://paciolan.com/.

20. "2012 CES Grows, Excites, and Catalyzes," January 13, 2012, http://www.cesweb.org.

21. Christine Comaford, "Sales Stuck? Try Sticking to a Script," *BusinessWeek,* April 4, 2008.

22. Steve Berkowitz, "Marketers Reshape How College Teams Sell Tickets," *USA Today,* August 5, 2011, http://www.usatoday.com.

23. "Accelerating the Trend toward Outsourcing Athletic Event Ticket Sales, Two More Universities Partner with IMG College," press release, May 31, 2011, http://www.imgworld.com.

24. IMG College, http://www.imgcollege.com.

25. Michael Levy and Barton A. Weitz, *Retailing Management,* 8th ed. (New York: McGraw-Hill/Irwin, 2011).

26. Christine Comaford-Lynch, "A Bad Lead Is Worse Than No Lead at All," *BusinessWeek,* March 26, 2008.

27. Barton A. Weitz, Harish Sujan, and Mita Sujan, "Knowledge, Motivation, and Adaptive Behavior: A Framework for Improving Selling Effectiveness," *Journal of Marketing,* October 1986, pp. 174–91.

28. Robert Keller, "Handling Objections in Today's Tough Environment," *SMM,* March 30, 2009.

29. http://www.quotedb.com/quotes/1303.

30. Mark W. Johnston and Greg W. Marshall, *Churchill/Ford/Walker's Sales Force Management,* 9th ed. (Burr Ridge, IL: McGraw-Hill/Irwin, 2009).

31. Susan Greco, "Personality Testing for Sales Recruits," *INC.,* March 1, 2009.

32. Barbara Chai, "Social Media Add Twist to Publicity Tango for 'Evita'," *The Wall Street Journal,* March 4, 2010, http://online.wsj.com.

33. Liz Wolf, "Selling via Social Network," *Star Tribune* (*Twin Cities*), March 15, 2012, http://www.startribune.com.

34. Fetherstonhaugh, Forbes.com, op. cit.

35. Johnston and Marshall, *Relationship Selling and Sales Management,* pp. 375–76; Johnston and Marshall, *Churchill/Ford/Walker's Sales Force Management.*

36. Rene Y. Darmon, "Where Do the Best Sales Force Profit Producers Come From?" *Journal of Personal Selling and Sales Management* 13, no. 3 (1993), pp. 17–29.

37. Julie Chang, "Born to Sell?" *Sales and Marketing Management,* July 2003, p. 36.

38. "Mary Kay: Where's the Money?" http://www.marykay.com; http://www.Marykay.com/lsoulier; "Mary Kay Museum," www.addisontexas.net.

39. Johnston and Marshall, *Relationship Selling and Sales Management.*

40. For a discussion of common measures used to evaluate salespeople, see Johnston and Marshall, *Churchill/Ford/Walker's Sales Force Management.*

41. Candace Jackson, "A Real Estate Star Is Born," *The Wall Street Journal,* August 1, 2013, http://online.wsj.com.

42. David H. Holtzman, "Big Business Knows Us Too Well," *BusinessWeek,* June 22, 2007.

43. Johnston and Marshall, *Churchill/Ford/Walker's Sales Force Management.*

44. "Ethical Breach," *Sales & Marketing Management,* July 2004.

45. Casey Donoho and Timothy Heinze, "The Personal Selling Ethics Scale: Revisions and Expansions for Teaching Sales Ethics" *Journal of Marketing Education* 33, no. 1 (April 2011), pp. 107–22.

credits

CHAPTER 1

Page 2, RED MANGO name, design and related marks are trademarks of Red Mango, Inc. ©2012 Red Mango, Inc. All rights reserved. P. 4, RED MANGO name, design and related marks are trademarks of Red Mango, Inc. ©2012 Red Mango, Inc. All rights reserved. P. 5, RED MANGO name, design and related marks are trademarks of Red Mango, Inc. ©2012 Red Mango, Inc. All rights reserved. P. 6, Rex Features via AP Images. P. 6, PRNewsFoto/PepsiCo; AP Photo. P. 7, Photo by Larry Busacca/Getty Images. P. 7, Courtesy So Delicious Dairy Free. P. 7, Courtesy The Haagen-Dazs Brand. P. 8, Photo by Julian Finney/Getty Images. P. 8, Photo by Tim Mosenfelder/Getty Images. P. 9, ©Paul Hoppe. P. 10, PRNewsFoto/Coty Beauty/AP Images. P. 11, ©2014 Brinker International. Chili's Brand Strategy/Used with permission. P. 12, Courtesy National Fluid Milk Processor Promotion Board; Agency: Lowe Worldwide, Inc. P. 12, Used by Permission of Deutsch Inc. as Agent for National Fluid Milk Processor Promotion Board. P. 12, H. Armstrong Roberts/Retrofile/Getty Images. P. 12, Jamie Grill/Iconica/Getty Images. P. 12, ©Ted Dayton Photography/Beateworks/Corbis. P. 12, Ciaran Griffin/Stockbyte/Getty Images. P. 12, Courtesy of Apple. P. 13, Courtesy Starwood Hotels & Resorts; Agency: Deutsch Inc./New York.; Photos: Augustus Butera for Marge Casey & ssociates. P. 14, Rex Features via AP Images. P. 15, Photo by Tim Boyle/Getty Images. P. 15, ©Michael Newman/PhotoEdit. P. 16, Photo by Spencer Platt/Getty Images. P. 16, Copyright® Intelity, LLC Inc. A Self-Service Software Solutions Company—IntelityCorp.com.P. 17, Infographic Brought To You By growing social/www.growingsocialmedia.com, surgegroup/www.surgegroup.com. Sources: GlobalWebindex Study, Visual.ly, Gigaom, www.jeffbullas.com P. 18, Digital Vision/Getty Images. P. 18, Jason Reed/Getty Images. P. 18, BananaStock/JupiterImages. P. 18, ©Edward Rozzo/Corbis. P. 18, ©Roy McMahon/Corbis. P. 18, Andrew Ward/Life File/Getty Images. P. 19, Courtesy BBH-Singapore. P. 20, ©M. Hruby. P. 21, AP Photo/Chris Pizzello. P. 21, ©Hero Images/Getty Images.

CHAPTER 2

Page 22, ©Brent Jones. P. 24, Photo by Jun Sato/WireImage/Getty Images. P. 27, ©Jeff Greenberg/Alamy. P. 27, Courtesy Netflix Inc. P. 30, Photographer: Robert Wilson. P. 30, Imago sportfotodienst/Newscom. P. 30, ©2012 Teach For America, Inc. P. 31, Photo by Larry Busacca/Getty Images for Nickelodeon. P. 32, Photo by Getty Images for Nike. P. 33, Both images: Courtesy The Hertz Corporation. P. 34, Photo by Jim Spellman/WireImage/Getty Images. P. 34, Photo by Christopher Lee/Getty Images for Nike. P. 34, Photo by Kohjiro Kinno/Sports Illustrated/Getty Images. P. 35, Courtesy Pizza Hut. P. 36, Courtesy Dyson, Inc. P. 37, Rex Features via AP Images. P. 38, Photo by Chung Sung-Jun/Getty Images. P. 40, ©Westmacott/Alamy. P. 41, Courtesy ©2008 The Goodyear Tire & Rubber Company. All rights reserved. Agency: McCann Erickson/New York, NY. Creative Director: Craig Markus; Art Director: Tim Dillingham; Copywriter: Mark Ronquillo; Photographer: ©2007 Graham Westmoreland/Friend and Johnson. P. 41, Both images: Courtesy of Apple. P. 42, Photo by Gilles Mingasson/Liaison/Getty Images. P. 43, Photo by Dowling/PictureGroup via AP Images. P. 44, Photo by Craig Barritt/Getty Images. P. 45, ©Hero Images/Getty Images.

CHAPTER 3

Page 46, ©Brent Jones. P. 48, ©Clayton Hauck Photography. P. 50, Chris Ryan/OJO Images/Getty Images. P. 51, Courtesy Staples, Inc. P. 53, Courtesy Canadian Mountain Holidays. P. 54, Courtesy The Home Depot. P. 56, ©incamerastock/Alamy. P. 57, ©M. Hruby. P. 58, ©2012 Google. P. 58, Photo by Dave M. Benett/Getty Images. P. 58, Courtesy HSN, Inc. P. 60, ©John Boud/Alamy. P. 62, Courtesy Crisp Social/Copenhagen, Denmark. P. 63, ©K. Rousonelos. P. 64, Courtesy foursquare ©2012. P. 64, Courtesy Left Brain Right Brain LLC. Used with permission. P. 66, Courtesy Salesforce Radian6. P. 70, Courtesy Applebee's Neighborhood Bar & Grill. P. 73, ©Hero Images/Getty Images.

CHAPTER 4

Page 74, Glowimages/Getty Images. P. 76, ©Joseph Sohm/Visions of America/Corbis. P. 76, AP Photo/CSPS. P. 77, GRANTLANDD®. Copyright Grantland Enterprises; www.grantland.net. P. 78, Dyamic Graphics/JupiterImages. P. 79, Photo Illustration by Brendan Smialowski/Getty Images. P. 80, ©2012 Wal-Mart Stores, Inc. P. 81, ©Dennis MacDonald/PhotoEdit. P. 82, ©2010 The Dannon Company, Inc., Reprinted with Permission. P. 82, AP Photo/US Coast Guard. P. 83, AP Photo/The Record-Eagle, Keith King. P. 87, Both images: ©Newman's Own, Inc. P. 88, Courtesy Ford Motor Company. P. 89, ©K. Rousonelos. P. 91, ©2010–2013 McDonald's. All Rights Reserved. P. 92, PRNewsFoto/Frito-Lay North America/AP Images. P. 93, Courtesy General Electric Company. P. 93, ©Hero Images/Getty Images.

CHAPTER 5

Page 94, BJI/Blue Jean Images/Getty Images. P. 95, Courtesy The Cool Hunter.net. P. 98, ©M. Hruby. P. 99, Courtesy Nau & Ben Moon. P. 100, Both ads: Courtesy MINI USA. P. 102, Jack Hollingsworth/Getty Images. P. 103, ©The McGraw-Hill Companies Inc./John Flournoy Photographer. P. 104, Photo by Brian Bahr/Getty Images. P. 105, Courtesy of Hammacher Schlemmer, www.hammacher.com. P. 106, ©2006 Oldemarak, LLC. Reprinted with permission. The Wendy's name, design and logo are registered trademarks of Oldemark, Llc and are licensed to Wendy's International, Inc. P. 106, Photo by Ian Walton/Getty Images or Nike. P. 107, Comstock/PictureQuest. P. 107, Courtesy Subway Franchise Advertising Fund Trust. P. 108, Newton Daly/Stockbyte/Getty Images. P. 109, ©Plush Studios/Blend Images LLC. P. 109, Warwick Lister-Kaye/Getty Images. P. 111, AP Photo/Ric Feld. P. 112, Carolina Ruiz Bega/La Nacion de Costa Rica/Newscom. P. 113, Kaz Chiba/Digital Vision/Getty Images. P. 114, Louis Gouliamaki/AFP/Getty Images. P. 115, ©Hero Images/Getty Images.

CHAPTER 6

Page 116, Courtesy Zipcar. P. 118, Courtesy Zipcar. P. 120, Courtesy BMW of North America, LLC. P. 120, Photo by Timothy A. Clary/AFP/Getty Images. P. 120, ©M. Hruby. P. 121, Photo by Amy Sussman/Getty Images. P. 122, Courtesy of Refinery29.com. P. 123, Courtesy mySugr/GmbH.—K. Rose. P. 125, Rebecca Sapp/Wireimage. P. 126, AP Photo/Ann Taylor. P. 126, AP Photo/Sang Tan. P. 126, All photos: ©M. Hruby. P. 127, Ramin Talale/Bloomberg via Getty Images. P. 129, Handout/MCT/Newscom. P. 130, Courtesy Whirlpool Corporation. P. 130, Richard B. Levine/Newscom. P. 132, Courtesy Taco Bell. P. 132, McGruff® and Scruff® are a part of

Images. P. 258, ©M. Hruby. P. 259, Frederic J. Brown/AFP/Getty Images. P. 259 Photo by Caroline Bittencourt/LatinContent/Getty Images. P. 260, Courtesy Apple, Inc. P. 260, ©Green Mountain Coffee Roasters, Inc. Used with permission. P. 261, ©GfK Custom Research, LLC. P. 261, AP Photo/Paul Sakuma. P. 263, ©K. Rousonelos. P. 264, ©1998–2012 Mozilla.org and Firefox®. P. 265, Odd Andersen/AFP/Getty Images. P. 266, Courtesy Balanced Body, Inc. P. 267, ©Richard Levine/Alamy. P. 268, ©M. Hruby. P. 268, Photo courtesy of Staples, Inc. P. 269, Photo by Dave Hogan/Getty Images. P. 270, AP Photo/Nick Wass. P. 271, Money Sharma/EPA/Newscom. P. 272, Photo by Keith Bedford/Bloomberg via Getty Images. P. 274, ZUMA Press/Newscom. P. 276, ©M. Hruby. P. 277, Courtesy Henkel Corporation. P. 278, Hallmark online ad courtesy of Hallmark Cards, Inc. P. 279, ©Hero Images/Getty Images.

CHAPTER 13

Page 280, Carolyn A. McKeone/Photo Researchers/Getty Images. P. 282, ©2012 Zappos.com. P. 283, Chris Clinton/Digital Vision/Getty Images. P. 283, Dynamic Graphics/Jupiter Images. P. 283, ©Jose Fuste Raga/CORBIS. P. 283, The McGraw-Hill Companies, Inc./Andrew Resek, Photographer. P. 283, John A. Rizzo/Getty Images. P. 283, ©Charles Bowman/Alamy. P. 283, ©Photodisc. P. 284, Ken James/Bloomberg via GettyImages. P. 285, Courtesy Carbonite, Inc. P. 286, Jupiterimages/Getty Images. P. 286, ©Buddy Mays/CORBIS. P. 288, ©iStockphoto LP. P. 290, Courtesy The Broadmoor. P. 292, McGraw-Hill Companies/Gideon Kindall. P. 293, Chris Ryan/OJO Images/Getty Images. P. 295, PRNewsFoto/PriceGrabber.com/AP Images. P. 296, Juanmonino/E+/Getty Images. P. 296, Keith Brofsky/Photodisc/Getty Images. P. 297, Courtesy L.L. Bean. Used with permission. P. 299, ©Dave Carroll. P. 301, ©Hero Images/Getty Images.

CHAPTER 14

Page 302, ©Brent Jones. P. 304, ©The McGraw-Hill Companies, Inc./Jill Braaten, photographer. P. 305, Everett Collection/Newscom. P. 305, ©The McGraw-Hill Companies, Inc./Jill Braaten, photographer. P. 307, ©M.Hruby. P. 308, *Both images:* Courtesy Paradigm Electronics, Inc. P. 308, Noah Berger/Bloomberg via Getty Images. P. 309, Photo by C.W. Griffin/Miami Hearalt/MCT via Getty Images. P. 310, Johnathan

Kitchen/Getty Images. P. 311, Photo by George Pimentel/WireImage/Getty Images. P. 311, The McGraw-Hill Companies/Bob Coyle, Photographer. P. 311, Foodcollection. P. 312, ©Tony Cenicola/The New York Times/Redux. P. 313, Photodisc/Getty Images. P. 317, Allan Danahar/Digital Vision/Getty Images. P. 317, Inti St Clair/Photodisc Red/Getty Images. P. 317, Steve Cole/Getty Images. P. 317, ©Corbis—All Rights Reserved. P. 317, Ingram Publishing/SuperStock. P. 317, ©Brand X Pictures/PunchStock. P. 319, Photo by Mike Mergen/Bloomberg via Getty Images. P. 319, Patrick Fallon/Bloomberg via Getty Images. P. 320, Courtesy Sears, Roebuck and Co. P. 320, ©Bill Aron/PhotoEdit. P. 321, Photo by Ethan Miller/Getty Images. P. 322, ©Alex Segre/Alamy. P. 323, ©Jeff Greenberg/PhotoEdit, Inc. P. 324, ©Tom Prettyman/PhotoEdit. P. 325, ©Hero Images/Getty Images.

CHAPTER 15

Page 327, Vesna Andjic/Vetta/Getty Images. P. 328, ©2012 Wal-Mart Stores, Inc. P. 329, ©M. Hruby. P. 331, ©Thinkstock/Alamy/Getty Images. P. 333, Courtesy The Stanley Works. P. 333, ©John Gress/Corbis. P. 335, ©Lana Sundman/Alamy. P. 336, ©Justin Kase zsixz/Alamy. P. 338, AP Photo/Kin Cheung. P. 340, Digital Vision/Punchstock. P. 341, ©Charlie Mayer. P. 345, ©Wal-Mart Stores, Inc. P. 345, Press Association via AP Images. P. 346, UPI/Brian Kersey/Newscom. P. 347, ©Hero Images/Getty Images.

CHAPTER 16

Page 349, A. Chederros/ONOKY/Getty Images. P. 350, AP Photo/HSN, Jason Henry. P. 351, ©Linda Matlow/Alamy. P. 352, AP Photo/Jeff Chiu. P. 353, ©Jeff Greenberg/PhotoEdit. P. 353, ©Susan Van Etten/PhotoEdit. P. 356, ©Daniel Koebe/Corbis. P. 356, Photo by David Paul Morris/Bloomberg via Getty Images. P. 357, ©Francis Dean/Corbis. P. 357, Daniel Acker/Bloomberg via Getty Images. P. 358, Photo by Rachel Murray WireImage/Getty Images. P. 358, AP Photo/MarkHumphrey. P. 359, Courtesy Prime Retail. P. 360, The McGraw-Hill Companies, Inc./Andrew Resek, photographer. P. 360, The White Castle images and materials and the "WHITE CASTLE®" mark are the exclusive property of White Castle Management Co. and are used under license. No use, reproduction or distribution is allowed. P. 361, ©Camera

Press/Redux. P. 362, ©Richard Levine/Alamy. P. 362, PRNewsFoto/Parago/AP Images. P. 363, ©K. Rousonelos. P. 363, Courtesy Walgreen Co. P. 364, Courtesy Bass Pro Shops. P. 365, ©M. Hruby. P. 365, Courtesy Mall of America. P. 366, Courtesy Bluefly, Inc. P. 367, Danny Johnston/AP Images. P. 368, *All images:* Courtesy Patagonia, Inc. P. 369, ©Hero Images/Getty Images.

CHAPTER 17

Page 370, ©Imaginechina/Corbis. P. 372, ©2006–2012 The Coca-Cola Company. P. 373, ©2006–2012 The Coca-Cola Company. P. 373, ©ZUMA Wire Service/Alamy. P. 374, ©2006–2012 The Coca-Cola Company. P. 375, Photo by Sonja Flemming/CBS via Getty Images. P. 376, ©2006–2012 The Coca-Cola Company. P. 377, Courtesy Peapod. P. 377, ©M. Hruby. P. 379, Images Courtesy of The Advertising Archives. P. 380, Photo by Ida Mae Astute/ABC via Getty Images. P. 380, Jeff Kowalsky/Bloomberg via Getty Images. P. 382, Photo by Fernanda Calfat/Getty Images. P. 385, PRNewsFoto/Choice Hotels International, Inc./AP Images. P. 385, ©2006 copyright 2006, The Knot, Inc. Reproduced by Permission. All Rights Reserved. P. 386, Courtesy RD2Inc via Southwest Airlines. P. 386, Photo by Albert L. Ortega/Getty Images. P. 387, Courtesy Southwest Airlines; Photographer: Irwin Thompson. P. 387, Courtesy Columbia Sportswear Company. P. 389, Nicole Weingart/Redux. P. 390, Courtesy Google, Inc. P. 391, ©Hero Images/Getty Images.

CHAPTER 18

Page 392, DC Hunter/Pacific Coast/Newscom. P. 394, ©Press 2000/Alamy. P. 394, Courtesy Tropicana Products, Inc. P. 396, Photo by Jun Sato/WireImage/Getty Images. P. 396, Joerg Carstensen/EPA/Landov. P. 397, PRNewsFoto/Chrysler Group LLC/AP Images. P. 398, ©The Procter & Gamble Company. Used by permission. P. 399, Courtesy Pepsi-Cola Company. P. 399, PRNewsFoto/Milk Processor Education Program/AP Images. P. 401, Courtesy Chrysler Group LLC. P. 402, ©General Motors LLC, 2010. P. 403, PRNewsFoto/Coty Inc./AP Images. P. 403, ©K. Rousonelos. P. 406, ©PRNewsFoto/Duluth Trading Company/AP Images. P. 407, ©Ford Motor Company. P. 407, © General Motors. P. 408, ©Newscom. P. 408, Photo by Gregg DeGuire/FilmMagic/Getty Images. P. 409,

©Bill Aron/PhotoEdit. P. 410, Photo by Jason Merritt/Getty Images. P. 411, Images used with permission of Chili's® Grill & Bar. P. 411, PRNewsFoto/Red Bull/AP Images. P. 413, Courtesy Payless Shoe Source, Inc. P. 413, Photo by Frederick M. Brown/Getty Images. P. 414, RNewsFoto/Nivea/AP Images. P. 415, PRNewFoto/AXE/AP Images. P. 416, ©Paramount Pictures/Photofest. P. 417, ©Hero Images/Getty Images.

CHAPTER 19

Page 418, John Giustina/The Image Bank/Getty Images. P. 420, Courtesy Ogilvy & Mather. P. 422, ©Royalty-Free/Corbis. P. 422, Mark Edward Atkinson/Blend Images/Getty Images. P. 422, Thinkstock/JupiterImages. P. 423, Hiroko Masuike/The New York Times/Redux. P. 425, AP Photo/Paul Sakuma. P. 425, Guillermo Legaria/AFP/Getty Images. P. 427, ©Royalty-Free/Corbis. P. 427, ©Susan Van Etten/PhotoEdit, Inc. P. 428, ©Digital-Vision/Getty Images. P. 429, ©Susan Van Etten/PhotoEdit, Inc. P. 431, ©Mark Tuschman. P. 432, Photo by Theo Wargo/Getty Images. P. 433, Photo by Gustavo Caballero/Getty Images for Vital Sports & Entertainment. P. 434, Ryan McVay/Getty Images. P. 434, Courtesy Awards Network. P. 435, Courtesy Mary Kay, Inc. P. 437, AP Photo/Charlie Riedel. ©Custom Medical Stock Photo. P. 437, ©Hero Images/Getty Images.

name index

A page number followed by an *e* indicates an exhibit; a page number with an *n* indicates a note.

A page number followed by an *e* indicates an exhibit; a page number with an *n* indicates a note.

A page number followed by an e indicates an exhibit.

CSR (corporate social responsibility), 20, 40, 81–83, 90–92
CTR (click-through rate), 390
Culture, 99–101, 136, 166–168, 169
Customer excellence, 25–27
Customer loyalty, 26, 130, 241, 244, 297
Customer orientation, 308
Customer relationship management (CRM)
  definition, 15–16
  integrated, 367–368
  loyalty and retention programs, 26, 244, 415
  personal selling and, 427
Customer satisfaction, 128–129
Customer service, 26–27, 283, 366, 367
Customers; see also 4E framework
  engagement of, 54, 58–61, 65–69
  expectations of, 353
  input from, 267–269
  lifetime value of, 26, 219, 298
  listening to, 298–299
  needs of, 256, 257
  pricing strategies for, 309–314
  salespeople and, 437
  as stakeholders, 92
  VOC programs, 291
Customer-to-customer (C2C) marketing, 10
Customs and Border Protection, 341

D

Data
  biometric, 230
  definition, 213
  panel, 216
  primary, 212, 219, 227
  scanner, 216
  secondary, 212, 214–219, 227
  syndicated, 215–217
Data analysis, 213–214
Data collection techniques
  experiments, 226–227
  focus groups, 223–224
  interviews, 223
  observation, 220
  panels and scanners, 226
  process overview, 212–213
  secondary data, 214–219, 227
  social media, 220–222
  surveys and questionnaires, 190–192, 213, 224–226
Data mining, 218
Data warehouses, 218, 340–342

Deals, 413
Deceptive advertising, 409–410
Deceptive price advertising, 322–323
Deciders, 151
Decision process
  alternatives evaluation, 124–128
  ethics and, 84–86, 124, 125, 127
  habitual decision making, 140–141
  information searches, 120–124
  involvement and, 139–141
  need recognition, 119–120
  postpurchase behavior, 128–130
  psychological factors in, 131–135
  purchase and consumption, 128
  situational factors in, 136–138
  social factors in, 135–136
Decision rules, 126–128
Decline stage, 275, 277–278
Decoding, 374
Delivery gap, 288, 293–295
Demand curve, 309–310
Democratic buying centers, 153
Demographic segmentation, 188–189
Demographics
  definition, 101
  education, 105–106
  ethnicity, 106–107
  gender, 106
  generational cohorts, 101–104
  income, 104–105, 164
Department stores, 357
Depth, 237–238
Derived demand, 145
Desire, in AIDA model, 379–380
Determinant attributes, 126
Differentiated targeting strategy, 197–199
Diffusion of innovation, 259–264
Digital Natives, 101–102
Direct investment, 175–176
Direct marketing, 383–384
Direct marketing channel, 331–332
Direct store delivery, 343–344
Distribution centers, 331, 343–346
Distribution intensity, 353–354
Distribution strategies, 181; see also Place
Distributive fairness, 299–300
Distributors, 146
Diversification strategy, 45, 257–258
Do Not Call Registry, 110
Dogs in portfolio analysis, 39e, 41–43
Do-Not-Call list, 426
Drugstores, 358
Duty, 165

E

Early adopters, 261–262
Early majority, 262–263
Economic situation, 113, 161–164
EDLP (everyday low pricing), 319
Education demographics, 105–106
Education of customers, 51, 59, 60, 61, 65
Elastic, 312
Electronic data interchange (EDI), 340–342
Electronic Privacy Information Center (EPIC), 228
Emotion, 402
Emotional appeals, 402
Emotional support, 294
Empathy, 289–291, 429, 433
Employees, 92, 294
Empowerment, 293–294
Encoding, 374
Engagement of customers, 54, 58–61, 65–69
Entrepreneurs, 19–21
Environmental Protection Agency (EPA), 110, 250
EPIC (Electronic Privacy Information Center), 228
Esteem needs, 133
Ethical climate, 78
Ethics
  business, 77
  censorship, 172
  corporate social responsibility, 20, 40, 81–83, 90–92
  fake consumer reviews, 296
  fast food diets, 124, 125
  global marketing, 152, 172, 271
  green marketing, 109–110
  Internet versus brick-and-mortar stores, 63
  introduction, 75–77
  marketing, 77
  marketing research, 221, 228–230
  marketing to children, 103, 109, 243, 382, 409–410
  packaging, 312
  personal, 80–81
  personal branding and, 72–73
  personal selling, 435–437
  pricing strategies, 322–325
  privacy concerns, 89, 103, 110, 228–230, 383
  product labeling, 127, 250, 251
  product testing, 271
  professional rankings, 77–78
  supply chain, 338
  workplace, 78–80

Private-label brands, 217, 245
PRIZM (Potential Rating Index by Zip Market), 194–195
Problem solving, 140–141, 300–301
Procedural fairness, 299–300
Product design, 270–271
Product development
    alpha and beta testing, 270–271
    compatibility, 264
    complexity, 264
    concept testing phase, 269–270
    definition, 270
    diffusion of innovation, 259–264
    evaluation phase, 274
    idea generation phase, 265–269
    introduction, 253–255
    market testing phase, 271–272
    in maturity stage, 277
    observability, 264
    pricing strategies, 321
    product launch phase, 272–274
    prototypes, 270
    reasons for, 255–259
    relative advantage, 264
    trialability, 264
Product development strategy, 44–45
Product excellence, 25, 27
Product launch, 272–274
Product life cycle, 275–279
Product lines, 39, 237–240
Product mix, 237–240
Product placement, 415–416
Product specification, 149
Product-focused advertisements, 398–399
Production-oriented era, 12–13
Products; see also Branding
    complementary, 313
    complexity of, 234–235
    definition, 7–9, 234
    failures, 260–262
    global strategies, 178–179
    introduction, 7–9, 233–234
    labeling, 127, 250, 251
    merchandise flows, 343–347
    mix and lines, 237–240
    packaging, 138, 249–251, 312
    prestige, 310
    retail strategies, 361–362
    services versus, 284–287
    substitute, 313
    types, 235–237
    value creation and, 35
Professional blogs, 61
Professional ethics, 77–78

Professionals, 55
Profit orientation, 306, 315–316
Profitable segments, 196–197
Promotion; see also Advertising; Integrated marketing communications; Personal selling
    global strategies, 181–183
    product development and, 273
    retail strategies, 362–364
    value communication and, 10, 36
Promotions, 137–138
Proposal analysis, 149
Prototypes, 270
"Proud Sponsor of Moms" campaign, 177
PSA (public service advertising), 399–400
Psychographics, 190–192
Psychological factors in decision process, 131–135
Psychological needs, 120
Psychological risk, 124
Public relations (PR), 381, 410–412
Public service advertising (PSA), 399–400
Puffery, 322, 410
Pull marketing strategy, 342–343, 396–397
Pulsing, 404–405
Purchase decisions, 128
Purchase situation, 136
Purchasing power parity (PPP), 162
Pure competition, 318
Push marketing strategy, 342–343, 396–397

Q

Qualify, 425, 426–427
Qualitative research, 219
Quantitative research, 219
Question marks in portfolio analysis, 39e, 41
Questionnaires, 190–192, 213, 224–226
Quick response (QR) systems, 347
Quotas, 165

R

Radio frequency identification (RFID) tags, 344
R&D (research and development), 265–266
Reach, 389
Reachable segments, 196
Real income, 164
Rebates, 415

Rebranding, 248
Receivers, 374, 377
Receiving, 344
Reference groups, 135–136
Reference price, 320, 322–323
Referent power, 335
Regional culture, 100–101
Regulatory environment, 113–115, 409–410
Related diversification, 45
Relational orientation, 15–16
Relationship building, 153–154, 259, 337–339, 424
Relationship selling, 424, 429
Relative market share, 39–40
Relevance, 390
Reliability, 289–291, 429
Reminder advertising, 398
Reps (manufacturer's representatives), 430–431
Request for proposals (RFP), 149
Research; see Marketing research
Research and development (R&D), 265–266
Resellers, 146–147
Reservations or objections, 428–429
Resilience, 433
Responsiveness, 289–291, 429
Retailer/store brands, 245
Retailing
    definition, 351
    introduction, 349–350
    multichannel, 352, 366–369
    partner choices, 352–354
    store benefits, 365–366
    strategy development and, 361–365
    types
        food, 355–357
        general merchandise, 357–359
        services, 359–360
Retrieval sets, 124–125, 126
Return on investment (ROI), 67, 390–391
Reverse engineering, 267
Reverse innovation, 179, 265
Reward power, 334
RFID (radio frequency identification) tags, 344
RFP (request for proposals), 149
Risk management, 257–258, 366
Risk types, 122–124
Robinson-Patman Act, 114, 324
ROI (return on investment), 67, 390–391
Role playing, 427
Rule-of-thumb methods, 388

Practice

▮ MARKETING

Real-world multiplayer games for practical learning

Practice Marketing is an online, interactive learning environment that simulates the full marketing mix including market segmentation, product, pricing, promotion, and place.

Engage your students through practical learning

McGraw-Hill Education's award-winning *Practice Marketing* is a 3D, multiplayer strategy game that allows you to engage your students with the key concepts of marketing in a compelling game environment while remaining academically and pedagogically sound. Students learn by doing what it takes to be an effective marketing manager.

IMMERSIVE.   ENGAGING.   PRACTICAL.

www.mhpractice.com